Visual Basic® 6
Database Programming

Visual Basic® 6 Database Programming

John W. Fronckowiak and David J. Helda

IDG Books Worldwide, Inc.
An International Data Group Company

Foster City, CA ◆ Chicago, IL ◆ Indianapolis, IN ◆ New York, NY

Visual Basic® 6 Database Programming

Published by
IDG Books Worldwide, Inc.
An International Data Group Company
919 E. Hillsdale Blvd., Suite 400
Foster City, CA 94404
www.idgbooks.com (IDG Books Worldwide Web site)

Library of Congress Catalog Card Number: 98-075154

ISBN: 0-7645-3254-5

Printed in the United States of America

10 9 8 7 6 5 4 3 2

1B/QX/RS/ZY/FC

Distributed in the United States by IDG Books Worldwide, Inc.

Distributed by Macmillan Canada for Canada; by Transworld Publishers Limited in the United Kingdom; by IDG Norge Books for Norway; by IDG Sweden Books for Sweden; by Woodslane Pty. Ltd. for Australia; by Woodslane (NZ) Ltd. for New Zealand; by Addison Wesley Longman Singapore Pte Ltd. for Singapore, Malaysia, Thailand, Indonesia, and Korea; by Norma Comunicaciones S.A. for Colombia; by Intersoft for South Africa; by International Thomson Publishing for Germany, Austria, and Switzerland; by Toppan Company Ltd. for Japan; by Distribuidora Cuspide for Argentina; by Livraria Cultura for Brazil; by Ediciencia S.A. for Ecuador; by Ediciones ZETA S.C.R. Ltda. for Peru; by WS Computer Publishing Corporation, Inc., for the Philippines; by Unalis Corporation for Taiwan; by Contemporanea de Ediciones for Venezuela; by Computer Book & Magazine Store for Puerto Rico; by Express Computer Distributors for the Caribbean and West Indies. Authorized Sales Agent: Anthony Rudkin Associates for the Middle East and North Africa.

For general information on IDG Books Worldwide's books in the U.S., please call our Consumer Customer Service department at 800-762-2974. For reseller information, including discounts and premium sales, please call our Reseller Customer Service department at 800-434-3422.

For information on where to purchase IDG Books Worldwide's books outside the U.S., please contact our International Sales department at 650-655-3200 or fax 650-655-3297.

For information on foreign language translations, please contact our Foreign & Subsidiary Rights department at 650-655-3021 or fax 650-655-3281.

For sales inquiries and special prices for bulk quantities, please contact our Sales department at 650-655-3200 or write to the address above.

For information on using IDG Books Worldwide's books in the classroom or for ordering examination copies, please contact our Educational Sales department at 800-434-2086 or fax 317-596-5499.

For press review copies, author interviews, or other publicity information, please contact our Public Relations department at 650-655-3000 or fax 650-655-3299.

For authorization to photocopy items for corporate, personal, or educational use, please contact Copyright Clearance Center, 222 Rosewood Drive, Danvers, MA 01923, or fax 978-750-4470.

 is a trademark under exclusive license to IDG Books Worldwide, Inc., from International Data Group, Inc.

ABOUT IDG BOOKS WORLDWIDE

Welcome to the world of IDG Books Worldwide.

IDG Books Worldwide, Inc., is a subsidiary of International Data Group, the world's largest publisher of computer-related information and the leading global provider of information services on information technology. IDG was founded more than 30 years ago by Patrick J. McGovern and now employs more than 9,000 people worldwide. IDG publishes more than 290 computer publications in over 75 countries. More than 90 million people read one or more IDG publications each month.

Launched in 1990, IDG Books Worldwide is today the #1 publisher of best-selling computer books in the United States. We are proud to have received eight awards from the Computer Press Association in recognition of editorial excellence and three from Computer Currents' First Annual Readers' Choice Awards. Our best-selling ...For Dummies® series has more than 50 million copies in print with translations in 31 languages. IDG Books Worldwide, through a joint venture with IDG's Hi-Tech Beijing, became the first U.S. publisher to publish a computer book in the People's Republic of China. In record time, IDG Books Worldwide has become the first choice for millions of readers around the world who want to learn how to better manage their businesses.

Our mission is simple: Every one of our books is designed to bring extra value and skill-building instructions to the reader. Our books are written by experts who understand and care about our readers. The knowledge base of our editorial staff comes from years of experience in publishing, education, and journalism — experience we use to produce books to carry us into the new millennium. In short, we care about books, so we attract the best people. We devote special attention to details such as audience, interior design, use of icons, and illustrations. And because we use an efficient process of authoring, editing, and desktop publishing our books electronically, we can spend more time ensuring superior content and less time on the technicalities of making books.

You can count on our commitment to deliver high-quality books at competitive prices on topics you want to read about. At IDG Books Worldwide, we continue in the IDG tradition of delivering quality for more than 30 years. You'll find no better book on a subject than one from IDG Books Worldwide.

John Kilcullen
Chairman and CEO
IDG Books Worldwide, Inc.

Steven Berkowitz
President and Publisher
IDG Books Worldwide, Inc.

Eighth Annual
Computer Press
Awards ≥1992

Ninth Annual
Computer Press
Awards ≥1993

Tenth Annual
Computer Press
Awards ≥1994

Eleventh Annual
Computer Press
Awards ≥1995

Credits

ACQUISITIONS EDITOR
John Osborn

DEVELOPMENT EDITOR
Laura E. Brown

TECHNICAL EDITOR
Chris Stone

COPY EDITORS
Bill McManus
Barry Childs-Helton

PROJECT COORDINATOR
Tom Debolski

PACKAGING COORDINATOR
Constance Petros

QUALITY CONTROL SPECIALISTS
Mick Arellano
Mark Schumann

**GRAPHICS AND
PRODUCTION SPECIALISTS**
Mario Amador
Jude Levinson
Linda Marousek
Dina F Quan

ILLUSTRATOR
Jesse Coleman

PROOFREADER
Jennifer K. Overmyer

INDEXER
Carol Burbo

BOOK DESIGNER
Jim Donohue

COVER DESIGN
©mike parsons design

About the Authors

John W. Fronckowiak is president and founder of IDC Consulting, Inc., which specializes in Internet/intranet consulting, application development, and network consulting. He has extensive experience with database application development, client/server networking, Internet and intranet presence development, application development, and project management. John's previous writing experience includes *Java Bible*, *COBOL For Dummies – Quick Reference*, and *Building an Intranet For Dummies* from IDG Books Worldwide. John lives in East Amherst, New York, with his wife Diane and their cat Eiffel and parrot Elmo.

    David J. Helda is a senior systems analyst at Frontier Science Research and Technology Foundation. He has extensive experience in application development, building distributed client/server database systems for the medical research community, and programming project management.

For Diane — *J.F.*

Preface

Visual Basic 6 Database Programming is a concise, professional guide for teaching experienced Visual Basic programmers how to design and build database applications using the Microsoft Visual Basic Enterprise Edition. As part of the Professional series from IDG Books Worldwide, this book explores support for database programming in Visual Basic 6, provides solutions for many of the problems that database programmers most frequently encounter, and shows how these techniques combine to create full-blown client/server and Web-based applications.

Visual Basic 6 Database Programming provides a comprehensive review of all the data access models supported by Visual Basic, including Data Access Objects (DAO), Remote Data Objects (RDO), ActiveX Data Objects (ADO), Open Database Connectivity (ODBC), and OLE DB. The purpose of this book is not to teach you the Visual Basic programming language, but rather, to leverage your existing knowledge as you create full-featured applications that provide database access.

Who Should Read This Book

Visual Basic 6 Database Programming is a one-stop reference for Visual Basic application developers who are using Visual Basic 6 to create and deploy client/server database applications. Visual Basic has become the most popular programming language used by programmers to develop client/server database applications. Visual Basic provides diverse data access methodologies: DAO, RDO, ADO, ODBC, and OLE DB; *Visual Basic 6 Database Programming* delves deep into each. Beginning with an introduction to client/server application development, you learn how to choose the data access methodology most appropriate for your applications. Whichever method you choose, you receive an in-depth, detailed review of its features.

What's Inside This Book

The book addresses eight major areas of consideration for Visual Basic 6 programmers.

Part 1: Overview

Part I provides an overview of the new features in Visual Basic 6. This part also introduces concepts for the design and development of Visual Basic 6 applications. You learn about the client/server database architecture, and review each of the data access methodologies provided by Visual Basic 6.

Part II: Design of Client/Server Applications

Part II provides an overview of the design and development process for Visual Basic 6 database applications. You also learn how to set up your client and server systems for database access applications. The SQL query language is introduced, and you learn how to design your queries and databases for optimal performance.

Part III: Data Access Objects API

Part III introduces the DAO API. The DAO is a set of DLLs (Dynamic Link Libraries) that form the core of the Jet database engine. The DAO supports two different types of database environments: (1) by using the Microsoft Jet database engine, the DAO is optimized for accessing local ISAM (Index Sequential Access Method) databases such as dBASE, Paradox, FoxPro, and others; (2) by using ODBCDirect the DAO is optimized for ODBC databases with minimal overhead. Each component of the DAO is reviewed in detail, and you learn how to design database applications for optimal performance with the DAO.

Part IV: Remote Data Objects API

Part IV introduces the RDO API. The RDO provides a set of objects that assists in the development of client/server applications by addressing their unique requirements. Unlike the DAO, which provides an interface to the Jet database engine, the RDO provides an object-oriented layer of abstraction that directly interfaces with the ODBC API – as does the ODBCDirect interface. The RDO uses the ODBC API and the database server drivers to create database server connections, create queries and cursors to navigate the resulting data sets, and execute complex procedures relying on the database server for the majority of the processing requirements. Unlike the DAO, which utilizes the Jet database engine for query preprocessing and connection management, the RDO directly interfaces to the database server. This makes the RDO particularly suited to client/server application development. Each component of the RDO is reviewed in detail, and you learn how to design database applications for optimal performance with the RDO.

Part V: ActiveX Data Objects API

Part V introduces the ADO, another API for developing applications that can access OLE DB data providers. The ADO is supported in a number of different programming languages, including Visual C++, VBScript, Visual J++, Visual Basic, and Active Server Pages. While using the OLE DB directly provided a very low-level approach to accessing OLE DB providers, the ADO provides a higher level and easier-to-understand mechanism. If you are familiar with the DAO and RDO APIs for application development, the ADO will seem similar, with good reason: It combines the best aspects of DAO and RDO, without relying as heavily on the object hierarchy as do either DAO and RDO. This means it is much easier to create and manipulate ADO objects because they can be created and managed directly. The ADO is specifically designed for client/server application development; because the ADO can be used from VBScript, it is also well suited for server-side Web/database integration. Each component of the ADO is reviewed in detail, and you learn how to design database applications for optimal performance with the ADO.

Part VI: ODBC API and OLE DB API

Part VI introduces the Open Database Connectivity (ODBC) API. ODBC provides a fast and efficient way to access server-side databases. This part reviews the needs and requirements for developing Visual Basic applications using this foundation of Windows-based client/server programming. Part VI also introduces the OLE DB API; in addition to the ways it differs from ODBC, you learn about the basic concepts that underlie this new data access methodology.

Part VII: Controls, Wizards, and DHTML

Part VII introduces data controls and wizards, new to Visual Basic 6, which can help you speed the process of creating your applications. Dynamic HTML (DHTML) support is also new to Visual Basic 6. This part introduces this new language and shows you how to put it to work with your database access applications in Visual Basic 6.

Part VIII: Accessing Other Data Sources

Part VIII reviews the major database sources used with Visual Basic 6 database access applications: Access 97, SQL Server 7, and Oracle8. You also learn how to choose the database access model most appropriate to the database server source you are using.

Appendixes

The appendixes provide a detailed reference to the DAO, RDO, and ADO APIs. Also provided is a detailed reference of Microsoft SQL Server 7 errors.

Visual Basic 6 Database Programming also includes a Quick Reference that highlights the most-used Visual Basic and Windows database features, as well as a glossary of special terms, and a detailed index.

Keep in Touch!

I love to hear from readers! Please let me know what you liked, disliked, or would like to see more of in this book. You can contact me in care of IDG Books Worldwide, 919 E. Hillsdale Blvd, Ste. 400, Foster City, CA 94404. You can also contact me directly though electronic mail at `john@idcc.net`.

Acknowledgments

I would like to thank everyone who helped to make this book possible: My wife Diane for putting up with me, and helping me work through the day-to-day ups and downs while keeping me focused on my larger goals. Thanks also to my family – Mom, Dad, Kim, Mike, Marie, Mom S., Alicia, and Becky – for understanding and supporting my desire to write.

I'd like to send special thanks to Studio B Productions, Inc. and David Rogelberg for presenting me with the opportunity to work on this project. Thanks also to John Osborn for giving me the opportunity to write this book, Laura Brown, and all the unseen individuals who helped turn this book into reality. Finally, thanks to my cat Eiffel and my Quaker parrot Elmo, for providing companionship (and loud meows and squawks) while I wrote.

– J.W.F.

Some might think the best thing about finishing a book is finishing the book. For me it's more of a moment of reflection and appreciation for all the people in my life who have provided unwavering support, understanding, and belief in my abilities. First and foremost, I'd like to thank my loving wife Karolyn for tolerating the long hours and taking care of everything while I was writing. Thanks to Justin, my wondeful two-year-old son, for providing the wisdom of enjoying life. Thanks to Greg Pavlov for pushing me to be my best in my career and writing. And special thanks to John Fronckowiak for being my mentor, confidant, and my best friend who's been there for it all. Finally, Johnny, it's time to ask the following question again: *What's so funny about Peace, Love, and Understanding?*

Thanks to one and all.
– D.J.H.

Contents at a Glance

Contents

Part VI   **ODBC and OLE DB API**

Appendixes

Part I

Overview

Chapter 1

Visual Basic 6 Overview

VISUAL BASIC 6 IS THE NEWEST version of Microsoft's rapid application-development tool. This chapter introduces the features and benefits found in this latest version, with special attention paid to the new data access features that are provided. Visual Basic is the fastest and easiest way to develop Windows applications. It evolved from the BASIC (Beginners All Purpose Symbolic Instruction Code) language that was popular in the earliest days of PC computing. Visual Basic has taken the BASIC programming language to a new level, providing developers with a tool to create powerful Windows 95/98- and Windows NT-compatible applications. Visual Basic has grown to become *the* choice for developers who need to develop and deploy client/server-based database applications quickly.

What's New with Visual Basic 6

Visual Basic 6 provides several new features that enhance the development process, including the following:

◆ **New data access features**: Support for the ActiveX Data Object (ADO) data access model; tools to manipulate and configure connections and commands; enhanced data-bound controls, which manage and display data source data, without requiring any complex programming; support for Object Linking and Embedding Databases (OLE DB) Component Object Model (COM) interfaces; tools to configure, manipulate, and view database schemas, queries, and stored procedures; a Data Report control, which enables you to create reports quickly, based on ordered record sets; and complete support for multitier data access architectures.

◆ **New controls**: An ADO data-bound control; an Internet Explorer-style toolbar control; a Grid control that can be bound to a data source; data-bound controls that can dynamically change data sources; a drop-down Calendar control for fast and easy entry of dates and times; flat-looking scroll bars; a Hierarchical Grid control that can display related record sets; a Month view control, which enables users to pick dates and date ranges quickly. New control features include enhanced handling when a control loses the input focus, the capability to add and remove controls dynamically through programming, and the capability to validate all controls on a form before the form is closed.

◆ **New Internet features**: The capability to write server-side applications for Internet Information Server (IIS); support for Dynamic HTML (DHTML); a Web-publishing wizard that simplifies packaging and delivery of your applications over the Internet; support for asynchronous operations; and the capability to store the state of ActiveX controls across a Web-browsing session.

◆ **New language features**: The capability to pass user-defined methods as procedure parameters and object properties; functions can return arrays as results; a new set of objects to support file-system access; the capability to access a property or method by using a string containing its name; the capability to create objects on remote machines; and enhanced string conversion features for internationalization.

◆ **New component-creation features**: The capability to create dynamically OLE DB consumer and data source controls; improved component debugging; improved object persistence – objects can be saved to a file for retrieval later; the capability to create ActiveX controls that support multithreading, for improved asynchronous operation; and automation for creating middle-tier data objects.

◆ **New wizards**: An enhanced Setup Wizard that provides support for easy Web distribution of your Visual Basic applications and components; a Data Form Wizard that can automatically create data forms from a data source; an improved Class-Building Wizard to automate the creation of Visual Basic classes; and a toolbar wizard that automates the creation of an application toolbar.

As shown in Figure 1-1, Visual Basic 6 provides a complete development environment, enabling programmers to design and implement their applications rapidly.

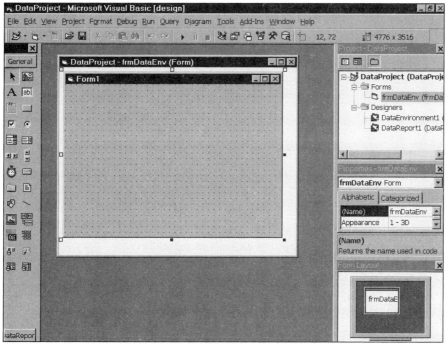

Figure 1-1: Using Visual Basic 6's application-development environment

Visual Basic 6 also provides these features:

◆ **Integrated Internet capabilities**: Enable you to create and distribute applications that can be deployed over the Internet and over your corporate intranet.

◆ **Complete ActiveX support**: Enables you to integrate and automate other applications, including Microsoft Word, Excel, and other Office and Windows applications.

◆ **Data access**: Enables you to develop complete client/server applications, manage data sources, and create server-side components (including stored procedures) for various database servers, including Microsoft SQL Server and Oracle.

◆ **Native executables**: Enable you to generate native executable (.exe) files, which can be distributed without restrictions.

Visual Basic Editions

Visual Basic 6 is available in three different versions: the Enterprise Edition, Professional Edition, and Learning Edition. Each edition is oriented toward a specific set of development environments.

Data access features available in Visual Basic 6 that are specific to a particular edition will be identified by an icon that indicates the edition.

Learning Edition

The Visual Basic Learning Edition enables programmers to create applications quickly for Microsoft Windows and Windows NT. This edition includes all intrinsic controls, plus grid, tab, and data-bound controls.

Professional Edition

Visual Basic Professional Edition provides a full-featured set of tools for professional programmers to develop Visual Basic solutions for others. This edition includes all the features of the Learning edition, plus additional ActiveX controls, the IIS Application Designer, Integrated Data Tools and Data Environment, Active Data Objects, and the Dynamic HTML Page Designer.

Enterprise Edition

The Enterprise Edition enables professionals to create robust distributed applications in a team setting. This edition includes all the features of the Professional edition, plus BackOffice tools, such as SQL Server, Transaction Server, IIS, Visual SourceSafe, SNA Server, and more.

System Requirements

Before you can install Visual Basic 6, your system must meet the following requirements:

- ◆ A Pentium processor, 90MHz or higher microprocessor
- ◆ A VGA-compatible video card, with a 640x480-resolution or higher display supported by Windows
- ◆ At least 24MB RAM for Windows 95, or at least 32MB for Windows NT

- ◆ Windows NT 3.51 or later, or Windows 95 or later

- ◆ Microsoft Internet Explorer version 4.01 or later (version 4.01 Service Pack 1 or later is required for DHTML application developers, and version 4.01 or later is required for application users)

- ◆ Disk–space requirements:

  - ■ Standard Edition: typical installation, 48MB; full installation, 80MB

  - ■ Professional Edition: typical installation, 48MB; full installation, 80MB

  - ■ Enterprise Edition: typical installation, 128MB; full installation, 147MB

- ◆ Additional components:

  - ■ Microsoft Developers Network (for documentation): 67MB

  - ■ Internet Explorer 4.01: approximately 66MB

- ◆ A CD-ROM

New Data Access Tools

Visual Basic 6 provides numerous new and important tools and features that enhance and simplify the development of data-enabled applications. Visual Basic 6 provides support for several data access models, including:

- ◆ Data Access Objects (DAOs), which are optimized to access single-user, standalone database sources. The DAO data access model is reviewed in detail in Part III.

- ◆ Remote Data Objects (RDOs), which are optimized to access Open Database Connectivity (ODBC) server-side database sources. The RDO data access model is reviewed in detail in Part IV.

- ◆ ActiveX Data Objects (ADOs), which provide access to OLE DB data sources. The ADO data access model is new to Visual Basic 6 and is reviewed in detail in Part V.

The ODBC and OLE DB data access methodologies are reviewed in Part VI. Visual Basic 6 enables you to use the ODBC and OLE DB APIs directly to develop and deploy applications that access your database source, but typically you will use either the DAO, RDO, or ADO data access model. Chapter 3 compares and contrasts each data access methodology.

OLE DB Support

Visual Basic 6 provides full support for the OLE DB and ADO data access methodologies, but what are ADO and OLE DB all about? Microsoft introduced ODBC with the promise of creating a singular common access methodology for databases. The earliest versions of ODBC suffered from inconsistent support and performance. In fact, ODBC was supported by very few database products, and those that did support ODBC also provided their own database drivers, which often were more reliable and faster. ODBC has come a long way from those early days. In its current form, two versions of ODBC are available – Version 2.0, which supports 16-bit applications, and, with the release of Windows 95, Version 3.0, which supports 32-bit applications. Today, almost every major database supports ODBC drivers, and third-party developers provide optimized driver versions. In fact, ODBC drivers have become as ubiquitous as video drivers and other Windows device drivers. Also, many data processing applications (such as Excel, Access, Lotus 1-2-3, and so forth) support ODBC data access. ODBC has become the omnipresent methodology for providing access to database sources.

The primary focus of ODBC is to provide a consistent interface to database data sources. OLE DB is designed with an even broader goal in mind: to provide a methodology to access data, regardless of the data source. OLE DB becomes the data access bridge for documents, e-mail systems, file systems, spread sheets, COM components, and other database sources that utilize ODBC drivers.

An OLE DB implementation basically is comprised of two components: a data provider and a data consumer. A *data provider* is an application that responds to queries and returns data in a usable form. An OLE DB data provider responds to various OLE DB calls that request the information it contains in a usable tabular form. For example, a spreadsheet OLE DB provider may allow access to a selection of cells or properties of the sheet, such as the creator, description, and date created.

A *data consumer* is an application or other COM component that utilizes the API of OLE DB to access a data source. A data consumer can be any application that requires access to data. OLE DB allows a data consumer to access the entire range of available enterprise data, regardless of where it is stored.

MAKING DATA SOURCES ACCESSIBLE

The key feature of OLE DB is that it lowers the requirements for implementing a data provider interface. Previously, to provide an ODBC interface, an application was required to implement a database engine that was capable of interpreting and executing SQL queries. With OLE DB, a data provider simply is required to return data in a tabular form. With OLE DB, a provider is not required to support a command interface. In conjunction with a query processor, OLE DB provides a unified way to access enterprise data.

A third component to an OLE DB implementation that hasn't been discussed is a *service provider*, which is a middleman in the OLE DB architecture. Acting as both a consumer of raw OLE DB data sources and as a provider to other OLE DB consumers, a service provider manipulates and processes the raw OLE DB data sources. OLE DB componentizes an application, providing diverse data source components, a query processing component, and an application. Because OLE DB provides a consistent data interface, any of the components can be exchanged without affecting functionality.

So, how is OLE DB different from ODBC connectivity? OLE DB extends the capabilities of ODBC, as discussed earlier, by providing the capability for less-sophisticated data applications to become data providers. This doesn't mean that the ODBC interface will be abandoned, however. ODBC will still be used to support database data sources, but instead of relying on the ODBC interface, applications will utilize the OLE DB interface to access these data sources. The OLE DB SDK contains an OLE DB provider for ODBC data, which enables you to access ODBC data sources from your OLE DB consumer applications.

EXAMINING THE COMPONENT OBJECT MODEL (COM)

The idea of component-based software was reviewed earlier. Microsoft has been working on developing this component-based model of application development for a long time. First came OLE, which facilitated interapplication communication by enabling application objects to be embedded in other applications. For example, a spreadsheet object could be placed in a word processing document, and a user was allowed to edit that object in place. Visual Basic Controls (VBXs) were introduced with Visual Basic. VBXs provided custom Windows controls that could be embedded in Visual Basic applications. These controls could be Windows interface elements, such as list boxes and buttons. VBXs could also provide specialized processing routines, such as specialized parsing and sorting routines. OLE and VBXs were Microsoft's first steps toward developing object-oriented application components. OLE and VBX were later merged into OLE Controls (OCXs, which are OLE-based custom controls). After OCX, the technology evolved into ActiveX, the key difference of which is that ActiveX controls are designed to function cross-platform. Microsoft has ported ActiveX to the Macintosh environment, and Sun has licensed ActiveX with an eye toward porting it to its architecture.

But just what is COM? COM is a specification for developing application components that can dynamically exchange data and that can be interchanged to support new functionality. COM employs object-oriented programming techniques to build encapsulated application components. These components provide an interface to an object. This interface is used to manipulate the object's state, and can be determined dynamically at run time. The COM architecture makes the development process an independent task by enabling components to work together, even if they have been developed with different programming languages and by different people. COM also provides the capability for components to work together in a distributed environment.

If you want more detailed information regarding the COM interface, the complete COM specification can be found on the Internet at `http://www.microsoft.com/olecom/title.htm`.

COM enables developers to create application components that can be pieced together to form new applications. These components can be developed independently and in different programming languages, and later may be easily reassembled to form a new application or a portion of an application. This componentization of application development helps to speed and simplify the development process. Unlike other models, the COM architecture may be used to develop a methodology for interapplication communication. After this communication methodology is established, applications can communicate directly with each other; the COM architecture doesn't impose any overhead.

The following are the key aspects of COM:

◆ Provides a strict set of rules that a component must follow, unlike earlier Windows-based component models, which provided functional repositories and communications methodologies, such as DDE and DLLs. COM isn't a way to develop an application; instead, it is a technology that enables a developer to build robust components that can evolve over time, which is made possible by the strict rules that define application components. COM components can be upgraded and can evolve without upgrading the applications in which they are utilized.

◆ COM components are independent, by nature. They can be developed with different programming languages, without requiring any specialized interface to bridge interapplication communications. This makes all COM components naturally compatible.

◆ COM components are truly object-oriented. They define an encapsulated object that presents a fixed set of interfaces, hiding the implementation details from the components' users.

◆ Provides mechanisms for encapsulating the life cycle of an object via reference counting.

◆ Employs the concept of Globally Unique Identifiers (GUIDs), which are used to identify a COM object uniquely. COM employs 128-bit identifiers, which ensure the uniqueness of each object.

◆ Security is inherent in the COM architecture. Basic operating system privileges are employed to ensure that a user has the rights to execute a component.

◆ Supports a distributed model, enabling components to be utilized in a networked environment and to be accessed and executed on remote systems.

OLE DB is what COM is all about, because it brings together numerous components – data providers and data consumers, which, when integrated together, can provide access to distributed enterprise-wide information. OLE DB is firmly based on the COM architecture and provides distributed data access by leveraging COM to glue together these application components.

ActiveX Data Objects (ADO) Support

ADO is another API for developing applications that can access OLE DB data providers. ADO is supported in various different programming languages, including Visual C++, VBScript, Visual J++, and Visual Basic, as well as in Active Server Pages. While using OLE DB directly provides a very low-level approach to accessing OLE DB providers, ADO provides a higher-level and easier-to-understand mechanism. If you are familiar with the DAO and RDO APIs for application development, ADO will seem very similar. ADO is a combination of the best aspects of DAO and RDO and doesn't rely as heavily on the object hierarchy as DAO and RDO. This means that manipulating and creating ADO objects is much easier, because they can be created and managed directly. ADO is specifically designed for client/server application development.

The key features of ADO include support for the following:

◆ Batch updating, in which multiple record updates are cached and transmitted simultaneously.

◆ All types of cursors, including forward only, key set, dynamic, and static.

◆ Server-side stored procedures, which can greatly improve application proficiency.

◆ Queries that return multiple record sets.

◆ Query goals, including limits on the number of records returned, active filtering of the records returned, and prepared statements.

Visual Database Tools

Visual Basic 6 includes support for several visually oriented database management tools, including Visual Data Manager, shown in Figure 1-2. Visual Data Manager can access server-side databases, including Microsoft SQL Server and Oracle, which provides the capability to create and change database tables, views, and queries, and to modify table column data types.

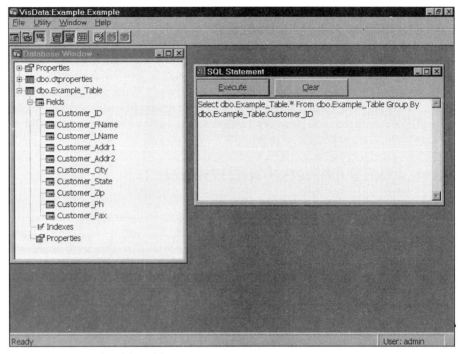

Figure 1-2: Using Visual Data Manager

Data Binding

Data binding to controls enables Visual Basic Controls to interact directly with data sources. Data-bound controls enable you to create and deploy data access applications quickly, with minimal programming. Visual Basic 6 has enhanced the data binding methodology, including the capability to bind controls to both ODBC and OLE DB data sources, and the capability to bind controls at run time (rather than at design time). Figure 1-3 illustrates the use of data-bound controls.

Data Report Control

Visual Basic 6 includes an integrated report design application. The Data Report control, shown in Figure 1-4, can create reports using numerous tables from any relational database. The Data Report control can access any OLE DB or ODBC data source. The primary features of the Data Report control include:

◆ Complete field drag-and-drop functionality during the design of your report.

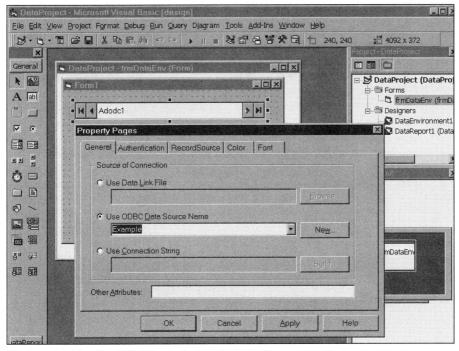

Figure 1-3: Using the ADO Data control while designing your application

- ◆ A complete set of dedicated report controls, including labels, shapes, list boxes, text boxes, lines, and images.

- ◆ The capability to preview a report on-screen before it's sent to the printer.

- ◆ The capability to print reports exactly as they appear on your screen.

- ◆ The capability to export reports into HTML (Hypertext Markup Language) and Text formats.

- ◆ The capability to print and export reports as independent tasks.

Data View Window

The Data View window, shown in Figure 1-5, enables you to view and manage the database to which you are connected. You can view and change database tables, views, and stored procedures for any database to which you have established a connection.

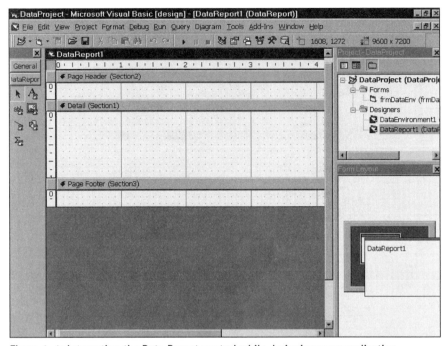

Figure 1-4: Integrating the Data Report control while designing your application

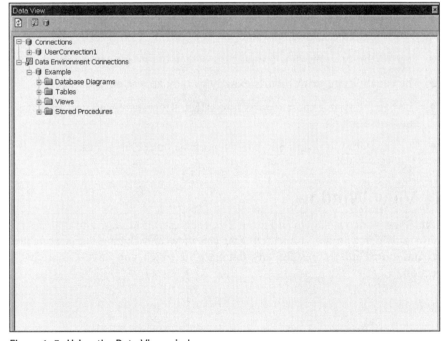

Figure 1-5: Using the Data View window

SQL Editor

SQL Editor, shown in Figure 1-6, enables you to add and modify stored procedures in your SQL Server and Oracle databases. Stored procedures are routines that manipulate the databases that are run directly on your database server. SQL Editor also enables you to create and modify database *triggers*, which are stored procedures that are automatically fired by your database manager whenever a specified event occurs (for example, the addition or deletion of a row in a table).

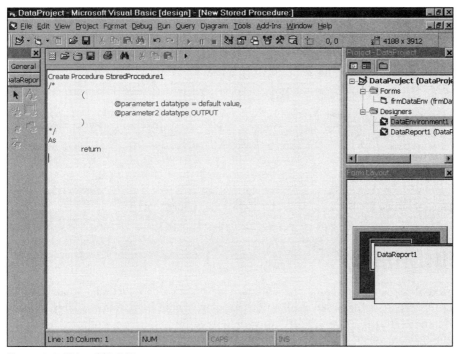

Figure 1-6: Using SQL Editor

Microsoft Developer Network

The Microsoft Developer Network (MSDN), shown in Figure 1-7, is included with the Professional and Enterprise editions of Visual Basic. MSDN provides a complete reference tool for all products that are included in the Visual Studio application-development suite (which includes Visual C++, Visual Basic, Visual InterDev, Visual FoxPro, and Visual J++). In addition to providing complete online documentation for all Visual Studio products, MSDN includes the complete Windows API documentation, Knowledge Base articles, technical articles, periodicals, and conference papers. MSDN is truly your one-stop information shopping source for all of your application-development needs.

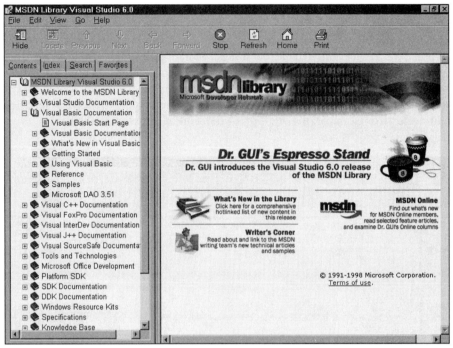

Figure 1–7: Using the Microsoft Developer Network reference tool

Summary

Visual Basic 6 has become the standard of choice for developers that need to develop client/server-based applications quickly. Visual Basic 6 is available in three different editions, each oriented toward a specific set of development environments. Visual Basic 6 provides numerous new tools to speed the development of data-access-oriented applications, including: support for the newest ADO and OLE DB data access models and the Data Environment tool, a visually based tool that enables you to create and manipulate ADO connections and commands.

The next two chapters in this overview section discuss the basic issues involved in the development and design of client/server applications using Visual Basic 6, including a detailed review of the data access programming interfaces that are available.

Chapter 2

Understanding Client/Server Architecture

IN THIS CHAPTER

◆ Understanding how the client/server architecture works

◆ Breaking down the client and server processes

◆ Reviewing multitiered architectures

◆ Asking the right questions before developing your own client/server applications

VISUAL BASIC 6 IS A KEY component to developing client/server-based data access applications. If you're new to developing data access applications, or new to developing applications that access a database server, this chapter introduces the basic concepts of client/server computing. Client/server computing has two distinct types of architectures — two-tier- and three-tier-based. This chapter explains both types of architectures and shows you how to design the client/server environment that's right for your application and company infrastructure. If you are already familiar with client/server computing, you may choose to jump ahead to Chapter 3, in which the Visual Basic 6 data access libraries are introduced.

Understanding the Architecture

Client/server computing is the logical extension of modular programming. Modular-based programming assumes that the separation of a large piece of software into its constituent parts, or *modules*, creates easier development and better maintainability. Client/server computing takes modular-based programming a step farther by recognizing that the modules don't all need to be executed within the same memory space. With this architecture, the calling module becomes the *client* (which requests a service), and the called module becomes the *server* (which provides the service).

The logical extension of client/server computing is to have clients and servers running on the appropriate hardware and software platforms for their functions. This includes database management system (DBMS) servers that run on platforms specially designed and configured to perform queries, or file servers that run on platforms with special elements for managing files.

The basic characteristics of client/server architectures are the following:

◆ Combination of a client (or *front-end* portion) that interacts with the user, and a server (or *back-end* portion) that interacts with the shared resource. The client process contains solution-specific logic and provides the interface between the user and the rest of the application system. The server process acts as a software engine that manages shared resources, such as databases, printers, modems, or high-powered processors.

◆ The front-end task and back-end task have fundamentally different requirements for computing resources, such as processor speeds, memory, disk speeds and capacities, and input/output devices.

◆ The environment is typically heterogeneous and multivendor. The hardware platform and operating system of client and server are not usually the same. Client and server processes communicate through a well-defined set of standard *application program interfaces* (APIs).

◆ An important characteristic of client/server systems is *scalability*. They can be scaled horizontally or vertically. *Horizontal scaling* means to add or remove client workstations with only a slight performance impact. *Vertical scaling* means to migrate to a larger and faster server machine or multiple servers.

Client Processes

The *client* is a process (program) that sends a message to a server process (program), requesting that the server perform a task (service). Client programs usually manage the user-interface portion of the application, validate data entered by the user, dispatch requests to server programs, and sometimes execute business logic. The client-based process is the front end of the application that the user sees and interacts with. The client process contains solution-specific logic and provides the interface between the user and the rest of the application system. The client process also manages the local resources that the user interacts with, such as the monitor, keyboard, workstation CPU, and peripherals. One of the key elements of a client workstation is the *graphical user interface* (GUI), which – normally as part of the operating system – detects user actions, manages the windows on the display, and displays the data in the windows.

Server Processes

A *server* is a process (program) that fulfills the client request by performing the task requested. Server programs generally receive requests from client programs, execute database retrievals and updates, manage data integrity, and dispatch responses to client requests. Sometimes, server programs execute common or complex business logic. The server-based process "may" run on another machine on the network. This server could be the host operating system or network file server; the server is then provided both file system services and application services. Or, in some cases, another desktop machine provides the application services. The server process acts as a software engine that manages shared resources, such as databases, printers, communication links, or high-powered processors. The server process performs the back-end tasks that are common to similar applications.

Two-Tiered Client/Server Architecture

The architecture and technology that evolved to answer application processing demands is the client/server architecture, in the guise of a two-tiered approach. By replacing the file server with a true database server, the network can respond to client requests simply by providing the answer to a query processed against a relational database server (rather than the entire file). One benefit to this approach, then, is to reduce network traffic significantly. Also, with a real database server, true multiuser updating is easily available to users on the network. This two-tiered approach has been widely implemented in many corporations.

In a two-tiered client/server architecture, as shown in Figure 2-1, remote calls or SQL commands typically are used to communicate between the client and server. The server likely supports stored procedures and triggers. Stored procedures enable the server to be programmed to implement business rules that are better suited to run on the server than on the client, resulting in a much more efficient overall system.

Since the early '90s, software vendors have developed and brought to market many toolsets to simplify development of applications for the two-tiered client/server architecture – such as Visual Basic, which has been, and continues to be, one of the leading development tools in this market. These modern, powerful tools, combined with literally millions of developers who know how to use them, means that the two-tiered client/server approach is a good and economical solution for certain classes of problems.

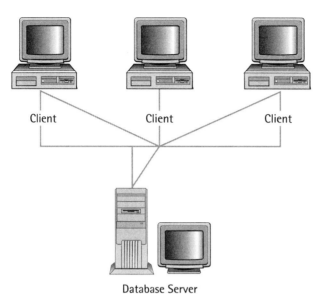

Database Server

Figure 2-1: The two-tiered client/server architecture

The two-tiered client/server architecture has proven to be very effective in solving workgroup problems. *Workgroup*, as used here, is loosely defined as 12 to 100 people interacting on a local area network (LAN). For bigger, enterprise-class problems or applications that are distributed over a wide area network (WAN), use of this two-tiered approach has generated some problems – which have been solved with three-tiered approaches.

Three-Tiered Client/Server Architecture

Typically, in a large enterprise environment with a client/server architecture, the performance of a two-tiered architecture deteriorates as the number of online users increases, due to the connection process of the database server. The database server needs to maintain a thread for each client that is connected to the server. Even when no work is being done, the client and server continuously exchange "keep alive" messages. If something happens to the connection, the client must go through a session reinitiating process. With 50 clients and current typical PC hardware, this process is hardly noticeable. With 2,000 or more clients on a single server, however, the resulting performance isn't likely to be satisfactory.

The data language used to implement server procedures in SQL server-type DBMSs is proprietary to each vendor. Microsoft, Oracle, Sybase, Informix, and IBM, for example, have implemented different language extensions for these functions. Proprietary approaches are fine from a performance point of view, but are a disadvantage for users who want to maintain flexibility and choice in which database server to use with their applications.

Another problem with the two-tiered approach is that current implementations provide no flexibility in "after-the-fact partitioning." After an application is already developed, splitting some of the program functionality from one server to another isn't easy, and requires manually regenerating procedural code. In some of the newer three-tiered approaches, tools offer the capability to drag and drop application code modules onto different computers.

The industry has responded to limitations in the two-tiered architecture by adding a third, middle tier between the client and the database server. This middle layer can perform numerous different functions – queuing, application execution, database staging, and so forth. The use of client/server technology with such a middle layer has proven to offer considerably more performance and flexibility than a two-tiered approach.

One advantage of a middle layer is that, if the middle tier can provide queuing, the synchronous process of the two-tiered approach becomes asynchronous. In other words, the client can deliver its request to the middle layer, disengage, and be assured that a proper response will be forthcoming. In addition, the middle layer adds scheduling and prioritization for the work in process. The use of an architecture with such a middle layer is called *three-tiered* or *multitiered*. These two terms are largely synonymous in this context.

However, the price for this added flexibility and performance is a development environment that is considerably more difficult to use than the very visually oriented development of two-tiered applications.

TRANSACTION PROCESSING MONITOR

The most basic type of middle layer (and the oldest, with the concept of mainframes dating from the early 1970s) is the *transaction processing monitor* (TP monitor), shown in Figure 2-2. You may think of a TP monitor as a kind of message queuing service. The client connects to the TP monitor instead of the database server. The transaction is accepted by the monitor, which queues it and then takes responsibility for managing it to correct completion.

TP monitors first became popular in the 1970s, on mainframes. Online access to mainframes was available through one of two implementations – time sharing or online transaction processing (OLTP). Time sharing was used for program development, and the computer's resources were allocated with a simple scheduling algorithm, such as round robin. OLTP scheduling was more sophisticated and priority-driven. TP monitors were almost always used in this environment, and the most popular of these TP monitors was IBM's CICS (Customer Information Control System).

As client/server applications gained popularity over the early 1990s, the use of TP monitors declined, principally because many of the services provided by a TP monitor were available as part of the database server. The TP services embedded in the database were suitable for use only with a relatively small number of clients connected.

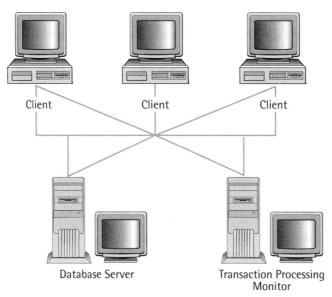

Figure 2-2: A three-tiered client/server architecture using a
transaction processing monitor

Full-service TP monitors have staged a comeback, because their queuing engines provide a funneling effect, thus reducing the number of threads that a database server needs to maintain. The client connects with the monitor, which accepts the message and queues it for processing against the database. After the monitor accepts the message, the client can be released for further processing. The synchronous session-based computing of a two-tiered architecture becomes asynchronous through the insertion of the TP monitor into the equation. The monitor smoothes out and lowers the overhead of accessing the database server.

Some other key services that a monitor provides are the following:

◆ The capability to update multiple database servers in a single transaction

◆ Connectivity to a variety of data sources, including flat files,
  a nonrelational database server, and the mainframe

◆ The capability to attach priorities to transactions

◆ Robust security

The net result of using a three-tiered client/server architecture with a TP monitor is that the resulting environment is much more scaleable than a two-tiered approach with a direct client-to-server connection. For really large (for example, 1,000 users) applications, a TP monitor is one of the most effective solutions.

However, network-based TP monitors have a downside. Currently, the major problem with using this approach is that the code to implement TP monitors is usually written in a lower-level language.

MESSAGE SERVER

Messaging provides still another technology to implement three-tiered computing, as shown in Figure 2-3. You can think of a messaging server as a kind of "second-generation" TP monitor, providing the same funneling process. Messages are processed asynchronously with the appropriate priority level, and, like a TP monitor, a messaging server provides connectivity to data sources other than database servers. The architecture of an application that uses messaging services looks similar to an approach that depends on distributed objects and object request brokers (ORBs) for communication.

A *message* is a self-contained object that carries information about what it is, where it needs to go, and what should happen when it reaches its destination. At least two parts exist to every message: the *header* contains the priority, address, and an ID number; the *body* contains the information being sent, which can include text, images, and transactions.

A primary difference between a message-server architecture and a TP-monitor environment is that the former is designed around intelligence in the message itself, and the latter places the system intelligence in the monitor or the process logic of the application server.

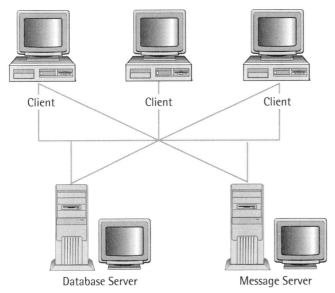

Figure 2-3: A three-tiered client/server architecture using a message server

In a TP-monitor environment, the transactions are simply dumb packets of data that travel over a preexisting and predefined connection to the TP monitor. The TP monitor interrogates and processes the transaction, usually submitting the request to a server-tier application. If the TP monitor doesn't understand the data, the data doesn't get processed. Ultimately, the TP monitor needs to know as much about the transaction as the server tier does.

By contrast, in a message-based architecture, intelligence is contained in the message itself. The message server becomes a container of messages and their stored procedures. The operations performed by the message server on the message are communications-related (for example, encrypt messages sent over one service and decrypt messages sent over another service). Generally, messages are treated as discrete objects. The message contains all the information needed to traverse network services. Because the message contains the intelligence, the middle tier of a message-based system is more flexible than a TP monitor. For one kind of message, the middle tier may simply serve as a routing point between two kinds of network services. For another kind of message, the middle tier may execute a stored procedure or business rule, as directed by the message. This abstraction of the middle tier away from the contents and behavior of the information flowing through it makes the system more portable to different environments and networks. The specifics of communicating the information are hidden underneath the messaging service.

Messaging systems are designed for robustness. By using store-and-forward logic, messaging systems provide message delivery after and around failures. They also provide independence from the enabling technologies, such as wired or wireless technologies or protocols. They don't require a persistent connection between the client and server. Because messaging systems support an emerging wireless infrastructure, they should become popular for supporting mobile and, occasionally, connected workers.

APPLICATION SERVER

When discussing a *three-tiered architecture*, most people usually are referring to applications servers, as shown in Figure 2-4. With this approach, most of the application's business logic is moved from the client into a common, shared host server. The client is used for presentation services – not unlike the role that a terminal plays on a mainframe. For this reason, it is termed a *thin client*.

The application-server approach is similar in overall concept to the X architecture that was developed at MIT in the 1980s. In X, the goal is to allow host-based computing with graphical interfaces on the desktop. The similarity between X and a three-tiered client/server architecture with an application server is that both architectures have the goal of pulling the main body of application logic from the desktop and running it on a shared host. Windows NT, Terminal Server Edition, will bring this type of shared host computing into the Windows computing world.

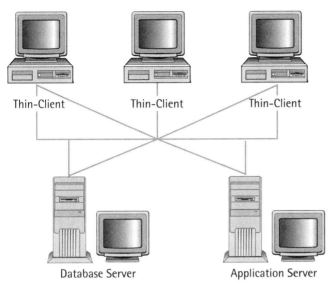

Thin-Client   Thin-Client   Thin-Client

Database Server   Application Server

Figure 2-4: A three-tiered client/server architecture using an application server

The application server is also similar to a mainframe, in that it doesn't need to worry about driving a GUI. Therefore, the application server is a shared business-logic, computation, and data-retrieval engine. The server is very scaleable in terms of performance. As new versions of the application software are developed and released, the installation of that software occurs on one server rather than on hundreds or thousands of clients.

Putting business logic on a server offers several important advantages to the application designer:

◆ Less software on the client means less worry about security, because the important software is on a server, in a more controlled environment.

◆ The resulting application is more scalable with an application server approach. For one thing, servers are far more scalable than PCs.

◆ The support and installation costs of maintaining software on a single server is much less than trying to maintain the same software on hundreds or thousands of PCs.

◆ With a middle application server tier, designing the application to be database server-independent is much easier. Switching to another database server vendor is more achievable with a single multithreaded application than with thousands of applications on clients.

◆ Most new tools for implementing a three-tiered application server approach offer "after-the-fact" application partitioning, which means that code and function modules can be reallocated to new servers after the application has been built. This offers important flexibility and performance benefits.

The major downside to the application-server approach is that the technology is much more difficult to implement than in a two-tiered approach.

DISTRIBUTED COMPONENTS

The next wave of three-tiered approaches, which is just beginning to be used with Internet-based application deployment, is *distributed components*, as shown in Figure 2-5. In this wave, applications are assembled from preexisting components. Vendors who want to create software components need to agree on the software object communication standard. Only two real candidates for such a standard exist: Microsoft's COM and DCOM, and Object Management Group's (OMG) implementations of CORBA and OpenDoc.

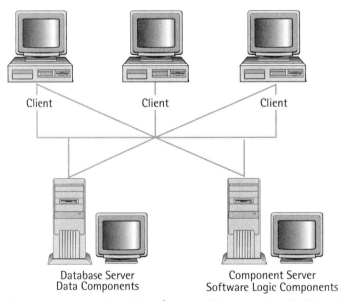

Client   Client   Client

Database Server   Component Server
Data Components   Software Logic Components

Figure 2-5: A three-tiered client/server architecture using distributed components

The distributed object implementation of client/server computing is going to change the way applications are built. Some very interesting advantages should be observed. First, if you need fault-tolerant computing, you could implement copies of objects onto multiple servers. That way, if any servers are down, you can go to another site for service. Second, because distributed objects are self-contained and executable (all data and procedures are present), a systems administrator can tune the performance of the network by moving those objects from overloaded hardware to underutilized computers. This approach is called *tuning through drag and drop*, referring to the method that the administrator uses on a workstation to move the components.

A distributed object architecture should offer other benefits for application developers, such as the following:

◆ The same interface is used to build a desktop, single-location application and a fully distributed application.

◆ The application can be developed and tested locally, ensuring that it will work fine when it's distributed — you depend on the known services of an ORB for distribution.

◆ Because the application developer deals with an ORB for transmission services, technical issues such as queuing, timing, and protocols aren't an issue for the application developer.

THE FUTURE

Client/server architectures are flexible and modular. They can be changed, added to, and evolved in numerous ways. All of the previously described three-tiered approaches can be mixed and matched in various combinations to satisfy almost any computing need. As the Internet becomes a significant factor in computing environments, client/server applications that operate over the Internet will become an important new type of distributed computing. This is probably an understatement, because the use of Internet- and intranet-based applications very soon will dwarf all past distributed computing initiatives.

The Internet will extend the reach and power of client/server computing. Through its promise of widely accepted standards, the Internet will ease and extend client/server computing, both intra- and intercompany. The movement in programming languages to the technology of distributed objects is going to happen fast — because of the Internet.

Client/server still remains the only and best architecture for taking advantage of the Internet and other new technologies that come along. Inevitably, changes will occur, but regardless of what changes take place, client/server computing is likely to remain the underpinning for most computing developments over the next decade.

Asking the Right Questions

Before you begin developing your own client/server applications, you must make the right network and system-design choices to ensure that your application will be suitable for your environment. During the design phase of your project, you might ask the following questions, which will help you create the best application for your needs:

- ◆ What type of architecture and DBMS is right for the performance needs of the application?

- ◆ Will the organization outgrow the architecture too quickly, or is the architecture too complex for the organization's current and future needs?

- ◆ Does the architecture fit the current corporate infrastructure?

- ◆ How many users will be supported by this application? Can the application and architecture handle the load?

- ◆ How should the application be developed? What tools and techniques will be used?

- ◆ Are the tools and techniques known by the developers?

- ◆ How long will developing the application take? How long do we have?

- ◆ If a prototyping approach is used, how will we prove that it will scale to our needs?

- ◆ Does a plan exist to test the application under heavy network loads and with numerous users before it is deployed?

- ◆ Is the application too sophisticated for the current users?

- ◆ Will the users be part of the design and development process? Remember that if they are included, you need to keep them focused on the function of the application and not necessarily on the details of the user interface.

- ◆ Does the design and development strategy fit with the tools and computing environment currently deployed?

- ◆ What new equipment will be required to support this application?

- ◆ How much will the design, development, and equipment cost? Is this in line with projections and budgets?

- ◆ How can the application be scaled to fit the current budgetary needs, but still be prepared for the future?

- ◆ Have you already implemented a similar system successfully? If not, do you know anyone who has?

Summary

Client/server computing is the logical extension of modular programming. Client/server computing furthers the modular approach by recognizing that this modularity can be extended to multiple systems. The basic characteristics of client/server architectures are the following:

◆ A client, or front-end portion, interacts with the user; a server, or back-end portion, interacts with the shared resource.

◆ The front-end task and back-end task have fundamentally different requirements for computing resources.

◆ The environment typically is heterogeneous and multivendor.

◆ The system is scalable.

Three-tiered client/server approaches help to address the scalability of client/server systems, and may be required for the successful deployment of large client/server applications. Now that you have a basic understanding of client/server computing, Chapter 3 introduces the data access methodologies provided by Visual Basic 6.

Chapter 3

Overview of Data Access Methodologies

IN THIS CHAPTER

- ◆ Examining DAO
- ◆ Delving in RDO
- ◆ Exploring ADO
- ◆ Using ODBC and OLE DB
- ◆ Comparing strategies

VISUAL BASIC 6 PROVIDES two different ways to provide data source connectivity in your applications: data-bound controls and data access APIs (Application Programming Interfaces). Data binding to controls allows Visual Basic controls to directly interact with data sources. Data-bound controls enable you to create and deploy data access applications quickly with minimal programming.

 The data-bound controls provided by Visual Basic 6 are reviewed in detail in Part VII of this book.

While data-bound controls can help to get your applications off the ground quickly, they usually aren't sufficient when you're trying to develop more-complex applications. Visual Basic 6 supports three distinct object-oriented data access APIs: *Data Access Objects* (DAO), *Remote Data Objects* (RDO), and *ActiveX Data Objects* (ADO). This chapter introduces these APIs and helps you choose the one that's right for your applications. Parts III, IV, and V explore each methodology in greater detail (these parts treat, respectively, the Data Access Objects API, the Remote Data Objects API, and the ActiveX Data Objects API).

Examining DAO

DAO, sometimes referred to as the *Jet Database Engine*, is a set of Dynamic Link Libraries (DLLs) that forms the core of the database engine.

Architecture Levels

The DAO application architecture has three levels, as shown in Figure 3-1.

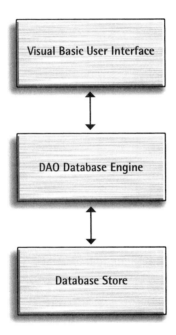

Figure 3-1: DAO application architecture

   The *User Interface* is developed by using Visual Basic; this contains all the necessary components for the user to interact with the database. The Jet Database Engine is provided by DAO; this provides the mechanisms to interact with the database. The *Database Store* is essentially the data repository, which simply stores the data that the application uses, in a form that the Database Engine can manipulate. The Database Store can be various different database types.

   The Database Store can be either local or remote when you use DAO. In the *local* setup, all the components of the DAO application architecture reside on the same computer, as shown in Figure 3-2.

CLIENT

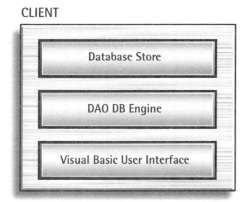

Figure 3-2: A local DAO application configuration

A *remote* Database Store has two further distinct configurations: a client/server database and a remote database. In a *client/server* configuration, the Database Engine and Database Store reside on the same server computer, while the User Interface resides on the client computer, as shown in Figure 3-3. The server computer can manage multiple client applications simultaneously.

SERVER

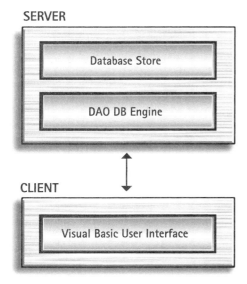

Figure 3-3: A client/server DAO application configuration

In a Remote database application configuration, the Database Store resides on a remote server computer, while the User Interface and the Database Engine reside on the same client computer, as shown in Figure 3-4. In this configuration, the server computer simply manages access to the Database Store files.

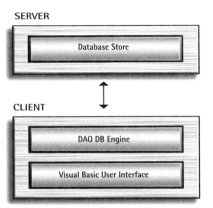

Figure 3-4: A remote DAO application configuration

A true client/server database engine simply serves as a communication layer between the database and the application. The DAO Database Engine is not a true client/server database engine. Each application that is developed by using DAO requires a local copy of the DAO DLL files to access the database, even if the application is running multiple client computers. However, you can use DAO to create client/server applications by connecting to Open Database Connectivity (ODBC) database sources.

The DAO classes are organized in a hierarchy, which is illustrated in Figure 3-5.

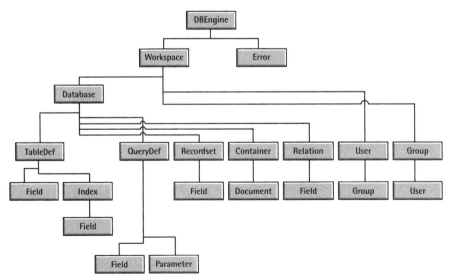

Figure 3-5: The DAO class hierarchy

Database Types

DAO can access data from several different database stores:

- ◆ Native DAO databases – Microsoft Access
- ◆ ODBC databases, which include Microsoft SQL Server, Oracle, Sybase, or any other client/server database that provides ODBC drivers
- ◆ FoxPro Versions 2.0, 2.5, and 2.6
- ◆ dBase III, IV, and V
- ◆ Paradox Versions 3.*x*, 4.*x*, and 5.*x*
- ◆ Btrieve Version 5.1.*x*
- ◆ Lotus spreadsheets
- ◆ Excel worksheets
- ◆ Text files

When DAO operates in its native mode, it creates databases that are directly accessible by Microsoft Access. Three ways exist to connect to external databases, which include opening the database directly, attaching the external database to a DAO native database, and creating queries that contain external database linkage information.

 Each DAO object is reviewed in detail in Part III, which discusses the Data Access Objects API.

Each of the database sources intrinsically provide different levels of security, performance, and requirements. The main concept of DAO is to abstract the application programmer from details of each database source and present a consistent API to the programmer.

JET DATA SOURCES

Jet-type database sources include those created by using the DAO API, Microsoft Access, and Microsoft Excel 5.0. Jet-type databases provide security methodologies, multiuser support, database replication, and methodologies to help ensure referential integrity.

INSTALLABLE INDEX SEQUENTIAL ACCESS METHOD (ISAM) DATA SOURCES

Using the ISAM access methodology of the DAO Database Engine can access Btrieve, dBase, Excel, FoxPro, Lotus, Paradox, and text files. The DAO abstracts the API requirements of each of these database sources from the applications programmer and presents a consistent API through the use of the DAO class objects.

ODBC DATA SOURCES

Using the ODBC access methodology, the DAO Database Engine can access client/server databases. ODBC databases can be accessed directly or connected to native Jet databases. Any client/server database that provides standard ODBC drivers can be accessed from DAO; these include Oracle, Sybase, and SQL Server.

Part II covers the special issues of designing and accessing client/server ODBC Database Stores.

Delving into RDO

RDO provides a set of objects that assists in the development of client/server applications by addressing their unique requirements. Unlike DAO, which provides an interface to the Jet Database Engine, RDO provides an object-oriented layer of abstraction that directly interfaces with the ODBC API. RDO uses the ODBC API and the database server drivers to create database server connections, create queries and cursors to navigate the resulting data sets, and execute complex procedures that rely on the database server for the majority of the processing requirements. Unlike DAO, which utilizes the Jet Database Engine for query preprocessing and connection management, RDO directly interfaces to the database server. This makes RDO particularly suited to client/server application development. Figure 3-6 illustrates the RDO class hierarchy.

RDO can interface with the server-side database at a lower level than DAO, as shown in Figure 3-7. RDO provides a thinly layered interface over the ODBC API. Unlike DAO, which routes all database access through the Jet Database Engine, RDO directly interfaces with the ODBC.

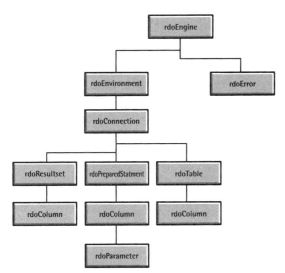

Figure 3-6: The RDO class hierarchy

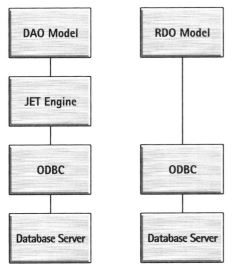

Figure 3-7: The layers of database connections
in the DAO and RDO models

DAO and RDO function pretty much in the same manner, though, enabling an application to connect to a database, submit a query, create a resulting data set or cursor, and manipulate the resulting data set. Both RDO and DAO provide access to server-side database views, stored procedures, and transaction management. The biggest difference in both database access models is in the details of how these tasks are accomplished.

The RDO database isn't designed for ISAM database access, which means that you shouldn't use the RDO database model to access dBase, FoxBase, or Paradox database sources. The RDO model is designed to access database server data sources, including Oracle, Sybase, and SQL Server database servers.

The RDO model utilizes more standard relational database terminology. In RDO, *fields* are referred to as *columns,* and *records* as *rows*.

The RDO model doesn't support any direct methods to perform database schema modification. The DAO model does enable an application to create and modify tables and indexes directly, through DAO methods. Previously, DAO supported database schema manipulation through SQL, which is the only methodology currently supported by RDO. Unlike DAO, however, new databases can't be created through the RDO interface. You must consult your database-server documentation for more information regarding the creation of a database and the manipulation of the database schema.

Because RDO isn't designed to support ISAM databases, heterogeneous database joins can't be performed, which means that, unlike with DAO, tables can't be joined from a Paradox database and an SQL Server database. When you use DAO, you can attach a table to an ISAM database source and work with both database sources as if they are one; this isn't possible with RDO.

RDO is supported only on 32-bit Windows environments (Windows 95 and Windows NT). DAO is supported on both 16-bit and 32-bit Windows environments.

RDO attempts to address the unique processing requirements of client/server applications in the following ways:

♦ **Faster data access** – Because RDO interfaces directly to the ODBC API, RDO can retrieve and manipulate data much more quickly than DAO. RDO relies on the processing power of the database server to perform complex queries and retrieve their results quickly. RDO is designed to utilize high-performance database servers, including Oracle and Sybase, and is especially engineered for optimal performance with SQL Server. Also, because the RDO interface is much smaller than DAO, your applications load much more quickly, providing access to your data faster.

◆ **Query result management** – RDO provides the capability to perform a query that returns several related data sets. RDO also allows the number of rows returned by a query to be limited. This can result in more predictable execution times when you access very complex queries. To utilize the row limitation option, the back-end database server must support it.

◆ **Stored procedure input parameter and output management** – RDO provides improved access to stored database server procedures. Output parameters are used to access the results of singleton queries and the results of administrative functions. Output parameters are also used to determine the execution results of a stored procedure.

◆ **Cursor utilization** – RDO supports the utilization of server-side cursors, which can greatly enhance application performance and reduce the resource requirements for the client workstation.

◆ **Asynchronous query execution** – When you process long-running query operations with DAO, your application is blocked from running any other queries or database operations until the initial query is complete. RDO provides an asynchronous query option that can be set before a query is executed. This allows a query to be processed in the background. RDO also provides a method to cancel an asynchronous query operation.

◆ **Batch query access** – RDO supports the execution of a batched set of queries that can return one or more resulting data sets. This can help to improve database server performance by reducing the number of query requests that need to be processed.

◆ **Direct access to the ODBC API** – RDO provides direct access to the ODBC API, including environment, connection, and statement handles. This provides access to the database driver and driver manager options.

◆ **Error management** – Database servers can generate a variety of informational errors of low severity that you may choose to ignore. RDO provides the capability to differentiate between low-severity informational errors and fatal errors that affect an operation being processed. RDO can set an error threshold, which determines the levels of errors that should be considered fatal.

◆ **Lower client memory requirements** — RDO interfaces directly with the ODBC API; it doesn't require the overhead of the Jet Database Engine (unlike DAO), resulting in a much smaller interface and lower memory requirements on the client. Also, RDO doesn't use client memory for low-level cursor management (unlike DAO), further decreasing client memory requirements.

Exploring ADO

ActiveX Data Objects (ADO) is another API for developing applications that can access OLE DB data providers. ADO is supported in several different programming languages, including Visual Basic, Visual C++, VBScript, Visual J++, and in Active Server Pages. While using the OLE DB directly provides a very low-level approach to accessing OLE DB providers, ADO provides a higher-level, easier-to-understand mechanism. If you are familiar with the DAO and RDO APIs for application development, ADO will seem very similar. ADO is a combination of the best aspects of DAO and RDO. ADO doesn't rely as heavily on the object hierarchy as DAO and RDO. This means that creating and manipulating ADO objects is much easier, because they can be created and managed directly. ADO is specifically designed for client/server application development, and because ADO can be used from VBScript, it is also well-suited for server-side Web/database integration. Figure 3-8 demonstrates the typical ADO application configuration.

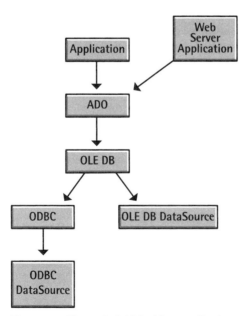

Figure 3-8: The typical ADO object application configuration

The key features of ADO include:

◆ Support for batch updating, in which several record updates are cached and transmitted simultaneously.

◆ Support for all types of cursors, including forward-only, keyset, dynamic, and static cursors.

◆ Support for server-side stored procedures, which can greatly improve application proficiency.

◆ Support for queries that return multiple record sets.

◆ Support for query goals, including limits on the number of records returned, active filtering of the records returned, and prepared statements.

While ADO supports all of these features, they still require the OLE DB provider to be used. By using the OLE DB ODBC provider, ADO can be used to access existing ODBC data sources.

ADO is comprised of the following objects: Command, Connection, Error, Field, Parameter, and Recordset. Figure 3-9 shows the hierarchy of the ADO objects, which do not function in a strict hierarchy, as do the DAO and RDO objects. This makes the ADO much easier to use, because all the ADO objects except for the Error and Field objects, can be created independently. The Command, Error, and Parameter objects are optional.

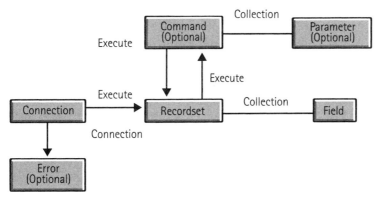

Figure 3-9: The ADO object hierarchy

Using ODBC and OLE DB

The Open Database Connectivity (ODBC) interface is an industry standard and a component of Microsoft Windows Open Services Architecture (WOSA). The ODBC interface enables applications to access data from a variety of database management systems (DBMSs). The ODBC interface permits maximum interoperability – an application can access data in diverse DBMSs through a single interface. Furthermore, that application is independent of any DBMS from which it accesses data. Users of the application can add software components called *drivers*, which create an interface between an application and a specific DBMS.

While the primary focus of ODBC is to provide a consistent interface to database data sources, OLE DB is designed with an even broader goal in mind: to provide a methodology to access data regardless of the data source. OLE DB becomes the data access bridge for documents, e-mail systems, file systems, spreadsheets, Component Object Model (COM) components, and other database sources that utilize ODBC drivers.

An OLE DB implementation is basically comprised of two components: a data provider and a data consumer. A *data provider* is an application that responds to queries and returns data in a usable form. An OLE DB data provider responds to various OLE DB calls to provide the information that it contains in a usable tabular form. For example, a spreadsheet OLE DB provider may allow access to a selection of cells or properties of the sheet, such as the creator, description, and date created.

A *data consumer* is an application or other COM component that utilizes the API of OLE DB to access a data source. A data consumer can be any application that requires access to data. OLE DB allows a data consumer to access the entire range of enterprise data available, regardless of where it is stored.

Comparing Strategies

ADO is very similar to the DAO Library. As the DAO object hierarchy in Figure 3.1 demonstrates, ADO and DAO share many similar objects. Unlike DAO, many of the ADO objects can be created directly, without requiring adherence to the strict object hierarchy. The methods provided by the ADO objects haven't been reviewed yet, but they are very similar to their DAO counterparts.

Although DAO does permit access to ODBC data sources, it actually is optimized for access to Access/Jet database sources. Because ADO utilizes OLE DB providers, ADO is geared more toward heterogeneous data access. ADO has built upon some of the key features of DAO and has added additional support for batch updating, independent object creation, and multithreaded support. If you are familiar with the DAO model, transition to the ADO interface should be fairly easy.

The similarities that exist between ADO and DAO are also apparent between ADO and RDO, but the relationship between ADO and RDO is even stronger. They both are optimized for accessing server-side data sources. As the RDO object hierarchy in Figure 3-6 shows, ADO also shares many similar object types.

Again, unlike RDO, ADO doesn't function in the same strict object hierarchy. They both share the capability to access server-side stored procedures, parameterized queries, support for multiple result sets, and support for server-side cursors. If you are familiar with the RDO model, the transition to ADO should also be fairly easy.

Knowing Which Methodology to Choose

With the number of data access methodologies available for Visual Basic 6, you may be wondering which is the right choice?

- ◆ **DAO** – The first object-oriented interface to expose the Microsoft Jet Database Engine (used by Microsoft Access) and enable Visual Basic developers to connect directly to Access tables – as well as other databases – through ODBC. DAO is best suited for either single-system applications or small, local deployments.

- ◆ **RDO** – An object-oriented data access interface to ODBC that is combined with the easy-to-use style of DAO, providing an interface that exposes virtually all of ODBC's low-level power and flexibility. RDO is limited, though, in that it doesn't access Jet or ISAM databases very well and can access relational databases only through existing ODBC drivers. However, RDO has proven to be the interface of choice for many developers of SQL Server, Oracle, and other large relational databases. RDO provides the objects, properties, and methods needed to access the more complex aspects of stored procedures and complex result sets.

- ◆ **ADO** – The successor to DAO/RDO. Functionally, ADO is very similar to RDO, and the two models generally have a similar mapping. ADO "flattens" the object model that is used by DAO and RDO, meaning that ADO contains fewer objects and more properties, methods (and arguments), and events. For example, ADO has no equivalents to the `rdoEngine` and `rdoEnvironment` objects, which expose the ODBC driver manager. Nor can you currently create ODBC data sources from ADO, despite the fact that your interface might be through the ODBC OLE DB service provider.

Microsoft has positioned ADO as its choice for the future of data access APIs. While that doesn't mean you should rush out and rewrite all of your existing applications that use DAO and RDO to use ADO; instead, you should seriously consider using ADO for any *new* application development. With the number of applications that have been developed using DAO and RDO, you should expect continued support for these models for some time.

ADO isn't automatically code-compatible with your existing data access applications. While ADO encapsulates the *functionality* of DAO and RDO, you must convert many of the language elements to ADO syntax. In some cases, this requires only a simple conversion of some functions of your existing code. In other cases, rewriting the application by using ADO's new features might be best.

Much of the functionality contained in the DAO and RDO models was consolidated into single objects, resulting in a much simpler object model. However, because of this consolidation, you initially might experience some difficulty finding the appropriate ADO object, collection, property, method, or event. Unlike DAO and RDO, although ADO objects are hierarchical, they can also be created outside the scope of the hierarchy.

You should note, however, that ADO currently doesn't support all of DAO's functionality. ADO mostly includes RDO-style functionality to interact with OLE DB data sources, plus remoting and DHTML technology.

Generally, it's probably too early in the evolution of ADO to migrate most DAO applications to ADO, because ADO doesn't currently support DDL, users, groups, and so forth. However, if you use DAO only for client-server applications and don't rely on the Jet Database Engine or use DDL, then you probably can migrate to ADO now. Eventually, Microsoft will provide an ADO DDL component to aid DAO-to-ADO migration and generic DDL support for OLE DB providers.

You can interact directly with the ODBC and OLE DB interfaces, but most Visual Basic applications are written using either DAO, RDO, or ADO. Using OLE DB and ODBC directly generally is reserved for C/C++ applications. Understanding these interfaces does help you get a feel for how data access works at its core.

 See Part VI for the details of using the ODBC API and OLE DB API Visual Basic interfaces.

Summary

Visual Basic 6 provides two different ways to provide data source connectivity in your applications: data bound controls and data access APIs. For the latest news and updates on the Microsoft data access technologies, go to the Web site at `http://www.microsoft.com/data`.

Part II

Design of Client/Server Applications

Chapter 4

Planning Your Application

IN THIS CHAPTER

- ◆ Designing Visual Basic 6 applications

- ◆ Centralizing the logic of your application

- ◆ Introducing data access cursors and buffers

- ◆ Using Rapid Application Development (RAD) techniques in your own applications

- ◆ Learning the seven important elements of using RAD in your development efforts

DESIGNING AND PLANNING your application before you begin actual implementation is important to any successful application-development effort, especially database applications. This chapter explores the general issues related to developing client/server applications by using Microsoft Visual Basic 6, including a key concept relative to using the Visual Basic 6 data access libraries – the use of cursors and buffers. By the end of this chapter, you will have a framework that you can use to design and develop your Visual Basic 6 database applications. As you work through the remainder of the book, make a special note to return to this chapter when you're ready to develop your own applications.

Application Design

If you expect your application-development efforts to be successful, you must begin with a plan. In this case, your plan begins with your application design efforts. Undoubtedly, you'll have numerous questions as you work through the actual implementation of your application. A good application design will help you to answer many of those questions *before* you confront them while coding your application. Because of the visual nature of application development with Visual Basic 6, you easily may perceive the design of your application as just the user interface. Actually, the design of a good database application involves much more than the user interface.

Until you thoroughly understand the data access models provided by Visual Basic 6, all the components that are required for a good application design may be unclear to you. Overall application design techniques are discussed later in this chapter, but this section presents a few basic questions that you should ask yourself before you begin to implement any application project. You may not understand the importance of each of these questions at this point – but as you work through each data access model, their significance will become clear. Likewise, many of these questions may have more than one clear answer. As you explore the data access models in the chapters ahead, I will point out how each data access model also influences your answers. The important design questions that you should ask include the following:

♦ How should connections to your database server be made? Should connections be created when a user first logs on and be kept until they are finished?

♦ Are resources limited? Do you need to manage connections to your database differently?

♦ How should queries and application logic be handled? Should they be built into your application, or centralized by using stored procedures or a transaction manager?

♦ How should data be retrieved? Should you use a buffer or cursor?

♦ Should rows be sorted, searched, and processed on the server, or should these operations be performed in your application after the rows have been retrieved?

♦ How should data be updated? Should you create updatable cursors, use special stored procedures, or use action queries?

♦ What type of multiuser access should you use? Can you lock an entire table while updates are made?

♦ How should your application handle different users having varying levels of access to your system?

♦ Must changes to a database be automatically visible to a user? If so, is the corresponding overhead on the server and workstation justified?

♦ How many users are expected to run your application at any one time? Can your database support enough connections to manage the load? Is enough disk space available on the server? Are any other applications, databases, or users accessing the server?

♦ How should database access security be handled? Should you design a front-end security model, or rely on your database server for security management?

◆ Can your application still be used if your database server is unavailable? Do you have a plan if your database server becomes unavailable while your application is running?

◆ Should your application consider using bound controls?

◆ Do you have a modular design for your application – so that multiple developers can work on it simultaneously?

Centralizing Your Application Logic

A key element in designing and deploying your applications is choosing where to store the logic that drives your application. Visual Basic 6 and its data access models enable you to locate the logic of your application in three places:

◆ **Integrated:** Application logic is contained completely within your Visual Basic application. This is the traditional model, which most developers are used to.

◆ **Stored procedures:** Most server-side databases (including Microsoft SQL Server and Oracle) allow you to create procedures that are stored and executed on the database server itself. This enables you to centralize your application logic on the database server and reuse that same logic in other applications. The use of stored procedures is discussed in conjunction with the coverage of each data access model.

Multitier: In multitier data access applications, you can store components of your applications in a centralized location – typically on a Transaction Server. Again, these components are executed on the Transaction Server, which enables you to centralize your application logic there and reuse that same logic in other applications. These transaction components can be created by using Visual Basic.

Multitier components are discussed in more detail in Part V, "*ActiveX Data Objects API*," and Part VI, "*ODBC API* and *OLE DB API*."

Choosing where to store you application logic may seem to be a complex choice at this point, but as you begin to explore the data access models provided by Visual Basic 6 and the requirements of your own application, this choice will become clearer. This issue, too, is discussed in conjunction with the coverage of each data access model, in the chapters ahead.

Introduction to Cursors and Buffers

If you haven't worked with client/server applications before, you may not know what cursors are or how they function in relation to databases. This section reviews database cursors and buffers, so that when you encounter them relative to each of the data access models, you will understand their purpose. This section also reviews the types of buffers that are supported by the data access models.

A *cursor* is simply a pointer. When you access data from a database, you may retrieve one or more rows. Only one row of this set of data can be accessed at a time – either for reading or updating. If you're using bound controls, such as a grid, you may actually be able to see more than one row at a time. On the other hand, buffers are temporary storage locations. When your application accesses a row of data from your database, it is read into the buffer, where it is available for your application. If you make a change to a row, it is first changed in the buffer, and then changed in the actual database.

The primary differences between the cursor types supported by the data access models are how they handle the rows that are retrieved and how data is sent to the client. A column is a member of a cursor if it is included in the set of rows that is retrieved as the result of a database query, as shown in Figure 4-1.

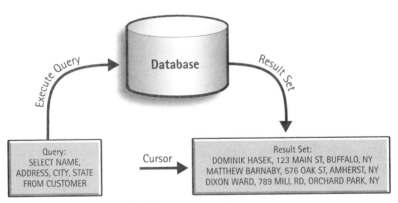

Figure 4-1: Viewing how database cursors work

Types of Cursors

With all the data access models provided by Visual Basic 6, four types of cursors can be used: keyset cursors, snapshot or static cursors, dynamic cursors, and mixed cursors. Each data access model supports cursors slightly differently, but all the data access models provide support for at least two of these basic cursor types. Table 4-1 lists the cursor and buffer types supported by all data access models, and how they apply to each particular data access model.

TABLE 4-1 THE CURSOR AND BUFFER TYPES SUPPORTED
          BY THE DATA ACCESS MODEL

Cursor/Buffer Types	DAO	RDO	ADO	ODBC	OLE DB
Keyset	Yes	Yes	Yes	Yes	Yes
Static	Yes	Yes	Yes	Yes	Yes
Dynamic	No	Yes	Yes	Yes	Yes
Mixed	No	No	Yes	Yes	Yes
Single-row buffer	No	Yes (forward only)	Yes	Yes	Yes
n-row buffer	No	No	No	Yes	Yes

KEYSET CURSORS

A keyset cursor stores a set of keys, which permits a selected row to be retrieved according to the row-specific information stored in those keys, precisely when it is actually required. The keyset cursor requires separate storage for the data in each of the keys that comprise it. This cursor's membership is fixed after the result set is created – this means that if the database changes after the cursor has been created, the changes can't be seen by this type of cursor, until it is recreated.

SNAPSHOT CURSORS

A snapshot or *static* cursor uses the same keyset accessibility as the keyset cursor, but the data retrieved from the database is also stored on the client. After the query runs, the result is buffered on the client, and any rows that are read as the result of the query are read from this buffer. If any changes are made to the database – even to rows that are members of the result set – these changes won't be seen by the client.

DYNAMIC CURSORS

Just like the keyset cursor, a dynamic cursor stores the keys that are required to retrieve the row. Each time that you access a row in the result set, the query is re-executed. This means that you always see the most current data in the database. The downside of using dynamic cursors is performance. They are typically very slow and expensive to implement. If you need access to the most current database data, though, dynamic cursors are the only way to go.

MIXED CURSORS

Mixed cursors are a hybrid of dynamic and keyset cursors. As a result, when a query is executed, the key information is buffered on the client, and that information is subsequently used when accessing the actual data in the database.

Types of Buffers

Two types of buffers are supported by the Visual Basic 6 data access models: single-row buffers and multirow buffers. Multirow buffers are supported only by the lower-level data access models, namely ODBC and OLE DB.

SINGLE-ROW BUFFERS

A single-row buffer is not a cursor, but it functions in the same way that the keyset cursor functions. With a single-row buffer, you can see only one row of a query result set at a time. When using a single-row buffer, data can be viewed in one direction only – as you move forward through the data contained in the result set.

MULTIROW BUFFERS

A multirow buffer expands the vision of a single-row buffer. With multirow buffers, a fixed set of rows from a query result set is retrieved and stored on the client. You can move in any direction through this multirow buffer. Only the low-level data access methodologies, namely ODBC and OLE DB, support multirow buffers.

Rapid Application Development Techniques

Corporate demand for large, highly visible client/server projects is increasing rapidly. Although the size and importance of the applications have grown, the demand for extremely rapid implementation has remained the same. Information Systems (IS) groups face the dilemma of trying to produce key applications quickly while ensuring that the applications fully support the organization's business needs.

Rapid Application Development (RAD) is a platform-independent software development approach that can potentially reduce the time required to deliver high-quality software, and most client/server IS groups claim that they use RAD. When asked how they are doing, however, these groups often describe the best intentions being followed by scenarios of impossible deadlines, hacked code, and stressed-out project teams.

Some organizations report outstanding, repeatable success using RAD for client/server applications. RAD originated in the microcomputer heyday of the mid-1980s – spurred by growing dissatisfaction with mainframe-oriented software development methodologies. These methodologies rigidly scheduled phase after phase of requirements collection, design, development, testing, and finally (sometimes years later), the delivery of the system.

Scott Shultz, a project manager at DuPont, created a new, extremely successful software development methodology that he called *rapid iterative productive prototyping* (RIPP). His idea was to deliver usable pieces of the final system every three to four months, in order of business priority, with each piece building on the last. This approach permitted ongoing feedback from users over the course of the system's development, rather than waiting until the system was complete. In the early 1990s, James Martin coined the acronym RAD and popularized the approach.

RAD relies heavily on a skilled team and software tools to facilitate data modeling, process modeling, prototyping, and code generation. The release of each piece of the system is rigidly scheduled, and careful measurements are recorded for each piece's quality and the effort expended to produce it. Features are added only when they fit into predetermined timeframes.

As client/server computing emerged, RAD was the natural choice for a development methodology. The marriage of client/server computing and RAD brought together the graphical user interface (GUI), quick client-PC computing, the ability to show results almost immediately, and a methodology built on quick deliverables. RAD became a symbol of hope for achieving better, faster, and cheaper results in the client/server environment.

This impression was reinforced by development-tool vendors who promised the capability to create – in half a day – usable, useful applications that might require writing just a few lines of code. Visual Basic 6 is an ideal application-development platform for implementing RAD techniques. It is well-suited to the incremental and multideveloper approach to application development.

Expectations

IS groups have adopted RAD as a superior alternative to traditional application-development methodologies. The RAD approach brings attractive promises:

- ◆ **Fast results:** Usable applications that can be delivered quickly.

- ◆ **Cost control:** With an incremental application due to be delivered on a specific time schedule, costs can be predicted and tightly controlled.

- ◆ **Greater user ownership:** RAD employs specific methods for involving users in the development process. For example, joint-application-design (JAD) sessions, in which users and developers work together to identify requirements and build and review the prototype iterations, are a key element of the RAD approach.

Reality

In the client/server world, the RAD approach often fails to live up to its promise. In application development, interest in RAD has focused almost entirely on speed of delivery – coupled with a willingness to sacrifice structure and methodology – which is probably based on the ease and freedom with which developing "quick and dirty" solutions is possible in the PC environment. Although RAD originated as a way to increase and control quality, it has been evolving into an excuse for eliminating design. The result is often low-quality, unstable, buggy applications that are expensive or nearly impossible to maintain.

A focus on speed alone often produces ad hoc development practices, which lead to applications with little or no consistency in appearance or navigation. This situation increases application difficulty and creates a need for more user training. In the mad dash for the finish line, database design often gets little attention. New databases (*data islands*) are created for every application. These islands seldom represent the enterprise's current information needs and are rarely reusable.

How do successful organizations overcome the challenges presented by client/server RAD to take advantage of its benefits?

Mistakes

The two biggest mistakes made with RAD are to underestimate the difficulty and complexity of RAD client/server projects and to confuse RAD with QADAD (quick and dirty application development).

An organization can't successfully declare a mainframe shop a "RAD shop," buy some tools, and "do RAD." Moving to a RAD methodology is a significant cultural change for most IS groups. Most successful RAD shops have met the challenges of working in a new environment without forgetting or discarding the wisdom and best practices of the past.

Several ways exist in which IS groups can lower the risk of moving to a client/server environment while enjoying the benefits of RAD, which are discussed next.

USE A FLEXIBLE APPROACH

Flexibility and responsiveness are critical success factors in business today. As an organization struggles to respond to changing business demands and new ideas, the IS group must be able to modify software development practices to support the organization's needs. New problems sometimes require solutions that may not fit well into an existing methodology.

RAD offers organizations the opportunity to interact continually with users, to be aware of their evolving business needs, to adjust the course, and to deliver results in two to four months.

DON'T REINVENT THE WHEEL

Use dependable, object-oriented class libraries and components in the RAD proto-typing and development process. Components and class libraries provide a development foundation and embody appropriate development and interface standards. Commercially available class libraries and components vary greatly in quality and style, so choose your class library carefully. It should set a high standard for quality, be easy to learn and use, and employ object-oriented methods.

USE THE RIGHT TOOLS

IS managers often make the shortsighted mistake of "economizing" by limiting software tool purchases. Effective tools can mean the difference between a dynamic, responsive RAD team and a struggling, stressed, ineffective team.

High-quality, "best-of-class" tools should be available for data modeling, process modeling, application development, project management, and automated application testing. Visual Basic 6 is clearly one of these "best-of-class" application-development tools.

BUY INTO STRATEGIC TRAINING AND EXPERTS

Appropriate user training and experience are as important as the tools themselves. An experienced team member can make the RAD process much more effective. If you bring in outside experts, make sure that they act as mentors to the IS staff.

One key to the RAD approach is heavy user involvement in a series of working sessions, which include such activities as developing a conceptual model and reviewing a prototype. RAD requires strong skills in process facilitation and business communications. If you can't find these skills in-house, you should provide training or bring in an experienced facilitator. Too often, IS shops make the same mistake of undervaluing these skills and assigning as facilitator an eager but untrained and inexperienced person. Facilitation is a learned, formal skill.

DESIGN A STRONG DATA MODEL
AND A WELL-DESIGNED DATABASE

Most IS professionals agree that building a sound database is an important investment in the support of enterprise information. The data model and physical database are foundations for current, as well as future, applications.

Under pressure to produce visible results, RAD teams too often neglect database design or eliminate it entirely. They cobble together databases to support the rapid development of a visible, sexy front-end application.

When insufficient attention is paid to database design up front, it becomes a painful recurring task. Every week brings new, significant database changes that require code rewrites. It is not unusual to see client/server projects in which the final testing process produces significant database changes. This is particularly deadly to RAD projects, in which time is critical.

INCLUDE QUALITY ASSURANCE TESTING

Quality assurance (QA) testing is particularly important in the client/server environment. The RAD prototyping approach produces a series of application releases over a short time. Because each release has more features and is more complex than its predecessor, each should be tested for original, as well as new, functionality. However, QA resources may be insufficient to test each release fully. Keep in mind, though, that RAD application releases may be deployed on hundreds or even thousands of desktops. The risk and cost of correcting a bug and redeploying are enormous.

Primarily because of our inability to produce testable software before the end of the development phase, applications developed by using traditional methodologies usually are completed before they are handed to the QA group. With the iterative RAD approach and client/server development tools, you can create functioning, testable parts of your final application fairly quickly and can begin formal QA testing almost simultaneously with the development process. Including QA testing as an integral part of each prototyping cycle may appear to increase project cost, but it is, in fact, a cost-effective strategy.

By including QA testing throughout the project, you have the opportunity to check the direction and progress of your project on a regular, frequent basis. Early course correction is, by far, the easiest and least expensive strategy.

The Seven Cs of RAD

No magic bullets or formulas are available in RAD, and nothing can substitute for planning and continuous improvement. The keys to successful RAD are to find a balance between structure and flexibility, put together a skilled team, and avoid the artificially structured, constrained practices of the traditional methodologies and the free-for-all, "quick and dirty" application-development tendencies in the PC environment.

The following list contains the seven reasons that RAD works for most development efforts, which I like to think of as the seven Cs of RAD:

- ◆ Competition
- ◆ Consistency
- ◆ Coherence
- ◆ Cost
- ◆ Conformity
- ◆ Complexity
- ◆ Cooperation

COMPETITION

Two good reasons to embrace seriously the RAD concept are to respond to competition or beat it to market. Speed of delivery is more important today than it was five years ago, and is not as important today as it will be five years from now.

"Speed" is gaining both momentum and mass as a critical success factor in business information systems (as long as quality doesn't diminish). Momentum comes from the need for increasingly quicker delivery; mass comes from the growing impact (mission-criticality) that rapidly developed applications have on the business.

Speed of delivery also requires smoother and quicker enhancement and maintenance of existing systems. Thus, the procedures and products that are used to develop should also be used integrally to deliver successive iterations.

Heading into the twenty-first century, increasingly more businesses will define their competitive edge in terms of their information systems (applications). Customers will be found, introduced, informed, sold, signed, delivered, surveyed, and serviced via applications. Literally every aspect of the customer relationship will be affected by applications. Clearly, not every application demands a crisis-mode development cycle. But, before you dismiss RAD as "quick and dirty" technology, consider the other reasons for using it – not as a supplement, but as a strategy.

CONSISTENCY

One of the most counterproductive application-development faults has been the failure to integrate languages and utilities into a seamless environment. RAD shouldn't require its practitioners to be fluent in some eclectic variety of programming languages and disconnected utilities. The only consideration should be whether the language-utilities environment can generate an application that works as intended. If it can generate such an application in a single, consistent language, then the development effort is just dollars and days ahead.

Contemporary RAD should have one uniform, consistent language. It should be used in data dictionary management, application management, maintenance, report writing, and ad hoc queries. Simply put, this language should be powerful enough to become a de facto standard.

The benefits of the language standard (providing it is powerful enough) are evident: flexibility, portability, productivity, power (usually with less code), speed of development, and less (and simpler) maintenance.

COHERENCE

One of the signal problems for RAD has been that earlier iterations of the technology automated only isolated phases of the development process. These earlier iterations lacked a coherent, logical, integrated system that took the developer from the design phase completely through the development phase and ultimately to completion of the deployment phase.

The final aspect—application deployment—becomes a bonus, inasmuch as it usually isn't part of conventional definitions of the "full life cycle." Yet, in the client/server world, in which it is necessary to develop applications that can run unmodified on multiple platforms, deployment capabilities are absolutely as valid as any other phase of the life cycle. The considerable advantages of new RAD technology would be completely nullified if separate development efforts were required to construct separate applications for different platforms. Deployment facilities are the solution.

COST

Even with the large number of mainframe, midrange, and PC applications in existence, most businesses—and all medium-sized and large businesses—need to cope with internal software development. They like the customized specificity of home-grown software, but they hate the spiraling cost of in-house-developed applications.

Properly executed, RAD has the potential to put a cap on those costs. Compared to conventional development costs, the savings usually average 25 to 40 percent per application (the costs between concept and delivery), and as much as 50 percent in maintenance and enhancement dollars. This doesn't mean building every application at a frantic pace. It means institutionally using RAD application-development technology to streamline some of the plodding processes that still encumber too many shops. If the end product of a one-year development effort is the same as the end product of a four-month development effort, which one does it make more sense to pay for?

CONFORMITY

In a world in which competing standards hamper, if not doom, the smooth application-development process, some sane conformity is needed. The best answer to conformity is openness.

Any RAD environment is going to suffer (to the point where "RAD" becomes an inappropriate designation) if the development products do not conform to key industry standards and strategically embrace openness. RAD in the client-server era means being able to provide hardware and database independence, links to other application-development tools, and "preintegration" with relevant new technologies that become available.

In short, RAD must eliminate the old excuses that previously slowed and even stopped application development. The reality is inescapable: we live in a heterogeneous world that isn't going to change any time soon. RAD technology that acknowledges that simple truth is the only path toward conformity—and away from chaos.

COMPLEXITY

Until recently, RAD technology has been called inadequate on a number of important counts. The biggest knock was that, while RAD could be used successfully on simple, single-platform PC applications, it was inadequate for the complex, multiplatform systems that typify a client/server environment.

Now, full-functioning application-development environments are emerging that enable RAD to be executed for extremely high-level applications. The key to this new technology is use of the Entity-Relationship (E-R) Model, which, at the application-design level, provides a clear and concise method for describing the data model.

Because the E-R Model has been established as the foundation for client-server, computer-aided software engineering (CASE) and strategic core technologies, such as IBM's Repository, it is instantly and massively relevant. The result is applications that far transcend RAD's old limitations. These applications include such developments as interactive customer information systems, advanced integrated manufacturing systems, and multiuser, multiplatform financial information systems – all in addition to the simpler software requirements for which every business needs to be prepared.

COOPERATION

While the world has long been promised user-friendly Application Development Environments (including some in which the user literally does all the application development), this hasn't happened. Thus, "user involvement" in the development process has taken the form of predevelopment requirement-analysis and postdevelopment review, skipping the vital middle stage of actual development, where user involvement is really needed.

Strategically, user involvement in the middle stage is a key to shortening the development cycle and managing costs. It is axiomatic that changes made to a completed application cost ten times as much as changes made during development. Thus, an ADE that embraces user-developer cooperation at the tactical level is essential.

Today, nontechnical users and business-area analysts can mold the application in-process. Using screen and report painters, they can literally settle on user screens and output before a line of code is written. They can easily and consistently express data (table) relationships, related integrity constraints, and business rules, which become a built-in part of the database. They can intermittently test the work in progress via prototypes, which provides a twofold value: the work is completed sooner, and the resulting application, packed with user-provided specificity, is of greater value.

Summary

This chapter presented the basic design issues that you need to consider when implementing any application – not just Visual Basic database applications. Many of the basic concepts and application design techniques of database applications were presented in this chapter. You should now understand the considerations of where to store your application logic, the basics of cursors and buffers, and how to employ RAD techniques to make your projects more successful. In the next chapter, you learn the first basic steps to accessing your database – establishing a connection using the ODBC and OLE DB models. General error-handling techniques are also reviewed.

Chapter 5

Connecting to Your Database

IN THIS CHAPTER

◆ Employing database security

◆ Creating ODBC data resources

◆ Finding and fixing connection errors

BEFORE YOU CAN BEGIN developing a client/server application with Visual Basic 6, you need to be able to communicate with your database server. This chapter reviews the basic issues involved with connecting to a database server, including security and troubleshooting. A step-by-step guide to creating and managing Open Database Connectivity (ODBC) and Object Linking and Embedding Database (OLE DB) client-side resources is also included.

Database Security

If your database contains important data, then it's worth protecting. Practically all database servers provide security mechanisms that you can employ to protect your data investment. The management of database server security is usually the responsibility of a database administrator. Users can be given varying levels of permissions to access various portions of a database, from a single table to a set of columns in a table.

Server-side database security is maintained primarily through the typical username and password mechanism. A full review of the user-management features of all server-side databases is beyond the scope of this book. You should consult your database-server documentation for more information on how to set up user accounts and grant permissions. This chapter does provide a brief discussion of how to manage users who are using Microsoft SQL Server 7.

Microsoft SQL Server User Management

Microsoft SQL Server provides an integrated Enterprise Manager, shown in Figure 5-1, which helps to manage all aspects of SQL Server. SQL Server can use either Windows NT integrated domain security or its own standalone security. I recommend using the Windows NT integrated domain security when you use SQL Server. With integrated domain security, after a user logs in to the Windows NT domain that contains SQL Server, they can access SQL Server services, without being required to enter yet another username and password.

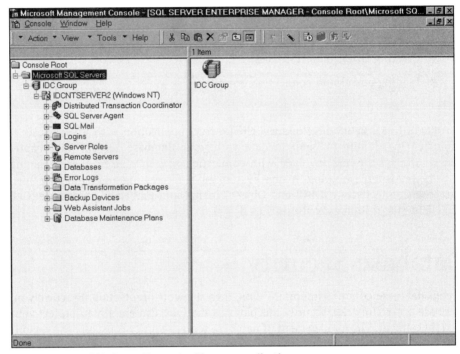

Figure 5-1: The SQL Server Enterprise Manager application

You add a new user in SQL Server 7 via the following steps:

1. From the SQL Server Enterprise Manager console, open your SQL Server group by double-clicking it.

2. Open the SQL Server that you want to manage by double-clicking it.

3. Open the Logins folder by double-clicking it.

4. To add a new user, choose Action → New Login.

5. The SQL Server Login Properties – New Login dialog box is displayed, as shown in Figure 5-2.

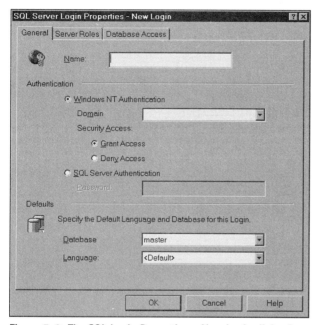

Figure 5-2: The SQL Login Properties – New Login dialog box

6. Enter the name, authentication, and default database for the user. If you select Windows NT Authentication, the name should be the same as an existing domain username.

7. If this new user is allowed to access additional databases, click the Database Access tab, to display the dialog box shown in Figure 5-3.

8. Click the Permit radio box in the database list box for each database that this user is permitted to access.

9. Click OK to complete the addition of this new user to your SQL 7 database server.

Figure 5-3: The SQL Login Properties – New Login dialog box,
Database Access tab view

Oracle Security

Oracle provides a command-line interface in the SQL*Plus application that enables
you to create tables and users. The SQL*Plus application uses standard SQL commands to create tables and users.

Chapter 6, *Creating Queries*, introduces the SQL language.

Oracle provides security at three levels: the Server, Database, and Object levels.
At the Server level, Oracle requires a username and password, before a connection
can be established. At the Database level, Oracle ensures that a user is allowed to
access a particular database. At the Object level, Oracle controls access to database
objects, such as tables and stored procedures.

Oracle also provides the capability to create groups (a *group* is a collection of
users) and apply database object permissions at a group level, which quickly gives
a group of users access to an object.

Creating ODBC Resources

Before a client can access a database server by using an ODBC method, you must configure an ODBC resource to be used by your application. This section walks you through the process of installing and configuring an ODBC resource for your application.

 Before you configure an ODBC resource for your database server, you must make sure that you install the client utilities for your database server. Consult your database-server documentation for more information on how to install the client utilities.

To configure an ODBC resource on a client computer, follow these steps:

1. Access the ODBC applet from the Control Panel, to display the ODBC Data Source Administrator dialog box, shown in Figure 5-4. The ODBC Data Source Administrator dialog box has the following tabs available:

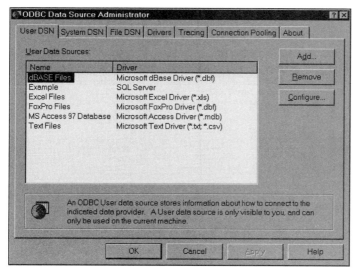

Figure 5-4: The ODBC Data Source Administrator dialog box

- **User DSN (Data Source Name)** – Adds, deletes, or configures a data source that is local to a computer and that may be used only by the current user

- **System DSN** – Adds, deletes, or configures a data source that is local to a computer and that may be used by any user of the computer

- **File DSN** – Adds, deletes, or configures a data source that is stored in a separate file. These files can be shared by users that have the same database drivers installed.

- **Drivers** – Lists the database drivers that are installed on the client computer

- **Tracing** – Helpful when debugging your database application. Traces the ODBC communications between a client and the database server.

- **Connection Pooling** – Allows multiple connections to be reused automatically by various applications. This helps to limit the communication overhead with the database server.

- **About** – Displays the versions of the key ODBC components

2. To set up and configure a System DSN, click the System DSN tab, which displays the dialog box, shown in Figure 5-5.

3. Click the Add button to add a new DSN. The Create New Data Source dialog box, shown in Figure 5-5, is displayed.

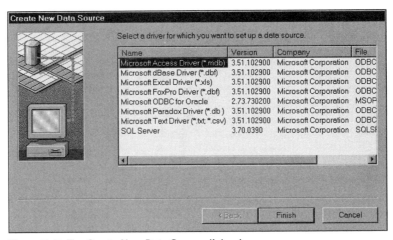

Figure 5-5: The Create New Data Source dialog box

4. Select the database server to which you want to set up an ODBC connection. This example sets up a connection to an SQL Server database. Click the Finish button to continue.

5. The Create a New Data Source to SQL Server dialog box is displayed, as shown in Figure 5-6. Enter the name of the data source, a short

description, and select the name of the database server to which you want to connect. Click the Next button to continue.

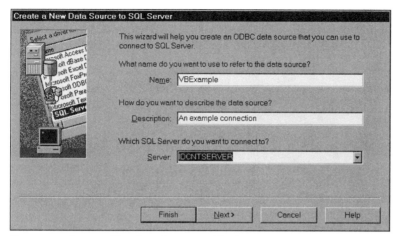

Figure 5-6: Create a New Data Source to SQL Server dialog box

6. The Create a New Data Source to SQL Server – Step 2 dialog box is displayed, as shown in Figure 5-7. Select the authentication mode used by your database server. Click the Next button to continue.

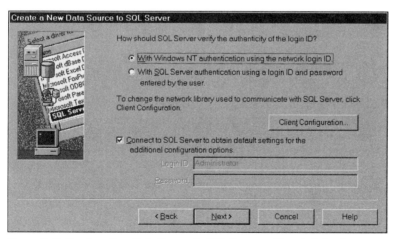

Figure 5-7: Create a New Data Source to SQL Server – Step 2 dialog box

7. The Create a New Data Source to SQL Server – Step 3 dialog box is displayed, as shown in Figure 5-8. To change the default database to connect to, click the Change Default Database To radio button and then select the default database from the drop-down list box. Unless your application has special needs, you should keep the default selections provided for saving stored procedures, quoted identifiers, and NULL handling. Click the Next button to continue.

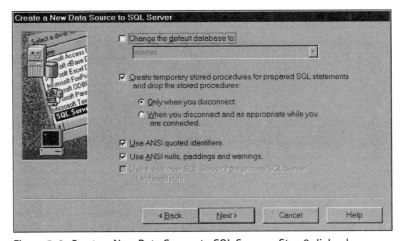

Figure 5-8: Create a New Data Source to SQL Server – Step 3 dialog box

8. The Create a New Data Source to SQL Server – Step 3 dialog box is displayed, as shown in Figure 5-9. If you need to create query logs or keep driver statistics for debugging purposes, click the appropriate radio buttons. Click the Finish button to complete the setup of your data source.

9. The ODBC Microsoft SQL Server Setup dialog box is displayed, as shown in Figure 5-10. Click the Test Data Source button to make sure that you have configured the ODBC DSN correctly. If your connection is configured correctly, the SQL Server ODBC Data Source Test dialog box is displayed, as shown in Figure 5-11. Click OK two times in a row to save your new System DSN. Finally, click OK to close the ODBC Data Source Administrator dialog box.

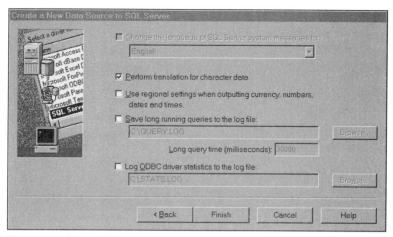

Figure 5-9: Create a New Data Source to SQL Server – Step 4 dialog box

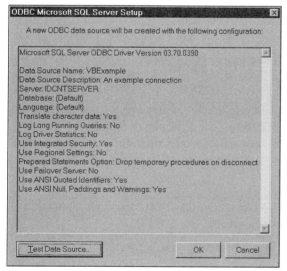

Figure 5-10: The ODBC Microsoft SQL Server Setup dialog box

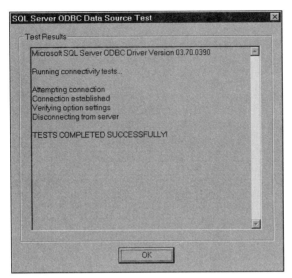

Figure 5-11: The SQL Server ODBC Data Source Test
dialog box

Error Troubleshooting

Undoubtedly, you'll develop a client/server application that eventually has a problem connecting to your database server. Don't worry — this doesn't happen too often, but you should have a bag of tricks available to diagnose potential connection problems. While each data access model provided by Visual Basic 6 handles errors differently, connection troubleshooting typically can be divided into four areas:

◆ **Application errors** — Errors that occur because your application didn't handle or anticipate an error

◆ **Network errors** — Errors related to your network

◆ **Connection and license errors** — Errors caused by the lack of available connections or user licenses on the server

◆ **Logon errors** — Errors related to incorrect database logins

Obviously, you should try to avoid these errors, but that probably isn't possible. Thus, you need strategies to diagnose and solve these errors quickly.

Application Errors

Application errors probably are some of the most typical errors that can occur when communicating with your database. Due to the inherent differences in error handling provided by the various database access strategies in Visual Basic 6, you may sometimes be very confused while trying to figure out what and where things went wrong with your application.

Communicating with your database server is as simple as talking on the telephone; you hardly notice the complex technologies involved until something goes wrong. When something does break down, asking yourself the following questions may be helpful to determine whether the error is related to your application or falls into another area:

- **Did your application connect in the past? What may have changed since that time?** If your application connected recently, something probably has changed since that time. Check to see whether the user has installed or removed any applications recently. You could be missing libraries or other application files. Ask your database administrator whether anything has changed on your database server.

- **What were the exact set of circumstances surrounding the inability to connect?** Re-creating the steps that the user took can help you to determine whether this is an isolated problem or a general application problem. Try to recreate the problem on another computer. If the same thing happens, it's probably an error in your application; otherwise, it may be a configuration error on the user's computer.

- **Did the application process the error or did it crash and burn?** Determine what happened when the error occurred. If the application simply crashed, an unanticipated error may have occurred, which means that it's time to break out your debugging hat and dig into the application.

- **Did the user receive any error messages? What did they say?** If an error message was displayed, it certainly may help lead you in the right direction to solve the problem. Unfortunately, not all error messages lead you in the right direction. Be prepared to step back and take another look at things if you believe that you may be headed down the wrong path.

- **Is the system connected to the network?** While this seems to be one of the most obvious problems, it is the problem that most often is overlooked. Before you break out the source code and start to dig in, make sure that your user can connect and communicate with other network resources.

Network Errors

Errors caused by your network can make connecting to your database server virtually impossible. At times, network errors can look like an application error, because the error message that you receive may be too generic – for example, Unable to Connect. To help determine whether an error is related to your network, ask yourself the following questions:

- ◆ **Can the user log on and access network resources?** If the user can't log on to the network or access other network resources, the user may have failed to log on to the network when starting their computer, the user's computer may not be connected to the LAN, or the user's password or permissions may have changed. Check the network connections and restart the computer to determine whether the user can access the network.

- ◆ **Is the network down? Did the system administrator take down the network for various reasons?** The database server may be down for routine maintenance. Check with your system administrator or another computer to determine whether you can connect to network resources.

- ◆ **Does the user have the proper permissions on the network and at the database server?** Check whether the user has permission to access the database server. The user may be a new user that wasn't set up properly, or the user's authority and responsibilities may have changed.

- ◆ **Is the user running other applications that are connected to the database server?** Typically, clients can't access an infinite number of resources – they usually have a limit on the number of connections that they can support at one time. Try closing other open applications and running the application again.

- ◆ **Has the database server run out of connections?** Again, the database server isn't an infinite resource. Most database servers have a limit on the number of simultaneous user connections they can support. Sometimes, database administrators limit the number of connections, to utilize memory more efficiently on the database server. It may be time to upgrade the number of available connections or database server resources.

Connection and License Errors

Database servers can support many connections, but they are not infinite resources. Database servers can be configured to limit the number of simultaneous connections. Before deploying your application, you should test it on a limited-connection database server to see how it reacts when the maximum number of connections are exceeded. Make sure that your application displays an understandable error message and that it handles this error gracefully.

Also, most database servers are on a per-user basis. When the maximum number of users is reached, no other users can access the database server. User licenses are a separate issue from connections, and are also managed separately. If your database server runs out of user licenses, you will have to purchase additional licenses. Microsoft SQL Server 7 works with the license manager that is built into Windows NT Server. You can access the License applet from the Control Panel, as shown in Figure 5-12.

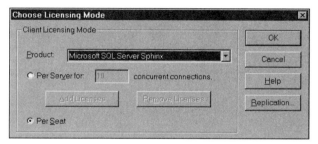

Figure 5-12: The Windows NT Choose Licensing Mode dialog box

Microsoft SQL Server uses per server and per seat license methods:

◆ **Per Server licensing** – Each Client Access License is assigned to your database server and allows one connection to that server for basic network services. You must have at least as many Client Access Licenses dedicated to the database server as the maximum number of client computers that will connect to the database server at any one time. If you select Per Server, you must specify the number of Client Access Licenses for concurrent connections that you have purchased for that server. Per Server often is more economical for networks in which clients tend to connect to only one occasional-use or special-purpose server.

◆ **Per Seat licensing** – Requires a Client Access License for each computer that will access SQL Server for basic network services. After a computer is licensed, it may access any computer that is running SQL Server on the network, at no additional charge. Per Seat often is more economical for networks in which clients tend to connect to more than one database server. If you are unsure of which licensing mode to choose, click Per Server. The license agreement allows you a one-time, one-way option to change from Per Server licensing mode to Per Seat licensing mode.

Logon Errors

Finally, when you connect to a database server, you typically must provide three pieces of information: a username, password, and the name of the server to connect to. If any one of these items is not supplied correctly, you won't be able to connect to your database server. If you decide to code the database server name into your application, be careful – if the name of your database server is changed, which does happen, your application will break. Remember, too, that all the data access models provide error information of one sort or another. While it may seem like a good idea to display this raw information to the user, be warned that this information often can be misleading – especially when you provide incorrect user, password, or database server name information. Beyond knowing that something has gone wrong, users really need to know how they can correct the problem. Make sure that your error messages tell the user how to proceed. This will save you countless hours of troubleshooting.

Summary

Accessing your database server is a task that involves several components, including user access security, creating resources to access your database from your clients, and troubleshooting common errors that can occur when connecting to your database server. This chapter reviewed how to manage and solve these basic tasks, which are a critical component to your client/server applications. Now that you have a greater understanding of how to design your database applications and how to initiate communications with your database server, you're ready to learn how to communicate with your database server, and to access and retrieve data. The next chapter takes a closer look at the Structured Query Language, which is the common dialect used to interact with relational databases.

Chapter 6

Creating Queries

UNDERSTANDING HOW TO retrieve data from your database is essential when you develop database applications. The data access models provided by Visual Basic 6 all utilize the Structured Query Language (SQL) to provide access to data. SQL is a standardized database language that is used to perform data manipulation and definition. The SQL query language is also a key component of almost all server-side databases. This chapter introduces the SQL query language and illustrates how you can use it to retrieve and manage your databases.

Introducing SQL

SQL is a standardized language that enables you to manipulate a database and, more importantly, the data that it contains. SQL was developed in the 1970s; its roots can be traced to E.F. Codd, the inventor of relational databases, and to work performed at IBM during the same period. Since that time, SQL has evolved into *the* standard for manipulating relational database information.

The American National Standards Institute (ANSI) is responsible for defining computer industry standards. Although different relational databases have slightly different versions of SQL, most comply to the ANSI SQL committee standards. The ANSI SQL-89 standard was established in 1989, and most relational databases comply with that standard. In 1992, the ANSI SQL-92 standard was introduced. All the data access models provided by Visual Basic 6 comply to the ANSI SQL-92 standard.

SQL provides two subsets of commands. One subset is used for data manipulation, and the other subset is used for data definition. *Data manipulation* commands facilitate the selection and modification of database data. *Data definition* commands provide the capability to change the database schema (tables, fields, and indices).

SQL Queries — Data Manipulation

The review of the SQL command language begins with the data manipulation command subset. The data manipulation commands are the most frequently used commands in SQL. This overview of SQL will also be applicable in other chapters in which the Visual Basic 6 data access models are discussed.

The intent of this discussion is to present an overview of SQL, not the entire SQL language. This chapter gives you a sufficient understanding of SQL to write most of the SQL commands that your applications require.

 When SQL keywords are utilized, they are presented in all capital letters. This is *not* a requirement of SQL, but it helps you to identify the keywords in the SQL statements that you will write in this chapter.

As the SQL language is discussed in this chapter, assume that you have a database named Customer, which contains tables named Customers, Order Details, and Order, as defined in Tables 6-1, 6-2, and 6-3, respectively.

TABLE 6-1 THE CUSTOMERS TABLE

Field	Type
CustomerID	Long integer
CompanyName	50-character string
ContactFirstName	30-character string
ContactLastName	50-character string
CompanyOrDepartment	50-character string
BillingAddress	255-character string

Field	Type
City	50-character string
StateOrProvince	20-character string
PostalCode	20-character string
Country	50-character string
ContactTitle	50-character string
PhoneNumber	30-character string
Extension	30-character string
FaxNumber	30-character string
EmailAddress	50-character string
Notes	Memo

TABLE 6-2 THE ORDER DETAILS TABLE

Field	Type
OrderDetailID	Long integer
OrderID	Long integer
ProductID	Long integer
DateSold	Date
Quantity	Double
UnitPrice	Currency
Discount	Double
SalePrice	Currency
SalesTax	Currency
LineTotal	Currency

TABLE 6-3 THE ORDER TABLE

Field	Type
OrderID	Long integer
CustomerID	Long integer
Required-byDate	Date
Promised-byDate	Date
ShipName	50-character string
ShipAddress	255-character string
ShipCity	50-character string
ShipState	50-character string
ShipStateOrProvince	50-character string
ShipPostalCode	20-character string
ShipCountry	50-character string
ShipPhoneNumber	30-character string
ShipDate	Date
ShippingMethodID	Long integer
FreightCharge	Currency
SalesTaxRate	Double

SELECT Statement

SELECT statements are used to retrieve subsets of records in the database, and to read data from the database; SELECT statements do not change any data. The most basic SELECT statement has the following form:

SELECT *fields* FROM *table*

in which the *fields* parameter represents the fields of the table that you want to access, and the *table* parameter represents the database table from which you want to access data. The *fields* parameter can be the actual name of each field in your table, separated by commas, or, if you want all the fields contained in the table, you can use the asterisk (*) instead. For example, to retrieve just the `CustomerID` and `CompanyName` fields from a table named `Customer`, the following `SELECT` statement is used:

```
SELECT CustomerID, CompanyName FROM Customer
```

To retrieve all the fields from the table named `Customer`, use the following `SELECT` statement:

```
SELECT * FROM Customer
```

Clauses

A few different clauses can be used in association with your SQL commands. These clauses can specify subsets of data to operate on, change the ordering and grouping of the data, and specify access to external databases. Each of these clauses is reviewed next, to show how they apply to the `SELECT` statement.

WHERE

The `WHERE` clause of a `SELECT` statement limits the set of records that are selected. Whereas the `SELECT` statement can control which fields are retrieved from a table — the `WHERE` clause filters which data is selected from a table. The `WHERE` clause can also be used to join two or more tables.

The `WHERE` clause can be used to filter the records that are selected. A `SELECT` statement with a `WHERE` clause has the following form:

```
SELECT fields FROM table
WHERE field COMPAREOP value {LOGICALOP field COMPAREOP value}...
```

You previously learned how to specify the `fields` and `table` parameters of the `SELECT` statement. The `field` parameter specifies the name of a field, and the `value` parameter specifies the value of the field that you are interested in. The `COMPAREOP` parameter is one of the SQL *comparison* operators, and the `LOGICALOP` parameter is one of the SQL *logical* operators. The portion of the `WHERE` clause that is contained in brackets is an optional expression, or it can be repeated (up to 40 expressions) to create complex `SELECT` statements. Several upcoming examples will make this clearer.

Table 6-4 summarizes the SQL comparison operators, and Table 6-5 summarizes the SQL logical operators. The logical and comparison operators, for the most part, should be familiar to any programmer that has constructed an `IF` statement. In fact, the `WHERE` clause can be thought of as an `IF` statement; after the data is retrieved from the table by the SELECT statement, the WHERE clause tests the actual data values that are retrieved against the logical WHERE clause statement. If the WHERE clause test passes, the record is included in the SELECT subset; otherwise, it is excluded.

TABLE **6-4 THE SQL COMPARISON OPERATORS**

Operator	Usage
=	Equal to
<	Less than
<=	Less than or equal to
>	Greater than
>=	Greater than or equal to
<>	Not equal to
LIKE	Used to match a pattern
BETWEEN...AND	Used to specify a range of values
IN	Used to specify a set of values

TABLE **6-5 THE SQL LOGICAL OPERATORS**

Operator	Usage
AND	Both conditions joined by the AND operator must be true for the WHERE clause to be true
OR	Either condition joined by the OR operator must be true for the WHERE clause to be true
NOT	Logical NOT

Expanding on the earlier example, to retrieve just the CustomerID and CompanyName fields from a table named Customer, in which the StateOrProvince is NY, use the following SELECT statement:

```
SELECT CustomerID, CompanyName FROM Customer
WHERE StateOrProvince = 'NY'
```

When you specify string literals in SQL, you may enclose them in either single quotes (') or double quotes ("). As explained later in this chapter, SQL commands are passed to the data access libraries as strings. Using single quotes, as in the examples, is easier than using double quotes, because double quotes must be specified as " " " in Visual Basic strings.

As illustrated by the previous query, a field included in a WHERE clause doesn't need to be included in the fields that are retrieved. A field in the WHERE clause *must* be a member of the table or tables from which you are retrieving data. You probably are familiar already with how the =, <=, >=, and <> comparison operators work.

The IN, BETWEEN, and LIKE comparison operators are described next. To retrieve all the fields from the Customer table, in which the StateOrProvince is NY, NJ, or CA, the following SELECT statement is used:

```
SELECT * FROM Customer
WHERE StateOrProvince IN ('NY', 'NJ', 'CA')
```

The IN operator requires a set of values to be defined. If the field's value is in the set that is specified, that record will be included in the resulting subset of data.

The BETWEEN operator is used to specify a range of values in which a field's value must fall. To retrieve all the Customer table fields in which the CustomerID is in the range of 1 to 1000, inclusive, use the following SELECT statement:

```
SELECT * FROM Customers
WHERE CustomerID BETWEEN 1 AND 1000
```

The previous two SELECT statements can also be combined to retrieve all the Customer table fields in which the CustomerID is between 1 and 1000, and the StateOrProvince is NY, NJ, or CA; the following SELECT statement is used:

```
SELECT * FROM Customers
WHERE StateOrProvince IN ('NY', 'NJ', 'CA')
AND   CustomerID BETWEEN 1 AND 1000
```

This example illustrates how the WHERE statement expressions can be combined to create complex filters. WHERE expressions are evaluated from left to right; parentheses may be used to control the evaluation order, if necessary.

The LIKE operator can be used in pattern matching. To specify a match to a single character, you use the ?. To specify a match to multiple characters, use the *. This is similar to wildcard matching with the DOS DIR command. Table 6-6 shows which values a sample LIKE statement will match.

TABLE **6-6** EXAMPLE LIKE STATEMENTS

Like Statement	Values Matched	Values Not Matched
LIKE('*A*')	CA, PA, CAN,	NY, NY, JOHN,
	DIANE, MARIE	Diane
LIKE('?A')	CA, PA, WA	MARIE, NY, NJ
LIKE('A?')	AL, AK	NY, NJ, WA

To retrieve all the fields from the `Customer` table in which the `StateOrProvince` begins with an *N*, use the following `SELECT` statement:

```
SELECT * FROM Customers
WHERE StateOrProvince LIKE('N*')
```

Now that you know how to use the `WHERE` clause to filter the data retrieved by the `SELECT` statement, you may proceed by looking at how the `WHERE` clause can be used to link together two or more tables into a single, resulting set of data.

The capability to join together multiple tables is the real power of relational databases. You don't have to worry about the details of how this is accomplished; SQL handles these details for you. A `SELECT` statement that joins together two or more tables has the simplest form:

```
SELECT table1.field1, table2.field2 FROM table1, table2
WHERE  table1.field1 = table2.field2
```

A few new concepts are introduced in this example. First, the `FROM` portion of the `SELECT` statement specifies more than one table. Second, the . operator is introduced in naming fields, as in `table1.field1`. `Field1` is a member of `table1`. If the fields that you are selecting have different names, the . operator isn't required. The . operator makes unique the name of the field that you are selecting. Although the . operator isn't required, it does help when you are creating complex queries. The . operator can also be combined with the * field specifier to retrieve all the fields from a table. The statement `table1.*` would retrieve all the fields from `table1`.

To retrieve from the sample database all of the customer's information, along with an order number for each associated order that the customer has placed, the following `SELECT` statement is used:

```
SELECT Orders.OrderID, Customer.*
```

```
WHERE   Orders.CustomerID = Customer.CustomerID
```

As you learned earlier, you don't need to include the `Orders.CustomerID` field in the set of fields that you are retrieving. You should also note that you *do* need to use the . operator in the example; if you don't, SQL can't determine which `CustomerID` field you're referencing – the one in the `Orders` table or the one in the `Customer` table.

The capability of the `WHERE` clause to filter selected data can be combined with its capability to join two or more tables. To extend the preceding `SELECT` statement to return only the records in which the `OrderID` is between 1 and 2000, use the following `SELECT` statement:

```
SELECT Orders.OrderID, Customers.* FROM Customers, Orders
WHERE   Orders.CustomerID = Customers.CustomerID
AND     Order.OrderID BETWEEN 1 AND 2000
```

Earlier, you learned how to use the `IN` comparison operator to specify a set of data for a field value. You can also create this subset of data for the `IN` operator by using another query. To select all the `Customer` fields that have an order `Promised-byDate` that is after 05/25/99, use the following `SELECT` statement:

```
SELECT Customers.* FROM Customers
WHERE CustomerID IN
        (SELECT Orders.CustomerID FROM Orders
         WHERE   Orders.Promised-byDate > #05/25/99#)
```

In Visual Basic 6, date literals must be enclosed by the pound sign (#), as shown in the preceding code. Also, date literals must be in U.S. format, even if a non-U.S. version of your database access methodology is being used.

As illustrated by this example, two `SELECT` statements are performed: one creates the set of `CustomerID`s from the `Orders` table that has a `Promised-byDate` greater than 05/25/99, and the other uses the results from the first `SELECT` statement, along with the `IN` logical operator, to filter the `Customer` records.

The general format for using subqueries is the following:

```
expression [NOT] IN (subquery)
comparison [ANY | ALL | SOME] (subquery)
[NOT] EXISTS (subquery)
```

This code uses the IN operator. The ANY, ALL, or SOME operators are used, respectively, to match any, all, or some of the fields in the *subquery*. The EXISTS operator checks whether any records are returned by the *subquery*.

AGGREGATE FUNCTIONS

Aggregate functions can be used in SELECT statements to return a result that applies to a group of records. Table 6-7 summarizes the aggregate functions that are available.

TABLE 6-7 SQL AGGREGATE FUNCTIONS

Function	Usage
AVG	Returns the average value of a field
COUNT	Returns the number of records
MAX	Returns the maximum value of a field
MIN	Returns the minimum value of a field
SUM	Returns the sum of the values of a field

To determine the total amount of all the orders in the Order Detail table, use the following SELECT statement:

```
SELECT SUM([Order Detail].LineTotal) FROM [Order Detail]
```

 The [] characters are used to enclose table or field names that contain a space or punctuation.

GROUP BY

The GROUP BY clause combines records with identical field values into a single record. The GROUP BY clause is useful with SQL aggregate functions. To retrieve the total amount of all orders for each CustomerID, you can use the following SELECT statement:

```
SELECT [Order Detail].CustomerID,
       SUM([Order Detail].LineTotal)
FROM   [Order Detail]
```

This SELECT statement works, but it returns duplicate records – one for each order that a customer has placed. The GROUP BY clause eliminates these duplicate records. To use the GROUP BY clause, this SELECT statement is rewritten as follows:

```
SELECT    [Order Detail].CustomerID,
          SUM([Order Detail].LineTotal)
FROM      [Order Detail]
GROUP BY [Order Detail].CustomerID
```

This returns a single record for each CustomerID. Each record will contain the CustomerID and a total of all orders in the Order Detail table for that CustomerID.

HAVING

The HAVING clause is used with the GROUP BY clause to filter the grouped data that results from the GROUP BY clause, in the same way that the WHERE clause filters the data of the SELECT statement. HAVING expressions are constructed in the same manner as WHERE expressions, and both types of expressions are limited to 40 expressions. To retrieve the total amount of all orders exceeding $1000 for each CustomerID, you can use the following SELECT statement:

```
SELECT    [Order Detail].CustomerID,
          SUM([Order Detail].LineTotal) AS TotalAmt
FROM      [Order Detail]
GROUP BY [Order Detail].CustomerID
HAVING    TotalAmt > 1000
```

ORDER BY

The ORDER BY clause is used to sort the SELECT statement resultant set of records. Multiple sort keys can be specified, and records can be sorted in ascending or descending order. To retrieve all the records in the Customer table, sorted by CompanyName in ascending order, use the following SELECT statement:

```
SELECT * FROM Customers
ORDER BY CompanyName ASC
```

To perform the same selection but sorted in descending order, the following SQL statement is used:

```
SELECT * FROM Customers
ORDER BY CompanyName DESC
```

To retrieve all the records in the Customer table, sorted by StateOrProvince in ascending order and then by CompanyName in ascending order, use the following:

```
SELECT * FROM Customers
ORDER BY StateOrProvince, CompanyName ASC
```

If the ordering directive (ASC or DESC) is omitted, the records are sorted in ascending order, by default.

DISTINCT AND DISTINCTROW

The DISTINCT clause is used to remove duplicate records from the resulting data set. To retrieve the unique customer-contact last names from the Customers table, the following SELECT statement is used:

```
SELECT DISTINCT ContactLastName FROM Customers
```

If more than one customer contact has the last name Jones, only one record is included in the resulting subset of data.

The DISTINCTROW clause can be used to select data that is distinct in any of the fields. To retrieve all the nonduplicate records in the Customers table, the following SELECT statement is used:

```
SELECT DISTINCTROW * FROM Customers
```

TOP

The TOP clause is used in conjunction with the ORDER BY clause. With the TOP clause, you can limit to the TOP *n* number of records the number of records that are returned, where *n* is specified in the SELECT statement. To retrieve the top 50 total amounts of all orders for each CustomerID, you can use the following SELECT statement:

```
SELECT   TOP 50 [Order Detail].CustomerID,
               SUM([Order Detail].LineTotal) AS TotalAmt
FROM     [Order Detail]
GROUP BY [Order Detail].CustomerID
ORDER BY TotalAmt
```

The TOP clause can also be used to specify a percent. To perform the same query to return the top 10 percent of total amounts, the following SELECT statement can be used:

```
SELECT   TOP 10 PERCENT [Order Detail].CustomerID,
               SUM([Order Detail].LineTotal)
                     AS TotalAmt
```

```
FROM    [Order Detail]
GROUP BY [Order Detail].CustomerID
ORDER BY TotalAmt
```

JOIN

Creating a join is one of the more powerful functions that can be performed with a relational database. The three types of joins that can be created are summarized in Table 6-8.

TABLE **6-8** THE THREE TYPES OF JOINS

Join Type	Result
INNER JOIN	Records are included in the resulting data set only when the field specified in the first table matches the field specified in the second table.
RIGHT OUTER JOIN	All the records from the second table (the rightmost table in the JOIN clause) are included with the matching records from both tables.
LEFT OUTER JOIN	All the records from the first table (the leftmost table in the JOIN clause) are included with the matching records from both tables.

The JOIN clause is used in the following manner:

```
FROM table1 [LEFT | RIGHT | INNER] JOIN table2
ON table1.field1 = table2.field2
```

Creating an INNER JOIN is the same as creating a join while using the WHERE clause. LEFT and RIGHT joins produce additional records, as specified in Table 6-8.

Earlier in this chapter, the following SELECT statement, which uses the WHERE clause, was used to retrieve all of the customer's information and the order numbers for each order that the customer has placed:

```
SELECT Orders.OrderID, Customers.* FROM Orders, Customers
WHERE  Orders.CustomerID = Customer.CustomerID
```

The same result can be produced by using the following SELECT statement with an INNER JOIN:

```
SELECT  Orders.OrderID, Customers.*
FROM    Orders INNER JOIN Customers
ON      Orders.CustomerID = Customer.CustomerID
```

Now that you have a basic understanding of how to use the SQL language to retrieve data from your databases, the next few sections look at other SQL commands that enable you to modify records in the database.

INSERT INTO

The INSERT INTO command is used to add records to a table. Records can be inserted from the result of another SELECT statement, or single records can be appended by specifying their values. To append records to the Customers table from a similarly structured Customer table, the following SQL statement is used:

```
INSERT INTO Customers
SELECT  CustomerID, CompanyName, ContactFirstName, ContactLastName,
        CompanyOrDepartment, BillingAddress, City, StateOrProvince,
        PostalCode, Country, ContactTitle, PhoneNumber, Extension,
        FaxNumber, EmailAddress
FROM    Customer
```

If any field is omitted from the target of the table insert, it becomes a NULL value. To append a single record to the Customers table, use the following SQL statement:

```
INSERT INTO Customers(CustomerID, CompanyName,
                      ContactFirstName,
                      ContactLastName,
                      CompanyOrDepartment,
                      BillingAddress, City,
                      StateOrProvince,
                      PostalCode, Country, ContactTitle,
                      PhoneNumber,
                      Extension, FaxNumber, EmailAddress)
VALUES (100, 'ABC Manufacturing', 'Marie', 'McCartan',
        'Executive','123 Main Street', 'Buffalo',
        'New York', '14225', 'USA', 'President',
        '716-555-1212', '123', '716-555-2121',
        'president@abcmfg.com')
```

UPDATE

The UPDATE command is used to modify records in a table, based on a specified criteria, and is useful for changing multiple records or fields in multiple tables. To update the sales-tax rate to six percent for all orders in the Orders table that are shipped to CA, use the following SQL statement:

```
UPDATE Orders
SET SalesTaxRate = 0.06
WHERE Orders.ShipState = 'CA'
```

DELETE

The DELETE command is used to remove from a table the records that meet a specified criteria. After the records are deleted, they can't be recovered. To delete all the records from the Customers table that represent customers from San Diego, CA, the following SQL statement is used:

```
DELETE FROM Customers
WHERE  Customers.City = 'San Diego' AND
       Customers.StateOrProvince = 'CA'
```

Using Data Definition with SQL

You have learned how to use the SQL language to retrieve, add, and modify records in database tables. SQL can also be used to make modifications to the schema of the database. The CREATE command is used to create tables and indices. The DROP command is used to delete tables. The ALTER command is used to modify table fields and indices.

CREATE

The CREATE command is used to create new tables and indices. The following example shows how you can create a new table named Products by using the CREATE command:

```
CREATE TABLE Products (ProductID INTEGER,
                       ProductDesc TEXT(50))
```

The new table contains two fields: ProductID and ProductDesc. As you can see, the type of the field is specified after the field name.

To create a new, unique index for the newly created Products table on the ProductID field, use the following SQL statement:

```
CREATE UNIQUE INDEX ProdIndex ON Products (ProductID)
```

ALTER

The ALTER command is used to add or remove fields and indices to and from a table. To add the new fields SupplierID and ProductColor to the Products table, the following SQL statement is used:

```
ALTER TABLE Products ADD COLUMN SupplierID INTEGER
ALTER TABLE Products ADD COLUMN ProductColor TEXT(30)
```

To remove the ProductColor field from the Products table, use the following SQL statement:

```
ALTER TABLE Products DROP COLUMN ProductColor
```

To add a secondary index on the SupplierID field in the Products table, use the following SQL statement:

```
ALTER TABLE Products ADD CONSTRAINT ProdSuppIdx
    FOREIGN KEY SupplierID
```

To delete the newly created index from the Products table, use the following SQL statement:

```
ALTER TABLE Products DROP CONSTRAINT ProdSuppIdx
```

DROP

The DROP command can be used to delete tables. The DROP command removes the table and its associated indices, unlike the DELETE command, which deletes the selected records from the table. Even if all the table records are deleted from a table by using the DELETE command, the table and associated indices are still present, even though they are empty. You *can't* recover a deleted table. To delete the Products table that you just created and modified, the following SQL statement is used:

```
DROP TABLE Products
```

Testing Your Queries

SQL queries are an important cornerstone in the development of your Visual Basic 6 data access applications. Sometimes, though, you may need to write an SQL command and you might not be sure whether it's right or how it will work. If you are new to SQL, or even if you're an old pro, you can save a lot of time during the implementation of your programs by testing your queries and SQL statements *before* you implement them in your applications. Fortunately, the Visual Basic 6 application-development environment provides a tool that you can use to test your queries, before you implement them in your application – Visual Data Manager. This section shows you how to use Visual Data Manager to connect to, and retrieve data from, your database server. Before you can access your database server, though, you need to establish an Open Database Connectivity (ODBC) resource.

To review the process of creating an ODBC resource, see Chapter 5.

After you establish and test an ODBC resource, you can follow these steps to get up and running with Visual Data Manager:

For this example, I created an SQL Server database, ExampleDB, which contains the `Customers`, `Order Detail`, and `Order` table, as previously illustrated in Tables 6-1, 6-2, and 6-3, respectively. I also created a System ODBC Data Source, called ExampleDB.

Also, while this example illustrates how to use ODBC to connect to a database server, you can also use Visual Data Manager to access dBase, FoxPro, Paradox, Excel, and Text files directly.

1. Start the Visual Basic 6 application-development environment. Select the Add-Ins → Visual Data Manager applications, to start Visual Data Manager, as shown in Figure 6-1.

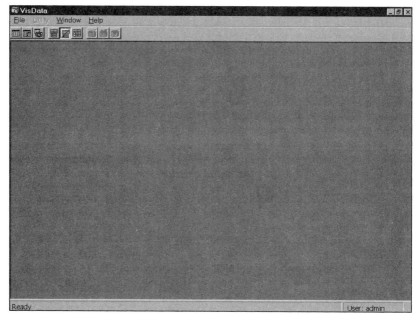

Figure 6-1: Starting Visual Data Manager

2. To open an ODBC data source, select File → Open Database → ODBC, to display the ODBC Logon dialog box, as shown in Figure 6-2. Enter the Data Source Name (DSN) and, if necessary, the UID (User ID), Password, and Database. Click the OK button to connect to your database server.

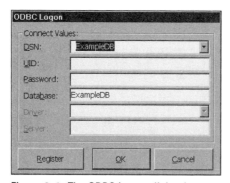

Figure 6-2: The ODBC Logon dialog box

3. After you connect to your database server, the Database and SQL Statement windows are displayed, as shown in Figure 6-3. The Database window shows all the tables that are available in the database. The SQL Statement window enables you to enter SQL statements that retrieve or manipulate data.

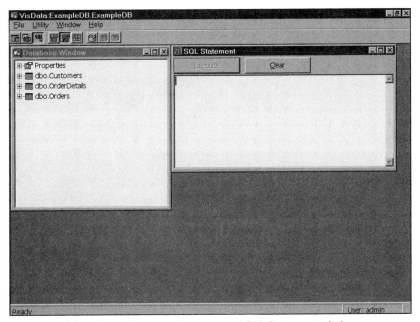

Figure 6-3: Visual Data Manager's Database and SQL Statement windows

4. In the Database window, if you click the plus sign, you can view the Fields, Indexes, and Properties of the table. Click the plus sign next to the Fields item to view the individual fields that comprise the table. Figure 6-4 illustrates how you can view the fields in the OrderDetails table.

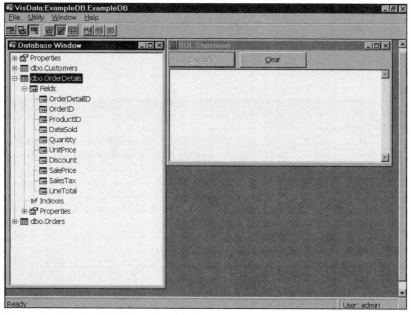

Figure 6-4: Viewing OrderDetails table fields from the Database window

5. To retrieve data from a table, you simply enter an SQL SELECT statement, as described in "Introduction to SQL," earlier in this chapter. For example, to retrieve all the items from the OrderDetails table for OrderID 1, enter the following SELECT statement, SELECT * FROM OrderDetails WHERE OrderID = 1, as shown in Figure 6-5.

6. After you enter the SQL command in the SQL Statement window, click the Execute button to run your query. The results of your SQL command are displayed in the SELECT window, as shown in Figure 6-6. You can use the Add, Edit, Delete, Move, and Find commands to explore the data that you have retrieved.

7. After you view the results of your query, you can click the Close button to close the SELECT window.

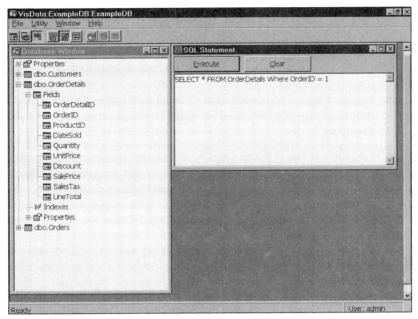

Figure 6-5: Entering an SQL SELECT statement in the SQL Statement window

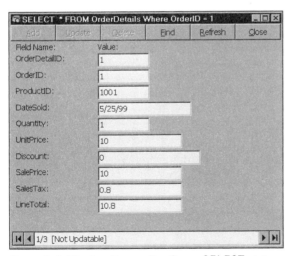

Figure 6-6: Viewing the results of your SELECT statement
in the SELECT window

Understanding Query Errors

Just as you've probably experienced with any other programming language that you have used, two types of errors can occur when writing SQL commands:

- ◆ **Syntax errors** – These errors are caused by incorrectly stating an SQL statement. Syntax errors are the most common errors that you will encounter.

- ◆ **Semantic errors** – These types of errors can be harder to uncover, because your SQL statement still runs – but the results returned aren't quite what you expect. You need to review the SQL command reference, covered earlier in this chapter, to make sure that you understand the SQL command that you used.

Syntax errors usually are the easiest to discover, because your queries won't run if syntax errors are encountered. When you use Visual Data Manager, and the SQL statement that you enter is incorrect, an error message dialog box is displayed, as shown in Figure 6-7.

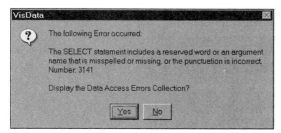

Figure 6-7: Viewing the Error dialog box

If you click the Yes button to display the Errors Collection, you retrieve more-detailed error information, as shown in Figure 6-8.

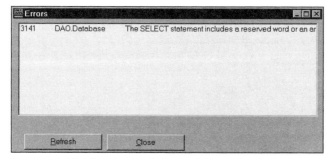

Figure 6-8: Viewing the detailed error information dialog box

Return to your SQL Statement window and carefully review your SQL command to determine whether you have omitted a phrase or typed your command incorrectly.

Summary

You now have a good foundation to begin developing your own data access applications by using Visual Basic 6. This chapter reviewed the Structured Query Language – which is a standardized language that facilitates database manipulation and, more importantly, the data that the database contains. This chapter showed you how to use SQL for data retrieval and data definition. The data manipulation commands are the most frequently used in SQL – they are used to retrieve the data that is stored in your database. SQL can also be used to make modifications to the schema (or structure) of the database. If you are new to SQL, or even if you're an old pro, you can save a lot of time during the implementation of your programs by testing your queries and SQL statements before you implement them in your applications. This chapter also demonstrated how you can use the Visual Data Manager application of Visual Basic 6 to test your queries before you implement them in your database.

Part III

Data Access Objects API

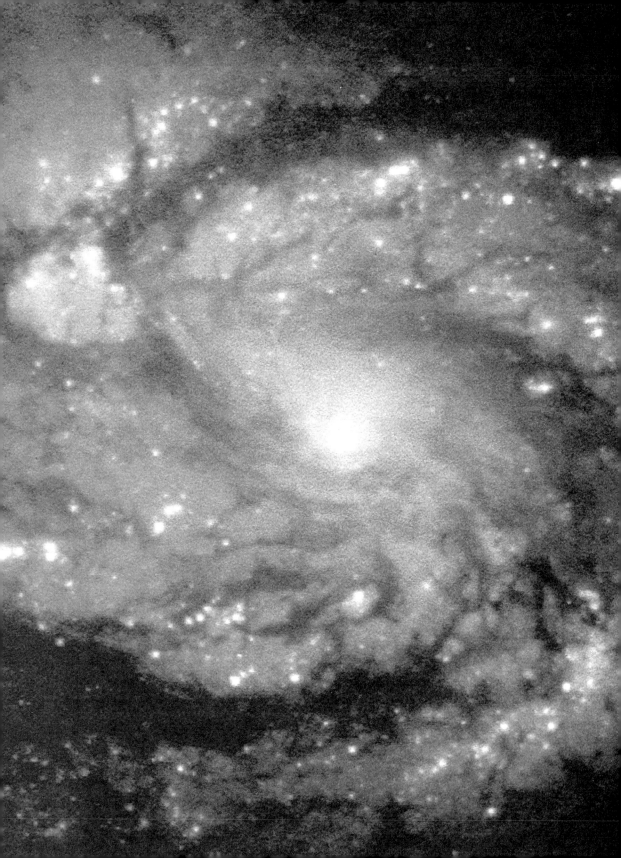

Chapter 7

Introduction to the DAO Object Library

IN THIS CHAPTER

- ◆ Using the DAO object hierarchy
- ◆ Accessing database types through DAO
- ◆ Connecting to a database
- ◆ Using the `DBEngine` and `Database` objects
- ◆ Incorporating DAO into your own applications

THIS CHAPTER BEGINS an in-depth review of the data access models provided by Visual Basic 6. In this chapter, and for the remainder of Part III, the first and oldest Visual Basic data access model – Data Access Objects (DAO) – is explored in depth. DAO can be used to access two distinct database environments: standalone index sequential databases (such as dBase, Paradox, and FoxPro) and client/server Open Database Connectivity (ODBC) databases (such as Microsoft SQL Server and Oracle) that use ODBCDirect. This chapter introduces the objects, including their properties and methods, that provide the foundation for DAO: `DBEngine`, `Database`, and `Workspace`.

Object Hierarchy

Now that you have a basic understanding of relational databases and their components, this section looks at the Data Access Object (DAO) Class Hierarchy and how DAO actually works.

MDAO is a set of *Dynamic Link Libraries* (DLLs) that forms the core of Microsoft's Jet Database Engine. DAO supports two different types of database environments: Using the Microsoft Jet Database Engine, DAO is optimized for accessing local *Index Sequential Access Method* (ISAM) databases, such as dBase, Paradox, FoxPro, and others; using ODBCDirect, DAO is optimized for ODBC databases with minimal overhead. The DAO application architecture has three levels, as shown in Figure 7-1.

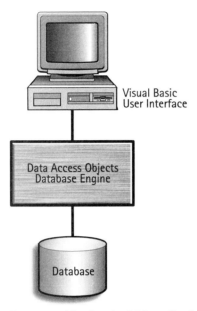

Figure 7-1: Viewing the DAO application
architecture

The User Interface, which is developed by using Visual Basic, contains all the
necessary components for the user to interact with the database. The Database
Engine, which is provided by DAO, provides the mechanisms to interact with the
database. The Database is essentially the data repository, which simply stores the
data that the application uses in a form that the Database Engine can manipulate.
The Database Store can be a variety of different database types, which are reviewed
in the "Database Types" section, later in this chapter.

Figure 7-2: Viewing a local DAO application
configuration

The Database Store can be located either locally or remotely when using DAO. In the local setup, all the components of the DAO application architecture reside on the same computer, as shown in Figure 7-2.

A remote Database Store can be broken down further into two distinct configurations: a client/server database and a remote database. In a client/server configuration, the Database Engine and the Database Store reside on the same server computer, while the User Interface resides on the client computer, as shown in Figure 7-3. The server computer can manage multiple client applications simultaneously.

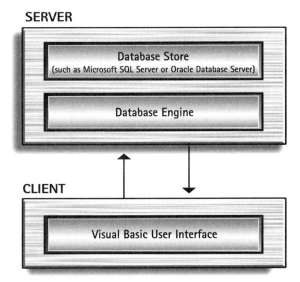

SERVER

Database Store
(such as Microsoft SQL Server or Oracle Database Server)

Database Engine

CLIENT

Visual Basic User Interface

Figure 7-3: Viewing a client/server DAO application configuration

In a Remote database application configuration, the Database Store resides on a remote server computer, while the User Interface and the Database Engine reside on the same client computer, as shown in Figure 7-4. In this configuration, the server computer simply manages access to the Database Store files.

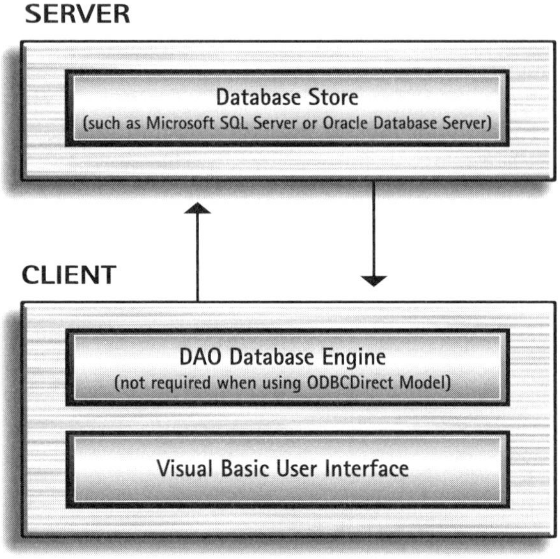

SERVER

Database Store
(such as Microsoft SQL Server or Oracle Database Server)

CLIENT

DAO Database Engine
(not required when using ODBCDirect Model)

Visual Basic User Interface

Figure 7-4: Viewing a remote DAO application configuration

A true client/server database engine serves simply as a communication layer between the database and the application. The DAO Jet Database Engine is not a true client/server database engine. Each application that is developed using the DAO Jet Database Engine requires a local copy of the DAO DLL files to access the database, even if the application is running multiple client computers. However, you can create client/server applications using DAO by connecting to ODBC database sources.

The DAO object classes are organized in a hierarchy, like other Visual Basic object classes that you have encountered. The class hierarchy of DAO is illustrated in Figure 7-5.

Each of the objects in the DAO class hierarchy are reviewed in depth throughout Part III of this book.

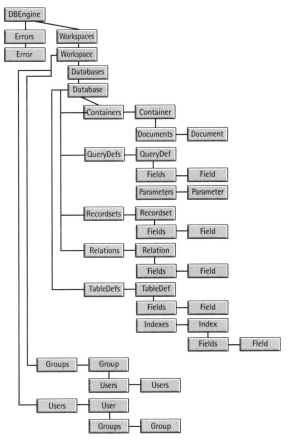

Figure 7-5: Viewing the DAO class hierarchy

Database Types

DAO can access data from numerous different database sources, listed as follows:

- ◆ Native DAO databases – Microsoft Access
- ◆ ODBC databases, which include Microsoft SQL Server, Oracle, Sybase, or any other client/server database that provides ODBC drivers
- ◆ FoxPro

- ◆ dBase III, IV, and V

- ◆ Paradox

- ◆ Btrieve

- ◆ Lotus spreadsheets

- ◆ Excel worksheets

- ◆ Text files

When operating in its native mode using the Jet Database Engine, DAO creates databases that are directly accessible by Microsoft Access. Three ways exist to connect to external databases, which include opening the database directly, attaching the external database to a DAO native database, and creating queries that contain external database linkage information.

 All three ways to connect to external databases are explored in more detail in Chapter 9.

Each of the database sources intrinsically provide different levels of security, performance, and requirements. The main concept of DAO is to abstract the application programmer from the details of each database source and present a consistent Application Programming Interface (API) to the programmer.

Jet

Jet-type database sources include those created using the DAO API, Microsoft Access, and Microsoft Excel. Jet-type databases provide security methodologies, multiuser support, database replication, and methodologies to help ensure referential integrity.

Installable ISAM

Using the ISAM access methodology of the DAO/JET database engine can access Btrieve, dBase, Excel, FoxPro, Lotus, Paradox, and text files. DAO abstracts the API requirements of each of these database sources from the applications programmer and presents a consistent API through the use of the DAO class objects.

ODBC

Using the ODBC access methodology, the DAO database engine can access client/server databases. ODBC databases can be accessed directly or connected to native Jet databases. Any client/server database that provides standard ODBC drivers can be accessed from DAO; these include Oracle, Sybase, and SQL Server.

Chapter 11 reviews the special issues surrounding access to client/server ODBC database stores.

Connecting to a Database

The first step in developing your database applications by using DAO involves initializing the database engine and establishing a connection to your database. Before you begin this first step, you need to understand how to use the three objects that form the foundation of DAO: DBEngine, Workspace, and Database. Each of these objects is explored in detail next, and then you learn how to put them together to begin communicating with your own databases.

To use DAO in your Visual Basic application, your application must include the DAO Object Library. To add the DAO Object Library to your application:

1. Open your Visual Basic project.

2. Select Project → References, to display the References dialog box, shown in Figure 7-6.

3. The latest version of the DAO Object Library is 3.51, which is the version that is discussed in the remainder of Part III of this book. Select Microsoft DAO 3.51 Object Library from the Available References list by clicking the checkbox next to the name entry.

4. Click OK to make the DAO Object Library available to your application.

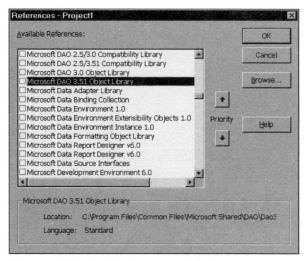

Figure 7-6: Viewing the References dialog box

DBEngine Object

As Figure 7-5 illustrated, DBEngine is the top-level object in the DAO class hierarchy. An overview of the objects, properties, and methods of DBEngine are shown in Table 7-1. "Putting Things Together," later in this chapter, reviews the details of the properties and methods; a complete DAO class reference can be found in Appendix A.

TABLE 7-1 DBENGINE OBJECTS, PROPERTIES, AND METHODS

Objects	Properties	Methods
Collection of Workspaces	Version	Idle()
Collection of Errors	LoginTimeout	CompactDatabase()
	IniPath	RepairDatabase()
	SystemDb	CreateWorkspace()
	DefaultUser	Rollback()
	DefaultPassword	CreateDatabase()
	DefaultType	OpenDatabase()

Objects	Properties	Methods
		RegisterDatabase()
		RepairDatabase()
		SetOption()
		OpenConnection()

When the engine is initialized, a default workspace is provided automatically. The DefaultType property can be used to specify the default Workspace type. If it is set to dbUseJet, the Jet Database Engine is used; if it is set to dbUseODBC, the ODBCDirect model is used. The DBEngine object is also used to specify the system parameters for the database engine. The DBEngine properties are used as follows:

◆ The Version property is used to obtain the DAO version number.

◆ The LoginTimeout property is used to obtain or set the ODBC login timeout, and the RegisterDatabase() method is used to provide ODBC information to the Jet Database Engine.

◆ The DefaultType property is used to set the default type of database connection that Workspace objects will use: Microsoft Jet or ODBCDirect.

◆ The DefaultPassword and DefaultUser properties are used to set the user identification and password when connecting to your database.

◆ The IniPath and SystemDB properties are used to specify the location of Microsoft Jet Windows Registry information and the Microsoft Jet workgroup information file. The SetOption() method is used to enable you to override Windows Registry settings for the Microsoft Jet Database Engine.

The DBEngine methods are used as follows:

◆ The CreateDatabase() method is used to create a new Microsoft Jet database.

◆ The Idle() method is used to enable the Microsoft Jet Database Engine to complete any pending tasks.

◆ The CompactDatabase() and RepairDatabase() methods are used to maintain database files.

Workspace Object

The Workspace object is a container for open databases. The Workspace provides a security context for the open database. An overview of the objects, properties, and methods of the Workspace object is shown in Table 7-2. "Putting Things Together," later in this chapter, reviews the details of the properties and methods; a complete DAO class reference can be found in Appendix A.

TABLE 7-2 WORKSPACE OBJECTS, PROPERTIES, AND METHODS

Objects	Properties	Methods
Collection of Databases	Name	BeginTrans()
Collection of Users	UserName	Close()
Collection of Groups	Password	CommitTrans()
Collection of Properties	IsolateODBCTrans	CreateUser()
	LoginTimeout	OpenDatabase()
	Type	CreateDatabase()
	DefaultCursorDriver	CreateGroup()
		Rollback()

A default Workspace object is automatically created when the DBEngine object is created. The Workspace object is used to specify the username and password for access to the database. The default Workspace is created when the DBEngine object is created, and is always available and can't be closed. The Workspace properties are used as follows:

◆ The Name, UserName, and Type properties are used to establish named sessions. The session creates a scope in which you can open multiple databases and conduct an instance of nested transactions.

◆ The IsolateODBCTrans property is used to isolate multiple transactions that involve the same Microsoft Jet-connected ODBC database.

◆ The Groups and Users collections are used to establish group and user access permissions to objects in the Workspace.

The Workspace methods are used as follows:

◆ The Close() method is used to terminate a session.

◆ The OpenDatabase() method is used to open one or more existing databases on a Workspace.

◆ The BeginTrans(), CommitTrans(), and Rollback() methods are used to manage nested transaction processing within a Workspace and several Workspace objects can be used to conduct multiple, simultaneous, and overlapping transactions.

Database Object

The Database object encapsulates the Database Store and defines the database's tables, relations, stored queries, and open records. An overview of the objects, properties, and methods of the Database object is shown in Table 7-3.

TABLE 7-3 DATABASE OBJECTS, PROPERTIES, AND METHODS

Objects	Properties	Methods
Collection of TableDefs	CollatingOrder	Close()
Collection of QueryDefs	Connect	Execute()
Collection of Relations	QueryTimeout	OpenRecordset()
Collection of Containers	Name	CreateProperty()
Collection of Recordsets	Transactions	CreateRelation()
Collection of Properties	Updatable	CreateTabledef()
	Version	CreateQuerydef()
	DesignMaster	Synchronize()
	Connection	MakeReplica()
	DesignMasterID	PopulatePartial()
	RecordsAffected	NewPassword()
	Replicable	
	ReplicaID	

The `Database` object is used to manipulate an open database. The `Database` object properties are used as follows:

♦ The `Connect` property is used to establish a connection to an ODBC data source.

♦ The `QueryTimeout` property is used to limit the time to wait for a query to execute in an ODBC data source.

♦ The `RecordsAffected` property is used to determine how many records were changed by an action query.

♦ The `Version` property is used to determine which version of a database engine created the database.

♦ The `CollatingOrder` property is used to establish the alphabetic sorting order for character-based fields in different languages.

The `Database` object methods are used as follows:

♦ The `Execute()` method is used to run an action query.

♦ The `OpenRecordset()` method is used to execute a select query and create a `Recordset` object.

♦ The `CreateTableDef()` and `CreateRelation()` methods are used to create tables and relations, respectively.

♦ The `CreateProperty()` method is used to define new `Database` object properties.

♦ The `CreateQueryDef()` method is used to create a persistent or temporary query definition.

♦ The `MakeReplica()`, `Synchronize()`, and `PopulatePartial()` methods are used to create and synchronize full or partial replicas of your database.

Putting Things Together

Now that you have a basic understanding of the key objects of DAO, you can begin to incorporate this library into your own applications. Before you can dig in and start accessing and manipulating database data, you need to establish a connection to your database. As mentioned earlier, you can access your databases using DAO in either of two ways: Use the Microsoft Jet Database Engine to access ISAM or ODBC data sources, or use ODBCDirect to access only ODBC data sources. To open a database, the `OpenDatabase()` method (described in Table 7-4) is employed as follows:

```
OpenDatabase(db, options, readonly, connect)
```

 See Chapter 5 for more detailed information on creating an ODBC data source.

TABLE **7-4 OPENDATABASE() METHOD PARAMETERS**

Argument	Description
db	The name of the database source that you want to open (a path name can be included, including a network path name, if necessary) or the data source name of an existing ODBC data source. db is a string.
options	When using the Jet Database Engine, the options parameter is a Boolean value that indicates whether the database should be opened in exclusive use mode. If false, the database is opened in a sharable manner. If exclusive is not specified, it is false by default. When using ODBCDirect, the options parameter determines whether and when to prompt the user for information to establish the connection, such as username, password, and driver.
readonly	A Boolean value that indicates whether the database can be read and written to after it is opened. If readonly is not specified, it is false by default, which means that the database can be read and written to.
connect	A string that specifies special parameters necessary for opening the database. These parameters include the type of the database, the driver, and ODBC connection information. When you open a Jet/Access-type database, this information is not required. Elements of the connect string are separated by semicolons.

Connect Using the Jet Database Engine

To connect to a database, the DBEngine object must be declared, and then the OpenDatabase() method is called. This creates a database in the default Workspace. If you plan to use the Jet Database Engine, you also must first set the DefaultType property to dbUseJet. Listings 7-1, 7-2, and 7-3 show you how to open a dBase, Paradox, and ODBC database, respectively, using the Jet Database Engine.

Listing 7-1: Using DAO to Connect to a dBase Database

```
Sub AccessDatabase()
  ' Create a Database Object
  Dim MyDatabase As Database

  ' Set the default database type to the
  ' Jet Engine
  DBEngine.DefaultType = dbUseJet

  ' Open A dBase database named OrderEntry
  Set MyDatabase = DBEngine.OpenDatabase(
                 "\\Database\\OrderEntry",
                 True, False, "DBase IV;")
  MyDatabase.Close()
End Sub
```

Listing 7-2: Using DAO to Connect to a Paradox Database

```
Sub AccessDatabase()
  ' Create a Database Object
  Dim MyDatabase As Database

  ' Set the default database type to the
  ' Jet Engine
  DBEngine.DefaultType = dbUseJet

  ' Open A Paradox database named OrderEntry
  Set MyDatabase = DBEngine.OpenDatabase(
                 "\\Database\OrderEntry",
                 True, False, "Paradox;")
  MyDatabase.Close()
End Sub
```

Listing 7-3: Using DAO to Connect to an ODBC Database

```
Sub AccessDatabase()
  ' Create a Database Object
  Dim MyDatabase As Database

  ' Set the default database type to the
  ' Jet Engine
  DBEngine.DefaultType = dbUseJet

  ' Open An ODBC database named OrderEntry
  Set MyDatabase = DBEngine.OpenDatabase(
                "\\Database\\OrderEntry",
                True, False,
                "ODBC;DSN=OrderEnt;DATABASE=Orders;
                UID=John;PWD=Password"")
  MyDatabase.Close()
End Sub
```

Basically, when opening different types of databases, the `OpenDatabase()` method is invoked in the same manner. The parameters of the connect string are different, though. Some things to consider: When you open a dBase or Paradox database, you are opening a single table, and the connect string specifies the database driver that is being used, which directly corresponds to the name and version number of the database manager used to create and manage the tables. When you connect to an ODBC data source, the name of the database is no longer specified in the db field. The connect string is more complex in this case. The first portion specifies the database driver being used – in this case, ODBC. The `DSN=` parameter provides the name of the database server computer – in this case, DBServer. The `DATABASE=` parameter specifies the name of the database located on the database server – in this case, MyDatabase. The `UID=` specifies the User ID to be used when accessing the database – in this case, John. Finally, the `PASSWORD=` parameter specifies the password of the user specified in the `UID=` parameter – in this case, Password.

Passwords as discussed in this section raise several security considerations, reviewed in detail in Chapter 11.

Connect Using ODBCDirect

Now that you understand how to use DAO to access ISAM and ODBC data sources using the Jet Database Engine, it's time to review how to use the ODBCDirect() method. When you use the ODBCDirect() method, the options parameter of the OpenDatabase() method can accept the values outlined in Table 7-5. Figure 7-7 illustrates the ODBC Select Data Source dialog box. Listing 7-4 illustrates how to open an ODBCDirect data source.

TABLE 7-5 LEGAL VALUES FOR THE OPTIONS PARAMETER
WHEN USING ODBCDIRECT

Constant	Description
dbDriverNoPrompt	The ODBC Driver Manager uses the connection string provided in the dbname and connect parameters. If you don't provide complete connection information, your application will experience a runtime error.
DbDriverPrompt	The ODBC Driver Manager always displays the ODBC Select Data Source dialog box, as shown in Figure 7-7. Any connect information that was provided in the dbname or connect parameters is displayed as the default. The connection is made using the information supplied in this dialog box.
DbDriverComplete	This is the default option. If the connect information provided in the dbname or connect parameters is complete, then the database connection is established. If any information is missing or incomplete, the ODBC Driver Manager is displayed, and the user must fill in any missing information required to connect to the database.
dbDriverCompleteRequired	This option is similar to the dbDriverComplete option, except that when the ODBC Device Driver dialog box is displayed, prompts are disabled for any information that is not required to complete the connection.

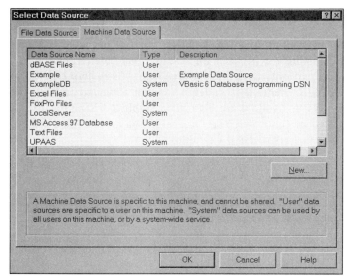

Figure 7-7: The ODBC Select Data Source dialog box

Listing 7-4: Using the ODBCDirect() Method to Open an ODBC Database

```
Sub AccessDatabase()
  ' Create a Database Object
  Dim MyDatabase As Database

  ' Set the default database type to the
  ' ODBCDirect method
  DBEngine.DefaultType = dbUseODBC

  ' Open An ODBC database named OrderEntry
  Set MyDatabase = DBEngine.OpenDatabase(
                "",
                dbDriverPrompt, False,
                "ODBC;DSN=OrderEnt;DATABASE=Orders;
                 UID=John;PWD=Password"")
  MyDatabase.Close()
End Sub
```

Dynamic Database Creation

Now that you know how to open an existing database, what if you want to create one dynamically instead? Listing 7-5 presents an example that creates and opens a database dynamically. You can only dynamically create Jet/MS Access-type databases. The `CreateDatabase()` method is called to create a new database. The `CreateDatabase` parameters that follow are detailed in Table 7-6. The locale sort order constants are detailed in Table 7-7. The `CreateDatabase()` method returns the open database that was just created, for example:

```
CreateDatabase(db, locale, options)
```

TABLE 7-6 THE CREATEDATABASE PARAMETERS

Argument	Description
db	The name of the database source that you want to create. This can include a path name (including a network path name, if necessary). db is a string.
locale	This specifies the sort order of the database. The locale sort order constants are detailed in Table 7-7.
options	This specifies the Jet/MSAccess database version to use when creating the database, and can also specify whether the database should be encrypted. The dbEncrypt constant is used to create an encrypted database. The dbVersion10, dbVersion11, dbVersion20, and dbVersion30 constants are used to specify the format of the database. Unless you need to support older applications, you should use the dbVersion30 constant, as this creates databases that are fully compliant with DAO Version 3.5.

TABLE 7-7 THE CREATEDATABASE SORT ORDER CONSTANTS

Constant	Sorting order
dbLangGeneral	English, German, French, Portuguese, Italian, and Modern Spanish
dbLangArabic	Arabic

Constant	Sorting order
dbLangChineseSimplified	Simplified Chinese
dbLangChineseTraditional	Traditional Chinese
dbLangCyrillic	Russian
dbLangCzech	Czech
dbLangDutch	Dutch
dbLangGreek	Greek
dbLangHebrew	Hebrew
dbLangHungarian	Hungarian
dbLangIcelandic	Icelandic
dbLangJapanese	Japanese
dbLangKorean	Korean
dbLangNordic	Nordic languages (only supported by the Microsoft Jet Database Engine Version 1.0)
dbLangNorwDan	Norwegian and Danish
dbLangPolish	Polish
dbLangSlovenian	Slovenian
dbLangSpanish	Traditional Spanish
dbLangSwedFin	Swedish and Finnish
dbLangThai	Thai
dbLangTurkish	Turkish

Listing 7-5: Using DAO to Connect to an ODBC Database

```
Sub CreateDatabase()
  ' Create a Database Object
  Dim MyNewDatabase As Database

  ' Set the default database type to the
  ' Jet Engine
  DBEngine.DefaultType = dbUseJet
```

```
' Open A JET database named OrderEntry
Set MyNewDatabase = DBEngine.CreateDatabase(
                              "MyNewDB",dbLangGeneral,
                              dbVersion30)

MyNewDatabase.Close()
End Sub
```

Summary

This chapter introduced the DAO Object Library. DAO is a set of DLLs that form the core of the Jet Database Engine. DAO supports two different types of database environments; Using the Microsoft Jet Database Engine, DAO is optimized for accessing local ISAM databases, such as dBase, Paradox, FoxPro, and others; using ODBCDirect, DAO is optimized for ODBC databases with minimal overhead. This chapter demonstrated how to use the objects that provide the foundation of the DAO Object Library: DBEngine, Workspace, and Database. Now that you understand how to establish a connection to your database, Chapter 8 shows you how to begin accessing the tables, fields, and indexes of your database.

Chapter 8

Integrating the DAO Object Library

IN THIS CHAPTER

◆ Reviewing `TableDef` and `TableDefs` objects

◆ Reviewing `Field` and `Fields` objects

◆ Using indexes and relations

◆ Retrieving database schema information

◆ Introducing the `Recordset` object

◆ Performing database maintenance with DAO

THIS CHAPTER INTRODUCES the `TableDef`, `Field`, `Index`, and `Relation` objects. You will learn how to put these objects together to create a Visual Basic 6 procedure that retrieves and displays a schema of a database, utilizing DAO. Next, you will explore the `Recordset` object, which is used for basic database navigation. Finally, you will review the mechanisms provided in DAO to perform the basic database maintenance operations of compacting, repairing, and encrypting.

TableDef and TableDefs Objects

The `TableDef` object is a container for the components that comprise a database table. A `TableDef` object contains the fields, indexes, and properties that define a database table. If the table defined by the `TableDef` object is not an attached table, the attributes of the `TableDef` object may be modified, and the actual database table will be modified accordingly. An overview of the `TableDef` objects, methods, and properties is shown in Table 8-1.

The `Database` object contains a collection of `TableDefs` in the `TableDefs` object. An overview of the `TableDefs` properties and methods is shown in Table 8-2.

TABLE 8-1 TABLEDEF OBJECTS, METHODS, AND PROPERTIES

Objects	Methods	Properties
Collection of Fields	CreateProperty()	Attributes
Collection of Indexes	OpenRecordset()	ConflictTable
Collection of Properties	CreateIndex()	Connect
	RefreshLink()	DateCreated
	CreateField()	LastUpdated
		KeepLocal
		Name
		RecordCount
		Replicable
		ReplicaFilter
		SourceTableName
		Updateable
		ValidationRule
		ValidationText

For an explanation of the Database object and the TableDefs object, see Chapter 7.

TABLE 8-2 METHODS AND PROPERTIES PROVIDED BY TABLEDEFS

Methods	Properties
Append()	Count
Delete()	
Refresh()	

In this chapter, you will work through the development of a Visual Basic procedure called Schema. A database schema is the information that defines the database itself – it is the definition of the tables, fields, indexes, and relations that comprise the database.

The Schema procedure that you develop in this chapter requires the information necessary to open the database. Chapter 7 discussed the four parameters that are required to open a database: a string that specifies the database name; a boolean that indicates whether the database should be opened for exclusive access; a boolean that indicates whether the database should be opened for read-only access; and a string specifying the connect string. For purposes of this class, you can assume that when you access the database for which you want to generate a schema, you will require only read access to the database, and that you don't want to have the database opened exclusively. The Schema procedure that you are going to develop requires two arguments: the name of the database and the connect string.

You'll begin by defining the Schema class. To this point, you have learned about the DBEngine, Database, TableDefs, and TableDef objects. So far, you have enough information to initiate the database engine, open the database, and access information attributes of the database itself and the tables that are contained in the database. Listing 8-1 presents the first step in defining the Schema class. The highlights of this class and its key components are discussed after the listing.

Listing 8-1: First Revision of the Schema Class

```
Sub Schema(DBName As String, ConnectString As String)
  Dim db As Database
  Dim tbls As TableDefs
  Dim tbl As TableDef

  Rem Open the Database
  Set db = DBEngine.OpenDatabase(DBName, True,
                                 True, ConnectString)

  Rem Print the Database Information
  List.AddItem "--------------------"
  List.AddItem "Database Information"
  List.AddItem ""
  List.AddItem "Database Name: " & db.Name
  List.AddItem "Version: " & db.Version
  List.AddItem "Connection String: " & db.Connect
  List.AddItem "Sorting Order: " & db.CollatingOrder
  List.AddItem "Supports Transactions: " &
                                 db.Transactions
  List.AddItem "Query Time Out: " & db.QueryTimeout
  List.AddItem "--------------------"
```

```
    List.AddItem ""

    Rem Print The Table Information
    List.AddItem "--------------------"
    List.AddItem "Database Tables"
    List.AddItem ""

    Rem Loop Through Each Table In The Database
    Set tbls = db.TableDefs
    For Each tbl In tbls

      Rem Display Table Information
      List.AddItem "**** BEGIN TABLE ***"
      List.AddItem "Table Name: " & tbl.Name
      List.AddItem "Date Table Created: " & tbl.DateCreated
      List.AddItem "Date Table Updated: " & tbl.LastUpdated
      List.AddItem "Can Update Table: " & tbl.Updatable
      List.AddItem ""

      Rem Display Table Attributes
      List.AddItem "Table Attributes:"
      If (tbl.Attributes And dbSystemObject) > 0 Then
        List.AddItem "System Object Table"
      End If
      If (tbl.Attributes And dbAttachedTable) > 0 Then
        List.AddItem "Attached Table"
      End If
      If (tbl.Attributes And dbAttachExclusive) > 0 Then
        List.AddItem "Attached Table Opened Exclusive"
      End If
      If (tbl.Attributes And dbAttachedODBC) > 0 Then
        List.AddItem "Attached ODBC Table"
      End If
      List.AddItem "*** END TABLE ***"
    Next tbl
    List.AddItem "--------------------"
    Rem Close The Database...We're Done For Now!
    db.Close
End Sub
```

As described earlier, the Schema procedure class takes two arguments: the name of the database and the connect string. The Schema procedure begins by opening the database with the parameters that are specified.

Next, the Schema procedure displays the attributes of the database as items in the list box List1. The Name property returns the name of the database. The Version property returns the version number of the database that is open. The Connect property displays the current value of the connect string. When accessing attached ODBC tables, the corresponding Connect property can be set to a value that can be used to establish the connect string parameters for the attached table. The Updatable property returns a boolean that indicates whether changes can be made to the database. Listing 8.1 specifies that the database is to be opened in read-only mode, so this will always return False. The CollatingOrder property returns the collating (sorting) order of the database. The Transactions property returns a boolean that indicates whether transaction-level processing is available on the database. If true, the database can support a series of operations on the database (appending records, deleting records, modifying records) that later can be committed (saved to the database) or rolled back (canceled). The QueryTimeout property returns the number of seconds the database engine will wait for an ODBC database operation to complete before it times out (quits due to excessive time). By default, this is 60 seconds. You can adjust this time by setting the QueryTimeout property to an alternative value.

Next, look at how to access the tables in the database. As stated earlier, the Database object contains a collection of TableDef objects that is encapsulated by the TableDefs object. To access this collection of tables, you can loop through the TableDefs object by using the For Each construct. After you have a TableDef object, you can begin to examine some of its attributes. The Name property returns the name of the table. You can set the Name property to an alternative value to change the name of the table. The next two properties, DateCreated and LastUpdated, return the date the table was created and updated, respectively.

The Updateable property returns a boolean that determines whether this table is updatable. The Attributes property returns a bit mask that you logically AND with the DAO constants that define these attributes:

- dbSystemObject indicates that this table is a system table.

- dbAttachedTable indicates that this is an attached table (a non-ODBC attached table).

- dbAttachExclusive indicates that the attached table is opened for exclusive access.

- dbAttachedODBC indicates that the table is an attached ODBC table.

If you are accessing an Access-type database, several tables are displayed that begin with mSys. These are Access system tables. You must not modify or delete these tables, because serious damage can result in the database.

The Schema procedure can now attach to a database, display attributes of the database, and display the database tables and their associated attributes. After a review of how to add and delete tables from a database, the Schema procedure will be expanded to display more of the components of a table, including the fields that comprise a table and the information about the table's associated indexes.

Creating Tables

The Database object provides a method to create a new database table. The CreateTableDef() method creates a new table in the database and returns a TableDef object. Table 8-3 presents the parameters required by the CreateTableDef() method, which is called as follows:

```
CreateTableDef(tablename, tableattrib,
               sourcetbl, connect)
```

TABLE 8-3 CREATETABLEDEF PARAMETERS

Argument	Description
tablename	The name of the table that you want to create. The tablename parameter is a string type.
tableattrib	The attributes for the table, including the constants used in the previous Schema procedure. These constants are assembled by the logical or-ing of these constants. The tableattrib parameter is an integer type.
sourcetbl	The name of the table from the externally attached database that contains the actual table data. The sourcetbl parameter is a string type.
connect	The connect string for the external database. Used for passthrough queries. The connect parameter is a string type.

Listing 8-2 shows how the CreateTableDef() method would be called from Visual Basic to create a table named Temp, which is a hidden table. Note that, because this isn't an attached table, the *sourcetble* and *connect* parameters are not required. Also, the Append() method of the TableDefs collection must be called to actually add the table to the database.

Listing 8-2: Creating a Hidden Table Named Temp

```
Dim tbl As TableDef
Dim tbls As TableDefs

Rem Access the TableDefs collection
Set tbls = db.TableDefs

Rem Create the Temp table using the hidden object
tbl = db.CreateTable("Temp",dbHiddenObject)

Rem Append the table to the collection
tbls.AppendTable(tbl)
```

Deleting Tables

Deleting a table is much easier than creating a table. You should take caution when deleting a table, because you can't undo this operation. When a table is deleted, its associated data and indexes are also deleted. To delete a table, the `Delete()` method of the `TableDefs` object is called. The `Delete()` method takes one parameter, a `String` that is the name of the table. Listing 8-3 illustrates how to delete the Temp table that was created in Listing 8-2.

Listing 8-3: Deleting the Temp Table

```
Dim tbls As TableDefs
Rem Access the TableDefs collection
Set tbls = db.TableDefs

Rem Delete the table named Temp
tbls.Delete("Temp")
```

Field and Fields Objects

A table without any associated fields is not of much use. The `Field` object provides the container for a table field and can also be used to add new fields to a table. A table holds a collection of fields in an associated `Fields` object, just like the `Database` object holds a collection of tables in its associated `TableDefs` object.

The `Fields` object provides the same properties and methods that the `TableDefs` object provides. Table 8-4 summarizes the objects, methods, and properties of the `Field` object.

TABLE 8-4 FIELD OBJECTS, METHODS, AND PROPERTIES

Objects	Methods	Properties
Collection of Properties	AppendChunk()	AllowZeroLength
	CreateProperty()	Attributes
	GetChunk()	CollatingOrder
		DataUpdatable
		DefaultValue
		FieldSize
		Name
		OrdinalPosition
		OriginalValue
		Required
		Size
		SourceField
		Type
		ValidationOnSet
		ValidationRule
		ValidationText
		Value
		VisibleValue

The Field object properties are used as follows:

◆ The OrdinalPosition property is used to set or return the presentation order of the Field object in a Fields collection.

◆ The Value property of a field in a Recordset object is used to set or return stored data.

◆ The `FieldSize` is used to get the length of an OLE object or Memo field of a `Recordset` object.

◆ The `Type`, `Size`, and `Attributes` properties are used to determine the type of data that can be stored in the field.

◆ The `SourceField` and `SourceTable` properties are used to determine the original source of the data.

◆ The `ForeignName` property is used to set or return information about a foreign field in a `Relation` object.

◆ The `AllowZeroLength`, `DefaultValue`, `Required`, `ValidateOnSet`, `ValidationRule`, or `ValidationText` properties are used to set or return validation conditions.

◆ The `DefaultValue` property of a field on a `TableDef` object is used to set the default value for this field when new records are added.

◆ The `Value`, `VisibleValue`, and `OriginalValue` properties are used to verify successful completion of a batch update.

The `Field` object methods are used as follows:

◆ The `AppendChunk()` and `GetChunk()` methods are used to get or set a value in an OLE Object or Memo field of a `Recordset` object.

Using Field Types

Before you continue your extension of the `Schema` procedure that you started earlier, take a look at field types. DAO provides a set of constants that define a field's type. Table 8-5 summarizes these types. A field's type determines what kind of data can be stored in it. For example, if the field's type is boolean, it stores true or false values. You use these field type constants with the `Type` property when you define a field.

To continue the definition of the `Schema` procedure that you started earlier, you will add the capability to display the fields that are contained in a table and their associated attributes. Listing 8-4 presents the modifications to the `Schema` procedure to display the `Field` type information.

TABLE 8-5 FIELD TYPE CONSTANTS

Constant	Type Definition
dbBoolean	Boolean
dbByte	Byte
dbInteger	Integer
dbLong	Long
dbCurrency	A floating-point value
dbSingle	Single-precision floating-point value
dbDouble	Double-precision floating-point value
dbDate	Dates
dbText	A string
dbLongBinary	Large binary values; for example, an image
dbMemo	A long string of text

Listing 8-4: Modified Schema Procedure to Display Table Field Information

```
Sub Schema(DBName As String, ConnectString As String)
  Dim db As Database
  Dim tbls As TableDefs
  Dim tbl As TableDef
  Dim flds As Fields
  Dim fld As Field

  Rem Open the Database
  Set db = DBEngine.OpenDatabase(DBName, True,
                                 True, ConnectString)

  Rem Print the Database Information
  List.AddItem "--------------------"
  List.AddItem "Database Information"
  List.AddItem ""
  List.AddItem "Database Name: " & db.Name
  List.AddItem "Version: " & db.Version
  List.AddItem "Connection String: " & db.Connect
  List.AddItem "Sorting Order: " & db.CollatingOrder
```

```
List.AddItem "Supports Transactions: " &
                                    db.Transactions
List.AddItem "Query Time Out: " & db.QueryTimeout
List.AddItem "--------------------"
List.AddItem ""


Rem Print The Table Information
List.AddItem "--------------------"
List.AddItem "Database Tables"
List.AddItem ""


Rem Loop Through Each Table In The Database
Set tbls = db.TableDefs
For Each tbl In tbls

  Rem Display Table Information
  List.AddItem "**** BEGIN TABLE ***"
  List.AddItem "Table Name: " & tbl.Name
  List.AddItem "Date Table Created: " & tbl.DateCreated
  List.AddItem "Date Table Updated: " & tbl.LastUpdated
  List.AddItem "Can Update Table: " & tbl.Updatable
  List.AddItem ""

  Rem Display Table Attributes
  List.AddItem "Table Attributes:"
  If (tbl.Attributes And dbSystemObject) > 0 Then
    List.AddItem "System Object Table"
  End If
  If (tbl.Attributes And dbAttachedTable) > 0 Then
    List.AddItem "Attached Table"
  End If
  If (tbl.Attributes And dbAttachExclusive) > 0 Then
    List.AddItem "Attached Table Opened Exclusive"
  End If
  If (tbl.Attributes And dbAttachedODBC) > 0 Then
    List.AddItem "Attached ODBC Table"
  End If
  List.AddItem ""

  Rem Display Table Field Information
  List.AddItem "Table Fields"
  j = 0
  Set flds = tbl.Fields
  For Each fld In flds
```

```
Rem Display Field Name, Size, and Type
List.AddItem "Field Name [" & j & "] = " &
             fld.Name
List.AddItem "Field Size [" & j & "] = " &
             fld.ActualSize
List.AddItem "Field Type [" & j & "] = "
Select Case fld.Type
  Case dbBoolean
    List.AddItem "Boolean"
  Case dbByte
    List.AddItem "Byte"
  Case dbInteger
    List.AddItem "Integer"
  Case dbLong
    List.AddItem "Long"
  Case dbCurrency
    List.AddItem "Currency"
  Case dbSingle
    List.AddItem "Single"
  Case dbDouble
    List.AddItem "Double"
  Case dbDate
    List.AddItem "Date"
  Case dbText
    List.AddItem "Text"
  Case dbLongBinary
    List.AddItem "Long Binary"
  Case dbMemo
    List.AddItem "Memo"
  Case Else
    List.AddItem "Unknown Type!!!"
End Select
Rem Display Other Field Attributes
List.AddItem "Field Allow Zero Length [" & j &
             "] = " & fld.AllowZeroLength
List.AddItem "Field Source Table [" & j &
             "] = " & fld.SourceTable
List.AddItem "Field Ordinal Position [" & j &
             "] = " & fld.OrdinalPosition
List.AddItem "Field Collating Order [" & j &
             "] = " & fld.CollatingOrder
```

```
        List.AddItem "Field Required [" & j &
                    "] = " & fld.Required
        List.AddItem ""
        j = j + 1
    Next fld

    List.AddItem "*** END TABLE ***"
  Next tbl

  List.AddItem "--------------------"
  Rem Close The Database...We're Done For Now!
  db.Close
End Sub
```

You begin the process of examining the fields of a table by accessing the Fields object of the TableDef object. The Fields property returns a Fields object that you will use to loop through to access each of the fields in a table. You access the Fields object in the same way that you accessed the TableDefs object.

The Name and Size properties of the Field object return the field's name and size, respectively. The Type property returns one of the Field type constants that were described earlier. Using this value, you can determine the type of the field.

Finally, you display some basic attributes of the field. The AllowZeroLength property determines whether a field is allowed to be blank. The SourceTable property contains the actual name of the attached table from which this field retrieves its data, if it is an attached table. The OrdinalPosition and CollatingOrder properties determine the order of the field in the table and the sorting order of the field, respectively. The Required property determines whether the field requires data.

Adding a Field to a Table

Just as the Database object's CreateTableDef() method allows tables to be added to a database, the TableDef object's CreateField() method that follows allows fields to be added to a table. Table 8-6 presents the parameters that are required by the CreateField() method.

```
CreateField(fieldname, fieldtype, fieldsize)
```

TABLE 8-6 CREATEFIELD PARAMETERS

Argument	Description
fieldname	The name of the field that you want to create. The fieldname parameter is a string type.
fieldtype	The type of the field that you want to create. The fieldtype value must be one of the field type constants that were discussed earlier. The fieldtype parameter is an integer type.
fieldsize	The size (in bytes) of the field. This parameter is not required if the type of this field has an inherent size (for example, an integer field has an inherent size). The fieldsize parameter is an integer type.

Listing 8-5 shows how the CreateField() method would be called from Visual Basic to add a field to a table. This example creates a 50-character text field, named Field1, and an integer field, named Field2. You will add these fields to a table named Example. The Append() method of the Fields object must be called to actually add the fields to the table.

Listing 8-5: Adding Fields to a Table

```
Dim tbls As TableDefs
Dim tbl As TableDef
Dim flds As Fields
Dim fld1 As Field
Dim fld2 As Field

Rem Create Field1 and Field2 in table Example
tbl = tbls("Example")
flds = tbl.Fields
fld1 = tbl.CreateField("Field1",dbText,50)
fld2 = tbl.CreateField("Field2",dbInteger)

Rem Append the Fields to the table
flds.Append(fld1)
flds.Append(fld2)
```

Take a close look at the previous example, to review how you obtain access to the Example table. You don't pass an integer index to the `TableDefs` object. Instead, you pass the actual name of the table that you want. This behavior of collection indexing extends throughout DAO when you use it in a collection.

Deleting a Field from a Table

You should note that after a field is added to a table by the `Append()` method, it may not be changed. A field can be deleted by using the `Delete()` method of the `Fields` object. A field can be deleted only if it's not a member of an `Index` or `Relation` object. The `Index` and `Relation` objects are reviewed next. Listing 8-6 presents an example of deleting a field from a table that is not part of an index or relation. This example deletes Field1 from the table that is named Example.

Listing 8-6: Deleting a Field from a Table

```
Dim tbls As TableDefs
Dim flds As Fields

Rem Delete Field1 from the table Example
tbl = tbls("Example")
flds = tbl.Fields
flds.Delete("Field1")
```

Index Object

The `Index` object contains information about a table's indexes. As Chapter 7 explained, a table index is used to speed up retrieval from a table by using a key field value. Before you integrate the `Index` object into the final form of your `Schema` procedure, you will also review the `Relation` object.

The `TableDef` object holds a collection of indexes, which are stored in the `Indexes` object. Again, the `Index` and `Indexes` objects are related in the same way as the `TableDefs` and `TableDef` objects and `Fields` and `Field` objects are related.

The `Indexes` object provides the same methods that the `TableDefs` and `Fields` objects provide. Table 8-7 summarizes the objects, methods, and properties of the `Index` object.

TABLE 8-7 THE INDEX OBJECT'S METHODS AND PROPERTIES

Objects	Methods	Properties
Collection of Fields	CreateProperty()	Clustered
Collection of Properties	CreateField()	DistinctCount
		Foreign
		IgnoreNulls
		Name
		Primary
		Required
		Unique

Adding Indexes

As you saw earlier, the `TableDef` object provides a `CreateIndex()` method, which simply creates the new index. As Listing 8-7 illustrates, you must call the `CreateField()` method of the `Index` object to specify the field on which you are indexing. Finally, you must append the index field to the `Index` object and the newly created index to the `TableDef` object. This example creates a new index for the table Example for Field1; the new index will be called Index1.

Listing 8-7: Creating a New Index

```
Dim tbls As TableDefs
Dim tbl As TableDef
Dim idxs As Indexes
Dim idx As Index
Dim flds As Fields
Dim fld As Field

Rem Access the Tables collection
Set tbls = db.TableDefs

Rem Access the Example table
Set tbl = tbls("Example")

Rem Access the table indexes
Set idxs = tbl.Indexes
```

```
Rem Access the table fields
Set flds = tbl.Fields

Rem Create the New Index
Set idx = tbl.CreateIndex("Index1")

Rem Create the index field
Set fld = CreateField("Field1")

Rem Append the new field and index to the table
flds.Append(fld)
idxs.Append(idx)
```

Deleting Indexes

Deleting an index is a simple procedure. Listing 8-8 removes the index named Index1 from the table named Example that was created in the previous example. An Index object, just like a Field object, can't be deleted if it is part of a relation.

Listing 8-8: Deleting an Index from a Table

```
Dim tbls As TableDefs
Dim tbl As TableDef
Dim idxs As Indexes
Dim idx As Index
Dim flds As Fields
Dim fld As Field

Rem Access the Tables collection
Set tbls = db.TableDefs

Rem Access the Example table
Set tbl = tbls("Example")

Rem Access the table indexes
Set idxs = tbl.Indexes

Rem Delete index Index1
idxs.Delete("Index1")
```

Relation Object

A Relation object can be used to enforce referential integrity. The next chapter discusses in more detail how to create and use relations. For now, Table 8-8 summarizes the objects, methods, and properties of the Relation object. The Database object contains a collection of relations in the Relations object. The Relations object provides the same methods as the TableDefs, Fields, and Indexes objects.

TABLE 8-8 RELATION OBJECTS, METHODS, AND PROPERTIES

Objects	Methods	Properties
Collection of Fields	CreateField()	Attributes
Collection of Properties		ForeignTable
		Name
		PartialReplica
		Table

Retrieving Table, Field, and Index Information

Listing 8-9 presents the Schema procedure in its final form. Additional code has been added to print index information for each table and information about the relations contained in the database.

Listing 8-9: The Schema Procedure in Its Final Form

```
Sub Schema(DBName As String, ConnectString As String)
  Dim db As Database
  Dim tbls As TableDefs
  Dim tbl As TableDef
  Dim flds As Fields
  Dim fld As Field
  Dim idxs As Indexes
  Dim idx As Index
  Dim rels As Relations
  Dim rel As Relation
  Dim relflds As Fields
```

```
Dim relfld As Field

Rem Open the Database
Set db = DBEngine.OpenDatabase(DBName, True,
                                 True, ConnectString)

Rem Print the Database Information
List.AddItem "--------------------"
List.AddItem "Database Information"
List.AddItem ""
List.AddItem "Database Name: " & db.Name
List.AddItem "Version: " & db.Version
List.AddItem "Connection String: " & db.Connect
List.AddItem "Sorting Order: " & db.CollatingOrder
List.AddItem "Supports Transactions: " &
                                 db.Transactions
List.AddItem "Query Time Out: " & db.QueryTimeout
List.AddItem "--------------------"
List.AddItem ""

Rem Print The Table Information
List.AddItem "--------------------"
List.AddItem "Database Tables"
List.AddItem ""

Rem Loop Through Each Table In The Database
Set tbls = db.TableDefs
For Each tbl In tbls

  Rem Display Table Information
  List.AddItem "**** BEGIN TABLE ***"
  List.AddItem "Table Name: " & tbl.Name
  List.AddItem "Date Table Created: " & tbl.DateCreated
  List.AddItem "Date Table Updated: " & tbl.LastUpdated
  List.AddItem "Can Update Table: " & tbl.Updatable
  List.AddItem ""

  Rem Display Table Attributes
  List.AddItem "Table Attributes:"
  If (tbl.Attributes And dbSystemObject) > 0 Then
    List.AddItem "System Object Table"
  End If
  If (tbl.Attributes And dbAttachedTable) > 0 Then
    List.AddItem "Attached Table"
```

```
End If
If (tbl.Attributes And dbAttachExclusive) > 0 Then
  List.AddItem "Attached Table Opened Exclusive"
End If
If (tbl.Attributes And dbAttachedODBC) > 0 Then
  List.AddItem "Attached ODBC Table"
End If
List.AddItem ""

Rem Display Table Field Information
List.AddItem "Table Fields"
j = 0
Set flds = tbl.Fields
For Each fld In flds
  Rem Display Field Name, Size, and Type
  List.AddItem "Field Name [" & j & "] = " & _
               fld.Name
  List.AddItem "Field Size [" & j & "] = " & _
               fld.ActualSize
  List.AddItem "Field Type [" & j & "] = "
  Select Case fld.Type
    Case dbBoolean
      List.AddItem "Boolean"
    Case dbByte
      List.AddItem "Byte"
    Case dbInteger
      List.AddItem "Integer"
    Case dbLong
      List.AddItem "Long"
    Case dbCurrency
      List.AddItem "Currency"
    Case dbSingle
      List.AddItem "Single"
    Case dbDouble
      List.AddItem "Double"
    Case dbDate
      List.AddItem "Date"
    Case dbText
      List.AddItem "Text"
    Case dbLongBinary
      List.AddItem "Long Binary"
    Case dbMemo
      List.AddItem "Memo"
    Case Else
```

```
        List.AddItem "Unknown Type!!!"
    End Select
    Rem Display Other Field Attributes
    List.AddItem "Field Allow Zero Length [" & j &
                "] = " & fld.AllowZeroLength
    List.AddItem "Field Source Table [" & j &
                "] = " & fld.SourceTable
    List.AddItem "Field Ordinal Position [" & j &
                "] = " & fld.OrdinalPosition
    List.AddItem "Field Collating Order [" & j &
                "] = " & fld.CollatingOrder
    List.AddItem "Field Required [" & j &
                "] = " & fld.Required
    List.AddItem ""
    j = j + 1
  Next fld

  List.AddItem ""
  If(tbl.Attributes & dbSystemObjects) <> 0) Then
    List.AddItem "Table Indicies:"
    Set idxs = tbl.Indexes
    For Each idx In idxs
      List.AddItem "Index Name = " & idx.Name
      List.AddItem "Index is Foreign? " & idx.Foreign
      List.AddItem "Index is Primary? " & idx.Primary
      List.AddItem "Index is Unique? " & idx.Unique
      List.AddItem "Index is Required? " & idx.Required
      List.AddItem ""
    Next idx
  End If
  List.AddItem "*** END TABLE ***"
Next tbl

List.AddItem ""
List.AddItem "*** BEGIN RELATIONS ***"
Set rels = db.Relations
For Each rel In rels
  List.AddItem "Relation Name: " & rel.Name
  List.AddItem "Relation Name: " & rel.Attributes
  List.AddItem "Relation Name: " & rel.Table
  List.AddItem ""
  List.AddItem "Relation Fields:"
  Set relflds = rel.Fields
  For Each relfld In relflds
```

```
        List.AddItem "Relation Field Name: " & relfld.Name
    Next relfld
    List.AddItem "--------------------"
  Next rel
  List.AddItem "*** END RELATIONS ***"
  List.AddItem "--------------------"
  Rem Close The Database...We're Done For Now!
  db.Close
End Sub
```

Recordset Object

Now that you have a good understanding of how to manipulate the database objects, it's time to begin looking at how you can actually access the data that is contained in the database. Start by taking a look at the different types of `Recordset` objects that exist in DAO:

◆ `TableDef` — A `Recordset` that is accessed from a `TableDef` object. From this `Recordset`, you can access all the data in a table.

◆ `Dynaset` — A `Recordset` that is accessed from a `Dynaset` object. A `Dynaset` is created as the result of a query. Chapter 9 discusses queries and the `Dynaset` object in more detail.

◆ `Snapshot` — A `Recordset` that is accessed from a `Snapshot` object. A `Snapshot` contains a copy of the actual records in the database, unlike a `Dynaset`, which accesses the actual database records. Chapter 9 discusses the `Snapshot` object in more detail.

This chapter reviews the `TableDef` type `Recordset`. Chapter 9 explains how to create queries by using SQL and DAO, and how to examine query results by using the `Dynaset` and `Snapshot` objects.

Now, you explore how to open a table type `Recordset` object, and then continue by reviewing how you can navigate the `Recordset` object to examine the data stored in a table.

Opening a Recordset Object

Before you can begin to access the records in a table, you must first open a `Recordset` object. Table 8-9 presents the parameters required by the `TableDef` object's `OpenRecordset()` method that follows:

```
OpenRecordset(recordtype, recordoptions)
```

TABLE 8-9 OPENRECORDSET METHOD PARAMETERS

Argument	Description
recordtype	Specifies the type of the Recordset. Three constants, dbOpenTable, dbOpenDynaset, dbOpenSnapshot, specify the Recordset type. The recordtype parameter is an integer and also an optional parameter. If omitted, a Tabledef type Recordset is created, if possible.
recordoptions	Specifies optional parameters for creating the Recordset. These constants are specified in more detail in Appendix C. The recordoptions parameter is an integer and is optional.

Listing 8-10 illustrates how to open a Recordset for the table named Example.

Listing 8-10: Opening a Recordset for a Table

```
Dim tbls As TableDefs
Dim tbl As TableDef
Dim rs As Recordset

Rem Access the Tables collection
Set tbls = db.TableDefs

Rem Access the Example table
Set tbl = tbls("Example")

Rem Open the Recordset
Set rs = tbl.OpenRecordset()

Rem Do something with the Recordset...

Rem Close the Recordset
rs.Close
```

Navigating the Recordset

Now that you know how to open a `Recordset` object, take a look at how to navigate through the `Recordset`. Table 8-10 summarizes the objects, methods, and properties of the `Recordset` object.

TABLE 8-10 RECORDSET OBJECTS, METHODS, AND PROPERTIES

Objects	Methods	Properties
Collection of Fields	AddNew()	AbsolutePosition
Collection of Properties	Cancel()	BatchCollisionCount
	CancelUpdate()	BatchCollisions
	Clone()	BatchSize
	Close()	BOF
	CopyQueryDef()	EOF
	Delete()	Bookmark
	Edit()	Bookmarkable
	FillCache()	CacheSize
	FindFirst()	CacheStart
	FindLast()	Connection
	FindNext()	DateCreated
	FindPrevious()	LastUpdated
	GetRows()	EditMode
	Move()	Filter
	MoveFirst()	Index
	MoveLast()	LastModified
	MoveNext()	LockEdits
	MovePrevious()	Name
	NextRecordset()	NoMatch
	OpenRecordset()	PercentPosition
	Requery()	RecordCount

Objects	Methods	Properties
	Seek()	RecordStatus
	Update()	Restartable
		Sort
		StillExecuting
		Transactions
		Type
		Updateable
		ValidationRule
		ValidationText

As indicated by the methods of the Recordset object, the MoveFirst(), MoveLast(), MoveNext(), and MovePrevious() methods move through the database, moving to the first, last, next, and previous records, respectively. The Recordset object also provides two methods to test whether the current position is at the beginning or end of the table. The BOF property tests whether the beginning of the Recordset has been reached. The EOF property tests whether the end of the Recordset has been reached.

If you attempt to move beyond the first or last record in the Recordset, an error results.

Chapter 12 discusses how to handle DAO errors.

Listing 8-11 illustrates how to open a Recordset for the table Example, and how to step through the records from beginning to end, one at a time, printing the value of the field labeled Field1.

Listing 8-11: Navigating a Recordset for a Table

```
Dim tbls As TableDefs
Dim tbl As TableDef
Dim rs As Recordset
Dim fld As Field

Rem Access the Tables collection
```

```
Set tbls = db.TableDefs

Rem Access the Example table
Set tbl = tbls("Example")

Rem Open the Recordset
Set rs = tbl.OpenRecordset()

Rem Access Field Field1
Set fld = rs.Fields("Field1")

Rem Loop through the Recordset
rs.MoveFirst
While (Not rs.EOF)
  FieldValue = fld.Value
  rs.MoveNext
Wend

Rem Close the Recordset
rs.Close
```

Database Maintenance

The DBEngine object presents a set of methods that perform basic database mainte-nance and security. The Database object provides two methods, CompactDatabase() and RepairDatabase(), which compact and repair the database, respectively. The CompactDatabase() method may also be used to encrypt or de-encrypt a database. The CompactDatabase() and RepairDatabase() methods are primarily used for Access/Native Jet-type databases.

Compacting and Repairing the Database

The RepairDatabase() method, the simplest of the two methods, attempts to repair a damaged database. A database may become damaged if an incomplete read or write operation is performed. The RepairDatabase() method can fix basic problems that can occur with an Access/Native Jet-type database. The RepairDatabase() method simply takes one parameter, which is the name of the database to repair, as a string:

```
dbEngine.RepairDatabase("TEST.MDB")
```

Because some fragments of no-longer-needed data may be left after a repair, the CompactDatabase() method should then be invoked to complete the process of fixing the database.

TIP

Because the `RepairDatabase()` method can fix only basic database problems, ensuring that proper backups are maintained is always a good idea.

The `CompactDatabase()` method that follows takes four parameters, which are summarized in Table 8-11. When invoked, the `CompactDatabase()` method removes deleted records from the database and reorganizes the table data in a contiguous fashion.

```
CompactDatabase(srcdatabase, destdatabase, local, options)
```

TABLE 8-11 COMPACTDATABASE PARAMETERS

Argument	Description
srcdatabase	The `srcdatabase` is the name of the database to compact. The `srcdatabase` parameter is a string.
destdatabase	The `destdatabase` is the name the `srcdatabase` will be compacted to. The `srcdatabase` and `destdatabase` must not be the same name.
local	The `local` parameter specifies the sorting order of the database. See the `CreateDatabase()` method from the previous chapter for more information. The `local` parameter is a string and is an optional parameter.
options	The `options` parameter specifies the options to use when creating the `destdatabase`. See the `CreateDatabase()` method from the previous chapter for more information. The `options` parameter is an integer and an optional parameter.

NOTE

When you use the `CompactDatabase()` method on a Microsoft Access database, you must note that Access objects will *not* be converted to the compacted database. Access objects include database forms and procedures.

The following code shows how the `CompactDatabase()` method could be used to finish the repairs of the Test database:

```
dbEngine.CompactDatabase("Test.MDB","FIXEDTEST.MDB")
```

Encrypting/De-Encrypting a Database

Utilizing the `options` parameter of the `CompactDatabase()`, you can encrypt and de-encrypt a database. DAO provides two constants to specify encryption and de-encryption of the database: `dbEncrypt` and `dbDecrypt`, respectively. The final example of this chapter shows how to encrypt a database named PUBLIC.MDB to a database named PRIVATE.MDB. As you can see from the following code, the `dbEncrypt` value is placed in the option field before the `CompactDatabase()` method is called. The following example shows how you could de-encrypt a database using the same methodology:

```
dbEngine.CompactDatabase("Test.MDB","FIXEDTEST.MDB",
                         dbLangGeneral, dbEncrypt)
```

Summary

In this chapter, you learned how to access the tables contained in a database by using the `TableDefs` object. You should now understand how to access the attributes and information contained in a database table by using the `TableDef` object. You reviewed how to use the `Fields` and `Field` objects to access the individual fields in a table; how the `Index` and `Indexes` objects are used to manage a table's indexes; and how the `Recordset` object (and its associated `Move` methods) is used to access records contained in a table. You should also understand how to use the database methods to encrypt, de-crypt, repair, and compact a database. Finally, this chapter created a `Schema` procedure that displays tables, fields, indexes, and relations contained in a database.

Chapter 9

Queries and Navigation

IN THIS CHAPTER

- ◆ Differences between ANSI and DAO SQL

- ◆ Integrating SQL and DAO

- ◆ Navigating the result of a query

THIS CHAPTER REVIEWS the Structured Query Language (SQL) and the differences between ANSI SQL and DAO SQL. SQL is an important component in the process of retrieving database data in DAO, and the `QueryDef` object plays an important role in this process. This chapter introduces the `QueryDef` object, reviews how to create `Snapshot` and `Dynaset Recordset` objects, and reviews the `Find()` and `Seek()` methods.

SQL Overview

SQL is a standardized language that allows manipulation of a database and, more importantly, the data it contains. SQL was developed in the 1970s; its roots can be traced to E. F. Codd, the inventor of relational databases, and work performed at IBM during the same period. Since that time, SQL has evolved into the standard for manipulating relational database information.

SQL provides two subsets of commands. One set of commands is used for data manipulation, and the other subset is used for data definition. Data manipulation commands enable you to select and modify database data. Data definition commands provide the capability to change the database schema (tables, fields, and indices).

SQL is reviewed in detail in Chapter 6.

Differences Between DAO and ANSI SQL

If you are familiar with ANSI SQL, you need to be aware of a few differences between DAO SQL and ANSI SQL:

◆ In the LIKE conditional operator, the wildcards in ANSI SQL that are used to match a single character and multiple characters are _ and %, respectively. In DAO SQL, they are ? and *, respectively.

◆ The ANSI SQL security commands COMMIT, GRANT, and LOCK are not supported in DAO SQL.

◆ DAO SQL does not allow DISTINCT to be used on aggregate function fields.

Integrating SQL with DAO

Refer to Chapter 6, *Creating Queries*, if you need to review the SQL command language. To follow this chapter, you should have a basic understanding of the SQL language, at least enough to begin creating queries and perform most of the operations that you'll need.

QueryDef Object

The QueryDef object can be used to create and store queries for later use. An overview of the QueryDef objects, properties, and methods is shown in Table 9-1.

As explained in Chapter 8, a Database object also contains a collection of QueryDefs. The QueryDefs object has the same methods as the TableDefs object, as reviewed in Chapter 6.

TABLE 9-1 QUERYDEF OBJECTS, METHODS, AND PROPERTIES

Objects	Methods	Properties
Collection of Fields	Cancel()	CacheSize
Collection of Properties	Close()	Connect

Objects	Methods	Properties
Collection of Parameters	CreateProperty()	DateCreated
	Execute()	LastUpdated
	OpenRecordset()	KeepLocal
		LogMessages
		MaxRecords
		Name
		ODBCTimeout
		Prepare
		RecordsAffected
		Replicable
		ReturnsRecords
		SQL
		StillExecuting
		Type
		Updateable

The QueryDef object properties are used as follows:

◆ CacheSize sets or returns the number of records retrieved from an ODBC data source that will be locally buffered.

◆ Connect sets or returns a value that provides information about the source of an open connection.

◆ DateCreated and LastUpdated set or return the date and time the query was created and last updated, respectively.

◆ KeepLocal sets or returns a value on the query that you don't want to replicate when the database is replicated.

◆ LogMessages sets or returns a value that determines whether error messages returned from an ODBC data source are saved.

◆ MaxRecords sets or returns the maximum number of records returned by a query.

◆ Name sets or returns the user-defined name for the query.

◆ ODBCTimeout sets or returns the amount of time to wait when executing a query on an ODBC data source.

◆ Prepare sets or returns a value that indicates whether the query should be saved as a stored procedure on the ODBC data source – applicable only when accessing a database server such as Oracle or Microsoft SQL Server.

◆ RecordsAffected returns the number of records affected by the query.

◆ Replicable sets or returns a value that indicates whether the query can be replicated.

◆ ReturnsRecords sets or returns a value that indicates whether an SQL query returns records.

◆ SQL sets or returns the actual SQL statement to be executed.

◆ StillExecuting returns a value that indicates whether the SQL query is still running.

◆ Type returns the data type that is returned by the query.

◆ Updatable sets or returns a value that indicates whether the query can be updated.

The QueryDef object methods are used as follows:

◆ OpenRecordset() is used to open the record set returned by the query.

◆ Cancel() stops the executing of a query running in the background.

◆ Close() closes an open query.

◆ CreateProperty() is used to create new query properties.

◆ Execute is used to run the actual SQL query.

The OpenRecordset() method returns a Recordset object that can be navigated, as reviewed in Chapter 8. The Execute() method can be used in conjunction with the data definition SQL commands. QueryDef objects are best used with queries that are repeated, because the SQL command needs to be interpreted only once and can just be executed on subsequent executions.

A QueryDef object is created by the CreateQueryDef() method of the Database object, as follows:

```
CreateQueryDef(qdname, sqlstmt)
```

Table 9-2 presents the parameters that are required by the `CreateQueryDef()` method.

TABLE 9-2 THE CREATEQUERYDEF PARAMETERS

Parameter	Description
qdname	The name of the query definition. If this is an empty string (for example, " "), this `QueryDef` object can't be appended to the `Database` collection of `QueryDefs`. Qdname is a string.
sqlstmt	A valid SQL statement. `sqlstmt` is a string.

Listing 9-1 shows you how to create a `QueryDef` object in Visual Basic.

Listing 9-1: Creating a Query Definition

```
Dim qd As QueryDef
Dim db As Database
Set qd = db.CreateQueryDef("All Customers",
        "SELECT * FROM CUSTOMERS WHERE CustID > 1000")
```

To retrieve a `QueryDef` for later use, it must be appended to the `QueryDefs` collection of the `Database` object. Listing 9-2 shows how to append the `QueryDef` object that was created in Listing 9-2 to the `Database QueryDefs` collection.

Listing 9-2: Appending the QueryDef Object to the QueryDefs Collection

```
Dim qds As QueryDefs
Rem Get the QueryDefs collection
Set qds = db.QueryDefs
qds.Append(qd)
```

Listing 9-1 creates a query where the `CustID` is greater than 1000. What if the value that you wanted to be greater than was in a string? Because the SQL `SELECT` statement is in a string, you can simply append this value to the `SELECT` statement string, as shown in Listing 9-3.

Listing 9-3: Creating a Dynamic SELECT Statement with a Variable Value

```
Dim qd As QueryDef
Dim db As Database
Rem Dynamically Create The Select Statement
```

```
query = "SELECT * FROM CUSTOMERS WHERE CustID > " & Value
Set qd = db.CreateQueryDef("Cust Query",Query)
             )
```

Listing 9-4 shows how the Execute() method of the QueryDef object can be used to drop a table from the database.

 Only SQL Data Definition commands need to be executed.

Listing 9-4: Dropping a Table with a QueryDef Object

```
Dim qd As QueryDef
Dim db As Database
Set qd = db.CreateQueryDef("Drop Cust Cmd",
                           "DROP Customers")
qd.Execute()
```

The Execute() method can take an optional parameter that specifies options that are to be carried out when executing the SQL command. Table 9-3 specifies the options that can be used with the Execute() command. The Execute() method is called as follows, in which *options* is a variant parameter that has one of the values shown in Table 9-3:

```
Execute(options)
```

TABLE 9-3 EXECUTE() METHOD OPTION PARAMETERS

Execute Parameter	Description
dbDenyWrite	Denies other users write permission.
dbInconsistent	Inconsistent updates; this is the default.
dbConsistent	Consistent updates.
dbSQLPassThrough	SQL pass through. The SQL statement is passed to an ODBC database for processing.
dbFailOnError	Rolls back updates if an error occurs.
dbSeeChanges	A runtime error is generated if another user is changing data that is being edited.

Dynaset Recordset Object

As discussed in the previous chapter, two other types of Recordset objects can be created. One of those types, the Dynaset Recordset, can be updated. To open a QueryDef Recordset object, the OpenRecordset() method of the Database object is called. Listing 9-5 shows how to open the result of a query definition as a Dynaset Recordset.

Listing 9-5: Opening a Dynaset Recordset

```
Dim qd As QueryDef
Dim db As Database
Dim rs As Recordset

Rem Create a Query
Set qd = db.CreateQueryDef("All Customers",
        "SELECT * FROM CUSTOMERS WHERE CustID > 1000")

Rem Open a Dynaset Recordset
Set rs = qd.OpenRecordset("All Customers", dbOpenDynaset)
```

After a Dynaset Recordset is opened, any field values that are changed are reflected in the table.

The Updatable property of the Recordset object can be used to determine whether the Recordset can be modified.

Snapshot Recordset Object

A Snapshot Recordset is essentially the same as a Dynaset Recordset, with one very important difference: A Snapshot Recordset contains a copy of the resultant query data. A Snapshot Recordset can't be updated and will not reflect any changes made to the database by other users after the query has been performed. Listing 9-6 shows how to open the result of a query definition as a Snapshot Recordset.

Listing 9-6: Opening a Dynaset Recordset

```
Dim qd As QueryDef
Dim db As Database
Dim rs As Recordset
```

```
Rem Create a Query
Set qd = db.CreateQueryDef("All Customers",
         "SELECT * FROM CUSTOMERS WHERE CustID > 1000")

Rem Open a Snapshot Recordset
Set rs = qd.OpenRecordset("All Customers",
                          dbOpenSnapshot)
```

More Recordset Navigation

The Recordset object provides two methods to search for data in Recordset. The first method is Find(), which enables you to specify a search criteria and moves you to the first, next, last, or previous matching records. The Seek() method enables you to search for records based on an index. First, take a look at the various Find() methods.

Find() Methods

The DAO provides four Find() methods:

- ◆ FindFirst() finds the first matching record, starting at the beginning of the Recordset.

- ◆ FindLast() finds the last matching record, starting at the end of the Recordset.

- ◆ FindNext() finds the next matching record, searching forward from the current record in the Recordset.

- ◆ FindPrevious() finds the previous matching record, searching backward from the current record in the Recordset.

Each of the Find() methods takes a single string parameter that specifies the record to find. Listing 9-7 shows how to Find the first record in the Customers table that has CustomerID 1001.

Listing 9–7: Using FindFirst() to Find the First Record with CustomerID = 1001 in the Customers Table

```
Dim tbls As TableDefs
Dim tbl As TableDef
Dim rs As RecordSet
Dim fld As Field

Rem Access the Tables collection
```

```
Set tbls = db.TableDefs

Rem Access the Example table
Set tbl = tbls("Customers")

Rem Open the RecordSet
Set rs = tbl.OpenRecordSet()

Rem Find the record where CustomerID = 1001
rs.FindFirst("CustomerID = 1001")
```

Seek() Method

The Seek() method works like the Find() methods, to locate records in the database. However, the Seek() method can be faster, because it utilizes an associated index. A table must be indexed on the field that you are searching to utilize the Seek() method.

Listing 9-8 shows how to utilize the Seek() method to find the first record in the Customers table that has CustomerID 1001, assuming the Customers table has an index named CustomerIDIndex. The Seek() method takes 1 string parameter and up to 13 key parameters. The first String parameter specifies the comparison operator. This can be either <, <=, =, >=, or >. The key parameters specify the values of the index key components. In this example, the CustomerIDIndex index is composed of one key, the CustomerID.

Listing 9-8: Using Seek() to Find the First Record with CustomerID = 1001 in the Customers Table

```
Dim tbls As TableDefs
Dim tbl As TableDef
Dim rs As RecordSet
Dim fld As Field

Rem Access the Tables collection
Set tbls = db.TableDefs

Rem Access the Example table
Set tbl = tbls("Customers")

Rem Open the RecordSet
Set rs = tbl.OpenRecordSet()

Rem Find the record where CustomerID = 1001
rs.Seek("=","1001")
```

Summary

This chapter reviewed the Structured Query Language, and the differences between ANSI SQL and DAO SQL. SQL is an important component to retrieving database data in DAO, and the `QueryDef` object plays a large part. This chapter reviewed the `QueryDef` object and how to create `Snapshot` and `Dynaset Recordset` objects. Finally, this chapter reviewed how to use the `Recordset Find()` and `Seek()` methods.

Chapter 10

Multiuser Database Considerations

IN THIS CHAPTER

◆ Using database locks

◆ Replicating a database for access in multiple locations

◆ Implementing security with DAO

◆ Accessing multiuser databases with DAO

◆ Maintaining referential integrity

◆ Using transactions

◆ Developing client/server applications with DAO

OVER THE LAST FEW chapters, you have learned a lot about how to use and integrate DAO into Visual Basic's programming environment and your applications. You have acquired a basic understanding of how to develop a database application by utilizing DAO with Visual Basic. This chapter begins coverage of the more complex issues regarding the development of a database application to be used by multiple users simultaneously.

To begin exploring multiuser-related issues when utilizing DAO, the first section covers locking considerations, including database, table, and page locking. Next, you are introduced to the concept of *database replication*, the process that enables a database to be shared and kept in synchronization in a distributed environment. Inevitably, with multiple users accessing a shared data source, you must consider database security. This chapter teaches you how to handle security considerations when using DAO. The topic of security continues in the discussion of database sharing and security with Access- and ODBC-connected databases.

The `Relation` object was introduced in the last chapter. This chapter reviews how database relations can be used to ensure referential integrity in a multiuser environment. You also learn how DAO database-transaction mechanisms can be used to manage database updates and deletes through the use of the `BeginTrans()`, `CommitTrans()`, and `Rollback()` methods. Finally, this chapter introduces the special issues surrounding client/server-based application development.

Locking

DAO provides three levels of database locking when utilizing native JET/Access databases. From the most restrictive locking to the least, the three levels are the following:

◆ **Database-level locking:** Restricts access to the entire database to one user at a time.

◆ **Table-level locking:** Restricts access to a database table to one user at a time.

◆ **Page-level locking:** Restricts access to database records to one user at a time when a user has the record open. This is the base-level locking that is inherently provided by the JET database engine.

Each of these locking methods helps to ensure database integrity by restricting access to the database to one user at a time, at different levels. Database- and table-level locking can be directly specified when a database and table are accessed. Page-level locking cannot be turned on and off by your application, but this chapter shows how you can control which strategy is employed when locking records.

When you utilize back-end database servers with DAO, locking considerations are handled differently. This is discussed in more detail in "Client/Server Applications," later in this chapter.

Database Locking

Database-level locking prevents all other users from accessing the database after it is opened by one user. This is the most restrictive form of database locking.

Chapter 7, which introduces *the DAO Library*, describes in detail how to open a database.

The second parameter of the DBEngine object's OpenDatabase() method specifies whether the database is opened in exclusive mode. Listing 10-1 shows how to open a database in exclusive mode with the OpenDatabase() method.

Listing 10-1: Opening a Database for Exclusive Access

```
Sub AccessDatabase()
  ' Create a Database Object
  Dim MyDatabase As Database

  ' Set the default database type to the
  ' Jet Engine
  DBEngine.DefaultType = dbUseJet

  ' Open A dBase database named OrderEntry For Exclusive
  ' Access - The Second Parameter Determines If The
  ' Database Should Be Opened Exclusively
  Set MyDatabase = DBEngine.OpenDatabase(
                    "\\Database\\OrderEntry",
                    True, False, "DBase IV;")
  MyDatabase.Close()
End Sub
```

After the database is open for exclusive access, no other user or application is allowed to access the database until it is closed. Why would you want to use this restrictive locking mode? When you create or modify tables, fields, indexes, and relations, you probably want to ensure that no one else tries to access the database simultaneously. You also may need to update key values in multiple database tables, perhaps in tables that are part of one-to-one and one-to-many relationships. If you want to ensure that no one else tries to access these values simultaneously, database-level locking is necessary.

For more about database-level locking when you perform maintenance on your database, review Chapter 8.

As discussed in Chapter 8, the DBEngine.CompactDatabase() can be used to defragment the database and to encrypt and decrypt the database. When you perform these maintenance tasks, ensuring that no other users are accessing the database is important.

If you attempt to access a database that is open for exclusive access with the database-locking mode, an error occurs. (Error handling with DAO is reviewed later in the book.)

Chapter 12 discusses how to handle DAO errors in Visual Basic.

Table Locking

Except when you're performing database maintenance, including compacting the database and schema changes, database-level locking is not an effective strategy for controlling multiuser access. Perhaps you need to update the price of a large group of items in a product table. Table-level locking can be used to prevent others from accessing a table while operations are being performed on it. For example, while the table is being updated to reflect the new pricing, the table-level lock prevents users from retrieving a mixture of old and new prices during the update process.

To turn on table-level locking in DAO, the dbDenyRead and dbDenyWrite constants must be passed to the OpenRecordset() method. As you may recall from earlier chapters, the last parameter of the OpenRecordset() method specifies certain characteristics for the Recordset. Listing 10-2 shows how to open a table-type Recordset for exclusive access.

For more about the OpenRecordset() method, see Chapters 8 and 9.

Listing 10-2: Opening a Recordset for Exclusive Access

```
Dim db as Database

Rem Open the RecordSet
Rem The dbDenyWrite and dbDenyRead constants prevent
Rem other users from reading or writing to the
Rem Customers table

Set rs = db.OpenRecordSet("Customers",
                          dbOpenTable,
                          dbDenyWrite + dbDenyRead)

Rem Perform operations on Recordset while
Rem exclusively opened

rs.Close
```

Listing 10-2 prevents others from opening the Customers table until the `Recordset` is closed. If a table is locked when you attempt to open it, the `OpenRecordset()` method causes an error.

Chapter 12 reviews how to handle DAO errors in Visual Basic.

Page Locking

Page-level locking is automatically handled by DAO; it can't be turned on and off like database- and table-level locking. However, you can control the type of strategy employed with page-level locking. When you access data that is stored in a native JET/Access-type database, you use a paging methodology. The entire database is partitioned into sections, each the same size, called *pages*. When you use native JET/Access-type databases, the page size is always 2K. You can't control the page size or specify which records appear on a page.

When many modifications are made to a database, the pages can become fragmented, with holes of data that no longer contain valid data. When the `CompactDatabase()` method is executed, these holes are coalesced, which can improve database performance. The number of records present on a page is dependent on the size of your database records. If your record size is smaller than 2K, several records may be present on a page. Also, you should remember that when you make data modifications, records that may appear adjacent to each other when you access a table sequentially are not necessarily adjacent to each other on a page.

Two page-level locking strategies are available: pessimistic locking and optimistic locking. DAO enables you to select which locking strategy is employed.

PESSIMISTIC LOCKING
When the pessimistic-locking strategy is employed, a page becomes locked whenever an `Edit()` or `AddNew()` method is called. The page-level lock is released when the `Cancel()` or `Update()` method is called. Pessimistic locking ensures database integrity at the highest level. Whenever a user attempts to add or modify database records, the associated data pages become locked. Pessimistic locking, though, can cause pages to remain locked for long periods of time, preventing other users from accessing the same table data. The pessimistic-locking strategy is the default. The optimistic-locking strategy attempts to address these shortcomings.

OPTIMISTIC LOCKING
When the optimistic-locking strategy is employed, a page becomes locked only when the `Update()` method is called. The `Edit()` and `AddNew()` methods can be called without creating a lock, so that a user can start making modifications

without locking a page. When the Update() method is called, an attempt is made to lock the affected pages, and if the lock is allowed, the affected data is written to the locked pages. Optimistic locking can keep pages locked for the shortest period of time, which can be very important when many users are accessing the database.

The biggest disadvantage of optimistic locking is that two users can begin to make modifications on the same record, and they do not find out that the record is locked or has already been changed until they attempt to commit their changes. (When the Update() method is invoked and the affected pages are already locked, an exception is thrown.)

If the data source you are connected to is an ODBC database, only the optimistic-locking strategy is employed. This issue is covered in more detail when client/server applications are discussed later in this chapter.

CONTROLLING LOCKS

You can use the LockEdits property, a Boolean, to change the page-level locking strategy employed from the Recordset object. If LockEdits is true, the pessimistic-locking strategy is employed; if false, the optimistic-locking strategy is used. Listing 10-3 demonstrates how to open the Customers table with optimistic locking. By default, when a Recordset is opened, the pessimistic-locking strategy is in effect. The locking strategy for the specified Recordset remains in effect until the Recordset is changed, either by changing the LockEdits property or closing the Recordset.

Listing 10-3: Opening the Customers Table and Turning On Optimistic Locking

```
Dim db as Database

Rem Open the RecordSet
Rem The dbDenyWrite and dbDenyRead constants prevent
Rem other users from reading or writing to the
Rem Customers table
Set rs = db.OpenRecordSet("Customers",
                          dbOpenTable)


rs.LockEdits = True


Rem Perform operations on Recordset while
Rem using optimistic locking


rs.Close
```

The `LockEdits` property sets or returns a Boolean that specifies which lock edit mode is currently being employed.

CHOOSING A LOCKING STRATEGY

The inevitable question is which locking strategy should you employ? Pessimistic locking warns of a potential update conflict as soon as the operation to modify a record is invoked. The optimistic-locking strategy doesn't detect potential conflicts until an attempt is made to commit the changes.

Pessimistic locking can cause locks to be held for longer periods of time. For example, a user could begin modifying a record and then get distracted by something else, without completing the operation. When pessimistic locking is employed, that record remains locked until the user commits or cancels the changes. The optimistic-locking strategy attempts to minimize the amount of time that a record is locked. If more than one user begins to edit a record with optimistic locking, the first user to save their changes will have them committed to the database. A user can make many changes to a record, only to be frustrated to find that the changes can't be committed, because someone else has already made and saved a change to the same record. Even with its disadvantages, the optimistic-locking strategy is usually the most efficient and effective page-level locking strategy.

Database Replication

Database replication can enable a native JET/Access database to be split into multiple copies that can be kept in synchronization. Database replication can enable a database to be used in a distributed environment, providing mechanisms to bring the distributed copies back into synchronization. Each copy of the database is called a *replica*, and the process of distributing database updates is called *synchronization*.

While database replication can provide database access in a distributed computing environment, it does have some limitations. Principally, database replication is not a viable solution if it is important for each database user to have access to the most up-to-date data, and if a lot of the data will be changing frequently. The process of synchronizing database records can take some time and usually is performed at specified intervals.

Making Replicas

Before a database can be replicated, it must be converted to a format that is replicable. The `Replicable` property of the database determines whether a database is replicable. When the `Replicable` property is set to `T`, the database is replicable. Listing 10-4 demonstrates how to convert a database into a replicable form. Before a database can be replicated, you must ensure that it is not password-protected. If the database is password-protected, you must convert it into a decrypted form before it can be replicated.

Listing 10-4: Converting the OrderEntry Database into a Replicable Form

```
' Create a Database Object
Dim MyDatabase As Database
Dim repprop As Property

' Open The OrderEntry Database For Exclusive
' Access - The Second Parameter Determines If The
' Database Should Be Opened Exclusively
Set MyDatabase = DBEngine.OpenDatabase(
                    "OrderEntry.MDB",
                    True, False)

' Create the replicable property
Set repprop = MyDatabase.CreateProperty("Replicable",
                                    dbText, "T")
' Append the replicable property
MyDatabase.Append repprop

' Set the Replicable property to True
MyDatabase.Properties("Replicable") = "T"
```

The database converted for replication becomes the master design database. Any changes to the database schema can be performed only in the master design database.

Preventing a Database Object from Being Replicated

After the database is converted into a replicable form, each object contained in the database (tables, queries, and so on) is converted to an object that is replicable. If you don't want certain tables to be accessed in the database replicas, you must set their KeepLocal property to T. Database objects that you want to keep local must have their KeepLocal property set to T before the database is converted into a replicable form. If a table is part of a relation, both tables in the relation must have their KeepLocal properties set to the same value. Listing 10-5 demonstrates how to keep the Customers table from being replicated.

Listing 10-5: Keeping the Customers Table from Being Replicated

```
' Create a Database Object
Dim MyDatabase As Database
Dim tblprop As Property
Dim tbl As TableDef
```

```
' Open The OrderEntry Database For Exclusive
' Access - The Second Parameter Determines If The
' Database Should Be Opened Exclusively
Set MyDatabase = DBEngine.OpenDatabase(
                    "OrderEntry.MDB",
                    True, False)

Set tbl = MyDatabase.TableDefs("Customers")

' Create the Local property
Set tblprop = tbl.CreateProperty("KeepLocal",
                                    dbText, "T")
' Append the KeepLocal property
tbl.Append repprop

' Set the Replicable property to True
tbl.Properties("KeepLocal") = "T"
```

 When you convert a database into a replicable form, `AutoNumber` fields of a table are converted from incremental to random. If an `AutoNumber` field is a primary key, this conversion helps to ensure that the keys are unique if new records are added to the database. However, duplicate random keys can be created in replica databases. You may have to use the `s_Guid` (a GUID is a *globally unique identifier*, which contains a unique 12-bit value) field, which is automatically created, to be sure that all keys are unique. If your application relies on the sequential nature of an `AutoNumber` field, the addition of a Time/Date stamp field can be used to order fields sequentially.

Making Replica Copies

Additional replica copies can be made only from other replica copies. Design changes can be made only in the master design database. When the original database was converted to a replicable form in Listing 10.4, the replica set had only one replica member. To make another database replica, the `MakeReplica()` method is called:

```
MakeReplica(replicaname, replicadesc, readonly)
```

Table 10-1 presents the parameters that are required by the `MakeReplica()` method. Listing 10-6 demonstrates how to make a replica of the OrderEntry database.

TABLE 10-1 MAKEREPLICA PARAMETERS

Argument	Description
replicaname	The file name of the replica database (including path). replicaname is a string.
replicadesc	A description of the replica database. replicadesc is a string and is optional.
Readonly	If the dbMakeRepReadOnly value is passed in this optional parameter, the new database replica will be read-only.

 If your database contains attached tables, you need to test your new replica to ensure that all attached table paths are still valid from the new replica location.

Listing 10-6: Making a Replica Copy of the OrderEntry Database

```
' Create a Database Object
Dim MyDatabase As Database

' Open The OrderEntry Database For Exclusive
' Access - The Second Parameter Determines If The
' Database Should Be Opened Exclusively
Set MyDatabase = DBEngine.OpenDatabase(
                    "OrderEntry.MDB",
                    True, False)

' Create a database replica called OrderEntRep
MyDatabase.MakeReplica("OrderEnterRep.MDB",
                    "Order Entry Replica")
MyDatabase.Close
```

Synchronizing

To synchronize database replicas, the Database.Synchronize() method is called. When replicas are synchronized, all database design changes are synchronized first. Changes to the database data are then communicated between the replicas until the replicas are brought into synch. The synchronization of replicas can be either one-way or bidirectional. The first parameter of the Synchronize() method specifies the name of the replica database to synchronize with, while the second parameter passed to the Synchronize() method specifies the type of synchronization to be performed. Table 10-2 summarizes the synchronization options.

TABLE **10-2 SYNCHRONIZE() METHOD OPTIONS**

Option	Description
dbRepExportChanges	Export changes from the current database to the replica.
dbRepImportChanges	Import changes from the replica into the current database.
dbRepImpExpChanges	Bidirectionally synchronize databases. This is the default.

Listing 10-7 demonstrates how to use the Synchronize() method to perform a bidirectional synchronization on database replicas. Even if one-way synchronization is specified, design changes are still brought into synchronization between the replicas.

Listing 10-7: Bidirectional Synchronization of Database Replicas

```
' Create a Database Object
Dim MyDatabase As Database

' Open The OrderEntry Database For Exclusive
' Access - The Second Parameter Determines If The
' Database Should Be Opened Exclusively
Set MyDatabase = DBEngine.OpenDatabase(
                    "OrderEntry.MDB",
                    True, False)

' Synchronize database with replica
MyDatabase.Synchronize("OrderEnterRep.MDB")
MyDatabase.Close
```

Conflicts

This section wraps up the discussion of database replicas by addressing how conflicts are handled when replica databases are synchronized. Two types of synchronization conflicts can occur: design and data conflicts.

Whenever an error occurs during synchronization, a record is created in the conflict table. The name of the conflict table is MSysErrors. The `getConflictTable()` method can also be used to retrieve the name of the conflict table. The conflict table contains the following fields:

◆ **TableGuid**: The name of the table involved in the conflict

◆ **RowGuid**: The record that contained the errors

◆ **LastChange**: Which replica changed the record last

◆ **Operation**: The type of the failed operation

◆ **Gen_ReasonText, ReasonText**: Why the operation failed

After each synchronization, you should examine the conflict table to determine whether any errors occurred. This can be performed either automatically by the application or manually by the database administrator. Performing automatic conflict resolution can be a complex task, because you must determine which replica version of the database to trust as being correct.

If a design conflict occurs, a record is created in the design conflict table. The name of the design conflict table is MSysSchemaProb. This table can be checked after a synchronization to determine whether any design conflicts have occurred. Resolving these conflicts manually is probably your best strategy. The design conflict table contains the following fields:

◆ The type of command that failed

◆ Why the operation failed

◆ The design version that had the design problem

◆ The names of the tables and columns in conflict

Security

To utilize database security with native JET/Access databases, you must have Access installed on your system. When Access is installed, it creates a file called SYSTEM.MDW that contains the user and group information.

When you use Access 97 and the 32-bit version of DAO (DAO 3.0 through 3.5), the security file is called SYSTEM.MDW. When you use the older, 16-bit (DAO 2.5) version of DAO and Access, this file is called SYSTEM.MDA. The only difference between the two files is their names.

To enable system security on native JET/Access databases when you use DAO, Microsoft Access is required. You must remember that all security information for a database is stored in the SYSTEM.MDW file. If that file is removed, database security is compromised. In a multiuser environment, locating the SYSTEM.MDW file in a read-only area – ideally in a read-only directory on the network – is important. Multiple SYSTEM.MDW files can be used for different applications. If multiple SYSTEM.MDW files are used, they should be stored in the same directory as the database.

Even if the SYSTEM.MDW file is present, any application accessing the shared database is not required to utilize it. An application can open and manipulate a database without even checking for the SYSTEM.MDW file.

Users and Groups

DAO provides four objects to manage users and groups: `User`, `Users`, `Group`, and `Groups`. The `Users` object allows access to the collection of database users. The `User` object encapsulates the information for a specific user. A group is a collection of users. Groups can be used to grant or disallow access to a group of database users. The `Groups` and `Group` objects are similar to the `Users` and `User` objects, encapsulating all the groups and a single group, respectively. Tables 10-3 and 10-4 present the objects, properties, and methods associated with the `User` and `Group` objects, respectively.

The `Users` and `Groups` objects have the same methods and properties as the `TableDefs`, `Fields`, and `Indexes` objects presented in Chapter 7.

TABLE 10-3 USER OBJECTS, METHODS, AND PROPERTIES

Objects	Methods	Properties
Collection of `Groups`	`CreateGroup()`	`Name`
Collection of `Properties`	`NewPassword()`	`Password`
		`PID`

TABLE 10-4 GROUP OBJECTS, METHODS, AND PROPERTIES

Objects	Methods	Properties
Collection of Users	CreateUser()	Name
Collection of Properties		PID

Listing 10-8 demonstrates how to use the Users and User objects to create and add a new user. The PID is a user-defined string that uniquely identifies a new user or group. The new user is also added to the group DBUsers, which, for purposes of this example, you can assume already exists. Listing 10-9 demonstrates how to create a new group.

Listing 10-8: Creating a New User

```
Dim ws As Workspace
Dim newuser As User
Dim g As Group

Rem Create the new user
Set ws = DBEngine.Workspace(0)
Set newuser = ws.CreateUser("Diane","102972","POKEY")
ws.Users.Append newuser
Rem Add the new user to the DBUser group
Set g = ws.Groups("DBUser")
g.Append newuser
```

Listing 10-9: Creating a New Group

```
Dim ws As Workspace
Dim newgroup As Group

Rem Create the new group
Set ws = DBEngine.Workspace(0)
Set newgroup = ws.Group("DBUser","DBU11111")

Rem Append the new group
ws.Groups.Append newgroup
```

Changing Permissions

The DAO has three objects — Document, Container, and Containers — which are used to specify permissions for Database objects. A Database object holds a collection of Container objects (which are accessed through the Containers object). The JET database engine defines three different types of container-type objects: Databases, Tables, and Relations. Each container-type object holds information about all of its associated objects as Document objects. For example, the Tables container holds a collection of Document objects that represent the tables in the database. Listing 10-10 demonstrates how these objects are used to allow only read access to the Customers database for the user Diane that was created in the previous examples. Table 10-5 lists the permission constants.

Listing 10-10: Changing the Customers Table to Read-Only for the New User Diane

```
' Create a Database Object
Dim MyDatabase As Database
Dim c As Container
Dim d As Document

' Open The OrderEntry Database
Set MyDatabase = DBEngine.OpenDatabase(
                    "OrderEntry.MDB",
                    False, False)

' Get the Tables container
Set c = MyDatabase.Containers("Tables")

' Get the Customers table document
Set d = c.Documents("Customers")

' Give the user Diane retrieve permissions
d.UserName = "Diane"
d.Permissions = dbSecRetrieveData
```

When you change permissions, the database must be opened. Also, when you set multiple permission attributes on a database object, the constants should be logically ordered together.

TABLE 10-5 DATABASE OBJECT PERMISSION CONSTANTS

ConstantName	Description
dbSecCreate	The user can create new document objects.
DbSecDBCreate	The user can create new databases.
DbSecDBExclusive	The user has exclusive access to the database.
dbSecDBOpen	The user can open the database.
dbSecDelete	The user can delete the specified database object.
DbSecDeleteData	The user can delete data.
dbSecFullAccess	The user has complete access to the database object.
DbInsertData	The user can add new data.
dbSecNoAccess	The user has no access to the database object.
DbSecReadDef	The user can read the table definition.
DbSecReadSec	The user can read security information.
dbSecReplaceData	The user can modify records.
DbSecRetrieveData	The user can retrieve data.
dbSecWriteDef	The user can write the table definition.
DbSecWriteOwner	The user can change the owner properties of the database object.
DbSecWriteSec	The use can write security information.

Opening a Secured Access Database

When you open a secured Access database, you must set the default user and password before initializing the DBEngine. Listing 10-11 shows how the user created earlier, Diane, can access the OrderEntry database.

Listing 10-11: Accessing a Secured Access Database

```
' Create a Database Object
Dim MyDatabase As Database
```

```
' Set the default username and password
DBEngine.DefaultUser = "Diane"
DBEngine.DefaultPassword = "POKEY"

' Open The OrderEntry Database
Set MyDatabase = DBEngine.OpenDatabase(
                    "OrderEntry.MDB",
                    False, False)
```

Opening a Secured ODBC Database

When you access ODBC data sources with DAO, the server security is not enforced or overridden. If a user performs an operation that violates the database server security, they may receive an error message from the database server.

 You may want to review the discussion of usernames and passwords in Chapter 7.

When you open an ODBC database, the username and password are specified in the `OpenDatabase()` method's connect string parameter. Listing 10-12 demonstrates how an ODBC database is opened, in which the connect string specifies the username and password. The `UID` parameter of the connect string specifies the username, and the `PWD` parameter specifies the user's password. You must consult your database server documentation to determine how to set up users and their associated passwords.

Listing 10-12: Specifying the Username and Password when Opening an ODBC Database

```
' Create a Database Object
Dim MyDatabase As Database
Dim Connect As String

' Open The ODBC Data Source
Connect = "ODBC;DSN=IDCNTSERVER;Database=MyDatabase;
UID=John;PWD=Password"
Set MyDatabase = DBEngine.OpenDatabase(
                    "",
                    False, Connect)
```

Database Sharing

When multiple users are accessing an Access database, the following things need to be considered:

◆ Files with the extension .LDB are created in the same directory as the database. The LDB files manage user locking of the database. They should not be deleted while a user is accessing the database.

◆ When you share a database, you need to make sure that enough file locks are available to access the SYSTEM.MDW file. If a lock can't be granted, error messages result stating that the SYSTEM.MDW is locked by another user. If the SYSTEM.MDW file is located on a file server, consult your server documentation to ensure enough file locks are available.

When multiple users are accessing the database, DAO collections (for example, `Relations`, `Fields`, `TableDefs`, `Indexes`, and so on) can become stale. That is, they might not have values that accurately reflect the current database state. These collections provide a `Refresh()` method, which will synchronize them to the current database state. You should call the `Refresh()` method only when needed, though, because it is a high-overhead operation.

Maintaining Referential Integrity

Table *relationships* link two tables in a relational database, to produce useful information. Two tables are related to each other through the use of common fields that are unique in identifying records. Using the DAO `Relation` object, these relations can be maintained by the database. When multiple users are accessing the database simultaneously, maintaining referential integrity becomes very important.

See Chapter 8 for more about table relationships.

Defining Relations

Looking back at the simple OrderEntry database in the previous chapter, you can see that the two tables, Customers and Orders, are related by the `CustomerID` key.

The customers table is defined as follows:

Field	Type
CustomerID	Long integer
CompanyName	50-character string
ContactFirstName	30-character string
ContactLastName	50-character string
CompanyOrDepartment	50-character string
BillingAddress	255-character string
City	50-character string
StateOrProvince	20-character string
PostalCode	20-character string
Country	50-character string
ContactTitle	50-character string
PhoneNumber	30-character string
Extension	30-character string
FaxNumber	30-character string
EmailAddress	50-character string
Notes	Memo

The Orders table is defined as follows:

Field	Type
OrderID	Long Integer
CustomerID	Long Integer
Required-byDate	Date
Promised-byDate	Date
ShipName	50-character string
ShipAddress	255-character string
ShipCity	50-character string

Field	Type
ShipState	50-character string
ShipStateOrProvince	50-character string
ShipPostalCode	20-character string
ShipCountry	50-character string
ShipPhoneNumber	30-character string
ShipDate	Date
ShippingMethodID	Long Integer
FreightCharge	Currency
SalesTaxRate	Double

The relationship between the tables is a one-to-many relationship. Only one customer relates to a `CustomerID` in the Customers table, but the `CustomerID` can appear many times in the Orders table (a customer may have placed many orders). When the `CustomerID` field appears in the Customers table, it is referred to as a *primary key*. When the `CustomerID` field appears in the Orders table, it is referred to as a *foreign key*, because it is a key to another table. The Orders table is also referred to as the *foreign table* in this relationship. The Customers table is referred to as the *primary table*. To define a relationship using the DAO `Relation` object, you must know two things: the names of the primary and foreign tables, and the name of the primary and foreign key field. The `Database.CreateRelation()` method is called to establish the relation:

```
CreateRelation(relname, primarytable, foreigntable, attributes)
```

Table 10-6 summarizes the parameters required by the `CreateRelation()` method. Listing 10-13 demonstrates how to create the relation between Customers and Orders tables.

When a foreign key appears in a table, it should have the same name as the primary key. As you can see, the CustomerID field has the same name in both tables. Not only is this a good database design practice, but it is also a requirement when establishing relations.

TABLE 10-6 CREATERELATION() METHOD PARAMETERS

Parameter	Description
relname	The name of the relation. relname is a string parameter.
primarytable	The name of the primary table. primarytable is a string parameter.
foreigntable	The name of the primary table. foreigntable is a string parameter.
attributes	Specifies the relation attributes (summarized in Table 10-7). attributes is an optional integer value.

Listing 10-13: Creating a Relation

```
' Create a Database Object
Dim MyDatabase As Database
Dim r As Relation
Dimd f As Field

' Open The OrderEntry Database
Set MyDatabase = DBEngine.OpenDatabase(
                 "OrderEntry.MDB",
                 False, False)

' Create the new relation
Set r = MyDatabse.CreateRelation("CustOrders",
                    "Customers",
                    "Orders",
                    dbUpdateCascade +
                    dbDeleteCascade)

' Create the relation field
Set f = r.CreateField("CustomerID")

' Append the field to the Relation
r.Fields.Append f

' Append the new relation
db.Relations.Append r
```

Delete and Update Cascading

You now know how to define a relation, but the key to the importance of a relation is found in its attributes. Table 10-7 summarizes the relation attribute constants.

TABLE 10-7 SUMMARY OF RELATION ATTRIBUTE CONSTANTS

Constant	Description
dbRelationUnique	Specifies a one-to-one relationship
dbRelationDontEnforce	Don't enforce referential integrity on the relation
dbRelationInherited	The relationship includes attached tables
dbRelationUpdateCascade	Updates will be cascading
dbRelationDeleteCascade	Deletes will be cascading

The example in Listing 10-13 specified the relation necessary to have update and delete cascading attributes. With update and delete cascading, whenever the CustomerID field is deleted or changed in the Customers table, the records in which that CustomerID appears in the Orders table is also modified (with the new data value) or deleted, as appropriate. Delete cascading should be used with care. In Listing 10-13, update cascading is a good attribute of this relation, but you might not want to delete all orders placed by a customer when you delete the customer. You probably want your application to check whether any associated orders for a customer exist before allowing the customer to be deleted. Instead, you might want to add a field to the Customers table, marking the customer as inactive, but maintaining the necessary referential integrity for any orders previously placed. This information could also be used later to generate historical reports that list deleted customers.

Transactions

Sometimes, treating a series of database operations in your application as a single operation is advantageous. The transaction methods of DAO enable you to do this. Transactions also help to maintain database integrity. With transaction processing, you can update a large number of records that span a few tables, and if any errors occur during your processing, transaction processing can undo your changes before they are applied to the database.

To initiate transaction processing with DAO, the `Workspace` object provides three methods. These methods encapsulate your transaction. The `BeginTrans()` method specifies the start of your transaction. After your transactions are specified, the end of your transactions are marked by either the `RollBack()` or `CommitTrans()` methods. The `RollBack()` method causes your transactions *not* to be applied to the database, whereas the `CommitTrans()` method causes your transactions to be applied to the database. If the `Workspace` object is closed and transactions are still pending, they are rolled back. Transactions can be nested, up to five levels deep. The current level of transaction must be saved or rolled back before a higher level of transactions can be committed or rolled back. Listing 10-14 demonstrates the use of transactions in their simplest form.

Listing 10-14: Using Transactions when Updating the Customers Table

```
Dim db As Database
Dim ws As Workspace
Dim rs As RecordSet

Rem Access the default workspace
Set ws = db.Workspaces(0)

Rem Open the RecordSet
Set rs = db.OpenRecordSet("Customers", dbOpenTable)

Rem Begin the transaction
ws.BeginTrans

Rem Loop through the record set
rs.MoveFirst
While (Not rs.EOF)
  Rem Modify the table records ...
  rs.MoveNext
Wend

Rem Commit the transaction
ws.CommitTrans

Rem Close the RecordSet
rs.Close
```

As previously stated, using transactions in your DAO application can help to ensure database integrity. They also can increase the performance of your application. Your transactions are buffered until the `CommitTrans()` method is called. This can greatly increase database performance, because transactions are written to the database in a batch instead of incrementally. Transactions can also assist in processing complex database queries. The next section, "Client/Server Applications," explains that complex database queries can cause locking conflicts. Also, transactions can't be nested when using ODBC database sources.

Not all databases support the DAO transaction mechanisms. Some externally attached databases do not support transaction mechanisms – for example, Paradox. To check whether a `Recordset` or `Database` supports transactions, check the `Transactions` property of that object; if it is true, transactions are supported. `Recordsets` resulting from an SQL statement that includes `JOIN` and `WHERE` clauses do not support transactions.

When you begin a set of transactions, they are buffered to your local disk until they are committed or rolled back. An error occurs if you run out of disk space while buffering transactions.

Client/Server Applications

Client/server applications usually employ a back-end database server. Each client application establishes a connection to the database server to gain access to the database. By their definition, client/server applications are primarily used in multi-user environments.

See Chapter 8 to review how DAO establishes a link between the client application and the database server through ODBC connectivity.

You've already learned how to establish a connection to an ODBC database server, and even how to connect to a database server in a secured environment. Still to be covered are some considerations regarding controlling locking from DAO with a database server, as well as some strategies to help maximize resource utilization and application performance.

Locking

A database server usually has its own mechanisms for locking database records. The following are some things to note regarding the earlier discussion of locking as it relates to a database server environment:

◆ Database-level locking can't be employed with a database server. The open-for-exclusive-use parameter of the `OpenDatabase()` method is ignored when connecting to an ODBC database server.

- ◆ Table-level locking is not recommended. Locking a table can have detrimental performance effects with a database server.

- ◆ You can't control page-level locking for a database server. When you work through DAO with an ODBC database server, the database server always employs optimistic page-level locking.

- ◆ Complex transactions that update large amounts of data simultaneously can lock affected tables until the transaction is complete. Performing these operations during off-peak hours is best.

- ◆ When you use the `ORDER BY` clause in an SQL query, a database server may lock access to the tables that are part of the query until the `ORDER BY` sorting is complete.

- ◆ Relying on the database server's native locking mechanisms is your best option when utilizing DAO. Your application should be designed to handle locking errors when they do occur.

 When you finish with a transaction, you should commit or roll back the transaction as soon as possible, to release the resources that are being tied up while the transaction is open.

Connection Strategies

Establishing a connection with a database server in a client/server application can take a long time. If your application utilizes an ODBC database server, you can employ the following strategies to maximize your database server utilization and client performance:

- ◆ Establish a connection to the database server when your application starts. Opening a connection to the database when the application begins, with the `OpenDatabase()` method, establishes an initial connection to the database server.

- ◆ Review your application to reduce the number of open server connections if your server cannot process multiple queries over a single connection.

- ◆ Limit the number of records returned at one time in a `Dynaset` `Recordset`. DAO can return 100 or fewer records with a single connection; if the number of records returned is greater, multiple connections are required.

- ◆ Establish connection time-outs during long periods of inactivity. By default, a connection times out after 10 minutes (600 seconds) of inactivity. This can be changed by editing the `ConnectionTimeout` parameter in the `Microsoft\Jet\3.5\Engines\ODBC` folder, located in the Windows Registry.

◆ Remember to release your connections when you're through. If you are accessing a small `Recordset`, you can use the `MoveLast()` method to cause the execution of your query to complete execution. Executing the `MoveLast()` method can result in a performance penalty. If you are finished with your `Recordset`, the `Close()` method also causes the connection to close.

Although establishing database server connections is a multiuser database issue, establishing good connection strategies is also a matter of improving performance. The next chapter examines the performance issues of your DAO applications, including how to optimize your DAO performance through database design techniques, code and query optimizations, and client/server optimizations.

Summary

In this chapter, you learned how to utilize the database-, table-, and page-level locking mechanisms of DAO. You also reviewed the process and considerations of creating database replicas, and how to handle conflicts when errors occur during synchronization. You learned how to create users and groups for use when accessing secured Access databases. This chapter also covered the process of creating and utilizing table relations to maintain referential integrity when updating and deleting related fields. Finally, this chapter addressed the considerations of creating client/server applications, including how to handle locking and how to employ connection strategies to minimize the use of database resources.

Chapter 11

Optimization Issues

IN THIS CHAPTER

- ◆ Introducing database normalization
- ◆ Optimizing your DAO code for faster performance
- ◆ Optimizing your DAO code for better performance with client/server applications

THIS CHAPTER REVIEWS optimization from several different perspectives. Optimization is not a single issue; it must be considered part of a unified approach. As the old saying goes, "A chain is only as strong as its weakest link." This chapter looks at different areas of optimization when utilizing DAO, but remember that each area is a component of your overall application performance. Many of the techniques discussed in this chapter are applicable to database programming in general. These techniques will be useful when you are designing your applications with RDO, ADO, OLE DB, and ODBC.

Database Normalization

The first step in designing any database application is proper database design. A key aspect to designing an optimal relational database is *normalization*. Normalization can best be described as the process of eliminating duplicate data in your database. A normalized database can reduce the amount of data that your application needs to retrieve, modify, and add to your database. Entire books have been dedicated to the subject of database normalization; this chapter presents the basic rules of normalization, along with examples of their application. The following are the five basic rules/levels of database normalization:

- ◆ Level 1: Remove groups of repeating data
- ◆ Level 2: Remove duplicate data
- ◆ Level 3: Remove columns of a table that aren't dependent on the primary key
- ◆ Level 4: Place independent multiple relationships in separate tables
- ◆ Level 5: Place dependent multiple relationships in separate tables

Although these rules initially may seem complex, you will find that by applying common sense toward the goal of removing redundant data in your tables, you will be able to design a database to Level 3 normalization, better known as *third normal form*. Next, these rules are described in more detail and applied through some sample applications.

Remove Groups of Repeating Data

This first level of database normalization helps to reduce wasted space in your tables by removing repeated data components into their own individual tables. Table 11-1 is a possible initial design for a table that stores a customer's order. This table is used to demonstrate some of the principals of database normalization.

TABLE 11-1 INITIAL DESIGN FOR A CUSTOMER ORDERS TABLE

Field	Type
CompanyName	50-character string
ContactFirstName	30-character string
ContactLastName	50-character string
CompanyOrDepartment	50-character string
BillingAddress	255-character string
City	50-character string
StateOrProvince	20-character string
PostalCode	20-character string
Country	50-character string
ContactTitle	50-character string
PhoneNumber	30-character string
Extension	30-character string
FaxNumber	30-character string
EmailAddress	50-character string
Notes	Memo
OrderID	Long integer
Required-byDate	Date
Promised-byDate	Date

Field	Type
ShipName	50-character string
ShipAddress	255-character string
ShipCity	50-character string
ShipState	50-character string
ShipStateOrProvince	50-character string
ShipPostalCode	20-character string
ShipCountry	50-character string
ShipPhoneNumber	30-character string
ShipDate	Date
ShippingMethod	50-character string
ShipperName	50-character string
FreightCharge	Currency
SalesTaxRate	Double
ProductID1	Long integer
Quantity1	Long integer
ProductID2	Long integer
Quantity2	Long integer
ProductID3	Long integer
Quantity3	Long integer
ProductID4	Long integer
Quantity4	Long integer
ProductID5	Long integer
Quantity5	Long integer
OrderTotal	Double

You may notice various problems with this table design. These problems will be addressed by applying the normalization rules. The first rule states that you should eliminate multiple repeating groups of data.

Using numbered fields in your table is the easiest way to spot repeating groups of data. In the Orders table, numbered fields identify each product and the associated quantity a customer has ordered.

In Table 11-1, some flaws exist in how the data is stored that tracks the items that a customer orders. If a customer orders five or fewer items, the data can be stored; but, if they order fewer than five items, space is wasted due to empty fields. Applying the first rule of normalization, the order items need to be moved. Thus, the ProductIDx and Quantityx fields are moved into a new OrderItems table, as shown in Table 11-2. Entries in the OrderItems table contain the foreign key OrderID, which links these items back to the updated Orders table, as shown in Table 11-3. The ProductID field links to a Products table that contains a product description and unit price.

TABLE 11-2 THE ORDERITEMS TABLE

Field

OrderID

ProductID

Quantity

TABLE 11-3 THE UPDATED ORDERS TABLE

Field

CompanyName

ContactFirstName

ContactLastName

CompanyOrDepartment

BillingAddress

City

StateOrProvince

PostalCode

Field

Country

ContactTitle

PhoneNumber

Extension

FaxNumber

EmailAddress

Notes

OrderID

Required-byDate

Promised-byDate

ShipName

ShipAddress

ShipCity

ShipState

ShipStateOrProvince

ShipPostalCode

ShipCountry

ShipPhoneNumber

ShipDate

ShippingMethod

ShipperName

FreightCharge

SalesTaxRate

OrderTotal

With the addition of the OrderItems, as shown in Table 11-2, you can store more than five items for a customer's order, without wasting any space when a customer orders fewer than five items. With these modifications, the database is considered to be in *first normal form*.

Remove Duplicate Data

The next step in the normalization process is to remove duplicate data. Storing duplicate data in the database not only wastes space, but it can also cause integrity problems. Two types of integrity problems are addressed in Level 2 normalization: update and delete integrity. Using the Orders table, Table 11-3, look at what occurs if a customer's address changes. The customer's information has been duplicated for each order, so if a customer changes an address, you need to update each customer order record with the new address. This can be a time-consuming and wasteful process.

What happens if a customer places just one order, and then decides to cancel it? If you delete the customer's order from the Orders table, you no longer have any information for that customer. Then, if the customer orders again, you have to obtain all the customer information again. Although the update integrity problems can be a wasteful process, you can overcome them. However, the delete integrity problems just described can't be overcome with the current table design.

You can apply the second rule of database normalization to help rectify the update and delete anomalies. You need to move the customer information into a separate table, adding a foreign key to the Orders table, CustomerID, which links back to the unique customer that placed the order. You can also apply these rules to the customer shipping information. Table 11-4 shows the new Customers table, Table 11-5 shows the new CustomerShip table, and Table 11-6 shows the updated Orders table. With these modifications, the database now is considered to be in *second normal form*.

TABLE 11–4 THE NEW CUSTOMERS TABLE

Field

CustomerID

CompanyName

ContactFirstName

ContactLastName

CompanyOrDepartment

BillingAddress

City

StateOrProvince

PostalCode

Country

Field

ContactTitle

PhoneNumber

Extension

FaxNumber

EmailAddress

Notes

TABLE **11-5** THE NEW CUSTOMERSHIP TABLE

Field

CustomerShipID

CustomerID

ShipName

ShipAddress

ShipCity

ShipState

ShipStateOrProvince

ShipPostalCode

ShipCountry

ShipPhoneNumber

TABLE **11-6** THE UPDATED ORDERS TABLE

Field

OrderID

CustomerID

Continued

TABLE 11-6 THE UPDATED ORDERS TABLE *(continued)*

Field

CustomerShipID

Required-byDate

Promised-byDate

ShipDate

ShippingMethod

ShipperName

FreightCharge

SalesTaxRate

OrderTotal

Remove Columns of a Table That Aren't Dependent on the Primary Key

Well, you have come a long way from your initial Orders table in developing an effective database design. Much of what you have done so far can be accomplished by applying common sense, combined with the goal of eliminating redundant data. The next level of optimization asks you to examine your tables in even more detail, in an effort to eliminate redundant data. When you apply this rule, you need to look at all the field that a table contains; if the field isn't directly associated with the primary key of the table, it probably should be moved to a separate table. Also, you should try to eliminate fields that are the result of calculations of other fields.

The updated Orders table, Table 11-6, shows that the ShippingMethod and ShipperName fields are stored in the Orders table, although they aren't specifically related to the Orders table. Thus, you should store the information contained in these fields in a separate table. Applying the third rule of normalization, you need to create a Shipper table and store a ShipperID foreign key in the Orders table. Also, you could calculate the OrderTotal amount by using the OrderItems and Product tables, so you should eliminate the OrderTotal field from the Orders table.

Thus, applying the third rule of normalization helps you to eliminate even more redundant data from your database. Table 11-7 shows the new Shipper table, and Table 11-8 shows the updated Orders table. With these modifications, the database is now considered to be in *third normal form.*

As you begin to apply the next levels of database normalization, a tradeoff between application performance and normalization may occur occasionally. For example, applying this level of normalization to the Orders table, you might decide to eliminate the `OrderTotal` field from the Orders table, because you could determine the order's total by using the Products and OrderItems table. However, this strategy has tradeoffs; calculating the order total may take time and numerous table accesses. Also, if the price of an item is changed after an order is placed, the `OrderTotal` field may not have the correct amount. Thus, you need to determine whether to update the order's total to the new amount if an item's price changes after a customer places an order. What if the price increases? What if it decreases? You need to examine your business rules and the requirements of your application to determine how to apply these normalization rules. The best way to do so isn't always clear, because it depends on your specific business requirements.

TABLE 11-7 THE NEW SHIPPER TABLE

Field

ShipperID

ShipperName

ShippingMethod

TABLE 11-8 THE UPDATED ORDERS TABLE

Field

OrderID

CustomerID

CustomerShipID

Required-byDate

Promised-byDate

Continued

TABLE 11-8 THE UPDATED ORDERS TABLE *(continued)*

Field

ShipDate

ShipperID

FreightCharge

SalesTaxRate

For many of your database applications, the first three normalization rules will be sufficient. The final two associated rules are used when your application contains related and unrelated one-to-many and many-to-many relationships.

Place-Independent Multiple Relationships in Separate Tables

The fourth step in the normalization process involves multiple independent relations. If a table has a one-to-many relationship that contains more than one independent relationship, the fourth level of normalization requires that these relationships be placed in separate tables.

This fourth rule is best illustrated by an example. Refer to Table 11-9, the CustomerShip table, which contains the shipping information for a customer. A customer could have more than one location where it receives shipments. Suppose the shipping department wants to keep track of the customer's preferred shipper. You might want to add a field to the CustomerShip table that contains a preferred ShipperID. However, this wouldn't be correct – even though the customer's shipping address and preferred shipper are related, they are independent of each other. In following the rules of the fourth level of normalization, a new table, PreferredShip, should be created, to contain the customer's preferred ShipperID. A database that follows these rules is considered to be in *fourth normal form.*

TABLE 11-9 THE NEW PREFERREDSHIP TABLE

Field

CustomerID

ShipperID

Place-Dependent Multiple Relationships in Separate Tables

Finally, the fifth step of normalization deals with the handling of multiple dependent relationships. The fifth step of normalization is used when the database contains multiple many-to-many relationships. The fifth level of normalization states that related many-to-many relationships should be placed in separate tables.

Again, this level of normalization is best illustrated by an example. Assume that you need to track information regarding product suppliers, and track suppliers that are preferred by customers. Table 11-10 shows the Suppliers table that is needed to hold the supplier information. Following the fifth rule of normalization, you will create two simple separate tables: CustSuppliers, as shown in Table 11-11, and ProductSuppliers, as shown in Table 11-12. The CustSuppliers table tracks which suppliers a customer prefers. A customer may prefer many suppliers, and many customers may prefer a single supplier. The ProductSuppliers table tracks which suppliers supply different products. Many suppliers may supply a single product, and a supplier may supply many products. Isolating these relationships into separate tables follows the fifth rule of normalization. A database that complies with these rules is considered to be in *fifth normal form*.

TABLE 11-10 THE SUPPLIERS TABLE

Field

SupplierID

SupplierName

SupplierAddress

SupplierCity

SupplierState

SupplierZip

SupplierPhoneNumber

TABLE 11-11 THE CUSTSUPPLIER TABLE

Field

CustomerID

SupplierID

TABLE 11-12 THE PRODUCTSUPPLIERS TABLE

Field

ProductID

SupplierID

General Design Issues

Examine the types and lengths of the fields in your tables. If you have a character field that requires only 25 characters, don't define it as a 50-character field; doing so can waste a lot of space. Also, examine the types of your fields. Can a numeric value that you're storing in a table as a floating point be represented as an integer? This can save space and be retrieved from the database more quickly, because an integer occupies fewer bytes.

You should be careful when you create indexes for your tables. Although indexes can speed access to your tables, they can also add significant overhead when you add, modify, and delete data while updating your indexes. You should create table indexes only where they are required and will be utilized. Also, you should include only the number of fields that are required to uniquely identify the record in your index. This will result in smaller, more efficient indexes.

Code Optimization

You can apply various programming techniques to your applications that can help to improve performance. You need to remember to balance these techniques with the requirements of your application. These techniques will help you to determine which areas of your application can be improved.

Using the Seek() Method

Utilizing an associated index, the `Seek()` method can locate a record faster than the `Find()` method can locate a record. The `Find()` method uses field indexes when possible, but is based upon Dynaset or Snapshot `Recordsets`. The `Seek()` method uses an associated table index to locate a record that you're searching for. Utilizing the `Seek()` method has a few limitations. First, the field for which you are searching must be indexed. Second, you can employ the `Seek()` method only with a Table-type `Recordset`. The `Seek()` method can't be used with attached tables, because they can't be opened as a Table-type `Recordset`. If your index utilizes multiple fields, the `Seek()` method can still be utilized if the preceding indexed fields are also specified — for example, if you want to search for a specific `CustomerID` in the Orders table (Table 11-8). Assuming that it has an associated index named `CustOrders`, which is an index made up of the `OrderID` and `CustomerID` fields, you need to specify both the `OrderID` and `CustomerID` to use `Seek()`.

Listing 11-1 demonstrates how to search the Orders table for the record with the `OrderID` **12345** and the `CustomerID` **78910**, using the `CustOrders` index.

Listing 11-1: Using Seek() to Find the Record With OrderID 12345 and CustomerID 78910

```
Dim tbl As TableDef

Set tbl = db.TableDefs("Orders")
Set rs = tbl.OpenRecordset()

REM Use the CustOrders Index
rs.Index = "CustOrders"

REM Search for record with OrderID = 12345 and
REM CustomerID = 78910

rs.Seek "=", 12345, 78910
```

Using Indexes

If an index is available, opening a Table-type `Recordset` with an index is more efficient than using the `Sort()` method to access a `Recordset` in an ordered manner. If an index is not available, creating an SQL `SELECT` statement with an `ORDER BY` clause is faster than employing the `Sort()` method.

Using Requery()

If you have a time-consuming query that you need to refresh, use the `Requery()` method of the `Recordset`, instead of creating a new `Recordset` object. Listing 11-2 demonstrates how to use the `Requery()` method. When you use the `Requery()` method, the SQL statement doesn't need to be reinterpreted; it can simply be quickly reexecuted.

Listing 11-2: Using the Requery() Method

```
DIM rs as Recordset

Set rs = db.OpenRecordset("SELECT CompanyName,_
     ContactFirstName,_
     ContactLastName FROM Customer")

REM Perform operations which affect the Customers table

REM Requery the Recordset
rs.Requery
```

Using Seek()/Query() Rather Than Filter

The `Filter` property of a `Recordset` can be used to select certain records from a `Recordset`. As just mentioned, utilizing an index to access a `Recordset` in an ordered manner is faster than using the `Sort()` method on the `Recordset`. Using the `Seek()` method to move to a specific record position, and then using the `Move()` methods, can be faster than using a `Filter`. You can also open a new `Recordset` by using an SQL `SELECT` statement with a `WHERE` clause, to retrieve the subset of data that you need if an index is not available.

Using Transactions

Transactions buffer database changes until they are committed or canceled. If many records are affected by the operation that is enveloped by the transaction, instead of writing the changes to each record as they are performed, the changes are buffered and performed in a single write operation.

As covered in Chapter 10, transactions can greatly improve application performance.

Transactions are first buffered to memory and then spill over to the disk, as needed. Large transactions can cause insufficient memory or fill up available disk space if the transactions are too large. Grouping very large transactions into smaller groups is better.

 As discussed in this Chapter, you should not make your transactions too big.

Using Bookmarks

Just as a bookmark in a book can help you return to a specific page, DAO bookmarks can be used to return to a specific location in a table. The Recordset object provides a property — Bookmark — to implement table bookmarks. Bookmarks can be utilized in conjunction with the Seek() and Find() methods. If you need to return to a record that has previously been searched for, bookmarks can return you to that location quickly, without the need to re-search for the specific record. Listing 11-3 demonstrates how the bookmark is used in conjunction with the Seek() method that was demonstrated in Listing 11-1.

Listing 11-3: Using DAO Bookmarks in Conjunction with the Seek() Method

```
Dim tbl As TableDef
Dim bm As Variant

Set tbl = db.TableDefs("Orders")
Set rs = tbl.OpenRecordset()

REM Use the CustOrders Index
rs.Index = "CustOrders"

REM Search for record with OrderID = 12345 and
REM CustomerID = 78910

rs.Seek "=", 12345, 78910

REM Create a bookmark
Set bm = rs.Bookmark

REM Perform operations which change the current record
REM location

REM Return to bookmarked record
Set rs.Bookmark = bm
```

Using SQL

When you perform operations that affect multiple records, performing the operation as an equivalent SQL statement, if possible, is faster than writing the equivalent code. For example, if you have a Product table that contains pricing information and you need to increase all prices by 10 percent, writing an SQL UPDATE statement is better than writing the equivalent loop in Visual Basic code or using cursors. You can perform various techniques when you design database queries that can help enhance the performance of your application. This section looks at some of these techniques.

Retrieve Only Required Fields

When you retrieve information from the database by using SQL SELECT statements, make sure to specify only the fields that you absolutely require. Accessing any more data than is required takes up unnecessary time. The use of the * qualifier to retrieve all columns of data should be rare. Frequently, when you access a database server, you don't have access to all table fields, due to security requirements.

Have the Server Run as Much of the Query as Possible

When you access a database that is stored on a database server, the most efficient technique is to have the database server perform as much of the query as possible. Some of the query operations that aren't usually supported by a database server are the following:

♦ Joining tables on fields of different types. Most database servers can't perform the necessary inherent-type conversions to perform this type of query. You must explicitly specify these types of conversions.

♦ Queries that contain the DISTINCT clause or calculations in subqueries.

♦ Joining attached tables with tables that are found on the database server.

♦ Queries that use the TOP or CROSSTAB clauses.

Parameterized Queries

As illustrated in previous examples, when you need to create a database query in your application, you can dynamically build into the application, and then execute, the SQL SELECT statement string. Typically, this is referred to as *dynamic SQL*. Listing 11-4 presents an example of a dynamic SQL query that retrieves the CompanyName, ContactFirstName, and ContactLastName values for the CustomerID 1000.

Listing 11-4: A Sample Dynamic SQL Query

```
Dim CustIDValue As Integer
Dim Query As String

CustIDValue = 1000

Set Query = "SELECT CompanyName, ContactFirstName,_
   ContactLastName FROM Customer WHERE_
   CustomerID = " & Str(CustIDValue)

Set rs = db.OpenRecordset(Query)
```

This example creates a `CustIDValue` string variable. This value is appended to the `SELECT` statement string that is passed to the `OpenRecordset()` method. If the query is not executed repeatedly, your use of dynamic SQL doesn't present much of a performance penalty. If this statement were to be used many times, inside a loop possibly, a *parameterized SQL* would be much more efficient. Listing 11-5 presents an example of a parameterized SQL query.

Listing 11-5: Performing a Parameterized SQL Query

```
Dim qd1 As QueryDef
Dim qd2 As QueryDef
Dim ps As Parameters
Dim p As Parameter
Dim rs As Recordset

REM Create the parameterized query
Set qd1 = db.CreateQueryDef("CustQuery", _
   "PARAMETER CustID Long; SELECT CompanyName,_
   ContactFirstName, ContactLastName From Customer _
   WHERE CustomerID = [CustID]")
qd1.Close()

REM Open the query
Set qd2 = db.OpenQueryDef("CustQuery")

REM Access the query parameters
Set ps = qd2.Parameters

REM Set the value of the CustID parameter
Set p = ps("CustID")
p.Value = 1000

REM Open the recordset
Set rs = qd2.OpenRecordset(dbOpenDynaset)
```

The advantage of using a parameterized SQL query rather than a dynamic SQL query is that the SQL statement in a parameterized SQL query is interpreted just once, when the query is created. When it subsequently is executed, it doesn't need to be interpreted again; it is just executed. Listing 11-5 introduced a few new components: the PARAMETER clause, and the CreateQueryDef() and OpenQueryDef() methods.

The PARAMETER clause comes before your SQL statement and specifies the names of the parameters in your SQL statement. The name and the type of each parameter is specified, followed by a semicolon. More than one parameter can be specified by specifying the parameter name and type again, followed by a semicolon. Table 11-13 presents the parameter types that are possible for SQL parameters.

TABLE 11-13 SQL PARAMETER TYPES

Type	Description
Boolean	A Boolean-type field
Byte	A byte-type field
Integer	An integer-type field
Long	A long-type field
Currency	A currency-type field
Single	A single-precision floating-point-type field
Double	A double-precision floating-point-type field
Date	A date/time-type field
Text	A string-type field

The CreateQueryDef() method looks like the following

```
CreateQueryDef(queryname, sqlstmt)
```

and takes the parameters that are specified in Table 11-14.

TABLE **11-14 PARAMETERS OF THE CREATEQUERYDEF() METHOD**

Parameter	Description
queryname	The name of the query. *queryname* is a string parameter.
sqlstmt	The SQL statement. *sqlstmt* is a string parameter that contains a valid SQL statement.

The OpenQueryDef() method, shown in the following syntax, has one parameter, *queryname*, which is the name of the query to open. *queryname* is a string parameter.

```
OpenQueryDef(queryname)
```

Both CreateQueryDef() and OpenQueryDef() are methods of the Database object.

The Parameter and Parameters objects were also used in the example shown in Listing 11-5. The Parameter object represents each parameter of the query and has the following methods: Name(), Value(), Properties(), and Type().

The Parameters object has the same methods and properties as the TableDefs, Fields, and Indexes objects, which were reviewed in earlier chapters.

Use SQL PassThrough

SQL PassThrough queries can improve application performance by bypassing the Jet Database Engine and directly accessing a back-end database server. SQL PassThrough can be use to perform the following:

◆ Execute an SQL query directly, using the native database server SQL syntax

◆ Perform a stored procedure

◆ Create and update database server rules, triggers, and stored procedures

◆ Create new tables, indexes, or devices on the database server

◆ Perform administrative tasks

◆ Perform multiple INSERT and UPDATE commands in a single batch

◆ Run database server maintenance procedures

SQL PassThrough queries can be executed directly or can be created as `QueryDef` objects and then executed as required, just like the parameterized SQL queries. A PassThrough query can't be a parameterized SQL query, though. The result of a PassThrough query is always stored in a Snapshot-type `Recordset`, which contains a copy of the actual database data. Listing 11-6 demonstrates how to execute directly an SQL PassThrough statement that decreases all product `Prices` in a Product table by 10 percent.

Listing 11-6: Executing a PassThrough SQL Statement

```
Dim db As Database

db.OpenDatabase("",False,False,"ODBC;DSN=ExampleDSN;_
    Database=ExampleDB;UID=John;PWD=Password")

db.Execute("UPDATE Products SET Prices = Price * _
          0.9",dbSQLPassThrough)
```

As this example demonstrates, the `Execute()` method is called with the `dbSQLPassThrough` option. Also, the ODBC database is opened with the connect string parameters. This passes the SQL statement directly to the database server for processing. The Jet Database Engine will not attempt to interpret the statement. Listing 11-7 demonstrates how to create a PassThrough query by using the `QueryDef` object of an attached ODBC database.

Listing 11-7: Creating a PassThrough SQL Query

```
Dim qd As QueryDef
Dim rs As Recordset

Set qd = db.CreateQueryDef("CustQuery",_
    "SELECT CompanyName,_
    ContactFirstName, ContactLastName From Customer _
    WHERE CustomerID = 1000")
qd.Connect = "ODBC;DSN=ExampleDSN;_
                Database=ExampleDB;UID=John;PWD=Password"
Set rs = _ qd.OpenRecordset(dbOpenSnapShot,dbSQLPassThrough)
```

This example shows that when the `QueryDef Recordset` is opened, it is specified as a Snapshot-type `Recordset`, and the `dbSQLPassThrough` option is also specified.

Client/Server Optimization

Client/server applications can present a different set of performance requirements than the set presented by standalone database applications. This section looks at specific methods that you can use to enhance client/server applications when you are utilizing DAO. Just like the optimization methods discussed previously, you need to experiment with these techniques to determine which are applicable to your situation.

CacheStart(), CacheSize(), and FillCache() Methods

The `Recordset` cache methods can be used to cache the results of a Dynaset-type `Recordset`. These cache methods are used with a `Recordset` that is a result of an attached table. The `CacheStart()` property is a bookmark parameter that specifies the first record in the cache. The `CacheSize()` property is an integer parameter that specifies the number of records to store in the cache. The `FillCache()` method takes two optional parameters: the first parameter is the cache start bookmark and the second is the number of records to cache. If these parameters are omitted, the values specified by the `CacheStart()` and `CacheSize()` properties are used. If the records are used repeatedly, caching their values can significantly improve performance. As with other caching operations with DAO, records are cached into memory first and then to disk if not enough memory is available.

You must consider thoroughly your use of the `Recordset` cache methods when you're developing a multiuser application. You could cache a stale record; that is, another user may change a record, and that change will not be reflected in the application's cached `Recordset`.

Listing 11-8 demonstrates how the `Recordset` cache methods are utilized with an attached ODBC Customers table.

Listing 11–8: Using the Recordset Cache Methods

```
Dim tbl As TableDef
Dim tbls As TableDefs
Dim rs As Recordset
Dim bm As Variant

Set tbl = db.CreateTableDef("AttachTable")
```

```
tbl.Connect = "ODBC;DSN=ExampleDSN;_
              Database=ExampleDB;UID=John;PWD=Password"
tbl.SourceTableName = "Customers"
tbls.Append(tbl)
Set rs = db.OpenRecordset("AttachTable")

REM Move to the first record
rs.MoveFirst()
REM Set a bookmark
Set bm = rs.Bookmark

REM Cache the first 25 records
rs.CacheStart = bm
rs.CacheSize = 25

REM Fill the cache
rs.FillCache()
```

Using Snapshot Recordsets Rather Than Dynaset Recordsets

If your application doesn't need to update a retrieved data set and it contains fewer than 500 records, a Snapshot-type Recordset is more efficient than a Dynaset-type Recordset. Listing 11-9 demonstrates how to open a Recordset by specifying that it is a Snapshot type.

Listing 11-9: Retrieving a Snapshot-Type Recordset

```
Dim tbl As TableDef
Dim tbls As TableDefs
Dim rs As Recordset

Set tbls = db.Tabeldefs
Set tbl = tbls("Orders")

Set rs = tbl.OpenRecordset(dbOpenSnapShot)
```

If the table contains memo or OLE object fields, accessing the table as a Dynaset-type Recordset is probably more efficient. If the number of fields and records is relatively small, a Snapshot-type Recordset can be much more efficient. Also, as noted earlier, you should always remember to retrieve only the columns of the table that you require. If all the fields in the Orders table aren't required in Listing 11-9, using an SQL SELECT statement on the Orders table, instead, is much more efficient.

Using dbForwardOnly

When you create a Snapshot-type `Recordset`, by default, you can move forward and backward through the data set that is returned. If you know that you will need to move through the data set in a forward direction only, the `dbForwardOnly` option can be used when you open the `Recordset`. This technique is more efficient, because the resulting data set is not buffered. Listing 11-10 demonstrates how to create a `dbForwardOnly`-type `Recordset`. The performance gain of a forward-only-type data set is more noticeable with an ODBC-type data source. Only the `MoveNext()` method may be used on the resulting `Recordset`.

Listing 11-10: Retrieving a ForwardOnly Snapshot-Type Recordset

```
Dim tbl As TableDef
Dim tbls As TableDefs
Dim rs As Recordset

Set tbls = db.Tabeldefs
Set tbl = tbls("Orders")

Set rs = tbl.OpenRecordset(dbOpenSnapShot,dbForwardOnly)
```

Important ODBC Enhancements

When you access an ODBC database in a client/server application, using the following methodologies will produce the most noticeable improvements in performance :

- ◆ Normalize your database.
- ◆ Use transactions.
- ◆ Use an index to access a `Recordset` in an ordered manner instead of using the `Sort()` method.
- ◆ Use the `Recordset` cache methods.
- ◆ Use the `Find()` method only with fields that are part of a index.
- ◆ Use `Seek()` or a `Query` instead of using the `Filter()` method.
- ◆ Use the SQL PassThrough queries.
- ◆ Retrieve only the fields that you require.
- ◆ Use the `Requery()` method to update a data set instead of creating a new `Recordset`.
- ◆ Use a Snapshot-type `Recordset` rather than a Dynaset-type `Recordset`.

◆ Use bookmarks.

◆ Use the `dbForwardOnly` option with Snapshot-type `Recordsets`.

◆ Use SQL statements and avoid as much code as possible.

◆ Use parameterized SQL queries rather than dynamic SQL queries.

◆ Use stored procedures if they are available. Stored procedures don't have to be compiled each time that they are used. Stored procedures often are available in cache memory and can be executed very quickly.

◆ Using cursors can tie up database server resources. The use of cursors should be avoided if possible. If cursors are needed, forward-only-type cursors use the least amount of resources. Also, you should use read-only-type result sets if the query result set data will not need to be updated.

◆ Create fields only of the size required.

Summary

This chapter just touches the surface of optimizing your Visual Basic DAO applications. You will have to experiment with these techniques to determine which of them are appropriate to your application and which of them increase your application's performance.

In this chapter, you learned how to use the rules of database normalization to optimize your database. This lesson reviewed many issues surrounding database optimization, including: the use of indexes to increase performance; how to use the `Seek()` and `Find()` methods for optimal performance; and how to create optimized queries. The `Bookmark` object was introduced, which you learned how to utilize to return quickly to a specific location in your database. This chapter also discussed how to utilize a back-end database server to enhance application performance. You learned how to create and utilize parameterized queries to enhance query performance, how to use the `Recordset` cache methods, and how to use the Snapshot `Recordsets` and the `dbForwardOnly` property to speed record retrieval. Finally, this chapter discussed which enhancements are the most effective when utilizing ODBC database sources.

Chapter 12

Error Handling

IN THIS CHAPTER

◆ Using the DAO `Error` and `Errors` objects

◆ DAO error numbers and their descriptions

◆ Handling errors in Visual Basic

THIS CHAPTER INTRODUCES the DAO error handling objects — `Error` and `Errors`. These two objects enable you to determine the source of an error that occurs when accessing a data source. This chapter also shows you how to capture errors when they occur in your Visual Basic applications, and the appropriate measures to take to keep your application running — if possible — when errors occur.

Error and Errors Object

DAO provides two related objects: the `Error` and `Errors` objects. The `Errors` object contains a collection of `Error` objects. The `Errors` object is a member of the `DBEngine` object. The `Error` object has the properties described in Table 12-1. The `Errors` object can contain several errors when they occur in DAO. The first item on the `Errors` collections contains the lowest-level error that occurred, and the subsequent `Error` items contain the higher-level errors, in succession. The `Errors` object has the same methods and properties as the `TableDefs`, `Indexes`, `Fields`, and `Relations` objects, which were covered earlier.

The `Description` property returns a string that contains a description of the error. The `Source` property returns a string that contains the name of the object that generated the error. The `Number` property returns an integer that represents the number of the error that was generated. Listing 12-1 illustrates how to display a simple pop-up message box that displays the error information contained in the `Error` object.

TABLE 12-1 ERROR OBJECT PROPERTIES

Properties	Description
HelpContext	The Help context ID that is used when accessing the appropriate Help file.
Source	The source of the error.
Description	A string that contains a description of the error that has occurred.
HelpFile	The Widows Help file that contains further DAO error information.
Number	The number of the error.

Remember that the Description property of the Error object can be used to retrieve a text message that describes the error. This text message can be displayed to a user to indicate what is happening.

Listing 12-1: Displaying the Contents of the Err Object

```
MsgBox "Number: " & CStr(Errors(0).Number) &
      " Description: " & Errors(0).Description &
      " Source: " & Errors(0).Source
```

Table 12-2 lists and describes the error numbers that can be generated by DAO – note that error numbers don't start at 1 and that not all the numbers between the first error number, 2421, and the last error number, 3660, are used.

TABLE 12-2 POSSIBLE DAO ERROR NUMBERS AND THEIR DESCRIPTIONS

Error Number	Description
2421	Syntax error in date.
2422	Syntax error in string.
2423	Invalid use of '.', '!', or '()'.

Error Number	Description
2424	Unknown name.
2425	Unknown function name.
2426	Function isn't available in expressions.
2427	Object has no value.
2428	Invalid arguments used with domain function.
2429	In operator without ().
2430	Between operator without And.
2431	Syntax error (missing operator).
2432	Syntax error (comma).
2433	Syntax error.
2434	Syntax error (missing operator).
2435	Extra).
2436	Missing),], or Item.
2437	Invalid use of vertical bars.
2438	Syntax error.
2439	Wrong number of arguments used with function.
2440	IIf function without ().
2442	Invalid use of parentheses.
2443	Invalid use of Is operator.
2445	Expression too complex.
2446	Out of memory during calculation.
2447	Invalid use of '.', '!', or '()'.
2448	Can't set value.
3000	Reserved error *Item*; no message exists for this error.
3001	Invalid argument.
3002	Couldn't start session.
3003	Couldn't start transaction; too many transactions already nested.

Continued

TABLE **12-2 POSSIBLE DAO ERROR NUMBERS AND THEIR DESCRIPTIONS** *(continued)*

Error Number	Description
3005	*Database name* isn't a valid database name.
3006	*Database name* is exclusively locked.
3007	Can't open library database *name*.
3008	The table *name* is already opened exclusively by another user, or it is already open through the user interface and can't be manipulated programmatically.
3009	You tried to lock table *table* while opening it, but the table can't be locked, because it is currently in use. Wait a moment and then retry the operation.
3010	Table *name* already exists.
3011	The Microsoft Jet Database Engine couldn't find the object *name*. Make sure that the object exists and that you spelled its name and the path name correctly.
3012	Object *name* already exists.
3013	Couldn't rename installable Index Sequential Access Method (ISAM) file.
3014	Can't open any more tables.
3015	*Index name* isn't an index in this table. Look in the `Indexes` collection of the `TableDef` object to determine the valid index names.
3016	Field won't fit in record.
3017	The size of a field is too long.
3018	Couldn't find field *name*.
3019	Operation invalid without a current index.
3020	You tried to call `Update` or `CancelUpdate` or attempted to update a `Field` in a Recordset without first calling `AddNew` or `Edit`.
3021	No current record.

Error Number	Description
3022	The changes that you requested to the table weren't successful, because they would create duplicate values in the index, primary key, or relationship. Change the data in the field or fields that contain duplicate data, remove the index, or redefine the index to permit duplicate entries, and then try again.
3023	`AddNew` or `Edit` already used.
3024	Couldn't find file *name*.
3025	Can't open any more files.
3026	Not enough space on disk.
3027	Can't update. Database or object is read-only.
3028	Can't start your application. The workgroup information file is missing or opened exclusively by another user.
3029	Not a valid account name or password.
3030	*Account name* isn't a valid account name.
3031	Not a valid password.
3032	Can't perform this operation.
3033	You don't have the necessary permissions to use the *name* object. Have your system administrator or the person who created this object establish the appropriate permissions for you.
3034	You tried to commit or roll back a transaction without first using `BeginTrans`.
3036	Database has reached maximum size.
3037	Can't open any more tables or queries.
3039	Couldn't create index; too many indexes already defined.
3040	Disk I/O error during read.
3041	Can't open a database created with a previous version of your application.
3042	Out of MS-DOS file handles.
3043	Disk or network error.

Continued

TABLE 12-2 POSSIBLE DAO ERROR NUMBERS AND THEIR DESCRIPTIONS *(continued)*

Error Number	Description
3044	*Path* isn't a valid path. Make sure that the path name is spelled correctly and that you are connected to the server on which the file resides.
3045	Couldn't use *name*; file already in use.
3046	Couldn't save; currently locked by another user.
3047	Record is too large.
3048	Can't open any more databases.
3049	Can't open database *name*. It may not be a database that your application recognizes, or the file may be corrupt.
3051	The Microsoft Jet Database Engine can't open the file *name*. It is already opened exclusively by another user, or you need permission to view its data.
3052	File sharing lock count exceeded.
3053	Too many client tasks.
3054	Too many Memo or OLE Object fields.
3055	Not a valid file name.
3056	Couldn't repair this database.
3057	Operation not supported on linked tables.
3058	Index or primary key can't contain a Null value.
3059	Operation canceled by user.
3060	Wrong data type for parameter *parameter*.
3061	Too few parameters. Expected *number*.
3062	Duplicate output alias *name*.
3063	Duplicate output destination *name*.
3064	Can't open action query *name*.
3065	Can't execute a select query.
3066	Query must have at least one destination field.
3067	Query input must contain at least one table or query.

Error Number	Description
3068	Not a valid alias name.
3069	The action query *name* can't be used as a row source.
3070	The Microsoft Jet Database Engine doesn't recognize *name* as a valid field name or expression.
3071	This expression is typed incorrectly or is too complex to be evaluated. For example, a numeric expression may contain too many complicated elements. Try simplifying the expression by assigning parts of the expression to variables.
3073	Operation must use an updatable query.
3074	Can't repeat table name *name* in FROM clause.
3075	*Message* in query expression *expression.*
3076	*Name* in criteria expression.
3077	*Message* in expression.
3078	The Jet Database Engine can't find the input table or query *name.* Make sure it exists and that its name is spelled correctly.
3079	The specified field *field* could refer to more than one table listed in the FROM clause of your SQL statement.
3080	Joined table *name* not listed in FROM clause.
3081	Can't join more than one table with the same name *name.*
3082	JOIN operation *operation* refers to a field that isn't in one of the joined tables.
3083	Can't use internal report query.
3084	Can't insert data with action query.
3085	Undefined function *name* in expression.
3086	Couldn't delete from specified tables.
3087	Too many expressions in GROUP BY clause.
3088	Too many expressions in ORDER BY clause.
3089	Too many expressions in DISTINCT output.
3090	Resultant table not allowed to have more than one AutoNumber field.

Continued

TABLE 12-2 POSSIBLE DAO ERROR NUMBERS AND THEIR DESCRIPTIONS *(continued)*

Error Number	Description
3092	Can't use HAVING clause in TRANSFORM statement.
3093	ORDER BY clause *clause* conflicts with DISTINCT.
3094	ORDER BY clause *clause* conflicts with GROUP BY clause.
3095	Can't have aggregate function in expression *expression*.
3096	Can't have aggregate function in WHERE clause *clause*.
3097	Can't have aggregate function in ORDER BY clause *clause*.
3098	Can't have aggregate function in GROUP BY clause *clause*.
3099	Can't have aggregate function in JOIN operation *operation*.
3100	Can't set field *name* in join key to Null.
3101	The Microsoft Jet Database Engine can't find a record in the table *name* with key matching field(s) *name*.
3102	Circular reference caused by *query reference*.
3103	Circular reference caused by alias *name* in query definition's SELECT list.
3104	Can't specify fixed column heading *value* in a crosstab query more than once.
3105	Missing destination field name in SELECT INTO statement *statement*.
3106	Missing destination field name in UPDATE statement *statement*.
3107	Record(s) can't be added; no insert permission on *name*.
3108	Record(s) can't be edited; no update permission on *name*.
3109	Record(s) can't be deleted; no delete permission on *name*.
3110	Couldn't read definitions; no read definitions permission for table or query *name*.
3111	Couldn't create; no modify design permission for table or query *name*.
3112	Record(s) can't be read; no read permission on *name*.
3113	Can't update *field name*; field not updatable.

Error Number	Description
3114	Can't include Memo or OLE Object when you select unique values *statement*.
3115	Can't have Memo or OLE Object fields in aggregate argument *statement*.
3116	Can't have Memo or OLE Object fields in criteria *criteria* for aggregate function.
3117	Can't sort on Memo or OLE Object *clause*.
3118	Can't join on Memo or OLE Object *name*.
3119	Can't group on Memo or OLE Object *clause*.
3120	Can't group on fields selected with '*' *table name*.
3121	Can't group on fields selected with '*'.
3122	You tried to execute a query that doesn't include the specified expression *name* as part of an aggregate function.
3123	Can't use '*' in crosstab query.
3124	Can't input from internal report query *name*.
3125	The database engine can't find *name*. Make sure it is a valid parameter or alias name, that it doesn't include invalid characters or punctuation, and that the name isn't too long.
3126	Invalid bracketing of name *name*.
3127	The INSERT INTO statement contains the following unknown field name: *field name*. Make sure that you typed the name correctly, and then retry the operation.
3128	Specify the table containing the records that you want to delete.
3129	Invalid SQL statement; expected 'DELETE', 'INSERT', 'PROCEDURE', 'SELECT', or 'UPDATE'.
3130	Syntax error in DELETE statement.
3131	Syntax error in FROM clause.
3132	Syntax error in GROUP BY clause.
3133	Syntax error in HAVING clause.

Continued

TABLE 12-2 POSSIBLE DAO ERROR NUMBERS AND THEIR DESCRIPTIONS *(continued)*

Error Number	Description
3134	Syntax error in `INSERT INTO` statement.
3135	Syntax error in `JOIN` operation.
3136	The `LEVEL` clause includes a reserved word or argument that is misspelled or missing, or the punctuation is incorrect.
3138	Syntax error in `ORDER BY` clause.
3139	Syntax error in `PARAMETER` clause.
3140	Syntax error in `PROCEDURE` clause.
3141	The `SELECT` statement includes a reserved word or an argument name that is misspelled or missing, or the punctuation is incorrect.
3143	Syntax error in `TRANSFORM` statement.
3144	Syntax error in `UPDATE` statement.
3145	Syntax error in `WHERE` clause.
3146	ODBC - call failed.
3151	ODBC - connection to *name* failed.
3154	ODBC - couldn't find DLL *name.*
3155	ODBC - insert on a linked table *table* failed.
3156	ODBC - delete on a linked table *table* failed.
3157	ODBC - update on a linked table *table* failed.
3158	Couldn't save record; currently locked by another user.
3159	Not a valid bookmark.
3160	Table isn't open.
3161	Couldn't decrypt file.
3162	You tried to assign the Null value to a variable that isn't a Variant data type.
3163	The field is too small to accept the amount of data that you attempted to add. Try inserting or pasting less data.
3164	The field can't be updated, because another user or process has locked the corresponding record or table.

Error Number	Description
3165	Couldn't open INF file.
3166	Can't locate the requested Xbase memo file.
3167	Record is deleted.
3168	Invalid INF file.
3169	The Microsoft Jet Database Engine couldn't execute the SQL statement, because it contains a field that has an invalid data type.
3170	Couldn't find installable ISAM.
3171	Couldn't find network path or username.
3172	Couldn't open Paradox.net.
3173	Couldn't open table 'MSysAccounts' in the workgroup information file.
3174	Couldn't open table 'MSysGroups' in the workgroup information file.
3175	Date is out of range or is in an invalid format.
3176	Couldn't open file *name*.
3177	Not a valid table name.
3179	Encountered unexpected end of file.
3180	Couldn't write to file *name*.
3181	Invalid range.
3182	Invalid file format.
3183	Not enough space on temporary disk.
3184	Couldn't execute query; couldn't find linked table.
3185	`SELECT INTO` on a remote database tried to produce too many fields.
3186	Couldn't save; currently locked by user *name* on machine *name*.
3187	Couldn't read; currently locked by user *name* on machine *name*.
3188	Couldn't update; currently locked by another session on this machine.

Continued

TABLE 12-2 POSSIBLE DAO ERROR NUMBERS AND THEIR DESCRIPTIONS *(continued)*

Error Number	Description
3189	Table *name* is exclusively locked by user *name* on machine *name*.
3190	Too many fields defined.
3191	Can't define field more than once.
3192	Couldn't find output table *name*.
3196	The database *database name* is already in use by another person or process. When the database is available, try the operation again.
3197	The Microsoft Jet Database Engine stopped the process, because you and another user are simultaneously attempting to change the same data.
3198	Couldn't start session. Too many sessions already active.
3199	Couldn't find reference.
3200	The record can't be deleted or changed, because table *name* includes related records.
3201	You can't add or change a record, because a related record is required in table *name*.
3202	Couldn't save; currently locked by another user.
3203	Subqueries can't be used in the expression *expression*.
3204	Database already exists.
3205	Too many crosstab column headers *value*.
3206	Can't create a relationship between a field and itself.
3207	Operation not supported on a Paradox table with no primary key.
3208	Invalid Deleted setting in the Xbase key of the Windows Registry.
3210	The connection string is too long.
3211	The database engine couldn't lock table *name*, because it's already in use by another person or process.
3212	Couldn't lock table *name*; currently in use by user *name* on machine *name*.
3213	Invalid Date setting in the Xbase key of the Windows Registry.

Error Number	Description
3214	Invalid Mark setting in the Xbase key of the Windows Registry.
3215	Too many Btrieve tasks.
3216	Parameter *name* specified where a table name is required.
3217	Parameter *name* specified where a database name is required.
3218	Couldn't update; currently locked.
3219	Invalid operation.
3220	Incorrect collating sequence.
3221	Invalid settings in the Btrieve key of the Windows Registry.
3222	Query can't contain a `Database` parameter.
3223	*Parameter name* is invalid, because it is too long or contains invalid characters.
3224	Can't read Btrieve data dictionary.
3225	Encountered a record-locking deadlock while performing a Btrieve operation.
3226	Errors encountered while using the Btrieve DLL.
3227	Invalid Century setting in the Xbase key of the Windows Registry.
3228	Selected collating sequence not supported by the operating system.
3229	Btrieve — can't change field.
3230	Out-of-date Paradox lock file.
3231	ODBC — field would be too long; data truncated.
3232	ODBC — couldn't create table.
3234	ODBC — remote query timeout expired.
3235	ODBC — data type not supported on server.
3238	ODBC — data out of range.
3239	Too many active users.
3240	Btrieve — missing Btrieve engine.
3241	Btrieve — out of resources.

Continued

TABLE **12-2 POSSIBLE DAO ERROR NUMBERS AND THEIR DESCRIPTIONS** *(continued)*

Error Number	Description
3242	Invalid reference in SELECT statement.
3243	None of the import field names match fields in the appended table.
3244	Can't import password-protected spreadsheet.
3245	Couldn't parse field names from the first row of the import table.
3246	Operation not supported in transactions.
3247	ODBC – linked table definition has changed.
3248	Invalid NetworkAccess setting in the Windows Registry.
3249	Invalid PageTimeout setting in the Windows Registry.
3250	Couldn't build key.
3251	Operation is not supported for this type of object.
3252	Can't open a form whose underlying query contains a user-defined function that attempts to set or get the form's RecordsetClone property.
3254	ODBC – can't lock all records.
3256	Index file not found.
3257	Syntax error in WITH OWNERACCESS OPTION declaration.
3258	The SQL statement couldn't be executed, because it contains ambiguous outer joins. To force one of the joins to be performed first, create a separate query that performs the first join, and then include that query in your SQL statement.
3259	Invalid field data type.
3260	Couldn't update; currently locked by user *name* on machine *name*.
3261	Table *name* is exclusively locked by user *name* on machine *name*.
3262	Couldn't lock table *name*; currently in use by user *name* on machine *name*.
3263	Invalid Database object.
3264	No field defined – can't append TableDef or Index.
3265	Item not found in this collection.

Error Number	Description
3266	Can't append a `Field` that is already part of a `Fields` collection.
3267	Property can be set only when the `Field` is part of a `Recordset` object's `Fields` collection.
3268	Can't set this property after the object is part of a collection.
3269	Can't append an `Index` that is already part of an `Indexes` collection.
3270	Property not found.
3271	Invalid property value.
3272	Object isn't a collection.
3273	Method not applicable for this object.
3274	External table isn't in the expected format.
3275	Unexpected error from external database driver *error number*.
3276	Invalid database object reference.
3277	Can't have more than ten fields in an index.
3278	The Microsoft Jet Database Engine has not been initialized.
3279	The Microsoft Jet Database Engine has already been initialized.
3280	Can't delete a field that is part of an index or is needed by the system.
3281	Can't delete this index or table. It is either the current index or used in a relationship.
3282	Operation not supported on a table that contains data.
3283	Primary key already exists.
3284	Index already exists.
3285	Invalid index definition.
3286	Format of memo file doesn't match specified external database format.
3287	Can't create index on the given field.
3288	Paradox index is not primary.

Continued

TABLE 12-2 **POSSIBLE DAO ERROR NUMBERS AND THEIR DESCRIPTIONS** *(continued)*

Error Number	Description
3289	Syntax error in CONSTRAINT clause.
3290	Syntax error in CREATE TABLE statement.
3291	Syntax error in CREATE INDEX statement.
3292	Syntax error in field definition.
3293	Syntax error in ALTER TABLE statement.
3294	Syntax error in DROP INDEX statement.
3295	Syntax error in DROP TABLE or DROP INDEX.
3296	Join expression not supported.
3297	Couldn't import table or query. No records found or all records contain errors.
3298	Several tables have that name. Please specify owner in the format *'owner.table'*.
3299	ODBC Specification Conformance Error *message*. Report this error to the developer of your application.
3300	Can't create a relationship.
3301	Can't perform this operation; features in this version aren't available in databases with older formats.
3302	Can't change a rule while the rules for this table are in use.
3303	Can't delete this field. It's part of one or more relationships.
3304	You must enter a personal identifier (PID) consisting of at least 4, and no more than 20, characters and digits.
3305	Invalid connection string in pass-through query.
3306	You've written a subquery that can return more than one field without using the EXISTS reserved word in the main query's FROM clause. Revise the SELECT statement of the subquery to request only one field.
3307	The number of columns in the two selected tables or queries of a union query don't match.
3308	Invalid TOP argument in select query.
3309	The property setting can't be larger than 2K.

Error Number	Description
3310	This property isn't supported for external data sources or for databases created with a previous version of Microsoft Jet.
3311	The property specified already exists.
3312	Validation rules and default values can't be placed on system or linked tables.
3313	Can't place this validation expression on this field.
3314	The field *name* can't contain a Null value, because the `Required` property for this field is set to `True`. Enter a value in this field.
3315	Field *name* can't be a zero-length string.
3316	*Table-level validation text.*
3317	One or more values are prohibited by the validation rule *rule* set for *name*. Enter a value that the expression for this field can accept.
3318	Values specified in a `TOP` clause are not allowed in delete queries or reports.
3319	Syntax error in union query.
3320	*Error* in table-level validation expression.
3321	No database specified in connection string or `IN` clause.
3322	Crosstab query contains one or more invalid fixed-column headings.
3323	The query can't be used as a row source.
3324	The query is a DDL query and can't be used as a row source.
3325	Pass-through query with `ReturnsRecords` property set to `True` didn't return any records.
3326	This `Recordset` is not updatable.
3334	Can be present only in version 1.0 format.
3336	Btrieve — invalid IndexDDF option in initialization setting.
3337	Invalid `DataCodePage` option in initialization setting.
3338	Btrieve — Xtrieve options aren't correct in initialization setting.

Continued

Table **12-2 POSSIBLE DAO ERROR NUMBERS AND THEIR DESCRIPTIONS** *(continued)*

Error Number	Description
3339	Btrieve — invalid `IndexDeleteRenumber` option in initialization setting.
3340	Query *name* is corrupt.
3341	The current field must match the join key *name* in the table that serves as the "one" side of one-to-many relationship. Enter a record in the "one" side table with the desired key value, and then make the entry with the desired join key in the "many-only" table.
3342	Invalid Memo or OLE Object in subquery *name*.
3343	Unrecognized database format *filename*.
3344	The database engine doesn't recognize either the field *name* in a validation expression or the default value in the table *name*.
3345	Unknown or invalid field reference *name*.
3346	Number of query values and destination fields aren't the same.
3349	Numeric field overflow.
3350	Object is invalid for operation.
3351	The `ORDER BY` expression *expression* includes fields that aren't selected by the query. Only those fields requested in the first query can be included in an `ORDER BY` expression.
3352	No destination field name in `INSERT INTO` statement *statement*.
3353	Btrieve — can't find file Field.ddf.
3354	At most, one record can be returned by this subquery.
3355	Syntax error in default value.
3356	You attempted to open a database that is already opened exclusively by user *name* on machine *name*. Try again when the database is available.
3357	This query is not a properly formed data-definition query.
3358	Can't open the Microsoft Jet Database Engine workgroup information file.
3359	Pass-through query must contain at least one character.
3360	Query is too complex.

Error Number	Description
3361	Unions not allowed in a subquery.
3362	Single-row update/delete affected more than one row of a linked table. Unique index contains duplicate values.
3364	Can't use Memo or OLE Object field *name* in the SELECT clause of a union query.
3365	Can't set this property for remote objects.
3366	Can't append a relation with no fields defined.
3367	Can't append. An object with that name already exists in the collection.
3368	Relationship must be on the same number of fields with the same data types.
3370	Can't modify the design of table *name*. It's in a read-only database.
3371	Can't find table or constraint.
3372	No such index *name* on table *name*.
3373	Can't create relationship. Referenced table *name* doesn't have a primary key.
3374	The specified fields are not uniquely indexed in table *name*.
3375	Table *name* already has an index named *name*.
3376	Table *name* doesn't exist.
3377	No such relationship *name* on table *name*.
3378	A relationship named *name* already exists in the current database.
3379	Can't create relationships to enforce referential integrity. Existing data in table *name* violates referential integrity rules in table *name*.
3380	Field *name* already exists in table *name*.
3381	No field named *name* exists in table *name*.
3382	Size of field *name* is too long.
3383	Can't delete field *name*. It's part of one or more relationships.
3384	Can't delete a built-in property.

Continued

TABLE 12-2 POSSIBLE DAO ERROR NUMBERS AND THEIR DESCRIPTIONS *(continued)*

Error Number	Description
3385	User-defined properties don't support a Null value.
3386	Property *name* must be set before using this method.
3388	Unknown function *name* in validation expression or default value on *name*.
3389	Query support unavailable.
3390	Account name already exists.
3393	Can't perform join, group, sort, or indexed restriction. A value being searched or sorted on is too long.
3394	Can't save property; property is a schema property.
3396	Can't perform cascading operation. Because related records exist in table *name*, referential integrity rules would be violated.
3397	Can't perform cascading operation. A related record must exist in table *name*.
3398	Can't perform cascading operation. It would result in a null key in table *name*.
3399	Can't perform cascading operation. It would result in a duplicate key in table *name*.
3400	Can't perform cascading operation. It would result in two updates to field *name* in table *name*.
3401	Can't perform cascading operation. It would cause field *name* to become Null, which isn't allowed.
3402	Can't perform cascading operation. It would cause field *name* to become a zero-length string, which isn't allowed.
3403	Can't perform cascading operation: *validation text*.
3404	Can't perform cascading operation. The value entered is prohibited by the validation rule *rule* set for *name*.
3405	Error *error text* in validation rule.
3406	The expression you're trying to use for the `DefaultValue` property is invalid, because of *error text*. Use a valid expression to set this property.

Error Number	Description
3407	The server's MSysConf table exists but is in an incorrect format. Contact your system administrator.
3409	Invalid field definition *name* in definition of index or relationship.
3411	Invalid entry. Can't perform cascading operation in table *name*, because the value entered is too large for field *name*.
3412	Can't perform cascading update on the table, because it is currently in use by another user.
3414	Can't perform cascading operation on table *name*, because it is currently in use.
3415	Zero-length string is valid only in a Text or Memo field.
3416	*reserved error alert*
3417	An action query can't be used as a row source.
3418	Can't open *tablename*. Another user has the table open, using a different network control file or locking style.
3419	Can't open this Paradox 4.*x* or 5.*x* table, because ParadoxNetStyle is set to 3.*x* in the Windows Registry.
3420	Object is invalid or no longer set.
3421	Data type conversion error.
3422	Can't modify table structure. Another user has the table open.
3423	You can't use ODBC to import from, export to, or link an external Microsoft Jet or ISAM database table to your database.
3424	Can't create database, because the locale is invalid.
3428	A problem occurred in your database. Correct the problem by repairing and compacting the database.
3429	Incompatible version of an installable ISAM.
3430	While loading the Microsoft Excel installable ISAM, OLE was unable to initialize.
3431	This is not a Microsoft Excel 5.0 file.
3432	Error opening a Microsoft Excel 5.0 file.

Continued

TABLE 12-2 POSSIBLE DAO ERROR NUMBERS AND THEIR DESCRIPTIONS *(continued)*

Error Number	Description
3433	Invalid setting in Excel key of the Engines section of the Windows Registry.
3434	Can't expand named range.
3435	Can't delete spreadsheet cells.
3436	Failure creating file.
3437	Spreadsheet is full.
3438	The data being exported doesn't match the format described in the Schema.ini file.
3439	You attempted to link or import a Microsoft Word mail merge file. Although you can export such files, you can't link or import them.
3440	An attempt was made to import or link an empty text file. To import or link a text file, the file must contain data.
3441	Text-file specification field separator matches decimal separator or text delimiter.
3442	In the text-file specification *name*, the *name* option is invalid.
3443	The fixed-width specification *name* contains no column widths.
3444	In the fixed-width specification *name*, column *column* doesn't specify a width.
3445	Incorrect version of the DLL file *name* was found.
3446	Jet VBA file (VBAJET.dll for 16-bit versions, or VBAJET32.dll for 32-bit versions) is missing. Try reinstalling the application that returned the error.
3447	The Jet VBA file (VBAJET.dll for 16-bit versions, or VBAJET32.dll for 32-bit versions) failed to initialize when called. Try reinstalling the application that returned the error.
3448	A call to an OLE system function wasn't successful. Try reinstalling the application that returned the error.
3449	No country code found in the connection string.
3452	You can't make changes to the design of the database at this replica.

Error Number	Description
3453	You can't establish or maintain an enforced relationship between a replicated table and a local table.
3455	Can't make the database replicable.
3456	The object named *name* in the *name* collection can't be made replicable.
3457	You can't set the KeepLocal property for an object that is already replicated.
3458	The KeepLocal property can't be set on a database; it can be set only on the objects in a database.
3459	After a database has been replicated, you can't remove the replication features from the database.
3460	The operation you attempted conflicts with an existing operation involving this member of the replica set.
3461	The replication property you are attempting to set or delete is read-only and can't be changed.
3462	Failure to load a DLL.
3463	Can't find the DLL *name*.
3464	Data type mismatch in criteria expression.
3465	The disk drive you are attempting to access is unreadable.
3468	Access was denied while accessing dropbox folder *name*.
3469	The disk for dropbox folder *name* is full.
3470	Disk failure accessing dropbox folder *name*.
3471	Failure to write to the Synchronizer log file.
3472	Disk full for path *name*.
3473	Disk failure while accessing log file *name*.
3474	Can't open the log file *name* for writing.
3475	Sharing violation while attempting to open log file *name* in Deny Write mode.
3476	Invalid dropbox path *name*.

Continued

TABLE 12-2 POSSIBLE DAO ERROR NUMBERS AND THEIR DESCRIPTIONS *(continued)*

Error Number	Description
3477	Dropbox address *name* is syntactically invalid.
3478	The replica is not a partial replica.
3479	Can't designate a partial replica as the Design Master for the replica set.
3480	The relationship *name* in the partial filter expression is invalid.
3481	The table name *name* in the partial filter expression is invalid.
3482	The filter expression for the partial replica is invalid.
3483	The password supplied for the dropbox folder *name* is invalid.
3484	The password used by the Synchronizer to write to a destination dropbox folder is invalid.
3485	The object can't be replicated, because the database isn't replicated.
3486	You can't add a second Replication ID AutoNumber field to a table.
3487	The database you are attempting to replicate can't be converted.
3488	The value specified is not a `ReplicaID` for any member in the replica set.
3489	The object specified can't be replicated, because it is missing a necessary resource.
3490	You can't create a new replica, because the *name* object in *name* container couldn't be replicated.
3491	The database must be opened in exclusive mode before it can be replicated.
3492	The synchronization failed because a design change couldn't be applied to one of the replicas.
3493	Can't set the specified Registry parameter for the Synchronizer.
3494	Unable to retrieve the specified Registry parameter for the Synchronizer.
3495	No synchronizations are scheduled between the two Synchronizers.

Error Number	Description
3496	Replication Manager can't find the ExchangeID in the MSysExchangeLog table.
3497	Unable to set a schedule for the Synchronizer.
3499	Can't retrieve the full path information for a member of the replica set.
3500	You can't specify two different Synchronizers to manage the same replica.
3502	The Design Master or replica is not being managed by a Synchronizer.
3503	The Synchronizer's Registry has no value set for the key you queried.
3504	The Synchronizer ID does not match an existing ID in the MSysTranspAddress table.
3506	The Synchronizer is unable to open the Synchronizer log.
3507	Failure writing to the Synchronizer log.
3508	No active transport exists for the Synchronizer.
3509	Could not find a valid transport for this Synchronizer.
3510	The member of the replica set that you are attempting to synchronize is currently being used in another synchronization.
3512	Failed to read the dropbox folder.
3513	Failed to write to the dropbox folder.
3514	Synchronizer couldn't find any scheduled or on-demand synchronizations to process.
3515	The Microsoft Jet Database Engine couldn't read the system clock on your computer.
3516	Could not find transport address.
3517	Synchronizer could not find any messages to process.
3518	Could not find Synchronizer in the MSysTranspAddress table.
3519	Failed to send a message.

Continued

TABLE **12-2 POSSIBLE DAO ERROR NUMBERS AND THEIR DESCRIPTIONS** *(continued)*

Error Number	Description
3520	The replica name or ID does not match a currently managed member of the replica set.
3521	Two members of the replica set can't be synchronized, because no common point exists from which to start the synchronization.
3522	Synchronizer can't find the record of a specific synchronization in the MSysExchangeLog table.
3523	Synchronizer can't find a specific version number in the MSysSchChange table.
3524	The history of design changes in the replica doesn't match the history in the Design Master.
3525	Synchronizer could not access the message database.
3526	The name selected for the system object is already in use.
3527	The Synchronizer or Replication Manager couldn't find the system object.
3528	No new data exists in shared memory for the Synchronizer or Replication Manager to read.
3529	The Synchronizer or Replication Manager found unread data in the shared memory. The existing data will be overwritten.
3530	The Synchronizer is already serving a client.
3531	The wait period for an event has timed out.
3532	Synchronizer could not be initialized.
3533	The system object used by a process still exists after the process has stopped.
3534	Synchronizer looked for a system event but didn't find one to report to the client.
3535	Client has asked the Synchronizer to terminate operation.
3536	Synchronizer received an invalid message for a member of the replica set that it manages.
3538	Can't initialize Synchronizer, because too many applications are running.

Error Number	Description
3539	A system error has occurred or your swap file has reached its limit.
3540	Your swap file has reached its limit or is corrupted.
3541	Synchronizer could not be shut down properly and is still active.
3542	Process stopped when attempting to terminate Synchronizer client.
3543	Synchronizer has not been set up.
3544	Synchronizer is already running.
3545	The two replicas you are attempting to synchronize are from different replica sets.
3546	The type of synchronization you are attempting is not valid.
3547	Synchronizer couldn't find a replica from the correct set to complete the synchronization.
3548	GUIDs do not match or the requested GUID could not be found.
3549	The file name you provided is too long.
3550	No index exists on the GUID column.
3551	Unable to delete the specified Registry parameter for the Synchronizer.
3552	The size of the Registry parameter exceeds the maximum allowed.
3553	The GUID could not be created.
3555	All valid nicknames for replicas are already in use.
3556	Invalid path for destination dropbox folder.
3557	Invalid address for destination dropbox folder.
3558	Disk I/O error at destination dropbox folder.
3559	Failure to write, because destination disk is full.
3560	The two members of the replica set you are attempting to synchronize have the same ReplicaID.
3561	The two members of the replica set you are attempting to synchronize are both Design Masters.

Continued

TABLE 12-2 POSSIBLE DAO ERROR NUMBERS AND THEIR DESCRIPTIONS *(continued)*

Error Number	Description
3562	Access denied at destination dropbox folder.
3563	Fatal error accessing a local dropbox folder.
3564	Synchronizer can't find the source file for messages.
3565	A sharing violation exists in the source dropbox folder, because the message database is open in another application.
3566	Network I/O error.
3567	Message in dropbox folder belongs to the wrong Synchronizer.
3568	Synchronizer could not delete a file.
3569	This member of the replica set has been logically removed from the set and is no longer available.
3571	The attempt to set a column in a partial replica violated a rule governing partial replicas.
3572	A disk I/O error occurred while reading or writing to the TEMP directory.
3574	The ReplicaID for this member of the replica set was reassigned during a move or copy procedure.
3575	The disk drive you are attempting to write to is full.
3576	The database you are attempting to open is already in use by another application.
3577	Can't update replication system column.
3578	Failure to replicate database; can't determine whether the database is open in exclusive mode.
3581	Can't open replication system table *name*, because the table is already in use.
3583	Can't make the *name* object in *name* container replicable.
3584	Insufficient memory to complete operation.
3586	Syntax error in partial filter expression on table *name*.
3587	Invalid expression in the `ReplicaFilter` property.
3588	Error when evaluating the partial filter expression.

Error Number	Description
3589	The partial filter expression contains an unknown function.
3592	You can't replicate a password-protected database or set password protection on a replicated database.
3593	You can't change the data master attribute for the replica set.
3594	You can't change the data master attribute for the replica set. It allows data changes only at the Design Master.
3595	The system tables in your replica are no longer reliable and the replica should not be used.
3605	Synchronizing with a nonreplicated database isn't allowed. The *name* database isn't a Design Master or replica.
3607	The replication property you are attempting to delete is read-only and can't be removed.
3608	Record length is too long for an indexed Paradox table.
3609	No unique index found for the referenced field of the primary table.
3610	Same table *table* referenced as both the source and destination in a make-table query.
3611	Can't execute data definition statements on linked data sources.
3612	Multilevel GROUP BY clause isn't allowed in a subquery.
3613	Can't create a relationship on linked ODBC tables.
3614	GUID not allowed in Find() method criteria expression.
3615	Type mismatch in JOIN expression.
3616	Updating data in a linked table is not supported by this ISAM.
3617	Deleting data in a linked table is not supported by this ISAM.
3618	Exceptions table could not be created on import/export.
3619	Records could not be added to exceptions table.
3620	The connection for viewing your linked Microsoft Excel worksheet was lost.
3621	Can't change password on a shared open database.

Continued

TABLE 12-2 POSSIBLE DAO ERROR NUMBERS AND THEIR DESCRIPTIONS *(continued)*

Error Number	Description
3622	You must use the dbSeeChanges option with OpenRecordset when accessing an SQL Server table that has an IDENTITY column.
3623	Can't access the FoxPro 3.0 bound DBF file *filename*.
3624	Couldn't read the record; currently locked by another user.
3625	The text file specification *name* doesn't exist. You can't import, export, or link using the specification.
3626	The operation failed. Too many indexes are on table *name*. Delete some of the indexes on the table and retry the operation.
3627	Can't find the executable file for the Synchronizer (mstran35.exe).
3628	Partner replica is not managed by a Synchronizer.
3629	This Synchronizer and Synchronizer *name* have the same File System dropbox — *name*.
3631	Invalid table name in filter.
3632	Remote Synchronizer is not configured for remote synchronization.
3633	Can't load DLL *name*.
3634	Can't create a replica using a partial replica.
3635	Can't create partial replica of a workgroup information file.
3636	Can't populate the replica or change the replica's filter, because the replica has conflicts or data errors.
3637	Can't use the crosstab of a nonfixed column as a subquery.
3638	You can't make a database replicable that is being used by a program that controls modification.
3639	Can't create a replica of a workgroup information file.
3640	The fetch buffer was too small for the amount of data you requested.
3641	Fewer records than you requested remain in the Recordset.
3642	A cancel was performed on the operation.
3643	One of the records in the Recordset was deleted by another process.

Error Number	Description
3645	One of the binding parameters is incorrect.
3646	The specified row length is shorter than the sum of the column lengths.
3647	A column requested is not being returned to the `Recordset`.
3648	Can't synchronize a partial replica with another partial replica.
3649	The language-specific code page was not specified or couldn't be found.
3650	Internet is too slow.
3651	Invalid Internet address.
3652	Internet login failure.
3653	Internet connection not set up.
3656	Error in evaluating a partial expression.
3660	Requested exchange failed because *description follows*.

Capturing Errors

Error handling is an essential part of any program. No program is complete unless it has good error handling. Developing applications in a way that reduces the potential for errors is important – but sometimes you can't plan for all contingencies – which is where good error handling can help. Good programs don't necessarily eliminate all errors, they just handle them better than other programs. Writing error handlers is not difficult. In fact, you can add consistent error handling to your program by adding only a few lines of code to each module. The difficult part of writing a good error handler is knowing what to expect and how to handle the unexpected.

Visual Basic Error Handling

Handling errors in Visual Basic programs is a bit different from what you may have experienced in other languages, because Visual Basic uses an event-driven programming model and a call stack to isolate local variables (this means that local variables that could help to resume execution after an error occurs can be lost when a routine terminates). The best way to handle errors in Visual Basic is to write short routines that handle errors within the routine for each routine in your application.

You can develop global Visual Basic error handlers. Visual Basic needs to traverse up the procedure stack to locate an error, which makes resumption of
application execution impossible. Because of this, I recommend that you
employ local error-handling routines.

VISUAL BASIC ERROR–HANDLING OBJECTS

Visual Basic has two built-in objects that can be used to manage application errors.
The `Err` object is available to any Visual Basic application and can be used to track
and report runtime errors. Whenever an error occurs in your application, the `Err`
object is filled with information that can help you to identify it. The other objects
that can be used to track DAO application errors are the `Errors` and `Error` objects
(described earlier in this chapter). The `Errors` and `Error` objects are much more
useful in handling DAO application errors, because they can provide more-detailed
error information. Also, when developing client/server applications, sometimes an
error can occur on your database server – only the `Errors` and `Error` objects can
be used to identify these types of errors.

ERR OBJECT

The built-in `Err` object can be used to identify and handle most common Visual
Basic application errors. This object holds all the information related to the most
recent application error that has occurred.

Whenever an error occurs in your application, the `Err` object is filled with information that identifies the details of the error. Your application can inspect these values to determine a course of action to take. If possible, the error may be correctable,
and the execution of your application can continue. Listing 12-2 illustrates how to
display a simple message box that shows the contents of the `Err` object.

Listing 12-2: Displaying the Contents of the Err Object

```
MsgBox "Number: " & CStr(Err.Number) &
       " Description: " & Err.Description &
       " Source: " & Err.Source
```

Using On Error Goto

The `On Error Goto` statement is used at the beginning of a subroutine or a function. This statement tells your application what to do when an error occurs. The
syntax of the `On Error GOTO` function is as follows:

```
ON ERROR GOTO label
```

The label parameter is a label in your subroutine or function to which the function jumps whenever an error is encountered. This label contains the error-handling routine, which can be very simple or very complex, depending on the needs of your application.

The other important component of handling an error is determining what the error handler should do after it's finished. Four different ways exist to terminate an error-handling routine.

♦ The Resume statement can be used to jump back to the statement where the error occurred.

♦ The Resume Next statement can be used to resume execution at the line immediately following the line that caused the error.

♦ The Resume label command can be used to jump to a specific location in your subroutine or function that caused the error.

♦ The Exit Sub or Exit Function statements can be used to immediately exit the subroutine or function where the error occurred.

Now that you understand the pieces required for handling errors, you're ready to put together your own error handler.

Error Handling in Your Own Applications

Finally, you're ready to begin handling errors in your own applications. Remember, you need to use the ON ERROR statement at the beginning of your routine and employ an exit methodology. Listing 12-3 illustrates how to integrate error handling into a Visual Basic DAO routine.

Listing 12-3: Adding Error Handling into Your DAO Routines

```
Sub AccessDatabase()
  '
  ' Add the Error Handling To This Subroutine
  '
  On Error Goto LocalError

  ' Create a Database Object
  Dim MyDatabase As Database

  ' Set the default database type to the
  ' Jet Engine
  DBEngine.DefaultType = dbUseJet

  ' Open A Dbase database named OrderEntry
```

```
  Set MyDatabase = DBEngine.OpenDatabase(
                    "\\Database\\OrderEntry",
                    True, False, "DBase IV;")
  MyDatabase.Close()
  '
  ' Exit this sub routine if there isn't an error
  '
  Goto LocalExit

LocalError:
  '
  ' Display an error message
  '
  MsgBox "Number: " & CStr(Errors(0).Number) &
        " Description: "
        & Errors(0).Description &
        " Source: " & Errors(0).Source
  '
  ' Continue When an Error Occurs
  '
  Resume Next

LocalExit:

End Sub
```

Exiting the Error Handler

The final piece of handling errors in your Visual Basic applications is exiting the error handler. Choosing the way your application exits the error handler depends on the type of error that occurred and whether resuming execution is possible after the error occurs. Some errors can be fatal, and you may not be able to continue your application. In that case, your best option is to display a message that tells the user how to fix things so that they can properly run your applications, and then terminate your application. The type of error can be determined by examining the Number property of the Err and Error objects.

RESUME

The simplest way to handle an application error is by using the Resume statement. When the Resume statement is encountered in your error handler, the statement that caused the error is returned to and retried. The Resume statement is best used when you are confident that the situation that caused the error can be corrected, and you want to continue with your application. Listing 12-4 illustrates how to use the Resume statement in your error handler.

Listing 12-4: Using the Resume Statement

```
Sub AccessDatabase()
  '
  ' Add the Error Handling To This Subroutine
  '
  On Error Goto LocalError

  ' Create a Database Object
  Dim MyDatabase As Database

  ' Set the default database type to the
  ' Jet Engine
  DBEngine.DefaultType = dbUseJet

  ' Open A Dbase database named OrderEntry
  Set MyDatabase = DBEngine.OpenDatabase(
                   "\\Database\\OrderEntry",
                   True, False, "DBase IV;")
  MyDatabase.Close()
  '
  ' Exit this sub routine if there isn't an error
  '
  Goto LocalExit

LocalError:
  '
  ' Display an error message
  '
  MsgBox "Number: " & CStr(Errors(0).Number) &
         " Description: "
         & Errors(0).Description &
         " Source: " & Errors(0).Source
  '
  ' Try Again!
  '
  Resume

LocalExit:

End Sub
```

RESUME NEXT

The Resume Next statement can be used to resume execution at the line immediately following the line that caused the error. This is probably the least desirable way to handle an error; you should use this method only if you are sure that the statement that caused the error can be skipped. Sometimes, this may not be possible. If your error-handling routine can fix the error, then the Resume Next statement is the appropriate course.

RESUME LABEL

The Resume label statement can be used to return to a fixed point in your application. This point can perform whatever operations are necessary to correct the error. The Resume label command can only be used to jump to a point within the current subroutine or function; you can't jump to another subroutine or location by using the Resume label command.

EXIT

Finally, sometimes your application can't continue at all when a critical error occurs. In that case, your best option is to end your application or subroutine by using the Exit() or End() methods. Before you exit your application due to a critical error, you should display some sort of message that indicates to the user how to correct the situation before they attempt to run your application again.

Summary

An essential part of any program is error handling, and no program is complete without good error handling. You need to develop your applications in a manner that reduces the potential for errors. However, you can't plan for all contingencies, which is why good error handling can really help. A good program doesn't necessarily eliminate all errors, it just handles them better than other programs. This chapter introduced Visual Basic error handling and the objects that are used to handle errors in your DAO applications. The Errors object contains a collection of Error objects. The Errors object is a member of the DBEngine object. These objects can be used to determine the type of error that has occurred in your database application. In conjunction with the On Error Goto statement, you can create your own error-handling routines in each of your procedures or functions that access DAO objects. Finally, the type of exit employed by your error handler determines how your application proceeds after an error is encountered.

Chapter 13

Using the Data Control Object

THIS CHAPTER BEGINS to wrap up the discussion of the DAO data access model. You have learned how to integrate the DAO objects, methods, and properties into your own applications. An easier way exists, though, to provide basic data access from your Visual Basic applications – the Data Control object. Visual Basic provides numerous controls that are considered *bound* – that is, they can be directly associated with a data source. This binding process can simplify your programming process. While bound controls may not be the answer in all circumstances, they can greatly speed up your development process and make your applications more robust. This chapter illustrates how to use the Data Control object in your own applications; how to access its properties, methods and events; and the advantages and disadvantages of using bound controls.

Introducing Bound Controls

Before introducing the specifics of the Data Control object, you need to understand more about bound controls and why they can be useful. Bound controls are just like any other Visual Basic form control (such as edit boxes, list boxes, and buttons), but they have additional properties, events, and methods that enable you to associate them with one or more data tables. The control itself handles the details of accessing and navigating your data source – without the need for any programming. This can greatly simplify the developmental effort. Bound controls can be used for the following:

♦ Quickly loading the contents of a table into a Visual Basic object

♦ Allowing the user to select and navigate a set of records

♦ Loading form controls with the values of the requested record or records

♦ Validating user input

♦ Enforcing database integrity

♦ Updating the data source with the contents of Visual Basic form controls

As you have seen throughout Part III, *Data Access Object API*, bound controls aren't required to access a data source, and using a bound control often can be faster and easier – but sometimes, circumstances are such that developing your own code is more suitable.

The Data Control is used to access a database table. As shown in Figure 13-1, the Data Control is a standard Visual Basic control. The control enables you to create and access a single Dynaset type `Recordset`. While only a single `Recordset` can be associated with a Data Control, you can have more than one Data Control object in your applications or forms. Like any other Visual Basic form control, a Data Control has its own set of properties, methods, and events. Table 13-1 and Table 13-2 list and describe the properties, and methods of the Data Control.

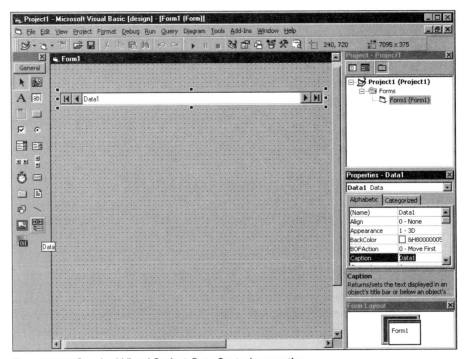

Figure 13-1: Standard Visual Basic 6 Data Control properties

TABLE 13-1 PROPERTIES SUPPORTED BY THE DATA CONTROL OBJECT

Property	Description
RightToLeft	When the RightToLeft property is set to True, the order of the navigation buttons is inverted to flow right to left. For example, the Move to first row, Move to previous row, Move to next row, and Move to last row triangle buttons flow from right to left across the navigation bar.
OLEDropMode	Returns or sets how a target component handles drop operations. If set to vbOLEDropNone, the target component does not accept OLE drops and displays the No Drop cursor; this is the default. If set to vbOLEDropManual, the target component triggers the OLE drop events, enabling the programmer to handle the OLE drop operation in code. If set to vbOLEDropAutomatic, the target component automatically accepts OLE drops if the DataObject object contains data in a format that it recognizes. No mouse or OLE drag/drop events on the target occur when OLEDropMode is set to vbOLEDropAutomatic.
BackColor	Returns or sets the background color of an object.
ForeColor	Returns or sets the foreground color used to display text and graphics in an object.
FontBold	Returns or sets the current font to a bold style.
FontItalic	Returns or sets the current font to an italic style.
FontStrikethru	Returns or sets the current font to a strikethrough style.
FontUnderline	Returns or sets the current font to an underline style.
FontName	Returns or sets the font used to display text in a control or in a runtime drawing or printing operation.
FontSize	Returns or sets the size of the font to be used for text displayed in a control or in a runtime drawing or printing operation.
Height	Returns or sets the height of the Data Control object.
Width	Returns or sets the width of the Data Control object.
Left	Returns or sets the distance between the internal left edge of an object and the left edge of its container

Continued

TABLE **13-1** PROPERTIES SUPPORTED BY THE DATA CONTROL OBJECT *(continued)*

Property	Description
Top	Returns or sets the distance between the internal top edge of an object and the top edge of its container.
Tag	Returns or sets an expression that stores any extra data needed for your program.
Visible	Returns or sets a value indicating whether an object is visible or hidden.
Align	Returns or sets a value that determines whether an object is displayed in any size anywhere on a form or whether it's displayed at the top, bottom, left, or right of the form and is automatically sized to fit the form's width.
DragIcon	Returns or sets the icon to be displayed as the pointer in a drag-and-drop operation.
DragMode	Returns or sets a value that determines whether manual or automatic drag mode is used for a drag-and-drop operation. If set to VbManual, requires using the Drag() method to initiate a drag-and-drop operation on the source control. If set to VbAutomatic, clicking the source control automatically initiates a drag-and-drop operation. OLE container controls are automatically dragged only when they don't have the focus.
MouseIcon	Returns or sets a custom mouse icon.
MousePointer	Returns or sets a value indicating the type of mouse pointer displayed when the mouse is over a particular part of an object at runtime.
Appearance	Returns or sets the paint style of controls on an MDIForm or Form object at design time. Read-only at runtime.
Caption	Determines the text displayed in the Data Control.
Enabled	Returns or sets a value that determines whether the Data Control can respond to user-generated events.
Index	Returns or sets the number that uniquely identifies the Data Control in a control array. Available only if the Data Control is part of a control array.
Name	Returns the name used in code to identify a Data Control. Read-only at runtime.

Property	Description
Parent	Returns the form, object, or collection that contains the Data Control.
Font	Identifies the specific Font object whose properties you want to use for the Data Control.
ToolTip	Returns or sets ToolTip text.
Database	Returns a reference to the Data Control's underlying Database object.
DatabaseName	Returns or sets the name and location of the source of data for the Data Control.
Exclusive	Returns or sets a value that indicates whether the underlying database for the Data Control is opened for single-user or multiuser access.
Options	Returns or sets a value that specifies one or more characteristics of the Recordset object in the control's Recordset property. The following constants may be added together to specify multiple attributes: dbDenyWrite, dbDenyRead, dbReadOnly, dbAppendOnly, dbInconsistent, dbConsistent, dbSQLPassThrough, dbForwardOnly, and dbSeeChanges.
ReadOnly	Returns or sets a value that determines whether the control's Database is opened for read-only access.
RecordSource	Returns or sets the underlying table, SQL statement, or stored procedure.
RecordSet	Returns or sets a Recordset object defined by the Data Control's properties or by an existing Recordset object.
BOFAction	Returns or sets a value indicating what action the Data Control takes when the beginning of the Recordset is reached.
EOFAction	Returns or sets a value indicating what action the Data Control takes when the end of the Recordset is reached.

Continued

TABLE 13-1 PROPERTIES SUPPORTED BY THE DATA CONTROL OBJECT *(continued)*

Property	Description
RecordsetType	Returns or sets the type of Recordset the Data Control creates. If set to vbRSTypeTable, a table Recordset is created. If set to vbRSTypeDynaset, a Dynaset type Recordset is created. If set to vbRSTypeSnapshot, a snapshot-type Recordset is created.
DefaultType	Returns or sets a value that determines the type of data source that is used by the Data Control. If set to dbUseODBC, use ODBCDirect to access your data. If set to dbUseJet, use the Microsoft Jet Database Engine to access your data.
CursorType	Controls what type of cursor driver is used on the connection (ODBCDirect only) created by the Data Control. If set to vbUseDefaultCursor, the ODBC driver determines which type of cursors to use. If set to vbUseODBCCursor, the ODBC cursor library is used. This option gives better performance for small result sets, but degrades quickly for larger result sets. If set to vbUseServerSideCursor, server-side cursors are used. For most large operations, this gives better performance, but might cause more network traffic.
WhatsThisHelpID	Returns or sets an associated context number for an object. Use to provide context-sensitive Help for your application using the "What's This" pop-up in Windows 95 Help.
Connect	Sets or returns a value that provides information about the source of an open connection, an open database, a database used in a pass-through query, or a linked table.
EditMode	Returns a value that indicates the state of editing for the current record. If set to dbEditNone, no editing operation is in progress. If set to dbEditInProgress, the Edit( ) method has been invoked and the current record is in the copy buffer. If set to dbEditAdd, the AddNew( ) method has been invoked, and the current record in the copy buffer is a new record that hasn't been saved in the database.

TABLE 13-2 METHODS SUPPORTED BY THE DATA CONTROL OBJECT

Method	Description
Refresh()	Forces a complete repaint of a form or control.
UpdateControls()	Gets the current record from a Data Control's Recordset object and displays the appropriate data in controls bound to a Data Control. Doesn't support named arguments.
UpdateRecord()	Saves the current contents of bound controls to the database during the Validate event, without triggering the Validate event again. Using this method avoids creating a cascading event. Has the same effect as executing the Edit() method, changing a field, and then executing the Update() method, except that no events occur.
Drag()	Begins, ends, or cancels a drag operation.
Move()	Moves the Data Control object.
Zorder()	Places the Data Control at the front or back of the z-order within its graphical level.
OLEDrag()	Causes the Data Control to initiate an OLE drag-and-drop operation.
ShowWhatsThis()	Displays a selected topic in a Help file by using the "What's This" pop-up window provided by Windows 95 Help.

Events Support

The Data Control Object supports numerous events that enable you to respond to different control conditions. Each of these events is described in this section, including a definition for each and an explanation of the parameters contained in the definition.

Error

The Error event occurs only as the result of a data access error that takes place when no Visual Basic code is being executed. If response is set to vbDataErrContinue, the application continues. If response is set to vbDataErrDisplay, the error message is displayed. The Error event is defined as follows:

```
Private Sub object_Error ([index As Integer,] dataerr As Integer,
response As Integer)
```

Parameters:

◆ object: Object expression that evaluates to an object in the Applies To list.

◆ index: Identifies the control if it's in a control array.

◆ dataerr: The error number.

◆ response: A number corresponding to the response that you want to take.

Reposition

The Reposition event occurs after a record becomes the current record. The Reposition event is defined as follows:

```
Private Sub object.Reposition ([index As Integer])
```

Parameters:

◆ object: Object expression that evaluates to an object in the Applies To list.

◆ index: Identifies the control if it's in a control array.

Validate

The Validate event occurs before a different record becomes the current record; before the Update() method (except when data is saved with the UpdateRecord() method); and before a Delete, Unload, or Close operation. It is defined as follows:

```
Private Sub object_Validate ([ index As Integer,] action As Integer,
save As Integer)
```

Parameters:

◆ object: Object expression that evaluates to an object in the Applies To list.

◆ index: Identifies the control if it's in a control array.

◆ action: Integer that indicates the operation causing this event to occur.

◆ save: A Boolean expression that specifies whether bound data has changed.

DragDrop

The DragDrop event occurs when a drag-and-drop operation is completed as a result of dragging a control over an object and releasing the mouse button or using the Drag() method with its action argument set to Drop. The DragDrop event is defined as follows:

```
Private Sub object_DragDrop([index As Integer,]source As Control, x
As Single, y As Single)
```

Parameters:

◆ object: Object expression that evaluates to an object in the Applies To list.

◆ index: An integer that uniquely identifies a control if it's in a control array.

◆ source: The control being dragged. You can include properties and methods in the event procedure with this argument.

◆ x, y: Numbers that specify the current horizontal (x) and vertical (y) position of the mouse pointer within the target form or control.

DragOver

The DragOver event occurs when a drag-and-drop operation is in progress. You can use this event to monitor the mouse pointer as it enters, leaves, or rests directly over a valid target. The mouse pointer position determines the target object that receives this event. The DragOver event is defined as follows:

```
Private Sub object_DragOver([index As Integer,]source As Control, x
As Single, y As Single, state As Integer)
```

Parameters:

◆ object: Object expression that evaluates to an object in the Applies To list.

◆ index: An integer that uniquely identifies a control if it's in a control array.

◆ source: The control being dragged. You can refer to properties and methods in the event procedure with this argument.

◆ x, y: Numbers that specify the current horizontal (x) and vertical (y) position of the mouse pointer within the target form or control.

◆ state: Integer that corresponds to the transition state of the control being dragged in relation to a target form or control: 0 = Enter (source control is being dragged within the range of a target). 1 = Leave (source control is being dragged out of the range of a target). 2 = Over (source control has moved from one position in the target to another).

MouseDown

The MouseDown event occurs when the user clicks a mouse button. It is defined as follows:

```
Private Sub object_MouseDown([index As Integer,]button As Integer,
shift As Integer, x As Single, y As Single)
```

Parameters:

◆ object: Object expression that evaluates to an object in the Applies To list.

◆ index: An integer that uniquely identifies a control if it's in a control array.

◆ button: An integer that identifies the button that was pressed (MouseDown) or released (MouseUp) to cause the event. The button argument is a bit field with bits corresponding to the left button (bit 0), right button (bit 1), and middle button (bit 2).

◆ shift: An integer that corresponds to the state of the Shift, Ctrl, and Alt keys when the button specified in the button argument is pressed or released. A bit is set if the key is down. The shift argument is a bit field with the least significant bits corresponding to the Shift key (bit 0), the Ctrl key (bit 1), and the Alt key (bit 2).

MouseUp

The `MouseUp` event occurs when the user releases a mouse button. It is defined as follows:

```
Private Sub object _MouseUp([index As Integer,]button As Integer,
shift As Integer, x As Single, y As Single)
```

Parameters:

- ◆ `object`: Object expression that evaluates to an object in the Applies To list.

- ◆ `index`: An integer that uniquely identifies a control if it's in a control array.

- ◆ `button`: An integer that identifies the button that was pressed (MouseDown) or released (MouseUp) to cause the event. The `button` argument is a bit field with bits corresponding to the left button (bit 0), right button (bit 1), and middle button (bit 2).

- ◆ `shift`: Returns an integer that corresponds to the state of the Shift, Ctrl, and Alt keys when the button specified in the button argument is pressed or released. A bit is set if the key is down. The `shift` argument is a bit field with the least significant bits corresponding to the Shift key (bit 0), the Ctrl key (bit 1), and the Alt key (bit 2).

MouseMove

The `MouseMove` event occurs when the user moves the mouse. It is defined as follows:

```
Private Sub object_MouseMove([index As Integer,] button As Integer,
shift As Integer, x As Single, y As Single)
```

Parameters:

- ◆ `object`: Object expression that evaluates to an object in the Applies To list.

- ◆ `index`: An integer that uniquely identifies a control if it's in a control array.

◆ button: An integer that corresponds to the state of the mouse buttons, in which a bit is set if the button is down. The button argument is a bit field with bits corresponding to the left button (bit 0), right button (bit 1), and middle button (bit 2). These bits correspond to the values 1, 2, and 4, respectively. It indicates the complete state of the mouse buttons; some, all, or none of these three bits can be set, indicating that some, all, or none of the buttons are pressed.

Resize

The Resize event occurs when an object is first displayed or when the window state of an object changes. It is defined as follows:

```
Private Sub object_Resize(height As Single, width As Single)
```

Parameters:

◆ object: Object expression that evaluates to an object in the Applies To list.

◆ height: A number specifying the new height of the control.

◆ width: A number specifying the new width of the control.

OLEDragComplete

The OLEDragComplete event occurs when a source component is dropped onto a target component, informing the source component that a drag action was either performed or canceled. It is defined as follows:

```
Private Sub object_OLECompleteDrag([effect As Long]
```

Parameters:

◆ object: Object expression that evaluates to an object in the Applies To list.

◆ effect: A long integer set by the source object identifying the action that has been performed. If set to VbDropEffectNone, the drop target can't accept the data, or the drop operation was canceled. If set to VbDropEffectCopy, the drop results in a copy of data from the source to the target. The original data is unaltered by the drag operation. If set to VbDropEffectMove, the drop results in data being moved from the drag source to the drop source. The drag source should remove the data from itself after the move.

OLEDragDrop

The OLEDragDrop event occurs when a source component is dropped onto a target component when the source component determines that a drop can occur. It is defined as follows:

```
Private Sub object_OLEDragDrop(data As DataObject, effect As Long,
button As Integer, shift As Integer, x As Single, y As Single)
```

Parameters:

- ◆ object: Object expression that evaluates to an object in the Applies To list.

- ◆ data: A DataObject object containing formats that the source provides, and possibly the data for those formats. If no data is contained in the DataObject, it's provided when the control calls the GetData method. The SetData and Clear methods can't be used here.

- ◆ effect: A long integer set by the target component identifying the action that has been performed (refer to the effect values under the OLEDragComplete event).

- ◆ button: An integer that acts as a bit field corresponding to the state of a mouse button when it is depressed. The left button is bit 0, the right button is bit 1, and the middle button is bit 2.

- ◆ shift: An integer that acts as a bit field corresponding to the state of the Shift, Ctrl, and Alt keys when they are depressed. The Shift key is bit 0, the Ctrl key is bit 1, and the Alt key is bit 2.

- ◆ x, y: Numbers that specify the current location of the mouse pointer.

OLEDragOver

The OLEDragOver event occurs when one component is dragged over another. It is defined as follows:

```
Private Sub object_OLEDragOver(data As DataObject, effect As Long,
button As Integer, shift As Integer, x As Single, y As Single, state
As Integer)
```

Parameters:

- ◆ object: Object expression that evaluates to an object in the Applies To list.

◆ `data`: A `DataObject` object that contains formats that the source provides, and possibly the data for those formats. If no data is contained in the `DataObject`, it is provided when the control calls the `GetData` method. The `SetData` and `Clear` methods can't be used here.

◆ `effect`: A `long` integer set by the target component identifying the action that has been performed (refer to the `effect` values under the `OLEDragComplete` event).

◆ `button`: An integer that acts as a bit field corresponding to the state of a mouse button when it is depressed. The left button is bit 0, the right button is bit 1, and the middle button is bit 2.

◆ `shift`: An integer that acts as a bit field corresponding to the state of the Shift, Ctrl, and Alt keys when they are depressed. The Shift key is bit 0, the Ctrl key is bit 1, and the Alt key is bit 2.

◆ `x`, `y`: Numbers that specify the current location of the mouse pointer.

◆ `state`: An integer that corresponds to the transition state of the control being dragged in relation to a target form or control. If set to `vbEnter`, the source component is being dragged within the range of a target. If set to `vbLeave`, the source component is being dragged out of the range of a target. If set to `vbOver`, the source component has moved from one position in the target to another.

OLEGiveFeedback

The `OLEGiveFeedback` event occurs after every `OLEDragOver` event. `OLEGiveFeedback` enables the source component to provide visual feedback to the user, such as changing the mouse cursor to indicate what will happen if the user drops the object, or providing visual feedback on the selection (in the source component) to indicate what will happen. The `OLEGiveFeedback` event is defined as follows:

```
Private Sub object_OLEGiveFeedback(effect As Long, defaultcursors As
Boolean)
```

Parameters:

◆ `object`: Object expression that evaluates to an object in the Applies To list.

◆ `effect`: A `long` integer set by the target component identifying the action that has been performed (refer to the `effect` values under the `OLEDragComplete` event).

◆ `defaultcursors`: A Boolean value that determines whether Visual Basic uses the default mouse cursor proved by the component or a user-defined mouse cursor.

OLESetData

The `OLESetData` event occurs on a source component when a target component performs the `GetData()` method on the source's `DataObject` object, but the data for the specified format hasn't been loaded yet. It is defined as follows:

```
Private Sub object_OLESetData(data As DataObject, dataformat As
Integer)
```

Parameters:

◆ `object`: Object expression that evaluates to an object in the Applies To list.

◆ `data`: A `DataObject` object in which to place the requested data. The component calls the `SetData()` method to load the requested format.

◆ `dataformat`: An integer specifying the format of the data that the target component is requesting.

OLEStartDrag

The `OLEStartDrag` event occurs when a component's `OLEDrag()` method is performed, or when a component initiates an OLE drag-and-drop operation when the `OLEDragMode` property is set to `Automatic`. It is defined as follows:

```
Private Sub object_OLEStartDrag(data As DataObject, allowedeffects
As Long)
```

Parameters:

◆ `object`: Object expression that evaluates to an object in the Applies To list.

◆ `data`: A `DataObject` object containing formats that the source provides, and optionally, the data for those formats. If no data is contained in the `DataObject`, it is provided when the control calls the `GetData()` method. The programmer should provide the values for this parameter in this event. The `SetData()` and `Clear()` methods can't be used here.

◆ `allowedeffects`: A `long` integer containing the effects that the source component supports.

Examining Properties

The following six properties of the Data Control play a primary role in data access:

◆ DatabaseName

◆ Exclusive

◆ Options

◆ ReadOnly

◆ RecordSource

◆ Connect

The DatabaseName property contains the name of the database that you want to access. For ISAM databases, this is the file name of the database, including the drive letter and path. When accessing ODBC data sources, the Connect property is used instead. The Connect property contains the name of the ODBC data source to which you want to connect.

The Connect property and ODBC data sources were discussed in Chapters 5 and 7, respectively.

The RecordSource property is used to determine the source of the records. The RecordSource property is a string, which can be the name of a table in the database that you are connected to, an SQL statement that accesses any of the tables in the database that you are connected to, or, if you are connected to a database server through ODBC, the name of a server-side stored procedure.

The ReadOnly and Exclusive properties are Boolean types that you can use to limit access to a database. When the Exclusive property is set to True, the database is opened for single-user exclusive access – which means that no one else will be able to access the database while you have it open. The ReadOnly property opens the database only for reading. You can't make any changes to the database while it is open for ReadOnly access.

Finally, the Options property is used to determine how the Recordset used by the Data Control is created. The following constants may be added together to specify multiple attributes:

◆ dbDenyWrite: In a multiuser environment, other users can't make changes to records in the Recordset.

- ◆ dbDenyRead: In a multiuser environment, other users can't read records.

- ◆ dbReadOnly: You can't make changes to records in the Recordset.

- ◆ dbAppendOnly: You can add new records to the Recordset, but you can't read existing records.

- ◆ dbInconsistent: Updates can apply to all fields of the Recordset, even if they violate the join condition.

- ◆ dbConsistent: Updates apply only to those fields that don't violate the join condition.

- ◆ dbSQLPassThrough: When using Data Controls with an SQL statement in the RecordSource property, sends the SQL statement to an ODBC database, such as an SQL Server or Oracle database, for processing.

- ◆ dbForwardOnly: The Recordset object supports forward-only scrolling. The only move method allowed is MoveNext(). This option can't be used on Recordset objects that are manipulated with the Data Control.

- ◆ dbSeeChanges: Generates a trappable error if another user is changing data that you are editing.

Using Methods and Events

As listed in Table 13-2, the Data Control supports numerous methods and events. Events occur each time something happens that is relevant to a control. When an event occurs, a message is sent to the control, which can respond to the message with a user-defined procedure. The following are three important data access events that you should be aware of:

- ◆ Reposition: Occurs each time the Data Control moves to a new record.

- ◆ Validate: Occurs each time the Data Control leaves the current record — this can be used to validate data before it is updated in the database.

- ◆ Error: Occurs whenever a database error occurs while the arrow buttons on the control are being used to move the record pointer.

Methods are special functions that are related to a control. While the Visual Basic Data Control has several methods, the following three are important for data access:

- ◆ Refresh(): Used any time that you change the Data Control. When called, the Refresh() method updates the Data Control and forces it to rebuild the Recordset. Calling the Refresh() method ensures that you have the most current set of records available.

◆ `UpdateControls()`: Used to update any bound input controls (bound input controls are reviewed in "Other Bound Controls," later in this chapter). This methods puts the current set of data in the input controls bound to the Data Control. Every time that you press one of the arrow buttons in the Data Control, the `UpdateControls()` method is automatically called.

◆ `UpdateRecord()`: Used to take the current set of data in any bound input controls associated with the Data Control, and use their data to update the database record.

Bound Data Entry Controls

The following three types of controls are useful in most data entry situations:

◆ `Text Control`: Used to access text or numeric field data.

◆ `CheckBox Control`: Used to access Boolean-type fields.

◆ `OLE Control`: Used to access binary type fields, such as images or sounds.

These controls are used for standard application data entry, but can also be bound to specific fields in a Data Control `Recordset`.

The following two properties of the preceding controls are relevant to data entry and binding to a Data Control:

◆ `DataSource`: The name of the Data Control that contains the `Recordset`.

◆ `DataField`: The name of the field in the `Recordset` that contains the data to be displayed in the associated control.

The next section takes you through the process of creating a basic data entry form, using the Data Control and bound data entry controls.

Integrating Bound Controls

To integrate a bound Data Control into your own Visual Basic applications, follow these steps to create a simple form that browses through a database (the complete source code is presented in Listing 13-2):

1. Open the Visual Basic development environment and begin creating a new application. After you open the new application, a blank form is displayed.

2. Select the Data Control object and place it on the form, as shown in Figure 13-2.

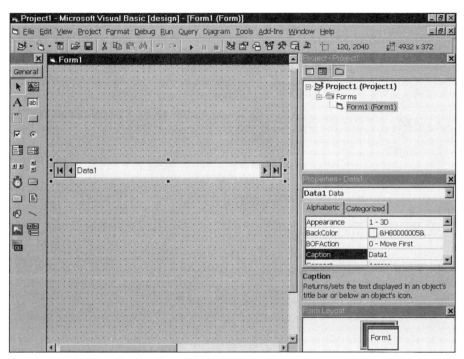

Figure 13–2: Placing the Data Control object on your form

3. This example accesses a simple Customers table that contains the fields CustFName and CustLName. So, you need to place two edit controls on the form that will be used to display the contents of these fields. You can also place labels on the form to label each field, as shown in Figure 13-3.

4. Set the `DatabaseName` property of the Data Control to the Customers database filename.

5. Set the `RecordSource` property to the Customers table name.

6. For each text field, set the `DataSource` property to the name of the Data Control, and the `DataField` name property to the first and last name field names.

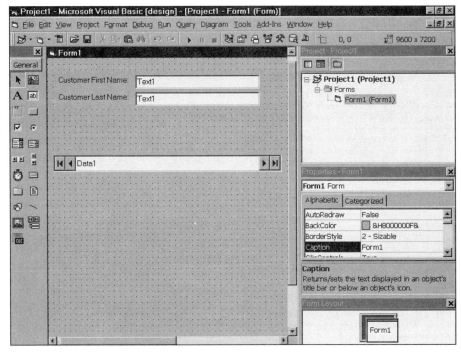

Figure 13-3: Placing the text-edit-box bound controls on your form

7. That's it; you can now run your application and review the data contained in the Customers table, as shown in Figure 13-4.

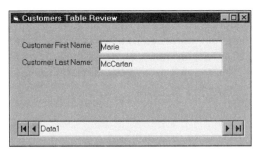

Figure 13-4: The completed Customers Table
Review application

Listing 13-1: The Customers Table Data Access Application

```
VERSION 5.00
Begin VB.Form Form1
   Caption         =   "Customers Table Review"
   ClientHeight    =   2556
   ClientLeft      =   48
   ClientTop       =   276
   ClientWidth     =   5148
   LinkTopic       =   "Form1"
   ScaleHeight     =   2556
   ScaleWidth      =   5148
   StartUpPosition =   3  'Windows Default
   Begin VB.TextBox Text2
      DataField    =   "CustLName"
      DataSource   =   "Data1"
      Height       =   288
      Left         =   1920
      TabIndex     =   3
      Text         =   "Text1"
      Top          =   720
      Width        =   2652
   End
   Begin VB.TextBox Text1
      DataField    =   "CustFName"
      DataSource   =   "Data1"
      Height       =   288
      Left         =   1920
      TabIndex     =   2
      Text         =   "Text1"
      Top          =   360
      Width        =   2652
   End
   Begin VB.Data Data1
      Caption      =   "Data1"
      Connect      =   "Access"
      DatabaseName =   "Customer.mdb"
      DefaultCursorType=  0  'DefaultCursor
      DefaultType  =   2  'UseODBC
      Exclusive    =   0   'False
      Height       =   372
      Left         =   120
      Options      =   0
      ReadOnly     =   0   'False
      RecordsetType =  1   'Dynaset
```

```
              RecordSource   =    "Customers"
              Top            =    2040
              Width          =    4932
          End
          Begin VB.Label Label2
              Caption        =    "Customer Last Name:"
              Height         =    252
              Left           =    240
              TabIndex       =    1
              Top            =    720
              Width          =    1572
          End
          Begin VB.Label Label1
              Caption        =    "Customer First Name:"
              Height         =    252
              Left           =    240
              TabIndex       =    0
              Top            =    360
              Width          =    1572
          End
      End
  End
  Attribute VB_Name = "Form1"
  Attribute VB_GlobalNameSpace = False
  Attribute VB_Creatable = False
  Attribute VB_PredeclaredId = True
  Attribute VB_Exposed = False
```

Summary

This chapter introduced bound controls, and more specifically, the Visual Basic Data Control. Bound controls are just like any other Visual Basic form control (such as edit boxes, list boxes, and buttons), but they have additional properties, events, and methods that enable you to associate them with one or more data tables. The control enables you to create and access a single Dynaset type `Recordset`. While only a single `Recordset` can be associated with a Data Control, you can have more than one Data Control object in your application, and on a form. This chapter described the important properties, methods, and attributes of the Data Control and showed you how to begin integrating the Data Control into your own applications.

Chapter 14

ODBCDirect and Jet Query Processor

IN THIS CHAPTER

- ◆ Overview of ODBCDirect data access using DAO
- ◆ Converting existing DAO applications to ODBCDirect
- ◆ Understanding the ODBCDirect `Connection` object
- ◆ Connecting to a database and executing queries with ODBCDirect
- ◆ Handling ODBCDirect `Recordsets` and asynchronous operations

ODBCDIRECT IS THE SECOND path that DAO provides to access remote data (the first and most widely used path is directly through the Jet Database Engine). This chapter explores the architecture of ODBCDirect data access, how to connect to remote data sources by using ODBCDirect, how to execute queries, and how to handle `Recordsets`. This chapter also reviews how to handle *asynchronous operations*, which return control to your application before your query or database process has completed. You also are given a few tips on how to convert your existing applications to use ODBCDirect. This chapter wraps up the discussion of the DAO data access methodology and starts the discussion of remote data access.

Remote data access is the primary focus of the next two parts — Part IV, *Remote Data Objects API*, and Part V, *ActiveX Data Objects API*.

Exploring the ODBCDirect Data Access Architecture

ODBCDirect, which was first introduced in Visual Basic version 5, uses a subset of the DAO data access interface and provides an easy path for moving existing DAO applications to Remote Data Object (RDO)-like interfaces.

 RDO is discussed in more detail in Part IV.

When you use the Jet Database Engine interface to access data through ODBC, DAO passes all calls to the Jet Database Engine, which takes your query and optimizes it, and then calls ODBC, as needed, to fetch your data. The resulting record sets are then passed back to the Jet Database Engine's cursor builder, which builds `Recordset` objects to pass back to the application. While this process provides access to your ODBC data sources, it isn't necessarily the most efficient path for accessing remote data sources. The Jet Database Engine provides a lot of functionality that simply isn't required. While applications are clearly easier to develop by using DAO and the Jet Database Engine, comparable applications that access the ODBC directly are much faster. ODBCDirect provides a simple way to have the speed of a direct interface to ODBC, with the simplicity of developing DAO applications.

ODBCDirect applications take less memory than comparable DAO applications, because ODBCDirect applications don't need to load the Jet Database Engine. When you choose the ODBCDirect methodology, though, you do give up some of the functionality provided by the Jet Database Engine, namely:

♦ The ability to join database tables stored in different back-end databases.

♦ ODBCDirect doesn't support the object data-definition capabilities provided with Jet, which means that you can't define new tables, indexes, or fields.

While these functions may not seem like a lot to give up for the speed of the ODBCDirect interface, the point is that the speed doesn't come without a price.

ODBCDirect is actually just a lighter version of the DAO interface. The object hierarchy of the ODBCDirect interface is illustrated in Figure 14-1. You've already encountered all of these objects earlier in this part of the book.

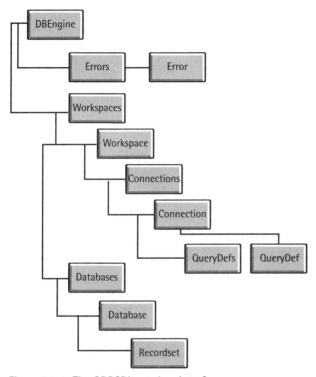

Figure 14-1: The ODBCDirect class interface

Converting Applications to ODBCDirect

To convert existing DAO applications to use the DAO model, you simply need to add one line of code:

```
DBEngine.DefaultType = dbUseODBC
```

This line should be inserted before you access any DAO objects. It can't be that easy, can it? Well, not quite. The catch is that your application uses only Recordset objects. While this may appear to be an impossible restriction, if you look closely at many client/server applications, they basically access data from the data source, update data as necessary, and return the data to the database server. These operations generally only require use of the Recordset object, anyway, so take a close look at your application – converting it to ODBCDirect might not be as difficult as you think. The remainder of this chapter reviews some of the special considerations that you may need to make when connecting to and accessing data sources by using ODBCDirect. "Tips for Converting Existing DAO Applications," at the end of this chapter, provides a checklist of things that you need to review in your application before completely converting it to the ODBCDirect model.

Understanding the Connection Object

A Connection is a nonpersistent object that represents a connection to a remote database. The Connection object is available only in ODBCDirect workspaces. Table 14-1 lists and describes the properties of the Connection object.

TABLE 14-1 CONNECTION OBJECT PROPERTIES

Property	Description
Connect	Sets or returns a value that provides information about the source of an open connection, an open database, a database used in a pass-through query, or a linked table.
Name	Sets or returns a user-defined name for the Collection object.
QueryTimeout	Sets or returns a value that specifies the number of seconds to wait before a timeout error occurs when a query is executed on an ODBC data source.
RecordsAffected	Returns the number of records affected by the most recently invoked Execute() method.
Updatable	Returns a value that indicates whether you can change the Connection object.
Transactions	Returns a value that indicates whether an object supports transactions.
Database	Returns the Database object that corresponds to the Connection object.
Executing	Indicates whether an asynchronous operation (a method called with the dbRunAsync option) has finished executing.

Connection Methods

The `Connection` object supports several methods that manage database access. Each of these methods is described in detail next.

CLOSE()

The `Close()` method, which has the following syntax, closes an open `Connection` object:

```
Close()
```

CREATEQUERYDEF()

The `CreateQueryDef()` method, which has the following syntax, creates a new `QueryDef` object in a specified `Connection`:

```
Set querydef = object.CreateQueryDef (name, sqltext)
```

Parameters:

♦ `querydef`: An object variable that represents the `QueryDef` object that you want to create.

♦ `object`: An object variable that represents an open `Connection` object that will contain the new `QueryDef`.

♦ `name`: A `Variant` (`String` subtype) that uniquely names the new `QueryDef`.

♦ `sqltext`: A Variant that is an SQL statement that defines the `QueryDef`. If you omit this argument, you can define the `QueryDef` by setting its SQL property before or after you append it to a collection.

EXECUTE()

The `Execute()` method, which has the following syntax, runs an action query or executes an SQL statement on a specified `Connection`:

```
object.Execute source, options
```

Parameters:

♦ `object`: A `Connection` object variable on which the query will run.

♦ `source`: A `String` that is an SQL statement or the `Name` property value of a `QueryDef` object.

◆ `options`: A constant or combination of constants that determines the data integrity characteristics of the query. If set to `dbRunAsync`, the query executes asynchronously. If set to `dbExecDirect`, the statement executes without first calling the `SQLPrepare` ODBC API function.

OPENRECORDSET()

The `OpenRecordset()` method creates a new `Recordset` object and appends it to the `Recordsets` collection. The `OpenRecordset()` method has the following syntax:

```
Set recordset = object.OpenRecordset (source, type, options,
lockedits)
```

Parameters:

◆ `recordset`: An object variable that represents the `Recordset` object that you want to open.

◆ `object`: An object variable that represents an existing object from which you want to create the new `Recordset`.

◆ `source`: A `String` that specifies the source of the records for the new `Recordset`. `source` can be a table name, a query name, or an SQL statement that returns records.

◆ `type`: A constant that indicates the type of `Recordset` to open. Settings follow:

■ `dbOpenDynamic`: Opens a dynamic-type `Recordset` object, which is similar to an ODBC dynamic cursor.

■ `dbOpenDynaset`: Opens a Dynaset-type `Recordset` object, which is similar to an ODBC keyset cursor.

■ `dbOpenSnapshot`: Opens a snapshot-type `Recordset` object, which is similar to an ODBC static cursor.

■ `dbOpenForwardOnly`: Opens a forward-only-type `Recordset` object.

◆ `options`: A combination of constants that specify characteristics of the new `Recordset`. Settings follow:

■ `dbRunAsync`: Runs an asynchronous query.

■ `dbExecDirect`: Runs a query by skipping `SQLPrepare` and directly calling `SQLExecDirect`.

◆ lockedits: A constant that determines the locking for the Recordset. If set to:

- dbOptimistic: Uses optimistic locking to determine how changes are made to the Recordset in a multiuser environment. The page containing the record is not locked until the Update() method is executed.

- dbOptimisticValue: Uses optimistic concurrency based on row values.

- dbOptimisticBatch: Enables batch optimistic updating.

CANCEL()

The Cancel() method cancels execution of a pending asynchronous method call. The Cancel() method has the following syntax:

```
Cancel()
```

Connecting to a Database

Before you establish a connection to a database using the ODBCDirect methodology, you must first select a cursor driver type. ODBCDirect has a global default cursor type that applies to every Recordset that is created. You can change the default cursor type by accessing the DefaultCursorDriver properties of the DBEngine object. By default, whenever a Recordset is created using ODBCDirect, the most appropriate cursor type for that Recordset is used. In most cases, the ODBCDirect model chooses to create server-side cursors, if they are supported by your database server.

After you establish a cursor model for your application, you are ready to connect to your database. In the Jet Database Engine model of DAO, you simply call the OpenDatabase() method, and a connection is automatically created for you. (Connecting to your data source form DAO is described in more detail in Chapter 7.) While ODBCDirect still supports this model for connecting to your database, you also have another choice – by using the Connection object.

The Connection object offers the advantage of running asynchronous queries and the ability to create temporary QueryDef objects. If you want to create code that is supported by both the ODBCDirect and Jet database engines, your best choice is to use just the Database object and the OpenDatabase() method. If you plan to support asynchronous queries or temporary QueryDefs, then you need to convert to the Connection object. Listing 14-1 demonstrates how to open a data source using the OpenDatabase() and OpenConnection() methods.

Listing 14-1: Opening a Database Using Both the OpenDatabase() and OpenConnection() methods

```
Dim db As Database
Dim con As Connection
Set db = OpenDatabase("",dbDriverRequired, false,
"ODBC;dsn=MyODBCSource;database=Customers;uid=sa;_
 pwd=mypassword;")
Set con = OpenConnection("",dbDriverNoPrompt, false,
"ODBC;dsn=MyODBCSource;database=Customers;uid=sa;pwd=mypassword;")
```

Executing Queries

After you establish a connection to your data source with ODBCDirect, you're ready to start submitting queries. In ODBCDirect, you work with `QueryDef` objects to create queries. ODBCDirect `QueryDef` objects are only temporary. After they fall out of a program's scope or are closed, they are lost. If you need to create parameterized queries, you need to use the `CreateQueryDef()` method of the `Connection` object; the ODBCDirect `Database` object doesn't support `QueryDef` objects. After you create a `QueryDef` object, you can set its parameters, execute it, access the resulting record set, and then do it all over again.

Unlike their Jet Database Engine equivalent, ODBCDirect `QueryDef` objects can't be saved in your database. `QueryDef` objects are powerful, because they preprocess your SQL command statements before they are executed, which means that they are interpreted once and optimized. By using the `Requery()` method, this interpretation and optimization process doesn't need to be carried out again. If you don't execute your queries more than once, you really don't gain any substantial benefit. When you create a `QueryDef` object using ODBCDirect, you are basically creating a temporary stored procedure on your database server (if you're using Microsoft SQL Server, these temporary stored procedures are created in the TempDB database).

When you access the `Parameters` collection of a `QueryDef` object, or execute a `QueryDef`, the temporary stored procedure is automatically created on the database server. You can access the parameters of a `QueryDef` object by using the same `Parameters` collection that is used in DAO. When you open the `Recordset` from the `QueryDef`, the temporary stored procedure is executed by the database server. Again, this stored procedure remains until you close the `QueryDef` object or it falls out of scope, in which case it is automatically closed for you. You can also control the number of records that are cached locally when you run your query by setting the `CacheSize` property of the `QueryDef` object. The more records that are cached locally, the fewer requests that are made of the database server, but if you are accessing a heavily changed table, the greater the chances are of having stale records in your cache. Listing 14-2 demonstrates how to create a `QueryDef` object and access the resulting `Recordset`. Except for the `Connection` object, this works just like the Jet engine methodology.

Listing 14-2: Creating a Query in ODBCDirect

```
Dim Query As QueryDef
Dim rs As Recordset

' Create the QueryDef
Set Query = connect.CreateQueryDef("MyQuery")

' Specify the Query
Query.SQL = "SELECT CustFName FROM Customers"

' Cached up to 50 Records locally
Query.CacheSize = 50

' Open the QueryDef Recordset
Set rs = Query.OpenRecordset()
```

Handling Recordsets

After you create and execute your query, you're ready to access and handle the resulting Recordsets. ODBCDirect Recordsets are handled much in the same ways as their DAO counterparts. The biggest difference is the type of cursors and locking that you can choose with ODBCDirect Recordsets. Table 14-2 lists and describes the type of cursors provided by ODBCDirect Recordsets.

TABLE 14-2 ODBCDIRECT RECORDSET CURSORS

Cursor Type	Description
dbOpenDynamic	Dynamic cursor
dbOpenDynaset	Keyset cursor
dbOpenSnapshot	Static cursor
dbOpenForwardOnly	Forward-only scrolling cursor
dbOptimisticBatch	Optimistic batch cursor

Table 14-3 lists and describes the type of locks that are supported by ODBCDirect Recordsets.

TABLE 14-3 ODBCDIRECT RECORDSET LOCK TYPES	
Locking Type	**Description**
dbOptimistic	Concurrent row version
dbPessimistic	Concurrent lock
dbOptimisticValue	Concurrent values
dbReadOnly	Read-only

Not all lock and cursor types are supported by all data sources. If the lock and cursor type that you request is not supported, your application creates an error when it tries to open the record set, so be prepared to trap these errors, if necessary. Remember, ODBCDirect uses the fastest cursor types by default – dbForwardOnly and dbReadOnly. If you need to do anything special with your record set – such as update or scroll bidirectionally – you need to specify that explicitly when you open the Recordset. Listing 14-3 shows how to open a Recordset with different cursors and locking options – again, this works the same as the Jet Database Engine.

Listing 14-3: Opening ODBCDirect Recordsets

```
Dim rs As Recordset

' Open a table - This will be a read-only, forward record set by
default
Set rs = db.OpenRecordset("SELECT * FROM Customers")

' Open a record set - with a dynamic cursor, and pessimistic locking
Set rs = db.OpenRecordset("SELECT * FROM Customers", dbOpenDynaSet,
0, dbPessimistic)

' Open a record set - with a dynamic cursor and optimistic locking -
using a connection
Set rs =
Connect.OpenRecordset("Customers",dbOpenDynamic,0,dbOptimistic)
```

Functionally, ODBCDirect Recordset objects work the same as they do when using the Jet Database Engine. Importantly, if you create a complex join query, more often than not, the resulting Recordset is not updateable. When you use the Jet Database Engine, this Recordset is updateable. If your application updates complex joins, you have to change your code to use SQL action-based queries instead (for example, use the SQL UPDATE command). Finally, ODBCDirect

Recordsets don't support the ISAM functionality, as does the Jet Database Engine. This means that you can't select indexes to use on table-based Recordset objects, and the Seek() method isn't supported. The FindFirst(), FindNext(), FindPrevious(), and FindLast() methods aren't supported either. This means that you have to provide this functionality by using SQL commands.

Multiple Recordsets

ODBCDirect provides the capability to run queries that return multiple Recordsets from a single SQL call. When you use multiple Recordset queries, you won't be able to update the resulting Recordsets. After you have multiple Recordsets being returned, you can use the NextRecordset() method to retrieve each Recordset individually. Calling the NextRecordset() method throws away the current Recordset and replaces it with the next Recordset. When the NextRecordset() method returns False, you have reached the end of the multiple Recordsets. Listing 14-4 illustrates how to open and access a multiple-Recordset query.

Listing 14-4: Opening Multiple Recordsets

```
Dim Connect As Connections
Dim rs as Recordset

' Use ODBCDirect

DefaultType = dbUseODBC

' Establish a Connection
Set Connect = OpenConnection("",dbDriverPrompt, False,
"ODBC;dsn=MyServer;Database=Customers")

' Open the Recordset
Set rs = Connect.OpenRecordSet("SELECT * FROM Customers; SELECT *
FROM Products")

' Loop through each field of the multiple Recordsets
Do
  While Not rs.EOF
    For Each fld In rs.Fields
      ' Access each Recordset field
    Next f
    rs.MoveNext
  Wend
' Loop until the last record set is reached
Loop Until (rs.NextRecordset() = False)
```

Using Asynchronous Operations

ODBCDirect provides the capability to run queries *asynchronously*, which means that control returns to your application before the query has completed processing so that you can continue with other operations. This can be very useful and efficient when you are working with applications that create complex queries. When you run an asynchronous query, you need to use the StillExecuting() method to check whether the query is still executing. As long as the StillExecuting() method returns True, the query is still executing. You can call the Cancel() method to abort an asynchronous query. If your query is updating your database, though, you need to make sure that you wrap your query in a transaction; otherwise, your update query will be aborted in the middle of its operation. A transaction enables you to roll back the query and undo any changes. Listing 14-5 illustrates how to use the StillExecuting() method.

Listing 14-5: Using the StillExecuting() Method

```
Dim Connect As Connections

' Use ODBCDirect

DefaultType = dbUseODBC

' Establish a Connection
Set Connect = OpenConnection("",dbDriverPrompt, False,
"ODBC;dsn=MyServer;Database=Customers")

Connect.Execute("DELETE * FROM Customers", dbRunAsync)

Do While Connect.StillExecuting()

  REM Perform another operation while query is
  REM Still executing

Wend
```

Converting Existing Applications

The following is a list of tips to help you convert your existing DAO applications to use the ODBCDirect model:

◆ First, move your applications to a database server, such as Microsoft SQL Server or Oracle. (Part VIII, *Accessing Other Data Sources*, provides in-depth coverage of how to access Microsoft SQL Server and Oracle databases.) You also need to create an ODBC resource on the client machine. (Creating and managing ODBC data sources is discussed in detail in Chapter 5, *Connecting to Your Database*.)

◆ Change the type of `Workspaces` you are using to the ODBCDirect type. Even if you don't use the `Workspace` object, you still need to tell the `DBEngine` to create ODBCDirect-type workspaces. This is accomplished by setting the `DefaultType` property of the `DBEngine` object to the `dbUseODBCDirect` constant. After you set this property, all subsequently created workspaces are of the ODBCDirect type. If your application calls the `CreateWorkspace()` method, the fourth parameter enables you to specify the type of `Workspace` to create. Again, use the `dbUseODBCDirect` constant to specify ODBCDirect-type workspaces.

◆ You need to change the arguments passed to the `OpenDatabase` command to use the new database that your are opening. Instead of passing the name of the database in the first parameter, you need to pass a connection string (which should begin with `ODBC;`) in the connection string, or the fourth parameter. You also may choose to use the `Connection` object instead of the connection string parameter.

◆ In ODBCDirect `Workspaces`, the `Database` object doesn't support the `CreateQueryDef()` method. This method instead is handled by the `Connection` object. You need to change your code so that all references to the `CreateQueryDef()` method are handled by the `Connection` property of the `Database` object, rather than directly by the `Database` object. `QueryDef` objects that are created by using ODBCDirect aren't stored in your database and are discarded each time that the object is closed.

◆ OBDCDirect `Recordsets` default to the fastest `Recordset` rather than the most useful `Recordset`-type objects, as when you use the Jet Database Engine. This is usually a `Recordset` that can't scroll backwards and is read-only. If you need to update your `Recordset` or scroll bidirectionally, you need to specify that in the `OpenRecordset()` method.

◆ ODBCDirect doesn't support named parameters. The syntax for specifying parameters in an ODBCDirect SQL statement is a ? rather than a name, as used with the Jet Database Engine. You need to fix any parameterized queries before you begin to use the ODBCDirect methodology.

♦ ODBCDirect doesn't support the `TableDefs` or `Indexes` collections. If you need to create any new tables or indexes while using the ODBCDirect methodology, you need to create them by using SQL commands rather than DAO objects. If this is too much work, you may be able to keep your existing code intact, by using a separate Jet Database Engine-based `Workspace` and then executing your data definition code in that separate `Workspace`.

Summary

This chapter reviewed the ODBCDirect data access methodology provided by DAO. ODBCDirect, which was first introduced in Visual Basic version 5, uses a subset of the DAO data access interface and provides an easy path for moving existing DAO applications to RDO-like interface. While applications are clearly easier to develop by using DAO and the Jet Database Engine, comparable applications that access the ODBC directly are much faster. ODBCDirect provides a simple way to have the speed of a direct interface to ODBC, with the simplicity of developing DAO applications. ODBCDirect applications take less memory than comparable DAO applications, because ODBCDirect applications don't need to load the Jet Database Engine. Converting existing DAO applications to use the ODBCDirect interface is a fairly simple process, requiring only that you set the `DefaultType` property of the `DBEngine` object to `dbUseODBC`, but you must also make sure that your application uses only the `Recordset`-type object. If your application uses other DAO objects, you have a little more work to do. Follow the tips provided in this chapter to add quickly the efficiency of the ODBCDirect interface into your existing DAO applications. This chapter concludes the discussion of the Data Access Objects API. The next chapter begins the review of the Remote Data Objects API.

Part IV

Remote Data Objects API

Chapter 15

Introduction to the RDO Object Library

IN THIS CHAPTER

♦ Introducing RDO

♦ Reviewing the `rdoEngine` and `rdoEnvironment` objects

♦ Establishing a connection with the `rdoConnection` object

THIS CHAPTER BEGINS our introduction to the Remote Data Object (RDO) Library. RDO utilizes remote procedure calls to access database servers that utilize Open Database Connectivity (ODBC). By utilizing RDO, you can access your ODBC database sources without using a local query processor. Unlike DAO, which uses the Jet Database Engine, RDO applications can have significantly better performance when accessing database server sources – just like the ODBCDirect methodology. RDO is particularly suited to client/server application development. RDO utilizes the power of the back-end database server for query processing and provides sophisticated methods to manipulate and navigate resulting query sets. RDO even permits asynchronous operations with the database server, allowing multiple operations to be performed on the database server simultaneously.

This chapter introduces the RDO Object Library and compares it to the DAO Object Library, presenting object equivalents to help introduce you to RDO. The advantages of using RDO in your applications are discussed. Finally, the review of RDO objects discusses the `rdoEngine`, `rdoEnvironment`, and `rdoConnection` objects, including their associated methods and properties.

RDO Overview

RDO provides a set of objects that assists in the development of client/server applications by addressing their unique requirements. Unlike DAO, which provides an interface to the Jet Database Engine, RDO provides an object-oriented layer of abstraction that directly interfaces with the ODBC API. The RDO operates just like the ODBCDirect interface. RDO uses the ODBC API and the database server drivers to create database server connections, create queries and cursors to navigate the resulting data sets, and execute complex procedures that rely on the database server for the majority of the processing requirements. Unlike DAO, which utilizes the Jet Database Engine for query preprocessing and connection management, RDO directly interfaces to the database server. This makes RDO particularly suited to client/server application development. Figure 15-1 illustrates the RDO class hierarchy.

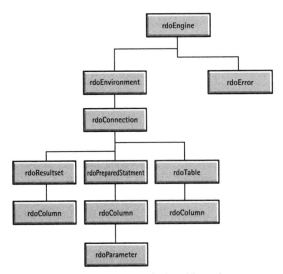

Figure 15-1: Viewing the RDO class hierarchy

Each of the objects in the RDO class hierarchy is discussed in more detail as you proceed through Part IV.

Comparing RDO and DAO

RDO can interface with the server-side database at a lower level than DAO. RDO provides a thinly layered interface over the ODBC API. Unlike DAO, which routes all database access through the Jet Database Engine, RDO directly interfaces with the ODBC.

DAO and RDO function pretty much in the same manner, though, allowing an application to connect to a database, submit a query, create a resulting data set or cursor, and manipulate the resulting data set. Both RDO and DAO allow access to server-side database views, stored procedures, and transaction management. The biggest difference in both database access models comes in the details of how these tasks are accomplished.

The RDO database isn't designed for ISAM database access, which means that you shouldn't use the RDO database model to access dBase, FoxBase, or Paradox database sources. The RDO model is designed very much toward accessing database server data sources, including Oracle, Sybase, and SQL Server database servers. Because RDO wasn't designed to access ISAM database sources, the Find() and Seek() methods supported by DAO Recordsets are not supported by RDO. Also, the RDO model doesn't support the DAO Index object, either. Instead of using the Seek() and Find() methods, the RDO model utilizes targeted database queries when searching for specific records.

The RDO model utilizes more of the relational database terminology than the DAO model. In the RDO, *fields* are referred to as *columns* and *records* are referred to as *rows*.

The RDO model doesn't support any direct methods to perform database schema modification. The DAO model enables an application to create and modify tables and indexes directly, through DAO methods. DAO did support database-schema manipulation through SQL, which is the only methodology that RDO supports. Unlike DAO, however, new databases can't be created through the RDO interface. You must consult your database-server documentation for more information regarding the creation of a database and the manipulation of the database schema.

Because RDO isn't designed to support ISAM databases, you can't perform *heterogeneous database joins*, which means that, unlike with DAO, you can't join tables from a Paradox database and SQL Server database with RDO. When you use DAO, you can attach a table to an ISAM database source and work with both database sources as if they are one; this isn't possible with RDO.

RDO is supported only on 32-bit Windows environments (Windows 95 and Windows NT). DAO is supported on both 16- and 32-bit Windows environments.

Discovering RDO's Advantages

RDO attempts to address the unique processing requirements of client/server applications in the following ways:

◆ **Faster data access:** RDO, which interfaces directly to the ODBC API, can retrieve and manipulate data much more quickly than can DAO. RDO relies on the processing power of the database server to perform complex queries and retrieve their results quickly. RDO is designed to utilize high-performance database servers, including Oracle and Sybase, and is especially engineered for optimal performance with SQL Server 6 enhancements. Also, because the RDO interface is much smaller than the DAO interface, your applications load much more quickly with RDO, permitting access to your data faster.

♦ **Query result management:** RDO provides the capability to perform a query that returns multiple related data sets. RDO also enables you to limit the number of rows returned by a query, which may result in more predictable execution times when you are accessing very complex queries. To utilize the row limitation option, the back-end database server must support it.

♦ **Batch-query access:** RDO enables you to execute a batched set of queries that can return one or more resulting data sets. This can help you to improve database server performance by reducing the number of query requests that need to be processed.

♦ **Stored procedure input parameter and output management:** RDO provides improved access to stored database server procedures. Output parameters are used to access the results of singleton queries and the results of administrative functions. Output parameters are also used to determine the execution results of a stored procedure.

♦ **Cursor utilization:** RDO supports the utilization of server-side cursors, which can greatly enhance application performance and reduce the resource requirements for the client workstation.

♦ **Asynchronous query execution:** When you process long-running query operations with DAO, your application is blocked from running any other queries or database operations until the initial query is complete. RDO provides an asynchronous query option that can be set before a query is executed. This allows a query to be processed in the background. RDO also provides a method to cancel an asynchronous query operation.

♦ **Error management:** Database servers can generate various informational errors of low severity that you may choose to ignore. RDO provides the capability to differentiate between low-severity, informational errors and fatal errors that will affect an operation being processed. RDO can set an error threshold, which determines the levels of errors that should be considered fatal.

♦ **Lower client memory requirements:** Because RDO interfaces directly with the ODBC API, it doesn't require the overhead of the Jet Database Engine (unlike DAO), resulting in a much smaller interface and lower memory requirements on the client. Also, RDO doesn't use client memory for low-level cursor management (unlike DAO), which further decreases client memory requirements.

◆ **Direct access to the ODBC API:** RDO provides direct access to the ODBC API, including environment, connection, and statement handles. This provides access to the database driver and driver manager options.

Discovering RDO and DAO Object Equivalents

RDO provides a set of objects that are very similar to the DAO objects. RDO provides a subset of the DAO objects. Because RDO relies on the back-end database server for much of its functionality, RDO objects are geared toward connection-oriented database interaction. Generally, the RDO interface is simpler than the DAO interface, and its implementation is fairly easy, especially if you are already familiar with DAO. Table 15-1 lists the RDO objects and their DAO equivalents.

TABLE 15-1 RDO AND DAO OBJECT EQUIVALENTS

RDO Object	DAO Object Equivalent
rdoEngine	DBEngine
Not applicable	User and Group
rdoEnvironment	Workspace
rdoConnection	Database
rdoTable	TableDef
Not applicable	Index
rdoResultset	Recordset
Not applicable	Table Type Recordset
Keyset Type rdoResultset	Dynaset Type Recordset
Static Type rdoResultset	Snapshot Type Recordset
Dynamic Type rdoResultset	Not applicable
Forward Only Type rdoResultset	Forward Only Snapshot Recordset
rdoColumn	Field
rdoPreparedStatement	QueryDef
rdoParameter	Parameter

Some of the objects available in DAO aren't supported by RDO. RDO follows more of a true relational database model; ISAM databases aren't supported by RDO. RDO strictly utilizes SQL when accessing and manipulating server-side databases. While the DAO model is geared toward abstracting a lot of the ODBC database access interface from your application, this comes at the cost of application performance. RDO is a lean and mean version of DAO, resulting in a database interface that is geared for performance; however, exposing more of the ODBC interface can provide a greater potential for introducing application errors. You must exercise a little extra care when you utilize RDO, but the result is greater application performance, which can certainly be worth the price.

rdoEngine Object

The rdoEngine object is analogous to the DBEngine object in DAO. The rdoEngine object is the top-level object in the RDO object hierarchy. An application should create only one rdoEngine object.

Learning the rdoEngine Object's Properties and Methods

The properties of the rdoEngine object are outlined in Table 15-2 and its methods are described in detail following the table.

TABLE 15-2 RDOENGINE OBJECT PROPERTIES

Property	Description
AbsolutePosition	Returns or sets the absolute row number of an rdoResultset object's current row
rdoDefaultCursorDriver	Returns or sets the cursor library used by the ODBC driver manager
rdoDefaultUser	Returns or sets the default username assigned to any new rdoEnvironment
rdoDefaultPassword	Returns or sets the default password assigned to any new rdoEnvironment
rdoDefaultErrorThreshold	Returns or sets a value that indicates the default value for the ErrorThreshold property for rdoQuery objects

Property	Description
rdoDefaultLoginTimeout	Returns or sets a default value that determines the number of seconds the ODBC driver waits before abandoning an attempt to connect to a data source
rdoLocaleID	Returns or sets a value that indicates the locale of the RDO library; if set to rdLocaleSystem, the system locale is used
rdoVersion	Returns a value that indicates the version of the RDO library that is associated with the object

RDOCREATEENVIRONMENT()

The rdoCreateEnvironment() method creates a new rdoEnvironment object. This method has the following syntax:

```
Set variable = rdoCreateEnvironment(name, user, password)
```

The variable parameter is an object expression that evaluates to an rdoEnvironment object. The Name parameter is a string variable that uniquely names the new rdoEnvironment object. The User parameter is a String variable that identifies the owner of the new rdoEnvironment object. The Password parameter is a String variable that contains the password for the new rdoEnvironment object. The password can be up to 14-characters long and can include any characters except ASCII character 0 (null).

RDOREGISTERDATASOURCE()

The rdoRegisterDataSource() method enters connection information for an ODBC data source into the Windows Registry. This method has the following syntax:

```
rdoRegisterDataSource DSN, driver, silent, attributes
```

The DSN parameter is a string expression that is the name used in the OpenConnection() method that refers to a block of descriptive information about the data source. The Driver parameter is a string expression that is the name of the ODBC driver. This isn't the name of the ODBC driver's dynamic link library (DLL) file. The Silent parameter is a Boolean value that is True if you don't want to display the ODBC driver dialog boxes that prompt for driver-specific information and False if you do want to display the ODBC driver dialog boxes. The Attributes parameter is a string expression that is a list of keywords to be added to the ODBC.INI file. The keywords are in a carriage-return-delimited string.

The rdoEngine object's methods utilize the ODBC driver to retrieve and set the appropriate information. The rdoEngine object isn't used to specify database-driver-specific information, because the database driver hasn't been selected at this point. The rdoEngine object is used to specify various default parameters. After an rdoEngine object is initialized, you can use the following properties:

◆ rdoDefaultCursorDriver: Used to retrieve or specify the default type of cursor used by RDO. If set to rdUseIfNeeded (default), RDO chooses the style of cursors most appropriate for the driver. Server-side cursors are used if they are available. If set to rdUseODBC, RDO uses the ODBC cursor library. This option gives better performance for small result sets, but degrades quickly for larger result sets. If set to rdUseServer, RDO uses server-side cursors. For most large operations, this gives better performance, but might cause more network traffic. If set to rdUseClientBatch, RDO uses the optimistic batch cursor library, as required by all batch mode operations and dissociate rdoResultset objects. If set to rdUseNone, RDO doesn't create a scrollable cursor. Basically, this is a forward-only, read-only result set with a RowsetSize set to 1. This type of result set performs faster than those that require the creation of a cursor.

◆ rdoDefaultErrorThreshold: Used to retrieve or specify the level of an error that will cause an error. If the number of the error is less than the value set for the rdoDefaultErrorThreshold, an error is generated. If this values is set to -1, no error threshold is used.

◆ rdoDefaultLoginTimout: Used to retrieve or specify the number of seconds that the ODBC driver waits while establishing a connection to a database server. If set to 0, RDO waits indefinitely for a database server. By default, this value is 15 seconds.

◆ rdoDefaultUser and rdoDefaultPassword: Used to retrieve or specify the default user and password used when creating new rdoEnvironment objects. When using domain-managed security, you may choose to leave these values at their default values, which are empty strings.

◆ rdoLocaleID: Used to retrieve or specify which language is used when generating error messages. By default, rdLocaleSystem is used, which specifies the default Windows system language to be used.

◆ rdoVersion: Returns a 5-character string that specifies the RDO library version.

◆ rdoEnvironments: Used to retrieve the collection of environments that the rdoEngine object has created.

Understanding Data-Source Registration

The rdoEngine object provides the rdoRegisterDataSource() method, which can be used to register new data sources. We suggest that you use the Control Panel ODBC Data Sources applet instead of this method when you create or modify data source entries. RDO can connect to any data source that provides an ODBC connectivity driver. You should note, though, that RDO has been specifically optimized to utilize SQL Server and Oracle database data sources.

Specifying the Default Cursor, User, and Password

Listing 15-1 demonstrates how to use the rdoEngine's rdoDefaultCursorDriver, rdoDefaultUser, and rdoDefaultPassword properties. This example changes the default cursor method so that it always uses server-side cursors, and sets the default username to "Diane" and the default password to "Pokey".

Listing 15-1: Changing the Default Cursor Method and Logon Information

```
With rdoEngine
 REM Set default cursor library
 .rdoDefaultCursorDriver = rdUseServer

 REM Set user name and password
 .rdoDefaultUser = "Diane"
 .rdoDefaultPassword = "Pokey"
End With
```

rdoEnvironment Object

The rdoCreateEnvironment() method of the rdoEngine object is used to create a new rdoEnvironment object. When the rdoEngine object is instantiated, a default rdoEnvironment is automatically created and appended to the rdoEngine object's environment collection. The rdoEnvironment object corresponds to the ODBC environment handle. The rdoEnvironment object is used to determine ODBC driver settings. Any option that can be specified by rdoEnvironment methods overrides any default values set by the rdoEngine methods.

The rdoEngine object's rdoCreateEnvironment() method requires the following parameters:

```
rdoCreateEnvironment envname, username, password
```

If the name of the environment is not specified, the environment created is said to be private. When a private rdoEnvironment object is created, it is not appended to the rdoEngine object's environment collection. After a private rdoEnvironment object is no longer referenced, all of its associated collections are automatically closed.

Table 15-3 describes the parameters required by the rdoEngine object's rdoCreateEnvironment() method.

TABLE 15-3 RDOCREATEENVIRONMENT() METHOD'S PARAMETERS

Parameter	Description
envname	The name of the new environment object. If the environment name is left blank, a private environment is created. envname is a String type.
username	The username to use when establishing connections. If the username is left blank, the username must be specified when you open a new connection. username is a String type.
password	The password to use when establishing connections. If the password is left blank, the password must be specified when opening a new connection. password is a String type.

You need to create a new rdoEnvironment object only if your application requires more than one transaction scope or a separate user and password context. As stated earlier, when the rdoEngine object is instantiated, a default rdoEnvironment object is created and appended to the rdoEngine's environment collection. Listing 15-2 demonstrates how to access the default rdoEnvironment object from the rdoEnvironments collection. The rdoEnvironments collection's objects provide Count and Item properties that function in the same manner as the DAO collection's objects: TableDefs, Indexes, Fields, and Relations. The Item property can be used to access an environment by name or index. The default environment is stored at index 0, and is named Default_Environment.

Listing 15-2: Accessing the Default rdoEnvironment Object

```
Dim en As rdoEnvironmentDim

REM Access the rdoEnvironment
en = rdoEngine.rdoEvironments(0)
```

Learning the rdoEnvironment Object's Properties and Methods

The properties and methods of the `rdoEnvironment` object are outlined in Tables 15-4 and 15-5, respectively.

TABLE 15-4 THE RDOENVIRONMENT OBJECT'S PROPERTIES

Property	Description
CursorDriver	Returns or sets a value that specifies the type of cursor to be created. If set to `rdUseIfNeeded`, the ODBC driver chooses the appropriate style of cursors. Server-side cursors are used if they are available. If set to `rdUseODBC`, the ODBC cursor library is used. If set to `rdUseServer`, server-side cursors are used. If set to `rdUseClientBatch`, RDO uses the optimistic batch cursor library.
hEnv	Returns a value corresponding to the ODBC environment handle.
LoginTimeout	Returns or sets a value that specifies the number of seconds the ODBC driver manager waits before a timeout error occurs when a connection is opened.
Name	Returns the name of a `RemoteData` object.
Password	Represents the password used during creation of an `rdoEnvironment` object.
UserName	Returns or sets a value that represents a user of an `rdoEnvironment` object. Use the `UserName` property with the `Password` property to connect to an ODBC data source.
Item	Returns a specific member of an RDO collection object, either by position or by key.
RdoConnections	Returns a specific member of an `rdoConnections` collection, either by position or by key.

TABLES 15-5 RDOENVIRONMENT OBJECT'S METHODS

Name	Syntax	Parameters	Description
BeginTrans()	BeginTrans	None	Begins a new transaction.
CommitTrans()	CommitTrans	None	Ends the current transaction and saves the changes.
Rollback Trans()	RollbackTrans	None	Ends the current transaction and restores the databases in the rdoEnvironment object to the state they were in when the current transaction began.
Close()	Close	None	Closes an open remote data object.
Open Connection ()	Set connection = environment. OpenConnection (dsName[, prompt[, readonly[, connect[, options]]]])	Connection: An object expression that evaluates to an rdoConnection object that you're opening. Environment: An object expression that evaluates to an existing rdo Environment object. DsName: A string expression that is the name of a registered ODBC data source name. Prompt: A Variant or constant that determines how the operation is carried out. Readonly: A Boolean value that is True if the	Opens a connection to an ODBC data source and returns a reference to the rdoConnection object that represents a specific database.

Name	Syntax	Parameters	Description
		connection is to be opened for read-only access, and `False` if the connection is to be opened for read/write access. `Connect`: A string expression used to pass arguments to the ODBC driver manager for opening the database. `Options`: A Variant or constant that determines how the operation is carried out.	
`Add()`	`object.Add item, key, before, after`	`Item`: An expression of any type that specifies the member to add to the collection. `Key`: A unique string expression that specifies a key string that can be used. `Before`: An expression that specifies a relative position in the collection. `After`: An expression that specifies a relative position in the collection.	Adds a member to a `Collection` object.
`Remove()`	`object.Remove index`	`Index`: An expression that specifies the position of a member of the collection.	Removes a member from a `Collection` object.

The `rdoEnvironment` object can be used to define a set of connections for a particular database server user. The `rdoEnvironment` object contains a collection of open connections, provides methods to manage database transactions, and helps to provide a context for database security. After an `rdoEnvironment` object is initialized, you can use the following methods and properties:

- The `LoginTimeout` property is used to retrieve or specify the number of seconds the ODBC driver waits while establishing a connection to a database server. By default, this value is set to the value specified by the `rdoEngine` default login timeout value.

- The `UserName` and `Password` properties are used to retrieve or specify the username and password to be used when establishing connections. You can override these values in the `OpenConnection()` method.

- The `hEnv` property returns the ODBC environment handle. This can be used by the ODBC API functions, which require the ODBC environment handle.

- The `Name()` method returns the name of the environment object.

- The `CursorDriver` property sets the type of cursors to be created for this environment. The `putCursorDriver()` method accepts the same parameters as the `putDefaultCursorDriver()` method of the `rdoEngine` object.

- The `BeginTrans`, `CommitTrans`, and `RollbackTrans` properties are used for transaction processing. Multiple `rdoEnvironment` objects can be used to perform multiple, simultaneous, and overlapping transactions.

- The `OpenConnection()` method is used to open one or more connections. Unlike DAO, which provides automatic connection and disconnection management, after a connection is closed in RDO, it is closed immediately.

- The `rdoConnections` property is used to access the collection of connections opened in the environment.

- The `Close()` method is used to close the environment object. After an environment is closed, all of its associated connections are also closed.

Understanding Transactions

If more than one username and password context is required, or if multiple transaction scopes are required, multiple environment objects should be created. As mentioned earlier, if the `rdoEnvironment` object isn't named, the environment object is private and not appended to the `rdoEngine`'s environment collection. You must also ensure that the name specified for a new environment is unique. If an existing environment object has the same name, an exception will be thrown.

When multiple rdoEnvironment objects are created, each can be used for independent transaction scopes. When the BeginTrans() method is called for an environment, all open connections in that environment are in the same transaction scope. When the RollBackTrans() or CommitTrans() methods are called, all pending operations for each connection are rolled back or committed. If multiple transaction scopes are required, you need to create additional rdoEnvironment objects.

Even though RDO supports multiple transaction scopes, it doesn't support nested transactions in a single scope. The BeginTrans() method sets a bit on the connection's handle. After the CommitTrans() or RollBackTrans() method is called, this bit is cleared.

Selecting a Cursor Driver

The rdoEnvironment object can be used to determine the type of the cursor driver that is used. If your application needs to manage multiple query result sets, it should be set to use the ODBC cursor library, using the rdUseODBC value. Using ODBC cursors can be very effective when you access small data sets, but performance can be affected quickly when you access larger data sets. The ODBC cursors also require more client-side resources than server-side cursors require.

If rdUseIfNeed is used, the ODBC driver determines the type of cursors to use. RDO utilizes server-side cursors if they are available on the database server. RDO can't determine whether your application will be requesting multiple data sets and, therefore, can't determine whether it should utilize ODBC cursors instead of server-side cursors.

If rdUseServer is used, server-side cursors will always be used if they are available. Server-side cursors are available on SQL Server and Oracle database servers. Using server-side cursors reduces the resources required on the client, but increases the amount of network traffic. When you use server-side cursors, they are maintained in a temporary space on the database server; if the server can't allocate any more space for cursor management, RDO drops back to using ODBC cursors, instead.

rdoConnection Object

The last RDO object considered in this chapter is the rdoConnection object. After the rdoEngine is initialized and the rdoEnvironment is created and properly configured, the rdoConnection object can be used to establish a connection with an ODBC data source. The rdoConnection object is used to manage connections with a single ODBC data source. Multiple connections can be used to access multiple ODBC data sources.

Establishing a Connection

The `OpenConnection()` method of the `rdoEnvironment` object is used to establish a connection to an ODBC data source, as follows:

```
OpenConnection datasrcname, prompt, readonly, connectstr
```

Table 15-6 describes the parameters required by the `OpenConnection()` method, which takes an ODBC connect string as its final parameter.

TABLE 15-6 OPENCONNECTION() METHOD PARAMETERS

Parameter	Description
`datasrcname`	Specifies the name of the ODBC data source. If the data source name isn't specified, the connect string is searched for the `DSN` parameter. `datasrcname` is a string type.
`prompt`	Specifies whether the user should be prompted if a data source name can't be found in the `datasrcname` parameter or on the connection string. If the `rdDriverNoPrompt` value is specified and a data source name isn't found, an exception is thrown. If the `rdDriverPrompt` value is specified, the user is prompted to specify the connect information in the ODBC Data Source dialog box. If the `rdDriverComplete` value is specified, the connect string information is used if the `datasrcname` is specified; otherwise, the user is prompted with the ODBC Data Source dialog box. If the `rdDriverCompleteRequired` is specified, the user is presented with the ODBC dialog box, but controls for information that isn't required to complete the connection are disabled.
`readonly`	If this value is `True`, the connection is opened only for read access; if `False`, the connection is opened for read/write access. By default, the connection is opened for read/write access. `readonly` is an optional parameter.
`connectstr`	Specifies the ODBC connect string. `connectstr` is a Variant type and is optional. If it is omitted, the environment default values are used when accessing the database source.

Table 15-7 presents a list of valid connect string parameters. Each connect string parameter is separated by a semicolon.

Table 15-7 CONNECT STRING PARAMETERS

Parameter	Description
DSN=	The name of the ODBC data source. This is not used if a driver name is specified in the OpenConnection() method.
DRIVER=	The name of the database driver. This is not required if the DSN is specified.
SERVER=	The network name of the ODBC data source server. The "(local)" name can be specified as the server name to use the ODBC data source on the current server.
UID=	Specifies the username. If this is an empty string, domain-managed security is employed, which passes your Windows NT username and password to the data source. Domain-managed security is easier to manage, because usernames and passwords are kept in a centralized location.
PWD=	Specifies the password. If this is an empty string, domain-managed security is used.
APP=	Specifies the name of the application; this is optional.
WSID=	Specifies the name of the workstation; this is optional.
DATABASE=	The name of the database server; this is optional.
LANGUAGE=	The language type to be used by the ODBC data source server; this is optional.

Now that you understand the parameters required by the OpenConnection() method and how to specify the connect string, take a look at how to put together all of this information to establish a connection. Listing 15-3 demonstrates how to create an rdoConnection object.

Listing 15-3: Connecting to an ODBC Data Source

```
Dim en As rdoEnvironment
Dim cn As rdoConnection
Set en = rdoEngine.rdoEvironments(0)
With en
  en.CursorDriver = rdUseODBC
  en.LoginTimeout = 5
  en.Name = "TestEnv"
```

```
Set cn = en.OpenConnection(dsname:="",
                prompt:=rdDriverNoPrompt,
                Connect:="UID=;PWD=;"
                driver={SQL Server};
                Server=MyServer;",
                Options:=rdAsyncEnable)
End With
```

 When you access an ODBC data source on a Windows NT server, be sure that user and group permissions are properly set up for the shared resource. Improper permissions can prevent your application from accessing the required data source.

Learning the rdoConnection Object's Properties and Methods

Now that you understand how to create an rdoConnection object, continue by reviewing Tables 15-8 and 15-9, which present the properties and methods of the rdoConnection object.

TABLE 15-8 RDOCONNECTION OBJECT PROPERTIES

Property	Description
AsyncCheckInterval	Returns or sets a value that specifies the number of milliseconds that RDO waits between checks to see whether an asynchronous query is complete.
Connect	Returns or sets a value that provides information about the source of an open rdoConnection. The Connect property contains the ODBC connect string. This property is always readable, but can't be changed after the connection is established.
CursorDriver	Returns or sets a value that specifies the type of cursor to create. If set to rdUseIfNeeded, the ODBC driver chooses the appropriate style of cursors. Server-side cursors are used if they are available. If set to rdUseODBC, RemoteData uses the ODBC cursor library. If set to rdUseServer, server-side cursors are used. If set to rdUseClientBatch, RDO uses the optimistic batch cursor library.

Property	Description
hDbc	Returns a value corresponding to the ODBC connection handle.
LoginTimeout	Returns or sets a value that specifies the number of seconds the ODBC driver manager waits before a timeout error occurs when a connection is opened.
LogMessages	Enables ODBC trace logging and returns or sets a value that indicates the path of the ODBC trace file, created by the ODBC driver manager to record all ODBC operations.
Name	Returns the name of a RemoteData object.
QueryTimeout	Returns or sets a value that specifies the number of seconds the ODBC driver manager waits before a timeout error occurs when a query is executed.
LastQueryResults	Returns a reference to the rdoResultset object generated by the last query, if any.
UpdateOperation	Returns or sets a value that specifies whether the optimistic batch update should use an Update statement or a Delete followed by an Insert. If set to rdOperationUpdate, an Update statement is used for each modified row. If set to rdOperationDelIns, a pair of Delete and Insert statements is used for each modified row.
RowsAffected	Returns the number of rows affected by the most recently invoked Execute() method.
StillExecuting	Returns a Boolean value that indicates whether a query is still executing.
Transactions	Returns a value that indicates whether an object supports the recording of a series of changes that can later be rolled back (undone) or committed (saved).
Version	Returns a value that indicates the version of the data source associated with the object.
StillConnecting	Returns a value that indicates if the connection has been established.

TABLE 15-9 RDOCONNECTION OBJECT METHODS

Method	Syntax	Parameters	Description
BeginTrans()	BeginTrans	None	Begins a new transaction.
CommitTrans()	CommitTrans	None	Ends the current transaction and saves the changes.
RollbackTrans()	RollbackTrans	None	Ends the current transaction and restores the databases in the rdoEnvironment object to the state they were in when the current transaction began.
Close()	Close	None	Closes an open remote data object.
Cancel()	Cancel	None	Cancels the processing of a query running in asynchronous mode, or cancels any pending results against the specified RDO object.
Execute()	connection. Execute source [, options]	Connection Query Source Options	Connection: An object expression that evaluates to the rdoConnection object on which the query will run. Query: An object expression that evaluates to the rdoQuery object whose SQL property setting specifies the SQL statement to execute. Source: A string expression that contains the action query to execute or the name of an rdoQuery. Options: A Variant or constant that determines how the query is run. If set to rdAsyncEnable, executes operation asynchronously. If set to rdExecDirect, bypasses creation of a stored procedure to execute the query.

Method	Syntax	Parameters	Description
			Runs an action query or executes an SQL statement that does not return rows.
OpenResultset()	Set variable = connection. OpenResultset (name [,type [,locktype [,option]]])	Connection: An object expression that evaluates to an existing rdo Connection object that you want to use to create the new rdoResultset. Name: A String that specifies the source of the rows for the new rdoResult set. Type: A Variant or constant that specifies the type of cursor to create. Locktype: A Variant or constant that specifies the type of concurrency control. Option: A Variant or constant that specifies characteristics of the new rdoResultset.	Creates a new rdoResultset object.

Continued

TABLE 15–9 **RDOCONNECTION OBJECT METHODS** *(continued)*

Method	Syntax	Parameters	Description
CreateQuery()	object. CreateQuery Name, SQLString	Object: An object expression that evaluates to an rdoConnection object. Name: A string expression that evaluates to the name for the new object. SQL String: SQL query for the new prepared statement.	Creates a new query object and adds it to the rdoQueries collection.
Establish Connection()	object. Establish Connection prompt, readonly, options	Object: An object expression that evaluates to an rdoConnection object. Prompt: Integer value indicating the ODBC prompting characteristic. Readonly: Boolean value that is True if you intend to use connection as read-only. Options: Integer value that indicates connection options.	Establishes a physical connection to an ODBC server.

After you create the rdoConnection object, it can be used to manipulate the database that is associated with the connection. The database server is not accessed until the connection is established. The following properties and methods can be used after you create the rdoConnection object:

◆ The `Transactions` property can be used to determine whether the connection supports transactions. If the connection does support transactions, the `BeginTrans()`, `CommitTrans()`, and `RollBackTrans()` methods can be used for transaction processing.

◆ The `Execute()` method can be used to perform an action or query an SQL statement. The `Execute()` method should not be used to perform queries that return rows. If the query returns any rows, an exception will be thrown. The `Execute()` method is most effective when you are adding, modifying, or deleting rows of data, or when you are performing SQL commands that affect the database schema. A command can be performed asynchronously if the `rdAsynchEnable` option is specified. The `RowsAffected` property is used to retrieve the number of rows affected by the most recently executed `Execute()` method.

◆ The `Cancel()` method can be used to stop the performance of all queries and statements that are currently running asynchronously. This can cause unpredictable results if the query or statement that is running affects multiple rows. Use the `Cancel` method with great caution.

◆ The `CreatePreparedStatement()` method is used to create stored SQL queries, which can be executed by specifying a set of parameters. Prepared queries were reviewed with DAO. When you create a prepared statement, it is appended to the `PreparedStatement` collection. The `getPreparedStatements()` method can be used to access this collection.

◆ The `AsyncCheckInterval()` method can be used to retrieve and specify the number of milliseconds that RDO waits between the times that it checks to see whether an asynchronous query has been completed. By default, this time is 500 milliseconds (or twice every second). Setting this value too low can cause increased network overhead.

◆ The `Connect` property returns the connect string that is used to establish the connection.

◆ The `hDbc()` method is used to retrieve the ODBC connection handle. This should be used only if you need to directly access the ODBC API.

◆ The `Name()` method returns the name of the connection.

◆ The `QueryTimeout` property is used to retrieve and specify the amount of time (in seconds) the connection waits for a query to complete. By default, this value is 0, which means that no timeout will occur. If a query exceeds the maximum time set, an exception will be thrown.

◆ The `rdoResultsets` property is used to retrieve the collection of result sets currently associated with the connection.

◆ The `rdoTables()` method is used to retrieve the collection of tables that is currently associated with the connection.

◆ The `StillExecuting` property is used to determine whether an asynchronous query is still executing.

◆ The `Updatable` property determines whether query result sets can be updated.

◆ The `Version` property returns a 10-character string that specifies the version number of the currently connected ODBC data source.

◆ The `OpenResultset()` methods is used to create a new `rdoResultset` cursor object. A cursor contains a subset of the database, which is specified by a query. A result set can be read-only or read/write. The next chapter explains the process of creating result sets by using the `OpenResultset()` method.

◆ The `Close()` method is used to close an open connection. After a connection is closed, it is automatically removed from the `rdoEnvironment`'s connection collection. If a connection is closed while any associated result sets are open, any changes made are automatically rolled back. Unlike DAO, RDO doesn't provide any automated connection management; you must explicitly close a connection when you are finished with it.

Finding a Named ODBC Database Source

Two procedures are recommended for finding a named ODBC database source on the client. The first procedure involves using the ODBC Control Panel applet. If you are installing your application on each client, you could use the ODBC Control Panel applet to set up the database source individually. This probably is not practical.

The second procedure can be more reliable: specify all the ODBC data source connection options on the command string. This assumes that the name of the ODBC data source server doesn't change. This is usually more reliable than permitting the user to select the ODBC data source manually by using the `rdDriverPrompt`.

Fixing Problems When Establishing Connections

Various problems may prevent your application from establishing a connection with an ODBC data source. If your application can't access the ODBC data source, be sure to check the following:

◆ Make sure the permissions on the ODBC data source server allow access to the data source.

◆ Make sure the network connections are functioning properly.

◆ Make sure the ODBC drivers are installed properly and that you are using the 32-bit version, not the 16-bit version, of the ODBC drivers.

◆ Make sure the data source is available. Some database servers limit the number of simultaneous connections, due to licensing restrictions.

Executing an SQL Command

Listing 15-4 demonstrates how to use the `rdoConnection` object to execute an SQL command asynchronously that deletes all the records in the table of customers who are from New York. Before you can execute this command, you must convert your request into SQL. The SQL command you want to perform is `DELETE * FROM Customers WHERE State = 'NY'`. When you call the `Execute()` method, you must pass the SQL command statement string and the option to execute the command asynchronously.

Listing 15-4: Executing an Asynchronous SQL Command

```
Dim en As rdoEnvironment
Dim cn As rdoConnection
Set en = rdoEngine.rdoEvironments(0)
With en
  en.CursorDriver = rdUseODBC
  en.LoginTimeout = 5
  en.Name = "TestEnv"
  Set cn = en.OpenConnection(dsname:="",
            prompt:=rdDriverNoPrompt,
            Connect:="UID=;PWD=;"
            driver={SQL Server};
            Server=MyServer;",
            Options:=rdAsyncEnable)
End With

cn.Execute "DELETE * FROM Customers Where State = 'NY'",
        rdAsnycEnable
```

Summary

This chapter introduced you to the RDO Object Library, including an RDO class hierarchy, and compared the RDO and DAO Object Libraries, including a discussion of the advantages of using the RDO Object Library. The RDO and DAO objects were compared, and a detailed look of the RDO objects began with the `rdoEngine`, `rdoConnection`, and `rdoEnvironment` objects. You learned how to utilize these objects to initialize the RDO Engine, create and configure the RDO environment, and open a database connection with the `OpenConnection()` method. Finally, this chapter discussed how RDO can be used to process asynchronous operations. The remainder of Part IV discusses in greater detail how to use RDO to perform database queries.

Chapter 16

RDO Database Navigation and Cursor Management

IN THIS CHAPTER

◆ Using RDO objects to access data

◆ Performing queries

◆ Handling multiple result sets

UP TO THIS POINT, you have reviewed the basic RDO elements and have learned how to initialize RDO and connect to your database server. You are ready to get down to the data. This chapter presents the RDO objects that you need to use to access data, perform queries, and navigate the resulting data sets by using cursors.

The rdoResultset object is used to access the results of a database query. The following four types of rdoResultset cursors can be created, each of which is reviewed in depth during this chapter:

◆ **Forward-only:** Not really a cursor as such, the resulting data set can be accessed only in a forward manner (similar to the ForwardOnly type in DAO).

◆ **Static:** Similar to the DAO Snapshot Recordset. A copy of the data that satisfies the query is retrieved.

◆ **Keyset:** Similar to the DAO Dynaset Recordset. The keys are retrieved that are necessary to retrieve the data requested, and as each resulting row of the query is accessed, the current database's data is retrieved. After the query result set is created, any database deletions or updates that satisfy the original query *are not* reflected in the resulting set.

◆ **Dynamic:** Just like the keyset cursor, except that the resulting data set always reflects the *current* database state.

As discussed in the last chapter, the following three different types of cursor drivers can be selected for the rdoEnvironment object:

◆ rdUseOdbc: ODBC cursors are used; this requires greater client overhead, but is the only cursor driver that supports multiple result sets.

◆ rdUseServer: Server-side cursors are used; this requires lower client overhead and can perform faster.

◆ rdUseIfNeeded: If the server supports cursors, they are used; otherwise, the ODBC cursors are used.

Later in this chapter, you will review the following three objects that can be used to access data using RDO:

◆ rdoResultSet: Analogous to the DAO Recordset object; used when you navigate a query result set.

◆ rdoPreparedStatement: Analogous to the DAO QueryDef object; can be used to create nonpersistent query definitions.

◆ rdoTable: Analogous to the DAO TableDef object; used in conjunction with the rdoTables object (similar to the DAO TableDefs object). Unlike in DAO, though, RDO doesn't automatically populate the rdoTable object.

The rdoResultset Object

The rdoResultset object is used to access the data set that results from a query. An SQL query generally results in an rdoResultset, which is the method of creating a result set that is discussed first. The OpenResultset() method of the rdoConnection object is used to create an rdoResultset object. Before the details of creating rdoResultset objects can be reviewed, you must first understand some of the important options of rdoResultset objects; namely, cursor types and page-locking options. These options can greatly affect the performance and resource utilization of your application.

Cursors

As already mentioned, RDO supports four different types of cursors. The choice of a cursor can greatly affect application performance. RDO utilizes the ODBC API to create cursors, according to your choice of options. You need to remember that RDO doesn't actually manage the cursors, but instead relies on ODBC to manage the cursors. When you choose the type of cursor that you are going to use in your application, you should consider the following key elements, keeping in mind that you may choose to utilize different types of cursors at varying points in your application:

◆ How should the resulting data set of the cursor be filled?

◆ Should changes in the database be reflected in the cursor result set after the selection is made, or does your application require a static, unchanging view of the data?

◆ What are the navigation requirements for the cursor? Will rows be accessed randomly, or sequentially from the beginning of the cursor to the end?

◆ Does your application need to update the cursor data?

◆ Can your application wait for the entire query result set to be created, or does it need to start accessing data immediately?

◆ What's the size of the query result set?

The advantages and disadvantages of each of the cursor type options that the `OpenRecordset()` method accepts are discussed next, as well as how the answers to the preceding list of questions should affect your choice of which cursor to use.

RDOPENFORWARDONLY CURSOR

The `rdOpenForwardOnly`-type cursor isn't really a type of cursor. It enables you to move sequentially through the query result data set only in a forward direction. You can't back up through the query result set. The `rdOpenForwardOnly`-type cursor is the fastest way to access your data.

RDOPENSTATIC CURSOR

The `rdOpenStatic`-type cursor retrieves a static snapshot of the resulting query data set. If any changes occur in the database that affect the members of the query set, those changes are not dynamically reflected in the cursor set. Static-type cursors aren't recommended for data sets that are constantly changing. The data contained in the static cursor is updated only when the cursor is closed and reopened. Depending on the ODBC data source, static cursors can be implemented in two ways:

◆ An actual copy of the query result set can be created and accessed by the static cursor.

◆ The records that are part of the query result set can be locked, disallowing other users from changing the records while the cursor is open.

You need to remember that Static-type cursors shouldn't be opened for too long, because the resulting data set can become stale and no longer reflect the current state of the database.

RDOPENKEYSET CURSOR

The `rdOpenKeyset`-type cursor is a dynamic type of cursor. With a Keyset-type cursor, if any members of the resulting query data set are changed, they are reflected dynamically when data is retrieved. If new records that fit the query criteria are added to the database, they are not reflected in the cursor's resulting data set. When a Keyset-type cursor is created, a key is created for each row of the query. Depending on the cursor library that is used, these values are stored either on the client or the database server. As each row of the query result set is accessed, the key value is accessed and the appropriate row is retrieved from the database. Retrieving just the key set of the query requires less overhead than retrieving a static copy. Depending on the cursor driver employed, enough space must be available on the client or server to store the key set.

If a record contained in the resulting data set is deleted or updated by another cursor, those rows appear as a hole in the data set. If a hole is encountered while navigating the data set, you need to be aware that an exception will be thrown.

 On some database servers, the Keyset-type cursor can detect when rows are modified with the `Execute()` method while the cursor is open. You must review your database-server documentation to see whether your server supports this feature.

RDOPENDYNAMIC CURSOR

The `rdOpenDynamic`-type cursor is very similar to the Keyset-type cursor. The difference with the Dynamic-type cursor is that it reflects all changes to the query result set as the changes occur. If any records are added or removed that are members of the resulting data set, they are reflected in the cursor. Dynamic cursors involve the most overhead, but you can access them faster initially than you can access Keyset-type cursors, because Dynamic cursors don't require a key set to be built.

MIXED-TYPE CURSORS

You can build a mixed cursor, which is a cross between a Dynamic and Keyset cursor type. This mixed-type cursor can merge the advantages of both types of cursors. The concept behind building mixed cursors is reviewed now – their actual implementation is reviewed later in this chapter.

You must utilize an `rdoPreparedStatement` to create a mixed-type cursor. By using the `rdoPreparedStatement` object's `KeySize` property, you can limit the size of the key set that is created for the query. To create a mixed-type cursor, the size of the key set must be smaller than the number of rows that you expect your query to generate, but larger than the Rowset size that determines the number of keyset rows to be buffered by the cursor. Don't worry if you don't understand these details now, because you will review the implementation details when the `rdoPreparedStatement` object is introduced later in the chapter.

Not all cursor driver/database server combinations support each type of cursor. You must test your cursor driver and cursor selection against potential database servers that your application may use. Consult your database-server documentation for more information regarding its cursor support. Due to the numerous different database servers, cursor drivers, and cursor types, listing all potential combinations and whether each is supported is impractical.

Page Locking

The last option to discuss regarding the creation of an `rdoResultset` object is the page locking options. When an `rdoResultset` is created, the database server places a share lock on all the rows that are part of the query result set. If the query is too complex and affects too many rows, a lock can be placed on a complete table. These locks are released only when all the rows of the query have been retrieved. If your application is used by multiple users — which it probably is if you require a database server — you must take these locking implications into account. These locks don't affect another user's ability to read the affected rows, but while the rows are locked, another user isn't permitted to change these affected rows.

One way to minimize the effect of record locking is to retrieve all the result set records as quickly as possible. The easiest way to do this is to move to the end of the cursor. The `MoveLast()` method quickly moves to the end of the resulting data set. Depending on the type of your cursor, this may involve significant overhead.

Another way to limit the effects of page locking is to limit the `RowsetSize`. As discussed with mixed cursors, limiting the `RowsetSize` is possible only with the `rdoPreparedStatement` object. By default, the `RowsetSize` is 100 rows; limiting this value may reduce the number of concurrent rows that are locked by the database server.

RDCONCURREADONLY-TYPE LOCKING

rdConcurReadOnly-type locking is the default. When this locking method is used, the result set is available for reading only. You may not update any of the result set rows.

RDCONCURLOCK-TYPE LOCKING

rdConcurLock-type locking employs the pessimistic-type locking scheme on the result set data. As you may recall, *pessimistic locking* ensures the greatest level of database integrity. Whenever a row is accessed, the page containing that row is exclusively locked, preventing all other users from accessing the data on that page. Again, the locks are released only after all the rows have been retrieved. This can be dangerous, because a page may be kept locked for a long time.

RDCONCURROWVER-TYPE LOCKING

rdConcurRowver-type locking employs optimistic-type page locking. With *optimistic locking*, an exclusive lock is placed on pages that contain result set data rows. rdConcurRowver-type locking is available for read access by other users while it is locked, and is made unavailable only when a row is updated. With optimistic locking, two users can start to modify the same row, and they won't find out that the record is locked – or has already been changed – until they attempt to commit their changes. The rdConcurRowver-type locking detects whether a change has occurred, based on a timestamp column.

RDCONCURVALUES-TYPE LOCKING

rdConcurValues-type locking employs optimistic page locking, just like rdConcurRowver-type locking. The difference is that rdConcurValues-type locking detects whether a change has been made, based on a comparison of the new and old row values.

Using the OpenResultset() Method

Now that you have a better understanding of the options available when creating an rdoResultset, you can now examine how to use the rdoConnections's OpenResultset() method to create an rdoResultset object. Table 16-1 presents the parameters that are required by the OpenResultset() method, which has the following syntax:

```
OpenResultset query, cursortype, locktype, exception
```

TABLE 16-1 PARAMETERS REQUIRED BY THE OPENRESULTSET() METHOD

Argument	Description
query	Describes the source for the rdoResultset object. Typically, this is an SQL statement that could return a resulting data set. This also could be the name of an rdoTable object (described later when the rdoTable object is reviewed). The query parameter is a string.
cursortype	Specifies the cursor type of the rdoResultset object. This can be rdOpenForwardOnly, rdOpenStatic, rdOpenKeyset, or rdOpenDynamic.
locktype	Specifies the locking type of the rdoResultset object. This can be rdConcurLock, rdConcurReadOnly, rdConcurRowver, or rdConcurValues.
exception	Specifies how to execute the query. RdAsyncEnable specifies the query to run asynchronously. RdExecDirect is most effective when the query will be run only once.

Listing 16-1 demonstrates how to open a new rdoResultset object, which selects all the fields from the Customers table from New York. The result set is opened with a dynamic-type cursor, for read-only access.

Listing 16-1: Opening an rdoResultset Object

```
Dim en As rdoEnvironment
Dim cn As rdoConnection
Dim Result As rdoResultSet

REM Create an Environment
Set en = rdoEngine.rdoEvironments(0)
With en
  en.CursorDriver = rdUseOdbc
  en.LoginTimeout = 5
  en.Name = "TestEnv"

  REM Establish a connection
  Set cn = en.OpenConnection("", rdDriverPrompt, True,
"DSN=MyDataSource;UID=Marie;PWD=Pooh;Database=Customers")

End With
```

```
REM Open the ResultSet with a Dynamic cursor and read-only access

Result = cn.OpenResultSet(
        "SELECT * FROM CUSTOMERS WHERE STATE='NY'",
        rdoOpenDynamic, rdConcurReadOnly)
```

rdoResultset Properties and Methods

The properties and methods of the rdoResultset object are presented in Tables 16-2 and 16-3.

TABLE 16-2 PROPERTIES OF THE RDORESULTSET OBJECT

Property	Description
AbsolutePosition	Returns or sets the absolute row number of an rdoResultset object's current row.
BOF	Returns a value that indicates whether the current row position is before the first row in an rdoResultset.
EOF	Returns a value that indicates whether the current row position is after the last row in an rdoResultset.
Bookmark	Returns or sets a bookmark that uniquely identifies the current row in an rdoResultset object. If you have a valid bookmark, you can use it to reposition the current row in an rdoResultset.
Bookmarkable	Returns a value that indicates whether an rdoResultset object supports bookmarks, which you can set by using the Bookmark property.
EditMode	Returns a value that indicates the state of editing for the current row. If set to rdEditNone, no editing operations are in progress. If set to rdEditInProgress, the Edit() method has been invoked, and the current row is in the copy buffer. If set to rdEditAdd, the AddNew() method has been invoked and the current row in the copy buffer is a new row that hasn't been saved in the database.
hStmt	Returns a value that corresponds to the ODBC statement handle.
LastModified	Returns a bookmark that indicates the most recently added or changed row.

Property	Description
LockType	Returns or sets a Long integer value that indicates the type of concurrency handling. If set to rdConcurReadOnly, the cursor is read-only and no updates are allowed. If set to rdConcurLock, pessimistic concurrency is used. If set to rdConcurRowver, optimistic concurrency is used, based on row ID. If set to rdConcurValues, optimistic concurrency is used, based on row values. If set to rdConcurBatch, optimistic concurrency using batch-mode updates is used.
LockEdits	Returns a Boolean value that indicates the type of locking that is in effect.
Name	Returns the name of a RemoteData object.
PercentPosition	Returns or sets a value that indicates or changes the approximate location of the current row in the rdoResultset object, based on a percentage of the rows in the rdoResultset.
BatchCollisionCount	Returns a value that specifies the number of rows that didn't complete the last batch-mode update.
BatchCollisionRows	Returns an array of bookmarks that indicates the rows that generated collisions in the last batch-mode update operation.
BatchSize	Returns or sets a value that specifies the number of statements sent back to the server in each batch.
Status	Returns or sets the status of the current row or column. If set to rdRowUnmodified, the row or column hasn't been modified or has been updated successfully. If set to rdRowModified, the row or column has been modified but not updated in the database. If set to rdRowNew, the row or column has been inserted with the AddNew() method, but hasn't been inserted yet into the database. If set to rdRowDeleted, the row or column has been deleted, but hasn't been deleted yet in the database. If set to rdRowDBDeleted, the row or column has been deleted locally and in the database.

Continued

TABLE 16-2 **PROPERTIES OF THE RDORESULTSET OBJECT** *(continued)*

Property	Description
UpdateCriteria	Returns or sets a value that specifies how the WHERE clause is constructed for each row during an optimistic batch-update operation. If set to rdCriteriaKey, just the key column(s) in the WHERE clause are used. If set to rdCriteriaAllCols, the key column(s) and all updated columns in the WHERE clause are used. If set to rdCriteriaUpdCols, the key column(s) and all the columns in the WHERE clause are used. If set to rdCriteriaTimeStamp, uses just the timestamp column, if available.
UpdateOperation	Returns or sets a value that specifies whether the optimistic batch update should use an Update statement or a Delete statement followed by an Insert. If set to rdOperationUpdate, uses an Update statement for each modified row. If set to rdOperationDelIns, uses a pair of Delete and Insert statements for each modified row.
Restartable	Returns a value that indicates whether an rdoResultset object supports the Requery() method, which reexecutes the query that the rdoResultset is based on.
RowCount	Returns the number of rows accessed in an rdoResultset object.
StillExecuting	Returns a Boolean value that indicates whether a query is still executing.
Transactions	Returns a value that indicates whether an object supports the recording of a series of changes that can later be rolled back (undone) or committed (saved).
Type	Returns or sets a value that indicates the type or data type of an object. (*Type constants* are defined later in this chapter.)
Updatable	Returns a Boolean value that indicates whether changes can be made to a remote data object.
ActiveConnection	Returns or sets an object reference that indicates the connection that this query should be associated with.

TABLE 16-3 METHODS OF THE RDORESULTSET OBJECT

Method	Syntax	Parameters	Description
AddNew()	AddNew	None	Creates a new row for an updatable rdoResultset object.
Cancel()	Cancel	None	Cancels the processing of a query running in asynchronous mode, or cancels any pending results against the specified RDO object.
CancelUpdate()	CancelUpdate	None	Cancels any pending updates to an rdoResultset object.
Close()	Close	None	Closes an open remote data object.
Delete()	Delete	None	Deletes the current row in an updatable rdoResultset object.
Edit()	Edit	None	Enables changes to data values in the current row of an updatable rdoResultset object.
GetRows()	array = object.GetRows (rows)	Array: The name of a Variant-type variable to store the returned data. Object: An object expression that evaluates to an object in the Applies To list. Rows: A Long value	Retrieves multiple rows of an rdoResultset into an array.

Continued

TABLE 16-3 **METHODS OF THE RDORESULTSET OBJECT** *(continued)*

Method	Syntax	Parameters	Description
		that indicates the number of rows to retrieve.	
`MoreResults()`	`MoreResults`	None	Clears the current result set of any pending rows and returns a Boolean value that indicates whether one or more additional result sets are pending.
`Move()`	`object.Move rows [, start]`	Object: An object expression that evaluates to an object in the Applies To list. Rows: A signed Long value that specifies the number of rows the position will move, as described in `Settings`. Start: A Variant value that identifies a bookmark, as described in `Settings`.	Repositions the current row pointer in an `rdoResultset` object.
`MoveFirst()`	`MoveFirst`	None	Move to the first record in the result set.
`MoveLast()`	`MoveLast`	None	Move to the last record in the result set.
`MoveNext()`	`MoveNext`	None	Move to the next record in the result set.
`MovePrevious()`	`MovePrevious`	None	Move to the previous record in the result set.

Method	Syntax	Parameters	Description
Requery()	object. Requery [options]	Object: The object placeholder represents an object expression that evaluates to an object in the Applies To list. Options: A Variant or constant that determines how the query is run; if set to rdAsyncEnable, the Execute operation is run asynchronously.	Execute the previous query again.
Update()	Update	None	Saves the contents of the copy buffer row to a specified updatable rdoResultset object and discards the copy buffer.
BatchUpdate()	object. BatchUpdate (SingleRow, Force)	Object: An object expression that evaluates to an object in the Applies To list. SingleRow: A Boolean value that is True if the update is done only for the current row, and False if the update applies to all rows in the batch. The default is False. Force:	Performs a batched optimistic update.

Continued

TABLE 16-3 METHODS OF THE RDORESULTSET OBJECT *(continued)*

Method	Syntax	Parameters	Description
		A Boolean value that is `True` if the row or batch of rows will overwrite existing rows in the database regardless of whether they cause collisions.	
`CancelBatch()`	`object.Cancel Batch (SingleRow)`	`Object:` An object expression that evaluates to an object in the Applies To list. `SingleRow:` A Boolean value that is `True` if the cancel action is done only for the current row, and `False` if the cancel action applies to all rows in the batch.	Cancels all uncommitted changes in the local cursor (used in batch mode).
`GetClipString()`	`Resultset String = object.Get ClipString (NumRows, [Column Delimiter], [Row Delimiter], NullExpr])`	`Resultset String:` A variable used to reference the entire result set as a delimited string. `Object:` An object expression that evaluates to an `rdoResultset` object. `NumRows:` Number of rows	The `GetClipString()` method returns a delimited string for 'n' rows in a result set.

Method	Syntax	Parameters	Description
		to copy into the clip string. `Column Delimiter:` String expression used to separate data columns. `RowDelimiter:` String expression used to separate data rows, as described in `Settings`. `NullExpr:` String expression used when `Null` values are encountered.	

After an `rdoResultset` object has been created, it can be used to manipulate the data contained in the query set, and the following methods can be utilized:

◆ The `Name` property returns the name of the `rdoResultset` object, which contains the first 256 characters of the SQL statement that was used to generate the result set.

◆ The `Move()`, `MoveFirst()`, `MoveLast()`, `MoveNext()`, and `MovePrevious()` methods can be used to navigate the resulting data set. When you use a forward-only-type cursor, the `MoveNext()` method can only be used.

◆ The `BOF` and `EOF` properties can be used to test whether the beginning or end, respectively, of the resulting data set has been reached. These methods work just like their DAO counterparts.

◆ The `RowCount` property returns the number of rows that have been accessed. After all the query result set rows have been accessed, the `RowCount` property reflects the total number of rows in the query result set.

◆ The `PercentPosition` property is used to retrieve and specify the relative position in a result set. This position is based upon the number of rows that have been retrieved at the time that the method is called. This can be useful when scrolling through a data set that is being displayed in a scrollable area (for example, a list box). The relative percent position is specified as a float value between 0.0 and 100.0.

◆ The `AbsolutePosition` property is used to retrieve and specify the absolute position in a result set. The absolute position methods aren't available when you use a forward-only-type cursor. By setting the absolute position to zero, the first row is accessed. When you retrieve the absolute position, a -1 is returned if no rows are in the query result set.

◆ The `Bookmarkable` property is used in conjunction with the `Bookmark` property. RDO bookmarks work just like DAO bookmarks. A bookmark can save a position in a resulting data set and then can be used to return quickly to that position. The `Bookmarkable` property returns `True` if the resulting data set supports bookmarks.

◆ The `LastModified` property returns a bookmark that points to the last query result set row that was modified.

◆ The `AddNew()`, `Delete()`, `Edit()`, and `Update()` methods are used to add, delete, and modify result set rows, respectively. The `Updatable` property can be used to determine whether the resulting data set can be modified. (Sometimes, though, the `Updatable` property may return `True` even though the resulting data set isn't updatable; for example, when creating a `JOIN`. Rely on the `getUpdatable()` method with caution.)

◆ The `CancelUpdate()` method can be used to cancel any updates pending on the resulting data set. The `EditMode` property can be used to determine whether any updates are pending that can be canceled.

◆ The `Requery()` method can be used to refresh the query result set, by reexecuting the original query. After a `Requery()` is executed, any bookmarks made on the original resulting data set become invalid. The `Restartable` property returns `True` if the result set supports the `Requery()` method, `False` otherwise.

◆ The `MoreResults()` method is used when a query returns multiple data sets. After the `MoreResults()` method is executed, the current result set buffer is cleared; if `True` is returned, additional result sets exist and are retrieved. `False` indicates that the query doesn't return any additional result sets.

- The LockEdits and Type properties return the type of locking and type of cursor, respectively, used to create the resulting data set. The LockEdits property returns True if pessimistic locking is being used, and False if optimistic locking is being used.

- The Transactions property indicates whether the query result set supports transactions.

- The StillExecuting property determines whether the query is still executing. This method is used when the asynchronous option of the OpenResultset() method is used.

- The rdoColumns property returns the collection of columns, as rdoColumn objects, that are contained in the resulting data set. The rdoColumns and rdoColumn objects are reviewed later in this chapter.

- The hStmt property returns the ODBC handle that corresponds to the rdoResultset object. As always, use the ODBC handles with great care.

- The Close() and Cancel() methods are used, respectively, to close and cancel rdoResultset objects. The Cancel() method is used when a query is generating asynchronously. If the query has pending updates, using the Cancel() method can produce unpredictable results.

Navigating the rdoResultset

After you create an rdoResultset object, you will want to access the individual rows of the query result set. Similar to DAO, RDO's Move() method and Bookmark property can be utilized to access each row of the query result set. Each result set contains a "pointer" to the current row; only the data contained in the row being accessed can be accessed. The Move() methods of the rdoResultset object are used to position the pointer in the query result set. The implementation details of these navigation methods are explored next.

MOVE() METHODS

Five different Move() methods are implemented by the rdoResultset object: the MoveNext(), MovePrevious(), MoveFirst(), and MoveLast() methods are fairly self-explanatory. The Move() method takes two parameters: the first parameter is an integer that specifies the relative number of rows to move from the current position. If this value is negative, the current position is moved toward the beginning of the data set; if positive, the current position is moved toward the end of the data set. The second parameter specifies a bookmark, which is used as the starting location of the move. If the row to which you are moving has been deleted by another user, an exception is thrown.

Just like in DAO, you can move past the beginning or end of the resulting data set. You must use the BOF and EOF properties, respectively, to determine whether you are positioned past the beginning or end of the data set.

Listing 16-2 expands the code in Listing 16-1 to show how you can use the Move() methods to loop through the customer records from New York, from the beginning to the end. Again, this is accomplished just like it is accomplished in DAO.

Listing 16-2: Navigating an rdoResultset Object by Using the Move() Methods

```
Dim en As rdoEnvironment
Dim cn As rdoConnection
Dim Result As rdoResultSet

Set en = rdoEngine.rdoEvironments(0)
With en
  en.CursorDriver = rdUseOdbc
  en.LoginTimeout = 5
  en.Name = "TestEnv"

  REM Establish a connection
  Set cn = en.OpenConnection("", rdDriverPrompt, True,
"DSN=MyDataSource;UID=Marie;PWD=Pooh;Database=Customers")

End With

REM Open the ResultSet with a Dynamic cursor and read only access

Result = cn.OpenResultSet(
        "SELECT *FROM CUSTOMERS WHERE STATE='NY'",
        rdoOpenDynamic, rdConcurReadOnly)

REM Loop Through the Record Set

DO WHILE (NOT Result.EOF)
  REM Access the rows values

  REM Move to the Next Row
  Result.MoveNext
WEND
```

As Listing 16-2 shows, looping through the rdoResultset one row at a time is a fairly straightforward process. An important detail was skipped in this example, though – how do you access the values of each column? That very important topic is reviewed following coverage of a few more important navigation techniques: bookmarks, absolute and relative positioning of the row pointer, and retrieving the number of rows accessed.

BOOKMARK PROPERTIES

Bookmarks can be used to return to saved positions in a resulting data set, just like they are used in DAO. Bookmarks are valid only from the time that they are created until an rdoResultset object is closed or is requeried. Bookmarks are utilized with the Move() method, to quickly return to a position in a query result set. The Move() method can also take a positive or negative offset from the bookmark location. If an offset is specified, you need to ensure that the record pointer is not moved past the beginning or end of the query result set. If you simply want to return to the exact bookmarked location, you can use the Bookmark property. Forward-only-type cursors don't support bookmarks.

To check whether a result set supports bookmarks, check the Bookmarkable() method before using the Bookmark() properties.

The AbsolutePosition property takes a single integer parameter that specifies an absolute location in a result set and moves the current record pointer to that location. You can use the AbsolutePosition property to move to a specific location in the result set, and you can save a bookmark to that location. Listing 16-3 demonstrates how to create a bookmark, and how to return to the bookmarked location by utilizing the Move() method.

Listing 16-3: Creating a Bookmark and Using the Move() Method to Return to the Bookmarked Location

```
Dim Result as rdoResultSet
Dim bm As Bookmark

REM Open the ResultSet
Set Result = RDOConnect.OpenResultset("SELECT *  FROM Customers _
     WHERE State = 'NY'",rdOpenDynamic, rdConcurReadOnly)

REM Move to the 10th record of the result set
Result.AbsolutePosition = 10
```

```
REM Bookmark the current location
If Result.Bookmarkable Then
  Set bm = Result.Bookmark
End If

REM Perform some methods which move the current record pointer
location

If Result.Bookmarkable Then
  Result.Move(0,bm)
End If
```

PERCENTPOSITION AND ROWCOUNT PROPERTIES

The last two rdoResultset navigation methods reviewed are PercentPosition and RowCount. The PercentPosition property is used to move to a relative position in a result data set. The PercentPosition property takes a float value, which specifies a percentage that represents a relative percentage position from the beginning of the data set. The record pointer is moved to that location. Note, however, that this relative position is based on the number of records that have been retrieved up to that time, not the total number of records that the query will return. After the PercentPosition property is set, the record pointer moves to the record that is closest to the specified relative percentage position from the beginning of the data set, and then the PercentPosition value is updated to reflect the *actual* percentage location that this record represents. The PercentPosition property returns a float value that represents this position. This property is very useful when you are navigating a data set that is displayed in a list box or window with a scroll bar, because it can ease the navigation of the result set in these situations.

The RowCount property returns the number of rows that have been retrieved to the point at which it is called. If you want to determine the number of rows in the record set, you need to use the MoveLast() method first and then call the RowCount property to determine how many records are in the record set. If the RowCount property returns 0, the query didn't return any rows. If the RowCount property returns -1, the data source is incapable of returning the number of query result rows. Listing 16-4 demonstrates how to utilize the PercentPosition and RowCount properties.

When you execute a query asynchronously, the RowCount() method will return 0 while the query is still executing. You must use the StillExecuting property before you use RowCount(). Also, some cursors (specifically the forward-only type) don't support the RowCount() method.

Listing 16-4: Using the PercentPosition() and RowCount() Methods

```
Dim Result as rdoResultSet
Dim NumRecs As Integer

REM Open the ResultSet
Set Result = RDOConnect.OpenResultset("SELECT *  FROM Customers _
     WHERE State = 'NY'",rdOpenDynamic, rdConcurReadOnly)

REM Determine the number of records in the query
Result.MoveLast
NumRecs = Result.RowCount

REM Move to the 1st record of the result set
Result.MoveFirst

REM Move to the middle of the record set - 50%
Result.PercentPosition = 50.0
```

The rdoColumns and rdoColumn Objects

Up to this point, you have learned how to create an rdoResultset object and how to use the rdoResultset methods to navigate the resulting data set. But how are the values in each row's columns accessed? The rdoResultset object provides the rdoColumns property to access the columns of the resulting data set.

The rdoColumns Object

The rdoColumns object contains a collection of rdoColumn objects. Table 16-4 presents the properties of the rdoColumns object.

After an rdoColumns object has been created, it can be used to manipulate a row's column data, using the following methods:

◆ The Count property returns the number of columns returned by the current query.

◆ The Item property is used to return an rdoColumn object. The Item() method takes a single Variant parameter, which is either the row index (in the range 0 to number of columns -1) or the actual name of the column.

◆ The Refresh() method is used to refresh the column collection, and is especially useful for multiuser environments in which the column structure may change.

TABLE 16-4 THE RDOCOLUMNS OBJECT PROPERTIES

Property	Description
Item	Returns a specific member of an RDO collection object, either by position or by key.
Count	Returns the number of objects in a collection.

The rdoColumn Object

Before you review the implementation details of accessing the rdoColumns object, take a look at the rdoColumn object, which encapsulates the actual columns of each row returned in the result set. The rdoColumn object is similar to the DAO Field object. Table 16-5 presents the properties provided by the rdoColumn object.

TABLE 16-5 THE RDOCOLUMN OBJECT PROPERTIES

Property	Description
AllowZeroLength	Returns a value that indicates whether a zero-length string ("") is a valid setting for the Value property of an rdoColumn object with a data type of rdTypeCHAR, rdTypeVARCHAR, or rdTypeLONGVARCHAR.
Attributes	Returns a value that indicates one or more characteristics of an rdoColumn object. If set to rdFixedColumn, the column size is fixed. If set to rdVariableColumn, the column size is variable. If set to rdAutoIncrColumn, the column value for new rows is automatically incremented to a unique value that can't be changed. If set to rdUpdatableColumn, the column value can be changed. If set to rdTimeStampColumn, the column is a timestamp value.
ChunkRequired	Returns a Boolean value that indicates whether data must be accessed by using the GetChunk() method.
Name	Returns the name of a RemoteData object.

Property	Description
OrdinalPosition	Returns the relative position of an rdoColumn object within the rdoColumns collection.
BatchConflictValue	Returns a value currently in the database that is newer than the Value property, as determined by an optimistic batch-update conflict.
KeyColumn	Returns or sets a value that specifies whether this column is part of the primary key.
Status	Returns or sets the status of the current row or column. If set to rdRowUnmodified, the row or column hasn't been modified or has been updated successfully. If set to rdRowModified, the row or column has been modified, but not updated in the database. If set to rdRowNew, the row or column has been inserted with the AddNew() method, but hasn't been inserted into the database yet. If set to rdRowDeleted, the row or column has been deleted, but hasn't been deleted in the database yet. If set to rdRowDBDeleted, the row or column has been deleted locally and in the database.
OriginalValue	Returns the value of the column as first fetched from the database.
Required	Returns a value that indicates whether an rdoColumn requires a non-Null value.
Size	Returns a value that indicates the maximum size, in bytes, of the underlying data of an rdoColumn object that contains text, or the fixed size of an rdoColumn object that contains text or numeric values.
SourceColumn	Returns a value that indicates the name of the column that is the original source of the data for an rdoColumn object.
SourceTable	Returns a value that indicates the name of the table that is the original source of the data for an rdoColumn object.

Continued

TABLE 16-5 THE RDOCOLUMN OBJECT PROPERTIES *(continued)*

Property	Description
Type	Returns or sets a value that indicates the type or data type of an object.
Updatable	Returns a Boolean value that indicates whether changes can be made to a remote data object.
Value	Returns or sets the value of the column.

APPENDCHUNK()

The AppendChunk() method appends data from a Variant expression to an rdoColumn object with a data type of rdTypeLONGVARBINARY or rdTypeLONGVARCHAR. The AppendChunk() method has the following syntax:

```
object ! column.AppendChunk source
```

The object parameter is an object expression that evaluates to the rdoResultset object containing the rdoColumns collection. The column parameter is an object expression that evaluates to an rdoColumn object whose ChunkRequired property is set to True. The source parameter is a string expression or variable that contains the data that you want to append to the rdoColumn object specified by column.

COLUMNSIZE()

The ColumnSize() method returns the number of bytes in an rdoColumn object with a data type of rdTypeLONGVARBINARY or rdTypeLONGVARCHAR. The ColumnSize() method has the following syntax:

```
varname = object ! column.ColumnSize( )
```

The Varname parameter is the name of a Long or Variant variable. The Object parameter is an object expression that evaluates to the rdoResultset object that contains the rdoColumns collection. The Column parameter is the name of an rdoColumn object whose ChunkRequired property is set to True.

GETCHUNK()

The GetChunk() method returns all or a portion of the contents of an rdoColumn object with a data type of rdTypeLONGVARBINARY or rdTypeLONGVARCHAR. The GetChunk() method has the following syntax:

```
varname = object ! column.GetChunk(numbytes)
```

The `Varname` parameter is the name of a Variant that receives the data from the `rdoColumn` object named by `column`. The `Object` parameter is an object expression that evaluates to an `rdoResultset` object containing the `rdoColumns` collection. The `Column` parameter is an object expression that evaluates to an `rdoColumn` object whose `ChunkRequired` property is `True`. The `Numbytes` parameter is a numeric expression that represents the number of bytes that you want to return.

After you have access to the `rdoColumn` object, you can use it to manipulate the actual data contained in the column of the current row pointer, using the following properties and methods:

♦ The `Attributes` property returns an integer bit mask that identifies characteristics of the current column. Table 16-6 displays the column attribute constants and their descriptions.

TABLE 16-6 ATTRIBUTE CONSTANT VALUES REPRESENTING COLUMN ATTRIBUTE
           BIT MASKS

Attribute Constant	Description
rdFixedColumn	The size of the column is fixed; this is the default for numeric fields.
rdVariableColumn	The size of the column is variable; this is the default for text fields.
rdAutoIncrColumn	The column is automatically incremented and can't be changed.
rdUpdatableCoumn	The column is writable.

♦ The `Name` property returns a string that represents the actual name of the field. If your query performs some aggregate function, such as an `AVG` like the following example: `SELECT_AVG(PRICE) AVGPRICE_FROM_PRODUCTS`, an empty string is returned if you don't specify a column name for the aggregate field, like `AVGPRICE`.

♦ The `OrdinalPosition` property returns the position of the column within the `rdoColumns` collection.

♦ The `Type` property returns a short value that represents the type of the field. Table 16-7 displays the data type constants and their associated descriptions. Use these constants to determine the field type.

TABLE 16-7 THE DATA TYPE CONSTANTS FOR EACH RDOCOLUMN TYPE

Field Type Constant	Description
RdTypeCHAR	A fixed-length character string. The getSize() method returns the length of the string.
RdTypeNUMERIC	A signed exact numeric value.
RdTypeDECIMAL	A signed exact numeric value.
RdTypeINTEGER	A signed exact numeric value in the range $-231*10^{10}$ to $231*10^{10}$ -1 when signed, and 0 to $232*10^{10}$ -1 when unsigned.
RdTypeSMALLINT	A signed exact numeric value in the range -32,768 to 32,767 when signed, and 0 to 65,535 when unsigned.
RdTypeFLOAT	A signed approximate numeric value in the range 10^{-308} to 10^{308}.
rdTypeREAL	A signed approximate numeric value in the range 10^{-38} to 10^{38}.
rdTypeDOUBLE	A signed approximate numeric value in the range 10^{-308} to 10^{308}.
rdTypeDATE	A date type; this value is dependent on the data source.
rdTypeTIME	A time type; this is dependent on the data source.
rdTypeTIMESTAMP	A timestamp type; this is dependent on the data source.
rdTypeVARCHAR	A variable-length character string, not exceeding 255 characters.
rdTypeLONGVCHAR	A variable-length character string, the length of which is determined by the data source.
rdTypeBINARY	A fixed-length binary field, not exceeding 25 bytes.
rdTypeVARBINARY	A variable-length binary field, the maximum length of which is 255 bytes.
rdTypeLONGVARBINARY	A variable-length binary field, the maximum size of which is determined by the data source.
rdTypeBIGINT	A signed exact numeric field in the range $-263*10^{19}$ to $263*10^{19}$ - 1 when signed, and 0 to $264*10^{20}$ - 1 when unsigned.

Field Type Constant	Description
rdTypeTINYINT	A signed exact numeric value in the range -128 to 127 when signed, and 0 to 255 when unsigned.
rdTypeBIT	A single binary digit.

◆ The Size property returns the size of text or fixed-length fields. For text fields, this method returns the maximum number of characters that the field can hold. For numeric fields, this method returns the number of bytes required to hold the numeric field.

◆ The ColumnSize property returns the number of bytes in a field of the type rdTypeLONVARBINARY or rdTypeLONGARCHAR. The ColumnSize() method can be used to determine the size of chunk fields.

◆ The AllowZeroLength property returns True if a character type field can use zero-length strings ("") to represent an empty value. If AllowZeroLength returns False, an empty value must be represented as a Null value.

◆ The Required property is used to determine whether a Null value is allowed in a field. If a Null value is allowed, the Required property returns False, and returns True otherwise. The Required property is used in conjunction with the AllowZeroLength property to determine whether a value is valid for a field.

◆ The Updatable property is used to determine whether a field is writable. If writable, the getUpdatable property returns True, and returns False otherwise.

◆ The SourceColumn and SourceTable properties are used to determine the original data source. These methods can be used to determine the original column and table names in queries in which their names may be unrelated to the names in the underlying table.

◆ The Value property is used to retrieve and specify a field's value.

◆ The AppendChunk() and GetChunk() methods are used to set and retrieve Long binary and Long character fields. Chunk fields can be a few bytes in size, up to 1.2GB. The ColumnSize property is used to determine the size of a Chunk field. An exception is thrown if a current row doesn't exist when these methods are called. The ChunkRequired property returns True if the AppendChunk() and GetChunk() methods must be used to access field values, and returns False otherwise.

Listing 16-1 opened an rdoResultset object, based on a query that selected some rows from the Customers table. Listing 16-2 showed you how to loop through the data set. Listing 16-5 extends this example, showing you how to print the names of each column and then the field's value for each row of the query result set.

Listing 16-5: Navigating an rdoResultset Object and Displaying the Values for Each Row

```
SUB DisplayTable
  Dim en As rdoEnvironment
  Dim cn As rdoConnection
  Dim Result As rdoResultSet
  Dim I As Integer

  Set en = rdoEngine.rdoEvironments(0)
  With en
    en.CursorDriver = rdUseOdbc
    en.LoginTimeout = 5
    en.Name = "TestEnv"

    REM Establish a connection
    Set cn = en.OpenConnection("", rdDriverPrompt, True,
 "DSN=MyDataSource;UID=Marie;PWD=Pooh;Database=Customers"   )

  End With

  REM Open the ResultSet with a Dynamic cursor and read
  REM only access

  Result = cn.OpenResultSet(
          "SELECT *FROM CUSTOMERS WHERE STATE='NY'",
          rdoOpenDynamic, rdConcurReadOnly)

  Result.MoveFirst();
  REM Display the column names...separated by tabs
  cols = RDOResult.rdoColumns
  FOR i = 0 To cols.Count - 1
    DispStr = Cols(i).Name & "      "
  NEXT I

  MsgBox DispStr

  REM Loop Through the Record Set

  DO WHILE (NOT Result.EOF)
    REM Access the rows values
```

```
FOR i = 0 To cols.Count - 1
  DispStr = cols(i).Value + "       "
Next I

MsgBox DispStr

REM Move to the Next Row
Result.MoveNext
WEND
END SUB
```

The rdoTables and rdoTable Objects

The rdoTable object represents a table or database view. The rdoTables object holds a collection of rdoTable objects and represents the collection of tables that are in your database. Because of the high overhead involved with populating the rdoTables collection, it isn't filled until it is accessed. Unlike in DAO, the RDO table objects can't be used to modify the database schema. Because of this fact, and because they require a large amount of overhead to fill, they aren't used very often. Regardless, these objects are presented here to complete the discussion of RDO objects.

The rdoTables and rdoTable classes can't be used to modify your database schema. If you need to make database schema changes, consult your database-server documentation and use the tools provided.

The rdoTables Object

As previously stated, the rdoTables object holds the collection of database tables and views. Table 16-8 presents the properties of the rdoTables object. After an rdoTables object is created, these methods can be used to perform the following:

◆ The Count property returns the number of tables and views stored in the collection.

◆ The Item property can be used to access an rdoTables object by the table name or, more commonly, by an index.

◆ The Refresh() method is used to update the rdoTables object with the latest database view. The rdoTables object is filled as each element of the collection is accessed or, alternatively, it can be completely filled by using the Refresh() method.

TABLE 16-8 THE RDOTABLES OBJECT PROPERTIES

Property	Description
Item	Returns a specific member of an RDO collection object, either by position or by key.
Count	Returns the number of objects in a collection.

The rdoTable Object

Now that you have an understanding of the rdoTables object and its methods, you are ready to review the rdoTable component objects. As stated earlier, the rdoTable object holds information about tables and views, including their name, columns collection, and type. Tables 16-9 presents the methods of the rdoTable object. The rdoTables method Item is used to access an individual rdoTable object. After an rdoTable object is available, its methods can be used to perform the following:

◆ The Name property returns the name of the database table or view associated with this object.

◆ The rdoColumns property returns an rdoColumns object. This can be used to access the names of the table's fields.

◆ The Type property returns the type of the table object. The following list summarizes the String-type table types returned by this method:

```
TABLE
VIEW
SYSTEM TABLE
GLOBAL TEMPORARY
LOCAL TEMPORARY
ALIAS
SYNONYM
```

◆ The `Updatable` property can be used to determine whether a table can be modified. Because an `rdoTable` object can't be changed, this method always returns `False`.

◆ The `OpenResultset()` method is used to access all the data contained in a table, by performing a `SELECT * FROM_table` query. If your table contains more than a few hundred records, this technique is a great way to slow down your database server — in other words, this method isn't very practical.

◆ The `RowCount` property returns the number of rows that are contained in the table or view object. If -1 is returned, the number of rows is not obtainable. If 0 is returned, the table or view doesn't contain any rows. Generally, only Jet-type tables support the `RowCount` property.

TABLE 16-9 THE RDOTABLE PROPERTIES

Property	Description
Name	Returns the name of a `RemoteData` object.
RowCount	Returns the number of rows accessed in an `rdoResultset` object.
Type	Returns or sets a value that indicates the type or data type of an object.
Updatable	Returns a Boolean value that indicates whether changes can be made to a remote data object.

OPENRESULTSET() METHOD

The `OpenResultset()` method is used to access all the data contained in a table. It has the following syntax:

```
Set variable = object.OpenResultset([type [,locktype [, option]]])
```

The `Variable` parameter is an object expression that evaluates to an `rdoResultset` object. The `Object` parameter is an object expression that evaluates to an existing `rdoQuery` or `rdoTable` object that you want to use to create the new `rdoResultset`. The `Name` parameter is a String that specifies the source of the rows for the new `rdoResultset`. This argument can specify the name of an `rdoTable` object, the name of an `rdoQuery`, or an SQL statement that might return rows. The

Type parameter is a Variant or constant that specifies the type of cursor to create. The LockType parameter is a Variant or constant that specifies the type of concurrency control. The Option parameter is a Variant or constant that specifies characteristics of the new rdoResultset.

The rdoPreparedStatement Object

The rdoPreparedStatement object is used to create a stored procedure that can be used to execute repeated stored queries. These prepared statements can also take an optional set of parameters. Two ways exist to create dynamic SQL queries. One way is to build the SQL select statement string dynamically at runtime. The State variable represents a String that specifies the name of the state in which customers need to reside to be included in the query result set.

Although building the SQL select statement string is effective when you are creating a one-time-only query, a prepared statement is much more efficient if you will be performing the same query or same type of query repeatedly.

The CreatePreparedStatement() method of the rdoConnection object is used to create an rdoPreparedStatement object. Table 16-10 details the parameters that are required by the CreatePreparedStatement() method, which has the following syntax:

CreatePreparedStatement name, sqlstmt

TABLE 16-10 PARAMETERS REQUIRED BY THE CREATEPREPAREDSTATEMENT()
            METHOD

Argument	Description
name	The name of the prepared statement; name is a String-type parameter. If a previously created prepared statement shares the same name with a prepared statement that is being created, an error will occur.
sqlstmt	A string expression that contains a valid SQL statement.

Before you review the details of implementing the CreatePreparedStatement() method, take a look at how to specify an SQL statement that accepts parameters. The syntax of how this is specified in RDO is slightly different than in DAO. Respecifying the SELECT statement used earlier in Listing 16-1 so that it accepts the State argument as a parameter is quite simple. You simply need to use the same query, but use a ? where you want a parameter to be substituted. The restructured query looks like this:

```
SELECT * FROM CUSTOMERS WHERE STATE = ?
```

The first thing you should notice is that, in contrast to DAO, you don't specify variables to be substituted in the SQL statement, which makes this syntax a bit easier than the syntax in DAO. Each parameter in the parameterized SQL statement is indexed based on where it occurs in the statement. You will review this in more detail when the rdoParameter object is discussed, but for now, note that this parameter will be at index 0.

Now that you know how to specify an RDO parameterized SQL statement, you are ready to convert the example presented in Listing 16-1 into a prepared statement query. Listing 16-8 demonstrates how this is accomplished.

Listing 16-8: Creating an rdoPreparedStatement Object

```
Dim en As rdoEnvironment
Dim cn As rdoConnection
Dim Result As rdoResultSet
Dim CustStmt As rdoPreparedStatement

Set en = rdoEngine.rdoEvironments(0)
With en
  en.CursorDriver = rdUseOdbc
  en.LoginTimeout = 5
  en.Name = "TestEnv"

  REM Establish a connection
  Set cn = en.OpenConnection("", rdDriverPrompt, True,
"DSN=MyDataSource;UID=Marie;PWD=Pooh;Database=Customers"  )

End With

Set CustStmt = cn.CreatePreparedStatement("CustSelect",
   "SELECT *  FROM CUSTOMERS WHERE STATE = ?")
```

The rdoConnection object provides a PreparedStatements property and keeps a collection of all the prepared statements that have been created since the rdoConnection object was created. After you create a prepared statement, it is automatically appended to this collection. The rdoPreparedStatements object is covered in more detail later in this chapter. After you create an rdoPreparedStatement object, as demonstrated, you can utilize its properties and methods to perform the following:

◆ The `BindThreshold` property is used to retrieve and specify the largest column that is automatically bound by using ODBC. This specifies the largest chunk size that can be handled when accessing column data. By default, this value is 1024 bytes.

◆ The `Connect` property is used to return the data source connect string. You can't change the connect string by using the `rdoPreparedStatement` object.

◆ The `ErrorThreshold` property is used to retrieve and specify the level of an error that caused an error event. The ODBC and database server can generate a variety of errors, many of which are informational only; the error threshold can be used to filter these errors. An exception is thrown only if its value exceeds the error threshold value that is set. If -1 is specified, all errors are filtered out.

◆ The `KeysetSize` property is used to retrieve and specify the number of key set rows to retrieve at one time for keyset and dynamic-type cursors. Recall the discussion of cursors from the previous chapter. Keyset-type cursors retrieve just the set of keys that is associated with the query and accesses the actual row data by using those keys when the corresponding row is actually accessed. The keyset size methods can be used to limit the number of rows in the keyset. By default, this value is zero. Specifying any other size creates a mixed-type cursor.

 Not all ODBC data sources support keyset-type cursors. Also, not all data sources support mixed-type cursors. Microsoft SQL Server 2.5 does not support mixed cursors and will generate an exception if one is used.

◆ The `LockType` property is used to specify the default locking type to use when you create an `rdoResultset` from a prepared statement. Refer to the previous chapter for a complete discussion of each locking type.

◆ The `LogMessages` property is used to retrieve and specify the path to the ODBC log file. If this file is specified as an empty string, no logging takes place. When logging is activated, the log file contains a record of all ODBC traffic, for debugging purposes.

◆ The `MaxRows` property is used to limit the number of rows returned by the query. When a query is executed, if the maximum number of rows is reached, no more rows will be returned. The `MaxRows` property also specifies the maximum number of rows to be processed by an action query; for example, an `INSERT`, `UPDATE`, or `DELETE`. This parameter can be used to limit the amount of resources required when executing a query. Tuning this parameter appropriately can help you to optimize your application. By default, this value is 100 rows, so make sure that you set this appropriately if you need to retrieve or affect more rows.

◆ The `QueryTimeout` property is used to retrieve and specify the number of seconds the ODBC driver waits before a query generates a timeout exception. By default, this value is 0, which indicates that a timeout will not occur. The query timeout does not function with asynchronous queries. This timeout parameter can be used to help balance your database server load from your application.

◆ The `RowsAffected` property is used to retrieve the number of rows modified by the most recently performed `Execute()` method. When you execute multiple-set queries, the `RowsAffected` value isn't changed.

◆ The `RowsetSize` property is used to retrieve and specify the number of rows in the result set cursor. The minimum number of rows is 1; by default, this value is 100. Minimizing this value can help to reduce client-side memory requirements.

◆ The `SQL` property is used to retrieve and specify the SQL statement that is used by the prepared statement when performing the `OpenResultset()` and `Execute()` methods. Table 16-12 presents the legal SQL statements.

TABLE 16-12 LEGAL SQL STATEMENTS

Statement	Description
A table name	Name of a table defined in an `rdoTables` collection `rdoTable` object. This retrieves all the rows of the table. A table name can't be used until the `rdoTables` collection has been filled.
An SQL statement	Some valid SQL statement.
An `rdoPrepared Statement`	The name of an `rdoPreparedStatement`.
Object name	The name of a previously created object.
An `rdoResultset`	The name of an `rdoResultset` already opened.
A stored procedure	The name of a database server stored procedure, preceded by the execute directive.

◆ The `Type` property is used to retrieve and specify the type of query that is specified by the prepared statement. Table 16-13 presents the possible `QueryTypeConstants` values. If you execute an action query, the `getType()` method incorrectly indicates a `SELECT` statement was specified; this is a known problem.

TABLE 16-13 TYPES OF QUERIES SPECIFIED IN THE RDOPREPAREDSTATEMENT

Type	Description
RdQSelect	A select-type query
RdQAction	An action-type query (for example, INSERT, UPDATE, DELETE)
RdQProcedure	A stored procedure

◆ The `Updatable` property is used to determine whether the result set returned from executing the query can be updated.

◆ The `Name` property returns the name of the prepared statement object. This is the name that was specified when the prepared statement was created.

◆ The `OpenResultset()` method is used to create an `rdoResultset` corresponding to the prepared statement query. A query can be run synchronously or asynchronously. The `OpenResultset()` method also accepts a parameter that specifies the cursor and locking type to be used when creating the `rdoResultset` object.

◆ The `Execute()` method is used to perform action queries, such as `INSERT`, `MODIFY`, or `DELETE`. An action query can be run synchronously or asynchronously.

◆ The `StillExecuting` property is used to determine whether a query or action query being performed asynchronously is still executing.

◆ The `Cancel()` method is used to stop the execution of a query or action statement that is executing asynchronously. When the `Cancel()` method is used with a synchronous query, the resources of the `rdoResultset` object are released and all buffers are flushed. When you use it with an action query executing asynchronously, unpredictable results may occur.

◆ The `rdoColumns` property is used to retrieve the collection of columns associated with the prepared statement.

◆ The rdoParameters property is used to retrieve the collection of parameters associated with the prepared statement. The rdoParameter object is reviewed later in this chapter.

◆ The hStmt property is used to retrieve the ODBC handle corresponding to the rdoResultset object created by the prepared statement.

◆ The Close() method is used to close a prepared statement. When a prepared statement is closed, it is automatically removed from the rdoPreparedStatements collection.

The rdoParameters and rdoParameter Objects

Before you can use the rdoPreparedStatment object to perform a stored query, you must first understand how to specify query parameters. The rdoParameter object is used to specify query parameter values. The rdoParameters object holds a collection of rdoParameter objects, one for each question mark specified in the query statement. The rdoParameters object is created only if a valid parameterized SQL statement is specified. Table 16-14 presents the rdoParameters properties.

TABLE 16-14 THE RDOPARAMETERS OBJECT PROPERTIES

Property	Description
Item	Returns a specific member of an RDO collection object, either by position or by key.
Count	Returns the number of objects in a collection.

An rdoParameters collection is created only when a valid parameterized SQL statement is specified. If the SQL statement is invalid, an exception is thrown when trying to access the rdoParameters collection, and not before.

The rdoParameters property of the rdoPreparedStatement object is used to access the rdoParameters object. The Count property returns the number of parameters specified by the query. The Item property is used to access the individual rdoParameter objects of the rdoParameters collection. Listing 16-9 demonstrates how to use the rdoParameters property to access the rdoParameters collection. After the rdoParameters collection is available, the Item property is used to access the rdoParameter object that represents the single ? parameter in the SELECT statement.

Listing 16-9: Accessing the rdoParameters Collection and the Single rdoParameter of the Query

```
Dim en As rdoEnvironment
Dim cn As rdoConnection
Dim Result As rdoResultSet
Dim CustStmt As rdoPreparedStatement
Dim params As rdoParameters
Dim param As rdoParameter

Set en = rdoEngine.rdoEvironments(0)
With en
  en.CursorDriver = rdUseOdbc
  en.LoginTimeout = 5
  en.Name = "TestEnv"

  REM Establish a connection
  Set cn = en.OpenConnection("", rdDriverPrompt, True,
"DSN=MyDataSource;UID=Marie;PWD=Pooh;Database=Customers"  )

End With

Set CustStmt = cn.CreatePreparedStatement("CustSelect",
   "SELECT *  FROM CUSTOMERS WHERE STATE = ?")

Set params = CustStmt.rdoParameters
Set param = params(0)
```

The rdoParameter object can be used to specify input and output query parameters. Table 16-15 presents the properties of the rdoParameter object.

TABLE 16-15 THE RDOPARAMETER OBJECT PROPERTIES

Property	Description
Direction	Returns or sets a value that indicates how a parameter is passed to or from a procedure. If set to rdParamInput, the parameter is used to pass information to the procedure. If set to rdParamInputOutput, the parameter is used to pass information both to and from the procedure. If set to rdParamOutput, the parameter is used to return information from the procedure, as in an output parameter in SQL. If set to rdParamReturnValue, the parameter is used to return the return status value from a procedure.
Name	Returns the name of a RemoteData object.
Type	Returns or sets a value that indicates the type or data type of an object.
Value	Returns or sets the value of an object.

APPENDCHUNK

The AppendChunk() method, which has the following syntax, appends data from a Variant expression to an rdoColumn object with a data type of rdTypeLONGVARBINARY or rdTypeLONGVARCHAR:

```
object ! column.AppendChunk source
```

The Object parameter is an object expression that evaluates to the rdoResultset object containing the rdoColumns collection. The Column parameter is an object expression that evaluates to an rdoColumn object whose ChunkRequired property is set to True. The Source parameter is a string expression or variable containing the data that you want to append to the rdoColumn object specified by column.

As demonstrated in Listing 16-9, the rdoParameter's Item property is used to access the individual parameter items of the query. After an rdoParameter object is accessed, its methods can be used for the following:

◆ The Direction property is used to retrieve and specify how the parameter is used. Table 16-16 presents the direction constants used to specify the direction.

TABLE 16-16 DIRECTION-TYPE CONSTANTS

Direction Types	Description
rdParamInput	Used to pass information to the query.
RdParamInputOutput	Used to pass information to the query and retrieve information from the query.
RdParamOutput	Used to retrieve information from the query as an SQL output parameter.
RdParamReturnValue	Used to pass the return value from a stored procedure.

◆ The Name property is used to retrieve and specify the name of the parameter. By default, parameters are given the name param*n*, in which *n* represents the parameter index.

◆ The Type property returns the type of the parameter.

◆ The Value property is used to retrieve and specify the value of a query parameter.

Creating Parameter Queries

Now that you have reviewed the objects necessary to create prepared statements and access their parameters, you are ready to look at the implementation details. When a prepared statement is created, a stored procedure that executes that query is temporarily created on the database server. Depending on the database server that you are using, these temporary procedures are created in the database or a temporary database on the database server. After the prepared statement or application is closed, these stored procedures are removed. When an application creates a stored procedure that corresponds to a prepared statement, that stored procedure can't be shared by other users. Generally, the overhead of creating a prepared statement doesn't improve application performance when the statement is executed only once. If the prepared statement is executed repeatedly, application performance can be greatly increased, because the database server does not need to interpret the SQL statement on subsequent execution.

Although you can use RDO to connect to any ODBC data source, RDO is geared toward the access of database server data sources. Prepared statements are an example of RDO objects that aren't supported by all ODBC data sources.

Listing 16-10 completes the task that you started earlier in this chapter of creating a prepared statement. Up to this point, you have modified the SQL statement to accept a parameter, by placing a question mark where you want the parameter located, and you have used the `rdoParameters` object to access the statement's single parameter. This example completes the task by specifying a value and direction for the query parameter and opening a result set. After the result set is open, the stored procedure created by the prepared statement is called, and the value that you specified for the parameter is replaced. One advantage of using the prepared statement is that quote problems are eliminated. When you specify the parameter's value, you simply use `NY` and you don't need to quote the value. Also note that the direction constant must be cast to a short when calling the `Direction` property.

Listing 16-10: Executing a Prepared Statement

```
Dim en As rdoEnvironment
Dim cn As rdoConnection
Dim Result As rdoResultSet
Dim CustStmt As rdoPreparedStatement
Dim params As rdoParameters
Dim param As rdoParameter

Set en = rdoEngine.rdoEvironments(0)
With en
  en.CursorDriver = rdUseOdbc
  en.LoginTimeout = 5
  en.Name = "TestEnv"

  REM Establish a connection
  Set cn = en.OpenConnection("", rdDriverPrompt, True,
"DSN=MyDataSource;UID=Marie;PWD=Pooh;Database=Customers")

End With
```

```
Set CustStmt = cn.CreatePreparedStatement("CustSelect",
   "SELECT *  FROM CUSTOMERS WHERE STATE = ?")

Set params = CustStmt.rdoParameters
Set param = params(0)

param.Direction = rdParamInput
param.Value = "NY"

REM Open the result set
Set Result= CustStmt.OpenResultset(rdOpenKeyset,
                    rdConcurReadOnly, rdExecDirect)
```

In this example, all the customers who live in New York are returned in the query result set. Listing 16-11 demonstrates how to call the prepared statement again, to retrieve all the customers who live in Washington (WA). Note that, because the prepared statement is already set up and the result set is opened, this is simply a matter of changing the parameter's value and requerying the result set.

Listing 16-11: Reexecuting a Prepared Statement

```
param.Value = "WA"

REM Execute the query again
Result.Requery()
```

Prepared statements require much less overhead on the database server and in your application. As Listing 16-11 demonstrates, executing a prepared statement is very easy after it has been set up; you just need to update the query's parameters and requery the result set.

Using prepared statements to create parameterized queries is only one use for the rdoPreparedStatement object. Prepared statements can also be used with SQL action queries. For example, you can create an SQL action query that adds a record to a table, utilizing parameters. As mentioned in the earlier discussion of SQL syntax, the INSERT statement is used to add new records to a table. You can create a prepared statement that uses the INSERT statement and takes a set of parameters that specify the field values of the new record. Listing 16-12 demonstrates how to create a prepared action statement that adds new records to the CUSTOMERS table. The new record's field values are specified as parameters. After the prepared statement is set up and field values are specified, the rdoPreparedStatement's Execute() method is used to perform the action query with the substituted parameter values.

Listing 16-12: Creating a Prepared Statement that Executes an Action Query

```
Dim ServerProc As rdoPreparedStatement
Dim params As rdoParameters
Dim param As rdoParameter

Set ServerProc = cn.CreatePreparedStatement("? = ServerProc(?)"

Set params = CustInsertStmt.rdoParameters

REM Specify parameters and directions
Set param = params(0)
param.Direction = rdParamReturnValue

Set param = params(1)
param.Direction = rdParamInputOutput
param.Value = 100

REM Execute the stored procedure
serverProc.Execute(rdDirectExec)
```

The ODBC interface helps you to handle the type conversions — and you don't have to worry about the quotes for the string parameters. Prepared statements don't have to be used just for queries; any SQL action statements can be used with prepared statements.

Using the rdoPreparedStatement to Call Stored Procedures

Prepared statements can be used for more than just creating queries and action queries. So far, you have reviewed how to use parameters to specify input variables. Prepared statements can be used to call server-side stored procedures, which return values but don't necessarily return rows-set information. Listing 16-13 demonstrates how to call a server-side procedure named ServerProc that takes two input parameters and one input/output parameter. The call to the server-side procedure must be enclosed in braces {}, and the name of the server-side procedure is preceded by the call directive. After the prepared statement is created, the direction of the parameters must be set up and then assigned values. The OpenResultset() method is used to call the server-side procedure with the specified parameters, using a static, read-only cursor. After the server-side procedure is called, the output parameters can be accessed.

Consult your database-server documentation for more information regarding creating server-side stored procedures.

Listing 16–13: Using a Prepared Statement to Call a Server–Side Stored Procedure

```
Dim CustInsertStmt As rdoPreparedStatement
Dim params As rdoParameters
Dim param As rdoParameter

Set CustInsertStmt = cn.CreatePreparedStatement("INSERT Customers
{CustID, Name, Address, City, State, ZipCode} VALUES (?, ?, ?, ?, ?,
?)"

Set params = CustInsertStmt.rdoParameters

REM Put CustID
Set param = params(0)
param.Direction = rdParamInput
param.Value = 1000

REM Put Name
Set param = params(1)
param.Direction = rdParamInput
param.Value = "Marie McCartan"

REM Put Address
Set param = params(2)
param.Direction = rdParamInput
param.Value = "123 Main Street"

REM Put City
Set param = params(3)
param.Direction = rdParamInput
param.Value = "Buffalo"

REM Put State
Set param = params(4)
param.Direction = rdParamInput
param.Value = "NY"
```

```
REM Put Zip
Set param = params(5)
param.Direction = rdParamInput
param.Value = "14000"

REM Execute the INSERT statement
CustInsertStmt.Execute(rdDirectExec)
```

Now that you know how to use prepared statements to call server-side procedures, you finally are going to learn how to call stock (predefined) server-side procedures. The next example demonstrates the SQL Server SP_PASSWORD procedure, which allows a user to change his or her password. This procedure takes two parameters: The first parameter is the SQL Server username, and the second parameter is the user's password. The SP_PASSWORD returns an integer value. If the return value isn't zero, the password-change operation was unsuccessful. Listing 16-14 demonstrates how to call the SP_PASSWORD procedure.

Review your database-server documentation to determine which stock (predefined) server-side procedures are provided.

Listing 16-14: Using a Prepared Statement to Call the SQL Server SP_PASSWORD Procedure

```
Dim en As rdoEnvironment
Dim cn As rdoConnection
Dim Result As rdoResultSet
Dim PasswordStmt As rdoPreparedStatement
Dim params As rdoParameters
Dim param As rdoParameter

Set en = rdoEngine.rdoEvironments(0)
With en
  en.CursorDriver = rdUseOdbc
  en.LoginTimeout = 5
  en.Name = "TestEnv"

  REM Establish a connection
  Set cn = en.OpenConnection("", rdDriverPrompt, True,
"DSN=MyDataSource;UID=Marie;PWD=Pooh;Database=Customers"  )
```

```
End With

Set PasswordStmt = cn.CreatePreparedStatement("PasswordStmt",
    "? = call SP_PASSWORD(?,?)")

Set params = CustInsertStmt.rdoParameters

REM Specify parameter directions and values
Set param = params(0)
param.Direction = rdParamReturnValue

Set params = CustInsertStmt.rdoParameters

Set param = params(1)
param.Direction = rdParamInput
param.Value = "John"

Set params = CustInsertStmt.rdoParameters

Set param = params(2)
param.Direction = rdParamInput
param.Value = "POKEY"

PasswordStmt.Execute(rdDirectExec)
```

rdoPreparedStatements Object

To complete the discussion of RDO objects, the rdoPreparedStatements object is reviewed. The rdoPreparedStatements object holds a collection of rdoPreparedStatement objects. The rdoConnection object provides the method getrdoPreparedStatements(), which returns an rdoPreparedStatements object. The rdoPreparedStatements collection object holds all rdoPreparedStatement objects that have been opened while the connection has been active. After an rdoPreparedStatement object is closed, it is removed from the rdoPreparedStatements collection. Table 16-17 presents the properties provided by the rdoPreparedStatements object.

TABLE 16-17 PROPERTIES OF THE RDOPREPAREDSTATEMENTS OBJECT

Property	Description
Item	Returns a specific member of an RDO collection object, either by position or by key.
Count	Returns the number of objects in a collection.

The Count property returns the number of prepared statements in the collection. The Item property is used to access a prepared statement, by ordinal number or by name. Listing 16-15 demonstrates how to access the rdoPreparedStatements object to retrieve the prepared statement with the name PasswordStmt.

Listing 16-15: Accessing the rdoPreparedStatements Object

```
Dim PrepStmts As rdoPreparedStatements
Dim Stmt As rdoPreparedStatment

Set PrepStmts = cn.rdoPreparedStatements

Set Stmt = PrepStmts("PasswordStmt")
```

Handling Multiple Result Sets

Multiple result sets are produced when several queries are strung together. Multiple SQL statements are separated by semicolons; for example: SQLSTMT1; SQLSTMT2; ... . Passing multiple statements can help to improve your application's efficiency, because a set of queries can be executed by creating a single prepared statement. The rdoResultset method MoreResults() is used to retrieve subsequent query results. Unfortunately, the RDO interface doesn't provide a method to determine how many result sets a query returns. So, the application developer must anticipate the number of result sets being returned. The MoreResults() method returns True if another result set is available and returns False otherwise.

When you create multiple result sets, you must use the ODBC cursor driver. Server-side cursors do not support multiple result sets. When you perform multiple SQL statements, if an action query is specified (for example, INSERT, MODIFY, or DELETE), the RowsAffected() method will not reflect the number of rows changed by the action query. Remember that action queries don't return any rows; using a Move() method when you access an action query result set causes an exception to be thrown. Listing 16-16 demonstrates how to create a query that returns and processes multiple result sets. A prepared statement is created that returns multiple result sets. The first result set is accessed and, when complete, the MoreResults() method is called to process the subsequent result sets. When the MoreResults() method is called for the final time, the resources required by the query are released.

Listing 16-16: Creating and Processing Multiple Result Set Queries

```
Dim en As rdoEnvironment
Dim cn As rdoConnection
Dim Result As rdoResultSet
Dim MultStmt As rdoPreparedStatement

Set en = rdoEngine.rdoEvironments(0)
With en
  en.CursorDriver = rdUseOdbc
  en.LoginTimeout = 5
  en.Name = "TestEnv"

  REM Establish a connection
  Set cn = en.OpenConnection("", rdDriverPrompt, True,
"DSN=MyDataSource;UID=Marie;PWD=Pooh;Database=Customers"  )

End With

Set MultStmt = cn.CreatePreparedStatement("CustSelect",
   "SELECT *  FROM CUSTOMERS; SELECT *    FROM ORDERS")

REM Open the result set
Set Result= CustStmt.OpenResultset(rdOpenKeyset,
                   rdConcurReadOnly, rdExecDirect)

DO WHILE (NOT Result.EOF)
  REM Process Each Row

  REM Move to the Next Row
  Result.MoveNext
WEND

REM Check for next result set
If Result.MoreResults Then
  DO WHILE (NOT Result.EOF)
    REM Process Each Row
```

```
      REM Move to the Next Row
      Result.MoveNext
   WEND
End If
```

Summary

During this chapter, you learned how the rdoResultset object is utilized to access the result of a query. After a query result set is available, a cursor is utilized to navigate the resulting records. This chapter reviewed the types of cursors that are supported by RDO: forward-only, static, keyset, dynamic, and mixed. Included in the cursor review was a discussion of how to choose the most appropriate cursor, based upon your application's requirements. This chapter also discussed the different page-locking mechanisms that are supported by RDO. You learned how to use the OpenResultset() method to specify an SQL query, cursor type, and page-locking scheme. You also learned how to use the rdoResultset Move(), including the absolute and relative positioning methods that are used to navigate a query result data set, and how to create and utilize bookmarks to facilitate your query navigation. You reviewed how to use the rdoColumn() and rdoColumns() methods to access field-level data, and the types of data that are supported by RDO fields. Finally, the rdoSchema class was created, which utilizes the rdoTable and rdoTables to access and display data-source schema information.

Chapter 17

RDO Error Handling

IN THIS CHAPTER

◆ Reviewing RDO error handling

◆ Overviewing `rdoError` and `rdoErrors` objects

◆ Viewing RDO error-handling examples

◆ Learning what to do when things go wrong

THIS CHAPTER REVIEWS RDO error handling. Basically, RDO handles exceptions in exactly the same way that DAO handles exceptions. Review Chapter 12, *Error Handling*, for a refresher on Visual Basic error handling. RDO uses the same Visual Basic `On Error` methodology to intercept RDO errors. The one difference with RDO error handling is its use of `rdoEngine`'s `rdoDefaultErrorThreshold` property. This property sets an *error threshold*, which means that an error is generated only if the error number value of the error is greater than the error threshold value. After an exception is caught, the `rdoError` and `rdoErrors` objects can be used to retrieve more information about the exception thrown. These objects are described in more detail shortly.

Review of RDO Exceptions

Before you review how to use the `rdoError` and `rdoErrors` objects to retrieve more information about an exception, and how to use the `rdoDefaultErrorThreshold` property to limit the errors generated, you need to review the exceptions that RDO can generate. Table 17-1 presents by error number the exceptions that are thrown by RDO. The table also includes a description of each RDO error.

 To control the errors that are generated by your database server, you should consult your database-server documentation. When you use SQL Server, the transact `SQL RAISERROR()` method is used to specify errors and other information.

The error numbers begin at 40000 and end at 40059. Some numbers in this range are *not* used; they are reserved for future and internal use.

TABLE 17-1 RDO-GENERATED EXCEPTIONS

Error Number	Description
40000	The `rdoRegisterDataSource ()` method failed. Check the parameters to be sure that they are valid.
40001	The SQL statement that was just executed did not return or affect any rows.
40002	The last method called generated an ODBC error. You must access the `rdoError getDescription()` method to determine the exact nature of the error.
40003	The parameter passed to the `putCursorDriver()` or `putrdoDefaultCursorDriver()` method is invalid. Remember, not all cursor drivers are supported for all data sources.
40004	An invalid ODBC handle was used by an ODBC operation. Unless you are directly using ODBC handles, you shouldn't experience this error with RDO.
40005	The connection string passed to the `OpenConnection()` method is invalid. Recheck and respecify your connection string.
40006	An unexpected error occurred. Check available resources and try again.
40008	When using a forward-only cursor, a move method other than `MoveNext()` was used. Only the `MoveNext()` method can be used with forward-only-type cursors.
40009	The `Edit()` method was called while on a row that has already been deleted, or the current row pointer is past the beginning or end of the result set. Be sure that you are on a valid row before you invoke the `Edit()` method.

Error Number	Description
40010	The AddNew() method was called while on a row that has already been deleted, or the current row pointer is past the beginning or end of the result set. Be sure that you are on a valid row before you invoke the AddNew() method. A row can also be invalid if the AddNew() or Edit() method is called without calling the Update() or Cancel() method to complete the operation.
40011	A method was called by an object that has already been closed or not allocated.
40014	The putValue() method was called with a field whose type does not match the column. Be sure that the types are correct when you access column values.
40016	The getrdoVersion() method was called and the VERSION.DLL was unavailable. Be sure that the VERSION.DLL is located in the Windows system directory before you make this call.
40017	An error occurred while attempting to create a prepared statement. Be sure to check the syntax of your prepared statement. Check the rdoErrorgetDescription() method for more information.
40018	The prepared statement being accessed was an empty screen. Be sure that the prepared statement is valid before you attempt to perform or execute the query.
40019	The lock type passed to the rdoPreparedStatement's OpenResultset() method is invalid. Remember that not all lock types are supported by all data sources.
40021	The getItem() method of a collection object was called with a text string. This collection doesn't support lookups by text strings; an ordinal value must be used to access collection items.
40022	You attempted to navigate an empty result set by using one of the Move methods. Check the RowCount() method before you attempt to navigate the result set.
40023	You attempted to navigate an invalid result set. A result set becomes invalid in the following situations: after it has been closed; when the MoreResults() method is called and it doesn't return any additional result sets; when an SQL error occurs.

Continued

TABLE 17-1 RDO-GENERATED EXCEPTIONS *(continued)*

Error Number	Description
40024	You attempted to call the `rdoResultset MoveNext()` method when the `EOF` property was set to `True`. To avoid this error, check the state of the `EOF` property before you call `MoveNext()`.
40025	An attempt was made to move past the beginning of the result set. Check the `getBOF()` method before you use the `MovePrevious()` method.
40026	An attempt was made to call the `Update()` method when pointing to an invalid row. A row is invalid in the following situations: if the current row pointer is past the beginning or end of the result set; if the `Cancel()` method is called for the current row; if the current row has been deleted already; if an SQL error occurs.
40027	The bookmark parameter passed to the `Move()` method is invalid.
40028	The bookmark parameter passed to the `Move()` method is not the right type. A bookmark must be an `int` or `byte` data type.
40029	A relative move was attempted with the `Move()` method when the current row pointer was past the beginning or end of the result set, or the result set is invalid.
40032	The `rdoRegisterDataSource()` method was called and the ODBCCP32.DLL file couldn't be accessed. Be sure that the ODBCCP32.DLL file is installed before you call this method.
40033	The `rdoEnvironment`'s `OpenConnection()` method was called with an invalid prompt constant. Check the `OpenConnection()` parameters and try again.
40034	The `OpenResultset()` method was called with an invalid cursor constant. Remember that not all cursor types are supported by all data sources.
40035	The result set contained a column with an unknown type. Check the column's type and the data source's documentation for more information.
40036	An attempt was made to access a BLOB (Binary Large Object) field with the `getValue()` methods. You must use the `GetChunk()` method when you access BLOB fields. Check the `GetChunkRequired()` method to determine whether the chunk methods are required.

Error Number	Description
40037	An attempt was made to access a BLOB field with the `putValue()` methods. You must use the `AppendChunk()` method when specifying BLOB field values. Check the `GetChunkRequired()` method to determine whether the chunk methods are required.
40038	An attempt was made to change a read-only field. Check the `Updatable()` method before changing values.
40039	An attempt was made to change a column's value before the `Edit()` or `AddNew()` method was called.
40040	A `Variant()`-type parameter was passed that contains an invalid data type. Make sure that you pass the correct data types when using `Variant()`-type parameters.
40041	When you attempted to access a collection with a text index, an index that matches the text index wasn't found. Use the ordinal value index or a text string that specifies a member of the collection to avoid this error.
40042	You attempted to change a parameter that hasn't been bound. Make sure that a previous error hasn't caused the object to be invalid.
40043	An attempt was made to set a value for an output parameter. Check the `getDirection()` method before you set a value for a parameter.
40045	A method or property was accessed while an asynchronous query was still executing. Check the `StillExecuting()` method to determine whether a query is still running, before you access other methods.
40046	An attempt was made to close an object that has already been closed.
40047	An invalid name was used when calling the `rdoCreateEnvironment()` method. The name can't be empty or a duplicate of an existing environment name.
40048	You attempted to create an environment either by using the `rdoCreateEnvironment()` method or by using a prepared statement with the `CreatePreparedStatement()` method and a duplicate name. Environments and prepared statements must have unique names.
40049	An attempt was made to change the contents of a collection. You can't modify the content of RDO collections.

Continued

TABLE 17-1 RDO-GENERATED EXCEPTIONS *(continued)*

Error Number	Description
40050	An error occurred while attempting to iterate through a collection; check available resources and try again.
40054	A value that was passed as a parameter to a method has an invalid type. Make sure that you use only proper data types when calling RDO methods.
40055	The method being accessed is not valid in the current context. Check the context of your operation.
40056	An attempt was made to move to a row which no longer exists — it has already been deleted using a bookmark operation.
40057	An attempt was made to execute a SELECT statement from the Execute() method. The Execute() method can be used only for SQL action statements; use the OpenResultset() method when you create queries.
40058	An attempt was made to modify a read-only result set. Check the lock type that is specified, before you attempt to modify a result set.
40059	The user clicked the Cancel button on an ODBC dialog box.

Table 17-2 lists and describes the most common SQL errors that can be generated when you access an SQL Server database server. The complete list of SQL Server errors is provided in Appendix D.

TABLE 17-2 MICROSOFT SQL SERVER ERRORS

Constant	Value	Error Message
SQLMEM	10000	Unable to allocate sufficient memory
SQLNULL	10001	Null DBOProcess encountered
SQLENLOG	10002	Null LoginRec encountered
SQLEPWD	10003	Login incorrect
SQLECONN	10004	Search on server failed
SQLEDDNE	10005	DBProcess is inactive or disabled

Constant	Value	Error Message
SQLENULLO	10006	Attempt to log in with Null Login record
SQLEMSG	10007	General SQL Server error has occurred
SQLEBTOK	10008	Bad token from SQL Server: data stream out of synch
SQLEREAD	10010	Read from SQL Server failed
SQLECNOR	10011	Column number out of range
SQLETSIT	10012	Attempt to call SQLTsPut with an invalid time stamp
SQLEPARAM	10013	Invalid parameter in DBLibrary function reference
SQLEAUTN	10014	Attempt to update time stamp of a table that has no time stamp column
SQLECOFL	10015	Data conversion resulted in overflow
SQLERDCN	10016	Requested data conversion does not exist
SQLEICN	10017	Invalid ComputeID or computer column number
SQLECLOS	10018	Error in closing network connection
SQLENTXT	10019	Attempt to get text identifier or text time stamp from a nontext column
SQLEDNTI	10020	Attempt to use SQLTxTsPut to put a new text time stamp into a column whose data type is neither text nor image
SQLETMTD	10021	Attempt to send too much text data by using SQLMoreText
SQLEASEC	10022	Attempt to send an empty command buffer to SQL Server
SQLENTLL	10023	Name too long for Login record
SQLETIME	10024	SQL Server connection timed out
SQLEWRIT	10025	Write to SQL Server failed
SQLEMODE	10026	Network connection not in correct mode; invalid SQL Server connection

Continued

TABLE 17-2 RDO-GENERATED EXCEPTIONS *(continued)*

Constant	Value	Error Message
SQLEOOB	10027	Error in sending out of band data to SQL Server
SQLEITM	10028	Illegal timeout value specified
SQLEDBPS	10029	Maximum number of SQL Server connections already allocated
SQLEIOPT	10030	Attempt to use invalid Visual Basic option
SQLEASNL	10031	Attempt to set fields in a NULL login record
SQLEASUL	10032	Attempt to set unknown Login record field
SQLENPRM	10033	Option can't have a NULL string as a parameter
SQLEDBOP	10034	Invalid or out-of-range parameter for the option
SQLENSIP	10035	Negative starting index passed to SQL string copy
SQLECNULL	10036	You have used 0 as an identifier for a text time stamp
SQLESEOF	10037	Unexpected EOF from the SQL Server
SQLERPND	10038	Attempt to initiate a new SQL Server query before processing the previous result set
SQLECSYN	10039	Attempt to convert data stopped by syntax error in source field
SQLENONE	10040	Network interface layer not in place
SQLEKBCO	10049	1000 rows successfully copied to host file
SQLEBBCI	10050	Batch successfully copied to SQL Server
SQLEKBCI	10051	1000 rows successfully copied to SQL Server
SQLEBCWE	10052	I/O error while writing BCP data
SQLEBCNN	10053	Attempt to bulk copy a Null value into an SQL Server column that doesn't accept Null values
SQLEBCOR	10054	Attempt to copy an oversized row to SQL Server
SQLEBCPI	10055	SQLBCPInit not called before BCP operation
SQLEBIVI	10059	Use SQLBCPColumns and SQLBCPColFmt only after SQLBCPInit

Constant	Value	Error Message
SQLEBCBC	10060	Use SQLBCPColumns before SQLBCPColFmt
SQLEBCFO	10061	Host files must contain at least one column
SQLEBCVH	10062	Call SQLBCPExec only after SQLBCPInit has been passed a valid host file
SQLEBCUO	10063	Unable to open host data file
SQLEBUOE	10064	Unable to open error file
SQLEBWEF	10065	I/O error writing BCP error file
SQLEBTMT	10066	Attempt to send too much data with BCP_moretext
SQLEBEOF	10067	Unexpected EOF encountered in BCP data file
SQLEBCSI	10068	Host file columns may be skipped only when copying to the SQL Server
SQLEPNUL	10069	Null program pointer encountered
SQLEBSKERR	10070	Cannot seek in data file
SQLEBDIO	10071	Bad bulk copy direction
SQLEBCNT	10072	Attempt to use bulk copy with nonexistent server table
SQLCRSINV	10075	Invalid cursor statement
SQLCRSCMD	10076	Attempt to call cursor function when commands are waiting to be executed
SQLCRSNOIND	10077	One of the tables involved in the cursor statement doesn't have an index
SQLCRSDIS	10078	Cursor statement contains one of the disallowed phrases — COMPUTER< UNION, FOR BROWSE, or SELECT INTO
SQLCRSAGR	10079	Aggregate functions not allowed in a cursor statement
SQLCRSORD	10080	Only fully keyset-driven cursors can have ORDER BY, GROUP BY, or HAVING phrases

Continued

TABLE 17-2 RDO-GENERATED EXCEPTIONS *(continued)*

Constant	Value	Error Message
SQLCRSMEM	10081	Keyset or window scroll size exceeds the memory limitations of this machine
SQLCRSBSKEY	10082	Keyset can't be scrolled backward in mixed cursors with a previous fetch type
SQLCRSNORES	10083	Cursor statement generated no results
SQLCRSVIEW	10084	A view can't be joined with another table or a view in a cursor statement
SQLCRSBUFR	10085	Row buffering shouldn't be turned on when using cursor APIs
SQLCRSFROWN	10086	Row number fetched is outside of valid range
SQLCRSBROL	10087	Backward-scrolling can't be used in a forward-scrolling cursor
SQLCRSFRAND	10088	Fetch types RANDOM and RELATIVE can be used only within the keyset of keyset-driven cursors
SQLCRSFLAST	10089	Fetch type LAST requires fully keyset-driven cursors
SQLCRSRO	10090	Data locking or modifications can't be made in a read-only cursor
SQLCRSTAB	10091	Table name must be determined in operations involving data locking or modifications
SQLCRSUPDATAB	10092	Update or insert operations using bind variables require single table cursors
SQLCRSUPNB	10093	Update or insert operations cannot use bind variables when binding type is NONBIND
SQLCRSVIIND	10094	The view used in the cursor statement doesn't include all the unique index columns of the underlying tables
SQLCRSNOUPD	10095	Update or delete operation did not affect any rows
SQLCRSOS2	10096	Cursors are not supported for this server

rdoError and rdoErrors Objects

The rdoError and rdoErrors objects are the last things that you need to review before you look at how exception handling is implemented in RDO. The rdoError object contains information, including an English description, for the exception that is thrown. The rdoErrors object holds a collection of rdoError objects. Importantly, an RDO method can, and often does, throw more than one exception when an error occurs. Therefore, you need to examine the entire contents of the rdoErrors object. The rdoEngine object provides the getrdoErrors() method, which returns the rdoErrors object that contains the errors generated by the last exception. The most detailed errors generated are placed at the beginning of the rdoErrors collection, and the most general errors are placed at the end of the rdoErrors collection. Table 17-3 presents the properties of the rdoError object.

TABLE 17-3 RDOERROR OBJECT PROPERTIES

Property	Description
Description	Returns a descriptive string associated with an error.
HelpContext	Returns a context ID for a topic in a Windows Help file.
HelpFile	Returns a fully qualified path to the Help file as a variable.
Number	Returns a numeric value that specifies a native error.
Source	Returns a value that indicates the source of a remote data access error.
SQLRetCode	Returns the ODBC error return code from the most recent RDO operation. If set to rdSQLSuccess, the operation is successful. If set to rdSQLSuccessWithInfo, the operation is successful and additional information is available. If set to rdSQLNoDataFound, no additional data is available. If set to rdSQLError, an error occurred performing the operation. If set to rdSQLInvalidHandle, the handle supplied is invalid.
SQLState	Returns a value corresponding to the type of error, as defined by the X/Open and SQL Access Group SQL.

The rdoError object is used to encapsulate an RDO error. An rdoError object is accessed from the rdoErrors collection, which is discussed next. After you have an rdoError object, its properties can be used to perform the following:

- ◆ The Description property returns a String that contains the English description of the error.

- ◆ The HelpContext and HelpFile properties return a Help context ID and the name of the Help file. They can be used to display more-detailed Help file information when an error occurs.

- ◆ The Number property returns an integer that is the number of the error. Refer to Table 17-1 for a list and description of error numbers.

- ◆ The Source property returns a string that identifies the source of the error.

- ◆ The SQLRetCode property returns the error return code from the most recent SQL command. Table 17-4 summarizes the SQL return code constants and their descriptions.

- ◆ The SQLState property returns a five-character error string, as defined by the X/Open and SQL Access Group. Values that begin with 01 indicate an error.

TABLE 17-4 SQL RETURN CODE CONSTANTS

Constant	Description
rdSQLSuccess	The SQL command was successful.
rdSQLSuccessWithInfo	The SQL command was successful and returned some extra information.
rdSQLNoDataFound	No extra information is available.
rdSQLError	The SQL command was not successful.
rdSQLInvalidHandle	An invalid handle was passed.

The rdoErrors object is used to access the individual rdoError objects and is accessed by calling the rdoEngine's getrdoErrors() method. Table 17-5 presents the properties provided by the rdoErrors object.

TABLE 17-5 RDOERRORS OBJECT PROPERTIES

Property	Description
Item	Returns a specific member of a Remote Data Objects (RDO) collection object, either by position or by key.
Count	Returns the number of objects in the rdoErrors collection.

The Clear() method is used to empty the rdoErrors collection. Usually, clearing the rdoErrors object isn't necessary, because it is cleared automatically each time that a new error occurs. The getCount() method returns the number of rdoError objects in the collection. The getItem() method is used to retrieve the individual rdoError objects of the collection. The getItem() method takes a single Variant parameter that specifies the index of the rdoError object to retrieve.

Error–Handling Example

Now that you understand the rdoError and rdoErrors objects, this section reviews how to put things together to check for errors when using the RDO library in Visual Basic. Listing 17-1 demonstrates how the RDO exception–handling techniques are applied to a sample application.

Listing 17-1: Applying Exception Handling with the RDO Library

```
REM Trap RDO Errors
On Error GoTo RDOErrHandlr
Dim en As rdoEnvironment
Dim cn As rdoConnection
Set en = rdoEngine.rdoEvironments(0)
With en
  en.CursorDriver = rdUseOdbc
  en.LoginTimeout = 5
  en.Name = "TestEnv"
  Set cn = en.OpenConnection(dsname:="",
                prompt:=rdDriverNoPrompt,
                Connect:="UID=;PWD=;"
                driver={SQL Server};
                Server=MyServer;",
                Options:=rdAsyncEnable)
End With
```

```
RDOErrHandlr:
    Dim RDOerr As rdoError
    REM Display a Message box for each error in the
    REM RDOErrors collection
    For Each RDOerr In rdoErrors
        MsgBox CStr(RDOerr.Number) & er.Description
    Next RDOerr
    Resume Next
```

When Things Go Wrong

No matter how well you design and develop your application, you're bound to experience errors occasionally. You may encounter a few tricky situations in your RDO applications – those applications that access your database server – that may cause you to experience errors. To help you understand and prepare for potential error situations, review the following list:

◆ **An added or updated row violates the unique key established for that row.** Rules that are defined on your database server limit the values occurring in a row to a set or combination of valid values; the row you're attempting to append to the database doesn't conform to these rules. You need to make sure that your front-end application also employs the same set of rules as defined in your back-end database – this ensures that the application won't attempt to add or update a row that is invalid.

◆ **An added or updated row violates one of the database server's validation rules.** This can be caused when another user adds a row that matches the same self-generated key and that user's row arrives before the records that you're attempting to add. When you create an application that generates its own keys, you must use transaction processing to prevent these types of errors.

◆ **One or more of the database pages are locked.** When this happens, your operation is hung up until the QueryTimeout period has elapsed; you can only abort or retry the operation.

◆ **The database server times out.** This can happen when your database QueryTimeout period isn't high enough to account for the amount of network traffic or the load on the database server. The server may be down or working on a very complex query. Again, you can only abort your operation or retry it.

◆ **The database server locks when executing your sequence of operations.** Occasionally, for unexplainable reasons, a series of operations may cause your process to hang. You need to review the sequence of operations that you're trying to perform and break them down into smaller steps, until you determine where the sequence hangs.

◆ **A table's insert trigger option finds an error and aborts your transaction.** Again, your database server table may have referential integrity rules or business logic that prevents invalid records from entering the database. Your application needs to edit for these errors before they are passed to the database server.

◆ **A connection error or another application error crashes your application.** This usually involves a network-type of error; perhaps the client workstation has lost its connection, a hub is down, or the database server is down for routine maintenance.

Summary

This chapter reviewed RDO error handling. The `rdoError` and `rdoErrors` objects are used to retrieve more information about the exception that is thrown. This chapter reviewed and explained the properties and methods of the `rdoError` and `rdoErrors` objects. The errors that can be generated by RDO – and, more specifi-cally, the errors that can be generated when accessing an SQL Server database – were defined and described in detail. You learned how to implement RDO error handing into your own applications through the example presented in this chapter. Finally, you can't escape all the scenarios that might cause your RDO applications to crash. Therefore, this chapter presented some common scenarios that cause crashes by RDO applications that access a centralized database server, and gave you some strategies for diagnosing and fixing these errors. In the next chapter, you learn how to implement RDO applications with less code – by using the Remote Data control.

Chapter 18

Using the Remote Data Control

IN THIS CHAPTER

◆ Introducing the Remote Data Control

◆ Integrating the Remote Data Control into your applications

THIS CHAPTER BEGINS to wrap up the discussion of the RDO data access model. You have learned how to integrate the RDO objects, methods, and properties into your own applications. However, an easier way exists to provide basic RDO data access from your Visual Basic applications – the Remote Data Control object. Visual Basic provides several controls that are considered to be *bound* – that is, they can be directly associated with a data source. This binding process can simplify your programming process. Although bound controls may not be the answer in all circumstances, they can greatly speed up your development process and make your applications more robust. This chapter illustrates how to use the Remote Data Control in your own applications and how to access its properties, methods, and events.

Introducing the Remote Data Control

The Remote Data Control (RDC) is analogous to the Data Control. As with the difference between DAO and RDO, the primary difference between the Data Control and the Remote Data Control is that the Data Control utilizes the Jet Database Engine.

Chapter 13 reviews the Data Control object.

Note, however, that when you utilize the ODBCDirect interface of DAO, you can bypass the Jet Database Engine with the Data Control, too, which somewhat clouds the issue of when you should choose to use the Remote Data Control. If you are developing an application that primarily utilizes RDO, however, the Remote Data Control is the more logical choice. Using the Remote Data Control in the following applications, among others, can help you to develop applications quicker:

◆ Filling a DBList with a list of valid field choices. A user can choose from a list of valid field choices during data entry. This can drastically increase the reliability of an application's data entry.

◆ Filling a DBCombo control with the results of a query.

◆ Displaying a picture in a Picture control from the result of a BLOB field in a single-row query.

◆ Binding a set of TextBox controls to the columns of a query result set.

The Remote Data Control is primarily used to access remote database sources (namely, database servers through ODBC). It provides an interface between Remote Data Objects (RDO) and data-aware bound controls. With the Remote Data Control, you can accomplish the following:

◆ Establish a connection to a data source, based on its properties

◆ Create rdoResultset objects

◆ Pass the current row's data to corresponding bound controls

◆ Permit the user to position the current row pointer

◆ Pass back to the data source any changes made to the bound controls

Properties

The Remote Data Control provides many properties, but a few in particular are especially important when you are developing data access applications. The Environment property of the RDC provides access to the underlying rdoEnvironment object. The following Remote Data Control properties determine how the default rdoEnvironment is set up:

◆ CursorDriver: Determines the type of cursor driver to use – a server-side cursor or one from the ODBC Cursor Driver Library.

Chapter 16 reviews each of the RDO cursor types in detail.

♦ LogMessages: Use to enable ODBC tracing – this normally is accessed through the rdoQuery object.

♦ Version: Use to determine the version of the RDO library that is being used. This normally is a property of the rdoEngine object.

The Connection property provides access to the underlying rdoConnection object. The following Remote Data Control properties determine how the rdoConnection environment is created:

♦ Connect: Specifies the ODBC connect string that is passed to the underlying OpenConnection() method.

♦ DataSourceName: Specifies the name of an ODBC Data Source Name, if you are using one. This, too, is passed to the underlying OpenConnection() method.

♦ LoginTimeout: Specifies how long to wait before the user's attempt to log in times out.

♦ UserName and Password: Specify the SQL Server login ID and password, respectively, if they haven't been specified in the ODBC connect string.

♦ Prompt: Specifies how the ODBC driver manager prompts the user at connect time if information is incomplete. This is the same type of argument passed to the OpenConnection() method.

♦ ReadOnly: Use to determine whether the ODBC connection is opened for read-only or read/write access. This is the same type of argument passed to the OpenConnection() method.

The ResultSet property provides access to the underlying rdoResultSet object. The following properties of the Remote Data Control are used to determine how the rdoResultSet is created or managed:

♦ BOFAction: Use to determine how the Remote Data Control reacts when the beginning of the record set is reached. If set to rdMoveFirst, the first row remains as the current row. If set to rdBOF, when moved past the beginning of the record set, the Validate event is called for the first row, followed by a Reposition event on the invalid BOF row – this causes the Move Previous button on the control to become disabled.

♦ EditMode: Use to determine whether the AddNew() or Edit() methods are active.

♦ EOFAction: Use to help when you are at the end of a result set or working with an empty result set, by automatically calling the AddNew() method when the end of the result set is reached. If set to rdMoveLast, the last row is kept as the current row. If set to `rdEOF`, moving past the end of the result set calls the `Validate` event for the last row, followed by a reposition on the invalid `EOF` row – this causes the Move Next button on the control to become disabled. If set to `rdAddNew`, moving past the end of the result set calls the `Validate` event for the last row, followed by a call to `AddNew`, followed by a repositioning to the new last row.

◆ `MaxRows`: Use to set the upper limit on the number of rows retrieved, inserted, updated, or deleted when you use the control.

◆ `Options`: Maps to the `OpenResultSet` options parameter. If set to `rdAsyncEnabled`, the query and any other operations run asynchronously. If set to `rdExecDirect`, the application pauses until the operation is completed.

◆ `QueryTimeout`: Determines how long a query can run before it is automatically timed out.

◆ `ResultSetType`: Use to access the underlying `edoResultSet` object that is created or will be created. You can use the `rdOpenStatic` and `rdoOpenKeyset` cursors only when you use the Remote Data Control.

◆ `RowsetSize`: Use to determine the row set size that is used by the Remote Data Control.

◆ `SQL`: Use to specify the query that will be run to fill the record set. Simply putting a table name in this property isn't advisable.

◆ `StillExecuting`: Use to determine whether an asynchronous operation has completed execution.

◆ `Transaction`: Use to determine whether the data source that you are connected to supports transactions – when you access a database server, such as Microsoft SQL Server or Oracle, this is always `True`.

Events

The following are the events supported by the Remote Data Control that are important for creating data access applications:

◆ The `QueryCompleted` event is triggered when an asynchronous query has been completed.

◆ The `Reposition` event is triggered whenever the current record in the record set is changed. This event occurs after the new row becomes current.

♦ The `Validate` event occurs before the current row is changed. This event can be used to perform calculations based on data in the current row or to ensure that the data in the current row is valid.

ERROR

The `Error` event occurs only as the result of a data access error that takes place when no Visual Basic code is being executed. It has the following syntax:

```
Private Sub object _Error([index As Integer,]Number As Long,
Description As String, Scode As Long, Source As String, HelpFile As
String, HelpContext As Long, CancelDisplay As Boolean)
```

The `Object` parameter is an object expression that evaluates to an object. The `Index` parameter identifies the control, if it's in a control array. `Number` is the native error number. The `Description` parameter describes the error. The `Scode` parameter is the ODBC error-return code. The `Source` parameter is the source of the error. The `HelpFile` parameter is the path to a Help file that contains more information about the error. The `HelpContext` parameter is the Help file context number. The `CancelDisplay` parameter is a number that corresponds to the action that you want to take: if set to `rdDataErrContinue`, continue running the application; if set to `rdDataErrDisplay`, display the error message.

REPOSITION

The `Reposition` event, which has the following syntax, occurs after a row becomes the current row:

```
Private Sub object.Reposition ([index As Integer])
```

VALIDATE

The `Validate` event occurs before a different row becomes the current row, before the `Update()` method (except when data is saved with the `UpdateRow()` method), and before a `Delete`, `Unload`, or `Close` operation. The `Validate` event has the following syntax:

```
Private Sub object_Validate ([index As Integer,] action As Integer,
reserved As Integer)
```

The `Reserved` parameter is an Integer argument that is preserved only for compatibility with RDO version 1.0, and is ignored by the Remote Data Control. The `Action` parameter is an integer or constant that indicates the operation causing this event to occur. Table 18-1 illustrates the use of the action parameter.

TABLE 18-1 RESULTS OF ACTION PARAMETER SETTINGS

If Action Parameter Set to . . .	The Result Is . . .
rRdActionCancel	Cancels the operation when the Sub exits.
rdActionMoveFirst	MoveFirst() method.
rdActionMovePrevious	MovePrevious() method.
rdActionMoveNext	MoveNext() method.
rdActionMoveLast	MoveLast() method.
rdActionAddNew	AddNew() method.
rdActionUpdate	Update() operation (not UpdateRow()).
rdActionDelete	Delete() method.
rdActionFind	Find() method (not implemented).
rdActionBookmark	The Bookmark property has been set.
rdActionClose	The Close() method.
rdActionUnload	The form is being unloaded.
rdActionUpdateAddNew	A new row was inserted into the result set.
rdActionUpdateModified	The current row changed.
rdActionRefresh	Refresh() method executed.
rdActionCancelUpdate	Update canceled.
rdActionBeginTransact	BeginTrans() method.
rdActionCommitTransact	CommitTrans() method.
rdActionRollbackTransact	RollbackTrans() method.
rdActionNewParameters	Change in parameters or order of columns or rows.
rdActionNewSQL	SQL statement changed.

QUERYCOMPLETED

The QueryCompleted event occurs after the query of an rdoResultset generated by a Remote Data Control returns the first result set. It has the following syntax:

```
Private Sub object.QueryCompleted ([index As Integer])
```

DRAGDROP

The DragDrop event occurs when a drag-and-drop operation is completed as a result of either dragging a control over an object and releasing the mouse button or using the Drag() method. It has the following syntax:

```
Private Sub object_DragDrop([index As Integer,]source As Control, x
As Single, y As Single)
```

The Source parameter identifies the control that is being dragged. The X and Y parameters are numbers that specify the current horizontal (*x*) and vertical (*y*) position of the mouse pointer within the target control.

DRAGOVER

The DragOver event occurs when a drag-and-drop operation is in progress. You can use this event to monitor the mouse pointer as it enters, leaves, or rests directly over a valid target. The mouse pointer position determines the target object that receives this event. It has the following syntax:

```
Private Sub object_DragOver([index As Integer,]source As Control, x
As Single, y As Single, state As Integer)
```

You can refer to properties and methods in the event procedure with Source parameter. The X and Y parameters are numbers that specify the current horizontal (*x*) and vertical (*y*) position of the mouse pointer within the target control. State is an integer that corresponds to the transition state of the control that is being dragged, relative to a target form or control: 0 = Enter (source control is being dragged within the range of a target); 1 = Leave (source control is being dragged out of the range of a target); 2 = Over (source control has moved from one position in the target to another).

MOUSEDOWN

The MouseDown event occurs when the user presses (MouseDown) a mouse button. It has the following syntax:

```
Private Sub object_MouseDown([index As Integer,]button As Integer,
shift As Integer, x As Single, y As Single)
```

The Button parameter returns an integer that identifies the button that was pressed (MouseDown) or released (MouseUp) to cause the event. The Button argument is a bit field with bits corresponding to the left button (bit 0), right button (bit 1), and middle button (bit 2). The Shift parameter returns an integer that corresponds to the state of the Shift, Ctrl, and Alt keys when the button specified in the Button argument is pressed or released. A bit is set if the key is down. The Shift argument is a bit field with the least significant bits corresponding to the Shift key (bit 0), Ctrl key (bit 1), and Alt key (bit 2). The X and Y parameters return a number that specifies the current location of the mouse pointer.

MOUSEUP

The MouseUp event occurs when the user releases (MouseUp) a mouse button. It has the following syntax:

```
Private Sub object _MouseUp([index As Integer,]button As Integer,
shift As Integer, x As Single, y As Single)
```

MOUSEMOVE

The MouseMove event occurs when the user moves the mouse. It has the following syntax:

```
Private Sub object_MouseMove([index As Integer,] button As Integer,
shift As Integer, x As Single, y As Single)
```

Methods

Again, although the Remote Data Control provides many methods and events, the following are critical when you are developing data access applications.

BEGINTRANS( ), COMMITTRANS( ), AND ROLLBACKTRANS( )

The BeginTrans(), CommitTrans(), and RollbackTrans() methods begin, commit, and undo a transaction (respectively). They have the following syntax:

```
BeginTrans()
CommitTrans()
RollbackTrans()
```

CANCEL( )

The Cancel() method cancels the processing of a query that is running in asynchronous mode or any pending results against the specified RDO object. It has the following syntax:

```
Cancel
```

REFRESH( )

The Refresh() method closes and rebuilds the rdoResultset object created by a Remote Data Contro or refreshes the members of the collections in the Applies To list. It has the following syntax:

```
Refresh
```

UPDATECONTROLS( )

The UpdateControls() method retrieves the current row from a Remote Data Control's rdoResultset object and displays the appropriate data in controls that are bound to a Remote Data Control. It has the following syntax:

```
UpdateControls
```

UPDATEROW( )

The UpdateRow() method saves to the database the current values of bound controls. It has the following syntax:

```
UpdateRow
```

DRAG( )

The Drag() method begins, ends, or cancels a drag operation of any control except the Line, Menu, Shape, Timer, or CommonDialog controls. This method doesn't support named arguments. It has the following syntax:

```
Drag action
```

The Action parameter is a constant or value that specifies the action to perform. If set to vbCancel, the drag operation is canceled. If set to vbBeginDrag, the object begins being dragged. If set to vbEndDrag, it ends dragging the object and drops it.

MOVE( )

The Move() method moves a control. It has the following syntax:

```
Move left, top, width, height
```

The Left parameter is a single-precision value that indicates the horizontal coordinate (x axis) for the left edge of the object. The Top parameter is a single-precision value that indicates the vertical coordinate (y axis) for the top edge of the object. The Width and Height parameters are single-precision values that indicate the new width and height, respectively, of the object.

ZORDER( )

The ZOrder() method places a specified control at the front or back of the z-order within its graphical level. This method doesn't support named arguments. It has the following syntax:

```
ZOrder position
```

The Position parameter is an Integer that indicates the position of an object, relative to other instances of the same object. If Position is 0 or omitted, the object is positioned at the front of the z-order. If Position is 1, the object is positioned at the back of the z-order.

SHOWWHATSTHIS( )

The ShowWhatsThis() method displays a selected topic in a Help file, using the "What's This" pop-up menu provided by Windows 95 Help. This method has the following syntax:

```
ShowWhatsThis
```

Integrating the Remote Data Control

To integrate a bound Remote Data Control into your own Visual Basic applications, follow these steps to create a simple form that browses through a database:

1. Open the Visual Basic Development Environment and begin creating a new application. After the new application is opened, a blank form is displayed.

2. Add the Remote Data Control to the control's toolbar by selecting Project → Components to display the Components dialog box, as shown in Figure 18-1. On the Controls tab, click the checkbox in front of the Microsoft Remote Data Control item in the list box. Click the OK button to continue.

3. Select the Remote Data Control object and place it on the form, as shown in Figure 18-2.

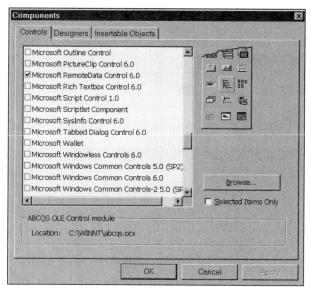

Figure 18-1: Using the Components dialog box

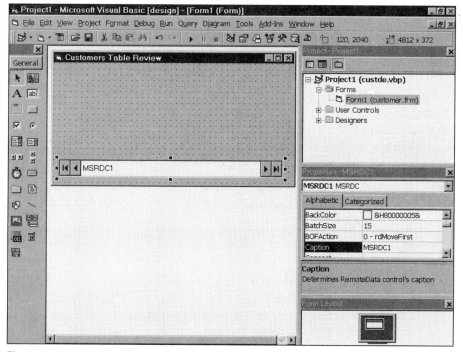

Figure 18-2: Adding the Remote Data Control to the form

4. This example accesses a simple Customer table from an SQL Server ODBC data source. The Customer table contains the fields `ContactFName` and `ContactLName`. You need to place two edit controls on the form, to be used to display the contents of these fields. You can also place labels on the form, to label each field, as shown in Figure 18-3.

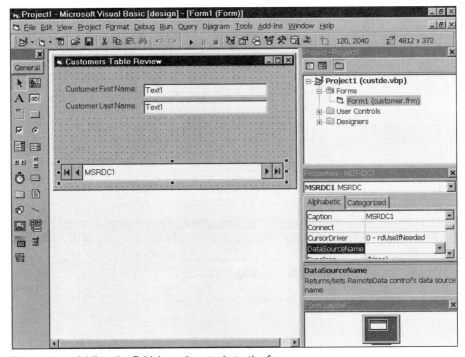

Figure 18-3: Adding the field-bound controls to the form

5. Set the `DataSourceName` of the Remote Data Control to an established ODBC data control.

6. Set the `SQL` property to a valid SQL query — in this case, a query that selects the records of the Customers table; for example, `SELECT * FROM CUSTOMERS`.

7. For each text field, set the `DataSource` property to the name of the Remote Data Control, and the `DataField` name property to the name of the first- and last-name fields.

8. You can now run your application and review the data contained in the Customers table, as shown in Figure 18-4.

Listing 18-1 shows the complete source code for integrating a bound Remote Data Control into your own Visual Basic applications.

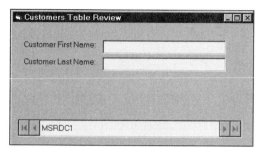

Figure 18-4: The running Customers application

Listing 18-1: The Customer Table Data Access Application

```
VERSION 5.00
Object = "{F6125AB1-8AB1-11CE-A77F-08002B2F4E98}#2.0#0";
"MSRDC20.OCX"
Begin VB.Form Form1
   Caption         =    "Customers Table Review"
   ClientHeight    =    2556
   ClientLeft      =    48
   ClientTop       =    276
   ClientWidth     =    5148
   LinkTopic       =    "Form1"
   ScaleHeight     =    2556
   ScaleWidth      =    5148
   StartUpPosition =    3   'Windows Default
   Begin VB.TextBox Text2
      DataField    =    "ContactLastName"
      DataSource   =    "MSRDC1"
      Height       =    288
      Left         =    1920
      TabIndex     =    1
      Text         =    "Text1"
      Top          =    720
      Width        =    2652
   End
   Begin VB.TextBox Text1
      DataField    =    "ContactLastName"
      DataSource   =    "MSRDC1"
```

```
        Height         =    288
        Left           =    1920
        TabIndex       =    0
        Text           =    "Text1"
        Top            =    360
        Width          =    2652
     End
     Begin MSRDC.MSRDC MSRDC1
        Height         =    372
        Left           =    120
        Top            =    2040
        Width          =    4812
        _ExtentX       =    8488
        _ExtentY       =    656
        _Version       =    393216
        Options        =    0
        CursorDriver   =    0
        BOFAction      =    0
        EOFAction      =    0
        RecordsetType  =    3
        LockType       =    1
        QueryType      =    0
        Prompt         =    3
        Appearance     =    1
        QueryTimeout   =    30
        RowsetSize     =    100
        LoginTimeout   =    15
        KeysetSize     =    0
        MaxRows        =    0
        ErrorThreshold =    -1
        BatchSize      =    15
        BackColor      =    -2147483643
        ForeColor      =    -2147483640
        Enabled        =    -1   'True
        ReadOnly       =    0    'False
        Appearance     =    -1   'True
        DataSourceName =    "ExampleDB"
        RecordSource   =    "SELECT * FROM CUSTOMERS"
        UserName       =    ""
        Password       =    ""
        Connect        =    ""
        LogMessages    =    ""
        Caption        =    "MSRDC1"
```

```
    BeginProperty Font {0BE35203-8F91-11CE-9DE3-00AA004BB851}
        Name            =    "MS Sans Serif"
        Size            =    7.8
        Charset         =    0
        Weight          =    400
        Underline       =    0    'False
        Italic          =    0    'False
        Strikethrough   =    0    'False
    EndProperty
End
Begin VB.Label Label2
    Caption         =    "Customer Last Name:"
    Height          =    252
    Left            =    240
    TabIndex        =    3
    Top             =    720
    Width           =    1572
End
Begin VB.Label Label1
    Caption         =    "Customer First Name:"
    Height          =    252
    Left            =    240
    TabIndex        =    2
    Top             =    360
    Width           =    1572
End
End
Attribute VB_Name = "Form1"
Attribute VB_GlobalNameSpace = False
Attribute VB_Creatable = False
Attribute VB_PredeclaredId = True
Attribute VB_Exposed = False
```

Summary

This chapter introduced the Visual Basic Remote Data Control, which works with other bound controls. Bound controls are just like any other Visual Basic form controls (such as edit boxes, list boxes, and buttons), but they have additional properties, events, and methods that enable you to associate them with one or more data tables. This chapter described the important properties, methods, and attributes of the Remote Data Control, and showed you how to begin integrating the Remote Data Control into your own applications.

Chapter 19

RDO Security Issues

THIS CHAPTER REVIEWS some of the issues surrounding the access of secured databases, including how security contexts are maintained using RDO, and the types of database permissions provided by most database servers. This chapter concludes by reviewing the specific security issues related to Microsoft SQL Server, including the security models provided, the types of protocols supported, and how to establish and maintain database permissions.

Users, Passwords, and Connection Strings

When you use the `OpenConnection()` method of the `rdoEnvironment` object to establish a database connection, the connection string parameter accepts two parameters — `UID` and `PWD` — that specify a username and password, respectively. Remember, the connection string isn't encrypted in any way, and if you hard-code into your application a connection string that contains a username and password in the connection string argument, your application may not be secure.

Chapter 15 reviewed in detail how to use the `OpenConnection()` method of the `rdoEnvironment` object.

Applications are available that can view a binary executable file, and potentially locate the encoded username and password. You also need to remember that, depending on the networking protocol that you are using, intercepting these arguments is theoretically possible, because the connect string parameters are not encrypted.

You must consult your database server documentation to see whether it provides any other methodologies to ensure secured access. When you utilize SQL Server and Windows NT Server on a local area network (LAN), you can rely on *domain-managed security*, which controls all access to network resources from a centralized point – Windows NT Server. When you use domain-managed security, after you log in to NT Server, you are granted access to any other network domain resources to which you have been granted access. With domain-managed security, you should leave blank the UID and PWD arguments of the connect string argument. When you attempt to make a connection, your Windows NT username and password are automatically passed to the database server.

Database Issues

Several permission levels are provided by most database servers. Generally, security is provided at three levels:

- **Server level**: Access to the database server is granted based on a username and password. Users without the proper username and password are not even allowed to establish a connection to a database server.

- **Database level**: A database server may contain many different databases. Using database server administrative utilities, a user is granted access to a database.

- **Table level**: A user may not have access to all the tables contained in a database. Generally, the GRANT and REVOKE commands are used to establish table- and field-level access. A user may either not be allowed to access a table, be given read-only access to a table, or be allowed to read and write to a table.

 When you develop your RDO applications, you must be aware of these restrictions and plan appropriately for them in your application. Many times, tables are defined in such a manner that not all of the fields are accessible. You should be aware of this, because a SELECT *-type of query on this type of table will fail.

SQL Server Issues

Many security issues are directly related to the specific database server that you are using. The remainder of this chapter focuses on security issues, while focusing specifically on SQL Server implementation details. SQL Server provides numerous stored procedures that can be used to determine who is currently connected, to create users and groups, and to change passwords. You will learn how to use the RDO interface to access these specific stored procedures. Finally, you will learn how to implement from RDO the GRANT and REVOKE SQL commands, which are used to set permissions on database tables and fields for specific users.

Security Models

Microsoft SQL Server implements the following three types of security models:

♦ **Standard:** SQL Server keeps a separate user account database. This model is implemented by default.

♦ **Integrated:** Domain-managed security is used. The users and groups created in the Windows NT domain are the same users and groups that are used by SQL Server to assign database permissions. When you use this model, you don't need to specify the UID and PWD parameters in the connect string.

♦ **Mixed:** Local SQL Server and domain-managed accounts are utilized. Depending on the user or group, a username and password may be required in the connect string.

You need to be aware of which type of model is implemented on your database server, because the security employed is dependent on the type of networking protocol that you are utilizing.

Protocols

SQL Server can support numerous different networking protocols. Two types of connections can be established between a client and the database server: trusted and untrusted. You need to be aware of which type of networking protocol is being utilized, because it affects the type of security model that you can employ.

Trusted connections can rely on the underlying protocol to validate that users are who they say they are. With *untrusted connections*, the underlying networking protocol can't determine whether a user is authentic. Untrusted networking protocols can utilize only the standard SQL Server security model. Trusted protocols can utilize any of the security models.

The following networking protocols are supported by SQL Server:

♦ **Named Pipes:** The networking protocol originally supported by SQL Server. It is the default protocol used by SQL Server and can be used over underlying NetBEUI, NWLink IPX/SPX, and TCP/IP protocol stacks. Named Pipes can be used to create trusted connections.

♦ **TCP/IP Sockets:** TCP/IP is a widely used protocol. SQL Server supports the use of TCP/IP Sockets by using the Windows-based socket interface. TCP/IP sockets create untrusted connections.

♦ **NWLink IPX/SPX:** When running in native Novell environments, SQL Server can use the NWLink IPX/SPX protocol to request transport services from IPX, similar to TCP/IP sockets. NWLink IPX/SPX creates untrusted connections.

♦ **Banyan VINES:** SQL Server can support the Banyan VINES networking protocol to create untrusted connections.

♦ **Multiprotocol RPC (Remote Procedure Call):** Multiprotocol RPC is the newest protocol supported by SQL Server. Multiprotocol RPC runs on top of Named Pipes, TCP/IP Sockets, and NWLink IPX/SPX, which is why it is called *multiprotocol.* When you use Multiprotcol RPC, trusted connections can be established over each of the previously listed protocols. More importantly, this protocol supports encrypted communication between the client and database server.

Stored Procedures

SQL Server provides various stored procedure queries that you can utilize in administrative functions. As long as the user you are logged in as has the appropriate permissions, these stored procedures are accessible from your RDO applications. This section looks at how the security-related SQL Server stored procedures can be accessed from RDO.

DETERMINING WHO'S LOGGED IN

Sometimes, determining who is currently connected to an SQL Server database server is important. SQL Server provides the SP_WHO stored procedure to determine which connections are currently active. Listing 19-1 demonstrates how the SP_WHO stored procedure can be called by using the RDO libraries. The SP_WHO procedure actually generates a system-level query, which returns the following columns:

♦ SPID: Process ID

♦ STATUS: Current process status

♦ LOGINAME: Username used to log in to SQL Server

- ◆ **HOSTNAME:** The hostname of the client

- ◆ **BLK:** Blocked status

- ◆ **DBNAME:** The name of the database connected to

- ◆ **CMD:** The current command being executed

Listing 19-1: Calling the SP_WHO Query from Visual Basic Using RDO

```
Dim en As rdoEnvironment
Dim cn As rdoConnection
Dim Result As rdoResultSet
Dim WhoStmt As Query
Dim rdoRes As rdoResultSet
Dim cl Ad rdoColumn

REM Create an Environment
Set en = rdoEngine.rdoEvironments(0)
With en
  en.CursorDriver = rdUseOdbc
  en.LoginTimeout = 5
  en.Name = "TestEnv"

  REM Establish a connection
  Set cn = en.OpenConnection("", rdDriverPrompt, True,
    "DSN=MyDataSource;UID=Marie;PWD=Pooh;Database=Customers")

End With

REM Call the Stored Procedure
Set WhoStmt = cn.CreateQuery("WhoStmt", "{ call SP_WHO }")

REM Open the result set
Set rdoRes = WhoStmt.OpenResultset(rdOpenKeyset, rdConcurReadOnly,
rdExecDirect)

REM Print Column Names
With rdoRes
 For Each cl In .rdoColumns
   Print cl.Name;
 Next cl
 .MoveNext
End With
```

```
Print

REM Print the values for each column and row
Do While NOT rdoRes.EOF
  With rdoRes
   For Each cl In .rdoColumns
     Print cl.Value
   Next cl
   .MoveNext
  End With
EndLoop
```

The SP_WHO procedure can be used to develop an application that monitors server connections, to determine who is logged in and what they are doing at a specific time.

DETERMINING THE LIST OF RECOGNIZED SQL SERVER USERS

The SYSUSERS table holds the names of the users that SQL Server recognizes. The UID field contains the numeric user ID. The NAME field contains the username. Listing 19-2 demonstrates how the SYSUSERS table can be queried.

Listing 19-2: Valid SQL Server Users

```
Dim en As rdoEnvironment
Dim cn As rdoConnection
Dim Result As rdoResultSet
Dim UsersStmt As Query
Dim rdoRes As rdoResultSet
Dim cl Ad rdoColumn

REM Create an Environment
Set en = rdoEngine.rdoEvironments(0)
With en
  en.CursorDriver = rdUseOdbc
  en.LoginTimeout = 5
  en.Name = "TestEnv"

  REM Establish a connection
  Set cn = en.OpenConnection("", rdDriverPrompt, True,

"DSN=MyDataSource;UID=Marie;PWD=Pooh;Database=Customers")

End With
```

```
REM Query the SYSUSERS table
Set UsersStmt = cn.CreateQuery("UsersStmt", "SELECT UID, NAME FROM
SYSUSERS")

REM Open the result set
Set rdoRes = Users.OpenResultset(rdOpenKeyset, rdConcurReadOnly,
rdExecDirect)

REM Print the values for each column and row
Do While NOT rdoRes.EOF
   Print rdoRes!UID, rdoRes!Name
   rdoRes.MoveNext
EndLoop
```

CREATING A NEW USER

The SP_ADDUSER stored procedure is used to add new users to SQL Server. This procedure takes three parameters: the username, the username in the database, and the group in which the user will be a member. Generally, the name in the database and the username are the same. Listing 19-3 demonstrates how the SP_ADDUSER procedure can be called to add a new user. In this example, the name in the database and the username are passed the same value.

Listing 19-3: Using the SP_ADDUSER Procedure to Add a New User

```
Dim en As rdoEnvironment
Dim cn As rdoConnection
Dim Result As rdoResultSet
Dim AddGrpStmt As Query
Dim rdoRes As rdoResultSet
Dim cl Ad rdoColumn

REM Create an Environment
Set en = rdoEngine.rdoEvironments(0)
With en
  en.CursorDriver = rdUseOdbc
  en.LoginTimeout = 5
  en.Name = "TestEnv"

  REM Establish a connection
  Set cn = en.OpenConnection("", rdDriverPrompt, True,

"DSN=MyDataSource;UID=Marie;PWD=Pooh;Database=Customers")

End With
```

```
REM Call the Stored Procedure
Set AddGrpStmt = cn.CreateQuery("AddGrpStmt", "{ ? = call
SP_ADDGROUP(?) }")

REM Access the parameters
AddGrpStmt.rdoParameters.Item(0).Direction = rdoParamReturnValue

AddGrpStmt.rdoParameters.Item(1).Direction = rdParamInput
AddGrpStmt.rdoParameters.Item(1).Value = "Admin"

AddGrpStmt.Execute

If (AddGrpStmt.rdoParameters.Item(0).Value = 0) Then
  Print "Group Added Successfully!"
Else
  Print "Group Not Added Successfully!"
End If
```

CREATING A GROUP

The SP_ADDGROUP stored procedure is used to add new SQL Server groups. This procedure takes a single parameter, which specifies the name of the group to add. After a group is created, it can be used when you specify database permissions. You can use a single command to grant permissions to all the members of a group, instead of setting permissions individually for each user. Listing 19-4 demonstrates how to create a new group by using the SP_ADDGROUP procedure.

Listing 19-4: Using the SP_ADDGROUP Procedure to Add a New Group

```
Dim en As rdoEnvironment
Dim cn As rdoConnection
Dim Result As rdoResultSet
Dim AddUserStmt As Query
Dim rdoRes As rdoResultSet
Dim cl Ad rdoColumn

REM Create an Environment
Set en = rdoEngine.rdoEvironments(0)
With en
  en.CursorDriver = rdUseOdbc
  en.LoginTimeout = 5
  en.Name = "TestEnv"

  REM Establish a connection
  Set cn = en.OpenConnection("", rdDriverPrompt, True,
```

```
                            "DSN=MyDataSource;UID=Marie;PWD=Pooh;Database=Customers")

End With

REM Call the Stored Procedure
Set AddUserStmt = cn.CreateQuery("AddUserStmt", "{ ? = call
SP_ADDUSER(?, ?, ?) }")

REM Access the parameters
AddUserStmt.rdoParameters.Item(0).Direction = rdParamReturnValue

REM User
AddUserStmt.rdoParameters.Item(1).Direction = rdParamInput
AddUserStmt.rdoParameters.Item(1).Value = "John"
AddUserStmt.rdoParameters.Item(2).Direction = rdParamInput
AddUserStmt.rdoParameters.Item(2).Value = "John"

REM Group
AddUserStmt.rdoParameters.Item(2).Direction = rdParamInput
AddUserStmt.rdoParameters.Item(2).Value = "Admin"

AddUserStmt.Execute

If (AddUserStmt.rdoParameters.Item(0).Value = 0) Then
  Print "User Added Successfully!"
Else
  Print "User Not Added Successfully!"
End If
```

ADDING A USER TO A GROUP

The SP_CHANGEGROUP stored procedure is used to add users to a group. This procedure takes two parameters: the first parameter specifies an existing group name and
the second parameter specifies an existing username. Listing 19-5 demonstrates
how the SP_CHANGEGROUP procedure is used to add a new group member.

SQL Server allows a user to be a member of only one custom group at a
time, due to the structuring of the SQL Server system tables. Every user is
always a member of the public group. Only the database owner (dbo) can
add users to a group. To change the group that a user is a member of, the
user has to be deleted from the group that they are currently in, before they
are added to a new group.

Listing 19-5: Using the SP_CHANGEGROUP Procedure to Add a User to a Group

```
Dim en As rdoEnvironment
Dim cn As rdoConnection
Dim Result As rdoResultSet
Dim ChangeGrpStmt As Query
Dim rdoRes As rdoResultSet
Dim cl Ad rdoColumn

REM Create an Environment
Set en = rdoEngine.rdoEvironments(0)
With en
  en.CursorDriver = rdUseOdbc
  en.LoginTimeout = 5
  en.Name = "TestEnv"

  REM Establish a connection
  Set cn = en.OpenConnection("", rdDriverPrompt, True,
"DSN=MyDataSource;UID=Marie;PWD=Pooh;Database=Customers")

End With

REM Call the Stored Procedure
Set ChangeGrpStmt = cn.CreateQuery("ChangeGrpStmt", "{ ? = call
SP_CHANGEGROUP(?, ?) }")

REM Access the parameters
ChangeGrpStmt.rdoParameters.Item(0).Direction = rdParamReturnValue

REM Group
ChangeGrpStmt.rdoParameters.Item(1).Direction = rdParamInput
ChangeGrpStmt.rdoParameters.Item(1).Value = "Admin"

REM User
ChangeGrpStmt.rdoParameters.Item(2).Direction = rdParamInput
ChangeGrpStmt.rdoParameters.Item(2).Value = "John"

REM Group
ChangeGrpStmt.rdoParameters.Item(2).Direction = rdParamInput
ChangeGrpStmt.rdoParameters.Item(2).Value = "Admin"

ChangeGrpStmt.Execute
```

```
If (ChangeGrpStmt.rdoParameters.Item(0).Value = 0) Then
  Print "User Added To Group Successfully!"
Else
  Print "User Not Added TO Group Successfully!"
End If
```

REMOVING A GROUP

The SP_DROPGROUP stored procedure is used to remove SQL Server groups. This procedure takes a single parameter: the name of the group to remove. Listing 19-6 demonstrates how the SP_DROPGROUP is used to remove a group.

 A group can be removed only if it does not contain any members!

Listing 19-6: Using the SP_DROPGROUP Procedure to Remove a Group

```
Dim en As rdoEnvironment
Dim cn As rdoConnection
Dim Result As rdoResultSet
Dim DropGrpStmt As Query
Dim rdoRes As rdoResultSet
Dim cl Ad rdoColumn

REM Create an Environment
Set en = rdoEngine.rdoEvironments(0)
With en
  en.CursorDriver = rdUseOdbc
  en.LoginTimeout = 5
  en.Name = "TestEnv"

  REM Establish a connection
  Set cn = en.OpenConnection("", rdDriverPrompt, True,
"DSN=MyDataSource;UID=Marie;PWD=Pooh;Database=Customers")

End With

REM Call the Stored Procedure
Set DropGrpStmt = cn.CreateQuery("DropGrpStmt", "{ ? = call
SP_DROPGROUP(?) }")

REM Access the parameters
DropGrpStmt.rdoParameters.Item(0).Direction = rdParamReturnValue
```

```
REM Group
DropGrpStmt.rdoParameters.Item(1).Direction = rdParamInput
DropGrpStmt.rdoParameters.Item(1).Value = "Admin"

DropGrpStmt.Execute

If (DropGrpStmt.rdoParameters.Item(0).Value = 0) Then
  Print "Group Removed Successfully!"
Else
  Print "Group Not Removed Successfully!"
End If
```

CHANGING PASSWORDS

The SP_PASSWORD stored procedure is provided to enable users to change their passwords. Listing 19-7 demonstrates how the SP_PASSWORD is used to change the current user's password.

Listing 19-7: Using the SP_PASSWORD Procedure to Change the Current User's Password

```
Dim en As rdoEnvironment
Dim cn As rdoConnection
Dim Result As rdoResultSet
Dim PassStmt As Query
Dim rdoRes As rdoResultSet
Dim cl Ad rdoColumn

REM Create an Environment
Set en = rdoEngine.rdoEvironments(0)
With en
  en.CursorDriver = rdUseOdbc
  en.LoginTimeout = 5
  en.Name = "TestEnv"

  REM Establish a connection
  Set cn = en.OpenConnection("", rdDriverPrompt, True,
"DSN=MyDataSource;UID=Marie;PWD=Pooh;Database=Customers")

End With

REM Call the Stored Procedure
Set PassStmt = cn.CreateQuery("PassStmt", "{ ? = call
SP_PASSWORD(?, ?) }")
```

```
REM Access the parameters
PassStmt.rdoParameters.Item(0).Direction = rdoParamReturnValue

REM User
PassStmt.rdoParameters.Item(1).Direction = rdParamInput
PassStmt.rdoParameters.Item(1).Value = "Marie"

REM Password
PassStmt.rdoParameters.Item(1).Direction = rdParamInput
PassStmt.rdoParameters.Item(1).Value = "Tigger"

PassStmt.Execute

If (PassStmt.rdoParameters.Item(0).Value = 0) Then
  Print "Password Changed Successfully!"
Else
  Print "Password Not Changed Successfully!"
End If
```

GRANTING PERMISSIONS

After you set up the appropriate users and groups with SQL Server, your next step is to assign the appropriate permissions to database objects. The GRANT statement, which has the following syntax, is used to assign permissions to database objects:

```
GRANT { ALL [privileges] | permission_list }
   ON { table_name [ ( column_list, . . . ) ] |
        view_name [ ( column_list, . . .) ] |
        stored_procedure_name }
   TO { group_name | user_name, . . . } [ options ]
```

The permission list can include SELECT, UPDATE, INSERT, DELETE, REFERENCES, and EXECUTE. The SELECT, UPDATE, INSERT, and DELETE permissions are fairly straightforward. The REFERENCES permission applies to SQL Server 6.0 and later, and to the ability to utilize declarative referential integrity. You can specify individual fields for tables and views. With the GRANT statement, you can specify that these permissions are applied to a number of users or groups simultaneously. When permissions are granted or revoked, these changes are reflected in the SYSPROTECTS system table.

You can change database permissions dynamically from your application by using RDO. Listing 19-8 demonstrates how to create a prepared statement that grants to the user or group passed as the second parameter all privileges for the table that is passed as the first parameter. All fields of the table passed in the first parameter are included.

Listing 19-8: Creating a Prepared Statement Using RDO to Grant All Permissions on a Table

```
Dim en As rdoEnvironment
Dim cn As rdoConnection
Dim Result As rdoResultSet
Dim GrantStmt As Query
Dim rdoRes As rdoResultSet
Dim cl Ad rdoColumn

REM Create an Environment
Set en = rdoEngine.rdoEvironments(0)
With en
  en.CursorDriver = rdUseOdbc
  en.LoginTimeout = 5
  en.Name = "TestEnv"

  REM Establish a connection
  Set cn = en.OpenConnection("", rdDriverPrompt, True,
"DSN=MyDataSource;UID=Marie;PWD=Pooh;Database=Customers")

End With

REM Call the Grant Command
Set GrantStmt = cn.CreateQuery("GrantStmt", "GRANT ALL ON ? TO ?")

REM Table
GrantStmt.rdoParameters.Item(0).Direction = rdParamInput
GrantStmt.rdoParameters.Item(0).Value = "Products"

REM User
GrantStmt.rdoParameters.Item(1).Direction = rdParamInput
GrantStmt.rdoParameters.Item(1).Value = "Marie"

GrantStmt.Execute
```

REVOKING PERMISSIONS

Finally, the REVOKE statement, which has the following syntax, can be used to remove permissions that have previously been granted:

```
REVOKE { GRANT OPTION FOR }
      { ALL [privileges] | permission_list }
    ON { table_name [ ( column_list, . . . ) ] |
        view_name [ ( column_list, . . .) ] |
        stored_procedure_name }
    TO { group_name | user_name, . . . } [ options ]
```

By using the REVOKE statement, you can revoke privileges to a database object. By using the GRANT OPTION, you can prevent a user from granting privileges to a database object. For example, if you want to prevent user John from granting SELECT privileges on the Products table, you would use the following command:

```
REVOKE GRANT OPTION FOR SELECT ON PRODUCTS TO JOHN
```

Listing 19-9 demonstrates how to create a prepared statement, using RDO, that can revoke all privileges to the user or group passed as the second parameter for the table that is passed as the first parameter.

Listing 19-9: Creating a Prepared Statement Using RDO to Revoke All Permissions on a Table

```
Dim en As rdoEnvironment
Dim cn As rdoConnection
Dim Result As rdoResultSet
Dim RevokeStmt As Query
Dim rdoRes As rdoResultSet
Dim cl Ad rdoColumn

REM Create an Environment
Set en = rdoEngine.rdoEvironments(0)
With en
  en.CursorDriver = rdUseOdbc
  en.LoginTimeout = 5
  en.Name = "TestEnv"

  REM Establish a connection
  Set cn = en.OpenConnection("", rdDriverPrompt, True,
"DSN=MyDataSource;UID=Marie;PWD=Pooh;Database=Customers")

End With

REM Call the Revoke Command
Set RevokeStmt = cn.CreateQuery("RevokeStmt", "REVOKE ALL ON ? TO
?")

REM Table
RevokeStmt.rdoParameters.Item(0).Direction = rdParamInput
RevokeStmt.rdoParameters.Item(0).Value = "Products"

REM User
RevokeStmt.rdoParameters.Item(1).Direction = rdParamInput
RevokeStmt.rdoParameters.Item(1).Value = "Marie"

RevokeStmt.Execute
```

The GRANT and REVOKE commands are very powerful, and, as you have seen in the two previous examples, they can be used to dynamically modify database permissions by using RDO's rdoPreparedStatement object. In conjunction with the SQL Server stored procedures, you can create applications that dynamically monitor and modify the security parameters of your SQL Server environment.

Summary

In this chapter, you learned how the RDO connection string is used to establish a security context. The network protocol affects how security issues are handled with RDO. If domain-managed security is in effect, the connection string does not require the username and password parameters. You learned about the general levels of database permissions provided by most database servers (Server, Database, and Table), and how the choice of SQL Server network protocols can affect the security of your RDO application. This chapter reviewed how SQL Server stored procedures can be used to do the following: determine who is currently connected; produce a list of valid SQL Server users; create a new user; create a new group; add a user to a group; remove a group; and change the current user's password. Finally, this chapter explained how to use the GRANT and REVOKE commands in conjunction with SQL Server to create security contexts for database server objects.

Part V

ActiveX Data Objects API

Chapter 20

Introduction to the ActiveX Data Object

IN THIS CHAPTER

- ◆ Introducing the COM and DCOM architectures
- ◆ Overviewing ActiveX
- ◆ Reviewing ADO and its objects
- ◆ Comparing ADO to DAO and RDO
- ◆ Redistributing the ADO components
- ◆ Converting applications from RDO to ADO
- ◆ Getting the latest ADO information on the Web

THIS CHAPTER OVERVIEWS the ActiveX Data Object (ADO), including a discussion of the technologies ADO is built upon — ActiveX, COM, and DCOM. The main objects that comprise ADO are reviewed, and ADO is compared with DAO and RDO application development. ADO can be used from Visual Basic, Visual Basic Scripting Language (VBScript), Active Server Pages, Visual C++, and Visual J++.

Outlining COM and DCOM

Microsoft has been working on developing the Distributed Component Object Model (DCOM), its component-based model of application development, for quite some time. First came Object Linking and Embedding (OLE), which facilitated inter-application communication by enabling application objects to be embedded in other applications. For example, a spreadsheet object could be placed into a word processing document, and a user could edit that object in place. Next, Visual Basic Controls (VBX) were introduced with Visual Basic. VBXs enabled custom Windows controls to be embedded into Visual Basic applications. These controls could be Windows interface elements, such as list boxes and buttons, or specialized processing routines, such as specialized parsing and sorting routines.

OLE and VBX were Microsoft's first steps toward developing object-oriented application components. OLE and VBX were later merged into OCX (OLE-based custom controls), and after OCX, the technology evolved into what is now ActiveX. The key difference between ActiveX and OCX controls is that ActiveX was designed to be cross-platform. Microsoft has ported ActiveX to the Macintosh environment, and Sun has licensed ActiveX for the purpose of porting it to Sun's architecture.

The Component Object Model (COM) is a specification for developing application components that can dynamically exchange data and that can be interchanged to support new functionality. COM employs object-oriented programming techniques to build encapsulated application components. These components provide an interface to an object. This interface is used to manipulate the object's state, and can be determined dynamically at runtime. The COM architecture makes the development process an independent task by enabling components to work together, even if they have been developed with different programming languages or by different people. COM also provides the capability for components to work together in a distributed environment.

 If you're interested in more-detailed information regarding the COM interface, the complete COM specification can be found on the Internet at `http://www.microsoft.com/com`.

COM enables developers to create application components that can be pieced together to form new applications. These components can be developed independently, in different programming languages, and can be easily assembled later to form a new application or a portion of an application. This componentization of application development can help to speed and simplify the development process. COM components can be used to facilitate the process of interapplication communication. Unlike other models, the COM architecture is used to develop a methodology for applications to communicate with one another. After this communication is established, applications can communicate directly with each other, and the COM architecture doesn't impose any overhead.

Key aspects of the Component Object Model include these:

◆ A strict set of rules that a component must follow, unlike earlier Windows-based component models, which provided functional repositories and communications methodologies, such as DDE (Dynamic Data Exchange) and DLLs. COM isn't a way to develop an application; instead, it is a technology that enables a developer to build robust components that can evolve over time, which is made possible by the strict rules that define application components. COM components can be upgraded and evolve without requiring the applications in which they are utilized to be upgraded.

♦ Naturally independent components. COM components can be developed with different programming languages, without requiring any specialized interface to bridge interapplication communications. This makes all COM components naturally compatible.

♦ Truly object-oriented components. COM components define an encapsulated object that presents a fixed set of interfaces, hiding the implementation details from users of the components.

♦ Mechanisms for encapsulating the life cycle of an object, via reference counting.

♦ Globally Unique Identifiers (GUIDs), which are used to identify a COM object uniquely. COM employs 128-bit identifiers, which ensure the uniqueness of each object.

♦ Inherent security. Basic operating system privileges are employed to ensure that a user has the rights to execute a component.

♦ Support for a distributed model, enabling components to be utilized in a networked environment. Components can be accessed and executed on remote systems.

Mastering ActiveX

This section explains ActiveX and how the ActiveX Data Object (ADO) API fits into server-side database programming. ActiveX actually is a set of technologies that is an extension of OLE and COM. COM provides the low-level object access infrastructure for OLE and ActiveX objects. ActiveX components are very much like OLE components, but ActiveX components are designed to be smaller and faster than OLE components, and are specifically designed to be embedded in Web pages. ActiveX components also are specifically designed for secure dynamic distribution over the Internet.

Currently, ActiveX components are supported on all Windows platforms, on Macintosh, and have recently been ported to UNIX. Microsoft is currently working on making ActiveX an open standard, administered by an independent standards body. Whether that effort will be successful, or how it will change the ActiveX standard, is unclear. ActiveX controls currently are directly supported only under the Internet Explorer Web browsers. However, plug-ins are available that enable ActiveX controls to be used from Netscape Navigator, such as ActiveScript by NCompass Labs, at http://www.ncompasslabs.com.

ActiveX actually is an umbrella term for several different technologies, which include the following:

◆ **ActiveX controls:** These controls are similar to their VBX/OCX counterparts, which can be embedded into HTML documents. ActiveX controls can be used to create Web sites that are more user-friendly and interactive.

◆ **ActiveX documents:** Enable non-HTML documents to be viewed from within a Web browser.

◆ **ActiveX scripting:** Enables the utilization of VBScript and JavaScript ActiveX controls and components to be controlled from within an HTML document.

◆ **ActiveX/COM components:** Include DAO and RDO, and other types of DLL-type components that can be developed in a large array of traditional programming languages.

◆ **ActiveX Server:** Includes various Internet Information Server (IIS) integrated functions, such as Active Server Pages.

Understanding ADO Components

ActiveX Data Objects (ADO) is another API that is used to develop applications that can access OLE DB data providers. ADO is supported in several different programming languages, including Visual C++, VBScript, Visual J++, and Visual Basic, and in Active Server Pages. While directly using the OLE DB provides a very low-level approach to accessing OLE DB providers, ADO provides a higher-level and easier-to-understand mechanism. If you are familiar with the Data Access Objects (DAO) and Remote Data Objects (RDO) APIs for application development, ADO will seem very similar. ADO is a combination of the best aspects of DAO and RDO, and doesn't rely as heavily on the object hierarchy as do DAO and RDO. This means that creating and manipulating ADO objects is much easier, because they can be created and managed directly. ADO is specifically designed for client/server application development, and because ADO can be used from VBScript, it is also well-suited for server-side Web/database integration. Figure 20-1 demonstrates the typical ADO application configuration.

ADO's Key Features

The key features of ADO include support for the following:

◆ Batch updating, in which a number of record updates are cached and transmitted simultaneously.

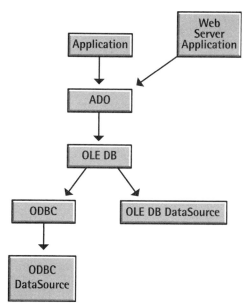

Figure 20-1: Viewing the typical ADO object application configuration

- ♦ All types of cursors, including forward-only, keyset, dynamic, and static.

- ♦ Server-side stored procedures, which can greatly improve application proficiency.

- ♦ Queries that return multiple record sets.

- ♦ Query goals, including limits on the number of records returned, active filtering of the records returned, and prepared statements.

While ADO supports all of these features, they still require use of the OLE DB provider. Using the OLE DB ODBC provider, ADO can be used to access existing ODBC data sources.

ADO Hierarchy

ADO consists of the following objects: Command, Connection, Error, Field, Parameter, and Recordset. Figure 20-2 shows the hierarchy of the ADO objects. The ADO objects don't function in a strict hierarchy like the DAO and RDO objects, which makes ADO much easier to use, because all the ADO objects, except for the Error and Field objects, can be created independently. The Command, Error, and Parameter objects are optional.

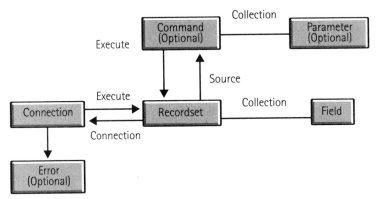

Figure 20-2: Viewing the ADO object hierarchy

CONNECTION OBJECT

The Connection object encapsulates a connection to a data source and allows commands to be executed by using the Execute() method. The Execute() command returns a Recordset object. The Connection object is used to configure a connection, define the isolation level, execute and control the execution of commands, manage transactions, and manage connection errors.

COMMAND OBJECT

The Command object encapsulates a command that can be interpreted by the data source. Command objects can be created independently of a Connection object and can be used for the following:

◆ To create Recordset objects by using data-manipulation commands, perform batch updates, and modify the data source schema by using data-definition commands.

◆ To open a connection to a data source, specify a command, execute stored procedures, and create prepared statements.

◆ To create parameterized commands, in conjunction with the Parameters object. The application can add parameters to the parameters collection, without requiring the data provider to fill the parameter collection beforehand.

The Command object is optional; it is supported only by OLE DB providers that support the command interface.

ERROR OBJECT

The `Error` object encapsulates errors returned from the data source. It is used to retrieve an error description, error number, the object that created the error, a Help file reference, and the current SQL state, if applicable. The `Error` object can support multiple errors. Before each ADO method is called, the `Error` collection is automatically cleared.

FIELD OBJECT

The `Field` object is used to encapsulate a column of a `Recordset`. A `Recordset` is comprised of a collection of `Field` objects. The `Field` object can be used to access the name of a column, the value of a column, and the type, precision, scale, and size of a column. The `Field` object can also be used to change the value of a field and access Binary Large Object (BLOB) fields. The `Field` object can be accessed only from a `Recordset` object. Depending on the OLE DB data provider, the `Field` object's capability may be limited.

PARAMETER OBJECT

The `Parameter` object encapsulates a command parameter, which can be an input, output, or input/output type. The `Parameter` object can be used to specify the name, value, attribute, direction, precision, scale, size, and type of a parameter. A `Parameter` object can also represent BLOB-type parameters. Parameters can be used with parameterized queries and stored procedures.

RECORDSET OBJECT

The `Recordset` object, which is the heart of ADO, can be created independently and can be used to access column-level data, specify a cursor, navigate a collection of records, update records in a batch mode, add and delete new records, and apply filters to records returned. The `Recordset` object can also be used to establish a direct connection with a data provider. The `Recordset` object encapsulates a collection of `Field` objects, which can be used to access column-level data.

Comparing ADO to DAO

ADO is very similar to the DAO library. As shown in the DAO object hierarchy in Figure 20-3, ADO and DAO share many similar objects. Unlike DAO, many of the ADO objects can be created directly, without requiring adherence to the strict object hierarchy. The methods provided by the ADO objects are very similar to their DAO counterparts.

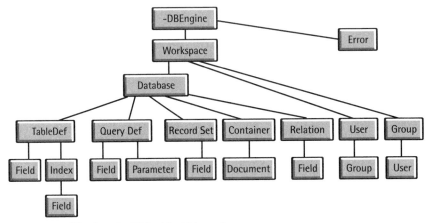

Figure 20-3: Viewing the DAO object hierarchy

Although DAO permits access to ODBC data sources, it is optimized for access to Access/Jet database sources. Because ADO utilizes OLE DB providers, it is geared more toward heterogeneous data access. ADO has built on some of the key features of DAO and has added additional support for batch updating, independent object creation, and multithreaded support. If you are familiar with the DAO model, transition to the ADO interface should be fairly easy.

Comparing ADO to RDO

The similarities that exist between ADO and DAO are also apparent between ADO and RDO, but the relationship between ADO and RDO is even stronger. ADO and RDO both are optimized to access server-side data sources. As the RDO object hierarchy in Figure 20-4 displays, ADO and RDO share many similar object types.

Again, unlike RDO, ADO doesn't function in the same strict object hierarchy They both have the ability to access server-side stored procedures and parameterized queries, and both support multiple result sets and server-side cursors. If you are familiar with the RDO model, the transition to ADO should be fairly easy.

Including ADO in Your Applications

Before you can begin to use ADO in your Visual Basic applications, you must make sure that your Visual Basic project includes the ADO Library. To add the ADO Library to your application:

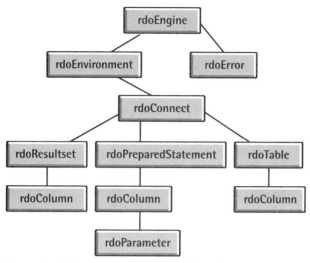

Figure 20-4: Viewing the RDO object hierarchy

1. Open your Visual Basic project.

2. Select Project → References, to display the References dialog box, shown in Figure 20-5.

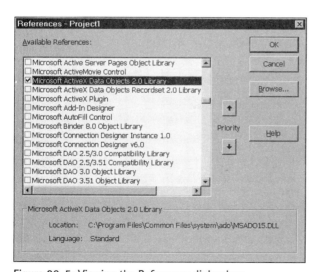

Figure 20-5: Viewing the References dialog box

3. The latest version of the ADO Library is 2.0. Select Microsoft ActiveX Data Objects 2.0 Library from the Available References list by clicking the checkbox next to its name.

4. Click the OK button to make the ADO Library available to your application.

Using Redistributable Components

To install the OLE DB and ADO components on a client, copy the following files to the `Program Files\Common Files\System\OLE DB` directory, as specified.

To provide data provider conversions:

◆ MSDAER.DLL*

◆ MSDAERR.DLL

To provide enumeration capabilities:

◆ MSDAENUM.DLL

◆ MSDATT.DLL*

◆ MSDATL.DLL

To provide OLE DB-provided conversions:

◆ MSDADC.DLL*

To support ADO:

◆ MSADO15.DLL*

◆ MSADER15.DLL*

To use the OLE DB ODBC Provider:

◆ MSDASQL.DLL*

◆ MSDASQLR.DLL

◆ MSDADC.DLL*

◆ MSDAER.DLL*

◆ MSDAERR.DLL

◆ MSDATL.DLL

◆ MSDATT.DLL*

The preceding file names that are marked with an asterisk must be registered on the client by using `RegSvr32`, which adds the appropriate entries for that component to the Registry. The `RegSvr32` application is found in the `SYSTEM` directory. Its command syntax is `RegSvr32 component_name`; for example, `RegSvr32 MSDAER.DLL`.

Converting from RDO to ADO

ADO isn't completely code-compatible with existing DAO and RDO data access applications. ADO encapsulates the functionality of DAO and RDO; however, you must convert many of the language elements to ADO syntax. In some cases, this requires only a simple conversion of some functions of your existing code. In other cases, your best option may be to rewrite the whole application by using ADO's new features.

Much of the functionality contained in the DAO and RDO models was consolidated into single objects, resulting in a much simpler object model. Because of this consolidation, you might initially experience difficulty finding the appropriate ADO object, collection, property, method, or event. Unlike DAO and RDO, ADO objects can also be created as standalone objects, even though they are hierarchical. The primary ADO objects can be related back to DAO and RDO equivalents, as follows:

◆ `Command` object: Contains information about a command, such as a query string, parameter definition, and so forth. The `Command` object is similar in functionality to RDO's `rdoQuery` object.

◆ `Connection` object: Contains information about a data provider. The `Connection` object is similar in functionality to RDO's `rdoConnection` object, and it contains the information on schema. It also contains some of the functionality of the `RDOEnvironment` object, such as transaction control.

◆ `Error` object: Contains extended information when an error occurs with a data provider. The `Error` object is similar in functionality to RDO's `rdoError` object. In comparison to RDO, however, the `Errors` collection is on the `Connection` object, whereas the `rdoErrors` collection is on the `rdoEngine` object.

◆ `Field` object: Contains information about a single column of data in a `Recordset`. The `Field` object is similar in functionality to RDO's `rdoColumn` object.

◆ `Parameter` object: Contains a single parameter for a parameterized `Command` object. The `Command` object has a `Parameters` collection to contain all of its `Parameter` objects. The `Parameter` object is similar in functionality to RDO's `rdoParameter` object.

◆ `Property` object: Contains a provider-defined characteristic of an ADO object. No RDO equivalent to this object exists, but DAO has a similar object.

◆ `Recordset` object: Contains records returned from a query, as well as a cursor into those records. The `Recordset` object is similar in functionality to RDO's `rdoResultset` object. You can open a `Recordset` (for example, perform a query) without explicitly opening a `Connection` object. If, however, you choose to create a `Connection` object, you can open multiple `Recordset` objects on the same connection.

ADO currently doesn't support all of DAO's functionality. ADO mostly includes RDO-style functionality to interact with OLE DB data sources. In general, migrating most DAO applications (except ones using ODBCDirect) to ADO right now is premature, because ADO doesn't support data definition language (DDL), users, and groups. However, if you use only DAO for client/server applications and don't rely on the Jet Database Engine or use DDL, then you can probably migrate to ADO now. Eventually, Microsoft will provide an ADO DDL component to aid DAO-to-ADO migration, and generic DDL support for OLE DB providers.

Using ADO/(Remote Data Services) RDS Internet Resources

Microsoft provides a few Web sites that you can utilize to stay informed regarding the latest developments of ADO and related technologies, including:

◆ `http://www.microsoft.com/rds`: Microsoft Remote Data Service (RDS)

◆ `http://www.microsoft.com/data/ado`: ADO API Web site

◆ `http://www.microsoft.com/oledev`: OLE Development information Web site — including DCOM information

◆ `http://www.microsoft.com/oledev/olecom/title.htm`: COM information

The following Internet news groups may also be helpful:

- `microsoft.public.oledb`: General OLE DB information, including ADO information

- `microsoft.public.activex.*`: A series of news groups related to the discussion of ActiveX components

- `microsoft.public.adc`: General ActiveX Data Connector discussions

Summary

This chapter reviewed the ActiveX Data Objects (ADO) and discussed how ADO is built on the ActiveX and COM/DCOM technologies. ADO is an Application Programming Interface (API) that is used to access OLE DB data sources. You also reviewed how ADO compares to the Data Access Object (DAO) and Remote Data Object (RDO) APIs.

Chapter 21

ADO Connection and Recordset Objects

IN THIS CHAPTER

◆ Using the Connection object

◆ Understanding the Connection object's methods and properties

◆ Using the Recordset object

◆ Understanding the Recordset object's methods and properties

THIS CHAPTER BEGINS a detailed review of ADO objects by looking at the Connection and Recordset objects, along with their methods and properties. The Connection object is used to establish and maintain a connection to an OLE DB data source, to provide a context for transactions, and to permit access to the ADO Error object.

The Error object is discussed in more detail in Chapter 24.

The Recordset object is the heart of ADO. In this chapter, you learn how to use the Connection and Recordset objects to connect to your OLE DB data source, how to create a query by using the Recordset object, and how to navigate the resulting query record set.

Connection Object

The Connection object provides a context for a connection with a data source. As you may recall, ADO doesn't require objects to be created in a strict hierarchy.

You're not required to create a `Connection` object to access a data source. This section shows how the ADO `Recordset` and `Command` objects can create their own internal `Connection` objects. If you plan to open multiple record sets or execute multiple commands on the same data source, you are recommended to create a `Connection` object, first. You can then use the `Connection` object in conjunction with the `Recordset` and `Command` objects that you subsequently create.

Each ADO object provides several methods and properties. *Properties* are used to set special object attributes. *Methods* are used to perform some function with an object. As you review each ADO object, each of the methods and properties supported by that object is reviewed in detail. Applicable code abstracts are provided, too, to demonstrate how an attribute or method is used.

 This chapter reviews all the properties and methods supported by the ADO objects. It is *very important* to realize that, ultimately, the methods and properties supported by an ADO object are dependent on the current data source that is being used. An OLE DB data source isn't required to support the complete functionality supported by the OLE DB specification. For example, not all OLE DB data sources may support transactions.

 Chapter 24 reviews how ADO error handling is used to trap the use of methods and properties that are not supported by the current data source.

Connection Methods

The `Connection` object methods are used to manage transactions, execute commands, and open and close the connection. Table 21-1 lists and briefly describes these methods.

TABLE 21-1 CONNECTION OBJECT METHODS

Method	Description
BeginTrans()	Begins a new transaction with the data source.
Close()	Closes a data source connection. Any resources in use are also freed.
CommitTrans()	Saves any changes that were made to the data source since the current nesting level was started (not all data sources support nested transactions).
Execute()	Executes a query or command that is supported by the data source and returns a Recordset object.
Open()	Opens a data-source connection.
RollbackTrans()	Throws away any changes made to the data source since the current nesting level was started (not all data sources support nested transactions).

USING THE OPEN() AND CLOSE() METHODS

The Open() and Close() methods are used to establish and break connections with a data source. The Open() method's syntax is

```
connect.Open ConnectionString, Username, Password
```

where connect represents a previously created Connection object. The ConnectString, Username, and Password parameters are optional. If they aren't provided, the Connection object uses the ConnectionString property value to establish the connection. The ConnectString is a String-type value that provides the data source connection string items. The connect string parameters supported by ADO are listed in Table 21-2. These are the only connect string parameters recognized by ADO. Any other arguments are passed directly to the data provider. Each connect string parameter is separated by a semicolon.

TABLE 21-2 ADO CONNECT STRING PARAMETERS

Parameter	Description
Provider=	The name of the OLE DB data provider.
Data Source=	The name of the connection data source.
User=	The username to use when accessing the OLE DB data source. If this is an empty string, domain-managed security is employed.
Password=	The password to use when accessing the OLE DB data source. If this is an empty string, domain-managed security is employed.
File Name=	The name of a file that contains connection information. An example of such a file is a streamed OLE DB data source object.

The Close() method is used to break the connection with an OLE DB. If any pending transactions are open when a data source is closed, they are rolled back. The Close() method syntax is

connect.Close

where *connect* represents a previously created Connection object. The Close() method should be called to ensure that any open resources are released. Calling the Close() method does not free the Connection object — it can be used again to open another data source. Listing 21-1 demonstrates how the Open() and Close() methods of the Connection object are used from Visual Basic. The Open() method is called for the data source IDCDatabase and the user "john." In this example, the password is omitted.

Listing 21-1: Using the ADO Connection Object's Open() and Close() Methods

```
DIM conn As ADODB.Connection

REM Open the Connection object, omit the password
conn.Open "data source=IDCDatabase", "john"

REM Use the Connection object here...

REM Close the Connection...
conn.Close
```

CONNECTING TO ODBC/OLE DB DATA SOURCES

If the OLE DB ODBC data provider is used, ADO can be used to access ODBC data sources. You must configure the ODBC data source by using your ODBC Control Panel applet. Table 21-3 lists the connect string parameters that are recognized by the OLE DB ODBC data source.

TABLE 21-3 OLE DB ODBC CONNECT STRING PARAMETERS

Parameter	Description
DSN=	The name of the ODBC data source. This isn't used if a driver name is specified in the OpenConnection() method.
DRIVER=	The name of the database driver. This isn't required if the DSN is specified.
SERVER=	The network name of the ODBC data source server. You can specify the "(local)" name as the server name, to use the ODBC data source on the current server..
UID=	Specifies the username. If this is an empty string, domain-managed security is employed. In domain-managed security, your Windows NT username and password are passed to the data source. Domain-managed security is easier to manage, because usernames and passwords are kept in a centralized location.
PWD=	Specifies the password. If this is an empty string, domain-managed security is employed.
APP=	Specifies the name of the application; this is optional.
WSID=	Specifies the name of the workstation; this is optional.
DATABASE=	The name of the database server; this is optional.
LANGUAGE=	The language type to be used by the ODBC data source server; this is optional.

EXECUTE() METHOD

The Execute() method is used to perform a data-definition command (such as CREATE TABLE), data-manipulation command (such as SELECT), or a server-side stored procedure. If the data provider supports it, the data-definition and data-manipulation commands can be SQL statements.

Chapter 23 reviews server-side stored procedures and parameters in more detail.

Upon return, the Execute() method can create and return a Recordset object, when executing a query that returns a record set. The Execute() method can simply be called when executing a data definition command. The Execute() method uses the following syntax:

```
Set rs = connect.Execute(Command, NumRecords, Options)
connect.Execute Command, NumRecords, Options
```

The connect identifier is the name of a valid open Connection object. If a data manipulation command is executed, rs represents the identifier for the returned Recordset object. The Command parameter is a String that contains the actual data definition or data manipulation command. The NumRecords parameter is a Long that returns the number of records retrieved or affected. Finally, the Options parameter is used to define the command-type options. The Options parameter, a CommandTypeEnum-type, can be used to optimize query processing, only if the contents of the Command parameter are known before the Execute() method is called. The NumRecords and Options parameters are optional. Table 21-4 lists and describes the CommandTypeEnum-type option constants. Listing 21-2 demonstrates how to open a Connection object and then perform a query and a data definition command. The Recordset object is reviewed in more detail later in this chapter.

The examples presented assume that the data provider supports SQL commands. You need to consult with the specific data provider that you are utilizing to determine whether it supports commands and, if so, the specifics of the commands that it supports.

TABLE 21-4 COMMAND-TYPE OPTIONS CONSTANTS

Constant Name	Value	Description
adCmdText	1	The command is an actual query or data definition statement.
adCmdTable	2	The command is just a table name.

Constant Name	Value	Description
adCmdStoredProc	4	The command refers to a server-side stored procedure.
adCmdUnknown	8	The content of the command is unknown.

Listing 21-2: Using the ADO Connection Object Execute( ) Method

```
Dim conn As ADODB.Connection
Dim rs As ADODB.Recordset

REM Open the Connection object, omit the password
conn.Open "data source=IDCDatabase", "john"

REM Execute a query...NumRecs Contains the Number of Records
Retrieved
set rs = conn.Execute("SELECT * FROM CUSTOMER",
                      NumRecs, 1)

REM Execute a command...NumRecs Contains the Number of Records
Deleted
conn.Execute "DELETE FROM Customers WHERE City = 'San Diego'",
NumRecs, 1

REM Close the Connection and Recordset...
conn.Close
rs.Close
```

BEGINTRANS( ), COMMITTRANS( ), AND ROLLBACKTRANS( ) METHODS

The last three methods supported by the `Connection` object are used to manage transactions. The `BeginTrans()` method is used to start a transaction. After a transaction is started, all the changes made on the data source are buffered until either the `CommitTrans()` or `RollbackTrans()` method is called. If the `CommitTrans()` method is called, all the buffered changes are applied to the data source; if the `RollbackTrans()` method is called, the changes are discarded. If the data source supports nesting, transactions can be nested. If transactions are currently nested, the `RollbackTrans()` or `CommitTrans()` method affects only the current transaction level, as shown in Figure 21-1.

Nested Transactions

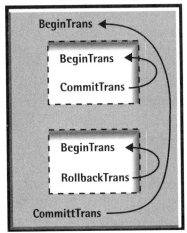

Figure 21-1: How nested transactions
function

The `CommitTrans()` or `RollbackTrans()` method affects only the operations
that occurred in the enclosing box. The `BeginTrans()`, `CommitTrans()`, and
`RollbackTrans()` methods use the following syntax:

```
TransLevel = connect.BeginTrans
connect.CommitTrans
connect.RollbackTrans
```

The *connect* identifier is the name of a valid open `Connection` object. The
`BeginTrans()` method returns an `Integer`-type value that indicates the current
transaction level. Calling either the `CommitTrans()` or `RollbackTrans()` method
causes an error to be generated if no open transaction is present. Listing 21-3
demonstrates how the transaction methods can be used.

Transactions can be used to increase application efficiency. Transactions are
buffered until they are either committed or discarded. You should realize
that in a client/server environment, the transactions are buffered on the
client side. When too many transactions are buffered, the client-side
resource requirements can increase greatly. As always, a tradeoff exists
between application efficiency and resource requirements.

Listing 21-3: Using the ADO Connection Object Transaction Methods

```
Dim conn As ADODB.Connection
Dim rs As ADODB.Recordset

NumRecs = 0
TransLevel = 0

REM Open the Connection object, omit the password
conn.Open "data source=IDCDatabase", "john"

REM Begin A Transaction
TransLevel = conn.BeginTrans

REM Execute a command...NumRecs Contains the Number of
REM Records Deleted
conn.Execute "DELETE FROM Customers WHERE City = 'San Diego'",
NumRecs, 1

REM Rollback the Transaction - The Delete is NOT
REM Applied!!
conn.RollbackTrans

REM Close the Connection...
conn.Close
```

Connection Properties

The Connection object supports numerous properties that can be used to manipulate the current state of the connection or retrieve some basic Connection object information. Some properties can be read only, while others can be read and written to. Table 21-5 lists the properties supported by the Connection object, each property's read/write status, and a property description.

TABLE 21-5 CONNECTION OBJECT PROPERTIES

Property	Read/Write	Description
Attributes	R/W	The Connection object attributes.
CommandTimeout	R/W	The number of seconds to wait for a command to execute; the default is 30 seconds.

Continued

TABLE 21-5 CONNECTION OBJECT PROPERTIES *(continued)*

Property	Read/Write	Description
ConnectionString	R/W	The string to use when connecting to a data source, when the ConnectString parameter is not passed to the Open( ) method.
ConnectionTimeout	R/W	The number of seconds to wait when establishing a connection to a data source; the default is 15 seconds.
DefaultDatabase	R/W	The default name of the database that is currently connected to, or the default name that is used in conjunction with the Open( ) method when a name is not specified.
IsolationLevel	R/W	How the Connection object handles transactions.
Mode	R/W	The sharing mode used when opening a new data source.
Provider	R/W	The name of the current data provider, or the name of the provider that is used in conjunction with the Open( ) method when a name is not specified.
Version	R	Returns the current ADO version number.

The use of the CommandTimeout, ConnectionString, ConnectionTimeout, DefaultDatabase, Provider, and Version properties are self-explanatory. The Attributes, Mode, and IsolationLevel properties require further explanation.

As with ADO methods, not all OLE DB data providers support all ADO object properties. You must consult your data provider to determine which ADO object properties it supports.

ATTRIBUTES PROPERTY

The `Attributes` property of the `Connection` object is used to determine how the `Connection` object handles transactions. The `Attributes` property is set to one of the `XactAttributeEnum` constant values. Table 21-6 lists and describes the `Connection` object's `Attributes` property value constants.

TABLE 21-6 CONNECTION OBJECT'S ATTRIBUTES PROPERTY VALUES CONSTANTS

Constant	Value	Description
adXactCommitRetaining	131072	After the `CommitTrans()` method is called, a new transaction is automatically started.
adXactAbortRetaining	262144	After the `RollbackTrans()` method is called, a new transaction is automatically started.

MODE PROPERTY

The `Mode` property determines the read, write, and sharing permissions that are used when opening the OLE DB data source. The `Mode` property is set to one of the `ConnectModeEnum` constant values. Table 21-7 lists and describes the `Connection` object's `Mode` property value constants.

TABLE 21-7 CONNECTION OBJECT'S MODE PROPERTY VALUES

Constant	Value	Description
adModeUnknown	0	The mode permissions haven't been specified.
adModeRead	1	The data source is opened only for read.
adModeWrite	2	The data source is opened only for write.
adModeReadWrite	3	The data source is opened for read and write.
adModeShareDenyRead	4	The data source is opened in a shared mode; other users are not allowed to open the data source for read.

Continued

TABLE 21-7 CONNECTION OBJECT'S MODE PROPERTY VALUES *(continued)*

Constant	Value	Description
adModeShareDenyWrite	8	The data source is opened in a shared mode; other users are not allowed to open the data source for write.
adModeShareExclusive	12	The data source is opened in a shared mode; other users are not allowed to open the data source for read and write.
adModeShareDenyNone	16	The data source is opened for exclusive use only.

The adModeRead, adModeWrite, and adModeReadWrite constants can be combined with the adShareDenyRead, adShareDenyWrite, adShareDenyExclusive, and adShareDenyNone constants by using the logical OR operation to specify the access and share modes.

ISOLATIONLEVEL PROPERTY

The IsolationLevel property determines whether record locking is applied for transactions. The IsolationLevel property is set to one of the IsolationLevelEnum constant values. Table 21-8 lists and describes the Connection object's IsolationLevel property value constants.

TABLE 21-8 THE CONNECTION OBJECT'S ISOLATIONLEVEL PROPERTY VALUES

Constant	Value	Description
adXactUnspecified	-1	The locking level has not been specified.
adXactChaos	16	If a change has been made in a higher-level transaction, it can't be overwritten in other transactions that employ a higher level of isolation.
adXactBrowse	256	Changes that haven't been committed to the data source can be viewed.

Constant	Value	Description
adXactReadUncommitted	256	Changes that haven't been committed to the data source can be viewed.
adXactCursorStability	4096	Only changes that have been committed can be viewed.
adXactReadCommitted	4096	Only changes that have been committed can be viewed.
adXactRepeatableRead	65536	Only changes that have been in the current transaction can be viewed.
adXactIsolated	1048576	Changes are made in complete isolation.
adXactSerializable	1048576	Changes are made in complete isolation.

Recordset Object

The Recordset object is used to encapsulate a set of data source records. A Recordset can be created as the result of a query, opening a table, or executing a stored procedure. The Recordset object represents a single record set at a time. The Recordset object can be used to open a data source directly, without the need for an associated Connection object. The Recordset object is the heart of ADO, because it allows direct access to a data source, creation of a set of data source records, and navigation of resulting record sets.

Recordset Methods

Table 21-9 lists and briefly describes the methods supported by the Recordset object. The Recordset object methods are used to add new records, manage batch updates, delete records, retrieve rows into an array, navigate the record set constants, update records, requery the data source, and resynchronize the current record set.

OPEN() AND CLOSE() METHODS

The Open() and Close() methods are used to open and close a Recordset specific connection. The syntax of the Recordset Open() and Close() methods is the following:

```
rs.Open RecordSource, Connection, Cursor, Lock, Options
rs.Close
```

TABLE 21-9 RECORDSET OBJECT METHODS

Method	Description
addNew()	Adds a new record to a record set.
CancelBatch()	Cancels a batch update, before the UpdateBatch is called.
CancelUpdate()	Cancels any changes made to a record, before the Update() method is called.
Clone()	Creates a new Recordset object that contains a copy of the current Recordset object.
Close()	Closes the current Recordset object connection.
Delete()	Deletes the current record.
GetRows()	Used to retrieve a number of rows from a record set into an array.
Move()	Used to move to a specific record.
MoveFirst()	Used to move to the first record of the record set.
MoveLast()	Used to move to the last record of the record set.
MoveNext()	Used to move to the next record of the record set.
MovePrevious()	Used to move to the previous record of the record set.
NextRecordset()	Retrieves the next record set of a query or stored procedure that returns multiple record sets.
Open()	Used to open a new Recordset object connection to a data source.
Requery()	Re-executes the current query.
Supports()	Determines whether a Recordset objects supports specific methods or properties.
Update()	Any changes to the current record are written back.
UpdateBatch()	Any changes to the current batch of records are written back.

The *rs* parameter is a valid `Recordset` object variable. The *RecordSource* parameter is a `Variant` type that specifies either a `Command` object, query command, table name, or stored procedure. The *Cursor* parameter is a `CursorTypeEnum`-type value that specifies the type of cursor used by the `Recordset` object. The *Lock* parameter is a `LockTypeEnum`-type value that specifies the type of locking used by the `Recordset` object. The *Options* parameter can be used to optimize query processing, if the content of the *RecordSource* parameter is known before the `Open()` method is called. All the `Open()` method parameters are optional. Listing 21-4 demonstrates how the `Recordset Open()` and `Close()` methods are utilized.

Listing 21-4: Using the Recordset Object's Open( ) and Close( ) Methods

```
DIM conn As String
DIM rs As ADODB.Recordset
DIM query As String


conn = "data source=IDCDatabase;user id=john;password=;"
query = "select * from customers"

REM Perform the Query
rs.Open query, conn

REM Use the Recordset Object Here...

REM Close the Recordset
rs.Close
```

ADDNEW( ) AND DELETE( ) METHODS

The `addNew()` and `Delete()` methods are used to add and delete records, respectively, from the current record set. The following is the syntax of the `addNew()` and `Delete()` methods:

```
rs.addNew Field, Value
rs.Delete AffectRecConstant
```

The *rs* parameter is a valid `Recordset` object variable. The *Field* parameter of the `addNew()` method is a Variant type that holds a single name or an array of field names or ordinal positions. The *Value* parameter of the `addNew()` method is a Variant type that holds a single value or an array of field values that have a one-to-one order correspondence to the *Field* array, which means that the first value of the *Field* array is assigned the first value in the *Value* array, and so on. The *Field* and *Value* parameters are optional. If they are omitted, the new record is provisionally added. Any field changes are buffered until the `Update()` or `UpdateBatch()` method is called.

The Delete() method takes a single optional parameter, AffectRecConstant, which is an AffectEnum-type value. This constant determines which records are actually deleted. Table 21-10 lists and describes the AffectEnum-type values. Listing 21-5 demonstrates how to use the addNew() and Delete() methods.

TABLE 21-10 AFFECTENUM TYPE CONSTANTS

Constant	Value	Description
adAffectCurrent	1	Only the current record is deleted. This is the default value.
adAffectGroup	2	All the records that match the currently applied filter are deleted.
adAffectAll	3	All the records in the Recordset are affected.

Listing 21-5: Using the addNew() and Delete() Methods

```
DIM conn As String
DIM rs As ADODB.Recordset
DIM query As String
DIM Fields(2) As String
DIM Values(2) As String

conn = "data source=IDCDatabase;user id=john;password=;"
query = "customers"

REM Perform the Query
rs.Open query, conn

REM Set the Field Names...
Fields(0) = "CUSTID"
Fields(1) = "CUSTNAME"

REM Set the Field Values
Values(0) = "99"
Values(1) = "Marie McCartan"

REM add a New Record
rs.addNew Fields, Values
```

```
REM Delete the Current Record
rs.Delete
```

```
REM Close the Recordset
rs.Close
```

CLONE( ) METHOD

The `Clone()` method is used to create a duplicate of the current `Recordset`. The following is the syntax of the `Clone()` method:

```
Set rscopy = rs.Clone
```

The `rs` parameter is a valid `Recordset` object variable. The `rscopy` variable will be a new `Recordset` object that is an exact copy of the current `rs` `Recordset`. When a `Recordset` clone is closed, its parent is *not* closed, and when a `Recordset` clone parent is closed, its clones are *not* closed. The `Clone()` method returns a new `Recordset` object that is an exact copy of the current `Recordset` object — it's not a reference to the parent `Recordset`.

 If the data provider doesn't support bookmarks for `Recordset` objects, the `Clone()` method is *not* supported. Consult your data provider to see whether it supports bookmarks. The `Bookmark()` method is reviewed later in this chapter.

GETROWS( ) METHOD

The `GetRows()` method is used to copy into an array a subset of records contained in the current record set. The resulting array may be two-dimensional: one dimension for each record retrieved and one dimension for each field. The `GetRows()` method just returns the data contained in the record set; it doesn't return any schema information. The syntax of the `GetRows()` method is the following:

```
Set RowArray = rs.GetRows(NumRows, StartRow, FieldArray)
```

The `rs` parameter is a valid `Recordset` object variable. The `RowArray` variable is the array that is created that contains the actual field data. The `NumRows` parameter is a Long type that determines the number of rows to retrieve. The `NumRows` parameter is optional; if it isn't specified, all rows are retrieved. By default, its value is -1. The `StartRow` parameter is a Variant type that is a *bookmark*, a reference value that points to a specific row in a record set. Bookmarks are reviewed in detail later in this chapter. The `StartRow` parameter is optional. The `FieldArray` parameter is a Variant type that holds a single name or an array of field names or ordinal positions. Only the fields named in the *FieldArray* are retrieved. The *FieldArray* parameter is optional; if it isn't specified, all fields are retrieved. Listing 21-6 demonstrates how to retrieve into an array all the records contained in the current record set.

Listing 21-6: Using the Recordset GetRows( ) Method

```
DIM conn As String
DIM rs As ADODB.Recordset
DIM query As String

conn = "data source=IDCDatabase;user id=john;password=;"
query = "select * from customers WHERE City = 'San Diego'"

REM Perform the Query
rs.Open query, conn

REM Retrieve Query Data Into The Customers Array
Set Customers = rs.GetRows

REM Close the Recordset
rs.Close
```

THE MOVE( ) METHODS

The Move( ) methods are used to navigate around a record set. When a record set is opened, you have a pointer to the current record. By default, when the record set is first opened, the pointer is positioned at the first record. The BOF and EOF properties are used to tell you whether the current record position is at the beginning or end, respectively, of the record set. They return True if the current record position is at or beyond the specified position. The following is the syntax of the Move methods:

```
rs.Move NumRecords, StartRow
rs.MoveFirst
rs.MoveLast
rs.MoveNext
rs.MovePrevious
```

The *rs* parameter is a valid Recordset object variable. The function of the MoveFirst( ), MoveLast( ), MoveNext( ), and MovePrevious( ) methods is self-evident. The Move( ) method has a little more depth. The *NumRecords* parameter determines how many positions to move from the current record position. If the value is positive, the current position is moved toward the end of the record set; if the value is negative, the current position is moved toward the beginning of the record set. The *StartRows* parameter specifies a bookmark starting value. If the Move() method is called with *NumRecords* of 0, with a *StartRows* bookmark value, the current record position moves to the bookmarked location. Listing 21-7 demonstrates how to use the Move() methods to loop through a data set.

Listing 21-7: Using the Recordset Move() Methods

```
DIM conn As String
DIM rs As ADODB.Recordset
DIM query As String

conn = "data source=IDCDatabase;user id=john;password=;"
query = "select * from customers WHERE City = 'San Diego'"

REM Perform the Query
rs.Open query, conn

REM Move To The First Record
rs.MoveFirst
REM Loop Through the Record Set Forwards
Do While (NOT rs.EOF)

    REM Do Something With Each Record

    REM Move to the Next Record…
    rs.MoveNext
Loop

REM Move To The First Record
rs.MoveFirst
REM Loop Through the Record Set Backwards
Do While (NOT rs.BOF)

    REM Do Something With Each Record

    REM Move to the Next Record…
    rs.MovePrevious
Loop

REM Close the Recordset And Connection
rs.Close
```

NEXTRECORDSET( ) METHOD

If your data provider supports multiple record sets, you can execute query or stored procedures that return multiple record sets. Even if your data provider supports multiple record sets, only one record set can be returned at a time. Multiple queries can be specified by separating them with a semicolon. The NextRecordset() method returns a new Recordset object containing the data of the next record set. The following is the syntax of the NextRecordset() method:

```
Set Nextrs = rs.NextRecordset(NumRows)
```

The rs parameter is a valid Recordset object variable. The Nextrs variable is assigned to a new Recordset object containing the data of the next record set. The NumRows parameter is a Long type that returns the number of rows contained in the next record set. The NumRows parameter is optional. Listing 21-8 demonstrates how to perform and access the results of a multiple record set query.

The NextRecordset() method can't be called if edits are pending on the current record set. Call the CancelUpdate() or Update() methods first.

Listing 21-8: Using the Recordset NextRecordset( ) Method

```
DIM conn As String
DIM rs As ADODB.Recordset
DIM query As String
DIM Prodrs As ADODB.Recordset

conn = "data source=IDCDatabase;user id=john;password=;"
query = "select * from customer;select * from products"

REM Perform the Query
rs.Open query, conn

REM Open the Product Query Recordset
Set Prodrs = rs.NextRecordset

REM Close the Recordsets
rs.Close
Prodrs.Close
```

REQUERY() METHOD

The `Requery()` method is used to refresh the contents of a record set, by re-executing the query or stored procedure that originally created the record set. The following is the syntax of the `Requery()` method:

```
rs.Requery
```

The *rs* parameter is a valid `Recordset` object variable.

 The `Requery()` method can't be called if edits are pending on the current record set. Call the `CancelUpdate()` or `Update()` methods first.

SUPPORTS() METHOD

The `Supports()` method is used to determine whether a `Recordset` object supports a specified functionality. The `Support()` method syntax is the following:

```
Set BoolVal = rs.Supports(Options)
```

The *rs* parameter is a valid `Recordset` object variable. *BoolVal* is a Boolean variable that returns `True` if the option is supported and `False` if it isn't. The *Options* parameter is a Long-type value that represents the option to check for support. The *Options* parameter is one of the `CursorOptionEnum`-type values. Table 21-11 lists and describes the `CursorOptionEnum`-type constants. Listing 21-9 demonstrates how to check whether a `Recordset` object supports the `addNew()` method.

 A query `Recordset` generally doesn't support the `addNew()` method. You must open the complete table to add new records.

TABLE 21-11 CURSORSOPTIONENUM TYPE CONSTANTS

Constant	Value	Description
adaddNew	16778240	Checks whether the `addNew()` method is supported.

Continued

TABLE 21-11 CURSORSOPTIONENUM TYPE CONSTANTS *(continued)*

Constant	Value	Description
adApproxPosition	16384	Checks whether the `AbsolutePosition` and `AbsolutePage` properties are supported
adBookmark	8192	Checks whether bookmarks are supported
adDelete	16779264	Checks whether the `Delete()` method is supported
adHoldRecords	256	Checks whether the other records can be retrieved while transactions are pending
adMovePrevious	512	Checks whether you can move backwards in the record set
adResync	131072	Checks whether the current record set can be updated with the most current data source data
adUpdate	16809984	Checks whether the `Update()` method is supported
adUpdateBatch	65536	Checks whether the `UpdateBatch()` method is supported

Listing 21-9: Using the Recordset Supports( ) Method

```
DIM conn As String
DIM rs As ADODB.Recordset
DIM query As String
conn = "data source=IDCDatabase;user id=john;password=;"
query = "customers"

REM Perform the Query
rs.Open query, conn

REM Check If addNew Method is Supported?
IF(rs.Supports(adaddNew)) THEN

   REM The addNew Method is Supported! add A New Record!

ENDIF
```

```
REM Close the Recordset and Connection
rs.Close
```

UPDATE( ), CANCELUPDATE( ), UPDATEBATCH( ) AND CANCELBATCH( ) METHODS

The Update( ) and UpdateBatch( ) methods are used to save any changes that were made to the current record or batch of records since the addNew( ) method was called. The CancelUpdate( ) and CancelBatch( ) methods are used to cancel any changes that were made to the current record or batch of records since the addNew( ) method was called. The following is the syntax of the Update( ), CancelUpdate( ), UpdateBatch( ), and CancelBatch( ) methods:

```
rs.Update Field, Value
rs.UpdateBatch AffectRecConstant
rs.CancelUpdate
rs.CancelBatch AffectRecConstant
```

The *rs* parameter is a valid Recordset object variable. The *Field* parameter of the Update( ) method is a Variant type that holds a single name or an array of field names or ordinal positions. The *Value* parameter of the Update( ) method is a Variant type that holds a single value or an array of field values that have a one-to-one order correspondence to the *Field* array, which means that the first value of the *Field* array is assigned the first value in the *Value* array, and so on. The *Field* and *Value* parameters are optional. The *AffectRecConstant* parameter of the UpdateBatch( ) and CancelBatch( ) methods is used to determine which records are actually updated, and if it contains one of the values found in Table 21-10. Listing 21-10 demonstrates how the Update( ) method is used to update the values of the current record.

If an update is pending, and you call one of the Move( ) methods to change the current record position, any pending update is automatically committed. Be sure to call the CancelUpdate( ) method to cancel any changes that you don't want applied, before moving the current record position.

Listing 21-10: Using the Recordset Update( ) Method

```
DIM conn As String
DIM rs As ADODB.Recordset
DIM query As String
DIM Fields(2) As String
```

```
DIM Values(2) As String

conn.Open "data source=IDCDatabase;user id=john;password=;"
query = "customers"

REM Perform the Query
rs.Open query, conn

REM Set the Field Names...
Fields(0) = "CUSTID"
Fields(1) = "CUSTNAME"

REM Set the Field Values
Values(0) = "99"
Values(1) = "Marie McCartan"

REM add a New Record
rs.Update Fields, Values

REM Close the Recordset
rs.Close
```

Recordset Properties

The Recordset object supports numerous properties that can be used to manipulate the record set page size, determine whether you're at the beginning or end of the Recordset, create bookmarks, determine the current edit mode, set filters, limit the number of records contained in the query, and determine other information about the current Recordset. Table 21-12 summarizes the Recordset properties. Some of the more important Recordset objects are reviewed in detail following Table 21-12.

TABLE 21-12 RECORDSET PROPERTIES

Property	Read/Write	Description
AbsolutePage	R/W	Used to set or determine the current record set page.
AbsolutePosition	R/W	Used to set or determine the current record position.

Property	Read/Write	Description
ActiveConnection	R/W	Used to set or determine the current Connection object.
BOF	R	Returns True if the current record position is at or before the beginning of the record set.
Bookmark	R/W	Used to set or return a bookmark to the current record.
CacheSize	R/W	Used to determine the number of records currently cached. When using forward-only-type cursors, this value is 1. With all other cursors, this value is 10.
CursorType	R/W	Used to set or determine the current cursor type.
EditMode	R	Used to determine the current edit mode.
EOF	R	Returns True if the current record position is after or at the end of the record set.
Filter	R/W	Used to specify a filter that is applied when navigating the record set.
LockType	R/W	Used to set or determine the current locking mode.
MaxRecords	R/W	Used to set or determine the maximum number of records returned by a query. By default, this value is 0, which indicates no limit.
PageCount	R	Used to determine the number of pages used by the record set.
PageSize	R/W	Used to set or determine the number of records.
RecordCount	R	Returns the number of records contained in the record set.
Source	R	Returns the source of the records contained in the record set.
Status	R	Returns the status of the current record.

BOOKMARK PROPERTY

Accessing the `Bookmark` property returns a Variant-type value that is an index to the current record. The bookmark value can be used with the `Move()` method to return quickly to the current record. If the `Recordset` is cloned, the bookmark value is valid across cloned `Recordset` objects. Listing 21-11 demonstrates how the `Bookmark` property is used in conjunction with the `Move()` method.

Listing 21-11: Using the Bookmark Property with the Move() Method

```
DIM conn As String
DIM rs As ADODB.Recordset
DIM query As String

conn = "data source=IDCDatabase;user id=john;password=;"
query = "select * from customers WHERE City = 'San Diego'"

REM Perform the Query
rs.Open query, conn

REM Move To The Fifth Record
rs.Move 5

REM Create A Bookmark
Set Bookmark = rs.Bookmark

REM Move To The First Record
rs.MoveFirst

REM Return To The Bookmarked Record
rs.Move 0, Bookmark

REM Close the Recordset
rs.Close
```

CURSORTYPE PROPERTY

The `CursorType` property determines the type of cursor to use when navigating the record set. The type of cursor determines how updates by other users are viewed, if at all. The following four types of `rdoResultset` cursors can be created, each of which is reviewed in depth during this chapter:

- ◆ **Forward-only:** This really isn't a cursor as such; the resulting data set can be accessed only in a forward manner.

- ◆ **Static:** A copy of the data that satisfies the query is retrieved.

◆ **Keyset:** The keys that are necessary to retrieve the data requested are retrieved. As each resulting row of the query is accessed, the current database's data is retrieved. After the query result set is created, any database deletions or updates that satisfy the original query aren't reflected in the resulting set.

◆ **Dynamic:** This is just like the Keyset cursor, except that the resulting data set always reflects the current state of the database.

Table 21-13 lists and describes the `CursorTypeEnum` constants.

Ways to optimize your ADO application are reviewed in Chapter 23. Selecting the cursor that has the exact functionality you require can greatly increase your application's performance. The forward-only-type cursor is the fastest type of cursor, and the dynamic-type cursor is the slowest.

TABLE 21-13 CURSORTYPEENUM CURSOR-TYPE CONSTANTS

Constant	Value	Description
adOpenForwardOnly	0	Specifies a forward-only-type cursor. You can move the record set only in a forward direction. Changes by other users are not visible.
adOpenKeyset	1	Specifies a keyset-type cursor. Records added by other users are not visible, but deletions and changes are visible.
adOpenDynamic	2	Specifies a dynamic-type cursor. All changes by other users are visible.
adOpenStatic	3	Specifies a static-type cursor. Changes by other users are not visible. The record set can be navigated forward and backwards.

EDITMODE PROPERTY

The `EditMode` property returns the current edit mode, which is one of the `EditModeEnum`-type values. Table 21-14 lists and describes the `EditModeEnum` constants.

TABLE 21-14 EDITMODEENUM CONSTANTS

Constant	Value	Description
adEditNone	0	No current edits exist.
adEditInProgress	1	The data contained in the current record has been changed.
adEditadd	2	An add operation is currently in progress.

FILTER PROPERTY

The `Filter` property is used to filter out records contained in the current record set. The `Filter` property contains a Variant-type value that can contain any one of the `FilterGroupEnum` constant values listed in Table 21-15, an array containing bookmarks, or a string containing a selection statement (equivalent to an SQL `SELECT` statement `WHERE` clause). Only the records that match the current filter are retrieved as the record set is navigated. Listing 21-12 demonstrates how a selection clause filter statement can be set and removed.

TABLE 21-15 FILTERGROUPENUM CONSTANTS

Constant	Value	Description
adFilterNone	0	Any filter currently in place is removed.
adFilterPendingRecords	1	Only records with changes pending are returned.
adFilterAffectedRecords	2	Only the records that were affected by the last call to the `Delete()`, `Resync()`, `UpdateBatch()`, or `CancelBatch()` methods are returned.
adFilterFetchedRecords	3	Only the most recently retrieved records are returned.

Listing 21-12: Using the Recordset Filter Property

```
DIM conn As String
DIM rs As ADODB.Recordset
DIM query As String

conn = "data source=IDCDatabase;user id=john;password=;"
query = "select * from customers"

REM Perform the Query
rs.Open query, conn

REM Set The Filter
rs.Filter = "City = 'San Diego'"

REM Loop Through the Record
REM Only The Filtered Records Will Be Viewed
Do While (NOT rs.EOF)
  REM Do Something With Each Record

  REM Move to the Next Record…
  rs.MoveNext
Loop

REM Remove The Filter
rs.Filter = adFilterNone

REM Close the Recordset
rs.Close
```

LOCKTYPE PROPERTY

The LockType property is used to specify the record-locking strategy that is employed by the Recordset object when navigating, adding, and modifying data. Four different locking types are used by ADO. Table 21-16 lists and describes the LockTypeEnum constant values.

PESSIMISTIC LOCKING   When the pessimistic-locking strategy is employed, a page becomes locked whenever a record is edited or the addNew() method is called. The page-level lock is released when the Cancel() or Update() method is called. Pessimistic locking ensures database integrity at the highest level. Whenever a user attempts to add or modify database records, the associated data pages become locked. Pessimistic locking, though, can cause pages to remain locked for long periods of time, preventing other users from accessing the same table data. The pessimistic-locking strategy is the default. The optimistic-locking strategy attempts to address these shortcomings.

TABLE 21-16 THE LOCKTYPEENUM CONSTANTS

Constant	Value	Description
adLockReadOnly	1	The current record set can only be read.
adLockPessimistic	2	Pessimistic record locking is employed.
adLockOptimistic	3	Optimistic record locking is employed.
adLockBatchOptimistic	4	Optimistic record locking is used for batch updates.

OPTIMISTIC LOCKING   When the optimistic-locking strategy is employed, a page becomes locked only when the Update() method is called. A change can be made to a record, or the addNew() method can be called, without creating a lock, so that a user can start making modifications without locking a page. After the Update() method is called, an attempt is made to lock the affected pages, and if it is allowed, the affected data is written to the locked pages. Optimistic locking can keep pages locked for the shortest period of time, which can be very important when many users are accessing the database. The biggest disadvantage of optimistic locking is that two users can begin to make modifications on the same record, and they don't find out that the record is locked or has been changed until they attempt to commit their changes. (When the Update() method is invoked and the affected pages are already locked, an exception is thrown.)

 If the data source that you are connected to is an ODBC database, only the optimistic-locking strategy is employed.

WHICH STRATEGY SHOULD I USE?   Inevitably, the question arises of which locking strategy to employ. Pessimistic locking can warn of a potential update conflict as soon as the operation to modify a record is invoked. Optimistic locking doesn't detect potential conflicts until an attempt is made to commit the changes.

Pessimistic locking can cause locks to be held for longer periods of time. For example, a user could begin the process of modifying a record and get distracted by something else, without completing the operation. When pessimistic locking is employed, that record remains locked until the user commits or cancels the changes. The optimistic-locking strategy attempts to minimize the amount of time that a record is locked. If more than one user begins to edit a record with optimistic locking, the first user to save their changes has them committed to the database. A user who makes many changes to a record, only to find that they can't be committed because someone else has already made a change to the same record, can become quite frustrated. Even with its disadvantages, the optimistic-locking strategy usually is the most efficient and effective page-level locking strategy.

SOURCE PROPERTY

The Source property is used to retrieve the source of the current record set. The Source property is a String-type value and can be either a query statement, table name, or stored procedure. The Source property is used when you attempt to determine the source of an error.

STATUS PROPERTY

Finally, the Recordset Status property is used to determine the status of the current record. The status is determined by logically ORing the RecordStatusEnum constant values in Table 21-17.

TABLE 21-17 THE RECORDSTATUSENUM CONSTANTS

Constant	Value	Description
adRecOK	0	This record was changed successfully.
adRecNew	1	This is a new record.
adRecModified	2	This record was changed.
adRecDeleted	4	This record was deleted.
adRecUnmodified	8	This record has not been modified.
adRecInvalid	16	This record has an invalid bookmark.
adRecMultipleChanges	64	This record was not saved, because the changes would have affected multiple records.
adRecPendingChanges	128	This record was not saved, due to a pending insert.
adRecCanceled	256	This record was not saved, because the Cancel() method was called.
adRecCantRelease	1024	A lock has prevented the record update.

Continued

TABLE 21-17 **THE RECORDSTATUSENUM CONSTANTS** *(continued)*

Constant	Value	Description
adRecConcurrencyViolation	2048	Optimistic locking has caused a record update to fail.
adRecIntegrityViolation	4096	Changes to the record were not saved, because integrity constraints were violated.
adRecMaxChangesExceeded	8192	Too many changes are pending to save the changes.
adRecObjectOpen	16384	An open storage object caused the record update to fail.
adRecOutOfMemory	32768	An out-of-memory error occurred wile attempting to update the record.
adRecPermissionDenied	65536	User permissions do not permit the record changes.
adRecSchemaViolation	131072	The record changes were not saved, due to a schema violation.
adRecDBDeleted	262144	The record was already deleted.

Summary

This chapter reviewed in detail how to access ADO. The detailed review of the ADO objects began with the Connection and Recordset objects. The Recordset object is the heart of ADO. You learned how to establish a connection with an OLE DB data source, create queries, and navigate the resulting record set. Finally, you reviewed the different types of Recordset objects that are provided by ADO. The next chapter continues your review of ADO with a discussion of the Command and Field objects. You will look in more detail at how to create record set queries and navigate the resulting record sets.

Chapter 22

ADO Command and Field Objects

IN THIS CHAPTER

◆ Using the Command object

◆ Using the Fields and Field objects to obtain database schema information

◆ Accessing Recordset fields

◆ Displaying Recordset schema information

IN THIS CHAPTER, you continue the review of ADO objects with the Command, Fields, and Field objects. The Command object is used to execute SQL queries, data definition commands, and stored procedures. The Fields collection object holds the collection of Fields that comprise a Recordset. The Field object is used primarily to access column-level Recordset data. The Field object can also be used to access Recordset metadata. This chapter presents a detailed review of how to use the Field object to access and convert data of different types, including Binary Large Objects (BLOB)-type information.

Command Object

The ADO Command object can be used to create and execute queries, data definition commands, and stored procedures for a data source. Typically, the Command object is used in conjunction with SQL commands, such as INSERT, DELETE, and CREATE. Data definition commands are used to create or modify tables or indexes, delete records, add records, and modify records. The Command object can also be used to execute server-side stored procedures, which are pieces of code that reside on the database server. Server-side stored procedures can increase application efficiency, because they are processed entirely on the server. In conjunction with the Parameter object, a Command object can be defined to accept parameters when it is executed. Chapter 23, *Parameter Object and Query Optimization*, reviews this in more detail. When you define a command or query, the data source receives the request, interprets it, and compiles it into something it can easily run. When you define a command, the `Command` object provides the option to keep around a compiled version for the duration of the connection. This precompiled version of the command is called a *prepared statement*.

If you expect to perform the same command or query more than once during a session, you can increase application performance greatly by saving it as a prepared statement. A data source can quickly execute a prepared statement, because it has already gone through the interpretation process.

Command Methods

Table 22-1 lists and briefly describes the methods provided by the `Command` object. You must associate a `Command` object with an open connection before a command can be performed. One way to do this is to assign the `Command` object's `ActiveConnection` property to an open `Connection` object.

TABLE 22-1 COMMAND OBJECT METHODS

Method	Description
CreateParameter()	Creates a new command `Parameter` object. Parameters can be used to specify a value that is passed to, or returned from, a command or stored procedure.
Execute()	Performs the specified command or stored procedure.

CREATEPARAMETER() METHOD

The `CreateParameter()` method is used to create a command parameter. A command parameter is used just like a parameter passed to a function. A parameter can be used to pass a value to a command, return a value from a command, or both; this is called the *parameters direction*. The following is the syntax of the `CreateParameter()` method:

```
Set param = cmd.CreateParameter(Name, Type, Direction, Size, Value)
```

The *cmd* parameter is a previously created Command object. The *param* parameter is the variable that the newly created Parameter object will be assigned. The *Name*, *Type*, *Direction*, *Size*, and *Value* parameters of the CreateParameter() method are used, respectively, to specify the name, data type, direction, size, and initial value of the Parameter object that is being created. The *Name* parameter is a String type. The *Type* parameter is an optional Long-type value that must be one of the DataTypeEnum constants shown in Table 22-2.

TABLE 22-2 DATATYPEENUM CONSTANTS

Constant	Value	Description
adBigInt	20	Signed integer (8 bytes).
adBinary	128	Binary value.
adBoolean	11	Boolean value.
adBSTR	8	Unicode character string that is null-terminated.
adChar	129	Null-terminated character string.
adCurrency	6	Currency value.
adDate	7	Date value.
adDBDate	133	Date value in the form *yyyymmdd*.
adDBTime	134	Time value in the form *hhmmss*.
adDBTimeStamp	135	Date-time value in the form *yyyymmddhhmmss*.
adDecimal	14	Fixed-precision floating-type value.
adDouble	5	Double-precision floating-point value.
adEmpty	0	Type has not been specified yet (default).
adError	10	Error-code type.
adGUID	72	Globally unique identifier (GUID)-type value.
adIDispatch	9	OLE IDispatch interface-type value.
adInteger	3	Signed integer (4 bytes).
adIUnknown	13	OLE IUnknown interface-type value.
adLongVarBinary	205	Long binary-type value. *Used only for Parameter objects.*

Continued

TABLE 22-2 DATATYPEENUM CONSTANTS *(continued)*

Constant	Value	Description
adLongVarChar	201	Long string-type value. *Used only for Parameter objects.*
adLongVarWChar	203	Long null-terminated character-string-type value. *Used only for Parameter objects.*
adNumeric	131	Exact numeric-type value with a fixed precision and scale.
adSingle	4	Single-precision floating-point-type value.
adSmallInt	2	Signed integer (2 bytes).
adTinyInt	16	Signed integer (1 byte).
adUnsignedBigInt	21	Unsigned integer (8 bytes).
adUnsignedInt	19	Unsigned integer (4 bytes).
adUnsignedSmallInt	18	Unsigned integer (2 bytes).
adUnsignedTinyInt	17	Unsigned integer (1 byte).
adUserDefined	132	User-defined type.
adVarBinary	204	Variable-length binary-type value. *Used only for Parameter objects.*
adVarChar	200	Variable-length character-string-type value. *Used only for Parameter objects.*
adVariant	12	OLE Variant-type value.
adVarWChar	202	Variable-length Unicode character string that is null-terminated. *Used only for Parameter objects.*
adWChar	130	Unicode character string that is null-terminated.

The *Direction* parameter is an optional Long-type value that must be one of the ParameterDirectionEnum constants shown in Table 22-3. The direction only needs to be specified if the data source cannot determine the direction itself. If you specify the direction, the data source won't have to determine the direction of the parameter, even if it can do so. The *Size* parameter is an optional Long-type value that specifies the size, in bytes, of the parameter. If the type of the parameter is variable-length, you must specify the size of the parameter. The *Value* is an optional Variant-type value that is used to set the initial value of the parameter. You may specify the type, direction, size, and value of the Parameter object after it has been created.

TABLE 22-3 PARAMETERDIRECTIONENUM CONSTANTS

Constant	Value	Description
adParamInput	1	Input-type parameter (default direction).
adParamOutput	2	Output-type parameter.
adParamInputOutput	3	Input-and-output-type parameter.
adParamReturnValue	4	Parameter is a return value.

Listing 22-1 demonstrates how to create a Command object, and a Parameter object by using the CreateParameter() method, from VBScript. The example creates an integer type, input/output parameter, named Param1. An initial value is not specified. Because an integer type has a fixed size, the size of the parameter is not required.

Listing 22-1: Creating a Parameter Object Using the CreateParameter() Method

```
DIM conn As ADODB.Connection
DIM cmd As ADODB.Command
Dim Param1 As ADODB.Parameter

REM Open the Connection object, omit the password
conn.Open "data source=IDCDatabase", "john"

REM One Way To Associate the Command with a Connection
cmd.ActiveConnection = conn

REM Create a Command Parameter
Set Param1 =
cmd.CreateParameter("Param1",adBigInt,adParamInputOutput)

REM Close the Connection...
conn.Close
```

EXECUTE() METHOD

The Execute() method can be used to perform a query – in which case, it returns a Recordset object containing the results – or it can be used to perform a data definition command or stored procedure. The Connection object also supports the Execute() method, but parameters can be used only with the Command object. The Execute() method has the following syntax:

```
Set rs = cmd.Execute(NumRecords, Params, Options)
cmd.Execute NumRecords, Params, Options
```

The *cmd* identifier is the name of a valid Command object that has been associated with a connection. If a data-manipulation command is executed, *rs* represents the identifier for the returned Recordset object. The *NumRecords* parameter is a Long that returns the number of records retrieved or affected. The *Options* parameter is used to define the command-type options. The *Params* parameter is a Variant array that is used to specify the initial parameter values. The *Params* array can't be used to return output parameter values. The *Options* parameter, a CommandTypeEnum -type, can be used to optimize query processing, if the contents of the *Command* parameter are known before the Execute() method is called. The *NumRecords*, *Params*, and *Options* parameters are optional. Table 22-4 lists and describes the CommandTypeEnum-type options constants. The CommandText is a String-type property that's used to specify the command to be performed. Listing 22-2 demonstrates how to create and execute a query and data definition command by using the Command object.

TABLE **22-4** COMMANDTYPEENUM OPTIONS CONSTANTS

Constant Name	Value	Description
adCmdText	1	The command is an actual query or data definition statement.
AdCmdTable	2	The command is just a table name.
adCmdStoredProc	4	The command refers to a server-side stored procedure.
adCmdUnknown	8	The content of the command is unknown.

Listing 22-2: Performing a Command Using the Execute() Method

```
DIM conn As ADODB.Connection
DIM cmd As ADODB.Command
DIM Param1 As ADODB.Parameter
DIM rs As ADODB.Recordset

REM Open the Connection object, omit the password
conn.Open "data source=IDCDatabase", "john"

REM One Way To Associate the Command with a Connection
cmd.ActiveConnection = conn

REM Execute a query...NumRecs Contains the Number of Records
Retrieved
cmd.CommandText = "SELECT * FROM CUSTOMER"
set rs = cmd.Execute(NumRecs)

REM Execute a command...NumRecs Contains the Number of
REM Records Deleted
cmd.CommandText =
  "DELETE FROM Customers WHERE City = 'San Diego'"
cmd.Execute NumRecs

REM Close the Connection...
rs.Close
conn.Close
```

Command Properties

The Command object supports several properties. These properties can be used to associate a connection with a Command, how long to wait for a command to execute, specify the actual command, the type of the command, and if the command should be saved as a prepared statement. Table 22-5 lists the properties supported by the Command object, the properties' read/write status, and a description of each property. You have already seen how the ActiveConnection property can be associated with an open Connection object, and how the CommandText property is used to specify the actual command.

TABLE 22-5 COMMAND OBJECT PROPERTIES

Property	Read/Write	Description
ActiveConnection	R/W	The connection associated with this command.
CommandText	R/W	The actual command text string.
CommandTimeout	R/W	The number of seconds to wait for the command to execute; the default is 30 seconds.
CommandType	R/W	The type of the command, as specified by one of the CommandTypeEnum constants in Table 22-4.
Prepared	R/W	A boolean value; if True, a prepared statement is created before the command is executed.

ACTIVECONNECTION PROPERTY

The ActiveConnection property is used to specify the connection associated with the Command object. Listing 22-1 assigned the ActiveConnection property to a Connection object. When accessing the ActiveConnection property, it returns a Connection object if the Command object has been associated with a connection. The ActiveConnection object can be assigned to a Connection object or a connect string. Connect strings and their parameters were reviewed in conjunction with the Connection object in Chapter 21, *Connection and Recordset Objects*. Listing 22-3 demonstrates opening a data source connection with a Command object by using a connect string. If the associated active Connection object is closed while the Command object is still active, you won't be able to execute a command. After a command connection is open, it can be used to create other Recordset and Command objects with the same connection, by using the ActiveConnection property.

 If a Command object connection is created by the Command object, it does not have to be closed explicitly. It is automatically closed when the Command object is released.

Listing 22-3: Using the ActiveConnection Property

```
DIM conn As ADODB.Connection
DIM cmd1 As ADODB.Command
DIM cmd2 As ADODB.Command
DIM rs As ADODB.Recordset

REM Use the Connect String to Create a New Connection
cmd1.ActiveConnection =
    "data source=IDCDatabase;user=john"

REM Execute a query...NumRecs Contains the Number of
REM Records Retrieved
cmd1.CommandText = "SELECT *FROM CUSTOMER"
set rs = cmd1.Execute(NumRecs)

REM Use the Same Connection for Cmd2
cmd2.ActiveConnection = cmd1.ActiveConnection

rs.Close
```

COMMANDTIMEOUT PROPERTY

The CommandTimeout property is used to specify the number of seconds to wait for a command while it's executing. By default, this property is set to 30 seconds. If the CommandTimeout property is 0, no limit is set on how long to wait while the command is executing. If the command takes longer than the amount of time specified, an error is generated. The Error object and error handling with ADO is discussed in more detail in Chapter 24, *ADO Error Handling*. Listing 22-4 demonstrates how to set the CommandTimeout property so that no limit exists on the time given to execute a command.

Not all data source providers support the CommandTimeout property. Be careful when giving a command an indefinite amount of time to execute. Without specifying a timeout period, you will not have a way to get control of the application while the command is executing. The CommandTimeout property should be set to a period that is reasonable to execute the command, depending on its complexity. If you can't determine the complexity of the command, 30 to 60 seconds usually is sufficient.

Listing 22-4: Using the CommandTimeout Property

```
DIM cmd As ADODB.Command
REM Use the Connect String to Create a New Connection
cmd.ActiveConnection =
  "data source=IDCDatabase;user=john"

REM Specify the CommandTimeout Period
cmd.CommandTimeout = 0
```

COMMANDTYPE PROPERTY

The CommandType property is used to specify the type of command that the Command object will execute. The CommandType property value must be one of the CommandTypeEnum constants shown in Table 22-4. The Command object uses this property to speed the interpretation of the command when it is executed. Listing 22-5 demonstrates how the CommandType property is used with different command types. By default, the command type is set to adCmdUnknown. Change this property only if you know the type of command that is being executed. If the CommandType property value doesn't match the command specified, an error will result.

Listing 22-5: Using the CommandType Property

```
DIM conn As ADODB.Connection
DIM cmd As ADODB.Command
DIM rs As ADODB.Recordset

REM Open the Connection object, omit the password
conn.Open "data source=IDCDatabase", "john"

REM Associate the Command with a Connection
cmd.ActiveConnection = conn

REM The Command Is Just a Table Name...All Table Records Are
Returned
cmd.CommandText = "CUSTOMER"
cmd.CommandType = adCmdTable
set rs = cmd.Execute(NumRecs)

REM Execute a command...NumRecs Contains the Number of Records
Deleted
cmd.CommandText =
  "DELETE FROM Customers WHERE City = 'San Diego'"
cmd.CommandType = adCmdText
cmd.Execute NumRecs
```

```
REM Close the Connection...
rs.Close
conn.Close
```

PREPARED PROPERTY

The `Prepared` property causes the data source to save a compiled version of the command. When the command is first executed, it may take a little longer. On subsequent executions, though, the command executes faster. Listing 22-6 demonstrates how to use the `Prepared` property. If the `Prepared` property is set to `True`, the compile version is saved. The prepared version of the command is kept only as long as the `Command` object is active. After the `Command` object is released, the prepared version of the command is also released.

Create a prepared version of a command only when you expect to execute a command more than once. After the prepared statement is generated, subsequent command executions will be faster.

Listing 22-6: Using the Prepared Property

```
DIM conn As ADODB.Connection
DIM cmd As ADODB.Command
DIM rs As ADODB.Recordset

REM Open the Connection object, omit the password
conn.Open "data source=IDCDatabase", "john"

REM Associate the Command with a Connection
cmd.ActiveConnection = conn

REM Specify the Query
cmd.CommandText = "SELECT * FROM CUSTOMER"
cmd.CommandType = adCmdText
cmd.Prepared = True
set rs = cmd.Execute(NumRecs)

REM Close the Connection...
rs.Close
conn.Close
```

Fields Collection Object

When a Recordset object is created, an associated Fields collection is also created. The Fields collection object holds a set of Field objects; one Field object for each column in the Recordset. Unlike the other ADO objects that you have reviewed so far, the Field object doesn't need to be created explicitly. It can be accessed from the Recordset object. The Fields object can be accessed through a column index or name.

A Recordset consists of a set of columns. The terms *field* and *column* are used interchangeably in this chapter.

Fields Refresh() Method

The Fields object provides a single method, Refresh(). The Refresh() method is used to update the Fields collection manually to reflect the current columns. You shouldn't need to use the Refresh() method with the Fields collection.

Fields Properties

The Fields object provides two properties. The Count property returns the number of Field objects contained in the collection. The Item property returns the Field object at the specified index. You don't need to use the Item method directly.

COUNT PROPERTY
The Count property simply returns the number of Field objects in the Fields collection, since the Fields collection can be accessed by a numeric index, and can be used to loop through the Fields collection. The previous listing, Listing 22-6, demonstrates how to use the Count property.

ITEM PROPERTY
The Item property can be used to access a Field object of the Fields collection. Listing 22-7 demonstrates how to access the fields contained in the Fields collection. As stated earlier, you don't need to use the Item property to access a Field contained in the Fields collection. You can access an item of the Fields collection in the following ways:

```
rs.Fields(index)
rs.Fields(name)
rs.Fields.Item(index)
```

```
rs.Fields.Item(name)
rs(index)
rs(name)
rs!name
```

rs is a valid `Recordset` object. The *index* parameter can be a numeric index. `Fields` collections are indexes from 0 to the `Count` property value − 1. When used as an index, the *name* parameter is a `String` that contains the name of the field.

Field Object

The `Field` object is used to access `Recordset` column-level data. Each `Field` object is stored in the `Recordset`'s `Fields` collection. The `Field` object is used to retrieve column schema information and actual column values. The `Field` object also provides methods to access BLOB-type fields, one piece at a time. When you make changes to record data, the `Field` object can also be used to retrieve the original column data, before it was changed.

Metadata Information

Field metadata is information about a field, including its type, name, size, precision, and scale. The `Field` object properties can be used to retrieve column-level metadata. Using column-level metadata, you can make your applications more dynamic in nature. You will present an example application that utilizes column-level metadata.

Field Methods

The `Field` object provides two methods that are used to store and retrieve large-text and binary-type column data. The `AppendChunk()` method is used to store large field data, and the `GetChunk()` method is used to retrieve large field data. These methods can be used to manipulate this data one piece at a time. The `AppendChunk()` and `GetChunk()` methods have the following syntax:

```
fld.AppendChunk ColData
Set ColData = fld.GetChunk(ByteSize)
```

Here *fld* is a valid `Field` object. The *ColData* parameter is the column data to set or retrieve. The *ByteSize* parameter of the `GetChunk()` method determines the number of bytes of data to retrieve at a time. The first time that the `AppendChunk()` method is called for a `Field`, any existing data is overwritten, and on subsequent calls, the data is appended to the column. The `GetChunk()` method is called for a `Field`, the first chunk of data is retrieved starting at the beginning of the column, and on subsequent calls, the data is retrieved where the last call left off.

Using the AppendChunk() and GetChunk() Methods

After the AppendChunk() or GetChunk() method is called for a field, data is appended or retrieved starting where you left off. If these methods are called for a different Field object, and then again for the original Field object, they will overwrite the current column data or start retrieving again at the beginning. This is illustrated in the following example:

```
REM Overwrite The Column 0 Data With The Data Value
rs.Fields(0).AppendChunk Data

REM Append The Data2 Value To The Column
rs.Fields(0).AppendChunk Data2

REM Overwrite The Column 1 Data With The Data3 Value
rs.Fields(1).AppendChunk Data3

REM Overwrite The Column 0 Data With The Data3 Value
REM This Data Is NOT APPENDED! It Will Be Over
REM Written!
rs.Fields(0).AppendChunk Data3
```

Field Properties

The Field object supports several properties. The Field object properties can be used to determine the column size, name, scale, value, original value, type, and current value. Table 22-6 lists the properties supported by the Field object, the properties' read/write status, and a description of each property.

TABLE 22-6 FIELD OBJECT PROPERTIES

Property	Read/Write	Description
ActualSize	R	The actual length of the column, if it's known.
Attributes	R	The properties of the field. Can be used to determine whether the field has a fixed length or can be set to a null value.
DefinedSize	R	The maximum length of the column.
Name	R	The name of the column.
NumericScale	R	The number of places to the right of the decimal in floating-point values.

Property	Read/Write	Description
OriginalValue	R	The original value of a column. This is the value the column had before any changes.
Precision	R	The total number of digits used to represent a numeric value.
Type	R	The type of the column, which *must* be one of the DataTypeEnum constants in Table 22-2.
UnderlyingValue	R	The current value that the column actually has at the data source. Use when synchronizing a column with transactions.
Value	R/W	The value of the field. Use to set and retrieve the column value.

FIELD SIZE

The Field object provides two size-related properties. The ActualSize property returns the size of the current column value. The DefinedSize property returns the maximum column size. If a column is defined as a 50-character column and contains only a 10-character string, the ActualSize property returns 10 and the DefinedSize property returns 50.

TYPE AND NUMERIC PROPERTIES

The Type property is used to determine the columns type. The column Type property will be one of the DataTypeEnum constants in Table 22-2. The NumericScale property determines the number of places to the right of the decimal point for floating-point values and is valid only for the adDecimal, adDouble, adNumeric, and adSingle types. The Precision property returns the number of places used to represent a numeric value and is valid only for numeric column types.

ATTRIBUTE PROPERTY

The Attribute property is used to determine special column attributes, including whether the field can be written to, can contain a null value, contains BLOB data, is cached, or is retrieved only when it is actually accessed. The Attribute property value *must* be one of the FieldAttributeEnum-type constants defined in Table 22-7. The Attribute value can be a combination of FieldAttributeEnum constants, which are combined by logically ORing together the values.

TABLE 22-7 FIELDATTRIBUTEENUM OPTIONS CONSTANTS

Constant Name	Value	Description
adFldMayDefer	2	The field is deferred. It is read from the data source only when the field is explicitly accessed.
adFldUpdatable	4	The field value can be changed.
adFldUnknownUpdatable	8	The data provider can't determine whether the field can be changed.
adFldFixed	16	The field contains fixed-length-type data.
adFldIsNullable	32	The field can be set to a Null value.
adFldMayBeNull	64	Indicates that you can read Null values from the field.
adFldLong	128	The field contains long text or binary information. The AppendChunk() and GetChunk() methods must be used to set and retrieve fields that have this attribute set.
adFldRowID	256	The field contains a record number, GUID, or other unique identifier.
adFldRowVersion	512	The field contains a time or date stamp that is used to track changes to a record.
adFldCacheDeferred	4096	The field value is cached by the provider.

FIELD VALUES

The Field property contains three different Value properties: OriginalValue, UnderlyingValue, and Value. The Value property is used to set and retrieve non-BLOB column values. The Attribute property must be checked to determine whether a field is writable. If the Field property does not possess the adFldUpdatable attribute, then the field value can only be read. The OriginalValue property holds the value that the field contained when it was first retrieved and can be used to undo changes. The UnderlyingValue property returns the field's current value at the data source. This is similar to calling the Resync() method for the Recordset, but in this case, only the field value is resynchronized.

Recordset Fields

This section looks at how to develop a function that can execute a query and display the results. This example demonstrates how to use the Fields object and the Count property to loop through the fields contained in a Recordset. The Field object Name property is used to display the name of the columns contained in the query. Listing 22-7 demonstrates how to display the results of a query.

Listing 22-7: Displaying the Results of a Query

```
DIM conn As ADODB.Connection
DIM cmd As ADODB.Command
DIM rs As ADODB.Recordset
DIM Msg As String

REM Open the Connection object, omit the password
conn.Open "data source=IDCDatabase", "john"

REM Associate the Command with a Connection
cmd.ActiveConnection = conn

REM Specify the Query
cmd.CommandText = "SELECT * FROM CUSTOMERS"
cmd.CommandType = adCmdText
set rs = cmd.Execute(NumRecs)

REM Loop Through and Display The Field Names
Msg = " "
For I = 0 To rs.Fields.Count - 1
  Msg = Msg & "|" & rs.Fields(I).Name
Next
MsgBox Msg

REM Loop Through and Display The Field Values For Each
REM Record
Msg = " "
rs.MoveFirst
Do While (Not rs.EOF)
  For I = 0 To rs.Fields.Count - 1
    Msg = Msg & "|" & rs.Fields(I)
  Next
  MsgBox Msg
  rs.MoveNext
Loop
```

```
REM Close the Connection...
rs.Close
conn.Close
```

When you access large text and binary fields by using the ADO `Field` object, you can't use the `Value` property — you must use the `GetChunk()` and `AppendChunk()` methods to access these fields. By checking the `Attribute` property, you can determine whether a field requires the use of the `GetChunk()` and `AppendChunk()` methods to retrieve field data. Listing 22-8 demonstrates how to retrieve a field value by utilizing the `Chunk` methods, when appropriate. In this example, the `GetChunk()` method is called to retrieve the entire field contents.

Listing 22-8: Using the GetColumn Function to Retrieve Field Values Appropriately

```
Function GetColumn(Field As ADODB.Field)
  If(Field.Attribute AND adFldLong) Then
    GetColumn = Field.GetChunk(Field.ActualSize)
  Else
    GetColumn = Field.Value
  End If
End Function
```

Recordset Schema Information

By using the `Field` object attributes, you can obtain `Recordset` schema information. This information can be used to determine the field name, type, and size; whether the field can be changed; how it is retrieved from the data source; and numeric attributes. The example in Listing 22-9 demonstrates how to retrieve and display the schema information for a query result `Recordset`.

Listing 22-9: Displaying Query Schema Information in a Table

```
DIM conn As ADODB.Connection
DIM cmd As ADODB.Command
DIM rs As ADODB.Recordset
DIM Msg As String

Sub DisplayType(TypeVal As LongInt)
  Select Case TypeVal
    Case 20
      MsgBox "adBigInt"
    Case 128
      MsgBox "adBinary"
```

```
Case 11
  MsgBox "adBoolean"
Case 8
  MsgBox "adBSTR"
Case 129
  MsgBox "adChar"
Case 6
  MsgBox "adCurrency"
Case 7
  MsgBox "adDate"
Case 133
  MsgBox "adDBDate"
Case 134
  MsgBox "adDBTime"
Case 135
  MsgBox "adDBTimeStamp"
Case 14
  MsgBox "adDecimal"
Case 5
  MsgBox "adDouble"
Case 0
  MsgBox "adEmpty"
Case 10
  MsgBox "adError"
Case 72
  MsgBox "adGUID"
Case 9
  MsgBox "adIDispatch"
Case 3
  MsgBox "adInteger"
Case 13
  MsgBox "adIUnknown"
Case 205
  MsgBox "adLongVarBinary"
Case 201
  MsgBox "adLongVarChar"
Case 203
  MsgBox "adLongVarWChar"
Case 131
  MsgBox "adNumeric"
Case 4
  MsgBox "adSingle"
Case 2
  MsgBox "adSmallInt"
```

```
    Case 16
      MsgBox "adTinyInt"
    Case 21
      MsgBox "adUnsignedBigInt"
    Case 19
      MsgBox "adUnsignedInt"
    Case 18
      MsgBox "adUnsignedSmallInt"
    Case 17
      MsgBox "adUnsignedTinyInt"
    Case 132
      MsgBox "adUserDefined"
    Case 204
      MsgBox "adVarBinary"
    Case 200
      MsgBox "adVarChar"
    Case 12
      MsgBox "adVariant"
    Case 202
      MsgBox "adVarWChar"
    Case 130
      MsgBox "adWChar"
  End Select
End Sub

Sub DisplayAttribute(Attrib)
  If(Attrib And 2) Then
    MsgBox "adFldMayDefer "
  End If
  If(Attrib And 4) Then
    MsgBox "adFldUpdatable "
  End If
  If(Attrib And 8) Then
    MsgBox "adFldUnknownUpdatable "
  End If
  If(Attrib And 16) Then
    MsgBox "adFldFixed "
  End If
  If(Attrib And 32) Then
    MsgBox "adFldIsNullable "
  End If
  If(Attrib And 64) Then
    MsgBox "adFldMayBeNull "
  End If
```

```
  If(Attrib And 128) Then
    MsgBox "adFldLong "
  End If
  If(Attrib And 256) Then
    MsgBox "adFldRowID "
  End If
  If(Attrib And 512) Then
    MsgBox "adFldRowVersion "
  End If
  If(Attrib And 4096) Then
    MsgBox "adFldCacheDeferred "
  End If
End Sub

REM Open the Connection object, omit the password
conn.Open "data source=IDCDatabase", "john", "john"

REM Associate the Command with a Connection
cmd.ActiveConnection = conn

REM Specify the Query
cmd.CommandText = "SELECT * FROM CUSTOMERS"
cmd.CommandType = adCmdText
set rs = cmd.Execute(NumRecs)

REM Loop Through and Display The Schema of Each Field
  For I = 0 To rs.Fields.Count - 1
    MsgBox rs.Fields(I).Name
    Call DisplayType(rs.Fields(I).Type)
    MsgBox rs.Fields(I).DefinedSize
    Call DisplayAttribute(rs.Fields(I).Attributes)
  Next

REM Close the Connection...
rs.Close
conn.Close
```

Summary

In this chapter, you learned how to utilize the `Command` and `Field` objects. You reviewed the `Field` and `Fields` objects in detail and learned how to navigate the results of a query `Recordset`. You learned how to use the `Field` object to access column-level data, including BLOB (Binary Large Object)-type column data, and created two example functions that display the result and schema of a query. The `Command` object was also reviewed in detail.

Chapter 23

Parameter Object and Query Optimization

IN THIS CHAPTER

- ◆ Using the `Parameter` object
- ◆ Implementing stored procedures
- ◆ Optimizing ADO queries

THIS CHAPTER CONCLUDES the review of primary ADO objects with coverage of the `Parameter` object. In Chapter 22, you learned how to use the `Command` object to create commands and queries. The real advantage of using the `Command` object, though, is its support of parameters. This chapter reviews how to create queries and commands, including stored procedures, which accept and return parameters.

ADO optimization issues are discussed in this chapter, as well. Optimization is not a single issue; it must be considered as part of a unified approach. Optimization is reviewed from several perspectives, including data source optimization, code optimization, client/server optimization, and general ADO optimization issues.

Parameter Object

In the last chapter, you learned how to create a `Parameter` object with the `Command` object's `CreateParameter()` method. Now you find out how to use the `Parameter` object, which is used to pass information to, or retrieve information from, a query, stored procedure, or command. An ADO `Parameter` object is used in the same manner that function and procedure parameters are used in traditional programming languages. You may have used the terms by reference and by value when it comes to passing parameters in traditional programming languages. ADO uses the term *direction*. An ADO `Parameter` can be either an input (by value), output (by reference, but just used on return), or input/output (by reference). After you review the `Parameter` object's methods and properties, you learn how to utilize parameters with queries, commands, and stored procedures.

Parameter AppendChunk() Method

The `Parameter` object provides just one method, the `AppendChunk()` method, which you have already reviewed. Parameters can be used to pass Binary Large Object (BLOB)-type information to commands and queries. The `AppendChunk()` method is used to store large text and binary information in a parameter. Before you use the `AppendChunk()` method, the `Parameter` object's `Attribute` property must set the `adFldLong` flag. The `Attribute` property is reviewed in more detail shortly. The following is the syntax of the `AppendChunk()` method:

param.AppendChunk *ParamData*

in which *param* is a valid `Parameter` object, and the *ParamData* parameter is the parameter data to set or retrieve. The first time that the `AppendChunk()` method is called by a `Parameter` object, any existing data is overwritten, and on subsequent calls, the data is appended to the parameter.

The `Parameter` object can use BLOB-type parameters only for input; you can't return BLOB-type output parameters with ADO.

Calling the `AppendChunk()` method with a NULL value results in an error. If you need to clear out the value of a BLOB-type parameter, simply set its `Value` property to an empty string.

Parameter Properties

The `Parameter` object provides several different properties, including its direction, if it supports a NULL value, name, size, type, numeric attributes, and value. Table 23-1 lists the properties supported by the `Parameter` object, the properties' read/write status, and a description of each property.

TABLE 23-1 PARAMETER OBJECT PROPERTIES

Property	Read/Write	Description
Attributes	R/W	The properties of the parameter. Can be used to determine whether the field has a fixed length or can be set to a null value.
Direction	R/W	Specifies whether the property is used for input, output, or input and output.
Name	R/W*	The name of the parameter. After a parameter has been added to the Parameters collection, its name can't be changed.
NumericScale	R/W	The number of places to the right of the decimal in floating-point values.
Precision	R/W	The total number of digits used to represent a numeric value.
Size	R/W	The maximum size of the parameter (in bytes).
Type	R/W	The type of the parameter, which *must* be one of the DataTypeEnum constants.
Value	R/W	The value of the parameter. Used to set and retrieve the non-BLOB parameter values.

ATTRIBUTE PROPERTY

The Attribute property of the Parameters object is used to specify that a parameter can accept a signed value, can be NULL, or contains a BLOB-type field. The Attribute property is a Long type; therefore it *must* be one of the ParameterAttributesEnum constants in Table 23-2. These attribute constant values can be combined with a logic ORing operation, to specify more than one attribute value for a parameter.

TABLE 23-2 PARAMETERATTRIBUTESENUM CONSTANTS

Constant	Value	Description
adParamSigned	16	The parameter value can be a signed numeric value (default).
adParamNullable	64	The parameter can accept a NULL value.
adParamLong	128	The parameter contains long text or binary information. The AppendChunk() method must be used to set parameters that have this attribute set.

DIRECTION PROPERTY

The Direction property of the Parameter object is used to specify whether the parameter is used to pass, retrieve, or pass and retrieve information to a query, command, or stored procedure. The Direction property *must* be one of the ParameterDirectionEnum constants shown in Table 23-3. You may have used the terms by reference and by value when it comes to passing parameters in traditional programming languages. ADO uses the term *direction*. An ADO Parameter can be either an input (by value), output (by reference, but just used on return), or input/output (by reference). The Parameter object also specifies another type of parameter, a return value, which is used to return a value from a call to a data source stored procedure.

TABLE 23-3 PARAMETERDIRECTIONENUM CONSTANTS

Constant	Value	Description
adParamInput	1	Input-type parameter (default direction).
adParamOutput	2	Output-type parameter.
adParamInputOutput	3	Input-and-output-type parameter.
adParamReturnValue	4	Parameter is a return value.

NAME AND OTHER SCHEMA-TYPE PROPERTIES

The `Parameter` object also supplies a group of properties. These properties describe the parameter and the type of information that it can contain. The `Name` property is used to set and retrieve the parameter name. After the `Parameter` is appended to the `Parameters` collection, which is discussed shortly, the parameter's name can't be changed. The `NumericScale` property defines the number of decimal places to the right of the decimal point in floating-type values. The `Precision` property defines the total number of digits used to represent a numeric value. The `Size` property is used to specify the maximum number of bytes used to define the parameter. The `Size` parameter is required only when using variable-length data types. The `Type` parameter, which defines the data type of the parameter, *must* be one of the `DataTypeEnum` constants shown in Table 23-4.

TABLE **23-4 DATATYPEENUM CONSTANTS**

Constant	Value	Description
adBigInt	20	Signed integer (8 bytes).
adBinary	128	Binary value.
adBoolean	11	Boolean value.
adBSTR	8	Unicode character string that is null-terminated.
adChar	129	Null-terminated character string.
adCurrency	6	Currency value.
adDate	7	Date value.
adDBDate	133	Date value in the form *yyyymmdd*.
adDBTime	134	Time value in the form *hhmmss*.
adDBTimeStamp	135	Date-time value in the form *yyyymmddhhmmss*.
adDecimal	14	Fixed-precision floating-type value.
adDouble	5	Double-precision floating-point value.
adEmpty	0	Type has not been specified yet (default).
adError	10	Error-code type.
adGUID	72	Globally unique identifier (GUID)-type value.

Continued

TABLE **23-4 DATATYPEENUM CONSTANTS** *(continued)*

Constant	Value	Description
adIDispatch	9	OLE IDispatch interface-type value.
adInteger	3	Signed integer (4 bytes).
adIUnknown	13	OLE IUnknown interface-type value.
adLongVarBinary	205	Long binary-type value. *Used only for Parameter objects.*
adLongVarChar	201	Long string-type value. *Used only for Parameter objects.*
adLongVarWChar	203	Long null-terminated character-string-type value. *Used only for Parameter objects.*
adNumeric	131	Exact numeric type value with a fixed precision and scale.
adSingle	4	Single-precision floating-point-type value.
adSmallInt	2	Signed integer (2 bytes).
adTinyInt	16	Signed integer (1 byte).
adUnsignedBigInt	21	Unsigned integer (8 bytes).
adUnsignedInt	19	Unsigned integer (4 bytes).
adUnsignedSmallInt	18	Unsigned integer (2 bytes).
adUnsignedTinyInt	17	Unsigned integer (1 byte).
adUserDefined	132	User-defined type.
adVarBinary	204	Variable-length binary-type value. *Used only for Parameter objects.*
adVarChar	200	Variable-length character-string-type value. *Used only for Parameter objects.*
adVariant	12	OLE Variant-type value.
adVarWChar	202	Variable-length Unicode character string that is null-terminated. *Used only for Parameter objects.*
adWChar	130	Unicode character string that is null-terminated.

VALUE PROPERTY

The Value property of the Parameter object is used to set and retrieve non-BLOB-type parameter values. The Value property can also be used to NULL out the value of a BLOB-type parameter, by setting the Value property to an empty string.

Parameters Collection

When a Command object is created, an associated Parameters collection is also created. The Parameters collection object holds a set of Parameter objects. You can create a Parameter object by using the CreateParameter() method of the Command object. A Parameter must be added to the Parameters collection before it is used by the Command object. The Parameters object can be accessed by its ordinal-number index or name.

Calling the CreateParameter object does not automatically append the newly created parameter to the Parameters collection. You must call the Append() method to append the new parameter manually.

Parameters Methods

The Parameters collection object provides several methods, which are listed and described in Table 23-5. The Parameters object methods can be used to add and remove parameters from the collection, and to synchronize the Parameters collection with the data source.

TABLE 23-5 PARAMETERS OBJECT METHODS

Property	Description
Refresh()	Retrieves provider parameter information for the stored procedure or parameterized query specified in the Command object.
Append()	Adds a new Parameter to the Parameters collection.
Delete()	Removes a Parameter from the Parameters collection.

REFRESH() METHOD

The Refresh() method is used to update the Parameters collection manually, to reflect the current parameter. The Refresh() method can be used with stored procedures to retrieve the parameters that are required by a data source stored procedure. Before the Refresh() method is called, you should assign the Command object to a valid connection.

When the Parameters collection is first accessed, it is automatically synchronized with the data source. You don't need to call the Refresh() method to populate the collection initially.

APPEND() METHOD

The Append() method is used to add a Parameter object to the Parameters collection. Manually creating and adding parameters is much more efficient than having the data source populate the Parameters collection. The following is the syntax of the Append() method:

```
params.Append param
```

The params parameter is a Parameters collection object. The param parameter is the Parameter object to append to the collection. After a Parameter object has been appended to a Parameters collection, its name can't be changed.

Not all data providers support parameterized queries or the automatic populations of the Parameters collection.

DELETE() METHOD

The Delete() method is used to remove a parameter from the Parameters collection. The Delete() method has the following syntax:

```
params.Append index
```

The params parameter is a Parameters collection object. The index parameter is the numeric index of the parameter to delete or the name of the parameter. After a Parameter object is deleted, it is automatically destroyed.

Parameters Properties

The `Parameters` object provides two properties: the `Count` property returns the number of `Parameter` objects contained in the collection, and the `Item` property returns the `Parameter` object at the specified index. You don't need to use the `Item()` method directly.

COUNT PROPERTY

The `Count` property simply returns the number of `Parameter` objects in the `Parameters` collection. Since the `Fields` collection can be accessed by a numeric index, and can be used to loop through the `Parameters` collection.

ITEM PROPERTY

The `Item` property can be used to access a `Parameter` object of the `Parameters` collection. You don't need to use the `Item` property to access a `Parameter` contained in the `Parameters` collection. You can access an item of the `Parameters` collection in the following ways:

```
command.Parameters(index)
command.Parameters(name)
command.Parameters.Item(index)
command.Parameters.Item(name)
command(index)
command(name)
command!name
```

The *command* is a valid `Command` object. The *index* parameter can be a numeric index. The `Parameters` collection contains indexes from 0 to the `Count` property value − 1. When used as an index, the *name* parameter is a String that contains the name of a parameter.

Parameterized Queries

Creating a query that accepts parameters is a fairly simple task. When you write your query, simply put a question mark where you would like your parameter to be replaced. For example, to create a query that retrieves all the fields in the CUSTOMERS table, for customers that live in a specific city, you write your query in the following parameterized form:

```
SELECT * FROM CUSTOMERS WHERE CITY = ?
```

While the ? parameter placeholder works with the OLE DB ODBC data source provider, you should consult the documentation when you use parameters with different OLE DB data providers.

The ? is replaced by a parameter value when it is executed. Listing 23-1 demonstrates how this query would be written. One parameter, named City, is created and appended to the Parameters collection of the command. The value of the parameter is substituted into the query at runtime, to search for all the customers that live in Buffalo. In this example, the City parameter is used only for input.

If you expect to use the query that you're creating only one time, you're probably better off dynamically creating the query string in your application. If you expect to use your query multiple times, a parameterized query is a better choice. If you do expect to use the query multiple times, you probably also want to make your query a prepared statement, by setting the Prepared property to True, to ensure faster query responses on subsequent executions (as shown in the example in Listing 23-1).

When the value of a string-type parameter is specified, you are *not* required to enclose the parameter in quotes, as you would if you were defining the query as one that didn't accept parameters. For example:

SELECT * FROM CUSTOMERS WHERE CITY = "Buffalo"

As you can see, Buffalo is enclosed in quotes here, but that is *not* required when it is used as a parameter value.

Listing 23-1: Creating a Parameterized Query

```
DIM conn As ADODB.Connection
DIM cmd As ADODB.Command
DIM rs As ADODB.Recordset
DIM Param1 As ADODB.Parameter

REM Open the Connection object, omit the password
conn.Open "data source=IDCDatabase", "john"

REM Associate the Command with a Connection
cmd.ActiveConnection = conn

REM Specify the Stored Procedure
```

```
cmd.CommandText =
   "SELECT *  FROM CUSTOMERS WHERE CITY = ?"

REM Save A Prepared Version Of This Query
cmd.Prepared = True
cmd.CommandType = adCmdText

REM Create The Command Parameters
Set Param1 = cmd.CreateParameter("City",adBSTR,adParamInput)

REM Serach For Customers In Buffalo
Param1.Value = "Buffalo"

REM Add The Parameters
cmd.Parameters.Append Param1

rs = cmd.Execute(NumRecs)

REM The rs Recordset Only Contains Customers That Live In
REM Buffalo

REM Close the Connection and Recordset...
rs.Close
conn.Close
```

SQL Server Stored Procedures

SQL Server provides several stored procedure queries that you can utilize in administrative functions. As long as the user that you are logged in as has the appropriate permissions, these stored procedures are accessible from your ADO applications. This section looks at how the security-related SQL Server stored procedures can be accessed from ADO. When calling a server-side stored procedure with SQL Server, the CommandType property must be assigned the adCmdStoredProc constant. A few of the commonly used administrative server-side stored procedures, provided by SQL Server, are listed in Table 23-6.

TABLE 23-6 ADMINISTRATIVE SERVER-SIDE STORED PROCEDURES

Stored Procedure	Description
SP_WHO	Performs a server-side stored procedure that returns the name of the user who is currently connected to the SQL Server database.
SP_ADDGROUP	Creates a new SQL Server group.
SP_ADDUSER	Creates a new SQL Server database user.
SP_CHANGEGROUP	Adds a user to an SQL Server group.
SP_DROPGROUP	Deletes an SQL Server group.
SP_PASSWORD	Changes the password of the current user.

Determining Who's Logged In

Sometimes, you need to determine who is currently connected to an SQL Server database server. SQL Server provides the SP_WHO stored procedure to determine which connections are currently active. Listing 23-2 demonstrates how the SP_WHO stored procedure can be called by using ADO. The SP_WHO procedure actually generates a system-level query, which returns the following columns:

◆ SPID: Process ID

◆ STATUS: Current process status

◆ LOGINAME: Username used to log in to SQL Server

◆ HOSTNAME: The hostname of the client

◆ BLK: Blocked status

◆ DBNAME: The name of the database connected to

◆ CMD: The current command being executed

In this example, the Field object is indexed by the column name, and not the ordinal index that you have used in the past.

Listing 23-2: Using the SP_WHO Stored Procedure

```
DIM conn As ADODB.Connection
DIM cmd As ADODB.Command
DIM rs As ADODB.Recordset
DIM Param1 As ADODB.Parameter

REM Open the Connection object, omit the password
conn.Open "data source=IDCDatabase", "john"

REM Associate the Command with a Connection
cmd.ActiveConnection = conn

REM Specify the Stored Procedure
cmd.CommandText = "SP_WHO"
cmd.CommandType = adCmdStoredProc

set rs = cmd.Execute(NumRecs)

REM Display The Login Name For Each Current User
rs.MoveFirst
Do While (NOT rs.EOF)
  MsgBox rs.Fields("LOGINAME")
  rs.MoveNext
Loop

REM Close the Connection...
rs.Close
conn.Close
```

Creating a Group

The SP_ADDGROUP stored procedure is used to add new SQL Server groups. The SP_ADDGROUP procedure takes a single parameter, which specifies the name of the group to add. After you create a group, you can use it when you specify database permissions. With a single command, all the members of a group can be granted the same permissions, instead of individually setting permissions for each user. Listing 23-3 demonstrates how to create a new group by using the SP_ADDGROUP procedure.

When you create parameterized queries, the ? placeholder is required, to specify where the query parameters should be replaced. When you call SQL Server server-side stored procedures, by using the OLE DB ODBC data provider, you don't need to specify the stored procedure's parameters with the ? placeholder.

Listing 23-3: Using the SP_ADDGROUP Stored Procedures

```
DIM conn As ADODB.Connection
DIM cmd As ADODB.Command
DIM rs As ADODB.Recordset
DIM Param1 As ADODB.Parameter
DIM Param2 As ADODB.Parameter

REM Open the Connection object, omit the password
conn.Open "data source=IDCDatabase", "john"

REM Associate the Command with a Connection
cmd.ActiveConnection = conn

REM Specify the Stored Procedure
cmd.CommandText = "SP_ADDGROUP"
cmd.CommandType = adCmdStoredProc

REM Create The Command Parameters
Set Param1 = cmd.CreateParameter("Return",
                  adInteger,adParamReturnValue)
Set Param2 = cmd.CreateParameter("GroupName",
                  adBSTR,adParamInput)
REM Create The ADMIN Group
Param2.Value = "ADMIN"

REM Add The Parameters
cmd.Parameters.Append Param1
cmd.Parameters.Append Param2

cmd.Execute(NumRecs)

If(Param1.Value = 0) Then
   MsgBox "The Group " & Param2.Value & " Was Added Successfully!"
Else
   MsgBox "The Group " & Param2.Value & " Was NOT Added
```

```
Successfully!"
End If

REM Close the Connection...
conn.Close
```

Creating a New User

The SP_ADDUSER stored procedure is used to add new users to SQL Server. The SP_ADDUSER procedure takes three parameters: the username, the username in the database, and the group in which the user will be a member. Generally, the name in the database and the username are the same. Listing 23-4 demonstrates how the SP_ADDUSER procedure can be called to add a new user. In this example, the name in the database and the username are passed the same value.

Listing 23-4: Using the SP_ADDUSER Stored Procedures

```
DIM conn As ADODB.Connection
DIM cmd As ADODB.Command
DIM rs As ADODB.Recordset
DIM Param1 As ADODB.Parameter
DIM Param2 As ADODB.Parameter
DIM Param3 As ADODB.Parameter
DIM Param4 As ADODB.Parameter

REM Open the Connection object, omit the password
conn.Open "data source=IDCDatabase", "john"

REM Associate the Command with a Connection
cmd.ActiveConnection = conn

REM Specify the Stored Procedure
cmd.CommandText = "SP_ADDUSER"
cmd.CommandType = adCmdStoredProc

REM Create The Command Parameters
Set Param1 = cmd.CreateParameter("Return",
                adInteger,adParamReturnValue)
Set Param2 = cmd.CreateParameter("UserName",
                adBSTR,adParamInput)
Set Param3 = cmd.CreateParameter("DBUserName",
                adBSTR,adParamInput)
Set Param4 = cmd.CreateParameter("GroupName",
                adBSTR,adParamInput)
```

```
REM Add The User Marie TO The ADMIN Group
Param2.Value = "MARIE"
Param3.Value = "MARIE"
Param4.Value = "ADMIN"

REM Add The Parameters
cmd.Parameters.Append Param1
cmd.Parameters.Append Param2
cmd.Parameters.Append Param3
cmd.Parameters.Append Param4

cmd.Execute(NumRecs)

If(Param1.Value = 0) Then
  MsgBox "User " & Param2.Value & " Was Added!!"
Else
  MsgBox "User " & Param2.Value & " Was NOT Added!"
End If

REM Close the Connection...
conn.Close
```

Adding a User to a Group

The SP_CHANGEGROUP stored procedure is used to add users to a group, The SP_CHANGEGROUP procedure takes two parameters: the first parameter specifies an existing group name, and the second parameter specifies an existing username. Listing 23-5 demonstrates how the SP_CHANGEGROUP procedure is used to add a new group member.

 SQL Server allows a user to be a member of only one custom group at a time, due to the structuring of the SQL Server system tables. All users are always a member of the public group. Only the database owner (dbo) can add users to a group. To change the group in which a user is a member, you need to delete the user from his or her current group, before you add them to a new group.

Listing 23–5: Using the SP_CHANGEGROUP Stored Procedures

```
DIM conn As ADODB.Connection
DIM cmd As ADODB.Command
DIM rs As ADODB.Recordset
```

```
DIM Param1 As ADODB.Parameter
DIM Param2 As ADODB.Parameter
DIM Param3 As ADODB.Parameter

REM Open the Connection object, omit the password
conn.Open "data source=IDCDatabase", "john"

REM Associate the Command with a Connection
cmd.ActiveConnection = conn

REM Specify the Stored Procedure
cmd.CommandText = "SP_CHANGEGROUP"
cmd.CommandType = adCmdStoredProc

REM Create The Command Parameters
Set Param1 = cmd.CreateParameter("Return",
                adInteger,adParamReturnValue)
Set Param2 = cmd.CreateParameter("GroupName",
                adBSTR,adParamInput)
Set Param3 = cmd.CreateParameter("UserName",
                adBSTR,adParamInput)

REM Add The User Marie TO The ADMIN Group
Param2.Value = "ADMIN"
Param3.Value = "MARIE"

REM Add The Parameters
cmd.Parameters.Append Param1
cmd.Parameters.Append Param2
cmd.Parameters.Append Param3

cmd.Execute(NumRecs)

If(Param1.Value = 0) Then
  MsgBox "User " & Param3.Value &
        " Was Added To The Group " &
          Param2.Value & " Successfully!"
Else
  MsgBox "User " & Param3.Value &
        " Was NOT Added To The Group " &
        Param2.Value & "!"
End If

REM Close the Connection...
conn.Close
```

Removing a Group

The SP_DROPGROUP stored procedure is used to remove SQL Server groups. The SP_DROPGROUP procedure takes a single parameter: the name of the group to remove. Listing 23-6 demonstrates how SP_DROPGROUP is used to remove a group.

 A group can be removed only if it does *not* contain any members.

Listing 23-6: Using the SP_DROPGROUP Stored Procedures

```
DIM conn As ADODB.Connection
DIM cmd As ADODB.Command
DIM rs As ADODB.Recordset
DIM Param1 As ADODB.Parameter
DIM Param2 As ADODB.Parameter

REM Open the Connection object, omit the password
conn.Open "data source=IDCDatabase", "john"

REM Associate the Command with a Connection
cmd.ActiveConnection = conn

REM Specify the Stored Procedure
cmd.CommandText = "SP_DROPGROUP"
cmd.CommandType = adCmdStoredProc

REM Create The Command Parameters
Set Param1 = cmd.CreateParameter("Return",
             adInteger,adParamReturnValue)
Set Param2 = cmd.CreateParameter("GroupName",
             adBSTR,adParamInput)

REM Remove The Admin Group
Param2.Value = "ADMIN"

REM Add The Parameters
cmd.Parameters.Append Param1
cmd.Parameters.Append Param2

cmd.Execute(NumRecs)
```

```
If(Param1.Value = 0) Then
  MsgBox "The Group " & Param2.Value & " Was Removed!"
Else
  MsgBox "The Group " & Param2.Value &
        " Was NOT Removed!"
End If

REM Close the Connection...
conn.Close
```

Changing a Password

The SP_PASSWORD stored procedure is provided to enable users to change their passwords. Listing 23-7 demonstrates how the SP_PASSWORD is used to change the current user's password. The SP_PASSWORD procedure takes two parameters: the
username and the user's new password.

Listing 23-7: Using the SP_PASSWORD Stored Procedures

```
DIM conn As ADODB.Connection
DIM cmd As ADODB.Command
DIM rs As ADODB.Recordset
DIM Param1 As ADODB.Parameter
DIM Param2 As ADODB.Parameter
DIM Param3 As ADODB.Parameter

REM Open the Connection object, omit the password
conn.Open "data source=IDCDatabase", "john"

REM Associate the Command with a Connection
cmd.ActiveConnection = conn

REM Specify the Stored Procedure
cmd.CommandText = "SP_PASSWORD"
cmd.CommandType = adCmdStoredProc

REM Create The Command Parameters
Set Param1 = cmd.CreateParameter("Return",
            adInteger,adParamReturnValue)
Set Param2 = cmd.CreateParameter("UserName",
            adBSTR,adParamInput)
Set Param3 = cmd.CreateParameter("GroupName",
            adBSTR,adParamInput)

REM Change The Password For The User Marie
```

```
Param2.Value = "MARIE"
Param3.Value = "POOH"

REM Add The Parameters
cmd.Parameters.Append Param1
cmd.Parameters.Append Param2
cmd.Parameters.Append Param3

cmd.Execute(NumRecs)

If(Param1.Value = 0) Then
  MsgBox "The Password Was Changed Successfully!"
Else
  MsgBox "The Password Was NOT Changed!"
End If

REM Close the Connection...
conn.Close
```

Query Optimization

Query optimization isn't a single process – several factors contribute to query processing and overall application efficiency. Query optimization can be broken down into these separate areas: data source, code, and client/server optimization issues. Each of these areas are covered in depth in this section. Depending on your particular needs and requirements, some of these tips and suggestions may not be possible to implement. However, this section will give you a good overall strategy for designing more efficient ADO applications and applets.

Data Source Optimization

The first step in designing an ADO application is a proper data source design, especially if your data source is a relational database. Depending on your data source, you might not be able to control the design of the data source. If you are using ADO to access a traditional data source, such as a relational database, you can do several things to help assure optimal data access. One key aspect to designing an optimal relational database is *normalization*, which can be described best as the process of eliminating duplicate data in your database. A normalized database can reduce the amount of data that your application needs to retrieve, modify, and add to your database. Entire books have been dedicated to the subject of database normalization; the following are the five basic rules/levels of database normalization:

- ◆ **Level 1:** Remove groups of repeating data
- ◆ **Level 2:** Remove duplicate data
- ◆ **Level 3:** Remove columns of a table that aren't dependent on the primary key
- ◆ **Level 4:** Place independent multiple relationships in separate tables
- ◆ **Level 5:** Place dependent multiple relationships in separate tables

These normalization rules are reviewed in detail in Chapter 12, *DAO Optimization.*

Field Types and Sizes

Your choice of field types and sizes is the last important aspect of designing your data source. Examine the types and lengths of the fields in your tables. If you have a character field that requires only 25 characters, don't define it as a 50-character field; doing so can waste a lot of space. Also, examine the types of your fields. Can a numeric value that you're storing in a table as a floating-point value be represented as an integer? If so, you can save space and achieve quicker retrieval from the database, because an integer occupies fewer bytes.

Code Optimization

A complete review of code optimization techniques could consume many books by itself. A few specific ADO techniques that can help to speed your application performance include: using transactions, using bookmarks, and letting an SQL statement do the work for you.

TRANSACTIONS

Transactions can greatly improve application performance. Transactions buffer database changes until they are committed or canceled. If many records are affected by an operation that is part of a transaction, instead of writing the changes to each record as they are performed, the changes are buffered and performed in a single write operation. You should not make transactions too big. Transactions are first buffered to memory and then spill over to the disk, as needed. Large transactions can cause insufficient memory or fill up available disk space if they are too large. You should group very large transactions into smaller groups.

BOOKMARKS

Just as a bookmark in a book helps you return to a specific page, ADO bookmarks are used to return to a specific location in a table. The `Recordset` object provides the `Bookmark` property, which returns a bookmark to the current record when accessed. When you assign a valid bookmark value to the `Bookmark` property, you can quickly return to the record that the bookmark references, which is much faster than looping back through a record set to find a specific record.

SQL INSTEAD OF CODE

When you perform operations that affect multiple records, performing the operation as an equivalent SQL statement, if possible, is faster than writing the equivalent code. For example, if you have a Product table that contains pricing information, and you need to increase all prices by ten percent, you are better served by writing an SQL `UPDATE` statement than writing the equivalent loop or use cursors.

Client/Server Optimization

Several different optimization issues can affect application performance when dealing with a server-side data source. Some of these client/server optimization issues include: retrieving only the fields that you require from a data source, allowing the server to run as much of your query as possible, and, if possible, using forward-only-type cursors.

TAKE ONLY WHAT YOU NEED

When you retrieve information from the database by using SQL `SELECT` statements, make sure to specify only the fields that you absolutely require. Accessing any more data than is required takes up unnecessary time. You rarely should use the * qualifier to retrieve all columns of data. Often, when you are accessing a database server, users don't have access to all table fields, due to security requirements.

LET THE SERVER DO THE WORK

When you access a database that is stored on a database server, your most efficient strategy is to have the database server perform as much of the query as possible. Some of the query operations that usually aren't supported by a database server are the following:

◆ Joining tables on fields of different types. Most database servers can't perform the necessary inherent-type conversions to perform this type of query. You must specify these types of conversions explicitly.

◆ Using queries that contain the `DISTINCT` clause or calculations in subqueries.

◆ Joining attached tables with tables found on the database server.

USE FORWARD-ONLY-TYPE CURSORS, IF POSSIBLE

When you create a `Recordset`, by default, you can move forward and backward through the data set that is returned. If you know that you need to move through the data set in a forward direction only, you can set the `CursorType` property to the `adOpenForwardOnly CursorTypeEnum` constant, to establish a forward-only-type cursor on the record set. This is more efficient, because the resulting data set is not buffered. The performance gain of a forward-only-type data set is more noticeable with an ODBC-type data source. Only the `MoveNext()` method may be used on the resulting `Recordset`.

Summary

This chapter reviewed the `Parameter` object in detail. You learned how to create parameterized queries and call SQL Server-stored procedures that accept and return parameters. Optimization techniques were also discussed. You learned how to apply database normalization techniques, to help ensure efficient data access, as well as how to apply code and client/server optimization techniques to your ADO applications and applets.

The next chapter wraps up the formal review of ADO objects with a discussion of the `Error` object and error-handling techniques. This should give you a full toolbox to create robust and efficient ADO applications.

Chapter 24

ADO Error Handling

IN THIS CHAPTER

♦ Using the ADO `Errors` collection

♦ Using the ADO `Error` object

♦ Capturing ADO errors in Visual Basic

♦ Overviewing the `Property` object

THIS CHAPTER WRAPS up the formal presentation of ADO objects with a detailed review of the `Error`, `Errors` collection, `Property`, and `Properties` collection objects. This chapter teaches you how to add robustness to your ADO applications. The `Error` and `Errors` objects are used to retrieve error information. An ADO error reference is also provided. Finally, the `Property` and `Properties` objects are reviewed. As discussed previously, not all OLE DB data sources support all ADO object properties. The `Property` and `Properties` object can report whether a property is available, whether it is required or optional, and whether it can be read or written. Knowing the availability and status of a property before it is utilized can add an extra level of robustness to your applications.

Errors Collection

When an error occurs while using an ADO object, multiple errors actually can be generated. An ADO error is contained in the `Error` object. The `Connection` object has an associated `Errors` collection. The `Errors` collection holds the collection of `Error` objects. Each `Error` object represents each individual error that is caused by an ADO object. While one ADO object is generating errors, they each become appended into the `Errors` collection. When a different ADO object generates an error, the `Errors` collection is automatically cleared. When an ADO error occurs, it actually is described by the collection of `Error` objects contained in the `Errors` collection. Examining each `Error` object can determine specifically what went wrong. The `Errors` object can be accessed from the `Connection` object in the same way that the `Fields` object is accessed from the `Recordset` object. For example:

```
Connect.Errors
```

in which `Connect` is a valid connection object. This section continues by reviewing the method and properties provided by the `Errors` collection.

Clear() Method

The `Errors` collection object provides a single method, `Clear()`, which is used to empty the `Errors` collection manually. As stated earlier, the `Errors` collection is automatically cleared when an ADO object generates its first error. Some `Recordset` methods and properties, though, can generate warnings. A warning will also generate an error object, even though it won't cause an application to stop. Before you call `Recordset` methods, such as `CancelBatch()`, `UpdateBatch()`, `Delete()`, and `Resync()`, you should clear the `Errors` collection. Remember that the `Errors` collection is associated with a `Connection` object. When you're using a `Recordset` or `Connection` object, the `Connection` object can be accessed by using the `ActiveConnection` property. For example, to call the `Errors` object `Clear()` method from a `Recordset` object, the following syntax would be used:

```
rsorcmd.ActiveConnection.Errors.Clear
```

in which *rsorcmd* is a valid `Recordset` or `Command` object. This works only if the `Recordset` or `Command` object has been assigned to a data source connection; otherwise, an error results.

Errors Properties

The `Errors` object provides two properties: the `Count` property returns the number of `Error` objects contained in the collection, and the `Item` property returns the `Error` object at the specified index. You don't need to use the `Item()` method directly.

COUNT PROPERTY

The `Count` property simply returns the number of `Error` objects in the `Errors` collection. Since the `Errors` collection can be accessed by a numeric index, and can be used to loop through the `Errors` collection.

ITEM PROPERTY

The `Item` property can be used to access an `Error` object of the `Errors` collection. You don't need to use the `Item` property to access an `Error` contained in the `Errors` collection. An item of the `Errors` collection can be accessed in the following ways:

```
connect.Errors(index)
connect.Errors.Item(index)
```

in which *connect* is a valid Connection object, and the *index* parameter is a numeric index. Errors collections are indexed from 0 to the Count property value − 1.

Error Object

The Error object is used to encapsulate an ADO error or warning. This error or warning can be generated by the ADO itself, by the data provider, or by the actual data source. The Error object enables you to access the information that is needed to interpret an error, and to take the necessary corrective actions, if possible. The Error object doesn't have any methods.

Error Properties

The Error object provides several properties. The Error properties can be used to obtain a text description of an error; a Help file reference; if applicable, the data source error message; an error number; the object that caused the error; and the ANSI-standard SQL error code. Table 24-1 lists and describes the properties provided by the Error object. All the Error object properties can only be read.

TABLE 24-1 ERROR OBJECT PROPERTIES

Property	Read/Write	Description
Description	R	Used to return a text message describing the error or warning.
HelpContext	R	Returns a Help file context that can be used to retrieve more information about the error that occurred.
HelpFile	R	Returns the name of the data source provider Help file.
NativeError	R	Used to return the data source error number that caused the error or warning. You must consult with your data source provider for more information.
Number	R	Returns ADO error constant value.
Source	R	Returns the name of the ADO object that caused the error or warning.
SQLState	R	Returns the ANSI SQL error code value. Not all data providers conform to the ANSI SQL error state standards.

DESCRIPTION PROPERTY

The Description property returns a String type that contains a text-based description of the error or warning that occurred. This description may come from the data source provider or ADO itself. The Description property will contain a short message that describes the error; for more detailed data source provider error or warning information, you need to consult the data provider documentation. If supported, the HelpContext and HelpFile properties, reviewed next, can assist in automating that process.

HELPCONTEXT AND HELPFILE PROPERTIES

The HelpFile and HelpContext properties are used to return the name and index, respectively, of a Windows Help file. Not all data providers supply this information. The HelpFile property is a String that contains the name of the Windows Help file. The HelpContext property contains a Long that is an index to a topic in the Help file that contains more information about the error or warning. Even if the data provider supplies this information, it probably is useful to you only if you're developing a complete application using ADO.

NATIVEERROR PROPERTY

The NativeError property returns a Long value, which is a data-source-specific error value. When you use the OLE DB ODBC data provider, this error value is the error value generated by the ODBC data source, such as Microsoft Access, Microsoft SQL Server, or Oracle.

 You must consult your data source documentation to interpret NativeError values. Generally, this value is useful only for debugging purposes.

NUMBER PROPERTY

The Number property returns a Long value, which is the actual ADO error value. While the NativeError property returns the data source error value or warning, the Number property contains a reference to an ADO error constant.

SOURCE PROPERTY

The Source property returns a String that contains the name of the ADO object that created the error. Because multiple Error objects can be in the Errors collection, the Source property helps to sort out the root of an error. Generally, the Source name is of the form ADODB.*objectname*, but when you use the lightweight Recordset object, the error Source may be of the form ADOR.*objectname*, in which *objectname* is the name of the ADO object that caused the error; for example, `Recordset`. The `Source` property can be very useful in determining how to correct automatically an error condition in your ADO applications.

SQLSTATE PROPERTY

The `SQLState` property is used to return an error code that describes why a query or command possibly failed. The `SQLState` property is a five-character String. Table 12-2 lists and describes the ANSI SQL State return codes, including errors and warnings that are returned by ODBC data sources. These values are returned only by data sources that comply to ANSI SQL standards. Data providers aren't required to comply to the ANSI standards.

 TIP You should consult with your data provider for more specific information regarding the SQL State return codes that it may return. A data source possibly won't even return an SQL State value.

An `SQLState` String is comprised of two parts: a two-character class value and a three-character subclass value. A class value of `01` indicates a warning. All other class values indicate an error, except for the `IM` class, which is a warning or error that is returned only by OLE DB ODBC data providers.

TABLE **24-2** ANSI SQL STATE RETURN CODES

SQL State Code	Description
00000	The operation completed successfully.
01002	An error occurred while disconnecting from a data source.
01004	While retrieving, data was truncated.
01006	Privilege not revoked for the specified command.
01S00	A connect string argument was invalid.
07001	The wrong number of parameters were specified when executing a query or command.
07006	The data being access is restricted.
08001	Could not connect to the specified data source.

Continued

TABLE **24-2 ANSI SQL STATE RETURN CODES** (continued)

SQL State Code	Description
08002	The data source connection is currently in use.
08003	Could not open a connection to the specified data source.
08004	The data source rejected the attempted connection.
08007	The data source connection failed during a transaction.
08S01	A communications error occurred while communicating with the data source.
21S01	The list of INSERT command values doesn't match the list of columns specified.
21S02	The derived table does not match the column list specified.
22001	String data was right-truncated while retrieving or setting a value.
22003	A numeric value is out of range.
22005	An assignment error occurred.
22008	A date or time field value caused an overflow condition.
22012	A divide-by-zero error occurred.
22026	A mismatch exists between string data and its allowed length.
23000	A data source integrity constraint has occurred.
24000	The current cursor is in an invalid state.
25000	The current transaction is in an invalid state.
28000	The authorization specified is not valid.
34000	The cursor name specified in not valid.
37000	A syntax or access violation error occurred.
3C000	A duplicate cursor name has been encountered.
40001	A data source serialization error occurred.
42000	A syntax or access violation error occurred.
70100	The current operation was aborted before completion.
IM001	The data source driver does not support this function.

SQL State Code	Description
M002	The data source name specified wasn't found. A default data source driver wasn't provided.
IM003	The driver specified by the data source name wasn't found or couldn't be loaded.
IM004	The data source driver method `SQLAllocEnv()` failed.
IM005	The data source driver method `SQLAllocConnect()` failed.
IM006	The data source driver method `SQLSetConnectOption()` failed.
IM007	A data source wasn't specified, and the option to prompt for a data source wasn't enabled.
IM008	A failure occurred when attempting to display a dialog box.
IM009	The data source translation DLL failed.
S0001	The table or view already exists.
S0002	The table specified was not found.
S0011	The index already exists.
S0012	The index specified was not found.
S0021	The column specified already exists.
S0022	The column specified was not found.
S1001	A memory allocation failure occurred.
S1002	The column number specified is invalid.
S1003	The type used is out of range.
S1004	The SQL data type used is invalid.
S1008	The operation has been canceled.
S1009	An invalid argument value was specified.
S1010	A function sequence error occurred.
S1012	An invalid transaction operation was specified.
S1015	The cursor name specified is not available.

Continued

TABLE **24-2** ANSI SQL STATE RETURN CODES *(continued)*

SQL State Code	Description
S1090	The buffer or string length specified is invalid.
S1091	The type descriptor is out of range.
S1092	The option type is out of range.
S1093	An invalid parameter number was specified.
S1094	The scale value specified is invalid.
S1095	The function type specified is invalid.
S1096	The information type specified is out of range.
S1097	The column type specified is out of range.
S1098	The scope type specified is out of range.
S1099	The nullable type specified is out of range.
S1100	The uniqueness option type specified is out of range.
S1101	The accuracy option type specified is out of range.
S1102	The table type specified is out of range.
S1103	The direction option specified is out of range.
S1106	The fetch type specified is out of range.
S1107	The row value specified is out of range.
S1108	The concurrency option specified is out of range.
S1109	The current cursor position is invalid.
S1110	The data source driver did not complete an operation correctly.
S1C00	The data source driver is not capable of the specified function.
S1DE0	The required parameter or column values are pending.
S1T00	The timeout period specified has elapsed.

The SQL State codes listed in Table 24-2 are all valid when you work with a Microsoft SQL Server data source and the OLE DB ODBC driver.

ADO Error Reference

ADO itself generates relatively few errors. These errors are indicated in the Error object Number property. Table 24-3 lists and describes the error constants and actual values generated by ADO.

TABLE 24-3 ERROR VALUE CONSTANTS RETURNED BY ADO

Constant	Value	Description
adErrInvalidArgument	3001	The arguments passed to a method are out of range, not the right type, or something else is wrong with them.
adErrNoCurrentRecord	3021	No current record exists. Either the current record has been deleted or you are past the beginning or end of the record set.
adErrIllegalOperation	3219	The method or property being accessed is not valid in the current context.
adErrInTransaction	3246	While a transaction is still open, you can't close the data source connection.
adErrFeatureNotAvailable	3251	The method or property isn't supported by the data provider.
adErrItemNotFound	3265	The collection item wasn't found. Check the index number or name.
adErrObjectNotSet	3420	This object is no longer valid.
adErrDataConversion	3421	The data being used with the current method or property could not be converted to the right type.

Continued

TABLE 24-3 ERROR VALUE CONSTANTS RETURNED BY ADO *(continued)*		
Constant	**Value**	**Description**
adErrObjectClosed	3704	The current operation is not allowed because the object has been closed.
adErrObjectOpen	3705	The current operation is not allowed because the object hasn't been opened.
adErrProviderNotFound	3706	The data provider specified could not be found.
adErrBoundToCommand	3707	This Recordset object is bound to a Command; its ActiveConnection property can't be changed.
adErrInvalidParamInfo	3708	The information provided for the parameter is not valid.
adErrInvalidConnection	3709	The current object isn't associated with a valid connection; the operation could not be performed.

The next step is to integrate the error-handling techniques provided by Visual Basic with the ADO Error and Errors objects. First, review how to integrate the ON ERROR RESUME NEXT statements, and the Error and Errors objects into a script that utilizes ADO. Listing 24-1 demonstrates a simple ADO application that checks for ADO errors.

Listing 24-1: Integrating Error Handling with ADO

```
Dim Conn As ADODB.Connection
DIM cmd As ADODB.Command
DIM rs As Recordset

REM *******************************
REM * Resume When An Error Occurs *
REM *******************************
ON ERROR RESUME NEXT

REM Open the Connection object, omit the password
conn.Open "data source=IDCDatabase", "john"
```

```
REM ******************************************************
REM * Check For A Connect Error - If The Error Count    *
REM * Is > 0                                            *
REM ******************************************************
If(conn.Errors.Count > 0) Then
  REM Just Display The First Error In The Collection
  MsgBox "Error: " & connect.Errors(0).Description,
         0, "Connect Error!"
End If

REM Associate the Command with a Connection
cmd.ActiveConnection = conn

REM Specify the Query
cmd.CommandText = "SELECT * FROM CUSTOMERS"
cmd.CommandType = adCmdText
set rs = cmd.Execute(NumRecs)

REM ******************************************************
REM * Check For A Execution Error - If The Error Count  *
REM * Is > 0                                            *
REM ******************************************************
If(rs.ActiveConnection.Errors.Count > 0) Then
  REM Just Display The First Error In The Collection
  MsgBox "Error: " & connect.Errors(0).Description,
         0, "Execute Error!"
End If

REM Loop Through and Display The Field Names
For I = 0 To rs.Fields.Count - 1
  MsgBox rs.Fields(I).Name
Next

REM Loop Through and Display The Field Values For Each
REM Record
rs.MoveFirst
Do While (Not rs.EOF)
  For I = 0 To rs.Fields.Count - 1
    MsgBox rs.Fields(I)
  Next
  rs.MoveNext
Loop

REM Close the Connection...
rs.Close
conn.Close
```

Take note of a few key points in this example. First, the ON ERROR RESUME NEXT statement is included at the beginning of the script. You should check for errors at two points: when the connection is opened, and when the query is executed. If the Errors object Count property is greater than 0, then the collection contains an Error object. In this basic example, only the description of the first error in the collection is displayed. Take special note of how, in the first error check, the *connect* object was used to access the Errors collection, and in the second error check, the Recordset ActiveConnection property was used to access the Errors collection.

Before the topic of ADO error handling and Visual Basic is closed, take a look at how to build a Visual Basic procedure that can check whether an error has occurred and display all the items in the Errors collection. Listing 24-2 displays the ADOError procedure, which displays each error contained in the Errors collection. If the user clicks the No button, the display of error messages is aborted.

Listing 24-2: Using the ADOError Procedure

```
Sub ADOError(Connect As ADODB.Connection)
  i = 0
  Quit = False
  REM Check For An Error
  If(Connect.Errors.Count > 0) Then
    REM Loop Through The Errors Collection
    Do While ((Not Quit) And
          (i < (Connect.Errors.Count - 1)))
      If(i = (Connect.Errors.Count - 1)) Then
        REM Just Display An OK Button For Last Error
        Title = "ADO Error"
      Else
        REM Display Error Count For Multiple Errors
        Title = "ADO Error # " & (i + 1) &
              " of " & Connect.Errors.Count & _
              " - Display Next Error?"
      End If
      RetVal = MsgBox Connect.Errors(i).Description
                & " Source: " & _
                Connect.Errors(i).Source, _
                Prompt + vbCritical, Title
      REM If The User Clicks No - Quit Displaying Errors
      If(RetVal = vbNo) Then
        Quit = True
      End If
      i = i + 1
    Loop
  End If
End Sub
```

Listing 24-3 demonstrates how the `ADOError()` method is integrated into a Visual Basic application.

Listing 24-3: Integrating the ADOError Procedure

```
ON ERROR RESUME NEXT

adCmdText = 1
REM Open the Connection object, omit the password
connect.Open "data source=IDCDatabase", "john"

REM Call The ADOError Procedure TO Check For Errors
ADOError(connect)
```

 TIP   Include the `ADOError` procedure at the beginning of your Visual Basic applications. Each time that you call an ADO object method, follow it with a call to the `ADOError` procedure. If an error hasn't occurred, nothing is displayed and execution continues.

Property Object

The `Property` object is used to determine whether a data provider supports an ADO object property, and to set and retrieve its value. While some of the ADO object properties are required, some objects provide optional properties. Each ADO object property is encapsulated by a `Property` object. Each of these property objects are contained in a `Properties` object collection. The `Properties` object is reviewed shortly. You will also learn how to check whether an ADO object supports a property while an application or applet is executing. First, the properties provided by the `Property` object are reviewed. The `Property` object does not have any methods.

The `Property` object provides properties that determine the special attributes of a property (if it is supported, required, or can be read and written), its name, type, and current value. Table 24-4 lists and describes the properties provided by the `Property` object.

TABLE 24-4 PROPERTY OBJECT PROPERTIES

Property	Read/Write	Description
Attribute	R	Describes the attributes of the property.
Name	R	Returns the name of the property.
Type	R	Returns the data type of the property value.
Value	R/W	Used to set or return the property's value.

Attribute Property

The Attribute property is used to determine whether a property can be read or written, and whether it's supported or required. The Attribute property value is a Long that is comprised of the PropertyAttributesEnum constants shown in Table 24-5. These values can be combined by logically ORing together the constant values.

TABLE 24-5 PROPERTYATTRIBUTESENUM CONSTANT VALUES

Constant	Value	Description
AdPropNotSupported	0	This property isn't supported for this object by the current data provider.
AdPropRequired	1	This property must have a value before the data source can be initialized.
AdPropOptional	2	This property is not required to have a value before the data source is initialized.
AdPropRead	512	This property value can be read.
AdPropWrite	1024	This property value can be written.

Name, Type, and Value Properties

The Name property simply returns a String that contains the proper name of the property. The Name value can be used to index the Properties collection (which is reviewed next). The Type property is used to determine the type of values that the property can accept. The ADO `DataTypeEnum` constants are listed and described in Table 24-6. The `Type` property is a Long-type value that *must* be one of `DataTypeEnum` constant values. The `Value` property simply is used to set a property value.

TABLE 24-6 DATATYPEENUM CONSTANTS

Constant	Value	Description
adBigInt	20	Signed integer (8 bytes).
adBinary	128	Binary value.
adBoolean	11	Boolean value.
adBSTR	8	Unicode character string that is null-terminated.
adChar	129	Null-terminated character string.
adCurrency	6	Currency value.
adDate	7	Date value.
adDBDate	133	Date value in the form *yyyymmdd*.
adDBTime	134	Time value in the form *hhmmss*.
adDBTimeStamp	135	Date-time value in the form *yyyymmddhhmmss*.
adDecimal	14	Fixed-precision floating-type value.
adDouble	5	Double-precision floating-point value.
adEmpty	0	Type has not been specified yet (default).
adError	10	Error-code type.
adGUID	72	Globally unique identifier (GUID)-type value.
adIDispatch	9	OLE IDispatch interface-type value.
adInteger	3	Signed integer (4 bytes).
adIUnknown	13	OLE IUnknown interface-type value.
adLongVarBinary	205	Long binary-type value. *Used only for Parameter objects.*

Continued

TABLE **24-6 DATATYPEENUM CONSTANTS** *(continued)*

Constant	Value	Description
adLongVarChar	201	Long string-type value. *Used only for Parameter objects.*
adLongVarWChar	203	Long null-terminated character-string-type value. *Used only for Parameter objects.*
adNumeric	131	Exact numeric-type value with a fixed precision and scale.
adSingle	4	Single-precision floating-point-type value.
adSmallInt	2	Signed integer (2 bytes).
adTinyInt	16	Signed integer (1 byte).
adUnsignedBigInt	21	Unsigned integer (8 bytes).
adUnsignedInt	19	Unsigned integer (4 bytes).
adUnsignedSmallInt	18	Unsigned integer (2 bytes).
adUnsignedTinyInt	17	Unsigned integer (1 byte).
adUserDefined	132	User-defined type.
adVarBinary	204	Variable-length binary-type value. *Used only for Parameter objects.*
adVarChar	200	Variable-length character-string-type value. *Used only for Parameter objects.*
adVariant	12	OLE Variant-type value.
adVarWChar	202	Variable-length Unicode character string that is null-terminated. *Used only for Parameter objects.*
adWChar	130	Unicode character string that is null-terminated.

Properties Collection

An ADO object can have, and almost always has, more than one property associated with it. The `Properties` collection is used to hold a collection of `Property` objects for an ADO object. Each ADO object has an associated `Properties` object. The `Properties` collection can be accessed in the following manner:

```
ADOObject.Properties
```

in which *ADOObject* is any valid ADO object that you're interested in. As you will see when you review the `Index` property of the `Properties` collection, a `Property` object in the `Properties` collection can be accessed by a numeric index or its name.

Properties Refresh() Method

The `Properties` object provides one method, `Refresh()`, which can be used to synchronize an ADO object's optional properties with a data provider. Calling the `Refresh()` method will fill the `Properties` collection. You do not need to call the `Refresh()` method explicitly, because the first time that you access the `Properties` collection, the collection becomes populated.

Properties Attributes

The `Properties` object provides two properties: the `Count` property returns the number of `Property` objects contained in the collection, and the `Item` property returns the `Property` object at the specified index. You don't need to use the `Item()` method directly.

COUNT PROPERTY
The `Count` property simply returns the number of `Property` objects in the `Properties` collection. The `Properties` collection can be accessed by a numeric index, and can be used to loop through the `Properties` collection.

ITEM PROPERTY
The `Item` property can be used to access a `Property` object of the `Properties` collection. You don't need to use the `Item` property to access a `Property` contained in the `Properties` collection. An item of the `Properties` collection can be accessed in the following ways:

```
ADOobject.Properties(index)
ADOobject.Properties.Item(index)
```

in which *ADOObject* is any valid ADO object, the *index* parameter is a numeric index or a property name, and the `Properties` collections are numerically indexed from 0 to the `Count` property value – 1.

Listing 24-4 demonstrates how to display the properties contained in the `Properties` collection for the `Connection` object, and their values.

Listing 24-4: Properties Provided by the Connect Object

```
For I = 0 To connect.Properties.Count - 1
  MsgBox connect.Properties(i).Name & " = " &
        connect.Properties(i).Value
Next
```

Summary

This chapter showed you how to use the ADO `Error` and `Errors` objects to add a level of robustness to your ADO applications. You also learned about the ADO `Property` and `Properties` objects, and how to dynamically access ADO object properties. Finally, an example function was developed that showed you the properties provided by the `Connection` object.

This wraps up the formal review of the ADO objects. The next chapter continues with a review of the Remote Data Services (RDS), which is a set of ActiveX components that automates the process of accessing database sources.

Chapter 25

Remote Data Services

IN THIS CHAPTER

◆ Overviewing RDS controls

◆ Comparing ADO and RDS

◆ Using RDS for data retrieval

◆ Getting the latest RDS information

REMOTE DATA SERVICES (RDS) is a set of ActiveX components that provides access to OLE DB data sources. RDS brings together several technologies to facilitate data access, including ActiveX, OLE DB, and ActiveX Data Objects (ADO). RDS operates in a three-tier client/server environment, which includes the traditional client- and server-side tiers, and a third, middle tier. The middle tier includes *business objects*, which are encapsulated applets that comprise specific rules, functions, and other discrete processes. This chapter reviews the RDS components and business objects. It also compares RDS and ADO. RDS brings together many Microsoft technologies, including Internet Information Server (IIS), the Distributed Component Object Model (DCOM), Microsoft Transaction Server, OLE DB, and SQL Server data sources, in an effort to provide seamless access to corporate data sources over the Internet and corporate intranets.

RDS Control Overview

RDS components include the Virtual Table Manager (VTM), which manages the OLE DB data source memory cache. The `RDS.DataControl` object provides data source binding and query management in a control. The `RDS.DataSpace` object provides the ability for the client tier to communicate with the middle tier. The `RDS.DataFactory` object provides the default business-object functionality, which provides the capability to retrieve and store data from the OLE DB data source. Advanced Data Internet Server API provides the functionality to Internet Information Server to communicate – and package – queries and parameters between a client and IIS. ADO `Recordset` marshaling provides the capability to communicate to `Recordset` objects over distinct thread and process boundaries by using HTTP and DCOM.

Figure 25-1 illustrates the three-tier nature of the Remote Data Services Model.

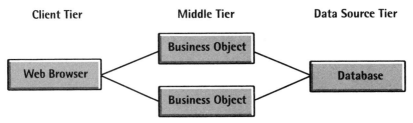

Figure 25-1: The three-tier nature of the Remote Data Services Model

The next section continues with a more detailed review of each RDS component.

Business Objects

Business objects are the middle-tier components in the RDS architecture. They provide read and write access to a data source. *Business objects* are encapsulated modules that cannot only provide data-source access, but can also provide business-specific validation rules and data-source authentication. Because business objects are part of the middle tier, they can also help to decrease resource requirements on the data source server. RDS provides a default business object, the RDS.DataFactory object, which simply provides the capability to communicate to a data source, and which can be the framework for building more-complex business objects. Because business objects provide their functionality in an encapsulated framework, they are completely reusable.

You can use Visual Basic and Visual C++ to create custom business objects.

Virtual Table Manager

Virtual Table Manager is not a directly accessible RDS component. The function of VTM is to provide an intelligent client-side cache for data source result sets and data modifications. VTM can store data source table and table schema information, and is a cache that functions exactly like the data source. VTM helps to minimize client/server communications through its capability to create temporary tables in a client-side cache and to collect data source modifications that can be transmitted in a batch mode. VTM ensures that the data source remains synchronized with client-side modifications. VTM is optimized to work with client-side Keyset cursors.

VTM implements the *tablegram communications protocol,* a proprietary communications format that is used to transmit table-based data-source record sets. The tablegram protocol utilizes the Internet standard MIME (Multipurpose Internet Mail Extensions) encoding to transmit record-set data to and from the data source, using the standard HTTP and DCOM communications protocols. The tablegram protocol takes advantage of data-source normalization, which can ensure that data-source tables are transmitted only when they are required.

ADO Recordset Marshaling

The last Advanced Data Control feature to discuss is ADO Recordset marshaling. *Marshaling* is the transmission of record-set data between the client and data source. As previously discussed, RDS uses the tablegram protocol to communicate record-set data. The Internet standard MIME protocol is used to encapsulate the data transmissions. The ADO Recordset objects are connected to the data source by using the server-side Advanced Data Internet Server API (ADISAPI) OLE DB provider mechanisms.

The ADODB.Recordset Object

The ADODB.Recordset object is the full-featured Recordset object that is supported only when you use the DCOM or Remote Procedure Call (RPC) protocols. When you communicate between the client and the middle tier, the ADODB.Recordset object is used.

The ADOR.Recordset Object

The ADOR.Recordset object — the lightweight version of the Recordset object — is used when you communicate between the server and the client. The ADOR.Recordset object is supported by HTTP. The ADOR.Recordset object supports a subset of the methods and properties provided by the full-blown Recordset object. Table 25-1 lists and describes the properties supported by the ADOR.Recordset object, and Table 25-2 lists and describes the methods provided. Remember that when you use RDS on the server side, the ADODB.Recordset object is used, and when you use RDS on the client side, the lighter-weight ADOR.Recordset object is used. The ADOR.Recordset on the client side is generally supported by a corresponding ADODB.Recordset on the server side.

You can access the lightweight version of the ADO `Recordset` for your ADO applications and applets, without using RDS. Generally, though, the lightweight version of the `Recordset` object is used only in conjunction with RDS.

TABLE 25-1 ADOR.RECORDSET PROPERTIES

Property	Description
BOF	A Boolean value that is `True` if the cursor is at or past the beginning of the record set.
EOF	A Boolean value that is `True` if the cursor is at or past the end of the record set.
Bookmark	A Long value that returns a bookmark to the current record.
MarshalOptions	Controls record set marshaling. Either all rows or only modified rows can be transferred between the client and server. Marshaling modified rows only can improve performance.

TABLE 25-2 ADOR.RECORDSET METHODS

Method	Description
Close()	Closes the `Recordset` object and releases the associated resources.
Move()	Use to move the cursor to a specified number of records or to a bookmarked location.
MoveFirst()	Use to move the cursor to the first record in the record set.
MoveLast()	Use to move the cursor to the last record in the record set.
MoveNext()	Use to move the cursor to the next record in the record set.
MovePrevious()	Use to move the cursor to the previous record in the record set.
Open()	Use to open a connection with a data source and then perform a query, perform a command, or open a table.

RDS and ADO Compared

Comparing RDS to ADO is like comparing ADO to OLE DB. ADO can be used to develop applications and applets that can access OLE DB data sources. ADO provides an abstracted interface to create an OLE DB data consumer. ADO utilizes the underlying OLE DB interface to perform its work. RDS provides the same layer of abstraction to ADO. RDS utilizes the ADO `Recordset` object to manage data source information, and provides the capability to hook a data source easily to other visually oriented controls, without the need for any complex programming.

Remote Data Services

Remote Data Services grew out of the Internet Data Connector, which originally was provided with IIS as a server-side means to access a database. RDS operates by using a distributed methodology. You can understand better how RDS is used for data access by understanding what RDS does, which is a combination of three things:

- ◆ Provides custom marshaling for `Recordset` objects. When discussing RDS, you will often hear the term *marshaling*, which is just a fancy name for passing data between the client and server. RDS can pass ADO `Recordset` objects between the client and the server on which the data source resides.

- ◆ Can be used on standard Internet communications protocols, such as HTTP (Hypertext Transfer Protocol) and HTTPS (Secured Hypertext Transfer Protocol). HTTP and HTTPS are the primary Web-based communications protocols.

- ◆ Provides the capability to bind data with other ActiveX controls. *Data binding,* another term that you will often hear associated with RDS, simply means that data contained in a record set can be automatically passed between a `Recordset` object and other ActiveX controls.

RDS provides server-side database control, with the capability to manipulate and control record sets on the client. Most importantly, the client side isn't required to have special drivers (such as ODBC) set up to access a database on the client side. Three main objects bring this functionality to RDS: `RDS.DataControl`, `RDS.DataSpace`, and `RDS.DataFactory`. Each of these objects is reviewed in detail next.

RDS.DataControl Object

The RDS.DataControl object is a nonvisual object that provides a context for binding with a data source and encapsulating the result of a query. The RDS.DataControl works in conjunction with the lightweight ADO Recordset (ADOR.Recordset). The resulting columns from an RDS.DataControl object query can be bound to other visual-data-aware controls – such as a text box, list box, or combo box – or third-party grid controls. When a column is bound to a control, its value automatically is transferred to the control. Table 25-3 lists the third-party data-aware controls that work with the RDS.DataControl object. The RDS.DataControl also provides the capability to specify a data source, the server on which the data source has been defined, the connect string for a data source, and a query. Each RDS.DataControl encapsulates the results of a single query.

TABLE 25-3 RDS.DATACONTROL OBJECT CONTROLS

Control	Manufacturer
DBListBox	Apex
	http://www.apexsc.com
	Provided with Visual Basic Enterprise Edition
DBComboBox	Apex
	http://www.apexsc.com
	Provided with Visual Basic Enterprise Edition
RichTextField	Microsoft Corporation
	Provided with Visual Basic Enterprise Edition
	http://www.microsoft.com
MhImage	MicroHelp
	http://www.microhelp.com
	Provided with Visual Basic Enterprise Edition
SSDBCombo	Sheridan
	http://www.shersoft.com
SSDBGrid	Sheridan
	http://www.shersoft.com

The `RDS.DataControl` object is the primary RDS object. It is used to establish a connection with a data source and to create a record set that is a result of a query. The `RDS.DataControl` can bind the columns of a query to other ActiveX objects. When a column is bound to an ActiveX control, such as an edit box, as you move through the query-result record set, the column's value is automatically placed in the control. When a column value is updated in a control, that value is also automatically updated in the record set, if the record set is writable. You will learn how to bind query results to various ActiveX controls later in this chapter. Before you learn how to use the `RDS.DataControl`, you first need to review the properties and methods that it provides.

RDS.DataControl Properties

Table 25-4 lists and briefly describes the properties provided by the `RDS.DataControl` object. These properties can be specified at the time an `RDS.DataControl` is created. You can specify control bindings, a data-source connection string, where server-side objects should be created, the query that is used to create a record set, and even whether to use a previously created ADO record set.

TABLE 25-4 RDS.DATACONTROL PROPERTIES

Property	Description
Bindings	Describes how query result columns are associated with other ActiveX controls.
Connect	Describes how to connect to a data source.
Recordset	Allows the `RDS.DataControl` to use record sets created by server-side business objects.
Server	Specifies where server-side objects are created and how to communicate with the server.
SQL	Specifies the query string to be executed.

BINDINGS PROPERTY

The `Bindings` property is a String type that is used to associate query-result columns with ActiveX controls. The `Bindings` property can be specified only when the `RDS.DataControl` object is created. Typical binding strings are of the form `Control.Text=Table.Column`; or simply `Control`; wherein `Control` is the name of an ActiveX control, `Table` is the name of the query table (optional), and `Column` is the name of a query-result column. The semicolon (;) is used to separate binding string statements. In the first form of the binding string, a single column value is bound to a control; in the second form, the complete query result is bound to a control (for example, a grid control). Don't worry if you don't understand all the parameters used – the remaining RDS.DataControl properties are reviewed next. Later in this chapter, you learn more about binding the RDS.DataControl to edit, list, and grid controls.

CONNECT PROPERTY

The Connect property is used to specify how to connect to a data source. The Connect property can be specified either at runtime or when the RDS.DataControl is created. Note especially how using RDS differs from using OLE DB or ADO to connect to a data source. Unlike OLE DB or ADO, using the RDS.DataControl doesn't require the presence of data-source drivers on the client. The Connect property is used to describe how to connect to the data source on the server side. Table 25-5 lists the connect string parameters. The name of the data source is the name of the ODBC data source on the server. To access an OLE DB data source, you need to create your own ADO record set and the Recordset property to use it.

TABLE 25-5 CONNECT STRING PARAMETERS

Parameter	Description
DSN=	The name of the ODBC data source.
UID=	Specifies the username. If this is an empty string, *domain-managed security* is employed, in which your Windows NT username and password are passed to the data source. Domain-managed security is easier to manage than data-source security, because usernames and passwords are kept in a centralized location.
PWD=	Specifies the password. If this is an empty string, domain-managed security is employed.

RECORDSET PROPERTY

The Recordset property is used to specify the ADOR.Recordset object that the RDS.DataControl should utilize. When the Recordset property is used, the query and connect strings are not required by the AdvancedDataControl. Listing 25-1 demonstrates how to use the Recordset property. By using the Recordset property, the RDS.DataControl can access an OLE DB data source.

Listing 25-1: Using the RDS.DataControl Recordset Property

```
REM Open the Connection object, omit the password
connect.Open "data source=IDCDatabase", "john"

REM Associate the Command with a Connection
cmd.ActiveConnection = connect

REM The Command Is Just a Table Name
REM All Table Records Are Returned
cmd.CommandText = "CUSTOMERS"
cmd.CommandType = adCmdTable
set rs = cmd.Execute(NumRecs)

AdvDataCtrl.Recordset = rs

REM Use the RDS.DataControl

REM Close the Record Set and Connection
rs.Close
connect.Close
```

SERVER PROPERTY

The Server property is used to specify where server-side objects are created. If this property is not specified, the server-side objects are created where the data source is located. The Server property can be specified either when the RDS.DataControl is created or during runtime. How you specify the server depends on the type of communications protocol that you are using. Table 25-6 summarizes how to specify the server when using HTTP, HTTPS, and DCOM, and when accessing a local data source.

TABLE 25-6 SPECIFYING THE SERVER PROPERTY VALUE FOR DIFFERENT
COMMUNICATIONS PROTOCOLS

Protocol	Design-Time Syntax
HTTP	http://WebServerName:Port
HTTPS	https://WebServerName:Port
DCOM	ServerName
Local	Empty string

WebServerName is the name of your Web server, *Port* is the Web-server port, and *ServerName* is the name of a server on your network.

SQL PROPERTY

The SQL property value is used to specify a query. This query string is executed by the Command object, to generate a record set. The SQL property can be specified either when the RDS.DataControl is created or during runtime.

RDS.DataControl Methods

Table 25-7 lists and briefly describes the methods provided by the RDS.DataControl object. These methods are used after an RDS.DataControl is created, to commit or abort changes, navigate the current record set, and synchronize the current record set with the data source.

TABLE 25–7 RDS.DATACONTROL METHODS

Method	Description
CancelUpdate()	Use to abort all pending record-set changes.
MoveFirst()	Use to move to the first record in the record set.
MoveLast()	Use to move to the last record in the record set.
MoveNext()	Use to move to the next record in the record set.
MovePrevious()	Use to move to the previous record in the record set.
Refresh()	Use to synchronize the data contained in the data source with the current record set.
SubmitChanges()	Use to commit any pending record-set changes.

CANCELUPDATE() METHOD

The CancelUpdate() method is used to abort all changes that are pending on the current record set. RDS keeps both the modified and original values for the record set. When the CancelUpdate() method is called, all the modified values are discarded. If the RDS.DataControl is bound to any other ActiveX controls, the values displayed automatically revert to the original record-set values.

MOVE() METHODS

The MoveFirst(), MoveNext(), MovePrevious(), and MoveLast() methods are used to navigate the current record set. If the record-set column values are bound to a control, the control values are automatically updated to contain the values of the current record.

By using the Recordset property, you can access the ADO Recordset associated with this RDS.DataControl, and you can determine whether you're at the beginning (BOF) or end (EOF) of the record set. You can also use the ADO Recordset object Move() methods to navigate the current record set.

You can use the ADO Recordset Clone() method to create a copy of the record set that is contained within an RDS.DataControl.

REFRESH() METHOD

The Refresh() method is used to synchronize the record set with the data source. Any pending record-set changes are discarded, and the record set is updated to contain the data that is currently contained at the data source. If the RDS.DataControl is bound to any other ActiveX controls, the values displayed are updated automatically to the current data-source values.

SUBMITCHANGES() METHOD

The SubmitChanges() method is used to commit all changes that are currently pending on the current record set. RDS keeps both the modified and original values for the record set. When the SubmitChanges() method is called, all the modified values are synchronized with the data source.

RDS.DataSpace Object

The RDS.DataSpace object serves as a client-side proxy when you communicate with business objects. It is a nonvisual control. The RDS.DataSpace object manages all communications with middle-tier business objects. Whenever a middle-tier business object is created on the client, the RDS.DataSpace proxy is automatically created to manage all communications between the client and middle tier.

The RDS.DataSpace object is used to create client-side proxies for business objects. A *proxy* is a client-side object that communicates with a server-side process, such as a business object. A proxy enables a client to communicate with a remote process, and is responsible for all client-side communications and parameter-passing with the server process. Business objects are the middle-tier components in the RDS architecture that provide read and write access to a data source. They are encapsulated modules which, in addition to providing data-source access, also provide business-specific validation rules and data-source authentication. Normally, you use the single-threaded version of the RDS.DataSpace. The RDS.DataSpace object does not provide any properties.

The RDS.DataSpace object provides a single method, CreateObject, which is used to create a business-object proxy. The CreateObject() method has the following form:

```
Set object = CreateObject(BusinessObject, ServerName)
```

in which object contains the new object proxy created, the BusinessObject parameter is a string that is the name of the business object to be created, and the ServerName parameter is a string that is the name of the server. Refer to Table 25-6 for more information on how to specify the server name. The RDS.DataFactory object is the default business object provided by RDS; it is examined in more detail next.

RDS.DataFactory Object

The RDS.DataFactory object is the default middle-tier business object provided by RDS. The AdvanceDataFactory, which resides on the server side, simply provides the means for a client to communicate with a data source. The RDS.DataFactory communicates with the server by using the Advanced Data Internet Server API (ADISAPI), discussed later in this chapter. The RDS.DataFactory can be used as the framework to build other, more advanced business objects.

The RDS.DataFactory is the default server-side business object. It is a very basic server-side object that enables you to read and write to a server-side data source and perform queries. The RDS.DataFactory communicates directly with the server-side data source, and communicates to the client through the RDS.DataSpace proxy. The RDS.DataFactory doesn't provide properties; its methods are discussed next.

The RDS.DataFactory is simply a pass-through business object. You can create your own server-side business objects to use for advanced data filtering or other specialized processing. The process of creating a custom business object is beyond the scope of the current discussion. Refer to the topic "Building Custom Business Objects" in the RDS online Help file for more information on creating custom business objects, which can be created with Visual Basic, Visual C++, or Active Server Pages.

Table 25-8 lists and briefly describes the methods provided by the RDS.DataFactory object. These methods are used after an RDS.DataFactory is created, to commit or abort changes, navigate the current record set, and synchronize the current record set with the data source.

TABLE 25-8 RDS.DATAFACTORY OBJECT METHODS

Method	Description
CreateRecordset()	Used to create an empty record set on the client. This record set can be filled by the server. Takes a single parameter that is an array that describes the schema of the record set to create.
Query()	Performs a query on the specified data source and returns a record set containing the requested server-side data.
SubmitChanges()	Used to apply changes made in a client-side record set back to the server-side data source.

CreateRecordset() Method

The CreateRecordset() method of the RDS.DataFactory object is used to create an empty ADODB (ADO Database) Recordset object. The CreateRecordset() method has the following form:

```
Set RecSet = AdvDataFact.CreateRecordset(Columns)
```

in which *RecSet* is the empty ADODB `Recordset` that will be created, *AdvDataFact* is a valid `RDS.DataFactory` object, and *Columns* is an array that describes the `Recordset` schema. Each element of the *Columns* array holds a smaller array that describes each column of the `Recordset` to be created. The following four elements are required to define a `Recordset` column:

◆ The column name; a string type

◆ The column type; an integer that is one of the type constants in Table 25-9

◆ The length of the column in bytes; an integer type

◆ A flag that indicates whether the column can contain a null value; a Boolean type

The length of the column is required only for variable-length types. If the column is a fixed-length type — a numeric or Boolean value, for example — the column length should be set to –1.

TABLE 25-9 THE RECORDSET COLUMN-TYPE CONSTANTS

Constant	Description
adBigInt	Signed integer (8 bytes)
adBinary	Binary value
adBoolean	Boolean value
adBSTR	Unicode character string that is null-terminated
adChar	Null-terminated character string
adCurrency	Currency value
adDate	Date value
adDBDate	Date value in the form *yyyymmdd*
adDBTime	Time value in the form *hhmmss*
adDBTimeStamp	Date-time value in the form *yyyymmddhhmmss*
adDecimal	Fixed-precision floating-type value
adDouble	Double-precision floating-point value

Constant	Description
adEmpty	Type has not been specified yet (default)
adError	Error-code type
adGUID	Globally unique identifier (GUID)-type value
adInteger	Signed integer (4 bytes)
adLongVarBinary	Long binary-type value
adLongVarChar	Long string-type value
adLongVarWChar	Long null-terminated character-string-type value
adNumeric	Exact numeric-type value with a fixed precision and scale
adSingle	Single-precision floating-point-type value
adSmallInt	Signed integer (2 bytes)
adTinyInt	Signed integer (1 byte)
adUnsignedBigInt	Unsigned integer (8 bytes)
adUnsignedInt	Unsigned integer (4 bytes)
adUnsignedSmallInt	Unsigned integer (2 bytes)
adUnsignedTinyInt	Unsigned integer (1 byte)
adUserDefined	User-defined type
adVarBinary	Variable-length binary-type value
adVarChar	Variable-length character-string-type value
adVariant	OLE Variant-type value
adVarWChar	Variable-length Unicode character string that is null-terminated
adWChar	Unicode character string that is null-terminated

Listing 25-2 demonstrates the process of creating a `Columns` array and calling the `CreateRecordset()` method.

Listing 25-2: Creating a Columns Array and Calling the CreateRecordset() Method

```
REM Create an RDS.DataFactory Object
set AdvDataFact = AdvDataSpace.CreateObject("RDS.DataFactory",_
                                    "IDCNTSERVER")


DIM Columns(2), Col1(3), Col2(3), Col3(3)

REM Define Column 1
Col1(0) = "ProductID"
Col1(1) = adInteger
Col1(2) = -1
Col1(3) = False

REM Define Column 2
Col2(0) = "ProductName"
Col2(1) = adChar
Col2(2) = 50
Col2(3) = False

REM Define Column 3
Col3(0) = "InStock"
Col3(1) = adBoolean
Col3(2) = -1
Col3(3) = False

REM Define Columns
Columns(0) = Col1
Columns(1) = Col2
Columns(2) = Col3

Set RecSet = AdvDataFact.CreateRecordset(Columns)
```

Query() method

The Query() method is used to execute a server-side query using the
RDS.DataFactory business object. The Query() method returns an ADODB
Recordset object. The Query() method has the following form:

```
Set RecSet = AdvDataFact.Query(ConnectString,Query)
```

in which *RecSet* is the empty ADODB Recordset that will be created, *AdvDataFact* is a valid RDS.DataFactory object, *ConnectString* is a string that establishes a data-source connection, and *Query* is a string that contains an SQL query command. Listing 25-3 demonstrates how to use the RDS.DataFactory's Query() method to create a Recordset object that contains the results of a server-side query.

Listing 25-3: Using the RDS.DataFactory's Query() Method to Create a Recordset Object

```
REM Create an RDS.DataFactory Object
set AdvDataFact = AdvDataSpace.CreateObject("RDS.DataFactory",_
"IDCNTSERVER")

REM Perform Query
set RecSet = AdvDataFact.Query("DSN=IDCDataSource;UID=John",_
                "SELECT * FROM CUSTOMERS")
```

SubmitChanges() Method

The SubmitChanges() method is used to apply to the server-side data source any changes made to a client-side record set. The SubmitChanges() method has the following form:

AdvDataFact.SubmitChanges(*ConnectString*,RecSet)

in which *AdvDataFact* is a valid RDS.DataFactory object, *ConnectString* is a string that establishes a data-source connection, and *RecSet* is a valid, updatable Recordset object that contains data to update. When a record set is updated at the data source, only the records that have been modified are sent back to the server. Listing 25-4 demonstrates how to use the SubmitChanges() method.

Each client-side record in the record set contains a *timestamp*, which determines when the record was retrieved from the server-side data source. Updating a record set doesn't affect the timestamps of the client-side records. After you update a record set, you need to call the Refresh() method of the Recordset object, to synchronize the client- and server-side timestamps.

Listing 25-4: Using the RDS.DataFactory SubmitChanges() Method

```
REM Create an RDS.DataFactory Object
set AdvDataFact = AdvDataSpace.CreateObject("RDS.DataFactory",_
                         "IDCNTSERVER")

REM Perform Query
set RecSet = AdvDataFact.Query("DSN=IDCDataSource;UID=John",_
                    "SELECT * FROM CUSTOMERS")

REM Make Modifications To RecSet

AdvDataFact.SubmitChanges("DSN=IDCDataSource;UID=John",
                     RecSet)
```

Database Data Retrieval

To retrieve server-side data with RDS, you need to use a business object. You can either use the default RDS.DataFactory business object or a custom business object that applies specific rules or filtering. The following steps are necessary to utilize a business object with RDS to retrieve database data:

1. Create an RDS.DataControl.

2. Create an RDS.DataSpace business object proxy.

3. Create the server-side business object by using the RDS.DataSpace object. You must specify the name of the server on which the business objects reside.

4. Use the business object to create a Recordset object. If you're using a custom business object, use the method that it provides for this purpose. If you're using the default business object, the RDS.DataFactory, you can use the Query() method to create a Recordset object that contains data-source data.

5. Set the RDS.DataControl's Recordset property to the Recordset object created by the business object.

Listing 25-5 demonstrates how each of these steps is implemented. As you can see, each RDS object is used to retrieve and utilize server-side data.

Listing 25-5: Retrieving Database Data Using the Remote Data Services Model

```
REM Step 1 - Create an RDS.DataControl object
DIM AdvDataControl As RDS.DataControl

REM Step 2 - Create an RDS.DataSpace object
DIM AdvDataSpace As RDS.DataSpace

REM Step 3 - Create an RDS.DataFactory Object
set AdvDataFact = AdvDataSpace.CreateObject("RDS.DataFactory",_
                            "IDCNTSERVER")

REM Step 4 - Use the RDS.DataFactory to Create A
REM RecordSet object
REM Which Contains Server Side Data
set RecSet = AdvDataFact.Query("DSN=IDCDataSource;UID=John",_
"SELECT * FROM CUSTOMERS")

REM Step 5 - Set The RDS.DataControl's Recordset
REM Property
AdvDataCtrl.Recordset = Recset
```

The Latest RDS Information

Microsoft provides Web-site and newsgroup resources to help you stay up to date with the latest RDS developments. These resources include:

- ◆ http://www.microsoft.com/data/rds — The Remote Data Services Web site.

- ◆ http://www.microsoft.com/iis — Internet Information Server Web site.

- ◆ http://www.microsoft.com/sql — Microsoft SQL Server Web site.

- ◆ http://www.microsoft.com/transaction — Microsoft Transaction Server Web site.

- ◆ microsoft.public.adc — The Remote Data Services news group.

- ◆ microsoft.public.adcbeta — The Remote Data Services beta release news group.

- ◆ microsoft.public.activex.* — A series of news groups related to the discussion of ActiveX components.

Summary

This chapter reviewed the Remote Data Services and its components. You learned how the RDS components work together to provide a three-tiered architecture that can utilize specialized business-object components that can, among other things, filter and validate data-source data. You learned about the requirements for installing the server- and client-side components. The installation process was reviewed, and you also learned how to test your installation. Finally, this chapter reviewed the Internet resources provided by Microsoft to keep you up to date with the latest RDS happenings.

Part VI

ODBC and OLE DB API

Chapter 26

ODBC Driver Manager

IN THIS CHAPTER

◆ Overviewing the ODBC driver

◆ Summarizing functions provided by ODBC 3.*x*

◆ Mapping ODBC 2.*x* functions to ODBC 3.*x*

◆ Determining driver capabilities using SQLGetInfo

◆ Obtaining error information in your applications

ODBC GIVES YOU ACCESS to a variety of databases with Visual Basic. The Structured Query Language (SQL) is the language that is used to access the database. Through the use of ODBC, an application may interact with numerous databases by using the same source code. This enables a developer to build and distribute a client/server application, without targeting a specific database management system (DBMS) or knowing specific details of various back-end data sources.

Introduction to the ODBC Driver

When an application needs to retrieve data from a data source, the application sends an SQL statement to Driver Manager, which then loads the driver that is required to talk to the data. The driver then translates the SQL sent by the application into the SQL used by the DBMS and sends it to the back-end database. The DBMS retrieves the data and passes it back to the application through the driver and Driver Manager.

ODBC is the database portion of Microsoft's Windows Open Services Architecture (WOSA), an interface that enables Windows-based applications to connect to multiple DBMSs without rewriting the application for each database.

The following are the components of ODBC:

◆ **ODBC API:** A library of function calls, a set of error codes, and a standard SQL syntax for accessing data on DBMSs.

◆ **ODBC Driver Manager:** A Dynamic Link Library (DLL) that loads ODBC database drivers on behalf of an application. This DLL is transparent to your application.

- ◆ **ODBC database drivers:** One or more DLLs that process ODBC function calls for specific DBMSs.

- ◆ **ODBC Cursor Library:** A DLL that resides between ODBC Driver Manager and the drivers and handles scrolling through the data.

- ◆ **ODBC Administrator:** A tool that is used to configure a DBMS to make it available as a data source for an application.

Developers can code directly to the API by declaring various functions and then using those functions to connect, send SQL statements, retrieve results, get errors, disconnect, and so forth. This technique is well documented and has been a very popular way of writing Visual Basic client/server applications. However, this technique is fairly difficult and involves a lot of code. Thus, to access ODBC data from applications, ADO, RDO, and DAO are used more often than this technique. ODBC has been the data access standard since 1992, and has played a very important role in enabling the development of client/server applications. Over 170 ODBC drivers are available. With well-written drivers, performance is excellent. ODBC, in the short and medium term, is the best way to access a broad range of relational data, due to its multitude of available drivers.

The assertion is false that ODBC's performance is always equal to, if not better than, all other solutions – a few instances exist where ODBC may be slower. For example, depending on the driver's implementation for loading and connecting, ODBC may take longer to connect to the data source than when using a proprietary API. This is related to the amount of behind-the-scenes work done during connection to support ODBC's capabilities.

Driver Manager

ODBC Driver Manager provides the interface from your application to the SQL Server ODBC driver. Driver Manager loads the SQL Server driver, initializes the interface, and determines the capabilities of the driver and parameter validation.

The purpose of the ODBC driver is to communicate with a particular back-end server, such as SQL server. The ODBC driver complements the back-end database by performing tasks that the database doesn't provide, and works with the back-end database to execute the functions that the database does provide. A *driver* is a DLL that implements ODBC function calls and interacts with a data source. Driver Manager loads a driver when the application calls the `SQLBrowseConnect`, `SQLConnect`, or `SQLDriverConnect` functions.

A driver performs the following tasks in response to ODBC function calls from an application:

- ◆ Establishes a connection to a data source

- ◆ Submits requests to the data source

- Translates data to or from other formats, if requested by the application

- Returns results to the application

- Formats errors into standard error codes and returns them to the application

- Declares and manipulates cursors, if necessary

- Initiates transactions, if the data source requires explicit transaction initiation

Driver Manager completely or partially implements various functions, and does the following to check for errors and warnings in those functions:

- Implements SQLDataSources and SQLDrivers, which check for all errors and warnings in these functions.

- Implements and checks for all errors and warnings in a selected driver if the driver doesn't implement SQLGetFunctions.

- Partially implements SQLAllocHandle, SQLConnect, SQLDriverConnect, SQLBrowseConnect, SQLFreeHandle, SQLGetDiagRec, and SQLGetDiagField and checks for some errors in these functions. Both the driver and Driver Manager may return the same errors for some of these functions, because they perform similar operations.

ODBC 3.X Functions

This section lists the functions, categorized by type, that are provided by ODBC 3.X. An application can call SQLGetFunctions to obtain information about support for a specific function in a driver.

Connecting to a Data Source

The following functions connect to a data source:

- SQLAllocHandle: Allocates an environment, connection, statement, or descriptor handle.

- SQLConnect: Establishes connections to a driver and a data source. The connection handle references to the data source the storage of all information about the connection, including status, transaction state, and error information.

- ◆ SQLDriverConnect: Like SQLConnect, this function connects to a driver and data source. It supports data sources that require more connection information than the three arguments in SQLConnect, dialog boxes to prompt the user for all connection information, and data sources that aren't defined in the system information.

- ◆ SQLBrowseConnect: Supports an iterative method of obtaining and enumerating the attributes and attribute values required to connect to a data source. Each call to the function returns successive levels of attributes and attribute values. After all attribute values are retrieved, a connection to the data source is made and a complete connection string is returned.

Obtaining Driver and Data-Source Information

The following functions obtain driver and data source information:

- ◆ SQLDataSources: Can be called multiple times to collect all data source names that are available to the application

- ◆ SQLDrivers: Returns the list of installed drivers, their descriptions, and their attribute keywords

- ◆ SQLGetInfo: Returns general information about a connection's driver and data source

- ◆ SQLGetFunctions: Returns information about whether a driver supports a particular function

- ◆ SQLGetTypeInfo: Returns information about data types supported by a data source

Setting and Obtaining Driver Attributes

These functions set and obtain driver attributes:

- ◆ SQLSetConnectAttr: Sets a connection attribute's value

- ◆ SQLGetConnectAttr: Returns a connection attribute's value

- ◆ SQLSetEnvAttr: Sets an environment attribute's value

- ◆ SQLGetEnvAttr: Returns an environment attribute's value

- ◆ SQLSetStmtAttr: Sets a statement attribute's value

- ◆ SQLGetStmtAttr: Returns a statement attribute's value

Setting and Obtaining Descriptor Fields

These functions set and obtain descriptor fields:

- ◆ SQLGetDescField: Returns the value of a single descriptor field.

- ◆ SQLGetDescRec: Returns the current values of multiple fields of a descriptor record. The fields returned describe the name, data type, and storage of column or parameter data.

- ◆ SQLSetDescField: Sets a single descriptor field.

- ◆ SQLSetDescRec: Sets multiple fields of a descriptor record.

Preparing SQL Statements

These functions help to prepare SQL statements:

- ◆ SQLPrepare: Prepares an SQL statement for execution

- ◆ SQLBindParameter: Assigns a buffer to a parameter in an SQL statement

- ◆ SQLGetCursorName: Returns the name of the cursor associated with a statement handle

- ◆ SQLSetCursorName: Specifies the cursor name for an associated statement handle

- ◆ SQLSetScrollOptions: Sets options that control cursor behavior

Submitting Requests

The following functions submit requests:

- ◆ SQLExecute: Executes a prepared statement

- ◆ SQLExecDirect: Executes a statement

- ◆ SQLNativeSql: Returns the driver's translation of an SQL statement

- ◆ SQLDescribeParam: Returns the description for a specific parameter in a prepared SQL statement

- ◆ SQLNumParams: Returns the number of parameters in an SQL statement

- ◆ SQLParamData: Used in conjunction with SQLPutData to supply parameter data at execution time

- ◆ SQLPutData: Sends part or all of a data value for a parameter during the execution of an SQL statement

Retrieving Results and Information About Results

The following functions retrieve results and their information:

◆ SQLRowCount: Returns the number of rows affected by an insert, update, or delete statement.

◆ SQLNumResultCols: Returns the number of columns in the result set.

◆ SQLDescribeCol: Returns the result descriptor record of a column in the result set.

◆ SQLColAttribute: Returns the attributes of a column in the result set.

◆ SQLBindCol: Assigns a buffer for a result column.

◆ SQLFetch: Retrieves the next row set of data from the result set and returns the data for all bound columns.

◆ SQLFetchScroll: Returns specified result rows.

◆ SQLGetData: Returns data for one column of one row of a result set.

◆ SQLSetPos: Sets the position of a cursor within a fetched data set. Data in the result set may be refreshed, updated, or deleted.

◆ SQLBulkOperations: Performs bulk insertions and bulk bookmark operations, including update, delete, and fetch by bookmark.

◆ SQLMoreResults: Determines whether more result sets are available and, if so, initializes processing for the next result set.

◆ SQLGetDiagField: Returns the value of a field of a diagnostic data record.

◆ SQLGetDiagRec: Returns the values of multiple fields of a diagnostic data record.

Obtaining Information About the Data Source's System Tables

The following functions obtain information about the data source's system tables:

◆ SQLColumnPrivileges: Returns a list of columns and associated privileges for the specified table.

◆ SQLColumns: Returns the list of column names in a specified table.

◆ SQLForeignKeys: Returns a list of column names that make up the foreign keys of a specified table.

- ◆ SQLPrimaryKeys: Returns the list of column names that make up the primary key for a table

- ◆ SQLProcedureColumns: Returns the list of input and output parameters, as well as the columns that make up the result set for the specified procedures

- ◆ SQLProcedures: Returns the list of procedure names stored in a specific data source

- ◆ SQLSpecialColumns: Returns information about either the set of columns that uniquely identifies a row in a specified table or the set of columns that is automatically updated when any value in the row is updated by a transaction

- ◆ SQLStatistics: Returns statistics about, and the indexes associated with, a single table

- ◆ SQLTablePrivileges: Returns a list of tables and the privileges associated with each table

- ◆ SQLTables: Returns the list of table names and table types stored in a specific data source

Terminating a Statement

The following functions terminate a statement:

- ◆ SQLFreeStmt: Ends statement processing, closes any associated cursors, discards pending results, and, optionally, frees all resources associated with the specified statement handle

- ◆ SQLCloseCursor: Closes a cursor that has been opened on a statement handle and discards pending results

- ◆ SQLCancel: Cancels the execution of an SQL statement

- ◆ SQLEndTran: Commits or rolls back a transaction

Terminating a Connection

The following functions deal with terminating a connection:

- ◆ SQLDisconnect: Closes the specified connection

- ◆ SQLFreeHandle: Releases an environment, connection, statement, or descriptor handle

Mapping ODBC 2.*x* Functions to ODBC 3.*x*

An ODBC 3.*x* application working through ODBC 3.x Driver Manager will work against an ODBC 2.*x* driver as long as no new features are used. However, both duplicated functionality and behavioral changes affect the way that the ODBC 3.*x* application works on an ODBC 2.*x* driver. When working with an ODBC 2.*x* driver, Driver Manager maps into the corresponding ODBC 2.*x* functions (as described in Table 26-1) the ODBC 3.*x* functions that have replaced one or more of the ODBC 2.*x* functions.

TABLE 26-1: MAPPING OF ODBC 2.X FUNCTIONS TO ODBC 3.X

ODBC 3.x Function	ODBC 2.x Function
SQLAllocHandle	SQLAllocEnv, SQLAllocConnect, or SQLAllocStmt
SQLBulkOperations	SQLSetPos
SQLColAttribute	SQLColAttributes
SQLEndTran	SQLTransact
SQLFetch	SQLExtendedFetch
SQLFetchScroll	SQLExtendedFetch
SQLFreeHandle	SQLFreeEnv, SQLFreeConnect, or SQLFreeStmt
SQLGetConnectAttr	SQLGetConnectOption
SQLGetDiagRec	SQLError
SQLGetStmtAttr	SQLGetStmtOption
SQLSetConnectAttr	SQLSetConnectOption
SQLSetStmtAttr	SQLSetStmtOption

SQLGetInfo

The function SQLGetInfo is a good starting point when you are attempting to interact with an ODBC driver, because SQLGetInfo provides detailed information regarding a driver's capabilities.

SQLGetInfo returns lists of supported options as an SQLUINTEGER bitmask. The bitmask for each option is used in conjunction with the flag to determine whether the option is supported.

Table 26-2 lists the property arguments and value descriptions that are returned by SQLGetInfo.

TABLE 26-2 PROPERTY ARGUMENTS AND VALUE DESCRIPTIONS RETURNED BY SQLGETINFO

Property	Value Returned by SQLGetInfo
SQL_ACCESSIBLE_PROCEDURES	Able to execute all procedures
SQL_ACCESSIBLE_TABLES	Able to retrieve data from all tables
SQL_ACTIVE_CONNECTIONS	Maximum number of active connections allowed
SQL_ACTIVE_STATEMENTS	Maximum number of active statements allowed
SQL_ALTER_TABLE	Clauses in ALTER TABLE allowed
SQL_BOOKMARK_PERSISTENCE	Functions through which bookmarks remain
SQL_COLUMN_ALIAS	Column aliases supported
SQL_CONCAT_NULL_BEHAVIOR	How concatenation of NULL is handled
SQL_CONVERT_FUNCTIONS	List of conversion functions available
SQL_CONVERT_type where type is the SQL datatype, such as CHAR	Data type allowed for CONVERT function
SQL_CORRELATION_NAME	Table-correlation names supported
SQL_CURSOR_COMMIT_BEHAVIOR	How cursors are affected by a COMMIT statement
SQL_CURSOR_ROLLBACK _BEHAVIOR	How cursors are affected by a ROLLBACK statement
SQL_DBMS_NAME	Name of current database

Continued

TABLE **26-2 PROPERTY ARGUMENTS AND VALUE DESCRIPTIONS RETURNED BY SQLGETINFO** *(continued)*

Property	Value Returned by SQLGetInfo
SQL_DEFAULT_TXN_ISOLATION	Default transaction isolation level supported
SQL_DRIVER_NAME	Driver filename
SQL_DRIVER_ODBC_VER	ODBC version that the driver supports
SQL_DRIVER_VER	Driver version
SQL_EXPRESSIONS_IN_ORDERBY	Expressions allowed in ORDER BY
SQL_FETCH_DIRECTION	List of fetch direction options
SQL_FILE_USAGE	How files in data source are treated
SQL_GETDATA_EXTENSIONS	List of extensions to SQLGetData
SQL_GROUP_BY	Relationship with GROUP BY columns
SQL_IDENTIFIER_CASE	Database case-sensitivity
SQL_IDENTIFIER_QUOTE_CHAR	SQL statement identifier delimiter
SQL_KEYWORDS	List of keywords
SQL_LIKE_ESCAPE_CLAUSE	Escape allowed in LIKE
SQL_LOCK_TYPES	List of supported lock types
SQL_MAX_BINARY_LITERAL_LEN	Maximum length of hexadecimal characters
SQL_MAX_CHAR_LITERAL_LEN	Maximum length of character literal
SQL_MAX_COLUMN_NAME_LEN	Maximum length of column name
SQL_MAX_COLUMNS_IN_GROUP_BY	Maximum number of columns in GROUP BY
SQL_MAX_COLUMNS_IN_INDEX	Maximum number of columns in index
SQL_MAX_COLUMNS_IN_ORDER_BY	Maximum number of columns in ORDER BY
SQL_MAX_COLUMNS_IN_SELECT	Maximum number of columns in a SELECT statement
SQL_MAX_COLUMNS_IN_TABLE	Maximum number of columns in a table
SQL_MAX_CURSOR_NAME_LEN	Maximum length of a cursor name
SQL_MAX_INDEX_SIZE	Maximum total size of fields in an index

Property	Value Returned by SQLGetInfo
SQL_MAX_OWNER_NAME_LEN	Maximum length of an owner name
SQL_MAX_PROCEDURE_NAME_LEN	Maximum length of a procedure name
SQL_MAX_QUALIFIER_NAME_LEN	Maximum length of a qualifier name
SQL_MAX_ROW_SIZE	Maximum length of a single row in a table
SQL_MAX_ROW_SIZE_INCLUDES_LONG	LONG values included in SQL_MAX_ROW_SIZE
SQL_MAX_STATEMENT_LEN	Maximum length of an SQL statement
SQL_MAX_TABLE_NAME_LEN	Maximum length of a table name
SQL_MAX_TABLES_IN_SELECT	Maximum number of tables in a SELECT
SQL_MAX_USER_NAME_LEN	Maximum length of a username
SQL_MULT_RESULT_SETS	Multiple result sets supported
SQL_MULTIPLE_ACTIVE_TXN	Multiple connection sets supported
SQL_NEED_LONG_DATA_LEN	Need length of long data value before value sent
SQL_NON_NULLABLE_COLUMNS	Non-nullable columns allowed
SQL_NULL_COLLATION	Sort order of NULLS in a list
SQL_NUMERIC_FUNCTIONS	List of numeric functions
SQL_ODBC_API_CONFORMANCE	Level of ODBC conformance
SQL_ODBC_SAG_CLI_CONFORMANCE	Level of compliance with SAG (SQL Access Group) specification
SQL_ODBC_SQL_CONFORMANCE	SQL grammar supported
SQL_ODBC_SQL_OPT_IEF	Integrity Enhancement Facility supported
SQL_ORDER_BY_COLUMNS_IN_SELECT	Need for ORDER BY columns in SELECT
SQL_OJ_CAPABILITIES	List of outer join capabilities
SQL_OUTER_JOINS	Outer joins supported
SQL_OWNER_TERM	Term for an owner

Continued

TABLE **26-2** PROPERTY ARGUMENTS AND VALUE DESCRIPTIONS RETURNED BY SQLGETINFO *(continued)*

Property	Value Returned by SQLGetInfo
SQL_OWNER_USAGE	Statements in which an owner can be used
SQL_POS_OPERATIONS	List of operations allowed in SQLSetPos
SQL_POSITIONED_STATEMENTS	List of positioned SQL statements allowed
SQL_PROCEDURE_TERM	Term for a procedure
SQL_PROCEDURES	Support for procedures and ODBC invocation syntax
SQL_QUALIFIER_LOCATION	Location of qualifier in qualifier table name
SQL_QUALIFIER_NAME_SEPARATOR	Separator between qualifier names
SQL_QUALIFIER_TERM	Term for a qualifier
SQL_QUALIFIER_USAGE	List of statements in which qualifier may be used
SQL_QUOTED_IDENTIFIER_CASE	Quoted identifier case-sensitivity
SQL_ROW_UPDATES	Driver supports row version maintenance
SQL_SCROLL_CONCURRENCY	Concurrency control options for scrollable cursors
SQL_SCROLL_OPTIONS	Scroll options supported for scrollable cursors
SQL_SEARCH_PATTERN_ESCAPE	Escape character for search patterns
SQL_SPECIAL_CHARACTERS	List of special characters allowed in object name
SQL_STATIC_SENSITIVITY	Application can detect changes made
SQL_STRING_FUNCTIONS	List of string functions
SQL_SUBQUERIES	List of predicates that support subqueries
SQL_SYSTEM_FUNCTIONS	List of system functions
SQL_TABLE_TERM	Term for a table
SQL_TIMEDATE_ADD_INTERVALS	List of timestamp intervals for TIMESTAMPADD
SQL_TIMEDATE_DIFF_INTERVALS	List of timestamp intervals for TIMESTAMPDIFF
SQL_TIMEDATE_FUNCTIONS	List of time and date functions

Property	Value Returned by SQLGetInfo
SQL_TXN_CAPABLE	Transaction support description
SQL_TXN_ISOLATION_OPTION	Transaction isolation levels available
SQL_UNION	UNION clause allowed

The ODBC SQL Server driver supports the new driver-specific SQLGetInfo value, (SQL_INFO_SS_NETLIB_NAME), which returns the name of the Net-Library DLL used to connect to SQL Server.

SQLError

SQLError returns error or status information, including detailed error information, when you call it after one of the other ODBC SQL functions fails. If SQLError itself fails, it can't return any error information.

If an ODBC function such as SQLExecQuery fails, the error information is defined and stored in memory. You can then make a call to the SQLError function and assign this information to an array variable. The information returned by SQLError has three formats:

- ◆ If no errors exist from a previous ODBC function call, SQLError returns only the #N/A error value to a one-dimensional array with one element. This error value may also be shown as "Error 2042" in the Debug window when you debug your macro.

- ◆ If only one error is reported, SQLError returns a one-dimensional array with three elements.

- ◆ If a function call generates multiple errors, SQLError returns a two-dimensional array in which each row describes a single error.

In the last two formats in the preceding list, each row has the following three fields:

- ◆ A character string that indicates the ODBC error class and subclass

- ◆ A numeric value that indicates the data source native-error code

- ◆ A text message that describes the error

The example in Listing 26-1 illustrates how to use the SQLError function to capture SQL errors.

Listing 26-1: Using SQLError to Capture SQL Errors

```
Sub SQLError_Example()
  'This example will return an error because
  'the data source being opened doesn't exist.

  'Declare variables
  Dim Channel As Variant       'Channel number
  Dim MyErrorArray As Variant 'Variable to store SQLError array
  Dim LF As String             'Line Feed variable

  LF = Chr(10)                  'Assign value for Line Feed

  'Open a channel to the Wind data source. This line will
  'produce an error because the data source 'Wind' doesn't exist.
  Channel = SQLOpen("DSN=Wind")

 'Check for possible error value in the Channel variable.
  If IsError(Channel) Then
  'Assign the elements of the SQLError array to MyErrorArray.
   MyErrorArray = SQLError()
   'Display the individual error elements of the MyErrorArray array.
   'Add Line Feed character for readability.
    MsgBox MyErrorArray(1) & LF & MyErrorArray(2) & LF &
MyErrorArray(3)

    'Exit sub procedure
    Exit Sub
   End If

  'Close the channel to Wind.
   SQLClose Channel
End Sub
```

When you run this example, you receive an error message that is similar to the following:

```
IM002
0
[Microsoft][ODBC DLL] Data source not found and no default driver
specified
```

In ODBC 3.*x*, calling SQLFetch or SQLFetchScroll populates the SQL_DESC_ARRAY_STATUS_PTR in the IRD, and the SQL_DIAG_ROW_NUMBER field of a given diagnostic record contains the number of the row in the row set to which this record pertains. Using this method, the application can correlate an error message with a given row position.

An ODBC 2.*x* driver is unable to provide this functionality. However, an ODBC 2.*x* driver will provide error demarcation with SQLSTATE 01S01 (error in row). An ODBC 3.*x* application that is using SQLFetch or SQLFetchScroll while going against an ODBC 2.*x* driver needs to be aware of this fact. Note also that such an application is unable to call SQLGetDiagField to get the SQL_DIAG_ROW_NUMBER field anyway. An ODBC 3.*x* application working with an ODBC 2.*x* driver is only able to call SQLGetDiagField with a *DiagIdentifier* argument of SQL_DIAG_MESSAGE_TEXT, SQL_DIAG_NATIVE, SQL_DIAG_RETURNCODE, or SQL_DIAG_SQLSTATE. ODBC 3.*x* Driver Manager maintains the diagnostic data structure when working with an ODBC 2.*x* driver, but the ODBC 2.*x* driver only returns these four fields.

When an ODBC 2.*x* application is working with an ODBC 2.*x* driver, if an operation can cause Driver Manager to return multiple errors, ODBC 3.*x* Driver Manager may return different errors than the errors returned by ODBC 2.*x* Driver Manager.

When an application calls SQLError through an ODBC 3.*x* driver, the call to

```
SQLError(henv, hdbc, hstmt, szSqlState, pfNativeError,
        szErrorMsg, cbErrorMsgMax, pcbErrorMsg)
```

is mapped to

```
SQLGetDiagRec(HandleType, Handle, RecNumber, szSqlstate,
             pfNativeErrorPtr, szErrorMsg,
             cbErrorMsgMax, pcbErrorMsg)
```

with the *HandleType* argument set to the value SQL_HANDLE_ENV, SQL_HANDLE_DBC, or SQL_HANDLE_STMT, as appropriate, and the *Handle* argument set to the value in *henv*, *hdbc*, or *hstmt*, as appropriate. The *RecNumber* argument is determined by Driver Manager.

SQLError returns SQLSTATE values, as defined by the X/Open and SQL Access Group SQL CAE draft specification (1991). SQLSTATE values are strings that contain five characters. Table 26-3 lists SQLSTATE values that a driver can return for SQLError.

The character string value returned for an SQLSTATE consists of a two-character class value, followed by a three-character subclass value. A class value of '01' indicates a warning and is accompanied by a return code of SQL_SUCCESS_WITH_INFO. Class values other than '01', except for the class 'IM', indicate an error and are accompanied by a return code of SQL_ERROR.

The class 'IM' is specific to warnings and errors that derive from the implementation of ODBC itself. The subclass value '000' in any class is for implementation-defined conditions within the given class. ANSI SQL2 defines the assignment of class and subclass values. Table 26-3 lists and describes the ANSI SQL error values.

TABLE 26-3 ANSI SQL ERROR VALUES

Return Value	Description	Functions Returning Value
00000	Success	SQLBrowseConnect, SQLError
01002	Disconnect error	SQLDisconnect
01004	Data truncated	SQLBrowseConnect, SQLColAttributes, SQLDataSources, SQLDescribeCol, SQLDriverConnect, SQLExtendedFetch, SQLFetch, SQLGetCursorName, SQLGetData, SQLGetInfo, SQLNativeSql
01006	Privilege not revoked	SQLExecDirect, SQLExecute
01S00	Invalid connection string attribute	SQLBrowseConnect, SQLDriverConnect
07001	Wrong number of parameters	SQLExecDirect, SQLExecute
07006	Restricted data type attribute violation	SQLExtendedFetch, SQLFetch, SQLGetData, SQLSetParam
08001	Unable to connect to data source	SQLBrowseConnect, SQLConnect, SQLDriverConnect
08002	Connection in use	SQLBrowseConnect, SQLConnect, SQLDriverConnect

Return Value	Description	Functions Returning Value
08003	Connection not open	SQLAllocStmt, SQLDisconnect SQLGetConnectOption, SQLGetInfo, SQLNativeSql, SQLSetConnectOption, SQLTransact
08004	Data source rejected establishment of connection	SQLBrowseConnect, SQLConnect, SQLDriverConnect
08007	Connection failure during transaction	SQLTransact
08S01	Communication link failure	SQLBrowseConnect, SQLColumnPrivileges, SQLColumns, SQLConnect, SQLDriverConnect, SQLExecDirect, SQLExecute, SQLExtendedFetch, SQLFetch, SQLForeignKeys, SQLFreeConnect, SQLGetData, SQLGetTypeInfo, SQLParamData, SQLPrepare, SQLPrimaryKeys, SQLProcedureColumns, SQLProcedures, SQLPutData, SQLSetConnectOption, SQLSetStmtOption, SQLSpecialColumns, SQLStatistics, SQLTablePrivileges, SQLTables

Continued

TABLE 26-3 ANSI SQL ERROR VALUES *(continued)*

Return Value	Description	Functions Returning Value
21S01	Insert value list does not match column list	SQLExecDirect, SQLPrepare
21S02	Degree of derived table does not match column list	SQLExecDirect, SQLPrepare
22001	String data right-truncation	SQLExecDirect, SQLExecute, SQLPutData
22003	Numeric value out of range	SQLExecDirect, SQLExecute, SQLExtendedFetch, SQLFetch, SQLGetData, SQLGetInfo, SQLPutData
22005	Error in assignment	SQLExecDirect, SQLExecute, SQLPrepare
22008	Datetime field overflow	SQLExecDirect, SQLExecute, SQLPutData
22012	Division by zero	SQLExecDirect, SQLExecute, SQLExtendedFetch, SQLFetch
22026	String data, length mismatch	SQLExecDirect, SQLPutData
23000	Integrity constraint violation	SQLExecDirect, SQLExecute
24000	Invalid cursor state	SQLColAttributes, SQLColumnPrivileges, SQLColumns, SQLDescribeCol, SQLExecDirect, SQLExecute, SQLExtendedFetch, SQLFetch, SQLForeignKeys, SQLGetData, SQLGetTypeInfo,

Return Value	Description	Functions Returning Value
		SQLPrepare, SQLPrimaryKeys, SQLProcedureColumns, SQLProcedures, SQLSetCursorName, SQLSetPos, SQLSetScrollOptions, SQLSpecialColumns, SQLStatistics, SQLTablePrivileges, SQLTables
25000	Invalid transaction state	SQLDisconnect
28000	Invalid authorization specification	SQLBrowseConnect, SQLConnect, SQLDriverConnect
34000	Invalid cursor name	SQLExecDirect, SQLPrepare, SQLSetCursorName
37000	Syntax error or access violation	SQLExecDirect, SQLNativeSql, SQLPrepare
3C000	Duplicate cursor name	SQLSetCursorName
40001	Serialization failure	SQLExecDirect, SQLExecute, SQLExtendedFetch, SQLFetch
42000	Syntax error or access violation	SQLExecDirect, SQLExecute, SQLPrepare
70100	Operation aborted	SQLCancel
IM001	Driver does not support this function	All ODBC functions except: SQLAllocConnect, SQLAllocEnv, SQLDataSources, SQLError, SQLFreeConnect, SQLFreeEnv, SQLGetFunctions

Continued

TABLE 26-3 ANSI SQL ERROR VALUES *(continued)*

Return Value	Description	Functions Returning Value
IM002	Data source name not found and no default driver specified	SQLBrowseConnect, SQLConnect, SQLDriverConnect
IM003	Driver specified by data source name could not be loaded	SQLBrowseConnect, SQLConnect, SQLDriverConnect
IM004	Driver's SQLAllocEnv failed	SQLBrowseConnect, SQLConnect, SQLDriverConnect
IM005	Driver's SQLAlloc Connect **failed**	SQLBrowseConnect, SQLConnect, SQLDriverConnect
IM006	Driver's SQLSet Connect — **Option failed**	SQLBrowseConnect, SQLConnect, SQLDriverConnect
IM007	No data source specified; dialog prohibited	SQLDriverConnect
IM008	Dialog failed	SQLDriverConnect
IM009	Unable to load translation DLL	SQLBrowseConnect, SQLConnect, SQLDriverConnect, SQLSetConnectOption
S0001	Base table or view already exists	SQLExecDirect, SQLPrepare
S0002	Base table not found	SQLExecDirect, SQLPrepare
S0011	Index already exists	SQLExecDirect, SQLPrepare
S0012	Index not found	SQLExecDirect, SQLPrepare
S0021	Column already exists	SQLExecDirect, SQLExecute, SQLPrepare

Return Value	Description	Functions Returning Value
S0022	Column not found	SQLExecDirect, SQLPrepare
S1000	General error	All ODBC functions except: SQLAllocEnv, SQLError
S1001	Memory allocation failure	All ODBC functions except: SQLError, SQLFreeConnect, SQLFreeEnv
S1002	Invalid column number	SQLBindCol, SQLColAttributes SQLDescribeCol, SQLExtendedFetch, SQLFetch, SQLGetData
S1003	Program type out of range	SQLBindCol, SQLGetData, SQLSetParam
S1004	SQL data type out of range	SQLGetTypeInfo, SQLSetParam
S1008	Operation canceled	All ODBC functions that can be processed asynchronously
S1009	Invalid argument value	SQLAllocConnect, SQLAllocStmt, SQLBindCol, SQLExecDirect, SQLForeignKeys, SQLGetData, SQLGetInfo, SQLNativeSql, SQLPrepare, SQLPutData, SQLSetConnectOption, SQLSetCursorName, SQLSetParam, SQLSetPos, SQLSetStmtOption

Continued

TABLE **26-3** ANSI SQL ERROR VALUES *(continued)*

Return Value	Description	Functions Returning Value
S1010	Function sequence error	SQLBindCol, SQLColAttributes, SQLColumnPrivileges, SQLColumns, SQLDescribeCol, SQLDescribeParam, SQLDisconnect, SQLExecDirect, SQLExecute, SQLExtendedFetch, SQLFetch, SQLForeignKeys, SQLFreeConnect, SQLFreeEnv, SQLFreeStmt, SQLGetConnectOption, SQLGetCursorName, SQLGetData, SQLGetFunctions, SQLGetInfo, SQLGetStmtOption, SQLGetTypeInfo, SQLMoreResults, SQLNumParams, SQLNumResultCols, SQLParamData, SQLParamOptions, SQLPrepare, SQLPrimaryKeys, SQLProcedureColumns, SQLProcedures, SQLPutData, SQLRowCount, SQLSetConnectOption, SQLSetCursorName, SQLSetParam, SQLSetPos, SQLSetScrollOptions, SQLSetStmtOption, SQLSpecialColumns, SQLStatistics, SQLTablePrivileges, SQLTables, SQLTransact

Return Value	Description	Functions Returning Value
S1012	Invalid transaction operation code specified	SQLTransact
S1015	No cursor name available	SQLGetCursorName
S1090	Invalid string or buffer length	SQLBindCol, SQLBrowseConnect, SQLColAttributes, SQLColumnPrivileges, SQLColumns, SQLConnect, SQLDataSources, SQLDescribeCol, SQLDriverConnect, SQLExecDirect, SQLExecute, SQLForeignKeys, SQLGetCursorName, SQLGetData, SQLGetInfo, SQLNativeSql, SQLPrepare, SQLPrimaryKeys, SQLProcedureColumns, SQLProcedures, SQLPutData, SQLSetCursorName, SQLSpecialColumns, SQLStatistics, SQLTablePrivileges, SQLTables
S1091	Descriptor type out of range	SQLColAttributes
S1092	Option type out of range	SQLFreeStmt, SQLGetConnectOption, SQLGetStmtOption, SQLSetConnectOption, SQLSetStmtOption
S1093	Invalid parameter number	SQLDescribeParam, SQLSetParam

(Continued)

Table **26-3** ANSI SQL ERROR VALUES *(continued)*

Return Value	Description	Functions Returning Value
S1094	Invalid scale value	SQLSetParam
S1095	Function type out of range	SQLGetFunctions
S1096	Information type out of range	SQLGetInfo
S1097	Column type out of range	SQLSpecialColumns
S1098	Scope type out of range	SQLSpecialColumns
S1099	Nullable type out of range	SQLSpecialColumns
S1100	Uniqueness option type out of range	SQLStatistics
S1101	Accuracy option type out of range	SQLStatistics
S1102	Table type out of range	SQLTables
S1103	Direction option out of range	SQLDataSources
S1106	Fetch type out of range	SQLExtendedFetch
S1107	Row value out of range	SQLExtendedFetch, SQLParamOptions, SQLSetPos, SQLSetScrollOptions
S1108	Concurrency option out of range	SQLSetScrollOptions
S1109	Invalid cursor position; no keyset defined	SQLSetPos
S1110	Invalid driver completion	SQLDriverConnect

Return Value	Description	Functions Returning Value
S1C00	Driver not capable	SQLBindCol, SQLColumnPrivileges, SQLColumns, SQLExtendedFetch, SQLFetch, SQLForeignKeys, SQLGetConnectOption, SQLGetData, SQLGetInfo, SQLGetStmtOption, SQLPrimaryKeys, SQLProcedureColumns, SQLProcedures, SQLSetConnectOption, SQLSetParam, SQLSetPos, SQLSetScrollOptions, SQLSetStmtOption, SQLSpecialColumns, SQLStatistics, SQLTablePrivileges, SQLTables, SQLTransact
S1DE0	No data at execution values pending	SQLParamData, SQLPutData
S1T00	Timeout expired	SQLBrowseConnect, SQLColAttributes, SQLColumnPrivileges, SQLColumnsSQLConnect, SQLDescribeCol, SQLDescribeParam, SQLDriverConnect, SQLExecDirect, SQLExecute, SQLExtendedFetch, SQLFetch, SQLForeignKeys, SQLGetData, SQLGetInfo, SQLGetTypeInfo, SQLMoreResults, SQLNumParams, SQLNumResultCols,

Continued

TABLE **26-3** ANSI SQL ERROR VALUES *(continued)*

Return Value	Description	Functions Returning Value
		SQLParamData, SQLPrepare, SQLProcedures, QLPutData, SQLSetPos, SQLStatistics, SQLTablePrivilege, SQLTables

Summary

ODBC provides a way to access data in a heterogeneous environment of relational and nonrelational database management systems. ODBC can do so in an efficient, high-performance manner. However, attaining this performance requires an understanding of the tools that are being used to access the data. As with any client/server application, the application needs to be tuned with the knowledge of the underlying tools, the database, and the user requirements.

The next chapter discusses working with connection handles to access a data source. How you connect to a data source by using ODBC functions is covered, as well as how you set various connection attributes.

Chapter 27

Connection Management

IN THIS CHAPTER

◆ Using `Environment` and `Connection` handles

◆ Connecting with a data source name

◆ Introduction to ODBC functions

◆ Understanding `Connection` options

◆ Closing a `Connection`

To COMMUNICATE WITH A remote server or database, you must choose an ODBC data source name or a connection name, which then is used as a pipeline to the remote server and your application. This name is referred to as the *connection handle*, a pointer to memory within the Windows environment. A connection handle is a value that refers to an object; in this case, the handle refers to a data source connection. To obtain a handle, you request a connection to the data source by using either the `SQLConnect()` or `SQLStringConnect()` function. If the connection is successful, your application receives a connection handle for use in subsequent Visual Basic calls.

To disconnect from a data source, you use the `SQLDisconnect()` function. Unlike the Microsoft Jet Database, no automatic connection timeout or reconnection occurs if the connection drops. These actions are left to the developer. Although this may seem like more work, in actuality, this allows you to develop your own connection management strategy. Your application can request multiple connections for one data source. You can also work with multiple ODBC data sources by requesting a connection to each data source that you want to access.

 Substantial changes exist between ODBC versions 1 and 2, as well as between versions 2 and 3. So, you should make sure to get a copy of *Microsoft ODBC 3.0 Programmer's Reference and SDK Guide*. The SDK comes with useful debugging tools, including ODBC Test, which enables you to test various function calls, and ODBC Spy, which logs the ODBC function calls.

Environment and Connection Handles

Three types of handles exist: environment, connection, and statement. This chapter covers environment and connection handles. Statement handles are discussed in Chapter 28.

The handles form a hierarchy. The connection handles in your application are associated with a single environment handle; hence, all connection handles must be freed before the environment handle is freed.

Your application can have virtually any number of connection handles at any given time.

To use any direct calls to functions in the ODBC API, you first must allocate memory and receive a handle from ODBC for a particular operation. Direct calls makes a request of the ODBC to set aside a small piece of memory, referred to as a *handle*. The handle is used to store information about the connection of the ODBC system. This is achieved with the SQLAllocHandle() function. The type of handle that SQLAllocHandle allocates must have one of the following values:

- ♦ SQL_HANDLE_ENV: An environment handle
- ♦ SQL_HANDLE_DBC: A database handle
- ♦ SQL_HANDLE_STMT: A statement handle
- ♦ SQL_HANDLE_DESC: A description handle

All ODBC handles must be released before you terminate your application; otherwise, no guarantee exists that the allocated memory will be released at the end of the application. Failing to release allocated memory in this manner is referred to as *memory leak*. If you grab enough handles and fail to release them, you will exhaust Windows' memory and cause Windows to shut down.

Connection Handles

The ODBC API uses a two-step process to create *connection handles*: allocating the handle and actually making the database connection. Inversely, to release the handle, you must disconnect and free the handle. You may think that the two steps should be collapsed into one step, but realistically, by breaking the process into two steps, the end-user has more power and control. Moreover, the end-user is able to develop customized functions (commonly referred to as *wrappers*). For example, you could simply disconnect a handle and then reuse the preexisting handle, instead of reallocating the handle each time and freeing the handle only when it's no longer needed.

Connection handles are used to connect your application to a particular database. The following code is an example of allocating a connection handle:

```
' Set connection handle
SQLAllocHandle(SQL_HANDLE_DBC, henv, hdbc)
```

If memory is successfully allocated for the handle, the function returns SQL_SUCCEED.

Environment Handles

The *environment handle* is used to manage the overall connection between your application and the ODBC system. The following code is an example of allocating an environment handle:

```
Dim iResult As Integer, hEnv As Long, hDbc As Long

' Set environment handle
iResult = SQLAllocHandle(SQL_HANDLE_ENV,
                         SQL_NULL_HANDLE, hEnv)
```

This is a generic function for allocating handles that replaces the ODBC 2.0 functions SQLAllocConnect, SQLAllocEnv, and SQLAllocStmt. To enable applications that call SQLAllocHandle to work with ODBC 2.*x* drivers, a call to SQLAllocHandle is mapped in Driver Manager to SQLAllocConnect, SQLAllocEnv, or SQLAllocStmt, as appropriate.

The SQLAllocHandle function returns one of the following result codes:

◆ SQL_SUCCESS

◆ SQL_SUCCESS_WITH_INFO

◆ SQL_INVALID_HANDLE

◆ SQL_ERROR

When allocating a handle, other than an environment handle, if SQLAllocHandle returns SQL_ERROR, the last parameter (*OutputHandlePtr*) is set to SQL_NULL_HDBC, SQL_NULL_HSTMT, or SQL_NULL_HDESC, depending on the value of the handle that you request. You can then obtain additional information from the diagnostic data structure associated with the handle.

When the system allocates memory for an environment handle, it actually is setting up information at two levels: within Driver Manager and within each driver. Hence, the error returned by SQLAllocHandle with a *HandleType* of SQL_HANDLE_ENV depends on the level in which the error occurred.

If Driver Manager fails to allocate memory for the environment output handle (SQLAllocHandle with a *HandleType* of SQL_HANDLE_ENV), or if you pass in a null pointer for *output handle*, SQLAllocHandle returns SQL_ERROR. Driver Manager sets the output handle to SQL_NULL_HENV (unless you provided a null pointer, which returns SQL_ERROR), which means that no handle is available with which to associate additional diagnostic information. Driver Manager doesn't allocate driver-level environment handles until your application calls SQLConnect, SQLBrowseConnect, or SQLDriverConnect. If an error occurs in the driver-level SQLAllocHandle function, then the Driver Manager-level SQLConnect, SQLBrowseConnect, or SQLDriverConnect function returns SQL_ERROR. Further information can be obtained through the diagnostic data structure, including the error state that the driver allocation failed (SQLSTATE IM004), followed by a driver-specific SQLSTATE value from the driver.

Data Source Name

A *data source* is an installed database server that ODBC has associated with a particular ODBC driver and a specific database located on your local hard drive or network. To make a connection to an ODBC data source, the ODBC system needs certain information to make the connection. The first piece of information, which is always needed, is the *data source name* (DSN). This is the descriptive name that ODBC uses to keep track of installed databases, and it is used any time that you are presented with a list of data sources. This information varies by database, driver, and your network setup.

When you open a connection to any database server with the ODBC API, you reference a DSN or specify the server, driver name, and default database in the connect string. Although you can create a DSN in code with the configDSN ODBC setup function, the easiest way to create or modify a DSN is by using the Control Panel ODBC Administrator program, which is already installed if you selected the ODBC option during your Visual Basic custom installation.

Connecting to a Data Source

ODBC connections start with a data source, an alias used by ODBC to refer a specific driver to a specified database. Fundamentally, an ODBC data source is a specific set of data, the information that is required to access that data, and the location of the data source, which can be described by using a DSN. From your program's point of view, the data source includes the data, the DBMS, the network (if any), and ODBC. A data source under Windows 95 and Windows NT is one of three types, as depicted in Table 27-1. You should consider the rules for each type, because each type will impact your application. For example, the User DSN will not work with another user logged in to the same machine, whereas the System DSN gives all users the same level of security access, and the File DSN is a one-on-one method.

TABLE 27-1 ODBC DATA SOURCE TYPES

Type	Description
System DSN	All users have access to the DSN, regardless of user security.
User DSN	Specific users have the right to use the DSN; this is the default setting.
File DSN	Any users that have the correct ODBC drivers installed can access the DSN.

As discussed earlier, to access data provided by a data source, your program must first establish a connection to the data source. After the environment and connection handles are allocated, data access can be managed through these connections. Moreover, you can add as many data connections to your project as you need. For example, if your application requires access to two different databases, you add two data connections. You can open multiple connections to the same database.

 At runtime, the server must have the appropriate ODBC driver to make the connection to the data source. Hence, if you deploy your applications to other servers, you must make sure that those servers also have the correct ODBC drivers.

To create the necessary parameters to establish a proper connection, you do the following:

1. Create an environment handle using `SQLAllocHandle(SQL_HANDLE_ENV, SQL_NULL_HANDLE,hEnv)`

2. Create a connection handle using `SQLAllocHandle(SQL_HANDLE_DBC, henv,hdbc)`

3. Create a registered DSN, corresponding to a DSN entry in the system registry

You also need the following information:

♦ A valid user ID, which is a logon ID or account name that is used to access the data source

♦ A valid password that corresponds to the user ID

♦ Any additional parameters that provide information to the driver

ODBC Functions

Three different functions are available in ODBC for connecting to data sources: `SQLConnect`, `SQLDriverConnect`, and `SQLBrowseConnect`. Each of these functions has varying arguments and operates at different levels of conformance, as set forth in Table 27-2.

TABLE 27-2 ODBC FUNCTIONS FOR CONNECTING TO DATA SOURCES

Function	ODBC version	Conformance	Main Arguments
SQLConnect	1.0	Core	hDbc, data source, user id, password
SQLDriver	1.0	1	hDbc, Window handle, input connect string, output connect string, completion option
SQLBrowseConnect	1.0	2	hDbc, input connect string, output connect string

SQLCONNECT

SQLConnect is the most basic way to connect to an ODBC data source. It is supported at all levels of conformance. Therefore, you are guaranteed that it will work with third-party ODBC drivers that comply with the standards. The connection handle references the storage of all information about the data source, including status, transaction state, and error information. The SQLConnect function takes in the following parameters: the connection handle; the server name; the server's name length; the username (user ID); the username length; and the user's password and password length. The following are the return codes from this function: SQL_SUCCESS, SQL_SUCCESS_WITH_INFO, SQL_ERROR, or SQL_INVALID_HANDLE.

When SQLConnect returns SQL_ERROR or SQL_SUCCESS_WITH_INFO, an associated SQLSTATE value can be obtained by calling SQLGetDiagRec with an SQL_HANDLE_DBC handle type and a ConnectionHandle handle.

SQLDRIVERCONNECT

SQLDriverConnect offers more flexibility than SQLConnect for making an ODBC connection. SQLDriverConnect supports: data sources that require more connection information than the three arguments in SQLConnect; dialog boxes to prompt the user for all connection information; and data sources that aren't defined in the system information (in the ODBC.INI or Registry).

SQLDriverConnect provides the following four connection attributes:

◆ Make a connection by using a connection string provided as a parameter in the function call that contains all the data that is needed for the connection, including the DSN, one or more user IDs, one or more passwords, and other custom information that is required by the database.

◆ Make a connection by using a partial connection string or no additional information; this enables ODBC Driver Manager and the driver to prompt the user for any additional information that is required to make the connection.

◆ Make a connection to a data source that isn't defined in the system information. If the application supplies a partial connection string, the driver can prompt the user for connection information.

◆ Make a connection to a data source by using a connection string that is constructed from the information in a DSN file.

If the connection is successful, the function returns SQL_SUCCESS and provides a completed connection string that can be used to make subsequent connections to the database.

SQLDriverConnect return codes are as follows: SQL_SUCCESS, SQL_SUCCESS _WITH_INFO, SQL_NO_DATA, SQL_ERROR, or SQL_INVALID_HANDLE. When SQLDriverConnect returns either SQL_ERROR or SQL_SUCCESS_WITH_INFO, an SQLSTATE value is available by calling SQLGetDiagRec with a handle type of SQL_HANDLE_DBC and the connection handle.

The valid additional arguments are:

◆ SQL_DRIVER_PROMPT: This option is used to display dialog boxes to prompt the user for connection information. Any values included in the function call are used to fill in the controls in the dialog box.

◆ SQL_DRIVER_COMPLETE: If enough information is contained in the function call, ODBC makes the connection. If some information is missing, the function pops up the dialog boxes, as with SQL_DRIVER_PROMPT, allowing the user to fill in the missing pieces of information.

◆ SQL_DRIVER_COMPLETE_REQUIRED: This is the same as SQL_DRIVER_COMPLETE except that the user can't change any information that has been provided by the function.

◆ SQL_DRIVER_NOPROMPT: If enough information is available in the function call, ODBC makes the connection; otherwise, it returns SQL_ERROR.

SQLBROWSECONNECT

SQLBrowseConnect, like SQLDriverConnect, uses a connection string. However, by using SQLBrowseConnect, an application can construct a complete connection string at runtime, which basically means that the function performs an interactive method of determining what it needs to connect to a database. When you call SQLBrowseConnect, the function returns additional attributes that are needed to make the connection. This enables you to do two things:

◆ Build your own dialog boxes to prompt for this information.

◆ Browse the system for data sources that can be used by a particular driver, possibly in several steps. For example, the user might first browse the network for servers and, after choosing a server, browse the server for databases that are accessible by the driver.

SQLBrowseConnect is a Conformance Level 2 function; your driver must support this level to make use of this function.

Connection Options

Use SQLSetConnectAttr to manage various aspects of your connection. An application can call SQLSetConnectAttr at any time between the time the connection is allocated and the time that it is freed. If a connection or statement attribute is successfully set by the application, its values persist until SQLFreeHandle is called on the connection. This means that if an application calls SQLSetConnectAttr before connecting to a data source, the attribute persists even if SQLSetConnectAttr fails in the driver when the application connects to the data source. If an application sets a driver-specific attribute, the attribute persists even if the application connects to a different driver on the connection.

Some connection attributes can be set only before or after a connection has been made, while others can be set at either time. Table 27-3 sets forth some of the most common attributes, their actions, and when they can be set.

TABLE **27-3 COMMON CONNECTION ATTRIBUTES**

Attribute	Description
SQL_ATTR_ACCESS_MODE	Used to set access mode to read-only or read-write. This mode can be used to optimize locking strategies, transaction management, or other areas that are appropriate to the driver or data source.
SQL_ATTR_ASYNC_ENABLE	Used to enable asynchronous connection setting.
SQL_ASYNC_ENABLE_ON	Enables asynchronous execution for all future statement handles allocated on this connection.
SQL_ATTR_AUTOCOMMIT	Turns on autocommit for transactions.
SQL_ATTR_CONNECTION_TIMEOUT	Sets the time for a connection to time out (this is a new feature under 3.x).
SQL_ATTR_CURRENT_CATALOG	A character string that contains the name of the catalog to be used by the data source.
SQL_ATTR_LOGIN_TIMEOUT	Sets the login timeout.
SQL_ATTR_ODBC_CURSORS	Controls how Driver Manager uses the ODBC Cursor Library.
SQL_ATTR_PACKET_SIZE	Sets the network packet size.
SQL_ATTR_QUIET_MODE	Enables or disables pop-up dialog boxes.
SQL_ATTR_TRACE	Turns on ODBC tracing.
SQL_ATTR_TRACEFILE	Specifies the location of the trace file.

The following code example is used to set the connection options:

```
result = SQLSetConnectAttr(hdbc, SQL_ATTR_ACCESS_MODE,
        SQL_MODE_READ_ONLY, 0)
result = SQLSetConnectAttr(hdbc, SQL_OPT_TRACEFILE,
        "C:\TRACE.OUT",SQL_NTS)
```

Retrieving

Use the `SQLGetConnectAttr` function to retrieve information regarding the connection. This function returns numeric codes or string values. The following example illustrates how to retrieve connection information:

```
Dim iVal As Long
Dim strVal  As string =512

result = SQLGetConnectionAttr(hDbc,SQL_ATTR_TRACE,iVal,0)
Debug.Print result, iVal

strVal = string$(512,0)
result = SQLGetConnectionAttr(hDbc,SQL_ATTR_TRACE,
        strVal,511);
Debug.Print result, strVal
```

Ending a Connection

To terminate a connection to a driver and SQL server, your application must perform the steps described in Table 27-4.

TABLE 27-4 STEPS REQUIRED TO TERMINATE A CONNECTION

Command	Description
SQLFreeStmt	Frees the statement handle and terminates all pending cursors.
SQLDisconnect	Closes the connection. The application can then use the handle to reconnect to the same data source or a different data source.

Command	Description
SQLFreeConnect	Frees the connection handle and all the resources associated with it.
SQLFreeEnv	Frees the environment handle and all the resources associated with it.

Summary

This chapter discussed the main building blocks required to make a connection to data sources through ODBC. Some ODBC databases support default drivers and data sources. These are created during the installation of the ODBC system driver. In most cases, you won't want to use these, but instead will want to connect to a specific driver and/or database. When you use Windows 95 or NT, you will find information in the Registry regarding the ODBC data sources, tuning parameter, and configuration.

Substantial changes exist between ODBC versions 1 and 2, and between versions 2 and 3. *Microsoft ODBC 3.0 Programmer's Reference and SDK Guide* is a good resource with which to confront these changes. Purchase the SDK; it comes with useful debugging tools, including ODBC Test and ODBC Spy.

Because you are allocating handles through the life of your application, make sure that you properly allocate, free, and release memory. Failure to do so results in memory leaks, which will cause a system crash if your application causes them enough times.

The next chapter puts together the concepts discussed in this chapter with an explanation of how to retrieve data from a database.

Chapter 28

Creating and Managing Result Sets

IN THIS CHAPTER

- ◆ Generating result sets

- ◆ Using statement handles

- ◆ Preparing and executing cursors

- ◆ Modifying result sets

- ◆ Handling errors

IN YOUR APPLICATION, each query that is submitted returns a *result set*, which is a set of rows on the data source that matches certain criteria. A result set is a conceptual table that is available to an application in tabular form. SELECT statements, catalog functions, and some procedures create result sets.

A result set can be empty, which is different from no result set at all. An empty result set is the same as any other result set, except that it has no rows. Therefore, the application can retrieve metadata for the result set, can attempt to fetch rows, and must close the cursor over the result set.

First, a little background concerning how result sets are created by using ODBC SQL. SQL is a way to communicate with a relational database that lets you define, query, modify, and control the data. Using SQL syntax, you can construct a statement that extracts a result set according to criteria that you specify.

Moreover, ODBC, which is the underlying method for connecting to the database, uses SQL to communicate with a data source through ODBC drivers. These drivers interpret the SQL and translate it, if necessary, for use with a particular database format.

ODBC defines the following extensions to SQL:

- ◆ Date, time, and timestamp data

- ◆ Scalar functions, such as numeric, string, and data type conversion functions

◆ Like predicate escape characters

◆ Outer joins

◆ Procedures

Statement Handles

The ODBC driver uses *statement handles* to access stored names, parameter information, error messages, and other information related to a statement-processing stream. Although a statement is often simply thought of as an SQL statement, such as a SELECT statement, it consists of much more. Included is all the information associated with that SQL statement, such as any result sets created by the statement, and execution parameters. A statement doesn't even require an application-defined SQL statement. Certain catalog functions execute a predefined SQL statement when called within an application.

A *statement handle* identifies each statement. A statement is associated with a single connection, which may have multiple statements on it. Some drivers limit the number of active statements that they support.

To obtain the number of active statements that a driver supports on a single connection, use the SQL_MAX_CONCURRENT_ACTIVITIES option in SQLGetInfo. A statement is considered to be "active" if it has results pending.

Within a piece of code that implements ODBC, the statement handle identifies a structure that contains statement information, such as the following:

◆ The statement's state

◆ The current statement-level diagnostics

◆ The addresses of the application variables that are bound to the statement's parameters and result set columns

◆ The current settings of each statement attribute

Most ODBC functions use statement handles. They are used in the functions to bind parameters and result set columns, prepare and execute statements, retrieve information about the data being collected, obtain results, and retrieve diagnostics. They are also used in catalog functions and several other functions.

Statement handles are allocated with SQLAllocHandle and freed with SQLFreeHandle.

Execution Strategies

The method by which you choose to execute an SQL statement should be based on whether you plan to execute the statement more than once. SQLPrepare and SQLExecute should be used when:

- You need to execute the statement multiple times.

- The statement to be executed contains parameters.

- You need information about the result set before the statement's execution.

Using SQLPrepare

Prepared execution is faster than direct execution for statements that are executed more than once, primarily because the statement is compiled only once; statements executed directly are compiled each time that they are executed. Prepared execution also can provide a reduction in network traffic, because the driver can send an access plan identifier (rather than an entire SQL statement) to the data source each time that the statement is executed – if the data source supports access plan identifiers.

The application can retrieve the metadata for the result set after the statement is prepared and before it is executed. However, returning metadata for prepared, unexecuted statements is expensive for some drivers and should be avoided by interoperable applications, if possible.

Prepared execution shouldn't be used for statements that are executed a single time. For such statements, prepared execution is slightly slower than direct execution, because prepared execution requires an additional ODBC function call.

Using SQLExecDirect

Use SQLExecDirect when

- You need to execute a statement only once.

- The statement to be executed does not contain parameters.

Direct execution is the simplest way to execute a statement. When the statement is submitted for execution, the data source compiles it into an access plan and then executes that access plan. Direct execution is commonly used by generic applications that build and execute statements at runtime, and works best for statements that will be executed a single time. Its major drawback is that the SQL statement is parsed every time that it is executed. In addition, the application can't retrieve information about the result set that is created by the statement (if any) until after the statement is executed; retrieval is possible if the statement is prepared and executed in two separate steps.

Parameters

A *parameter* is a variable in an SQL statement. Parameters are needed in situations where the syntax of an SQL statement in an application remains the same, but the associated data values for that syntax may change. In these instances, you can't hard-code the SQL statement and you don't need to completely build the SQL statement dynamically.

You use parameters by replacing the elements of a VALUES clause with question marks, or parameter markers. The parameter markers are then bound to application variables. Within the application, the variables are given values and the statement is executed. The driver then retrieves the current values of the variables and sends them to the data source. Statements that are to be executed multiple times can be made even more efficient by being prepared.

For any application, parameters ease the difficulty of constructing SQL statements at runtime by avoiding conversions to and from text.

Parameters are legal only in certain places in SQL statements. For example, they aren't allowed in the select list (the list of columns to be returned by a SELECT statement), nor are they allowed as both operands of a binary operator, such as the equals sign (=), because determining the parameter type would be impossible. In general, parameters are legal only in Data Manipulation Language (DML) statements, and not in Data Definition Language (DDL) statements.

An application should use parameter markers instead of literal values when:

♦ The same prepared statement will be executed with different parameter values.

♦ The values of the parameters are not known at the time the statement is prepared.

♦ Data type conversion is necessary to convert the data type of the parameters.

Ending Statements

SQLFreeStmt stops all processing associated with a specific statement, closes any open cursors associated with the statement, discards pending results, or, optionally, frees all resources associated with the statement handle. This function contains the options listed in Table 28-1.

TABLE 28-1 SQLFREESTMT OPTIONS

SQLFreeStmt option	Purpose
SQL_CLOSE	Closes the cursor and discards all pending results. The application can reopen this cursor later by executing a SELECT statement again with the same or different parameter values.
SQL_DROP	This option is deprecated. A call to SQLFreeStmt with this option is mapped in Driver Manager to SQLFreeHandle.
SQL_UNBIND	Releases all column buffers bound by SQLBindCol for the given statement handle.
SQL_RESET_PARAMS	Releases all parameter buffers set by SQLBindParameter for the given statement handle.

Retrieving Result Set Data

The process of retrieving rows from the data source and returning them to the application is called *fetching*. SQLBindCol is used to associate, or *bind*, columns in the result set to data buffers and length/indicator buffers in the application. When the application calls SQLFetch, SQLFetchScroll, or SQLSetPos to fetch data, the driver returns the data for the bound columns in the specified buffers.

Columns don't have to be bound to retrieve data from them. SQLGetData can also be used to retrieve data from columns. SQLGetData retrieves data for a single column in the result set, and can be called multiple times to retrieve variable-length data in parts. SQLGetData returns the data in a specified column. SQLGetData can be called only after one or more rows have been fetched from the result set by SQLFetch, SQLFetchScroll, or SQLExtendedFetch. If variable-length data is too large to be returned in a single call to SQLGetData, SQLGetData can retrieve it in parts. You can bind some columns in a row and call SQLGetData for others, although this is subject to some restrictions.

If the driver doesn't support extensions to SQLGetData, the function can return data only for unbound columns with a number greater than that of the last bound column. Furthermore, within a row of data, the value of the *ColumnNumber* argument in each call to SQLGetData must be greater than or equal to the value of *ColumnNumber* in the previous call; that is, data must be retrieved in increasing column-number order. Finally, if no extensions are supported, SQLGetData can't be called if the rowset size is greater than 1.

SQLGetData can be used to retrieve data in parts from a column that contains variable-length data. Such is the case when the identifier of the SQL data type of the column is SQL_CHAR, SQL_VARCHAR, SQL_LONGVARCHAR, SQL_WCHAR, SQL_WVARCHAR, SQL_WLONGVARCHAR, SQL_BINARY, SQL_VARBINARY, SQL_LONG-VARBINARY, or is a driver-specific identifier for a variable-length type.

To retrieve data in parts from a column, the application calls SQLGetData multiple times in succession for the same column. On each call, SQLGetData returns the next part of the data. The application is responsible for reassembling the parts. If more data exists to return, SQLGetData returns SQL_SUCCESS_WITH_INFO and SQLSTATE 01004 (data truncated). When SQLGetData returns the last part of the data, it returns SQL_SUCCESS. If SQLGetData is called after this point, it returns SQL_NO_DATA.

To retrieve column data successfully, the application must determine correctly the length and starting point of the data in the application buffer. When the application specifies an explicit target data type, errors in an application can be more easily detected. If the target data type of SQL_DEFAULT is used, SQLBindCol can be applied to a column inappropriately. In this situation, the application may fail to determine the start or length of the fetched column data. This can lead to unreported data errors or memory violations.

Accessing Metadata

SQLDescribeCol and SQLColAttribute are used to retrieve result set metadata. The difference between these two functions is that SQLDescribeCol always returns the same five pieces of information (a column's name, data type, precision, scale, and nullability), while SQLColAttribute returns a single piece of information requested by the application. However, SQLColAttribute can return a much richer selection of metadata, including a column's case sensitivity, display size, updatability, and searchability.

Many applications, especially ones that only display data, require only the metadata returned by SQLDescribeCol. For these applications, using SQLDescribeCol is faster than using SQLColAttribute, because the information is returned in a single call. Other applications, especially ones that update data, require the additional metadata returned by SQLColAttribute, thus use both functions. In addition, SQLColAttribute supports driver-specific metadata.

An application can retrieve result set metadata at any time after a statement has been prepared or executed, and before the cursor over the result set is closed. Very few applications require result set metadata after the statement is prepared and before it is executed. If possible, applications should wait to retrieve metadata until after the statement is executed, because some data sources can't return metadata for prepared statements, and emulating this capability in the driver is frequently a slow process.

Metadata is often expensive to retrieve from the data source. Because of this, drivers should cache any metadata that they retrieve from the server and hold it for as long as the cursor over the result set is open. Also, applications should request only the metadata that they absolutely need.

In most situations, application programmers know whether the statements that their application executes will create a result set — especially when the application uses hard-coded SQL statements written by the programmer, and usually when the application constructs SQL statements at runtime. The programmer can easily include code that flags whether a SELECT statement or an INSERT statement is being constructed. In a few situations, the programmer can't possibly know whether a statement will create a result set. This is true when the application provides a way for the user to enter and execute an SQL statement, and when the application constructs a statement at run time to execute a procedure.

In such cases, the application calls SQLNumResultCols to determine the number of columns in the result set. If this number is 0, the statement did not create a result set; if it is any other number, the statement did create a result set.

The application can call SQLNumResultCols at any time after the statement is prepared or executed. However, because some data sources can't easily describe the result sets that will be created by prepared statements, performance suffers if SQLNumResultCols is called after a statement is prepared, but before it is executed.

Some data sources also support determining the number of rows that an SQL statement returns in a result set. To make this determination, the application calls SQLRowCount. Exactly what the row count represents is indicated by the setting of the SQL_DYNAMIC_CURSOR_ATTRIBUTES2, SQL_FORWARD_ONLY_CURSOR_ATTRIBUTES2, SQL_KEYSET_CURSOR_ATTRIBUTES2, or SQL_STATIC_CURSOR_ATTRIBUTES2 option (depending on the type of the cursor) that is returned by a call to SQLGetInfo. This bitmask indicates, for each cursor type, whether the row count returned is exact, approximate, or unavailable. Whether row counts for static or keyset-driven cursors are affected by changes made through SQLBulkOperations or SQLSetPos, or by positioned update or delete statements, depends upon other bits returned by the same option arguments listed previously.

Cursors

ODBC Driver Manager always creates a cursor whenever the query returns a row-containing result set. Each time that your code calls SQLFetch, the driver positions the current row pointer at the next row in the cursor and retrieves the data for that row. By default, cursors are read-only and forward-scrolling-only. After you position the current row pointer past a row, that row is no longer available. Therefore, you must reexecute the query to retrieve it.

`SQLSetConnectOption` and `SQLSetStmtOptions` can be used to obtain OBDC driver information and statement information, respectively, such as the following:

◆ Whether an operation is asynchronous

◆ Whether SQL statements are scanned for escape clauses

◆ The length of a query timeout

◆ Whether a cursor is forward-only, static, keyset, or dynamic

◆ Whether bookmarks will be used with a cursor

◆ Whether a result set is read-only or read-write

◆ The size of the cursor keyset

◆ The number of rows in the cursor row set

◆ The maximum number of rows retrieved

◆ The maximum length of the data retrieved

◆ Whether binding is by row or by column

◆ The locking and concurrency attributes of a cursor

The ODBC API supports the following four types of cursors:

◆ Static cursors

◆ Dynamic cursors

◆ Keyset-driven cursors

◆ Mixed cursors (keyset/dynamic)

These are discussed in greater depth in the following sections.

Static Cursors

A static cursor is one in which the result set appears to be static. A static cursor doesn't usually detect changes made to the membership, order, or values of the result set after the cursor is opened. For example, if a static cursor fetches a row, and another application subsequently modifies that row, if the static cursor refetches the row, the values it sees are unchanged, despite the changes made by the other application.

Static cursors may detect their own updates, deletes, and inserts, although they aren't required to do so. Whether a particular static cursor detects these changes is reported through the `SQL_STATIC_SENSITIVITY` option in `SQLGetInfo`. Static cursors never detect other updates, deletes, and inserts.

The row status array specified by the SQL_ATTR_ROW_STATUS_PTR statement attribute can contain SQL_ROW_SUCCESS, SQL_ROW_SUCCESS_WITH_INFO, or SQL_ROW_ERROR for any row. It returns SQL_ROW_UPDATED, SQL_ROW_DELETED, or SQL_ROW_ADDED for rows updated, deleted, or inserted by the cursor, assuming that the cursor is capable of detecting such changes.

Dynamic Cursors

The result set of a dynamic cursor is changeable. The cursor can detect any changes made to the membership, order, and values of the result set after the cursor is opened. Dynamic cursors detect all updates, deletes, and inserts, both their own and those made by others. This type of cursor is the most expensive and the most difficult to implement.

Keyset-Driven Cursors

A keyset-driven cursor, like a static cursor, does not always detect changes to the membership and order of the result set. Like a dynamic cursor, however, a keyset-driven cursor does detect changes to the values of rows in the result set.

When a keyset-driven cursor is opened, it saves the keys for the entire result set; this fixes the apparent membership and order of the result set. As the cursor scrolls through the result set, it uses the keys in this *keyset* to retrieve the current data values for each row.

Mixed Cursors

A mixed cursor is a combination of a keyset-driven cursor and a dynamic cursor. It is used when the result set is too large reasonably to save keys for the entire result set. Mixed cursors are implemented by creating a keyset that is smaller than the entire result set but larger than the row set.

As long as the application scrolls within the keyset, the behavior is keyset-driven. When the application scrolls outside the keyset, the behavior is dynamic. The cursor fetches the requested rows and creates a new keyset. A mixed cursor is equivalent to a keyset-driven cursor when the keyset size is equal to the result set size, and is equivalent to a dynamic cursor when the keyset size is equal to 1.

Cursor Characteristics and Cursor Type

An application can specify the characteristics of a cursor instead of specifying the cursor type. To do so, the application selects the cursor's scrollability (by setting the SQL_ATTR_CURSOR_SCROLLABLE statement attribute) and sensitivity (by setting the SQL_ATTR_CURSOR_SENSITIVITY statement attribute) before opening the cursor on the statement handle. The driver then chooses the cursor type that most efficiently provides the characteristics that the application requested.

Whenever an application sets any of the statement attributes SQL_ATTR_CONCURRENCY, SQL_ATTR_CURSOR_SCROLLABLE, SQL_ATTR_CURSOR_SENSITIVITY, or SQL_ATTR_CURSOR_TYPE, the driver makes any required change to the other statement attributes in this set of four attributes, so that their values remain consistent. As a result, when the application specifies a cursor characteristic, the driver can change the attribute that indicates the cursor type, based on this implicit selection; when the application specifies a type, the driver can change any of the other attributes to be consistent with the characteristics of the selected type.

An application that sets statement attributes to specify both a cursor type and cursor characteristics runs the risk of obtaining a cursor that isn't the most efficient method available on that driver to meet the application's requirements.

The implicit setting of statement attributes is driver-defined, except it must follow these rules:

◆ Forward-only cursors are never scrollable.

◆ Insensitive cursors are never updatable (thus their concurrency is read-only); this is based on their definition of insensitive cursors in the ISO SQL standard.

The attributes used to modify cursor characteristics, and the version of ODBC in which the attributes were introduced, are shown in Table 28-2.

TABLE 28-2 ATTRIBUTES USED TO MODIFY CURSOR CHARACTERISTICS

Attribute	ValuePtr Contents
SQL_ATTR_CONCURRENCY (ODBC 2.0)	An SQLUINTEGER value that specifies the cursor concurrency.
	SQL_CONCUR_READ_ONLY = Cursor is read-only. No updates are allowed.
	SQL_CONCUR_LOCK = Cursor uses the lowest level of locking that is sufficient to ensure that the row can be updated.
	SQL_CONCUR_ROWVER = Cursor uses optimistic concurrency control, comparing row versions such as SQLBase ROWID or Sybase TIMESTAMP.
	SQL_CONCUR_VALUES = Cursor uses optimistic concurrency control, comparing values.
	The default value for SQL_ATTR_CONCURRENCY is SQL_CONCUR_READ_ONLY.

Attribute	ValuePtr Contents
	This attribute can't be specified for an open cursor.
SQL_ATTR_CURSOR_SCROLLABLE (ODBC 3.0)	An SQLUINTEGER value that specifies the level of support that the application requires. Setting this attribute affects subsequent calls to SQLExecDirect and SQLExecute.
	SQL_NONSCROLLABLE = Scrollable cursors aren't required on the statement handle. If the application calls SQLFetchScroll on this handle, the only valid value of FetchOrientation is SQL_FETCH_NEXT. This is the default.
	SQL_SCROLLABLE = Scrollable cursors are required on the statement handle. When calling SQLFetchScroll, the application may specify any valid value of FetchOrientation, achieving cursor positioning in modes other than the sequential mode.
SQL_ATTR_CURSOR_SENSITIVITY (ODBC 3.0)	An SQLUINTEGER value that specifies whether cursors on the statement handle make visible the changes made to a result set by another cursor. Setting this attribute affects subsequent calls to SQLExecDirect and SQLExecute. An application can read back the value of this attribute to obtain its initial state or its state as most recently set by the application.
	SQL_UNSPECIFIED = The cursor type is unspecified, and cursors on the statement handle may make visible none, some, or all the changes made to a result set by another cursor. This is the default.
	SQL_INSENSITIVE = All cursors on the statement handle show the result set, without reflecting any changes made to it by any other cursor. Insensitive cursors are read-only. This corresponds to a static cursor, which has a concurrency that is read-only.

Continued

TABLE **28-2** ATTRIBUTES USED TO MODIFY CURSOR CHARACTERISTICS *(Continued)*

Attribute	ValuePtr Contents
	SQL_SENSITIVE = All cursors on the statement handle make visible all changes made to a result set by another cursor.
SQL_ATTR_CURSOR_TYPE (ODBC 2.0)	An SQLUINTEGER value that specifies the cursor type:
	SQL_CURSOR_FORWARD_ONLY = The cursor scrolls forward only.
	SQL_CURSOR_STATIC = The data in the result set is static.
	SQL_CURSOR_KEYSET_DRIVEN = The driver saves and uses the keys for the number of rows specified in the SQL_ATTR_KEYSET_SIZE statement attribute.
	SQL_CURSOR_DYNAMIC = The driver only saves and uses the keys for the rows in the row set.
	The default value is SQL_CURSOR_FORWARD_ONLY. This attribute can't be specified after the SQL statement has been prepared.
	If the specified cursor type isn't supported by the data source, the driver substitutes a different cursor type and returns SQLSTATE 01S02 (option value changed). For a mixed or dynamic cursor, the driver substitutes, in order, a keyset-driven or static cursor. For a keyset-driven cursor, the driver substitutes a static cursor.

Modifying Results

One purpose of accessing a result set is to change some of its values. Data may be modified in one of three ways:

◆ Execute positioned UPDATE and DELETE statements by using a named cursor

◆ Use SQLSetPos with a named cursor

◆ Process multiple result sets with SQL statements that update or delete rows, based on the key values extracted from the result set

Executing Positioned UPDATE and DELETE Statements by Using a Named Cursor

The current row in the cursor result set may be updated or deleted. Statements that do this are referred to as *positioned* UPDATE or DELETE statements. After a SELECT statement is executed and a result set is obtained, SQLFetch may be called to position the cursor on the row to be modified. An UPDATE or DELETE statement may then be executed to make the modifications that you want.

To execute a positioned UPDATE or DELETE statement, the following must be true:

◆ A FOR UPDATE clause must be included in the SELECT statement that creates the result set.

◆ The cursor names used in the SELECT statement must be the same as the cursor names used in the UPDATE or DELETE statement.

◆ Different statement handles must be used for the SELECT statement and the UPDATE or DELETE statement.

◆ The statement handles for the SELECT statement and the UPDATE or DELETE statement must be on the same connection.

Using SQLSetPos with a Named Cursor

The cursor may also be positioned on a record using SQLExtendedFetch in conjunction with SQLSetPos by using the SQL_POSITION option. The update operation of SQLSetPos makes the data source update one or more selected rows of a table, using data in the application buffers for each bound column (unless the value in the length/indicator buffer is SQL_COLUMN_IGNORE). Columns that are not bound are not updated.

To update rows with SQLSetPos, the application does the following:

1. Places the new data values in the rowset buffers.

2. Sets the value in the length/indicator buffer of each column, as necessary.

3. Sets the value in the length/indicator buffer of those columns that aren't to be updated to SQL_COLUMN_IGNORE. Although the application can skip this step and resend existing data, this is inefficient and risks sending values to the data source that were truncated when they were read.

4. Calls `SQLSetPos` with *Operation* set to `SQL_UPDATE` and *RowNumber* set to the number of the row to update. If *RowNumber* is 0, all rows in the row set are updated.

After `SQLSetPos` returns, the current row is set to the updated row. The delete operation of `SQLSetPos` makes the data source delete one or more selected rows of a table. To delete rows with `SQLSetPos`, the application calls `SQLSetPos` with *Operation* set to `SQL_DELETE` and *RowNumber* set to the number of the row to delete. If *RowNumber* is 0, all rows in the row set are deleted.

After `SQLSetPos` returns, the deleted row is the current row and its status is `SQL_ROW_DELETED`. The row cannot be used in any further positioned operations, such as calls to `SQLGetData` or `SQLSetPos`.

When deleting all rows of the row set (*RowNumber* is equal to 0), the application can prevent the driver from deleting certain rows by using the row operation array, in the same way as the update operation of `SQLSetPos`.

Every row that is deleted should be a row that exists in the result set. If the application buffers were filled by fetching, and if a row status array has been maintained, the row's values at each of these row positions shouldn't be `SQL_ROW_DELETED`, `SQL_ROW_ERROR`, or `SQL_ROW_NOROW`.

Transactions

Transactions are sequential processing steps that result in a specific function or activity being completed, ensuring that a set of actions is treated as a single unit of work.

When you use transaction processing, you must design transactions to minimize the impact that they have on other users. To minimize the impact of transactions, design them so that they begin and end as close as possible to the actual data update; the ideal transaction contains only data-update statements.

When an application uses autocommit mode, each SQL statement is a complete transaction that is automatically committed. In manual-commit mode, a transaction may consist of more than one SQL statement. The application is responsible for either committing or rolling back the transaction by using `SQLEndTran`.

In manual-commit mode, applications must explicitly complete transactions by calling `SQLEndTran` to commit or roll back the transactions. This is the normal transaction mode for most relational databases.

Transactions in ODBC don't have to be initiated explicitly. Instead, a transaction begins implicitly whenever the application starts operating on the database. If the data source requires explicit transaction initiation, the driver must provide it whenever the application executes a statement that requires a transaction and no current transaction exists.

To set the transaction mode, use the `SQLSetConnectAttr` function with the `SQL_ATTR_AUTOCOMMIT` option.

Applications specify the transaction mode with the SQL_ATTR_AUTOCOMMIT connection attribute. By default, ODBC transactions are in autocommit mode. Switching from manual-commit mode to autocommit mode automatically commits any open transaction on the connection.

Schemas

A database *schema* describes the contents of a database – its table, fields, field types, field sizes, indexes, and so forth. The functions listed in Table 28-3 are provided to access a database schema from ODBC.

TABLE 28-3 DATABASE SCHEMA FUNCTIONS

Function	Information Returned
SQLColumns	Names of columns in one or more tables.
SQLColumnPrivileges	Privileges associated with each column in a single table.
SQLForeignKeys	Names of columns in a single table that are foreign keys; names of columns in other tables that refer to the primary key of the specified table.
SQLPrimaryKeys	Names of columns that comprise the primary key of a single table.
SQLProcedures	Names of procedures stored in a data source.
SQLProceduresColumns	A list of the input and output parameters, as well as the names of columns in the result set, for one or more procedures.
SQLSpecialColumns	Information about the optimal set of columns that uniquely identifies a row in a single table, or the columns in the table that are automatically updated when any value in the row is updated by a transaction.
SQLStatistics	Statistics about a single table and its associated indexes.
SQLTables	Names of tables stored in a data source.
SQLTablePrivileges	Privileges associated with one or more tables.

Server–Side Cursors

To use server-side cursors, an application must use level-2-compliant drivers. Use the `SQLSetConnectAttr` function with the `SQL_ATTR_ODBC_CURSORS` option to make Driver Manager use server-side cursors.

The server-side cursor library maintains the cursor keyset on the server, which eliminates the need to transmit the keyset to the workstation, where it consumes needed resources. However, the cursor driver consumes space on the remote server, so the database must be expanded to meet this requirement. Cursors created with the server-side driver can't contain more than one `SELECT` statement — if they do, a trappable error is fired. You can still use the server-side cursor driver with multiple result set queries, if you disable the cursor by creating a forward-only, read-only cursor with a rowset size of 1. Not all remote servers support server-side cursors.

When server-side cursors are used, the database engine uses its own resources to store cursor keyset values. Data values are still transmitted over the network, as with client-side cursors, but the impact on local workstation memory and disk space is reduced. For SQL Server, server-side cursors aren't used if the cursor is read-only and forward-only.

Stored procedures are a precompiled collection of SQL statements and optional control-of-flow statements that is stored under a name and processed as a unit. This collection is stored within a database and can be executed with one call from an application. Stored procedures allow user-declared variables, conditional execution, and other powerful programming features.

Stored procedures can make managing your database and displaying information about that database and its users much easier. Stored procedures can contain program flow, logic, and queries against the database, and can accept parameters, output parameters, return single or multiple result sets, and return values.

You can use stored procedures for any purpose for which you would use SQL statements, with these advantages:

♦ You can execute a series of SQL statements in a single stored procedure.

♦ You can reference other stored procedures from within your stored procedure, which can simplify a series of complex statements.

♦ The stored procedure executes faster than individual SQL statements execute.

The functionality of a stored procedure is dependent on the features offered by your database. For more details about what a stored procedure can accomplish for you, see your database documentation.

Table 28-4 contains a list of functions that return information regarding the stored procedures used within an application.

TABLE **28-4 STORED PROCEDURE FUNCTIONS**

Function	Purpose
dbhasretstat	Determines whether a stored procedure generates a return status number
dbnumrets	Calculates the number of returned parameter values generated by a stored procedure or a remote stored procedure
dbretdata	Returns a pointer to a return-parameter value generated by a stored procedure
dbretlen	Determines the length of a return-parameter value generated by a stored procedure
dbretname	Determines the name of a return parameter of a stored procedure
dbretstatus	Determines the stored-procedure status number returned by a stored procedure
dbrettype	Determines the data type of a stored procedure's return-parameter value
dbrpcexec	Executes a single stored procedure or a batch of stored procedures on SQL Server
dbrpcinit	Initializes a stored procedure
dbrpcparam	Adds a parameter to a stored procedure
dbrpcsend	Sends a single stored procedure or a batch of stored procedures to SQL Server to be executed

Error Handling

When an ODBC API function terminates, it returns a code that indicates success or failure. Not all errors are fatal, so your application must examine the result codes carefully and determine whether a problem exists. Table 28-5 lists the most common result codes that are returned.

TABLE **28-5** COMMON RESULT CODES

Result Code	Meaning
SQL_SUCCESS	Successful termination of function
SQL_SUCCESS_WITH_INFO	Successful termination of function; plus additional information is available
SQL_ERROR	Function failed

If additional information is available, the details may be obtained by calling the SQLError function.

Summary

This chapter introduced result sets. When a database query is issued, the results are returned together in a result set. The ODBC API provides various functions that you can use to create, access, and close a result set. You must create a statement handle before you can retrieve a result set. A statement handle contains the state, diagnostics, bound variables, and current settings of a statement. A statement can contain parameters or be executed directly. The SQLBindCol function is used to retrieve the results of a query into an application buffer. ODBC Driver Manager always creates a cursor when a result set is returned. Each time the SQLFetch command is called, the next row of the result set is returned. Finally, after each call to an ODBC API function, you must check its result. When SQL_ERROR is returned, the function has failed, and you must take the appropriate steps to correct the error.

Chapter 29

Introducing OLE DB

IN THIS CHAPTER

◆ Taking the next logical step forward from ODBC

◆ Creating universal data sources

◆ Reviewing the Component Object Model (COM)

◆ Overview of the OLE DB components

◆ Understanding the flow of OLE DB applications

THIS CHAPTER INTRODUCES Object Linking and Embedding Databases (OLE DB) and discusses how OLE DB fits into Microsoft's philosophy of universal data distribution. This chapter introduces the concept of the Component Object Model (COM) and explains how OLE DB becomes an integral part of this framework. You also review the OLE DB object hierarchy and the principal components of the OLE DB architecture.

ODBC – The Next Step – OLE DB

Microsoft introduced Open Database Connectivity (ODBC) with the promise of creating a singular common access methodology for databases. The earliest versions of ODBC suffered from inconsistent support and performance. In fact, very few database products supported ODBC, and those that did provided their own database drivers, which often were more reliable and faster than ODBC's drivers. ODBC has come a long way from those early days. In its current form, two versions of ODBC are available – version 2.0, which supports 16-bit applications, and with the release of Windows 95, version 3.0, which supports 32-bit applications. Today, almost every major database supports ODBC drivers, and third-party developers provide optimized driver versions. In fact, ODBC drivers have become as ubiquitous as video drivers and other Window's device drivers. Also, many data processing applications (such as Excel, Access, Lotus 1-2-3, and so forth) support ODBC data–access. ODBC has become the omnipresent methodology for providing access to database sources.

ODBC's primary focus is to provide a consistent interface to database data sources. OLE DB is designed with an even broader goal: to provide a methodology to access data, regardless of the data source. As Figure 29-1 shows, OLE DB becomes the data access bridge for documents, e-mail systems, file systems, spreadsheets, COM components, and other database sources that utilize ODBC drivers.

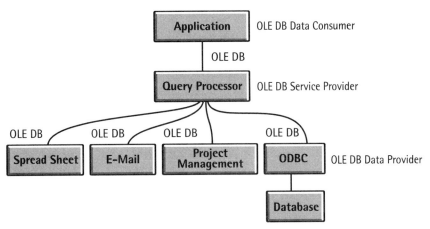

Figure 29-1: OLE DB application topology

An OLE DB implementation basically is comprised of two components: a data provider and a data consumer. A *data provider* is an application that responds to queries and returns data in a usable form. An OLE DB data provider responds to various OLE DB calls by providing the information that it contains in a usable tabular form. For example, a spreadsheet OLE DB provider may allow access to a selection of cells or properties of the sheet, such as the creator, description, and date created.

A *data consumer* is an application or other COM component that utilizes the API of OLE DB to access a data source. A data consumer can be any application that requires access to data. OLE DB gives a data consumer access to the entire range of enterprise data that is available, regardless of where the data is stored.

Making Data Sources Accessible

The key feature of OLE DB is that it lowers the requirements for implementing a data provider interface. Previously, to provide an ODBC interface, an application was required to implement a database engine that was capable of interpreting and executing SQL queries. With OLE DB, a data provider is only required to return data in a tabular form, and isn't required to support a command interface. In conjunction with a query processor, OLE DB provides a unified way to access enterprise data.

A third component to an OLE DB implementation is a *service provider*. As previously shown in Figure 29-1, a service provider is a middleman in the OLE DB architecture. Acting both as a consumer of raw OLE DB data sources and as a provider to other OLE DB consumers, a service provider manipulates and processes the raw OLE DB data sources. OLE DB modularizes an application, providing diverse data source components, a query processing component, and an application. Because OLE DB provides a consistent data interface, any of the components can be exchanged without affecting functionality.

OLE DB is different from ODBC connectivity: OLE DB extends the capabilities of ODBC by enabling less-sophisticated data applications to become data providers. However, this doesn't mean that the ODBC interface will be abandoned. ODBC will still be used to support database data sources, but instead of relying on the ODBC interface, applications will utilize the OLE DB interface to access these data sources. The OLE DB SDK contains an OLE DB provider for ODBC data, which enables you to access ODBC data sources from your OLE DB consumer applications.

Component Object Model

Microsoft has been developing a component-based model of application development for a long time. First came Object Linking and Embedding (OLE), which facilitated interapplication communication by enabling application objects to be embedded in other applications. For example, a spreadsheet object could be placed into a word processing document, and a user could edit that object in place.

Visual Basic Controls (VBXs) were next introduced, with Visual Basic. VBXs provide custom Windows controls to embed in Visual Basic applications. These controls included Windows interface elements, such as list boxes and buttons, and also could provide specialized processing routines, such as specialized parsing and sorting routines.

OLE and VBX were Microsoft's first steps toward developing object-oriented application components. OLE and VBX were later merged into OLE Controls (OCXs, which are OLE-based custom controls). After OCX, the technology evolved into ActiveX, the key difference of which is that ActiveX controls are designed to function cross-platform. Microsoft has ported ActiveX to the Macintosh environment, and Sun has licensed ActiveX with an eye toward porting it to its architecture.

The Component Object Model is a specification for developing application components that can dynamically exchange data and that can be interchanged to support new functionality. COM employs object-oriented programming (OOP) techniques to build encapsulated application components that provide an interface to an object. This interface is used to manipulate the object's state, and can be determined dynamically at runtime. The COM architecture makes the development process an independent task by enabling components to work together, even if they have been developed with different programming languages and by different people. COM also provides the capability for components to work together in a distributed environment.

More detailed information regarding the COM interface, including complete COM specifications, can be found on the Internet at this site: `http://www.microsoft.com/olecom/title.htm`.

COM enables developers to create application components that can be pieced together to form new applications. These components can be developed independently and in different programming languages, and later may be easily assembled to form a new application or a portion of an application. This "componentization" of application development can help to speed and simplify the development process. Unlike other models, the COM architecture is used to develop a methodology for applications to communicate with one another. After this communication methodology is established, applications can communicate with each other directly – COM doesn't impose any overhead.

The following are the key aspects of COM:

♦ Provides a strict set of rules that a component must follow, unlike earlier Windows-based component models, which provided functional repositories and communications methodologies, such as DDE and DLLs. COM isn't a way to develop an application. Instead, COM technology enables a developer to build robust components that can evolve over time, which is made possible by the strict rules that define application components. COM components can be upgraded and evolve without requiring the applications on which they are utilized to be upgraded.

♦ Naturally independent components that can be developed with different programming languages, without requiring any specialized interface to bridge interapplication communications, which makes all COM components naturally compatible.

♦ Truly object-oriented components, which define an encapsulated object that presents a fixed set of interfaces, hiding the implementation details from the components' users.

♦ Provides mechanisms for encapsulating the life cycle of an object via reference counting.

♦ Employs the concept of Globally Unique Identifiers (GUIDs), which are used to identify a COM object uniquely. COM uses 128-bit identifiers, which ensure the uniqueness of each object.

♦ Inherent security, by using basic operating system privileges to ensure that a user has the rights to execute a component.

◆ Supports a distributed model, enabling components to be used in a networked environment and to be accessed and executed on remote systems.

OLE DB is what COM is all about, because it brings together numerous components – data providers and data consumers – which can, when integrated together, provide access to distributed, enterprise-wide information. OLE DB is firmly based on the COM architecture and provides distributed data access by leveraging COM to glue together these application components.

Component Overview

The OLE DB interface is composed of a few major objects: TDataSource, TSession, TCommand, TRowset, TIndex, TError, and TTransaction. Figure 29-2 shows the hierarchy of the OLE DB objects, each of which is given a brief overview next.

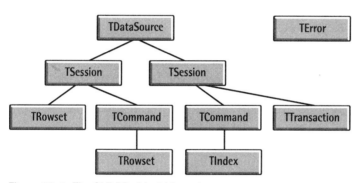

Figure 29-2: The OLE DB object hierarchy

Data Source

To connect to a data provider, a data consumer uses a TDataSource object. A data provider can be an OLE DB application, database, or an ODBC data source when using the OLE DB ODBC data source provider. When you connect to a database, a TDataSource object encapsulates the environment and connection information, including a username and password. A TDataSource object can be made persistent by saving its state to a file.

Session

A TSession object is used to provide a context for transactions. Sessions are used to create an environment in which to encapsulate transactions, generate rows of data from a data source, and generate commands that can query and manipulate the data source. A TSession object is created by a TDataSource object, which can create multiple TSession objects.

Command

A TCommand object is used to process commands. An OLE DB data provider is *not* required to process commands. A TCommand object can be used to create commands that can query or manipulate a data source. The result of a query creates a TRowset object. A TCommand object can be used to create multiple row sets. When you access a database data source, TCommand objects can be utilized to create prepared statements and queries that return multiple-row sets.

Rowset

A TRowset object is used to access information from a data source in a tabular form. A TRowset object can be created as the result of executing a command. If the data provider doesn't support commands (which it isn't required to support), a row set can be generated directly from the data provider. The capability to create row sets directly is a requirement of all data providers. A TRowset object is also used when accessing data source schema information. Depending on the functionality of the data provider, a TRowset object can also be used to modify, insert, and delete rows.

Indexes

A TIndex object is a special case of a TRowset object. A TIndex object is used to create a row set that uses an associated index, which allows ordered access to a data source row set.

Errors

A TError object is used to encapsulate errors that occur when you access a data provider. A TError object can be used to obtain extended return codes and status information. OLE DB TError objects use the standard OLE Automation methodology of error handling. While all OLE DB methods return error codes that indicate the success or failure of the method call, they aren't required to support the extended information provided by the TError object.

Transactions

A `TTransaction` object is used to encapsulate transactions within a data source. A transaction is used to buffer changes to the data source, giving the application the opportunity to commit or abort these changes. You can use transactions to improve application performance when accessing a data source. Distributed transactions are supported if the OLE DB provider supports them. This is where multiple OLE DB data consumers participate in a shared transaction. An OLE DB provider is not required to support the transaction interface.

Data Consumers and Providers

OLE DB applications, in their simplest form, are comprised of a data provider and a data consumer. A data provider is a COM component that provides an OLE DB-compliant interface. A data consumer is an application or component that utilizes an OLE DB interface to access a data source. As shown in Figure 29-3, OLE DB applications are structured in a give-and-take manner, with a data provider providing access to a data source through an interface, and a data consumer taking the data from the data source by utilizing the same interface.

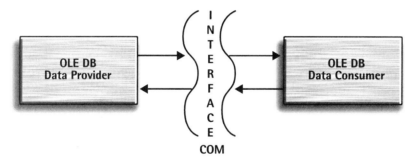

Figure 29-3: The give-and-take nature of OLE DB applications

OLE DB uses key COM concept – a well-defined and well-structured mechanism for application components to "talk" with each other – and extends this concept to include the task of providing access to enterprise data. An OLE DB data provider isn't required to support the complete OLE DB interface; for example, a data provider does *not* have to support commands. Lowering this barrier makes becoming an OLE DB provider much easier for an application. When you write an application, you can determine which OLE DB components are supported by the data provider that you are using, as well as how to write your application to take advantage of those components, through the interface layer of the COM architecture, which is discussed next.

Interfaces

To understand how to utilize OLE DB in your applications, you need to understand the concept of interfaces and COM components. A good real-world example of an interface is the standard electrical outlet in your wall. The outlet provides power to electrical devices through a three-pronged outlet. The top two holes in the outlet provide the power to an electrical device. The bottom hole provides grounding to an electrical device. Any electrical device that utilizes a plug that fits into the electrical outlet can use it as a source for power. Because an electrical outlet is a *standard* interface, it can support the power needs of any device that conforms to its standards — basically, a plug that fits into the holes that it provides. If the device can use the 120 volts of power provided in a standard electrical outlet and has a compatible plug, it can use the electrical outlet to provide the power that it requires.

An electrical outlet can provide power to a diverse set of devices — from a device as simple as a toaster, to complex devices, such as a personal computer. Any electrical device that includes a plug that complies with the electrical-outlet standards can be used anywhere that a standard outlet is available. Like any well-designed application component, an electrical outlet may be used by any existing or future device that conforms to its standards. Another key aspect of an electrical outlet is the provision of a hole that provides access to a ground. Not every electrical device utilizes the ground provided by the outlet, but that doesn't prevent the device from being able to use the outlet. Like a well-designed software component, an electrical outlet provides a set of required features and some extra features that aren't required.

Interfaces are the key aspect of the COM architecture. As Figure 29-4 demonstrates, the interfaces provided by COM components are essential. These interfaces describe the functionality provided by the component, and also provide the structured mechanism that these components use to talk to each other. You can think of the role of a component as a collection of code that is used to support the functionality described by the interface. This code is separate from the interface, and the details are abstracted from the end-user of the component. If you have OOP experience, a COM component should sound a lot like the description of an object, because a COM component is an object that uses the rules of the COM specification to provide access to interfaces provided by the component.

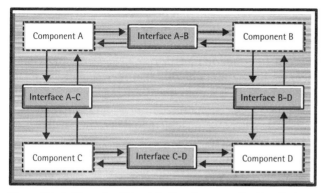

Figure 29-4: The role of the interface in an application that uses COM components

Interface factoring

One of the most important aspects of COM interfaces is that they don't change. Once a COM component interface is published, it remains static. When a new version of a component is released, a new interface is created, but the old version of the interface is still supported. Like the three-pronged electrical outlet that has two interfaces — one for two-pronged devices and another for three-pronged devices — a COM component can support multiple interfaces (in fact, a COM component theoretically can support an unlimited number of interfaces). These multiple interfaces enable a COM component to be upgraded with additional functionality and still be usable by older applications, developed before the component was upgraded and thus unaware of the component's additional features. As shown in Figure 29-5, an application that utilizes the COM architecture is defined by a set of components, each of which provides a set of interfaces — and each interface within the components defines a set of functions that is specific to that interface.

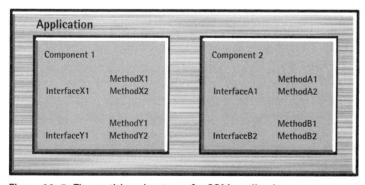

Figure 29-5: The partitioned nature of a COM application

The interfaces supported by a COM component can be determined by calling the QueryInterface() method. After an application determines whether a component supports a specific interface, the component is guaranteed to include the functionality of that interface. Because an interface defines a complete set of functions, interfaces are separated, or *factored*, by the functionality that they support. OLE DB uses this interface factoring extensively. Certain interfaces are required by the OLE DB specification, but OLE DB objects can support additional functionality. The QueryInterface() method is used by OLE DB consumers to determine the level of functionality that is supported by a component.

If you have experience with OOP, you may recall the aspect of object *polymorphism*, which is the concept of using the same methods when accessing different methods. COM components' capability to support multiple interfaces helps to facilitate polymorphism. As Figure 29-6 shows, OLE DB applications that are designed to support the base level of functionality can be used with different OLE DB data providers. As with an electrical outlet, different OLE DB providers can be *plugged* into the same application and still be guaranteed to work.

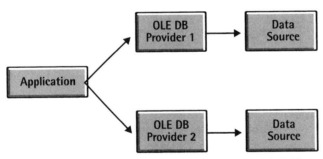

Figure 29-6: The plug-in orientation of COM and the OLE DB architecture

Interface negotiations

An application determines which interfaces are supported by an object by using the QueryInterface() method of the COM IUnknown interface. The QueryInterface() method returns a pointer to the interface if it is supported, and returns NULL otherwise. By using this mechanism, an application can determine the interface functionality supported by a component. Every COM component is required to support, at a minimum, the IUnknown interface (it must support other interfaces, too, to have any functionality). All interfaces are inherited from the IUnknown interface.

Application Flow

This section reviews the OLE DB objects in greater detail. Figure 29-7 illustrates the typical flow of an OLE DB application. An `Enumerator` object is used to determine which OLE DB data source providers are available. Using the data source name returned by using the `ISourcesRowset` and `IParseDisplayName` interfaces, a Data Source object can be created, which is then used to define both the data source access and a security context. Using the `IDBCreateSession` interface of the Data Source object, the `CreateSession()` method can be used to create a `Session` object, which then provides a logical scope for transactions and permits access to data source row sets and schema information. Using the `IDBCreateCommand` interface of the `Session` object, the `CreateCommand()` method can be used to create a `Command` object, which is used to perform provider-specific commands. For example, if the provider is a database that can interpret SQL statements, these commands may be SQL commands. Using the `ICommand` interface of the `Command` object, the `Execute()` method can be used to create a `TRowset` object. A `TRowset` object permits access to data source data in a tabular form.

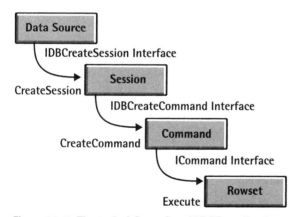

Figure 29-7: The typical flow of an OLE DB application

Latest OLE DB Information

Microsoft provides the following Web sites that you can use to stay informed regarding the latest developments in OLE DB and related technologies:

- ◆ `http://www.microsoft.com/data/oledb`: Contains all the latest OLE DB information

- ◆ `http://www.microsoft.com/data/oleddb/oledb20`: Contains the OLE DB Version 2.0 documentation

◆ `http://www.microsoft.com/data/RDS`: Remote Data Services Web site

◆ `http://www.microsoft.com/ado`: Advanced Data Object API Web site

◆ `http://www.microsoft.com/iis`: Internet Information Server Web site

◆ `http://www.microsoft.com/ntserver/info/indexserver.htm`: Microsoft Index Server Web site

◆ `http://www.microsoft.com/transaction`: Microsoft Transaction Server Web site

◆ `http://www.microsoft.com/oledev`: OLE Development information Web site

◆ `http://www.microsoft.com/oledev/olecom/title.htm`: Component Object Model information.

The following Internet news groups may also be helpful:

◆ `microsoft.public.oledb`: General OLE DB information

◆ `microsoft.public.oledb.sdk`: Specific OLE DB SDK-related information

◆ `microsoft.public.oledb.specification`: Information related to the OLE DB specifications

◆ `microsoft.public.activex.*`: A series of news groups related to the discussion of ActiveX components

◆ `microsoft.public.adc`: General ActiveX Data Connector discussions

Summary

This chapter presented an overview of OLE DB, including how OLE DB is the next logical step of ODBC, providing a consistent mechanism for universal access to enterprise-wide data. The topology of OLE DB applications was presented, including a discussion of how OLE DB makes a data source accessible. The Component Object Model, which is the basis of OLE DB, was also reviewed, and you saw how OLE DB fits into this model. The principal OLE DB objects and their hierarchy were also presented in this chapter.

Part VII

Controls, Wizards, and DHTML

Chapter 30

Using Visual Basic 6 Data Controls

IN THIS CHAPTER

- ◆ `DataGrid` control
- ◆ `DataList` control
- ◆ `DataCombo` control
- ◆ `DataRepeater` control
- ◆ `FlexGrid` control
- ◆ `RemoteData` control
- ◆ `DataReport` control

AS DISCUSSED IN PREVIOUS CHAPTERS, controls are the main method for a user to interact with your application. The user types, clicks, or moves through various controls on the application form and, through this process, manipulates their data. Basically, two types of controls are included on your forms: those bound to data and those not bound to data. When using a *bound control*, the values that are entered or chosen are stored in the data source, which can be a cursor field, table field, or a variable. You bind a control to data by setting its `ControlSource` property, or, in the case of grids, its `RecordSource` property. If you don't set the `ControlSource` property of a control, the value is only stored in memory and isn't written to disk. This chapter highlights the specific properties, methods, and events of each control.

Starting at the top level of the controls, two properties are used by all the controls: `DataField` and `DataSource`. Table 30-1 lists and describes the properties of the `DataField` and `DataSource` controls.

TABLE **30-1** DATAFIELD AND DATASOURCE PROPERTIES

Property	Description
DataField	The name of a field in the result set specified by the DataSource property. This field is used to determine which field in the currently accessed record will be highlighted. If a new selection is made, this field is updated when you move to a new record.
DataSource	Specifies the name of the RemoteData control (data source) to which the control is bound.

The steps to add a bound control to your application are as follows:

1. Draw the control on the same form as the RemoteData control to which it will be bound.

2. Set the DataSource property to specify the RemoteData control to which it will be associated.

The following sections look at the various bound controls and how they work.

DataGrid Control

The DataGrid control is a data-bound control that acts like a spreadsheet. It displays and enables data manipulation for a series of rows and columns representing records and fields from a CrdoResultset object. When you set the DataGrid control's DataSource property, the control is automatically filled and its column headers are automatically entered from a DataGrid control's Recordset object. This is a powerful feature that enables your users to browse and edit complete database tables or query results. The DataGrid control's Row and Col properties specify the current cell in a grid. Each cell can store either text or picture values. If a cell's text is too long to be displayed in the cell, the text wraps to the next line within the same cell. To display the wrapped text, you must increase the cell's Column object's Width property and/or the DataGrid control's RowHeight property. The DataGrid control can have numerous rows and as many columns as your system resources can support — up to 32,767 columns.

Users can either edit individual cells, by setting the focus to an individual cell and editing it, or select entire rows of cells on a per-column basis. At design time, you can set each column to have its own font, word-wrap, border, color width, and height. This is very useful in presenting information and, moreover, preventing the end-user from changing the forDEing properties at runtime.

To add a DataGrid control to your project, follow these steps:

1. Add a RemoteData control to a new dialog box and then set its properties to the database and table that you want to display.

2. Add a DataGrid control to the form and then set its DataSource property to the RemoteData control that you created in the preceding step.

3. Run the application.

Your program should now display the specified database table in the DataGrid control, complete with column headers and scroll bars. You can scroll through all the records and fields of the table and edit any cell in the table; the cell is updated automatically when you move to a new row. Additionally, with the AllowAddNew and AllowDelete properties set to True, you can delete records by selecting and deleting the entire row. Tables 30-2 and Table 30-3 describe the properties and events, respectively, of the DataGrid control.

TABLE **30-2 DATAGRID CONTROL PROPERTIES**

Property	Description
ApproxCount	Returns the approximate number of rows in the grid. It is used to improve the accuracy of the vertical scroll bar. You can use this property when you know the number of rows in advance.
CurrentCellModified	Sets or returns the modification status of the current cell. You can use this property to cancel any changes the user has made to the current text.
CurrentCellVisible	Sets or returns the visibility of the current cell. This causes the grid to scroll so that the current cell is brought into view.
AllowAddNew	Sets or returns a value indicating whether the user can add new records to the Recordset object bound to the DataGrid.

Continued

TABLE 30-2 **DATAGRID CONTROL PROPERTIES** *(continued)*

Property	Description
AllowDelete	Sets or returns a value indicating whether the user can delete records from the Recordset object bound to the DataGrid control. Use this property to prevent the user from deleting records.
AllowUpdate	Sets or returns a value indicating whether a user can modify any data in the DataGrid control. This enables users to scroll through the DataGrid control and select data, but not change any of the values.
AllowRowSizing	Sets or returns a value indicating whether a user can resize the rows of the DataGrid control or Split object at runtime.
ColumnHeaders	Sets or returns a value indicating whether the column headers are displayed in a DataGrid control.
DataChanged	Sets or returns a value indicating that the data in the bound control has been changed by some process other than that of retrieving data from the current record.
Column	Sets or returns the current data column in the data grid.
BoundText	Sets or returns the value of the field specified by the BoundColumn property.
Bookmark	Sets or returns a bookmark for the specified row within a RowBuffer object in an unbound DataGrid control.
AddNewMode	Returns a value that describes the location of the current cell with respect to the grid's AddNew row.
AllowArrows	Sets or returns a value that determines whether the control uses the arrow keys for grid navigation.
CurrentCellVisible	Sets or returns the visibility of the current cell.

TABLE **30-3 DATAGRID CONTROL EVENTS**

Event	Description
Validate	Occurs before the focus shifts to a (second) control that has its CausesValidation property set to True.
DblClick	Occurs when the user presses and releases a mouse button and then presses and releases it again over an object.

DataList and DataCombo Controls

The DataList and DataCombo controls serve related functions and have parallel sets of properties and events.

DataList Control

The DataList control is a data-bound list box that is automatically populated from a field in an attached data source. A common use of this control is to build a list of items, based on a database query, from which a user can select or enter a value. When an item in the list is selected, its associated BoundColumn value is made available to the RemoteData control specified by the DataSource property. This type of control is useful in a relational database, to use one table's data to supply values to be input into a second (related) table. For example, in an employee database, the name of each employee is stored in one table, with each employee's social security number as their unique ID. Another table, showing department rosters, uses the unique ID to designate which employee is in which department. You would use the DataList control to show the name of the employee, while (invisibly) supplying the ID of the employee to the department table.

DataCombo Control

The DataCombo control, like the DataList control, is similar to the standard combo box controls. The major difference (as with any data-bound control) is that the DataCombo control is filled automatically from a database field from the data control to which it is bound. This control is useful for providing the user with a predefined selection, loaded from a data source, for which the user may need to perform editing on the data. Like any other Visual Basic form controls, the DataList control and DataCombo control each has its own set of properties, methods, and events, which are set forth in Table 30-4.

TABLE **30-4 DATALIST AND DATACOMBO CONTROL PROPERTIES**

Property	Description
BoundColumn	Sets or returns the name of the source field in a Recordset object that is used to supply a data value to another Recordset. Generally, when you work with the DataList and DataCombo controls, you use two Data controls: one to fill the list, as designated by the ListField and RowSource properties, and one to update a field in a database, specified by the DataSource and DataField properties.
ListField	Sets or returns the name of the field in the Recordset object, specified by the RowSource property, used to fill the DataCombo or DataList control's list portion.
RowSource	Sets a value that specifies the Data control from which the DataList and DataCombo controls' list is filled.
SelectedItem	Returns a value containing a bookmark for the selected record in a DataCombo control; or, when you select an item in the list portion of the control, this property contains a bookmark that you can use to reposition to the selected record in the Recordset of the Data control specified by the RowSource property.
VisibleItems	Returns an array of bookmarks (which can be used to gather records), one for each visible item in the DataCombo or DataList control's list.
VisibleCount	Returns a value indicating the number of visible items in the list portion of the DataCombo or DataList control.
MatchEntry	Sets or returns a value indicating how the DataCombo or DataList control performs searches based on user input.
MatchedWithList	Returns True if the current content of the BoundText property matches one of the records in the list portion of the control.
Locked	Sets or returns a value indicating whether any data in the object can be modified.
RowMember	Sets or returns the data member to be used to qualify which data set to bind to the row and display-list text.
BoundText	Sets or returns the value of the field specified by the BoundColumn property.

The ReFill() method can be used for the DataList and DataCombo controls. It re-creates the list of a DataList or DataCombo control and forces a repaint.

DataRepeater Control

The DataRepeater control is a fast and powerful way to display several instances of the UserControl, each in its own row, and each bound to a different record in the database. Some possible uses are the following:

◆ To create a personal time manger

◆ To create an inventory application

◆ To create a custom data-bound grid that includes ComboBox controls

The DataRepeater control functions as a scrollable, data-bound container of any user data-bound user controls that you create. To use the DataRepeater control, you must first create a data-bound user control and compile it into an OCX. After you create the user control, the following basic steps must be taken: After compiling the control into an OCX, the DataRepeater control's Repeated ControlName property is set to the user control. The DataRepeater is then bound to a data source, such as the ADO Data Control, which sets up a connection between the user control and the employee database.

 At runtime, the user can scroll through a record set by using the Home, End, PgUp, PgDn, and arrow keys.

To add a DataRepeater control to your project, follow these steps:

1. Add the UserControl to the project by using the Components dialog box.

2. In the Properties window, click RepeatedControlName and then select the UserControl from the drop-down list.

3. Add a data source, such as the ADO Data control, to the form and connect it to a data source.

4. Set the DataRepeater control's DataSource property to the data source.

5. Right-click the DataRepeater control and then click DataRepeater Properties.

6. Click the RepeaterBindings tab.

7. Set the `PropertyName` to an appropriate `DataField` property and then click the Add button.

 The `DataRepeater` control displays only a single `UserControl` — the active control; this saves computer resources. The other controls displayed are simple images that don't maintain individual connections to the data source. Like any other Visual Basic form control, a `DataRepeater` control has its own set of properties, methods, and events. Tables 30-5 and 30-6, respectively, list and describe the properties and events of the Data control.

TABLE **30-5** DATA CONTROL PROPERTIES

Property	Description
RepeaterBinding	Used to change the contents of a `DataRepeater` control by changing how fields are bound.
CurrentRecord	Returns the bookmark of the current record.
PropertyNames	Returns an array of property names of the repeated control.
RepeatedControlName	Sets or returns the programmatic ID of the repeated control.
RepeaterBindings	Returns a reference to the `RepeaterBindings` collection of `RepeaterBinding` objects.
RepeatedControl	Returns a reference to the repeated control.
CaptionStyle	Sets or returns a value that determines the style of the caption, including alignment and visibility.
RowDividerStyle	Sets or returns a value that determines the appearance of the row divider.
RowIndicator	Sets or returns a value that determines whether the row indicator (a solid-black triangle) is drawn on the control. The indicator identifies the active record.
RecordCount	Returns the number of records in the record set.
ActiveRow	Sets or returns the row index where the current record will be positioned.

Property	Description
IntegralHeight	Sets or returns a value that determines whether the control displays partial rows.
VisibleRecords	Sets or returns the bookmark of the record to be displayed at the specified row index.
DataFields	Returns an array of DataField names of the DataSource. The DataFields array contains the names of all bindable properties of the repeated control.
ScrollBars	Sets or returns a value that determines the scroll bar style.

TABLE 30-6 DATA CONTROL EVENTS

Event	Description
ActiveRowChanged	Occurs when the ActiveRow property is set.
VisibleRecordChanged	Occurs when the VisibleRecords property changes.
DataUpdate	Occurs when a field is edited either programmatically or by a user.
CurrentRecordChanged	Occurs when the current record changes to a different record.
RepeatedControlLoaded	Occurs after the RepeatedControl has been created and initialized.
RepeatedControlUnLoaded	Occurs when the RepeatedControl is about to be unloaded.

Hierarchical FlexGrid and FlexGrid Control

The Microsoft Hierarchical FlexGrid and FlexGrid controls present Recordset data from one or more tables, in a grid format. These controls enable complete flexibility to sort, merge, and format tables containing strings and pictures. When bound to a Data control, these controls display read-only data. You can put text, a picture, or both, in any cell of these controls. If the text in a cell is too long to display in the cell, and the WordWrap property is set to True, the text wraps to the next line within the same cell. The Hierarchical FlexGrid control provides you with advanced features for displaying data in a grid. It is similar to the Microsoft Data Bound grid (DataGrid) control, but with the distinct difference that the Hierarchical FlexGrid control doesn't allow the user to edit data. This control, therefore, enables you to display data to the user, while ensuring that the original data remains secure and unchanged. However, you can also add cell-editing features to your Hierarchical FlexGrid control by combining it with a text box.

The Hierarchical FlexGrid and FlexGrid controls both can be used in the following scenarios:

◆ To implement a "sorting and merging" data display that groups information by category, enabling the user to modify the order in which information is presented.

◆ To create a spreadsheet with in-cell editing using standard Visual Basic controls.

◆ To implement an outline-style display, with heading items that can be collapsed or expanded with the mouse.

Both FlexGrid controls also support the following features, except for the features denoted with an asterisk at the end, which are available only in the Hierarchical FlexGrid version:

◆ Read-only data binding

◆ Rearrangement of columns and rows at runtime

◆ Regrouping of data during column adjustment

◆ Backward compatibility for Visual Basic code using the DataGrid control

◆ Each cell may contain text, a picture, or both

◆ Dynamic changing of current cell text in code

◆ Reading data automatically when the Hierarchical FlexGrid is assigned to a data control

◆ Word-wrap for text within cells

◆ ActiveX data binding when the DataSource and DataMember properties of the control are bound to a specific data provider

◆ Binding via the Data Binding Manager in Visual Basic

◆ Binding directly to grouped and related ADO Recordsets

◆ Additional display options when the Hierarchical FlexGrid is bound to a hierarchy of Recordsets

To access the FlexGrid controls, follow these steps:

1. On the Project menu, select Components.

2. On the Controls tab, select either of the FlexGrid controls. The control is added to the Visual Basic toolbox.

3. On the Visual Basic toolbox, click the control and then drop it on a Visual Basic form.

Like any other Visual Basic form control, a DataGrid control has its own set of properties, methods, and events. Tables 30-7 and 30-8, respectively, list and describe the properties and methods of the Hierarchical FlexGrid and FlexGrid controls.

TABLE 30-7 HIERARCHICAL FLEXGRID AND FLEXGRID CONTROL PROPERTIES

Property	Description
MergeCells	Sets or returns a value that determines whether cells with the same contents should be grouped in a single cell spanning multiple rows or columns.
MouseCol, MouseRow	Returns the current mouse position, in row and column coordinates. Use these properties programmatically to determine the mouse location.
Name	Sets or returns the name of the aggregate field or the field by which to group. This property cannot have the same name as the field in which the aggregate will be created.
Picture	Returns a picture of your grid.
PictureType	Sets or returns the type of picture to be generated by the Picture property.
Redraw	Sets or returns a value that determines whether the grid should be automatically redrawn after each change.
RowHeight	Sets or returns the height of the specified row, in twips.
RowHeightMin	Sets or returns the minimum row height for the entire control, in twips.
RowIsVisible	Sets or returns a value that determines whether a specified row is visible.

Continued

TABLE 30-7 HIERARCHICAL FLEXGRID AND FLEXGRID CONTROL PROPERTIES
(continued)

Property	Description
RowPos	Returns the distance, in twips, between the upper-left corner of the grid and the upper-left corner of a specified row.
ScrollBars	Sets or returns a value that determines whether a grid has horizontal and/or vertical scroll bars.
ScrollTrack	Sets or returns a value that determines whether the grid should scroll its contents while the user moves the scroll box along the scroll bars.
SelectionMode	Sets or returns a value that determines whether a grid should allow regular cell selection, selection by rows, or selection by columns.
Sort	Sets a value that sorts selected rows according to selected criteria.
Text	Sets or returns the text content of a cell or range of cells.
TextMatrix	Sets or returns the text contents of an arbitrary cell.
TextStyle, TextStyleBand, TextStyleFixed, TextStyleHeader	Sets or returns the three-dimensional style for text within a specific cell or range of cells.
TopRow	Sets or returns the uppermost visible row (other than a fixed row).
Version	Returns the version that is currently loaded in memory.
WordWrap	Sets or returns a value that determines whether a cell displays multiple lines of text or one long line of text.
ColPos	Returns the distance, in twips, between the upper-left corner of the control and the upper-left corner of a specified column.
ColPosition	Sets the position of a column, enabling you to move columns to specific positions.
RowPosition	Sets the position of a row, enabling you to move rows to specific positions.

Property	Description
Cols	Sets or returns the total number of columns.
Rows	Sets or returns the total number of rows. The Rows property also sets or returns the total number of columns in each band.
ColSel	Sets or returns the start or end column for a range of cells.
RowSel	Sets or returns the start or end row for a range of cells.
ColWidth	Sets or returns the width of the column in the specified band, in twips.
FillStyle	Sets or returns a value that determines whether setting the Text property, or one of the cell forDEing properties, applies the change to all selected cells within the grid.
FixedCols	Sets or returns the total number of fixed columns.
FixedRows	Sets or returns the total number of fixed rows.
FocusRect	Sets or returns a value that determines whether to draw a focus rectangle around the current cell.
FontWidth, FontWidthBand, FontWidthFixed, FontWidthHeader	Sets or returns the width, in points, of the font to be used for text, or for the grid's band, fixed, or header area.
ForeColor, ForeColorBand, ForeColorFixed, ForeColorHeader, ForeColorSel	Sets or returns the colors used to draw text.
FormatString	Sets the column width, alignment, fixed row text, and fixed column text
GridColor, GridColorBand, GridColorFixed, GridColorHeader, GridColorIndent, GridColorUnpopulated	Sets or returns the line color used between the cells, bands, headers, indents, or unpopulated areas of the grid.

Continued

TABLE **30-7** HIERARCHICAL FLEXGRID AND FLEXGRID CONTROL PROPERTIES
(continued)

Property	Description
GridLines, GridLinesBand, GridLinesFixed, GridLinesHeader, GridLinesIndent, GridLinesUnpopulated	Sets or returns a value that determines whether lines are drawn between cells, bands, headers, indents, or unpopulated areas. These properties also determine the type of lines that are drawn in the grid.
GridLineWidth, GridLineWidthBand, GridLineWidthFixed, GridLineWidthHeader, GridLineWidthIndent, GridLineWidth Unpopulated	Sets or returns the width, in pixels, of the lines displayed between cells, bands, headers, indents, or unpopulated areas.
HighLight	Determines whether selected cells appear highlighted.
LeftCol	Sets or returns the leftmost visible nonfixed column.
AllowBigSelection	Sets or returns a value that determines whether clicking a column or row header should cause the entire column or row to be selected.
AllowUserResizing	Sets or returns a value that determines whether the user can use the mouse to resize rows and columns.
BackColor, BackColorBkg, BackColorFixed, BackColorSel	Sets or returns the background color of various elements.
CellAlignment	Sets or returns a value that determines the horizontal and vertical alignment of data within the current cell.
CellBackColor	Sets or returns the background colors of individual cells or cell ranges.
CellForeColor	Sets or returns the foreground colors of individual cells or cell ranges.
CellFontBold	Sets or returns the bold style for the current cell text.
CellFontItalic	Sets or returns the italic style for the current cell text.

Property	Description
ColIsVisible	Sets or returns a value indicating whether a specified column is currently visible.

TABLE 30-8 HIERARCHICAL FLEXGRID AND FLEXGRID CONTROL METHODS

Method	Description
RemoveItem()	Removes a row from a grid at runtime.
CollapseAll()	Collapses all rows of the specified band within the grid.
ExpandAll()	Expands all rows of the specified band within the grid.
Clear()	Clears the contents of the grid (text, pictures, and cells).
ClearStructure()	Clears any mapping information from the grid regarding the order and name of the displayed columns.
RowColChange()	Occurs when the currently active cell changes to a different cell.
Scroll()	Occurs when the contents of the grid are scrolled.
SelChange()	Occurs when the selected range changes to a different cell or range of cells.
Collapse()	Occurs when the user collapses a row within the grid.
Compare()	Occurs when the Sort property for the grid is set to Custom Sort (9), so that the user can customize the sort process.
EnterCell()	Occurs when the currently active cell changes to a different cell.
Expand()	Occurs when the user expands a row within the grid.
LeaveCell()	Occurs immediately before the currently active cell changes to a different cell.

RemoteData Control

The RemoteData control implements data access by using the Microsoft Remote Data Objects (RDO). This gives you access to many standard database formats and enables you to create data-aware applications, without writing any code. The

`RemoteData` control is typically used with larger client/server databases such as Open Database Connectivity (ODBC) databases, Microsoft SQL Server, and Oracle.

> The `Data` control, `RemoteData` control, and the ADO `Data` control all connect a data source to a data-bound control. All three are similar; that is, each has a set of four buttons that enables the user to go immediately to the beginning or end, or scroll backwards and forwards, through the record set.

To add a `RemoteData` control, follow these steps:

1. Check if the `RemoteData` control is not in the Toolbox, (press Ctrl+T to display the Components dialog box.) In the Components dialog box, click Microsoft RemoteData Control. Click OK to add it to the Toolbox.

2. Draw a `RemoteData` control on the form.

3. Click the `RemoteData` control and then press F4 to display the Properties window.

4. Set the `DataSourceName` property to the DSN of the database.

5. On the Properties window, click the `SQL` property and then type an SQL statement; for example: **SELECT * FROM TestTbl**

6. Draw a `TextBox` control on the form.

7. Click the `TextBox` control and set the `DataSource` property to the `RemoteData` control on the Properties window.

8. Set the `DataField` property to the name of the field that you want in the database.

9. Repeat Steps 5, 6, and 7 for each additional field that you want to access.

10. Press F5 to run the application.

Like any other Visual Basic form control, a `Remote Data` control has its own set of properties, methods, and events. Tables 30-9, 30-10, and 30-11, respectively, list and describe the properties, methods, and events of the `RemoteData` control.

TABLE 30-9 REMOTEDATA CONTROL PROPERTIES

Property	Description
Connect	A string that can contain all the information necessary to make a connection.
UserName	Identifies a user to a protected database. The user must also supply a valid password that the DBMS recognizes.
Password	Allows the user to access protected data.
SQL	Contains the SQL statement used to retrieve a result set.
RowSetSize	Sets the number of rows returned in a result set, if the cursor is a keyset.
ReadOnly	Sets whether the data is read-only or can be modified.
CursorDriver	Specifies the location and type of driver.
LockType	Determines how the data is locked when others attempt to change the data.
BOFAction, EOFAction	Determine what occurs when the control is at the beginning and end, respectively, of the cursor. Choices include staying at the beginning or end, moving to the first or last record, or adding a new record (at the end only).
ResultSetType	Sets whether the cursor is static or a keyset type.
KeySetSize	Used to fine-tune the size of your result set, which is the set of key values used to identify specific rows in a cursor.
LoginTimeout	Sets the number of seconds to wait until an error is returned.
MaxRows	Defines the size, in rows, of the cursor.
Options	Specifies whether the control executes queries asynchronously.
Prompt	Determines whether dialog boxes are used to prompt the user.
QueryTimeout	Sets the number of seconds to wait for a query to complete before returning an error.
BatchSize	Determines how many statements can be sent in a batch.

(Continued)

TABLE 30-9 REMOTEDATA CONTROL PROPERTIES *(continued)*

Property	Description
Resultset	Sets or returns an `rdoResultset` object defined by a `RemoteData` control or as returned by the `OpenResultset()` method.
DataSourceName	Sets or returns the data source name for a `RemoteData` control.
Environment	Returns a reference to a `RemoteData` control's underlying `rdoEnvironment` object.
Name	Returns the name of a `RemoteData` object. `rdoTable` and `rdoQuery` objects can't share the same name. You can use the `Name` property to map database table and column names.
EditMode	Returns a value that indicates the state of editing for the current row.
BatchCollisionCount	Returns a value that specifies the number of rows that did not complete the last batch-mode update.
BatchCollisionRows	Returns an array of bookmarks indicating the rows that generated collisions in the last batch-update operation.
UpdateCriteria	Sets or returns a value that specifies how the SQL WHERE clause is constructed for each row during an optimistic batch-update operation.
UpdateOperation	Sets or returns a value that specifies whether the optimistic batch update should use an `update` statement or a `delete` statement followed by an `insert`.
LogMessages	Enables ODBC trace logging.
Version	Returns a value that indicates the version of the data source associated with the object.

TABLE **30-10** REMOTEDATA CONTROL METHODS

Method	Description
BeginTrans(), CommitTrans(), RollbackTrans()	The transaction methods manage transaction processing during a session represented by the object placeholder, as follows: BeginTrans begins a new transaction; CommitTrans ends the current transaction and saves the changes; RollbackTrans releases the changes made in a transaction.
Cancel()	Cancels the processing of a query running in asynchronous mode, or cancels any pending results against the specified RDO object.
Refresh()	Closes and rebuilds the rdoResultset object created by a RemoteData control or refreshes the members of the collections in the Applies To list.
UpdateControls()	Gets the current row from a RemoteData control's rdoResultset object and displays the appropriate data in controls bound to a RemoteData control.
UpdateRow()	Saves the current values of bound controls to the database.

TABLE **30-11** REMOTEDATA CONTROL EVENTS

Event	Description
Error	Occurs only as the result of a data access .
Reposition	Occurs after a row becomes the current row.
Validate	Occurs before a different row becomes the current row; before the Update() method (except when data is saved with the UpdateRow() method); and before a Delete, Unload, or Close operation.
QueryCompleted	Occurs after the query of an rdoResultset generated by a RemoteData control returns the first result set.

Data Report

As with most applications, data reports usually need to be generated. Microsoft Data Report Designer is a flexible data report generator that has the added feature of being able to create banded hierarchical reports. Coupled with a data source, this enables you to create reports from many different relational tables. In addition to creating printable reports, you can export the reports to HTML or text files.

Data Report Designer Features

Data Report Designer has several features:

♦ **Drag-and-drop functionality for fields:** Drag fields from Microsoft Data Environment Designer to Data Report Designer. A text box control is created on the data report and sets the `DataMember` and `DataField` properties of the dropped field.

♦ **Toolbox controls:** Data Report Designer features its own set of controls, which are created automatically on a new Toolbox tab when you add Data Report Designer to a project. These controls function similarly to Visual Basic intrinsic controls.

♦ **Print preview:** Preview the report within its own window by using the `Show()` method.

♦ **Print reports:** Within your application, you can make a call to the function `PrintReport`

♦ **File export:** Export the data report information by using the `ExportReport()` method. Formats for export include HTML and text.

♦ **Export templates:** You can create a collection of file templates to be used with the `ExportReport()` method. This is useful for exporting reports in a variety of formats, each tailored to the report type.

♦ **Asynchronous operation:** Using the `ProcessingTimeout` event, you can monitor the state of these operations and cancel any that are taking too long.

Parts of Data Report Designer

Data Report Designer consists of the following objects:

♦ `object`: This object is similar to a Visual Basic form; the object has both a visual designer and a code module.

♦ `Section` object: Data Report Designer breaks down each section of a report into a `Section` object in a `Sections` collection. Each section is represented by a header that you can click to select the section, where you can then place and position controls.

♦ **Data Report controls:** Special controls that work only on Data Report Designer.

Sections of Data Report Designer

The default Data Report Designer contains these sections:

♦ **Report Header:** Contains the text that appears at the beginning of a report, such as the report title, author, or database name.

♦ **Page Header:** The information that appears at the top of every page, such as the report's title.

♦ **Group Header/Footer:** Contains a "repeating" section of the data report.

♦ **Details:** Contains the innermost "repeating" part (the records) of the report.

♦ **Page Footer:** The information that goes at the bottom of every page; for example, the page number.

♦ **Report Footer:** Contains the text that appears at the very end of the report, such as summary information or an address or contact name. The Report Footer appears between the last Page Header and Page Footer.

Data Report Controls

When a new Data Report Designer is added to a project, the following controls are automatically placed in the Toolbox tab:

♦ `TextBox` **control:** Enables you to format text or assign a `DataFormat`.

♦ `Label` **control:** Enables you to place labels on the report, to identify fields or sections.

♦ `Image` **control:** Enables you to place graphics on your report. Note that this control cannot be bound to a data field.

♦ `Line` **control:** Enable you to draw rules on the report, to further distinguish sections.

♦ `Shape` **control:** Enables you to place rectangles, triangles, or circles (and ovals) on a report.

◆ `Function` **control:** A special text box that calculates values as the report is generated.

Like any other Visual Basic form control, a `DataReport` control has its own set of properties, methods, and events. Table 30-12 describes the properties of the `DataReport` control.

TABLE **30-12** DATAREPORT CONTROL PROPERTIES

Property	Description
`GridX, GridY`	Used as an aid in aligning controls.
`ReportWidth`	Sets or returns the width of the report, in twips.
`DataSource`	Sets or returns a data source through which a data consumer is bound to a database.
`Font`	Returns a `Font` object. Use the `Font` property of an object to identify a specific `Font` object whose properties you want to use.
`DataMember`	Sets or returns a specified data member from among several offered by the data provider.
`AsyncCount`	Returns the number of asynchronous operations still executing.
`Title`	Sets or returns the title of the report.
`Sections`	Returns a reference to the `Sections` collection.
`ReportWidth`	Sets or returns the width of the report, in twips.
`ExportFormats`	Returns a reference to the `ExportFormats` collection.
`BottomMargin, TopMargin`	Returns or sets, in twips, the height of the bottom and top margins, respectively.

Creating Reports

You now are going to create a simple data report by using a Data Environment Designer as a data source. The Data Environment Designer uses the example database to create a simple hierarchical cursor. The cursor contains two tables, Example1 and Example2, and uses the `CustomerID` field to link the two.

To create a simple hierarchical cursor in the Data Environment Designer, follow these steps:

1. On the Project menu, click Add Data Environment to add a designer to your project. If the designer is not listed on the Project menu, click Components. Click the Designers tab and then click Data Environment to add the designer to the menu.

2. In the Connection1 Properties dialog box, type **Northwind** in the Connection Name box. This name is used to identify the connection.

3. Click Use Connection String and then select Build.

4. Right-click the Commands folder and then click Add Command, to display the Command1 dialog box. In the dialog box, set the properties as follows:

Property	Setting
Command Name	**Example1**
Connection	**MyData**
DataBase Object	**Table**
Object Name	**Test1**

5. Click OK to close the dialog box.

6. Right-click the Example1 command, and then click the Add Child Command, to display the Command2 dialog box. In the dialog box, set the properties as follows:

Property	Setting
Command Name	**Example2**
Connection	**MyData**
DataBase Object	**Table**
Object Name	**Test2**

7. Click the Relation tab. The Relate to a Parent Command Object check box should be checked. The Parent box should contain Example1.

8. Click Add. Click OK to close the dialog box.

9. Clicking the Add button adds the relation to the `Command` object. After closing the dialog box, Data Environment Designer reflects the relationship by displaying the two commands as a hierarchy.

10. Set the properties of the project and designer according to the settings in the next section, and then save the project.

CREATING THE DATA REPORT

After you create the Data Environment Designer, you can create a data report. Because not all the fields in the data environment will be useful in a report, the following series of steps creates a limited report that displays only a few fields:

1. On the Project menu, click Add Data Report to instruct Visual Basic to add it to your project. If the designer is not on the Project menu, click Components. Click the Designers tab and then click Data Report, to add the designer to the menu.

2. Right-click the Data Report designer and then click Retrieve Structure.

3. From the Data Environment Designer, drag the structure onto the Group Header section.

4. Delete the `Label` control (`rptLabel`) named `Label1`.

5. Save the project.

PREVIEWING THE DATA REPORT USING THE SHOW METHOD

Now that you have created the data environment and the data report objects, you are almost ready to run the project. One step remains: writing code to show the data report.

To show the data report at runtime:

1. On the Project Explorer window, double-click the frmShowReport icon to display Form Designer.

2. On the Toolbox, click the General tab.

3. Click the CommandButton icon and draw a `CommandButton` on the form.

4. Set the properties of the `Command1` control as follows:

Property	Setting
Name	cmdShow
Caption	Show Report

5. In the button's `Click` event, paste the following code:

```
Private Sub cmdShow_Click()
rptNwind.Show
End Sub
```

6. Save and run the project.

7. Click Show Report to display the report in print-preview mode.

You should now understand how to add, customize, and preview reports by using the `DataReport` control. Use the `DataReport` control to add reports quickly and easily to your applications, with minimal programming.

Summary

This chapter discussed several data-bound controls, which are just like any other Visual Basic form control; the main difference is that they have additional properties, methods, and events that enable you to associate them with one or more data tables. The controls themselves encapsulate the details for accessing the data and greatly simplify accessing and navigating your data source – without the need for programming. Bounded controls can be used to do the following:

◆ Load the contents of the table into a Visual Basic object

◆ Allow the user to select and navigate a set of records

◆ Load form controls with values of the requested records

◆ Validate user input

◆ Enforce database integrity

◆ Update the data source with the contents of Visual Basic form controls

Chapter 31

Data Access Wizards

IN THIS CHAPTER

- ◆ Using Add-Ins
- ◆ Exploring the Data Object Wizard
- ◆ Examining the Data Form Wizard

WIZARDS ARE TOOLS you can use to provide data access quickly in your Visual Basic applications. This chapter introduces and explores the Data Object and Data Form Wizards. The Data Object Wizard helps you to create custom data sources and user controls that display and manipulate data through stored procedures. The Data Form Wizard helps you to generate automatically Visual Basic forms that contain the necessary bound controls.

Add-Ins Introduction

The Data Object and Data Form Wizards are provided to Visual Basic 6 as *Add-Ins*, which are extensions to Visual Basic that add extra capabilities to the Visual Basic development environment. Add-Ins can be accessed through the Add-Ins menu option in the Visual Basic development environment. Before you can begin to use the Data Form and Data Object Wizards, you need to add them to the Add-Ins menu. The Visual Basic Add-In Manager – which enables you to add or remove Visual Basic Add-Ins – can be used to add these wizards to the Add-Ins menu item, by following these steps:

1. From the Visual Basic development environment, select Add-Ins → Add-In Manager. The Visual Basic Add-In Manager dialog box is displayed, as shown in Figure 31-1.

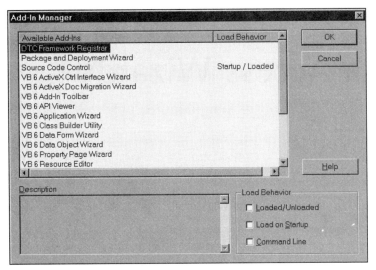

Figure 31-1: Viewing the Add-In Manager dialog box

2. The Available Add-Ins list contains all the Add-Ins that are available to you. To add the Data Form and Data Object Wizards to the Add-Ins menu item, select them from the Available Add-Ins list, and then click the Loaded/Unload and Load on Startup radio buttons, as shown in Figure 31-2.

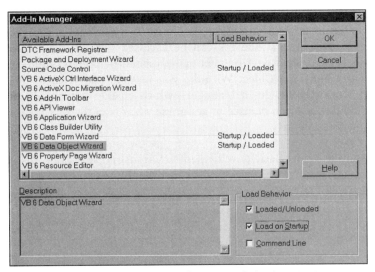

Figure 31-2: Viewing the wizard set for automatic load on startup

3. After you modify the startup behavior of each wizard, click the OK button. The Data Form and Data Object Wizards are now being added to the Add-Ins menu item.

Next, you will review in detail how to use each of these wizards.

Data Object Wizard

The Data Object Wizard automates the process of generating code to create custom data sources and user controls, to display and manipulate data through stored procedures. Before you can use the Data Object Wizard, you must create a Data Environment, which, at a minimum, contains a SELECT statement that creates the data set with which you want to work. The Data Object Wizard can be used to do the following:

♦ Create updateable record sets from stored procedures

♦ Create user controls to display and manipulate data

♦ Generate Visual Basic code that reflects relationships between data

♦ Create user controls that display, and allow you to interact with, lookup relationships

♦ Provide meaningful text descriptions rather than cryptic lookup values

♦ Provide meaningful text for NULL values

To use the Data Object Wizard to create a class object to which other objects can bind data, you must first create a Data Environment, by following these steps:

1. From an open Microsoft Visual Basic application, select Project → Add Data Environment.

2. The DataEnvironment window is displayed, as shown in Figure 31-3.

3. Right-click the Connection1 object and then select the Properties menu item, to display the Data Link dialog box, as shown in Figure 31-4.

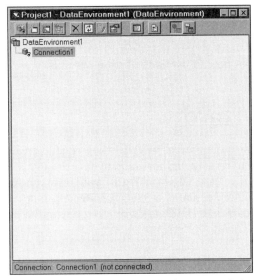

Figure 31-3: Viewing the DataEnvironment window

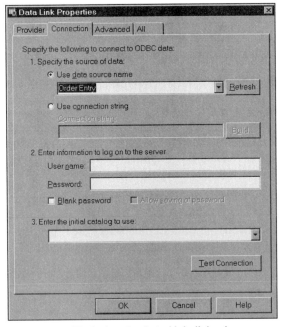

Figure 31-4: Displaying the Data Link dialog box

4. Click the Connection tab and select the OLE DB data provider or ODBC resource to which you want to connect. After you specify the connection information, click the OK button to continue.

5. Right-click the Connection1 object and then select the Refresh menu item, to establish a connection to the data source.

6. To add a command to your connection, right-click the DataConnection1 object and select the Add Command menu item. The new command is displayed in the DataEnvironment window.

7. Right-click the new command object and then select the Properties menu item, to display the Command Properties dialog box, as shown in Figure 31-5.

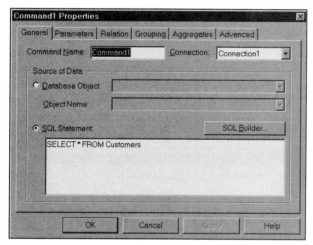

Figure 31-5: Displaying the Command Properties dialog box

8. Specify the Command Name, select the connection the command is associated with (a Data Environment can have more than one connection object), and then specify the SQL command or stored procedure to execute that creates a new data set. Click the OK button to save your command properties.

Now that you have created a Data Environment, Connection, and Command, you can use the data environment with the Data Object Wizard. To create a new data object by using the Data Object Wizard, follow these steps:

1. Select Add-Ins → VB 6 Data Object Wizard, to display the Data Object Wizard – Introduction dialog box, as shown in Figure 31-6. Click Next to continue.

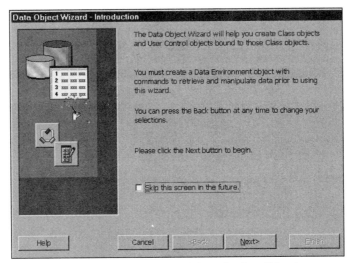

Figure 31-6: The Data Object Wizard's Introduction dialog box

2. The Data Object – Create Object dialog box is displayed, as shown in Figure 31-7. Select the type of object that you want to create: a new class object or a user control object. Click Next to continue.

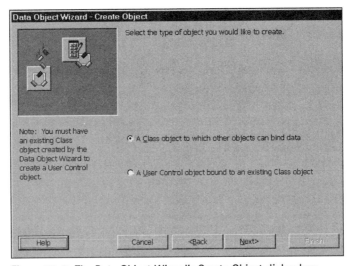

Figure 31-7: The Data Object Wizard's Create Object dialog box

3. The Data Object – Select Data Environment Command dialog box is displayed, as shown in Figure 31-8. Select the Data Environment command that you want to use as the record source, and then click Next to continue.

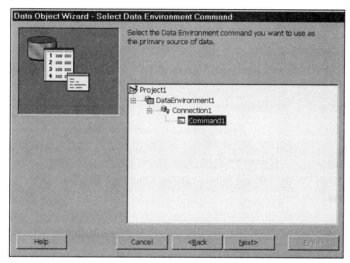

Figure 31-8: The Data Object Wizard's Select Data Environment dialog box

4. The Data Object – Define Class Field Information dialog box is displayed, as shown in Figure 31-9. Select the fields that can have blank values (nullable) and the primary keys of the data set. Click Next to continue.

5. The Data Object – Define Lookup Table Information dialog box is displayed, as shown in Figure 31-10. Lookup fields can be used to translate field codes into more meaningful information. You can define the source fields and lookup commands. After you complete your definitions, click Next to continue.

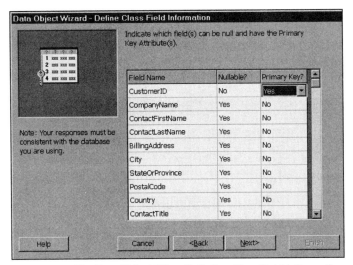

Figure 31-9: The Data Object Wizard's Define Class Field Information dialog box

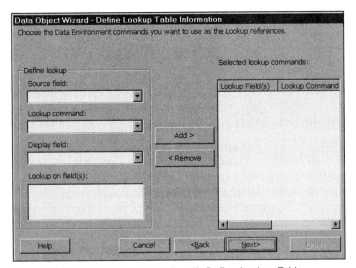

Figure 31-10: The Data Object Wizard's Define Lookup Table Information dialog box

6. The Data Object – Define and Map Insert Command dialog box is displayed, as shown in Figure 31-11. You can select the data environment command that will be used to insert new records into the database. After you select a command, click Next to continue.

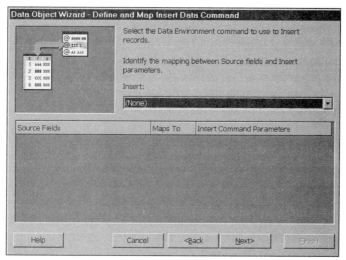

Figure 31-11: The Data Object Wizard's Define and Map Insert
Command dialog box

7. The Data Object – Define and Map Update Command dialog box is
   displayed, as shown in Figure 31-12. You can select the data environment
   command that will be used to update records in the database. After you
   make a selection, click Next.

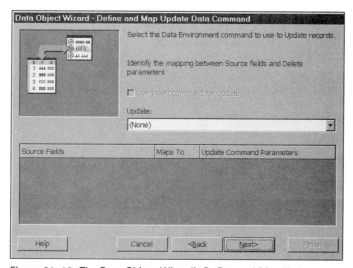

Figure 31-12: The Data Object Wizard's Define and Map Update
Command dialog box

8. The Data Object – Define and Map Delete Command dialog box is displayed, as shown in Figure 31-13. You can select the data environment command that will be used to delete records in the database. After you select, click Next.

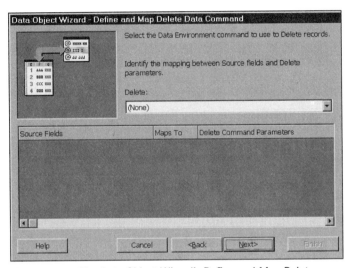

Figure 31-13: The Data Object Wizard's Define and Map Delete Command dialog box

9. The Data Object – Finished! dialog box is displayed, as shown in Figure 31-14. Give a name to your new Class and click Finish to complete the Data Object Wizard.

You now have created a Visual Basic 6 object that you can use in your applications to access the data generated by the `Command` object that you created in your application's Data Environment.

Data Form Wizard

The Data Form Wizard is used to create quickly Visual Basic 6 forms that can be used to access the data in a database. To use the Data Form Wizard, follow these steps:

1. From an open Microsoft Visual Basic application, select Add-Ins → Data Form Wizard. The Data Form Wizard Introduction dialog box is displayed, as shown in Figure 31-15.

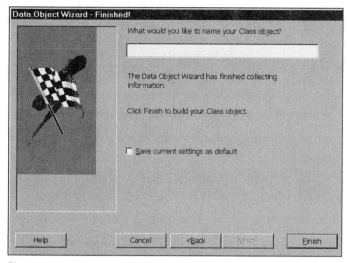

Figure 31-14: The Data Object Wizard's Finished! dialog box

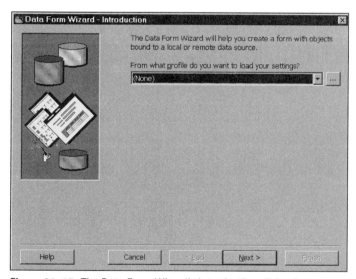

Figure 31-15: The Data Form Wizard's Introduction dialog box

2. You can select a profile that will be used to create your new form. If you don't select a profile, the default form layout is used. Click Next to continue.

3. The Data Form Wizard – Database Type dialog box is displayed, as shown in Figure 31-16. Select the database type that you are using and then click Next to continue.

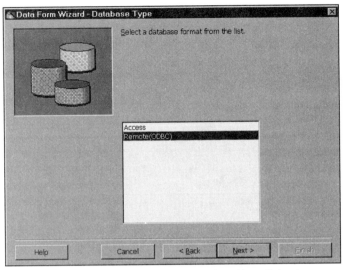

Figure 31-16: The Data Form Wizard's Database Type dialog box

4. This example selects a Remote (ODBC) data source. The Data Form Wizard – Connection Information dialog box is displayed, as shown in Figure 31-17. Specify the necessary ODBC connection information and then click Next to continue.

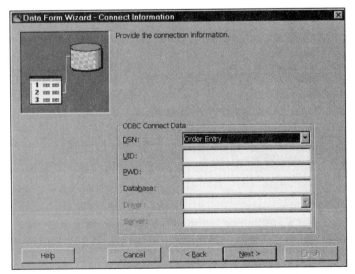

Figure 31-17: The Data Form Wizard's Connection Information dialog box

5. The Data Form Wizard – Form dialog box is displayed, as shown in Figure 31-18. Specify the name of the form, the type of layout that you want to use, and the ADO binding type to use. Click Next to continue.

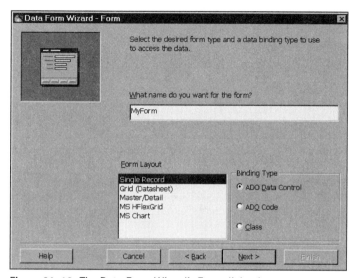

Figure 31-18: The Data Form Wizard's Form dialog box

6. The Data Form Wizard – Record Source dialog box is displayed, as shown in Figure 31-19. Select the record source and fields that you want to display on your form. Click Next to continue.

7. The Data Form Wizard – Control Selection dialog box is displayed, as shown in Figure 31-20. Select the controls that you want to have available on the form. Click Next.

8. The Data Form Wizard – Finished! dialog box is displayed, as shown in Figure 31-21. You can save your selection in a profile by entering a profile name. Click Finish to complete the Data Form Wizard.

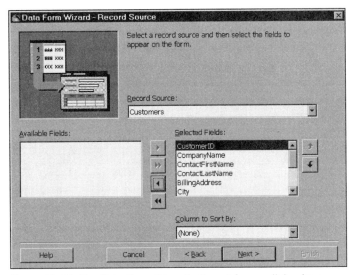

Figure 31-19: The Data Form Wizard's Record Source dialog box

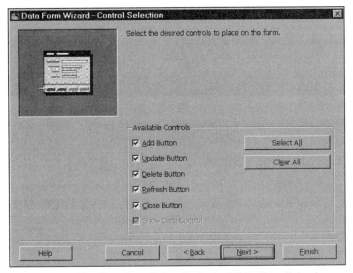

Figure 31-20: The Data Form Wizard's Control Selection dialog box

A new Visual Basic data form has been created, as shown in Figure 31-22. This form contains the complete code to support the buttons displayed. You can use this form anywhere in your application to access your database quickly.

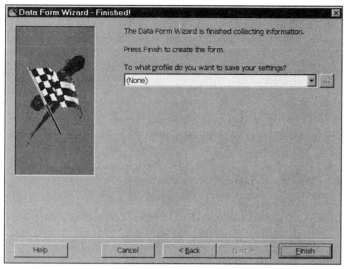

Figure 31-21: The Data Form Wizard's Finished! dialog box

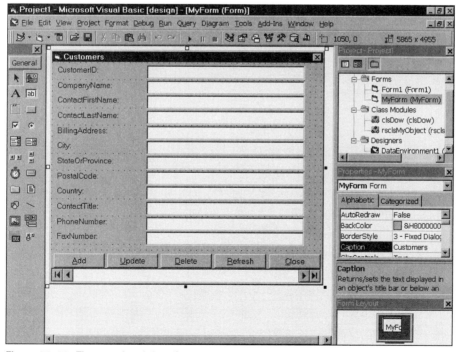

Figure 31-22: The completed data form

Summary

This chapter introduced and reviewed the Data Form and Data Object Wizards. The Data Form Wizard helps you to generate automatically Visual Basic forms that contain the necessary bound controls. The Data Object Wizard helps you to create custom data sources and user controls that display and manipulate data through stored procedures. Use these wizards to quickly get your Visual Basic data access applications up and running.

Chapter 32

DHTML, Data Access, and Visual Basic 6

IN THIS CHAPTER

♦ Introducing DHTML

♦ Integrating DHTML and Visual Basic

♦ Accessing data from Visual Basic 6 and DHTML

DYNAMIC HTML, OR *DHTML*, is a set of HTML extensions that enables programmers to change dynamically the rendering and content of a document. DHTML also gives authors the capability to create visually outstanding HTML documents that interact with the user, without the burden of relying on server-side programs or complicated sets of HTML pages to achieve special effects.

Introduction to DHTML

Dynamic HTML enables you to add effects to your documents that were previously difficult to achieve. For example, you can do the following:

♦ **Hide text and images in a document.** These hidden portions may remain hidden for a specified period of time or until the user interacts with the page.

♦ **Animate text and images** in a document.

♦ **Create a ticker** that automatically refreshes its content with the latest news, stock quotes, or other data.

♦ **Create a form,** and then instantly read, process, and respond to the data that the user enters in the form.

To achieve these effects, DHTML modifies the current document and automatically reformats and redisplays it. Therefore, you are able to see changes without having to reload the document, load a new document, or wait for a server to create new information. DHTML takes advantage of the user's computer by allowing it to determine and produce changes, which means that a user doesn't have to wait for text and data to be sent back and forth to a server. Usually, DHTML documents use styles and a bit of script to process user input and manipulate directly the HTML tags, attributes, styles, and text in the document. Applets or embedded controls aren't needed to make changes to the document.

The HTML elements, attributes, and styles in DHTML are based on existing HTML and Cascading Style Sheet (CSS) specifications. Documents created with DHTML can be viewed through any browser. If the browser doesn't support DHTML, the dynamic and interactive components won't be fully functional.

DHTML works well with applets, ActiveX controls, and other embedded objects. You can use existing applets and controls, or you can create new ones that specifically take advantage of the features of DHTML.

The following are key topics that you should understand when working with DHTML, each of which is explained in this section:

◆ Dynamic styles

◆ Dynamic content

◆ Positioning and animation

◆ Filters and transitions

◆ Font download

◆ Data binding

◆ Dynamic HTML Object Model

Dynamic Styles

Dynamic styles are among the primary features of DHTML. Using styles and style sheets, you can quickly modify the appearance of components on a document. This helps keep documents small, which means the scripts that process the document can be fast.

Styles are accessed through the DHTML Object Model. Using simple script-based programming, you can modify the inline styles of individual elements and the style rules in a document's CSS.

Dynamic Content

The content of a document can be modified after it is loaded with DHTML. An extensive set of properties and methods is provided with Internet Explorer to create and modify documents dynamically.

The DHTML Object Model provides access to all elements in the document. Document elements can be easily altered with minimal code.

Positioning and Animation

Positioning is the ability to place an HTML element at a particular location in a document by assigning *x*- and *y*-coordinates and a *z*-plane to that element. You can set the position of an element by setting the appropriate CSS attributes for that element.

Because you can easily set an element's position, you can modify an element's position in response to specific user interaction, or animate an object by slightly modifying its position at designated intervals.

Filters and Transitions

Through CSS properties, you can specify filters and transitions. You can use visual filters to apply visual effects to an element, which doesn't require any scripts. Transitions are effects that you can apply when you change the way an element is displayed.

Font Download

Using the @font-face style attribute, a document can reference a font, which then is automatically downloaded, used for the current page only, and discarded after the page is no longer displayed.

Data Binding

DHTML data binding permits individual elements (such as a document) to be bound to data from another source, such as a database or comma-delimited text file. When the document is loaded, the data is automatically retrieved from the source and formatted and displayed within the element.

A simple syntax is used to display data using standard HTML elements, without resorting to complex scripting. Instead of using the traditional method of merging the data with the HTML – through server-side templates or Common Gateway Interface (CGI) scripts – before sending the page to the browser, data binding performs this operation on the client after a page is received.

Data binding differs from traditional data-publishing methodologies, because data binding uses standard HTML as a template for the data, and then merges the data with the template asynchronously as the data is transmitted to the client – like rendering a GIF – rather than building the entire page on the server. This results in a page that displays data incrementally as it's transmitted to the client, for faster initial response time.

Dynamic HTML Object Model

The DHTML Object Model is the foundation of DHTML, providing the interface that enables scripts and components to access DHTML features. Anything within the document can be accessed and manipulated through the Object Model. Because each of the HTML elements in the document is available as an individual object, the document's attributes can be modified by reading and setting properties and by calling methods.

The DHTML Object Model also makes user actions available as events that can be captured and processed.

DHTML and Visual Basic 6

The default Microsoft Visual InterDev HTML editor provides three modes for working with Web pages:

- **Design view**: The editor is displayed onscreen in a manner that is similar to how a word processor is displayed, as text with character and paragraph formatting.

- **Source view**: The editor shows HTML tags, text, and script. The HTML tags and text are highlighted.

- **Quick view**: The editor displays HTML pages as they will appear in Internet Explorer.

The HTML editor provides various document outlines that provide quick and easy access to a document. In the Design and Source views, the HTML elements and objects in a page are shown in a hierarchical view, called the *HTML Outline window*. In Source view, the *Script Outline window* shows a tree view of all scriptable elements on the page, and for each element, the events for which you can write scripts. Existing scripts are indicated in bold.

When you select an element in either of the outline windows, you move to that element in the page.

HTML Outline Window

The HTML Outline window provides both an overview of the HTML elements on a page and a convenient way of navigating between them. In the HTML Outline window, you can do the following:

- Display a tree view of elements in the body portion of your page

- Navigate quickly to an object in the HTML editor (in either Design or Source view)

♦ Click an element in the HTML Outline window to select it in the HTML editor

The HTML Outline window displays the most commonly used elements in a document. To avoid making the view too complex, the HTML Outline window doesn't show every possible element – for example, it doesn't show individual paragraph tags (`<P>`) or table cell tags (`<TD>`). The complete list of elements that can appear in the HTML Outline window appears in Table 32-1.

TABLE 32-1 HTML OUTLINE WINDOW ELEMENTS

Element	HTML Tag
Body	`<BODY>`
Form	`<FORM>`
Text box	`<INPUT>` or `<INPUT TYPE="text">`
Text area	`<TEXTAREA>`
Password field	`<INPUT TYPE="password">`
File field	`<INPUT TYPE="file">`
Hidden field	`<INPUT TYPE="hidden">`
Checkbox	`<INPUT TYPE="checkbox">`
Radio button	`<INPUT TYPE="radio">`
Submit button	`<INPUT TYPE="submit">` or `<INPUT TYPE="image">` or `<BUTTON TYPE="submit">`
Reset button	`<INPUT TYPE="reset">` or `<BUTTON TYPE="reset">`
Button	`<INPUT TYPE="button">` or `<BUTTON TYPE="button">` or `<BUTTON>`
Combo box	`<SELECT>`
Listbox	`<SELECT SIZE=2>`
Link	`<A HREF="URL">`

Continued

TABLE 32-1 HTML OUTLINE WINDOW ELEMENTS *(continued)*

Element	HTML Tag
Bookmark	`<A NAME="name">`
Image	`<IMG>`
Marquee	`<MARQUEE>`
IFrame	`<IFRAME>`
Table	`<TABLE>`
Table row	`<TR>`
Control	`<OBJECT>`
Java applet	`<APPLET>`
Division	`<DIV>`
Span	`<SPAN>`
Horizontal rule	`<HR>`

Objects appear in the HTML Outline window only if they are between the `<BODY>` and `</BODY>` tags in the page. The tree view displays objects by using the document's hierarchy. For example, if a table appears within a form, the HTML Outline window places the table as a node under the node for the form.

The tree view displays the element's ID, if it has one, or its name, if it has no ID. If the element has neither an ID nor a name, the outline shows the element's type.

The Toolbox

In Design view or Source view, the Toolbox can be used to add objects by dragging-and-dropping them onto a page. The Toolbox displays a preselected set of controls that is currently available on the computer.

The Toolbox can also be used to store any pieces of text from the editor, which are then referred to as *scraps*.

Adding Objects and Controls

Visual InterDev is part of the Visual Studio product family. Visual Studio helps to manage Web-based application development, by seamlessly integrating Visual Studio programming environments, such as Visual Basic and Visual Studio. When you are working in Visual InterDev, the Toolbox lists the controls that you can use on your page, including these:

- ◆ **Visual InterDev design-time controls**: User interface controls, such as text boxes and buttons, that enable you to use standard object-oriented techniques for creating and scripting Web pages.

- ◆ **ActiveX controls**: Controls that are registered on your computer.

- ◆ **HTML intrinsic controls**: Standard HTML controls, such as text areas and buttons.

- ◆ **Server components**: A list of the components and objects supported on Microsoft Internet Information Server (IIS) that you can use in server script, which includes ActiveX Data Objects (ADO) and Index Server objects.

Most controls and objects are displayed graphically in the HTML editor in both Design view and Source view. In Source view, the text version of an object can be requested.

Design View

Design view makes viewing and editing HTML text easy, in a format that is similar to what the text looks like in a browser. The page is displayed with all the character and paragraph formatting that is specified, much like in a browser. In Design view, properties for elements on the page can be set. If the Property window is displayed, it displays properties for the currently selected element on the page.

Although Design view is similar to how a page looks in a browser, it differs from a browser view in the following ways:

- ◆ Character and paragraph formatting might appear different, because each browser can implement formatting differently.

- ◆ Client scripts do not run.

- ◆ Links are not live.

Glyphs are used to represent certain elements, such as scripts, comments, and unrecognized HTML tags, so that you can clearly see that they are included on the page. Invisible elements can be displayed with a border, so that their location is known.

In Design view in the HTML editor:

- ◆ A page may be viewed and edited in a WYSIWYG-like environment.

- ◆ HTML controls can be manipulated by using the visual representation that they will have in the browser.

- ◆ Menu and toolbar commands can be used to apply certain types of formatting that are not available in Source view.

◆ Menu and toolbar commands can be used to add and edit certain elements that must be edited as HTML text in Source view.

◆ Absolutely positioned elements may be dragged to reposition them.

◆ The Properties window and customized properties dialog boxes can be used to edit the appearance and behavior of HTML text and controls on the page.

◆ The HTML Outline window can be used to jump to any element in the page.

◆ Only the body of a document is displayed. Information in the <HEAD> block must be accessed by using the Source view or the elements' property pages.

◆ Web pages are formatted and displayed the way they would be in Internet Explorer 4.0, even if a different browser normally is used.

EDITING

You can edit in Design view in much the same way that you edit in a word processing program. In general, to format elements, you select text and use the HTML toolbar, Design toolbar, or menu commands to apply formats. You can add elements — such as HTML controls, applets, paragraph and line breaks, and horizontal lines — by dragging them from the Toolbox onto the page. You can change a selected element's appearance by setting values in the Properties window.

VISUAL DIFFERENCES

A document displayed in Design view differs from one displayed in a browser in the following ways:

◆ Character and paragraph formatting might appear different, because each browser can implement formatting differently.

◆ Links are not live.

◆ Client scripts do not run.

◆ Marquee elements do not scroll.

◆ Elements that support alternate text (such as images) don't display the alternate text in ToolTips when the pointer is over them.

◆ Certain design-time controls, such as a Recordset control, appear in Design view so that you can edit them, but they don't appear in the browser.

◆ Design view can display glyphs for some elements, such as HTML comments or scripts, that aren't normally visible in the browser.

Source View

The HTML of a page can be viewed and edited in Source view. In addition, you can access scripts and either graphical or textual representations of Visual InterDev design-time controls, ActiveX controls, and Java applets.

Objects or HTML elements are edited by selecting them and then setting their properties through the Properties window or a customized property pages window. Modifications made in these windows are reflected in the HTML source code for those objects. Scripts can be edited through the Source view or directly.

Source view in the HTML editor enables you to do the following:

◆ View and edit text and HTML tags.

◆ View and edit scripts in the page.

◆ Work with design-time controls, Java applets, and most other objects by using the visual representation that they will have in the browser. (Intrinsic HTML controls are displayed as HTML text.)

◆ Use the Properties window and customized properties dialog boxes to edit the appearance and behavior of HTML text and controls on the page.

◆ Use the HTML Outline window to jump to any element in the page.

◆ Use the Script Outline window to view and create scripts for elements in the page.

◆ Perform debugger functions, such as setting breakpoints and viewing the current line indicator.

Source view is useful for working directly with "raw" HTML text. However, by default, objects can be accessed visually.

EDITING

When you work in Source view, the editor colors text to show its function. For example, by default, HTML tags are displayed in brown, tag attributes in red, attribute value in blue, and so on. If your page contains script, the script is colored according to the rules for the language of that script.

To move between scripts, you use the Script Outline window. Simply click the name of a script to place the insertion point in that script. If you are working on a script in the page and want to see where you are in the Script Outline window, right-click the script block and choose Synch Outline.

SCRIPT OUTLINE WINDOW

The Script Outline window displays scriptable elements and existing scripts in a page when you are working in Source view of the HTML editor. In the Script Outline window, you can do the following:

◆ Display a tree view of all elements on your page that have their ID or NAME attribute set.

◆ Display events for each element.

◆ Navigate quickly to any script in the page.

◆ Quickly create new handlers for events on the page.

The Script Outline window is available in Source view of the HTML editor. In its initial state, the tree view displays the following four nodes:

◆ **Client Objects and Events**: A hierarchy of the elements that support client script or have client script attached. Under the node for each element is a list of the events for which you can write handlers.

◆ **Client Scripts**: A set of nodes for each client script on the page. A node exists for each script block on the page, and a separate node exists for each function or subroutine defined within a script block. A node also exists for inline scripts that are defined as part of a control definition, as in this example:

```
<INPUT TYPE="button"
NAME="button1"
ONCLICK="alert('Clicked!')">
```

◆ **Server Objects and Events**: A list of nodes for each element that supports server script or that has server script attached. Under each node is a list of the events for which you can write handlers. The IIS object model also is displayed, including the Session object, Application object, and so on. These objects don't support events and, thus, are displayed for informational purposes only.

◆ **Server Scripts**: A set of nodes for each server script on the page. Functions and subroutines are identified by name. Inline server script appears in tree view, but isn't identified by name.

DEBUGGING

Source view enables you to execute debugger commands, such as setting breakpoints, by choosing commands from the Debug menu or the Debug toolbar. The left margin of the edit window displays glyphs, indicating breakpoints.

When the debugger is running, the current page is displayed in Source view, so that you can see individual lines of script. The current line is indicated in the margin with an arrow indicator.

Quick View

Quick view in the HTML editor offers these features:

◆ HTML files may be viewed in a manner similar to how they will look in a browser.

◆ Client elements of ASP files may be viewed.

◆ Results of the most recent changes can be viewed instantly, without saving the document.

◆ Runtime elements of a page can be tested, such as links, bookmarks, marquees, and client scripts.

◆ The tabs at the bottom of the editor window can be used to switch to Quick view.

Quick view differs from Design view, because the Quick view page is interactive. Links or HTML controls can be clicked and the results viewed. In addition, the page is displayed in a manner that more closely resembles the way it will look in Internet Explorer.

HTML Editor Tasks

If you are creating pages that will be displayed using Internet Explorer 4.0 DHTML, you can place elements on your page and position them absolutely — that is, you can assign them a position that uses x- and y-coordinates relative to the window in which they appear. (In contrast, elements that aren't positioned absolutely appear inline in the page, with the HTML text around them.) Because you can place absolutely positioned elements anywhere on the page, you can also layer them.

Container objects, such as tables and divisions (DIVs), can also be absolutely positioned. The objects in the container are then absolutely positioned with respect to the container.

In the editor, you use Design view to work with absolutely positioned elements. In Design view, you can convert elements to be absolutely positioned and then drag them into position.

Inserting Scrolling Text

You can add scrolling text to your page by using a marquee control, which moves your specified text across the page in ticker-tape fashion. To insert scrolling text, in either Design view or Source view, first select the text that you want to scroll. The text doesn't have to be in a paragraph by itself, but when the marquee is displayed, the text will be on its own line in the browser window. Then, from the HTML menu, choose Marquee.

Select the marquee text and then, in the Properties window, set the properties to determine how the text scrolls. Table 32-2 sets forth the property choices for your scrolling text,

---

TABLE 32-2 TEXT SCROLLING PROPERTIES

Property	Description
behavior	SCROLL: Scroll onto the page, and then off the page. SLIDE: Stop when text touches far edge. ALTERNATE: Bounce between edges.
direction	LEFT or RIGHT, indicating the side from which the scroll text should start.
loop	How many times to repeat; use -1 to repeat indefinitely.
scrollamount	The number of pixels that the text jumps for each scroll increment. The lower this number, the more smoothly the text scrolls, but the more slowly it moves across the page.
scrolldelay	Number of milliseconds that the marquee waits between scroll increments. The lower this number, the faster the text scrolls.
width	Width of the scroll area, in pixels or as a percentage of screen width.

Inserting Links and Bookmarks

A link is a "hot" area (link) on your page that causes an action when the user clicks it. You can use links to do the following:

♦ Jump to another location, including a different Web page, a specific location (bookmark) on the current page, or a bookmark on another page

♦ Launch e-mail and prepare a message for the recipient that you specify

♦ Download and open or run a document or other file

♦ Access other Internet resources by using the FTP, gopher, TelNet, and WAIS protocols

Links can jump from text, an image, or another HTML element, such as a marquee. The link typically is marked in the browser with an alternative color and underlining, depending on the user's settings for the browser.

The following table lists the types of links that are available, as well as the protocol to use:

Link Type	Select This Protocol
Jump to another Web page	`http:`
Jump to a bookmark on the current page	Leaves the protocol blank
Download a file and open it	`file:`
Create a link that sends e-mail	`mailto:`
Access other Internet resources	The protocol (such as `ftp`) that is required for that resource

In the URL box, type the destination for the type of link that you are creating, as described in the following table:

Link Type	Specify This in the URL Box
Jump to another Web page	The URL of the page to link to
Jump to a bookmark on the current page	A hash mark (#) followed by the name of the bookmark (for example, `#part2`)
Jump to a bookmark on another page	The URL of the destination page, and then add a hash mark (#), and then the name of the bookmark to jump to (for example, `mypage.htm#part2`)
Download a file and open it	The path or URL of the file
Create a link that sends e-mail	The full e-mail address of the recipient (for example, `ann@mycompany.com`)

Applying Styles

In addition to simply formatting individual characters or paragraphs in your HTML document, you can apply *styles*, or predefined formatting instructions. In the HTML editor, you can define and apply styles by using the following techniques:

◆ Reference a Cascading Style Sheet. This technique is useful if you want to use the same styles for multiple documents.

◆ Create a document-specific style block. This is similar to using a style sheet, but the style definitions apply only to that document.

◆ Apply styles individually to elements, such as paragraphs, or to collections of elements in divisions or spans.

You can apply styles in the following different ways:

◆ **Implicitly.** If you have referenced a style sheet or included a STYLE block in the document, styles that match existing tags in your document apply automatically. For example, if your style sheet or style block defines the style H2 as being 14-point, bold, and sans serif, then all paragraphs tagged with H2 will have those attributes (unless you override the attributes explicitly).

◆ **By applying a style class to an individual element, span, or division.** The style sheet or style block must contain class definitions. A span of text differs from a division in that a division is always set off from the rest of the document as separate paragraphs.

◆ **By setting inline style properties for any HTML element.** This technique doesn't reference any style sheet or style block. If the element's style is already defined in a style sheet or style block, setting inline style attributes overrides the inherited style.

Summary

DHTML provides authors with total creative control over all aspects of an HTML document. It extends traditional HTML and CSS to enable you to access and manipulate all elements of a document – tags, attributes, styles, images, objects, and text – creating, moving, and modifying these elements, as needed. Building a DHTML application in Visual Basic provides several advantages over other methods of Internet development. DHTML applications give you the following:

◆ Full access to the richness of DHTML, integrated with the power of Visual Basic code and controls.

◆ Better use of server resources, because each request or user action doesn't have to be routed through the Web server.

◆ Fewer refreshes, faster responses.

◆ Direct manipulation of any element on the page and the ability to create and manage new elements dynamically

◆ Storage of state between requests, without using the server, which means that you can develop applications without requiring server interaction, complex URL-based state, or cookies.

◆ Better security, because your code is compiled, it is not part of the HTML page itself, and cannot be tampered with as easily.

In short, DHTML eliminates the shortcomings of previous browser technologies. Authors can create innovative Web sites, whether on the Internet or an intranet, without having to sacrifice performance for interactivity and special effects. Not only does DHTML enhance the user's perception of your documents, it also improves server performance by reducing requests to the server and, consequently, server load.

Part VII

Accessing Other Data Sources

Chapter 33

Microsoft Access 97 Considerations

IN THIS CHAPTER

♦ Overviewing Access 97

♦ Using the Jet Database Engine with Access 97

♦ Accessing Access 97 databases from Visual Basic 6

THIS CHAPTER BEGINS the review of different databases that are commonly accessed from Visual Basic applications. Part VIII reviews Microsoft Access 97, Microsoft SQL Server 7, and Oracle 8. Special considerations affect the accessing of each database type discussed here; these are reviewed, in addition to each type of database and its features.

This chapter reviews Access 97, the primary database component of the Microsoft Office suite of products. Access 97 relies on the Jet Database Engine as its data access engine, which is also covered in this chapter. Finally, this chapter explores different data access methodologies and their applicability to accessing Access 97 databases.

Access 97 Overview

Access 97 (shown in Figure 33-1) is the primary database component of the Microsoft Office suite of products. It also is the primary database type accessed when using the Data Access Object (DAO) data access model. Access 97 has all the features of a typical relational database management system (DBMS). Access 97 can also be used to build applications, by using a built-in language that is a subset of Visual Basic itself (Visual Basic for Applications). If you're building very simple data-entry-oriented applications and are considering using Access 97 databases, you may first want to review the option of building your application in Access 97. Access 97 includes a rich set of wizards that walk you through the process of creating tables and queries and customizing a wide variety of forms and reports. You can also use Access 97 to access database files in other formats, including dBase, Paradox, FoxPro, and other ODBC (Open Database Connectivity) data sources.

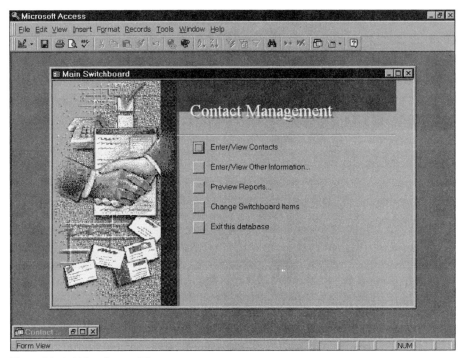

Figure 33-1: Using Access 97

Uses of Access 97

Access 97 can be used to create a wide variety of applications, including for the following purposes:

♦ **Small businesses:** You can use Access 97 to create applications to manage small business. Numerous third-party tools are available that work with Access 97 to help you run your small business.

♦ **Sales and marketing tool:** Marketing and sales representatives can use Access 97 to access and analyze quickly customer and product information.

♦ **Workgroup applications:** Access 97 can be used to develop applications used by small workgroups. Because you can use Access 97 to access a wide variety of data sources, workgroups can create their own data stores and tap into enterprise data sources when needed.

♦ **Information processing systems:** In corporate environments, Access 97 is commonly used as a simple front-end tool to access enterprise-wide data sources.

A Brief Tour of Access 97

The following are the five major components of Microsoft Access 97:

- ◆ **Tables:** The key component of any relational database system. Access 97 supports a wide variety of table field data types.

- ◆ **Forms:** Used to create a user interface to Access 97 tables.

- ◆ **Queries:** Used to view, change, and analyze data in a wide variety of formats. Queries can also be used as a source of records for forms and reports.

- ◆ **Reports:** Used to present data in a printed manner. Access reports enable you to control every aspect of everything on a report, including size and appearance.

- ◆ **Macros, Modules, and Events:** Macros are a series of actions that perform a particular operation – they are analogous to `sub` routines in the Visual Basic programming language. Modules are similar to modules in the Visual Basic programming language – they contain a collection of declarations and procedures that are stored together. Events are actions that occur on or with a specific object – such as mouse clicks, data changes, or forms opening and closing.

Jet Database Engine

The Jet Database Engine provides support for Microsoft Access databases. The DAO access methodology is optimized for accessing Jet-type databases. Recall that DAO is a set of DLLs (Dynamic Link Libraries) that forms the core of the Jet Database Engine. DAO supports two different types of database environments:

- ◆ Using the Microsoft Jet Database Engine, DAO is optimized for accessing local ISAM (Index Sequential Access Method) databases, such as dBase, Paradox, FoxPro, and others.

- ◆ Using ODBCDirect, DAO is optimized for accessing ODBC databases, with minimal overhead.

The DAO Jet Database Engine is not a true client/server database engine. Each application that is developed using the DAO Jet Database Engine requires a local copy of the DAO DLL files to access the database, even if the application is running multiple client computers. However, you can create client/server applications using DAO by connecting to ODBC database sources. When operating in its native mode, using the Jet Database Engine, DAO creates databases that are directly accessible by Microsoft Access.

Jet-type database sources include those created by using the DAO API, Microsoft Access, and Microsoft Excel. Jet-type databases provide security methodologies, multiuser support, database replication, and methodologies to help ensure referential integrity.

Data Access Models

When you are developing an application that will use Access 97 databases, the DAO data access methodology is clearly the development choice. You can create an ODBC data source for Access 97 databases and access them by using RDO or ADO.

Considerations

When you develop a data access application that is designed for Access 97 databases, the following are the primary things that you should consider:

◆ Access 97 databases can be used when you develop small workgroup applications. Access/Jet-type databases aren't designed for a large number of users. You need to consider early in the design process the scalability of your applications and the maximum number of users they will support. If you anticipate your application growing beyond a few users – you may want to consider moving to SQL Server or Oracle databases.

◆ If you're not sure whether your application will grow beyond a few users, you may want to consider using the RDO data access model, and access your Access 97 databases through ODBC. Although DAO provides richer support than ODBC for Access 97-type databases, scaling up your application to SQL Server or Oracle will be easier if you use the RDO or ADO data access methodology.

◆ If you decide to use the DAO model with your Access database applications, you need to remember to distribute the appropriate DLLs. Unfortunately, the DAO model DLLs are not redistributable – but they are installed wherever Microsoft Office is installed.

◆ If you're building a simple data access application, you should consider using Access 97 itself to develop your applications.

Summary

Access 97 is the primary database component of the Microsoft Office suite of products. Access 97 has all the features of a typical relational database system, and can also be used to build applications – using a built-in language that is a subset of Visual Basic. The Jet Database Engine provides support for Microsoft Access databases, and the DAO access methodology is optimized for accessing Jet-type databases. DAO is a set of DLLs that forms the core of the Jet Database Engine. When developing applications that will use Access 97 databases, the DAO data access methodology is clearly the development choice.

Chapter 34

SQL Server 7 Considerations

IN THIS CHAPTER

- ◆ Introducing the new features of SQL Server 7

- ◆ Overviewing the SQL Server 7 architecture

- ◆ Exploring the SQL Server database engine

- ◆ Understanding the major components of SQL Server 7

- ◆ Choosing the appropriate SQL Server 7 data access model

IF YOU'RE USED to standalone database systems, such as Microsoft Access, you'll find SQL Server 7 to be a similar, but much more powerful and scalable, solution to managing your data. Unlike Microsoft Access and other standalone databases, SQL Server doesn't provide a single, all-encompassing application-development environment. SQL Server also enables you to convert your standalone and multiuser Access applications to the much more powerful data management services found in SQL Server.

This chapter reviews the features of Microsoft SQL Server 7, with special emphasis on its new and improved features, for those who are previous SQL Server users. An overview of the major management and development tools that are provided by SQL Server 7 is also included in this chapter. This chapter wraps up with an overview of the system requirements for installing and deploying SQL Server 7, and the issues that you should consider when developing data access applications.

Microsoft SQL Server 7 is a highly scalable, fully relational, high-performance, multiuser database server that can be used by large and small enterprises to manage large amounts of data for client/server applications. The major features of SQL Server 7 include:

- ◆ **Multiuser support**: The capability to support concurrent database usage for both large and small enterprises.

- ◆ **Scalability**: The capability to take advantage of built-in Windows NT scalability – including support both for multiple processors and databases over a terabyte in size.

679

◆ **SQL-92 standard**: Transact SQL is completely compliant with the ANSI SQL-92 standards.

◆ **A complete management and development toolset**: SQL Server 7 provides various tools to manage single and multiple SQL Servers, including Microsoft Management Console (MMC) for integrated management.

◆ **Parallel database backup and restore**: The capability to back up and restore databases and transaction logs, and the integrated capability to recover automatically from media, user, and server-downing errors.

◆ **Data replication**: The process of duplicating tables and transactions from one database to another.

◆ **Data warehousing**: The capability to manage and store large amounts of data. SQL Server 7 breaks the terabyte barrier for database size.

◆ **Distributed queries**: The capability to run queries automatically on multiple SQL Servers, to improve performance.

◆ **Distributed transactions**: The capability to create, manage, and coordinate transactions that use two or more SQL Servers.

◆ **Internet access**: Complete integration with Internet Information Server and Visual InterDev.

◆ **Integrated Windows NT security**: The capability to utilize Windows NT domain security – including users and groups.

◆ **Mail integration**: Complete integration with Microsoft Exchange Server for the automatic distribution of alert and error messages.

What's New with SQL Server 7

SQL Server version 7 offers a significant advance in the SQL Server lineage. The following is a summary of the major new features found in SQL Server version 7, each of which is explored in this chapter as new topics are introduced:

◆ The capability to run under Windows NT *and* Windows 95/98

◆ Improved scalability, including support for databases over a terabyte in size

◆ Full row-level and dynamic locking for improved performance

◆ New and improved administrative features, including integration with MMC

◆ Improved multiserver management

◆ The new Microsoft English Query – which automatically translates English-based queries into SQL

◆ Improved index design

◆ Parallel execution of a single query across multiple processors

◆ Enhanced security architecture that is better integrated with Windows NT and provides increased flexibility

◆ Complete compliance with the ANSI/ISO SQL-92 standard

◆ New and improved replication services – including update replication

◆ Complete support for ODBC version 3.5 and OLE DB interfaces

◆ Integrated HTML-based monitoring pages

◆ Support for 64-bit memory when Windows NT 5.0 is introduced

Architecture Examination

Microsoft SQL Server is an SQL-based, client/server relational database server. To understand the architecture of Microsoft SQL Server, you need to know what the following are: a database, a relational database, SQL, and client/server.

In a client/server database architecture, the database files and DBMS application reside on a server computer. A client interface is provided so that applications can run on separate client computers and communicate with the server over a network. This client interface also enables an application running on the server to communicate with the DBMS server application.

The DBMS server application is usually capable of working with several clients simultaneously. SQL Server can work with thousands of client applications simultaneously. The database server is also responsible for preventing multiple users from trying to update the same row in a table at the same time.

To work with the data in a database, you must use a set of commands, defined by the DBMS application. This set of commands is the *language* of the DBMS. Several different languages exist that can be used with relational databases, the most common of which is SQL. Both the American National Standards Institute (ANSI) and the International Standards Organization (ISO) have defined standards for SQL.

Difference Between SQL and SQL Server

With all the SQL terms being thrown around, you might have difficulty determining the difference between SQL Server and SQL itself. SQL Server is a relational database management system, also called an RDBMS, which is used to manage large amounts of data in a multiuser distributed client/server environment. SQL is a standardized language that allows manipulation of a database and, more importantly, the data contained in that database. SQL was developed in the 1970s; its roots can be traced back to E. F. Codd, the inventor of relational databases, and work performed at IBM during the same period. Since that time, SQL has evolved into the standard for manipulating relational database information.

ANSI is responsible for defining computer industry standards. Although different relational databases have slightly different versions of SQL, most comply to the ANSI-SQL committee standards. Most relational databases comply with the 1989 standard, ANSI SQL-89. In 1992, the ANSI SQL-92 standard was introduced. SQL is really an API that is used by SQL Server. Actually, SQL Server uses a variation of SQL-89/SQL-92 called Transact SQL.

SQL Server was built from the ground up to take special advantage of Windows NT. Windows NT Server is Microsoft's highest-end operating system, providing a true application server for high-end environments. Windows NT Server provides a true, 32-bit operating system with preemptive scheduling, protected memory, and support for symmetric multiprocessing in the operating system kernel. The primary features of the Windows NT operating system include:

◆ **32-bit architecture:** Windows NT 4.0 is built on a 32-bit memory-access architecture, which means that Windows NT can easily handle and manipulate large amounts of data, and 32-bit programs can take full advantage of the power behind the latest Intel processors.

Windows NT 5.0 will be built on a 64-bit architecture, which means that it will be able to manipulate even larger amounts of data, more efficiently. Windows NT 5.0 will also take advantage of the 64-bit features that will be available in the next generation of Intel processors, currently code-named Merced.

◆ **Built-in networking:** Complete support for multiprotocol networking is built into Windows NT. This provides many performance advantages, including the tolerance of communication issues that occur when applications request resources over busy networks.

◆ **Interoperability with NetWare, Macintosh, and UNIX networks:** Windows NT provides networking that is compatible with UNIX, NetWare, and even Macintosh-based networks. Windows NT provides file sharing, print sharing, and application-to-application interfaces.

◆ **Symmetric multiprocessing:** One of the most important features provided by Windows NT, and one that clearly differentiates it from Windows 95/98. With its support of symmetric multiprocessing, Windows NT can balance evenly across multiple processors the execution of multiple processes. Windows NT 4.0 is designed to use up to four processors optimally.

Windows NT 5.0 is designed to raise the bar for multiprocessor support, with plans by Microsoft to provide optimal support for up to eight processors.

◆ **Support for multiple platforms:** Windows NT 4.0 can run on different architectures. Windows NT was designed with portability in mind. By using a traditional kernel-based architecture, NT can be ported to different processor platforms with a rewrite of just the kernel functionality. Windows NT 4.0 currently runs under the Intel, DEC Alpha, MIPS, and Power PC architectures. Recently, though, future support for the MIPS and Power PC architectures has been phased out.

◆ **Preemptive multitasking:** Windows NT, like many other high-end operating systems, offers preemptive multitasking. *Multitasking* means that the operating system can perform multiple jobs simultaneously and keep track of the data, program, queue, and input/output requests of each job. *Preemptive* means that the operating system can switch between these multiple tasks, but it doesn't give a fixed amount of time to each job before it switches to the next. Instead, an operating system that offers preemptive multitasking can designate certain jobs as more important – such as critical OS tasks or networking components – and give more time to those tasks instead of lower priority tasks.

◆ **Backward compatibility with Windows 95 applications:** Window NT has backward compatibility with Windows 95 and earlier Windows versions. Most applications that normally run under Windows 95 and earlier will also run under Windows NT. The most notable exception here is games, because they seem to always push the boundaries of the operating system.

Windows NT 5.0 and Windows 98 will share an even higher level of compatibility. Many of the operating system features found on Windows 95, such as the DirectX graphics interface, will be completely available on Windows NT 5.0.

SQL Server Database Engine

To utilize multiple processors efficiently, SQL Server employs the Symmetric Server Architecture and native thread-level multiprocessing, which are described as follows:

◆ **Symmetric Server Architecture:** SQL Server runs as a single, multithreaded process, which helps to reduce memory usage and system overhead.

◆ **Native thread-level multiprocessing:** SQL Server uses multiple processors through the use of threads, as shown in Figure 34-1. This is one of the key features found in Windows NT, because it maintains the most efficient usage of multiple processors.

A *thread* is an application task (a few commands) that can be performed independently. When an operating system shares multiple CPUs through the use of threads, it is considered *multithreaded*. Multithreaded operating systems make the most efficient use of multiple processors, because the processors don't spend a lot of time waiting for their next task.

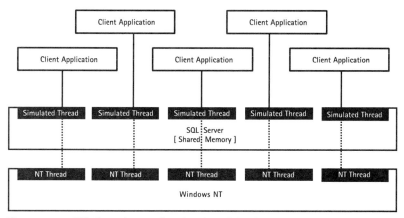

Figure 34-1: SQL Server's use of native thread-level multiprocessing

To better appreciate the efficiency of Windows NT and SQL Server's approach to multiprocessing, you need to understand how other operating systems/database systems manage multiple processors. In operating systems that don't support threading, such as some versions of UNIX, database servers that want to use multiple processors are run as separate processes, each assigned to a different processor. The disadvantage of this approach is the high memory and system usage required to manage each individual process. The database server must try to balance the load against the multiple processes, which makes balancing the processing load evenly on the multiple processors almost impossible. Windows NT and SQL Server use the single process, threaded approach. SQL Server actually uses native operating system threads, which means that it doesn't have to worry about the complexities of balancing the processing load – that's left up to the operating system, which can handle it most efficiently.

SQL Server can be tuned to specify that certain threads are assigned to, or prohibited from, specific processors. This optimization can help you to ring out the highest level of system performance.

Because SQL Server is run as a single process, processes don't need to be coordinated through shared memory. Each thread has access to the memory shared by the single process. Because SQL Server uses native Windows NT multithreading, it provides greater fault isolation and smoother task switching. Also, a custom SQL Server executable isn't required; the same application can run on both single- and multiprocessor systems. SQL Server always uses multiple threads, even on single-processor systems.

SQL Server has a pool of 1,024 *worker threads*, which wait for connection requests. However, SQL Server can support even more than 1,024 simultaneous connections, because it can share its pool of worker threads with multiple connections. SQL Server has another set of up to 255 threads, one for each device supported by SQL Server (a *device* is the physical location where data is stored). SQL Server also has different thread pools for different purposes, such as table scanning, backup striping, disk management, and user connections. SQL Server also supports multiple threads for query execution. This dramatically increases system performance, especially for multiprocessor systems, because queries can be scheduled dynamically across the multiple processors.

Component Applications

Management of SQL Server is accomplished through a set of component applications. SQL Server 7 introduces several new-and-improved management tools. This section provides a brief introduction to these management tools, beginning with the most important – SQL Server Enterprise Manager.

A great source of SQL Server information is included with SQL Server itself. The SQL Server Books Online application provides a full reference to SQL Server and its management components. SQL Server Books Online can be accessed from the SQL Server 7 program group, or from the Microsoft SQL Server Master Setup application — which is automatically started when you place your SQL Server 7 CD in your CD-ROM drive.

Microsoft Management Console

Instead of having a separate Enterprise Management application, SQL Server 7 Enterprise Manager is now a component of the Microsoft Management Console. The MMC is a common management application. It provides a consistent framework that can be used for all network administration under Windows NT and Windows 95/98. MMC provides a single, integrated management tool for administrators. MMC utilizes snap-ins, which work within MMC to manage various network services. All future releases of Microsoft BackOffice products (Exchange Server, IIS, SNA Server, Systems Management Server, Index Server, Proxy Server, Merchant Server, and Transaction Server) and Windows NT itself will use MMC as a single management tool for network applications. SQL Server Enterprise Manager, shown in Figure 34-2, is used to perform the following tasks:

◆ Manage and group multiple SQL Servers.

◆ Manage and create SQL Server users and user groups, including object-level security permissions.

◆ Manage and create database devices, databases, tables, indices, triggers, views, and stored procedures.

◆ Back up databases and transaction logs.

◆ Monitor the current server activity, with the capability to view, by user, a table of tasks.

◆ Schedule tasks to minimize the impact of systems administration on normal operation of the server. Tasks might include creating a device, reindexing a database, importing or exporting data – or any other task that doesn't have an immediate need.

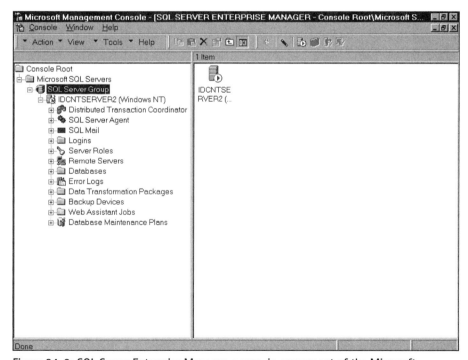

Figure 34-2: SQL Server Enterprise Manager, a snap-in component of the Microsoft Management Console

♦ Customize, view, and monitor alerts and error logs. Alerts are messages that are sent by pager or mail when a specified event occurs. The error log tracks most system events and messages.

♦ Duplicate tables and transactions from one database to another, which is known as *replication management.*

SQL Server Performance Monitor

SQL Server Performance Monitor, shown in Figure 34-3, is used to provide real-time activity and performance statistics. Performance Monitor is the ideal tool to diagnose and track system problems, and can also be used to tune your SQL Server installation for optimal performance.

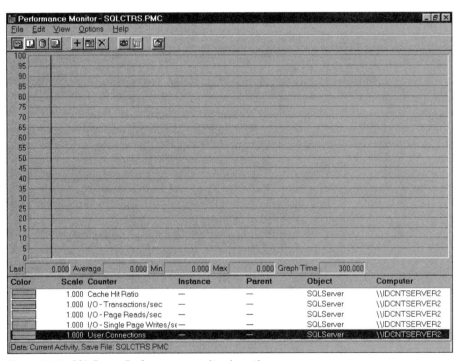

Figure 34-3: SQL Server Performance monitor in action

SQL Server Profiler

SQL Server Profiler, shown in Figure 34-4, is used to capture a continuous, real-time record of server activity. SQL Server Profiler can be used to monitor events and event categories, filter events, and output traces to a file, printer, or another SQL Server.

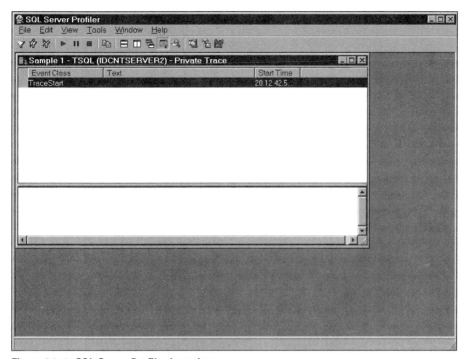

Figure 34-4: SQL Server Profiler in action

SQL Server Query Analyzer

The SQL Server Query Analyzer application replaces the ISQLW application found in previous versions. SQL Server Query Analyzer, shown in Figure 34-5, can be used to create and run a SQL query; view the results in a spreadsheet-like format; obtain Transact SQL help; analyze a query plan; view server statistics; and manage and execute multiple Transact SQL query scripts and stored procedures simultaneously.

SQL Server Service Manager

SQL Server Service Manager, shown in Figure 34-6, is used to start, stop, and pause Microsoft SQL Server, SQL Server Agent, and Distributed Transaction Coordinator (DTC). SQL Server Service Manager installs itself as an application installed on the system taskbar.

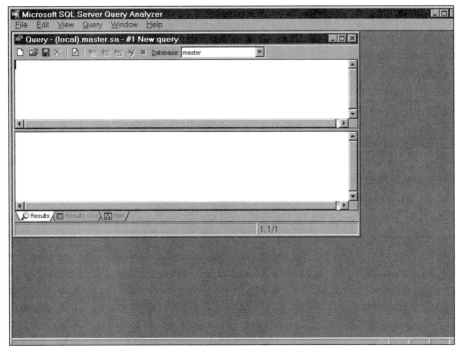

Figure 34-5: Viewing SQL Server Query Analyzer

Figure 34-6: Viewing SQL Server Service Manager

SQL Server Setup

The SQL Server Setup application, shown in Figure 34-7, is used to install and reconfigure an SQL Server installation. The Setup application can be used to change network support options; add a language; rebuild the master database; change the default character set and sort order; change server and security options; and remove an SQL Server installation.

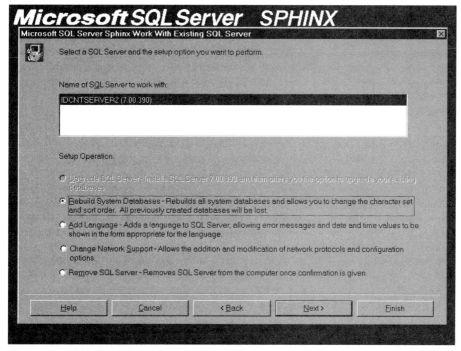

Figure 34-7: SQL Server Setup in action

SQL Server Wizards

SQL Server 7 provides numerous wizards that can help administrators through complex tasks. The wizards provided with SQL Server 7 are set forth in Table 34-1.

TABLE 34-1 SQL SERVER 7 WIZARDS

Wizard Name	Task
Create Alert Wizard	Create an alert
Create Database Wizard	Create a database
Create Index Wizard	Create a table index
Create Job Wizard	Create and schedule a job
Create Stored Procedures Wizard	Create a stored procedure

Continued

TABLE **34-1** SQL SERVER 7 WIZARDS *(continued)*

Wizard Name	Task
Create View Wizard	Create a database view
Database Maintenance Plan Wizard	Create a maintenance routine that can be run on a regularly scheduled basis
Distributed Transaction Services Export Wizard	Create a distributed transaction services transaction that exports data from an SQL Server database
DTS Import Wizard	Create a distributed transaction services transaction that imports data into an SQL Server database
Index Tuning Wizard	Tune a table index to achieve maximum performance
ODBC Driver Wizard	Create and install an ODBC data source and driver
Register Server Wizard	Register your SQL Server in a multiserver environment
Security Wizard	Implement security
Version Upgrade Wizard	Upgrade previous SQL Server versions to version 7
Web Assistant Wizard	Create a Web task that creates an HTML page from the data generated from a query

Data Access Models

All the data access models that have been reviewed – DAO, RDO, and ADO – may be used to access SQL Server database sources. Because Microsoft SQL Server is a server-side database source, RDO and ADO are more applicable for developing data access applications. Also, Microsoft SQL Server 7 is the first major data provider to provide native OLE DB data access – ADO will become an increasingly important methodology for accessing SQL Server 7 databases.

Choosing

RDO and ADO are the two primary data access models used to access SQL Server 7 databases. These data access models are optimized for accessing client/server types of databases. The DAO ODBCDirect mode can also be used for optimal access of SQL Server 7 databases. If you require fine-tuned performance, you can also access the ODBC interface directly, as defined in Part VI, *ODBC API and OLE DB API*.

Optimization

When you access server-side databases, a primary way to increase application performance is to employ server-side stored procedures, which execute completely on the database server. When you deal with a server-side data source, various different optimization issues can affect application performance, including

- Retrieving only the fields that you require from a data source

- Allowing the server to run as much of your query as possible

- Using forward-only-type cursors, if possible

TAKE ONLY WHAT YOU NEED

When you retrieve information from the database by using SQL SELECT statements, make sure to specify only the fields that you absolutely require. Accessing any more data than is required takes up unnecessary time. The use of the * qualifier to retrieve all columns of data should be rare. In many cases, when you are accessing a database server, you usually don't have access to all table fields, due to security requirements.

LET THE SERVER DO THE WORK

When you access a database that is stored on a database server, having the database server perform as much of the query as possible is most efficient. Some of the query operations that aren't usually supported by a database server are the following:

- Joining tables on fields of different types. Most database servers can't perform the necessary inherent-type conversions to perform this type of query. You must explicitly specify these types of conversions.

- Queries that contain the DISTINCT clause or calculations in subqueries.

- Joining attached tables with tables found on the database server.

USE FORWARD-ONLY-TYPE CURSORS, IF POSSIBLE

When you create a `Recordset`, you can move forward and backward, by default, through the data set returned. If you know that you will need to move through the data set only in a forward direction, the `CursorType` property can be set to the `adOpenForwardOnly CursorTypeEnum` constant, to establish a forward-only-type cursor on the record set. This is more efficient, because the resulting data set is not buffered. The performance gain of a forward-only-type data set is more noticeable with an ODBC-type data source. Only the `MoveNext()` method may be used on the resulting `Recordset`.

Summary

Microsoft SQL Server 7 is a highly scalable, fully relational, high-performance, multiuser database server that can be used by enterprises large and small to manage large amounts of data for client/server applications. The major new features of SQL Server 7, the new data access models supported, and their applicability to accessing SQL Server 7 databases – were reviewed in this chapter.

Chapter 35

Oracle8 Considerations

THIS CHAPTER PROVIDES an overview of Oracle8 for Windows NT, including a discussion of its major components. This chapter also reviews the major considerations required when designing and developing Visual Basic 6 database applications that access Oracle8 databases.

Introduction to Oracle8

Oracle8 for Windows NT (referred to simply as *Oracle8* in this chapter) provides a simple, powerful, reliable, and secure database for network computing. Oracle8 provides an advanced, scalable architecture that can support the most demanding and complex database applications. Oracle8 provides

◆ **Ease of use:** Oracle8 provides an easy-to-use interface that makes it suitable for practically any computing environment.

◆ **Multithreaded architecture:** Oracle8 delivers maximum performance and scalability through close integration with the Windows NT multithreaded architecture. Oracle8 for Windows NT is optimized to take full advantage of NT's multitasking and input/output capabilities.

◆ **Windows NT integration:** Oracle8 offers tight integration with Windows NT Registry, Windows NT Performance Monitor, Windows NT Event Viewer, Windows NT Service, and Windows NT Security Login.

Oracle8 provides complete support for online transaction processing (OLTP) and decision-support systems, and includes all the necessary tools to develop enterprise-critical applications, provide efficient and reliable data access, and manage corporate data completely.

Oracle's open, standards-based Network Computing Architecture (NCA) reduces the time that organizations have to spend on interoperability issues. Oracle8 is a major component of NCA and is designed to meet the demands of network-centric computing and object-oriented development methods. NCA is based on open industry standards, such as CORBA (Common Object Request Broker Architecture) and IIOP (Internet Inter ORB Protocol).

Online Transaction Processing

Working in conjunction with Oracle8's parallel architecture and Windows NT's multitasking, multithreaded environment, Oracle8 provides OLTP applications with the scalability to support thousands of users and extremely high-volume transaction workloads.

OLTP applications take advantage of Oracle8's parallel architecture by distributing tasks, or worker threads, across multiple processors or machines, improving individual transaction response times and overall system throughput. Oracle8 efficiently prioritizes the threads to achieve maximum performance. Windows NT automatically balances workload processing evenly across the allocated hardware and operating system resources.

Oracle8 also includes support for Oracle's multithreaded, multiserver (MTS) architecture, which can coordinate thousands of simultaneous user requests. Individual requests are queued and serviced by a minimum of server threads, which provides efficient memory utilization.

Oracle8 also includes complete caching of database blocks, SQL execution plans, and executable stored procedures which takes maximum advantage of available server memory. You can control and allocate available system resources to optimize performance and system capabilities on a dynamic basis. Input/output (I/O) operations use asynchronous and multiblock reads and writes to improve response times and overall system throughput for all users and all requests. Stored procedures and database triggers are stored in compiled form, enabling them to be executed directly, without recompilation or parsing, resulting in optimum runtime performance.

Oracle8 efficiently uses operating system and networking resources, enabling numerous concurrent users to connect over multiple network protocols. Connection pooling temporarily drops the physical connection for idle users (and transparently reestablishes the connection, when needed), which increases the number of users that can be supported. Connection Manager multiplexes several user sessions over one network connection, which reduces resource requirements, especially for multitier applications.

Large Database Support

Partitioned tables and indexes divide large tables and indexes into pieces that can be separately managed, instead of managing the entire table as one large object. Partitions provide a divide-and-conquer technique, which improves performance for a system that has large amounts of data. Partitioning decreases the time that is required for administrative tasks, by applying the operations to smaller units of storage, which improves performance through increased parallelism.

Oracle8 provides complete parallelism for insert, update, and delete operations, as well as queries. All queries can be run in parallel, including those based on an index scan, single-partition scan, or full-partition scan.

Oracle8 provides an object-relational model for complex applications. This improves the way in which data structures are defined and allows developers to define business entities directly, within Oracle8.

Manageability

Oracle8 provides many ease-of-use features that make installation and setup simple. A simple-to-use install procedure provides all that you need to get a pretuned and preconfigured Oracle8 database installed and running.

Oracle Enterprise Manager provides a single, integrated management console for central administration of multiple remote servers. Enterprise Manager enables administrators to perform complex management tasks through an easy-to-use graphical interface. Enterprise Manager can schedule and automate jobs and events on both specific objects and groups of objects, greatly simplifying management operations.

Oracle8 provides various wizards that can simplify the tasks involved with managing complex databases. The wizards provided by Oracle8 include:

◆ **Oracle Database Assistant:** An easy-to-use wizard that helps you to create databases quickly and automatically.

◆ **Oracle Data Migration Assistant:** Automatically migrates your existing Oracle 7 for Windows NT database to Oracle8 for Windows NT.

◆ **Oracle Web Publishing Assistant:** Provides a simple and efficient way to publish your Oracle databases on the Web. Knowledge of SQL or HTML syntax is not required.

◆ **Oracle Migration Assistant for Microsoft Access:** Provides an easy way to migrate a database schema or data, or both, from Microsoft Access databases to Oracle8.

◆ **Oracle INTYPE File Assistant:** Provides an easy way to generate the input files that are necessary for the *Object Type Translator*, a tool that you can use in conjunction with Oracle development environments to build rapid, object-based applications.

◆ **Oracle Net 8 Assistant:** A fast and simple way to configure networking for Oracle8.

Oracle8 includes several other management capabilities, including the following:

◆ Sites supporting Microsoft SMS (Systems Management Server) for software distribution can distribute Oracle8 client software and Oracle8. Predefined Oracle packages are provided to simplify software distribution through SMS.

◆ You can start or shut down the Oracle8 instance simply by going to the Windows NT Service Control Panel and selecting the appropriate service action.

◆ Oracle8 uses an integrated security login model. Administrators can grant access to Oracle8 via secured access to NT domains.

Data Access

Oracle8 supports open data access through a variety of standard data access methods, including Open Database Connectivity (ODBC), Oracle Objects for OLE, JDBC (Java Database Connectivity), and native Oracle drivers. Oracle Objects for OLE provides a custom control (OCX or ActiveX) combined with an OLE in-process server that lets you plug native Oracle8 functionality into your Windows applications.

Key Features

The key system-integration features of Oracle8 include:

◆ Windows NT Performance Monitor integration

◆ Windows NT Event Viewer integration

◆ Windows NT Registry support

◆ Windows NT Service integration

◆ Native Win32 administration utilities

◆ Native support for symmetric multiprocessors (SMP)

◆ Single-process, multithreaded, parallel architecture

- Dynamic load balancing for high loads

- Windows NT dynamic synchronization

- Security integration

- Automatic operating system authentication and operating system role management

- Raw device support

- Asynchronous I/O for high-performance data access

- Winsock 2.0 support

- SMS-enabled

The key networking features of Oracle8 include support for the following:

- Net 8

- TCP/IP

- IPX/SPX

- Named pipes

- DECNet

- DCE

- NDS

- LU6.2

The key management features of Oracle8 include:

- Oracle Database Assistant

- Oracle Data Migration Assistant

- Oracle Web Publishing Assistant

- Oracle Migration Assistant for Microsoft Access

- Oracle INTYPE File Assistant

- Oracle8 Net Assistant

- NT Backup/Recovery Manager

- Start/Stop Oracle Instance from NT Service

The key transaction-processing features of Oracle8 include:

◆ Multithreaded Server Architecture

◆ Scalable SMP performance

◆ Shared database buffer cache

◆ Shared SQL cache (SQL statements, PL/SQL procedures, functions, packages, and triggers)

◆ Shared dictionary cache

◆ Fast and group Commits

◆ Deferred writes

◆ Serializable transactions

◆ Queuing

The key transactional-data-access features of Oracle8 include:

◆ B-tree single-column and concatenated-column indexes

◆ Clustered tables, hash clusters, application-specific hash functions

◆ Query results directly from index lookup

◆ Integrated bitmapped indexes

◆ Index-organized tables

The key very-large-database support features of Oracle8 include:

◆ Table partitioning

◆ Index partitioning

◆ Partition-aware optimizer

◆ Concurrency control and reliable results

◆ Unrestricted row-level locking

◆ No lock escalation

◆ Contention-free queries

◆ Unique sequence number generation

◆ Nonblocking, multiversion, read-consistent query results

The key parallel data access support features of Oracle8 include:

◆ Parallel execution of SELECT, INSERT, UPDATE, and DELETE commands

◆ Parallel sorts, joins, and aggregates

◆ Parallel inserts, updates, and deletes

◆ Parallel direct database reads and direct database writes

◆ Parallelization of user-written code

◆ Parallel CREATE INDEX and CREATE TABLE AS SELECT commands

◆ Parallel direct-path data loading

◆ Oracle8 Parallel Server for SMP and MPP architectures

◆ Fully integrated parallel query architecture

◆ Application transparency

◆ Support for standard server features/options

◆ Dynamic workload balancing

The key critical-support-management features of Oracle8 include:

◆ Online backup by file, table-space, or database

◆ Online recovery

◆ Parallel recovery

◆ Parallel backup/restore utility

◆ Point-in-time database, tablespace recovery

◆ Incremental backup

◆ Read-only tablespaces

◆ Mirrored multisegment log files

◆ Checksums on database and redo log file blocks

◆ Dynamic resizing of database files

◆ Oracle8 Parallel Server for highly available applications

◆ Third-party integration of tape backup

The key distributed query and transaction support features of Oracle8 include:

◆ Transparent remote and distributed queries

◆ Distributed, optimized joins

◆ Location and network transparency

◆ Integrated distributed query architecture

◆ Transparent, multisite distributed transactions

◆ Distributed SQL updates and remote procedure calls (RPCs)

◆ Commit transparency

◆ Automatic failure detection and resolution

The key data replication features of Oracle8 include:

◆ Multiple, read-only snapshots (basic primary site replication)

◆ Symmetric replication

◆ Updateable snapshots (both master and snapshot tables updateable)

◆ Multiple master configurations (full table replication between master sites) and hybrid configurations (combine snapshot and multiple master configurations)

◆ Fail-over configuration support

◆ Automatic conflict detection and resolution

◆ Distributed schema management

◆ Synchronous and asynchronous replication support

◆ Subquery snapshots

◆ Object-relational database

The key view support features of Oracle8 include:

◆ Relational and object views over relational and object data

◆ INSTEAD OF triggers to update views

The key large object binary (LOB) support features of Oracle8 include:

◆ Large binary and character objects with random, piece-wise access

◆ BLOB storage inside or outside the database application development

The key SQL support features of Oracle8 include:

♦ 100 percent ANSI/ISO SQL 92 entry-level compliant – NIST (National Institues of Standards and Technology) tested

♦ ANSI/ISO standard precompilers applications interface (API)

♦ Robust SQL extensions, including UNION, INTERSECT, MINUS, outer join, and tree-structured queries (CONNECT BY)

♦ SQL3 inline views (query in the FROM clause of another query)

♦ Updatable join views

The key data integrity features of Oracle8 include:

♦ 100 percent ANSI/ISO standard declarative entity and referential integrity constraints

♦ CHECK, DEFAULT, not NULL constraints

♦ PRIMARY, FOREIGN, UNIQUE keys

♦ Optional DELETE CASCADE

♦ Constraint checking at end of statements or end of transactions

The key stored procedure support features of Oracle8 include:

♦ PL/SQL procedural extension to ANSI/ISO standard SQL strongly typed variable declarations (SQL datatypes)

♦ Block structure flow control, including FOR and WHILE loops and IF...THEN...ELSE SQL cursor support

♦ Static and dynamic SQL support

♦ Robust exception handling

♦ JSQL Java-stored procedures and triggers

♦ Subprogram types: procedures, functions, and packages

♦ Subprograms stored in shared, compiled form

♦ Called from Oracle and third-party tools, Oracle Precompilers, Oracle Call Interface, and other stored procedures and database triggers

♦ Remote procedure calls (RPCs) protected by a transparent two-phase commit

♦ User-defined PL/SQL functions in SQL

◆ Cursor variables for easy retrieval of multirow result sets

◆ Wrapper-utility hiding of PL/SQL application code in binary source format

◆ External procedure callouts

◆ Server-side file I/O

The key database trigger support features of Oracle8 include:

◆ Procedural code executed automatically on INSERT, UPDATE, or DELETE

◆ Triggers execute either BEFORE or AFTER operations

◆ Triggers fire once per statement or once per row

◆ Modeled after ANSI/ISO SQL3 specification

Data Access Models

Just like Microsoft SQL Server, all the data access models reviewed – DAO, RDO, and ADO – may be used to access Oracle8 database sources. Because Oracle8 is a server-side database source, RDO and ADO are more applicable for access. Unlike Microsoft SQL Server 7, though, Oracle8 doesn't yet provide native support for OLE DB data access.

Choosing

The two primary data access models used to access Oracle8 database are RDO and ADO. These data access models are optimized for accessing client/server types of databases. DAO ODBCDirect mode can also be used for optimal access of Oracle8 databases. If you require fine-tuned performance, you can also access the ODBC interface directly, as defined in Part VI, *ODBC API and OLE DB API*.

Optimization

When you access server-side databases, a primary way to increase application performance is to employ server-side stored procedures, which execute completely on the database server. Several different optimization issues can affect application performance when dealing with a server-side data source. Some of these client/server optimization issues include:

◆ Retrieving only the fields that you require from a data source

◆ Allowing the server to run as much of your query as possible

◆ Using forward-only-type cursors, if possible

TAKE ONLY WHAT YOU NEED

When you retrieve information from the database by using SQL `SELECT` statements, make sure to specify only the fields that you absolutely require. Accessing any more data than is required takes up unnecessary time. The use of the `*` qualifier to retrieve all columns of data should be rare. In many cases, when you are accessing a database server, you usually do not have access to all table fields, due to security requirements.

LET THE SERVER DO THE WORK

When you access a database that is stored on a database server, having the database server perform as much of the query as possible is most efficient. Some of the query operations that aren't usually supported by a database server are the following:

- Joining tables on fields of different types. Most database servers can't perform the necessary inherent-type conversions to perform this type of query. You must explicitly specify these types of conversions.

- Queries that contain the `DISTINCT` clause or calculations in subqueries.

- Joining attached tables with tables found on the database server.

USE FORWARD-ONLY-TYPE CURSORS, IF POSSIBLE

When you create a `Recordset`, you can move forward and backward, by default, through the data set returned. If you know that you will need to move through the data set only in a forward direction, the `CursorType` property can be set to the `adOpenForwardOnly CursorTypeEnum` constant, to establish a forward-only-type cursor on the record set. This is more efficient, because the resulting data set is not buffered. The performance gain of a forward-only-type data set is more noticeable with an ODBC type data source. Only the `MoveNext()` method may be used on the resulting `Recordset`.

Summary

This chapter provided an overview of Oracle8 for Windows NT, including a discussion of its major components. You also learned about the major considerations required when designing and developing Visual Basic 6 database applications that access Oracle8 databases.

This chapter concludes Visual Basic 6 Database Programming. You have reviewed all the data access methodologies provided by Visual Basic 6, including DAO, RDO, and ADO. The appendixes at the end of this book provide a complete reference to each of these data access methodologies. Remember, all the code presented in this book is provided on this book's included CD-ROM, along with applications that you will find useful when developing Visual Basic 6 applications. We hope you enjoyed this book — good luck, and good programming!

Quick Reference

ADO

ActiveX Data Objects (ADOs) are the distinctive feature of an API for developing applications that can access OLE DB data providers. ADO is supported in several different programming languages, including Visual C++, VBScript, Visual J++, Visual Basic, and in Active Server Pages. Using OLE DB directly to access OLE DB providers is a very low-level approach, compared to using ADO, which provides a higher-level and easier-to-understand mechanism. The Data Access Objects (DAO) and Remote Data Objects (RDO) APIs for application development are very similar to ADO. ADO is a combination of the best aspects of the DAO and RDO APIs. ADO doesn't rely on the object hierarchy as heavily as DAO and RDO do, which means that creating and manipulating ADO objects is much easier, because they can be created and managed directly. ADO is specifically designed for client/server application development, and because ADO can be used from VBScript, it is also well suited for server-side Web/database integration.

Connection Object

The `Connection` object encapsulates a connection to a data source and also enables commands to be executed using the `Execute()` method. The `Execute()` command returns a `Recordset` object. The `Connection` object is used to configure a connection, define the isolation level, execute commands and control their execution, manage transactions, and manage connection errors.

Command Object

The `Command` object encapsulates a command that can be interpreted by the data source. `Command` objects can be created independently of a `Connection` object. You can use the `Command` object to issue data-manipulation commands that create `Recordset` objects. In addition, you can use it to perform batch updates, issue data-definition commands to modify the data-source schema, open a connection to a data source, specify a command, execute stored procedures, and create prepared statements. The `Command` object can be used in conjunction with the `Parameters` object, to create parameterized commands. The application can add `Parameter` objects to the `Parameters` collection without requiring the data provider to fill the `Parameters` collection beforehand. The `Command` object is optional – supported only by OLE DB providers that support the command interface.

Error Object

The Error object encapsulates errors that are returned from the data source. The Error object is used to retrieve an error description, error number, the object that created the error, a Help file reference, and the current SQL state, if applicable. The Error object can support multiple errors. Before each ADO method is called, the Errors collection is automatically cleared. The Errors object provides two properties. The Count property returns the number of Error objects contained in the collection. The Item property returns the Error object at the specified index. Using the Item() method directly isn't necessary. The Errors collection object provides a single method, Clear(), which is used to empty the Errors collection manually.

Field Object

The Field object is used to encapsulate a column of a Recordset. A Recordset is comprised of a collection of Field objects. The Field object can be used to access the name, value, type, precision, scale, and size of a column. The Field object can also be used to change the value of a field and to access Binary Large Object (BLOB) fields. The Field object can be accessed only from a Recordset object. Depending on the OLE DB data provider, the Field object's ability may be limited. The Fields object provides two properties. The Count property returns the number of Field objects contained in the collection. The Item property returns the Field object at the specified index. Using the Item() method directly isn't necessary. The Fields object provides a single method, Refresh(), which is used to update the Fields collection manually, to reflect the current columns. You shouldn't need to use the Refresh() method with the Fields collection. The Field object provides two methods that are used to store and retrieve large text and binary-type column data. The AppendChunk() method is used to store large field data, and the GetChunk() method is used to retrieve large field data. These methods can be used to manipulate this data one piece at a time.

Parameter Object

The Parameter object encapsulates a command parameter. A command parameter can be an input, output, or input/output type. The Parameter object can be used to specify the parameter's name, value, attribute, direction, precision, scale, size, and type. A Parameter object can also represent BLOB-type parameters. Parameters can be used with parameterized queries and stored procedures. The Parameter object provides two properties. The Count property returns the number of Parameter objects contained in the collection. The Item property returns the Parameter object at the specified index. Using the Item() method directly isn't necessary. The Parameter object provides just one method, AppendChunk(), which is discussed under the `Field` object. Parameters can be used to pass BLOB-type information to commands and queries. The `AppendChunk()` method is used to store large text and binary information in a parameter. Before the `AppendChunk()` method can be used though, the `Parameter` object's `Attribute` property must have the `adFldLong` flag set.

Property Object

The `Property` object is used to determine whether a data provider supports an ADO object property and to set and retrieve its value. While some of the ADO object properties are required, some objects provide optional properties. Each ADO object property is encapsulated by a `Property` object. Each of these property objects are contained in a `Properties` object collection. The `Property` object does not provide any methods. The `Properties` object provides two properties. The `Count` property returns the number of `Property` objects contained in the collection. The `Item` property returns the `Property` object at the specified index. Using the `Item()` method directly isn't necessary. The `Properties` object provides one method, `Refresh()`, which can be used to synchronize an ADO object's optional properties with a data provider. Calling the `Refresh()` method fills the `Properties` collection. Explicitly calling the `Refresh()` method isn't necessary, because accessing the `Properties` collection for the first time also causes the collection to be populated.

Recordset Object

The `Recordset` object, which is the heart of ADO, can be created independently. The `Recordset` object can be used to do the following:

◆ Access column-level data

◆ Specify a cursor

◆ Navigate a collection of records

◆ Update records in a batch mode

◆ Add and delete new records

◆ Apply filters to records returned

◆ Establish a direct connection with a data provider

◆ Access column-level data, through the collection of `Field` objects that a `Recordset` object encapsulates

DAO

The Data Access Objects (DAO) model is a set of DLLs (Dynamic Link Libraries) that form the core of the Jet Database Engine. DAO supports two different types of database environments:

◆ Using the Microsoft Jet Database Engine, DAO is optimized for accessing local ISAM (Index Sequential Access Method) databases, such as dBase, Paradox, FoxPro, and others.

◆ Using ODBCDirect, DAO is optimized for accessing ODBC databases, with minimal overhead.

Table QR-1 lists the DAO collections and objects and their respective descriptions:

TABLE QR-1 DAO COLLECTIONS AND OBJECTS

Collection/Object	Description
Connections	Collection that contains the current Connection objects of a Workspace object.
Connection	Nonpersistent object that represents a connection to a remote database. Available only in ODBCDirect workspaces.
Containers	Collection that contains all the Container objects that are defined in a database.
Container	Groups together similar types of Document objects.
Databases	Collection that contains all open Database objects that have been opened or created in a Workspace object.
Database	Represents an open database.
DBEngine	The top level object in the DAO object model.
Documents	Collection that contains all the Document objects for a specific type of object.
Document	Includes information about one instance of an object. The object can be a database, saved table, query, or relationship.
Errors	Collection that contains all stored Error objects, each of which pertains to a single operation involving DAO.

Collection/Object	Description
Error	Contains details about data access errors, each of which pertains to a single operation involving DAO.
Fields	Collection that contains all stored Field objects of an Index, QueryDef, Recordset, Relation, or TableDef object.
Field	Represents a column of data with a common data type and a common set of properties.
Groups	Collection that contains all stored Group objects of a Workspace or user account.
Group	Represents a group of user accounts that have common access permissions when a Workspace object operates as a secure workgroup.
Indexes	Collection that contains all the stored Index objects of a TableDef object.
Index	Specifies the order of records accessed from database tables and whether duplicate records are accepted; this provides efficient access to data. For external databases, Index objects describe the indexes established for external tables.
Parameters	Collection that contains all the Parameter objects of a QueryDef object.
Parameter	Represents a value supplied to a query. The parameter is associated with a QueryDef object created from a parameter query.
Properties	Collection that contains all the Property objects for a specific instance of an object.
Property	Represents a built-in or user-defined characteristic of a DAO object.
QueryDefs	Collection that contains all QueryDef objects of a Database object in a Microsoft Jet database, and all QueryDef objects of a Connection object in an ODBCDirect workspace.
QueryDef	A stored definition of a query in a Microsoft Jet database, or a temporary definition of a query in an ODBCDirect workspace.
Recordsets	Collection that contains all open Recordset objects in a Connection or Database object.
Recordset	Represents the records in a base table or that result from running a query.

Continued

TABLE QR-1 DAO COLLECTIONS AND OBJECTS (CONTINUED)

Relations	Collection that contains stored Relation objects of a Database object.
Relation	Represents a relationship between fields in tables or queries.
TableDefs	Collection that contains all stored TableDef objects in a database.
TableDef	Represents the stored definition of a base table or a linked table.
Users	Collection that contains all stored User objects of a Workspace or Group object.
User	Represents a user account that has access permissions when a Workspace object operates as a secure workgroup.
Workspaces	Collection that contains all active, unhidden Workspace objects of the DBEngine object.
Workspace	Defines a named session for a user. It contains open databases, provides mechanisms for simultaneous transactions, and, in Microsoft Jet workspaces, provides mechanisms for secure workgroup support. It also controls whether you go through the Microsoft Jet Database Engine or ODBCDirect to access external data.

RDO

The Remote Data Objects (RDO) model provides a set of objects that assists in the development of client/server applications by addressing their unique requirements. Unlike DAO, which provides an interface to the Jet Database Engine, RDO provides an object-oriented layer of abstraction that directly interfaces with the ODBC API — just like the ODBCDirect interface. RDO uses the ODBC API and the database server drivers to create database server connections, create queries and cursors to navigate the resulting data sets, and execute complex procedures that rely on the database server for the majority of their processing requirements. Unlike DAO, which utilizes the Jet Database Engine for query preprocessing and connection management, RDO directly interfaces to the database server. This makes RDO particularly suited to client/server application development.

rdoColumn

The `rdoTable`, or `rdoResultset` object's `rdoColumns` collection, represents the `rdoColumn` object in a row of data. You can use the `rdoColumn` object in an `rdoResultset` to read and set values for the data columns in the current row of the object. However, in most cases, references to the `rdoColumn` object is only implied, because the `rdoColumns` collection is the `rdoResultset` object's default collection.

rdoColumns

The `rdoTable`, or `rdoResultset` object's `rdoColumns` collection, represents the `rdoColumn` objects in a row of data. You use the `rdoColumn` object in an `rdoResultset` to read and set values for the data columns in the current row of the object.

rdoConnection

Generally, an `rdoConnection` object represents a physical connection to the remote data source and corresponds to a single ODBC `hDbc` handle. A connection to a remote data source is required before you can access its data. You can open connections to remote ODBC data sources and create `rdoConnection` objects with either the `RemoteData` control or the `OpenConnection()` method of an `rdoEnvironment` object.

rdoEngine

The `rdoEngine` object can represent a remote database engine or another data source managed as a database by the ODBC Driver Manager. The `rdoEngine` object is a predefined object; therefore, you can't create additional `rdoEngine` objects and it isn't a member of any collection.

rdoEnvironment

An `rdoEnvironment` object defines a logical set of connections and transaction scope for a particular username. It contains both open and allocated but unopened connections, provides mechanisms for simultaneous transactions, and provides a security context for data manipulation language (DML) operations on the database.

rdoEnvironments

`rdoEnvironment` objects are created with the `rdoCreateEnvironment()` method of the `rdoEngine` object. Newly created `rdoEnvironment` objects are automatically appended to the `rdoEnvironments` collection, unless you don't provide a name for the new object when you use the `rdoCreateEnvironment()` method or simply declare a new `rdoEnvironment()` object in code. The `rdoEnvironments` collection is automatically initialized with a default rdoEnvironment object, based on the default properties set in the rdoEngine object.

rdoErrors

Any operation involving remote data objects can generate one or more errors. As each error occurs, one or more rdoError objects are placed in the rdoErrors collection of the rdoEngine object. When another RDO operation generates an error, the rdoErrors collection is cleared, and the new set of rdoError objects is placed in the rdoErrors collection. RDO operations that don't generate an error have no effect on the rdoErrors collection.

rdoError

Any operation involving remote data objects can potentially generate one or more ODBC errors or informational messages. As each error occurs or as messages are generated, one or more rdoError objects are placed in the rdoErrors collection of the rdoEngine object. When a subsequent RDO operation generates an error, the rdoErrors collection is cleared, and the new set of rdoError objects is placed in the rdoErrors collection. RDO operations that don't generate an error have no effect on the rdoErrors collection. To make error handling easier. you can use the Clear() method to purge the rdoErrors collection between operations.

rdoParameters

The rdoParameters collection provides information only about marked parameters in an rdoQuery object or stored procedure. You can't append objects to, or delete objects from, the rdoParameters collection.

When the rdoParameters collection is first referenced, RDO and the ODBC interface parse the query, searching for parameter markers – the question mark (?). For each marker found, RDO creates an rdoParameter object and places it in the rdoParameters collection. However, if the query can't be compiled or otherwise processed, the rdoParameters collection is not created and your code will trigger a trappable error, indicating that the object does not exist. In this case, check the query for improper syntax, permissions on underlying objects, and proper placement of parameter markers.

rdoParameter

When working with stored procedures or SQL queries that require the use of arguments that change from execution to execution, you should create an rdoQuery object to manage the query and its parameters. For example, if you submit a query that includes information provided by the user, such as a date range or part number, RDO and the ODBC interface can insert these values automatically into the SQL statement at specific positions in the query.

rdoPreparedStatement

An `rdoPreparedStatement` object is a prepared query definition.

rdoPreparedStatements

An `rdoPreparedStatements` collection contains all `rdoPreparedStatement` objects in an `rdoConnection`.

rdoQueries

Contains `rdoQuery` objects that have been added to the `rdoQueries` collection, either automatically via the `CreateQuery()` method or with the `Add()` method.

rdoQuery

The `rdoQuery` object is used to manage SQL queries requiring the use of input, output, or input/output parameters. Basically, an `rdoQuery` object functions as a compiled SQL statement. When you work with stored procedures or queries that require use of arguments that change from execution to execution, you can create an `rdoQuery` object to manage the query parameters. If your stored procedure returns output parameters or a return value, or if you want to use `rdoParameter` objects to handle the parameters, you must use an `rdoQuery` object to manage it. For example, if you submit a query that includes information provided by the user, such as a date range or part number, RDO can substitute these values automatically into the SQL statement when the query is executed.

rdoResultset

When you use remote data objects, you interact with data almost entirely by using `rdoResultset` objects, which are created by using the `RemoteData` control or the `OpenResultset()` method of the `rdoQuery`, `rdoTable`, or `rdoConnection` object.

When you execute a query that contains one or more SQL `SELECT` statements, the data source returns zero or more rows in an `rdoResultset` object. All `rdoResultset` objects are constructed using rows and columns.

A single `rdoResultset` can contain zero or any number of result sets — so-called "multiple" result sets. After you complete processing the first result set in an `rdoResultset` object, use the `MoreResults()` method to discard the current `rdoResultset` rows and activate the next `rdoResultset`. You can process individual rows of the new result set just as you processed the first rdoResultset. You can repeat this until the `MoreResults()` method returns `False`.

rdoResultsets

The rdoResultsets collection contains all open rdoResultset objects in an rdoConnection. A new rdoResultset is automatically added to the rdoResultsets collection when you open the object, and it's automatically removed when you close it. Several rdoResultset objects might be active at any one time.

rdoTables

The rdoTables collection contains all stored rdoTable objects in a database.

rdoTable

An rdoTable object represents the stored definition of a base table or an SQL view.

Appendix A

DAO API Reference

THE DATA ACCESS OBJECT MODEL is a set of DLLs that forms the core of the Jet Database Engine. DAO supports two different types of database environments. Using the Microsoft Jet Database Engine, DAO is optimized for accessing local Index Sequential Access Method (ISAM) databases, such as dBase, Paradox, FoxPro, and others. Using ODBCDirect, DAO is optimized for ODBC databases, with minimal overhead. The DAO User Interface, which is developed by using Visual Basic, contains all the necessary components for the user to interact with the database. The Database Engine, which is provided by DAO, encompasses the mechanisms needed to interact with the database. The Database Store is essentially the data repository, storing all the data that the application uses, in a form that the Database Engine can manipulate.

The Database Store can be one of a variety of different database types, which are reviewed in the "Database Types" section later in this appendix. The Database Store can be located either locally or remotely when using DAO:

- **Local Database Store**: All the components of the DAO application architecture reside on the same computer.

- **Remote Database Store**: Can be broken down further into two distinct configurations:

    - **Client/server database configuration**: The Database Engine and Database Store reside on the same server computer, while the User Interface resides on the client computer. The server computer can manage multiple client applications simultaneously.

    - **Remote database configuration**: The Database Store resides on a remote server computer, while the User Interface and the Database Engine reside on the same client computer. In this configuration, the server computer simply manages access to the Database Store files.

A true client/server database engine simply serves as a communication layer between the database and the application. The DAO Jet Database Engine is not a true client/server database engine.

Each application that is developed using the DAO Jet Database Engine requires a local copy of the DAO DLL files, to access the database, even if the application is running multiple client computers. However, you can create client/server applications using DAO by connecting to Open Database Connectivity (ODBC) database sources.

Each of the DAO objects is described in detail in this appendix, including its properties and methods. These objects are also reviewed in Part III, *Data Access Objects API.*

Connection Object

A Connection is a non-persistent object that represents a connection to a remote database. The Connection object is only available in ODBCDirect workspaces. Table A-1 lists and describes the properties of the Connection object.

TABLE A-1 **CONNECTION OBJECT PROPERTIES**

Property	Description
Connect	Sets or returns a value that provides information about the source of an open connection, an open database, a database used in a pass-through query, or a linked table. For Database objects, new Connection objects, linked tables, and TableDef objects not yet appended to a collection, this property setting is read/write. For QueryDef objects and base tables, this property is read-only.
Name	Sets or returns a user-defined name for a DAO object. For an object not appended to a collection, this property is read/write.
QueryTimeout	Sets or returns a value that specifies the number of seconds to wait before a timeout error occurs when a query is executed on an ODBC data source.
RecordsAffected	Returns the number of records affected by the most recently invoked Execute() method.
Updatable	Returns a value that indicates whether you can change a DAO object.
Transactions	Returns a value that indicates whether an object supports transactions.
Database	Returns the Database object that corresponds to this connection.
StillExecuting	Indicates whether an asynchronous operation has finished executing.

Table A-2 lists and describes the methods of the `Connection` object.

TABLE A-2 CONNECTION OBJECT METHODS

Method	Syntax	Parameters	Description
`Close()`	`object.` `Close`	None	Closes an open DAO object.

`CreateQuery`
`Def()`
	`Set querydef`
	`= object.`
	`CreateQuery`
	`Def (name,`
	`sqltext)`
		`querydef:` An object variable that represents the `QueryDef` object that you want to create. `Object:` An open `Connection` or `Database` object that will contain the new `Query Def. Name:` Uniquely names the new `Query Def. Sqltext:` An SQL statement defining the `QueryDef.`	Creates a new `QueryDef` object in a specified `Connection` or `Database` object.

`Execute()`	`object.`
	`Execute`
	`source,`
	`options`
		`Object:` A `Connection` or `Database` object variable on which the query will run. `Source:` An SQL statement or the `Name` property value of a `Query Def` object. `Options:` A constant or combination of	Runs an action query or executes an SQL statement on a specified `Connection.`

Continued

TABLE A-2 **CONNECTION OBJECT PROPERTIES** *(continued)*

Method	Syntax	Parameters	Description
		constants that determines the data integrity characteristics of the query.	
Open Record set()	Set recordset = object.Open Recordset (source, type, options, lockedits)	recordset: An object variable that represents the Recordset object that you want to open. Object: An object variable that represents an existing object from which you want to create the new Record set. Source: A string specifying the source of the records for the new Recordset. Type: A constant that indicates the type of Record set to open. Lock edits: A constant that determines the locking for the Recordset.	Creates a new Recordset object and appends it to the Recordsets collection.
Cancel()	Cancel	None	Cancels execution of a pending asynchronous method call.

Connections Object

A Connections collection contains the current Connection objects of a Workspace object. The Connections object has one property, Count, which returns the number of objects in a collection. The Connections object has one method, Refresh(), whose syntax is Refresh, with no parameters. This method updates the objects in a collection to reflect the current database's schema.

Containers Object

A Containers collection contains all the Container objects that are defined in a database. The Containers object has one property, Count, which returns the number of objects in a collection. The Containers object has one method, Refresh(), whose syntax is Refresh, with no parameters. This method updates the objects in a collection to reflect the current database's schema.

Container Object

A Container object groups similar types of Document objects together. Table A-3 lists and describes the properties of the Container object.

TABLE A-3 CONTAINER OBJECT PROPERTIES

Property	Description
AllPermissions	Returns all the permissions that apply to the current UserName property of the Container or Document object, including permissions that are specific to the user, as well as the permissions that a user inherits from memberships in groups.
Inherit	Sets or returns a value that indicates whether new Document objects will inherit a default Permissions property setting.
Name	Sets or returns a user-defined name for a DAO object. For an object not appended to a collection, this property is read/write.
Permissions	Sets or returns a value that establishes the permissions for the user or group identified by the UserName property of a Container or Document object.

Continued

TABLE A-3 **CONTAINER OBJECT PROPERTIES** *(continued)*

Property	Description
Owner	Sets or returns a value that specifies the owner of the object.
UserName	Sets or returns a value that represents a user, a group of users, or the owner of a Workspace object.

Databases Object

A Databases collection contains all open Database objects opened or created in a Workspace object. The Databases object has one property, Count, which returns the number of objects in a collection. The Databases object has one method, Refresh(), whose syntax is Refresh, with no parameters. This method updates the objects in a collection to reflect the current database's schema.

Database Object

A Database object represents an open database. Table A-4 lists and describes the properties of the Database object. Table A-5 lists and describes the methods of the Database object.

TABLE A-4 **DATABASE OBJECT PROPERTIES**

Property	Description
CollatingOrder	Returns a value that specifies the sequence of the sort order in text for string comparison or sorting.
Connect	Sets or returns a value that provides information about the source of an open connection, an open database, a database used in a pass-through query, or a linked table. For Database objects, new Connection objects, linked tables, and TableDef objects not yet appended to a collection, this property setting is read/write. For QueryDef objects and base tables, read-only.

Property	Description
Name	Sets or returns a user-defined name for a DAO object. For an object not appended to a collection, this property is read/write.
QueryTimeout	Sets or returns a value that specifies the number of seconds to wait before a timeout error occurs when a query is executed on an ODBC data source.
RecordsAffected	Returns the number of records affected by the most recently invoked Execute() method.
Version	Returns the version of DAO currently in use.
V1xNullBehavior	Indicates whether zero-length strings ("") used in code to fill Text or Memo fields are converted to Null.
Updatable	Returns a value that indicates whether you can change a DAO object.
Transactions	Returns a value that indicates whether an object supports transactions.
Replicable	Sets or returns a value that determines whether a database or object in a database can be replicated.
ReplicaID	Returns a 16-byte value that uniquely identifies a database replica.
Connection	On a Database object, returns the Connection object that corresponds to the database.

TABLE A-5 DATABASE OBJECT METHODS

Method	Syntax	Parameters	Description
Close()	Close	None	Closes an open DAO object.
Create Property()	Set property = object.Create Property (name, type, value, DDL)	Property: An object variable that represents the Property object	Creates a new user-defined Property object.

Continued

TABLE A-5 **DATABASE OBJECT METHODS** *(continued)*

Method	Syntax	Parameters	Description
		that you want to create. Object: An object variable that represents the Database, Field, Index, QueryDef, Document, or Table Def object you want to use to create the new Property object. Name: A String that uniquely names the new Property object. Type: A constant that defines the data type of the new Property object. Value: A Variant containing the initial property value. DDL: A Boolean that indicates whether the Property is a DDL object.	
CreateQuery Def()	Set querydef = object.Create QueryDef (name, sqltext)	Querydef: An object variable that represents the Query Def object you want to create. Object: An object variable that represents an open Connection or Database object that will contain the new QueryDef. Name: A String that	Creates a new QueryDef object in a specified Database object.

Method	Syntax	Parameters	Description
		uniquely names the new QueryDef. Sqltext: A String that is an SQL statement defining the QueryDef.	
CreateTable Def()	Set tabledef = database. CreateTableDef (name, attri- butes, source, connect	Tabledef: An object variable that represents the Table Def object that you want to create. Database: An object variable that represents the Database object that you want to use to create the new TableDef object. Name: A String that uniquely names the new TableDef object. Attributes: A constant or combination of constants that indicates one or more characteristics of the new TableDef object. Source: A String containing the name of a table in an external database. Connect: A String containing information about the source of an open database.	Creates a new TableDef object.
Execute()	object.Execute source, options	Object: A Connection or Database object variable on which	Runs an action query or executes an SQL statement on a specified Database.

Continued

TABLE **A-5 DATABASE OBJECT METHODS** *(continued)*

Method	Syntax	Parameters	Description
		the query will run. `Querydef:` An object variable that represents the `QueryDef` object whose SQL property setting specifies the SQL statement to execute. `Source:` A String that is an SQL statement or the `Name` property value of a `Query Def` object. `Options:` A constant or combination of constants that determines the data integrity characteristics of the query.	
`Create Relation()`	`Set relation = database. CreateRelation (name, table, foreigntable, attributes)`	`Relation:` An object variable that represents the `Relation` object that you want to create. `Database:` An object variable that represents the `Database` object for which you want to create the new `Relation` object. `Name:` A String that uniquely names the new `Relation` object. `Table:` A	Creates a new `Relation` object.

Method	Syntax	Parameters	Description
		String that names the primary table in the relation. Foreigntable: A String that names the foreign table in the relation. Attributes: A constant or combination of constants that contains information about the relationship type.	
NewPassword()	object. NewPassword oldpassword, newpassword	Object: An object variable that represents the User object or a Microsoft Jet 3.x Database object whose Password property you want to change. Oldpassword: A String that is the current setting of the Password property of the User or Jet 3.x Database object. Newpassword: A String that is the new setting of the Password property of the User or Jet 3.x Database object.	Changes the password of an existing user account or Microsoft Jet database.
MakeReplica()	database. MakeReplica replica, description, options	Database: An object variable that represents an existing Database that is a replica. Replica: A String that is the path and file	Makes a new replica from another database replica.

(Continued)

TABLE **A-5 DATABASE OBJECT METHODS** *(continued)*

Method	Syntax	Parameters	Description
		name of the new replica. Description: A String that describes the replica that you are creating. Options: A constant or combination of constants that specifies characteristics of the replica that you are creating.	
Synchronize()	database. Synchronize pathname, exchange	Database: An object variable that represents a Database object that is a replica. Pathname: A String that contains the path to the target replica with which the database will be synchronized. Exchange: A constant indicating which direction to synchronize changes between the two databases.	Synchronizes two replicas.
OpenRecordset()	Set recordset = object.Open Recordset (source, type, options, lockedits)	Recordset: An object variable that represents the Recordset object that you want to open. Object: An object variable that represents an existing object from which you want to create the new Recordset. Source: A String specifying the source of the records for the new	Creates a new Recordset object and appends it to the Recordsets collection.

Method	Syntax	Parameters	Description
		Recordset. Type: A constant that indicates the type of Recordset to open. Lockedits: A constant that determines the locking for the Recordset.	
Populate Partial()	database. Populate Partial dbname	Database: An object variable that references the partial replica Database object that you want to populate. Dbname: A string specifying the path and name of the full replica from which to populate records.	Synchronizes any changes in a partial replica with the full replica, clears all records in the partial replica, and then repopulates the partial replica based on the current replica filters.

DBEngine Object

The DBEngine object is the top-level object in the DAO object model. Table A-6 lists and describes the properties of the DBEngine object. Table A-7 lists and describes the methods of the DBEngine object.

TABLE A-6 DBENGINE OBJECT PROPERTIES

Property	Description
DefaultUser	Sets the username used to create the default Workspace when it is initialized.
DefaultPassword	Sets the password used to create the default Workspace when it is initialized.
IniPath	Sets or returns information about the Windows Registry key that contains values for the Microsoft Jet Database Engine.

Continued

TABLE A-6 DBENGINE OBJECT PROPERTIES *(continued)*

Property	Description
LoginTimeout	Sets or returns the number of seconds before an error occurs when you attempt to log on to an ODBC database.
Version	Returns the version of DAO currently in use.
SystemDB	Sets or returns the path for the current location of the workgroup information file.
DefaultType	Sets or returns a value that indicates what type of workspace will be used by the next Workspace object created.

TABLE A-7 DBENGINE OBJECT METHODS

Method	Syntax	Parameters	Description
Compact Database()	DBEngine. CompactDatabase olddb, newdb, locale, options, password	Olddb: A String that identifies an existing, closed database. Newdb: A String that is the file name (and path) of the compacted database that you're creating. Locale: A Variant that is a string expression that specifies a collating order for creating newdb, as specified in Settings. If you omit this argument, the locale of newdb is the same as olddb. Options: A constant or combination of constants that indicates one or more options.	Compacts the specified database.

Method	Syntax	Parameters	Description
Create Database()	Set database = workspace. CreateDatabase (name, locale, options)	Database: An object variable that represents the Database object that you want to create. Workspace: An object variable that represents the existing Workspace object that will contain the database. Name: A String, up to 255 characters long, that is the name of the database file that you're creating. It can be the full path and filename. Locale: A string expression that specifies a collating order for creating the database. Options: A constant or combination of constants that indicates one or more options.	Creates a new Database object, saves the database to disk, and returns an opened Database object.
Create Workspace()	Set workspace = CreateWorkspace (name, user, password, type)	Workspace: An object variable that represents the Workspace object that you want to create. Name: A String that uniquely names the new Workspace object. User: A String that identifies the owner of the new Workspace object. Password: A String containing the password for the new	Creates a new Workspace object.

Continued

TABLE **A-7 DBENGINE OBJECT METHODS** *(continued)*

Method	Syntax	Parameters	Description
		Workspace object. The password can be up to 14 characters long and can include any characters except ASCII character 0 (null). Type: A constant that indicates the type of workspace.	
Idle()	DBEngine.Idle	None	Suspends data processing, enabling the Microsoft Jet Database Engine to complete any pending tasks, such as memory optimization or page timeouts.
Open Database()	Set database = workspace. OpenDatabase (dbname, options, read-only, connect)	Database: An object variable that represents the Database object that you want to open. Workspace: An object variable that represents the existing Workspace object that will contain the database. Dbname: A String that is the name of an existing Microsoft Jet database file, or the data source name (DSN) of an ODBC data source. Options: A Variant that sets various options for the database. Read-only: A Boolean value that is True if you want to open the database with read-only access.	Opens a specified database in a Workspace object and returns a reference to the Database object that represents it.

Method	Syntax	Parameters	Description
		Connect: A String that specifies connection information, including passwords.	
Register Database()	DBEngine. Register Database dbname, driver, silent, attributes	Dbname: A String that is the name used in the OpenDatabase() method. It refers to a block of descriptive information about the data source. Driver: A String that is the name of the ODBC driver. Silent: A Boolean that is True if you don't want to display the ODBC driver dialog boxes that prompt for driver-specific information; or False if you want to display the ODBC driver dialog boxes. Attributes: A String that is a list of keywords to be added to the Windows Registry. The keywords are in a carriage-return–delimited string.	Enters connection information for an ODBC data source in the Windows Registry. The ODBC driver needs connection information when the ODBC data source is opened during a session.
SetOption()	DBEngine. SetOption parameter, newvalue	Parameter: A Long constant. Newvalue: A Variant value that you want to set parameter to.	Temporarily overrides values for the Microsoft Jet Database Engine keys in the Windows Registry.

Continued

TABLE A-7 DBENGINE OBJECT METHODS *(continued)*

Method	Syntax	Parameters	Description
Open Connection()	Set connection = workspace. OpenConnection (name, options, readonly, connect)	Connection: A Connection object variable to which the new connection will be assigned. Workspace: Variable of a Workspace object data type that references the existing Workspace object that will contain the new connection. Name: A string expression. Options: A Variant that sets various options for the connection. Readonly: A Boolean value that is True if the connection is to be opened for read-only. Connect: An ODBC connect string.	Opens a Connection object on an ODBC data source.

Documents Object

A Documents collection contains all the Document objects for a specific type of object. The Documents object has one property, Count, which returns the number of objects in a collection. The Documents object has one method, Refresh(), whose syntax is Refresh, with no parameters. This method updates the objects in a collection to reflect the current database's schema.

Document Object

A `Document` object includes information about one instance of an object. The object can be a database, saved table, query, or relationship. Table A-8 lists and describes the properties of the `Document` object. The `Document` object has one method, `CreateProperty()`, which creates a new user-defined `Property` object. It has the following syntax:

```
Set property = object.CreateProperty (name, type, value, DDL)
```

The `Property` parameter is an object variable that represents the `Property` object that you want to create. The `Object` parameter is an object variable that represents the `Database`, `Field`, `Index`, `QueryDef`, `Document`, or `TableDef` object that you want to use to create the new `Property` object. The `Name` parameter is a String that uniquely names the new `Property` object. The `Type` parameter is a constant that defines the data type of the new `Property` object. The `Value` parameter is a Variant containing the initial property value. The `DDL` parameter is a Boolean that indicates whether the `Property` is a `DDL` object.

TABLE A-8 DOCUMENT OBJECT PROPERTIES

Property	Description
Container	Returns the name of the `Container` object to which a `Document` object belongs.
AllPermissions	Returns all the permissions that apply to the current `UserName` property of the `Container` or `Document` object, including permissions that are specific to the user, as well as the permissions that a user inherits from memberships in groups.
DateCreated	Returns the date and time that an object was created, or the date and time that a base table was created if the object is a table-type `Recordset` object.
Name	Sets or returns a user-defined name for a DAO object. For an object not appended to a collection, this property is read/write.
Permissions	Sets or returns a value that establishes the permissions for the user or group identified by the `UserName` property of a `Container` or `Document` object (Microsoft Jet workspaces only).

Continued

TABLE A-8 DOCUMENT OBJECT PROPERTIES *(continued)*

Property	Description
Owner	Sets or returns a value that specifies the owner of the object (Microsoft Jet workspaces only).
UserName	Sets or returns a value that represents a user, a group of users, or the owner of a Workspace object.
Replicable	Sets or returns a value that determines whether a database or object in a database can be replicated.
KeepLocal	Sets or returns a value on a table, query, form, report, macro, or module that you do not want to replicate when the database is replicated.

Errors Object

An Errors collection contains all stored Error objects, each of which pertains to a single operation involving DAO. The Errors object has one property, Count, which returns the number of objects in a collection. The Errors object has one method, Refresh(), whose syntax is Refresh, with no parameters. This method updates the objects in a collection to reflect the current database's schema.

Error Object

An Error object contains details about data access errors, each of which pertains to a single operation involving DAO. Table A-9 lists and describes the properties of the Error object.

TABLE A-9 ERROR OBJECT PROPERTIES

Property	Description
HelpContext	Returns a context ID, as a Long variable, for a topic in a Microsoft Windows Help file.
HelpFile	Returns a String that is a fully qualified path to the Help file.

Property	Description
Description	Returns a descriptive string associated with an error. This is the default property for the Error object.
Number	Returns a numeric value specifying an error.
Source	Returns the name of the object or application that originally generated the error.

Fields Object

A Fields collection contains all stored Field objects of an Index, QueryDef, Recordset, Relation, or TableDef object. The Field object has one property, Count, which returns the number of objects in a collection. Table A-10 lists and describes the methods of the Fields object.

TABLE A-10 ERROR OBJECT PROPERTIES

Method	Syntax	Parameters	Description
Append()	collection. Append object	Collection: An object variable that represents any collection that can accept new objects. Object: An object variable that represents the object being appended, which must be of the same type as the elements of collection.	Adds a new DAO object to a collection.

Continued

TABLE A-10 ERROR OBJECT PROPERTIES *(continued)*

Method	Syntax	Parameters	Description
Delete()	collection. Delete object name	collection: An object variable that represents a collection from which you are deleting object name. Objectname: A String that is the Name property setting of an object in collection.	Deletes a persistent object from a collection.
Refresh()	Refresh	None	Updates the objects in a collection to reflect the current database's schema.

Field Object

A Field object represents a column of data with a common data type and a common set of properties. Table A-11 lists and describes the properties of the Field object. Table A-12 lists and describes the methods of the Field object.

TABLE A-11 FIELD OBJECT PROPERTIES

Property	Description
CollatingOrder	Returns a value that specifies the sequence of the sort order in text for string comparison or sorting.
Attributes	Sets or returns a value that indicates one or more characteristics of a Field, Relation, or TableDef object.
AllowZeroLength	Sets or returns a value that indicates whether a zero-length string ("") is a valid setting for the Value property of the Field object with a Text or Memo data type.
DataUpdatable	Returns a value that indicates whether the data in the field represented by a Field object is updatable.

Property	Description
ForeignName	Sets or returns a value that specifies the name of the `Field` object in a foreign table that corresponds to a field in a primary table for a relationship.
DefaultValue	Sets or returns the default value of a `Field` object. For a `Field` object not yet appended to the `Fields` collection, this property is read/write.
OrdinalPosition	Sets or returns the relative position of a `Field` object within a `Fields` collection. For an object not yet appended to the `Fields` collection, this property is read/write.
Name	Sets or returns a user-defined name for a DAO object. For an object not appended to a collection, this property is read/write.
Required	Sets or returns a value that indicates whether a `Field` object requires a non-`Null` value or whether all the fields in an `Index` object must have a value.
Size	Sets or returns a value that indicates the maximum size, in bytes, of a `Field` object.
SourceField	Returns a value that indicates the name of the field that is the original source of the data for a `Field` object.
SourceTable	Returns a value that indicates the name of the table that is the original source of the data for a `Field` object.
Type	Sets or returns a value that indicates the operational type or data type of an object.
ValidateOnSet	Sets or returns a value that specifies whether the value of a `Field` object is immediately validated when the object's `Value` property is set.
Value	Sets or returns the value of an object.
ValidationText	Sets or returns a value that specifies the text of the message that your application displays if the value of a `Field` object doesn't satisfy the validation rule specified by the `ValidationRule` property setting.
ValidationRule	Sets or returns a value that validates the data in a field as it's changed or added to a table.

Continued

TABLE **A-11** FIELD OBJECT PROPERTIES *(continued)*

Property	Description
OriginalValue	Returns the value of a Field in the database that existed when the last batch update began.
FieldSize	Returns the number of bytes used in the database (rather than in memory) of a Memo or Long Binary Field object in the Fields collection of a Recordset object.
VisibleValue	Returns a value currently in the database that is newer than the OriginalValue property, as determined by a batch update conflict.

TABLE **A-12** FIELD OBJECT METHODS

Method	Syntax	Parameters	Description
AppendChunk()	recordset ! field.Append Chunk source	Recordset: An object variable that represents the Recordset object containing the Fields collection. Field: An object variable that represents the name of a Field object. Source: A String expression or variable containing the data that you want to append to the Field object specified by field.	Appends data from a string expression to a Memo or Long Binary Field object in a Recordset.
Create Property()	Set property = object.Create Property (name, type, value, DDL)	Property: An object variable that represents the Property object that you want to create. Object: An object variable that represents the Database, Field, Index, QueryDef,	Creates a new user-defined Property object.

Method	Syntax	Parameters	Description
		`Document`, or `TableDef` object that you want to use to create the new `Property` object. Name: A String that uniquely names the new `Property` object. Type: A constant that defines the data type of the new `Property` object. `Value`: A Variant containing the initial property value. `DDL`: A Boolean that indicates whether the `Property` is a DDL object.	
`GetChunk()`	`Set variable = recordset ! field.Get Chunk (offset, numbytes)`	Variable: A String that receives the data from the `Field` object named by `field`. Recordset: An object variable that represents the `Recordset` object containing the `Fields` collection. `Field`: An object variable that represents a `Field` object. `Offset`: A Long value equal to the number of bytes to skip before copying begins. `Numbytes`: A Long value equal to the number of bytes you want to return.	Returns all or a portion of the contents of a Memo or Long Binary Field object in the `Fields` collection of a `Recordset` object.

Groups Object

A `Groups` collection contains all stored `Group` objects of a `Workspace` or user account. The `Groups` object has one property, `Count`, which returns the number of objects in a collection. Table A-13 lists and describes the methods of the `Groups` object.

TABLE A-13 GROUPS OBJECT METHODS

Method	Syntax	Parameters	Description
Append()	collection. Append object	Collection: An object variable that represents any collection that can accept new objects. Object: An object variable that represents the object being appended, which must be of the same type as the elements of collection.	Adds a new DAO object to a collection.
Delete	collection. Delete objectname	Collection: An object variable that represents a collection from which you are deleting objectname. Objectname: A String that is the Name property setting of an object in collection.	Deletes a persistent object from a collection.
Refresh	Refresh	None	Updates the objects in a collection to reflect the current database's schema.

Group Object

A Group object represents a group of user accounts that have common access permissions when a Workspace object operates as a secure workgroup. Table A-14 lists and describes the properties of the Group object. The Group object has just one method, CreateUser(), which creates a new User object. It has the following syntax:

```
Set user = object.CreateUser (name, pid, password)
```

The User parameter is an object variable that represents the User object that you want to create. The Object parameter is an object variable that represents the Group or Workspace object for which you want to create the new User object. The Name parameter is a String that uniquely names the new User object. The pid parameter is a String containing the PID of a user account. The Password parameter is a String containing the password for the new User object. The password can be up to 14 characters long and can include any characters except the ASCII character 0 (null).

TABLE A-14 GROUP OBJECT PROPERTIES

Property	Description
Name	Sets or returns a user-defined name for a DAO object. For an object not appended to a collection, this property is read/write.
PID	Sets the personal identifier (PID) for either a group or a user account.

Indexes Object

An Indexes collection contains all the stored Index objects of a TableDef object. The Indexes object has one property, Count, which returns the number of objects in a collection. Table A-15 lists and describes the methods of the Indexes object.

TABLE A-15 INDEXES OBJECT METHODS

Method	Syntax	Parameters	Description
Append()	collection. Append object	Collection: An object variable that represents any collection that can accept new objects. Object: An object variable that represents the object being appended, which must be of the same type as the elements of collection.	Adds a new DAO object to a collection.
Delete()	collection. Delete objectname	collection: An object variable that represents a collection from which you are deleting objectname. Objectname: A String that is the Name property setting of an object in collection.	Deletes a persistent object from a collection.
Refresh()	Refresh	None	Updates the objects in a collection to reflect the current database's schema.

Index Object

Index objects specify the order of records accessed from database tables and whether duplicate records are accepted, providing efficient access to data. For external databases, Index objects describe the indexes established for external tables. Table A-16 lists and describes the properties of the Index object. Table A-17 lists and describes the methods of the Index object.

Table A-16 INDEX OBJECT PROPERTIES

Property	Description
Clustered	Sets or returns a value that indicates whether an Index object represents a clustered index for a table.
Foreign	Returns a value that indicates whether an Index object represents a foreign key in a table.
DistinctCount	Returns a value that indicates the number of unique values for the Index objects that are included in the associated table.
IgnoreNulls	Sets or returns a value that indicates whether records that have Null values in their index fields have index entries.
Name	Sets or returns a user-defined name for a DAO object. For an object not appended to a collection, this property is read/write.
Primary	Sets or returns a value that indicates whether an Index object represents a primary key index for a table.
Required	Sets or returns a value that indicates whether a Field object requires a non-Null value or whether all the fields in an Index object must have a value.
Unique	Sets or returns a value that indicates whether an Index object represents a unique (key) index for a table.

Table A-17 INDEX OBJECT METHODS

Method	Syntax	Parameters	Description
Create Field()	Set field = object.Create Field (name, type, size)	Field: An object variable that represents the Field object that you want to create. Object: An object variable that represents the Index, Relation,	Creates a new Field object.

Continued

TABLE A-17 INDEX OBJECT METHODS *(continued)*

Method	Syntax	Parameters	Description
		or TableDef object for which you want to create the new Field object. Name: A Variant (String subtype) that uniquely names the new Field object. Type: A constant that determines the data type of the new Field object. Size: A Variant (Integer subtype) that indicates the maximum size, in bytes, of a Field object that contains text.	
Create Property()	Set property = object. CreateProperty (name, type, value, DDL)	Property: An object variable that represents the Property object that you want to create. Object: An object variable that represents the Database, Field, Index, QueryDef, Document, or Table Def object that you want to use to create the new Property object. Name: A Variant (String subtype) that uniquely names the new Property object. Type: A constant that defines the data type of the new Property object. See the Type property for valid data types. Value: A Variant containing the initial	Creates a new user-defined Property object.

Method	Syntax	Parameters	Description
		property value. See the `Value` property for details. `DDL`: A Variant (Boolean subtype) that indicates whether the `Property` is a DDL object. The default is `False`. If DDL is `True`, users can't change or delete this `Property` object unless they have `dbSecWriteDef` permission.	

Parameters Object

A `Parameters` collection contains all the `Parameter` objects of a `QueryDef` object. The `Parameters` object has one property, `Count`, which returns the number of objects in a collection. The `Parameters` object has one method, `Refresh()`, whose syntax is `Refresh`, with no parameters. This method updates the objects in a collection to reflect the current database's schema.

Parameter Object

A `Parameter` object represents a value supplied to a query. The parameter is associated with a `QueryDef` object created from a parameter query. Table A-18 lists and describes the properties of the `Parameter` object. The `Parameter` object does not have any methods.

TABLE A-18 PARAMETER OBJECT PROPERTIES

Property	Description
`Name`	Sets or returns a user-defined name for a DAO object. For an object not appended to a collection, this property is read/write.

Continued

TABLE **A-18 PARAMETER OBJECT PROPERTIES** *(continued)*

Property	Description
Type	Sets or returns a value that indicates the operational type or data type of an object.
Value	Sets or returns the value of an object.
Direction	Sets or returns a value that indicates whether a Parameter object represents an input parameter, an output parameter, both, or the return value from the procedure.

Properties Object

A Properties collection contains all the Property objects for a specific instance of an object. The Properties Object has one property, Count, which returns the number of objects in a collection. Table A-19 lists and describes the methods of the Properties object.

TABLE **A-19 PROPERTIES OBJECT METHODS**

Method	Syntax	Parameters	Description
Append()	collection. Append object	Collection: An object variable that represents any collection that can accept new objects. Object: An object variable that represents the object being appended, which must be of the same type as the elements of collection.	Adds a new DAO object to a collection.

Method	Syntax	Parameters	Description
Delete()	collection. Delete object name	collection: An object variable that represents a collection from which you are deleting objectname. Objectname: A String that is the Name property setting of an object in collection.	Deletes a persistent object from a collection.
Refresh()	Refresh	None	Updates the objects in a collection to reflect the current database's schema.

Property Object

A Property object represents a built-in or user-defined characteristic of a DAO object. Table A-20 lists and describes the properties of the Property object.

TABLE A-20 PROPERTY OBJECT PROPERTIES

Property	Description
Inherited	Returns a value that indicates whether a Property object is inherited from an underlying object.
Name	Sets or returns a user-defined name for a DAO object. For an object not appended to a collection, this property is read/write.
Type	Sets or returns a value that indicates the operational type or data type of an object.
Value	Sets or returns the value of an object.

QueryDefs Object

A QueryDefs collection contains all QueryDef objects of a Database object in a Microsoft Jet database, and all QueryDef objects of a Connection object in an ODBCDirect workspace. The QueryDefs object has one property, Count, which returns the number of objects in a collection. Table A-21 lists and describes the methods of the QueryDefs object.

TABLE A-21 QUERYDEFS OBJECT METHODS

Method	Syntax	Parameters	Description
Append()	collection. Append object	Collection: An object variable that represents any collection that can accept new objects. Object: An object variable that represents the object being appended, which must be of the same type as the elements of collection.	Adds a new DAO object to a collection.
Delete()	collection. Delete objectname	collection: An object variable that represents a collection from which you are deleting objectname. Objectname: A String that is the Name property setting of an object in collection.	Deletes a persistent object from a collection.
Refresh()	Refresh	None	Updates the objects in a collection to reflect the current database's schema.

QueryDef Object

A `QueryDef` object is a stored definition of a query in a Microsoft Jet database, or a temporary definition of a query in an ODBCDirect workspace. Table A-22 lists and describes the properties of the `QueryDef` object. Table A-23 lists and describes the methods of the `QueryDef` object.

TABLE A-22 QUERYDEF OBJECT PROPERTIES

Property	Description
Connect	Sets or returns a value that provides information about the source of an open connection, an open database, a database used in a pass-through query, or a linked table. For `Database` objects, new `Connection` objects, linked tables, and `TableDef` objects not yet appended to a collection, this property setting is read/write.
CacheSize	Sets or returns the number of records retrieved from an ODBC data source that will be cached locally.
DateCreated	Returns the date and time that an object was created, or the date and time a base table was created if the object is a table-type `Recordset` object.
LastUpdated	Returns the date and time of the most recent change made to an object, or to a base table if the object is a table-type `Recordset` object.
LogMessages	Sets or returns a value that specifies whether the messages returned from a Microsoft Jet-connected ODBC data source are recorded.
Name	Sets or returns a user-defined name for a DAO object. For an object not appended to a collection, this property is read/write.
ReturnsRecords	Sets or returns a value that indicates whether an SQL pass-through query to an external database returns records.
ODBCTimeout	Indicates the number of seconds to wait before a timeout error occurs when a `QueryDef` is executed on an ODBC database.

Continued

TABLE A-22 QUERYDEF OBJECT PROPERTIES *(continued)*

Property	Description
RecordsAffected	Returns the number of records affected by the most recently invoked Execute( ) method.
SQL	Sets or returns the SQL statement that defines the query executed by a QueryDef object.
Updatable	Returns a value that indicates whether you can change a DAO object.
Type	Sets or returns a value that indicates the operational type or data type of an object.
Replicable	Sets or returns a value that determines whether a database or object in a database can be replicated.
KeepLocal	Sets or returns a value on a table, query, form, report, macro, or module that you don't want to replicate when the database is replicated.
Prepare	Sets or returns a value that indicates whether the query should be prepared on the server as a temporary stored procedure, using the ODBC SQLPrepare API function, prior to execution.
StillExecuting	Indicates whether an asynchronous operation (that is, a method called with the dbRunAsync option) has finished executing.
MaxRecords	Sets or returns the maximum number of records to return from a query against an ODBC data source.

TABLE A-23 QUERYDEF OBJECT METHODS

Method	Syntax	Parameters	Description
Close( )	Close	None	Closes an open DAO object.
Create Property( )	Set property = object. CreateProperty (name, type, value, DDL)	Property: An object variable that represents the Property object that you want to create.	Creates a new user-defined Property object.

Method	Syntax	Parameters	Description
		Object: An object variable that represents the Database, Field, Index, QueryDef, Document, or Table Def object that you want to use to create the new Property object. Name: A String that uniquely names the new Property object. Type: A constant that defines the data type of the new Property object. Value: A Variant containing the initial property value. DDL: A Boolean that indicates whether or not the Property is a DDL object.	
Execute()	object. Execute source, options	Object: A Connection or Database object variable on which the query will run. Query def: An object variable that represents the QueryDef object whose SQL property setting specifies the SQL statement to execute. Source: A String that is an SQL statement or the Name property value of a QueryDef object. Options: A constant or combination of	Runs an action query or executes an SQL statement on a specified Connection.

Continued

TABLE A-23 **QUERYDEF OBJECT METHODS** *(continued)*

Method	Syntax	Parameters	Description
		constants that determines the data integrity characteristics of the query.	
Open Recordset()	Set recordset = object.Open Recordset (source, type, options, lockedits)	Recordset: An object variable that represents the Recordset object that you want to open. Object: An object variable that represents an existing object from which you want to create the new Recordset. Source: A String specifying the source of the records for the new Recordset. The source can be a table name, a query name, or an SQL statement that returns records. Type: A constant that indicates the type of Recordset to open. Lockedits: A constant that determines the locking for the Recordset.	Creates a new Recordset object and appends it to the Recordsets collection.
Cancel()	Cancel	None	Cancels execution of a pending asynchronous method call.

Recordsets Object

A `Recordsets` collection contains all open `Recordset` objects in a `Connection` or `Database` object. The `Recordsets` object has one property, `Count`, which returns the number of objects in a collection. The `Recordsets` object has one method, `Refresh()`, whose syntax is `Refresh`, with no parameters. This method updates the objects in a collection to reflect the current database's schema.

Recordset Object

A `Recordset` object represents the records in a base table or the records that result from running a query. Table A-24 lists and describes the properties of the `Recordset` object. Table A-25 lists and describes the methods of the `Recordset` object.

TABLE A-24 RECORDSET OBJECT PROPERTIES

Property	Description
AbsolutePosition	Sets or returns the relative record number of a `Recordset` object's current record.
BOF	Returns a value that indicates whether the current record position is before the first record in a `Recordset` object.
EOF	Returns a value that indicates whether the current record position is after the last record in a `Recordset` object.
CacheSize	Sets or returns the number of records retrieved from an ODBC data source that will be cached locally.
Bookmark	Sets or returns a bookmark that uniquely identifies the current record in a `Recordset` object.
Bookmarkable	Returns a value that indicates whether a `Recordset` object supports bookmarks, which you can set by using the `Bookmark` property.
EditMode	Returns a value that indicates the state of editing for the current record.
Filter	Sets or returns a value that determines the records included in a subsequently opened `Recordset` object.

Continued

TABLE **A-24 RECORDSET OBJECT PROPERTIES** *(continued)*

Property	Description
Index	Sets or returns a value that indicates the name of the current Index object in a table-type Recordset object.
DateCreated	Returns the date and time that an object was created, or the date and time that a base table was created if the object is a table-type Recordset object.
LastUpdated	Returns the date and time of the most recent change made to an object, or to a base table if the object is a table-type Recordset object.
Restartable	Returns a value that indicates whether a Recordset object supports the Requery() method, which re-executes the query on which the Recordset object is based.
PercentPosition	Sets or returns a value indicating the approximate location of the current record in the Recordset object, based on a percentage of the records in the Recordset.
Name	Sets or returns a user-defined name for a DAO object. For an object not appended to a collection, this property is read/write.
LockEdits	Sets or returns a value indicating the type of locking that is in effect while editing.
LastModified	Returns a bookmark indicating the most recently added or changed record.
RecordCount	Returns the number of records accessed in a Recordset object, or the total number of records in a table-type Recordset.
NoMatch	Indicates whether a particular record was found by using the Seek() method or one of the Find() methods.
Sort	Sets or returns the sort order for records in a Recordset object.
Updatable	Returns a value that indicates whether you can change a DAO object.

Property	Description
Type	Sets or returns a value that indicates the operational type or data type of an object.
Transactions	Returns a value that indicates whether an object supports transactions.
ValidationText	Sets or returns a value that specifies the text of the message that your application displays if the value of a Field object doesn't satisfy the validation rule specified by the ValidationRule property setting.
ValidationRule	Sets or returns a value that validates the data in a field as it's changed or added to a table.
UpdateOptions	Sets or returns a value that indicates how the WHERE clause is constructed for each record during a batch update, and whether the batch update should use an UPDATE statement or a DELETE followed by an INSERT.
Connection	Returns the Connection object that owns the Recordset.
CacheStart	Sets or returns a value that specifies the bookmark of the first record in a Dynaset-type Recordset object containing data to be locally cached from an ODBC data source.
BatchCollisionCount	Returns the number of records that did not complete the last batch update.
RecordStatus	Returns a value indicating the update status of the current record, if it is part of a batch update.
StillExecuting	Indicates whether an asynchronous operation has finished executing.
BatchSize	Sets or returns the number of statements sent back to the server in each batch.
BatchCollisions	Returns an array of bookmarks indicating the rows that generated collisions in the last batch-update operation.

TABLE A-25 RECORDSET OBJECT METHODS

Method	Syntax	Parameters	Description
Clone()	Set duplicate = original. Clone	Duplicate: An object variable identifying the duplicate Recordset object that you're creating. Original: An object variable identifying the Recordset object that you want to duplicate.	Creates a duplicate Recordset object that refers to the original Recordset object.
Close()	Close	None	The object placeholder is an object variable that represents an open Connection, Database, Recordset, or Workspace object.
CopyQuery Def()	Set querydef = recordset. CopyQueryDef	Querydef: An object variable that represents the copy of a QueryDef object that you want to create. Recordset: An object variable that represents the Recordset object created with the original QueryDef object.	Returns a QueryDef object that is a copy of the QueryDef used to create the Recordset object represented by the recordset placeholder.
AddNew()	AddNew	None	Creates a new record for an updatable Recordset object.

Method	Syntax	Parameters	Description
Cancel Update()	recordset. CancelUpdate type	Recordset: An object variable that represents the Recordset object for which you are canceling pending updates. Type: A constant indicating the type of update; if set to dbUpdate Regular, cancels pending changes that aren't cached; if set to dbUpdateBatch, cancels pending changes in the update cache.	Cancels any pending updates for a Recordset object.
Edit()	Edit	None	Copies the current record from an updatable Recordset object to the copy buffer for subsequent editing.
FillCache()	recordset. FillCache rows, start bookmark	Recordset: An object variable that represents a Recordset object created from an ODBC data source. Rows: An Integer that specifies the number of rows to store in the cache. Start bookmark: A String that specifies a bookmark.	Fills all or part of a local cache for a Recordset object that contains data from a Microsoft Jet-connected ODBC data source.

Continued

TABLE A-25 RECORDSET OBJECT METHODS *(continued)*

Method	Syntax	Parameters	Description
Delete()	Delete	None	Deletes the current record in an updatable Recordset object. For ODBCDirect workspaces, the type of driver determines whether Recordset objects are updatable, and therefore support the Delete() method.
FindFirst()	FindFirst	None	Locates the first record in a dynaset- or snapshot-type Recordset object that satisfies the specified criteria and then makes that record the current record.
FindLast()	FindLast	None	Locates the last record in a dynaset- or snapshot-type Recordset object that satisfies the specified criteria and then makes that record the current record.
FindNext()	FindNext	None	Locates the next record in a dynaset- or snapshot-type Recordset object that satisfies the specified criteria and then makes that record the current record.
FindPrevious()	FindPrevious	None	Locates the previous record in a dynaset- or snapshot-type Recordset object that satisfies the specified criteria and makes that record the current record.
MoveFirst()	MoveFirst	None	Move to the first record in a specified Recordset object and make that record the current record.

Method	Syntax	Parameters	Description
MoveLast()	MoveLast	None	Move to the last record in a specified Recordset object and make that record the current record.
MoveNext()	MoveNext	None	Move to the next record in a specified Recordset object and make that record the current record.
Move Previous()	Move Previous	None	Move to the previous record in a specified Recordset object and make that record the current record.
GetRows()	Set varArray = recordset. GetRows (numrows)	VarArray: A Variant that stores the returned data. Recordset: An object variable that represents a Recordset object. Numrows: A Variant that is equal to the number of rows to retrieve.	Retrieves multiple rows from a Recordset object.
Move()	recordset. Move rows, start	Recordset: An object variable that represents the Recordset object whose current record position is being moved. Rows: A signed Long value that specifies the number of rows the position will move. If rows is greater than zero, the position	Moves the position of the current record in a Recordset object.

Continued

TABLE A-25 RECORDSET OBJECT METHODS *(continued)*

Method	Syntax	Parameters	Description
		is moved forward (toward the end of the file). If rows is less than zero, the position is moved backward (toward the beginning of the file). Start bookmark: A Variant (String subtype) value identifying a bookmark. If you specify start bookmark, Move begins relative to this bookmark. Otherwise, Move begins from the current record.	
Seek()	recordset. Seek comparison, key1, key2 ...key13	Recordset: An object variable that represents an existing table-type Recordset object that has a defined index, as specified by the Recordset object's Index property. Comparison: One of the following string expressions: <, <=, =, >=, or >. Key1, key2... key13: One or more values corresponding to fields in the Recordset object's current index, as specified by its Index property setting. You can use up to 13 key arguments.	Locates the record in an indexed table-type Recordset object that satisfies the specified criteria for the current index and then makes that record the current record.

Method	Syntax	Parameters	Description
Open-Recordset()	Set recordset = object.Open Recordset (source, type, options, lockedits)	Recordset Source Type Lockedits	Recordset: An object variable that represents the Recordset object that you want to open. Object: An object variable that represents an existing object from which you want to create the new Recordset. Source: A String specifying the source of the records for the new Recordset. The source can be a table name, a query name, or an SQL statement that returns records. Type: A constant that indicates the type of Recordset to open. Lockedits: A constant that determines the locking for the Recordset. Creates a new Recordset object and appends it to the Recordsets collection.
Update()	recordset. Update (type, force)	Recordset: An object variable that represents an open, updatable Recordset object. Type: A constant indicating the type of update. Force: A Boolean value indicating whether to force the changes into the database.	Saves the contents of the copy buffer to an updatable Recordset object.

Continued

TABLE A-25 RECORDSET OBJECT METHODS *(continued)*

Method	Syntax	Parameters	Description
Requery()	recordset. Requery newquerydef	Recordset: An object variable that represents an existing Microsoft Jet dynaset-, snapshot-, or forward-only–type Recordset object, or an ODBCDirect Recordset object. Newquerydef: A Variant that represents the Name property value of a QueryDef object.	Updates the data in a Recordset object by re-executing the query on which the object is based.
Cancel()	Cancel	None	Cancels execution of a pending asynchronous method call.
Next Recordset()	Next Recordset	None	Gets the next set of records, if any, returned by a multipart select query in an OpenRecordset call, and returns a Boolean value indicating whether one or more additional records are pending.

Relations Object

A Relations collection contains stored Relation objects of a Database object. The Relations object has one property, Count, which returns the number of objects in a collection. Table A-26 lists and describes the methods of the Relations object.

TABLE **A-26 RELATIONS OBJECT METHODS**

Method	Syntax	Parameters	Description
Append()	collection. Append object	Collection: An object variable that represents any collection that can accept new objects. Object: An object variable that represents the object being appended, which must be of the same type as the elements of collection.	Adds a new DAO object to a collection.
Delete()	collection. Delete objectname	collection: An object variable that represents a collection from which you are deleting objectname. Objectname: A String that is the Name property setting of an object in collection.	Deletes a persistent object from a collection.
Refresh()	Refresh	None	Updates the objects in a collection, to reflect the current database's schema.

Relation Object

A Relation object represents a relationship between fields in tables or queries. Table A-27 lists and describes the properties of the Relation object. The Relation object has just one method, CreateField(), which creates a new field. It has the following syntax:

```
Set field = object.CreateField (name, type, size)
```

The Field parameter is an object variable that represents the Field object that you want to create. The Object parameter is an object variable that represents the Index, Relation, or TableDef object for which you want to create the new Field object. The Name parameter is a String that uniquely names the new Field object. The Type parameter is a constant that determines the data type of the new Field object. The Size parameter is an Integer that indicates the maximum size, in bytes, of a Field object that contains text.

TABLE A-27 RELATION OBJECT PROPERTIES

Property	Description
Attributes	Sets or returns a value that indicates one or more characteristics of a Relation.
ForeignTable	Sets or returns the name of the foreign table in a relationship.
Name	Sets or returns a user-defined name for a DAO object. For an object not appended to a collection, this property is read/write.
Table	Indicates the name of a Relation object's primary table.
PartialReplica	Sets or returns a value on a Relation object, indicating whether that relation should be considered when populating a partial replica from a full replica.

TableDefs Object

A TableDefs collection contains all stored TableDef objects in a database. The TableDefs object has one property, Count, which returns the number of objects in a collection. Table A-28 lists and describes the methods of the TableDefs object.

TABLE A-28 TABLEDEFS OBJECT METHODS

Method	Syntax	Parameters	Description
Append()	collection. Append object	Collection: An object variable that represents any collection that can	Adds a new DAO object to a collection.

Method	Syntax	Parameters	Description
		accept new objects. `Object`: An object variable that represents the object being appended, which must be of the same type as the elements of `collection`.	
`Delete()`	`collection.Delete objectname`	`collection`: An object variable that represents a collection from which you are deleting `objectname`. `Objectname`: A String that is the `Name` property setting of an object in `collection`.	Deletes a persistent object from a collection.
`Refresh()`	`Refresh`	None	Updates the objects in a collection to reflect the current database's schema.

TableDef Object

A `TableDef` object represents the stored definition of a base table or a linked table. Table A-29 lists and describes the properties of the `TableDef` object. Table A-30 lists and describes the methods of the `TableDef` object.

TABLE A-29 TABLEDEF OBJECT PROPERTIES

Property	Description
Connect	Sets or returns a value that provides information about the source of an open connection, an open database, a database used in a pass-through query, or a linked table.
Attributes	Sets or returns a value that indicates one or more characteristics of a TableDef object.
ConflictTable	Returns the name of a conflict table containing the database records that conflicted during the synchronization of two replicas.
DateCreated	Returns the date and time that an object was created, or the date and time a base table was created if the object is a table-type Recordset object.
LastUpdated	Returns the date and time of the most recent change made to an object, or to a base table if the object is a table-type Recordset object.
Name	Sets or returns a user-defined name for a DAO object. For an object not appended to a collection, this property is read/write.
RecordCount	Returns the number of records accessed in a Recordset object, or the total number of records in a TableDef object.
SourceTableName	Sets or returns a value that specifies the name of a linked table or the name of a base table.
Updatable	Returns a value that indicates whether you can change a DAO object.
ValidationText	Sets or returns a value that specifies the text of the message that your application displays if the value of a Field object doesn't satisfy the validation rule specified by the ValidationRule property setting.
Replicable	Sets or returns a value that determines whether a database or object in a database can be replicated.
KeepLocal	Sets or returns a value on a table, query, form, report, macro, or module that you do not want to replicate when the database is replicated.

Property	Description
ReplicaFilter	Sets or returns a value on a `TableDef` object within a partial replica that indicates which subset of records is replicated to that table from a full replica.

TABLE **A-30 TABLEDEF OBJECT METHODS**

Method	Syntax	Parameters	Description
CreateIndex()	`Set index = tabledef. CreateIndex (name)`	Index: An object variable that represents the index that you want to create. `Tabledef`: An object variable that represents the `TableDef` object that you want to use to create the new `Index` object. Name: A Variant (String subtype) that uniquely names the new `Index` object.	Creates a new `Index` object.
CreateField()	`Set field = object. CreateField (name, type, size)`	Field: An object variable that represents the `Field` object that you want to create. `Object`: An object variable that represents the `Index, Relation,` or `TableDef` object for which you want to create the new `Field` object. Name:	Creates a new `Field` object.

Continued

TABLE A-30 TABLEDEF OBJECT METHODS *(continued)*

Method	Syntax	Parameters	Description
		A Variant (String subtype) that uniquely names the new Field object. Type: A constant that determines the data type of the new Field object. Size: A Variant (Integer subtype) that indicates the maximum size, in bytes, of a Field object that contains text.	
Create Property()	Set property = object. Create Property (name, type, value, DDL)	Property: An object variable that represents the Property object that you want to create. Object: An object variable that represents the Database, Field, Index, QueryDef, Document, or TableDef object that you want to use to create the new Property object. Name: A String that uniquely names the Property object. Type: A constant that defines the data type of the new Property object. Value: A Variant containing the initial	Creates a new user-defined Property object.

Method	Syntax	Parameters	Description
		property value. DDL: A Boolean that indicates whether the Property is a DDL object.	
Open Recordset()	Set recordset = object.Open Recordset (source, type, options, lockedits)	Recordset: An object variable that represents the Recordset object that you want to open. Object: An object variable that represents an existing object from which you want to create the new Recordset. Source: A String specifying the source of the records for the new Recordset. Type: A constant that indicates the type of Recordset to open. Lockedits: A constant that determines the locking for the Recordset.	Creates a new Recordset object and appends it to the Recordsets collection.
RefreshLink()	RefreshLink	None	Updates the connection information for a linked table.

Users Object

A Users collection contains all stored User objects of a Workspace or Group object. The Users object has one property, Count, which returns the number of objects in a collection. Table A-31 lists and describes the methods of the Users object.

TABLE A-31 USERS OBJECT METHODS

Method	Syntax	Parameters	Description
Append()	collection. Append object	Collection: An object variable that represents any collection that can accept new objects. Object: An object variable that represents the object being appended, which must be of the same type as the elements of collection.	Adds a new DAO object to a collection.
Delete()	collection. Delete object name	Collection: An object variable that represents a collection from which you are deleting object name. Objectname: A String that is the Name property setting of an object in collection.	Deletes a persistent object from a collection.
Refresh()	Refresh	None	Updates the objects in a collection to reflect the current database's schema.

User Object

A User object represents a user account that has access permissions when a Workspace object operates as a secure workgroup. Table A-32 lists and describes the properties of the User object. Table A-33 lists and describes the methods of the User object.

TABLE A-32 USER OBJECT PROPERTIES

Property	Description
Name	Sets or returns a user-defined name for a DAO object. For an object not appended to a collection, this property is read/write.

Property	Description
Password	Sets the password for a user account.
PID	Sets the personal identifier (PID) for either a group or a user account.

TABLE A-33 USER OBJECT METHODS

Method	Syntax	Parameters	Description
Create Group()	Set group = object. CreateGroup (name, pid)	Group: An object variable that represents the Group that you want to create. Object: An object variable that represents the User or Workspace object for which you want to create the new Group object. Name: A Variant (String subtype) that uniquely names the new Group object. See the Name property for details on valid Group names. Pid: A variant (string subtype) containing the PID of a group account. The identifier must contain from 4 to 20 alphanumeric characters.	Create a new group.
New Password()	object. NewPassword oldpassword, newpassword	Object: An object variable that represents the User object or a Microsoft	Changes the password of an existing user account or Microsoft Jet database

(Continued)

TABLE A-33 USER OBJECT METHODS *(continued)*

Method	Syntax	Parameters	Description
		Jet 3.*x* Database object whose Password property you want to change. Oldpassword: A String that is the current setting of the Password property of the User or Jet 3.*x* Database object. Newpassword: A String that is the new setting of the Password property of the User or Jet 3.*x* Database object.	

Workspaces Object

A Workspaces collection contains all active, unhidden Workspace objects of the DBEngine object. The Workspaces object has one property, Count, which returns the number of objects in a collection. Table A-34 lists and describes the methods of the Workspaces object.

TABLE A-34 WORKSPACES OBJECT METHODS

Method	Syntax	Parameters	Description
Append()	collection. Append object	Collection: An object variable that represents any collection that can accept new objects. Object: An object variable that represents	Adds a new DAO object to a collection.

Method	Syntax	Parameters	Description
		the object being appended, which must be of the same type as the elements of collection.	
Delete()	collection. Delete objectname	Collection: An object variable that represents a collection from which you are deleting objectname. Objectname: A String that is the Name property setting of an object in collection.	Deletes a persistent object from a collection.
Refresh()	Refresh	None	Updates the objects in a collection to reflect the current database's schema.

Workspace Object

A Workspace object defines a named session for a user. It contains open databases, and provides mechanisms for simultaneous transactions, and, in Microsoft Jet workspaces, for secure workgroup support. A Workspace object also controls whether you are going through the Microsoft Jet Database Engine or ODBCDirect to access external data. Table A-35 lists and describes the properties of the Workspace object. Table A-36 lists and describes the methods of the Workspace object.

TABLE A-35 WORKSPACE OBJECT PROPERTIES

Property	Description
IsolateODBCTrans	Sets or returns a value that indicates whether multiple transactions that involve the same Microsoft Jet-connected ODBC data source are isolated.

Continued

TABLE A-35 WORKSPACE OBJECT PROPERTIES *(continued)*

Property	Description
Name	Sets or returns a user-defined name for a DAO object. For an object not appended to a collection, this property is read/write.
LoginTimeout	Sets or returns the number of seconds before an error occurs when you attempt to log on to an ODBC database.
Type	Sets or returns a value that indicates the operational type or data type of an object.
UserName	Sets or returns a value that represents a user, a group of users, or the owner of a Workspace object.
DefaultCursorDriver	Sets or returns the type of cursor driver used on the connection created by the OpenConnection() or OpenDatabase() methods.

TABLE A-36 WORKSPACE OBJECT METHODS

Method	Syntax	Parameters	Description
Begin Trans()	Begin Trans	None	Begins a new transaction.
Commit Trans()	Commit Trans	None	Ends the current transaction and saves the changes.
Rollback()	Rollback	None	Rollback() ends the current transaction and restores the databases in the Workspace object to the state they were in when the current transaction began.
Close()	Close	None	Closes an open DAO object.

Method	Syntax	Parameters	Description
Create Group()	Set group = object. Create Group (name, pid)	Group: An object variable that represents the Group that you want to create. Object: An object variable that represents the User or Workspace object for which you want to create the new Group object. Name: A Variant (String subtype) that uniquely names the new Group object. See the Name property for details on valid Group names. Pid: A Variant (String subtype) containing the PID of a group account. The identifier must contain from 4 to 20 alphanumeric characters.	Creates a new database group.
Create Database()	Set database = workspace. CreateData base (name, locale, options)	Database: An object variable that represents the Database object that you want to create. Workspace: An object variable that represents the existing Workspace object that will contain the database. Name: A String, up to 255 characters long, that is the name of the database file that you're creating. Locale: A string expression that	Creates a new Database object, saves the database to disk, and returns an opened Database object.

Continued

TABLE A-36 **WORKSPACE OBJECT METHODS** *(continued)*

Method	Syntax	Parameters	Description
		specifies a collating order for creating the database. Options: A constant or combination of constants that indicates one or more options.	
Create User()	Set user = object. CreateUser (name, pid, password)	User: An object variable that represents the User object that you want to create. Object: An object variable that represents the Group or Workspace object for which you want to create the new User object. Name: A String that uniquely names the new User object. Pid: A String containing the PID of a user account. Password: A String containing the password for the new User object.	Creates a new User object.
Open Database()	Set database = workspace. OpenDatabase (dbname, options, read-only, connect)	Database: An object variable that represents the Database object that you want to open. Workspace: An object variable that represents the existing Workspace object that will contain the database. Dbname: A String that is the name of an existing Microsoft Jet database file, or the data source name (DSN)	Opens a specified database in a Workspace object and returns a reference to the Database object that represents it.

Method	Syntax	Parameters	Description
		of an ODBC data source. Options: A Variant that sets various options for the database. Read-only: A Boolean value that is True if you want to open the database with read-only access. Connect: A String that specifies various connection information, including passwords.	
Open Connection ()	Set connection = workspace. Open Connection (name, options, readonly, connect)	Connection: A Connection object variable to which the new connection will be assigned. Workspace: Variable of a Workspace object data type that references the existing Workspace object that will contain the new connection. Name: A string expression. Options: A Variant that sets various options for the connection. Readonly: A Boolean value that is True if the connection is to be opened for read-only access and False if the connection is to be opened for read/write access. Connect: An ODBC connect string.	Opens a Connection object on an ODBC data source.

Appendix B

RDO API Reference

THE REMOTE DATA OBJECT model provides a set of objects that assists in the development of client/server applications by addressing their unique requirements. Unlike DAO, which provides an interface to the Jet Database Engine, RDO provides an object-oriented layer of abstraction that directly interfaces with the ODBC API — as does the ODBCDirect interface. RDO uses the ODBC API and the database server drivers to create database server connections, create queries and cursors to navigate the resulting data sets, and execute complex stored procedures that rely on the database server for the majority of the processing requirements. Unlike DAO, which utilizes the Jet Database Engine for query preprocessing and connection management, RDO directly interfaces to the database server, which makes RDO particularly suited to client/server application development. This appendix provides a complete reference for the objects provided by RDO and their methods and properties.

rdoColumn

The `rdoTable`, or `rdoResultset` object's `rdoColumns` collection, represents the `rdoColumn` object in a row of data. You can use the `rdoColumn` object in an `rdoResultset` to read and set values for the data columns in the current row of the object. However, in most cases, references to the `rdoColumn` object is only implied because the `rdoColumns` collection is the `rdoResultset` object's default collection. Table B-1 lists and describes the properties of the `rdoColumn` object. Table B-2 lists and describes the methods of the `rdoColumn` object.

TABLE **B-1** THE RDOCOLUMN OBJECT PROPERTIES

Property	Description
AllowZeroLength	Returns a value that indicates whether a zero-length string ("") is a valid setting for the Value property of an rdoColumn object with a data type of rdTypeCHAR, rdTypeVARCHAR, or rdTypeLONGVARCHAR.

Continued

TABLE **B-1** **THE RDOCOLUMN OBJECT PROPERTIES** *(continued)*

Property	Description
Attributes	Returns a value that indicates one or more characteristics of an rdoColumn object. It can be a sum of the following constants: rdFixedColumn — the column size is fixed (default for numeric columns). For example, Char, Binary. rdVariableColumn — the column size is variable. For example, VarChar and LongVarChar, VarBinary and LongVarBinary columns. rdAutoIncrColumn — the column value for new rows is automatically incremented to a unique value that can't be changed. rdUpdatableColumn — the column value can be changed. rdTimeStampColumn — the column is a timestamp value. This attribute is set only for rdClientBatch cursors.
ChunkRequired	Returns a Boolean value that indicates whether data must be accessed by using the GetChunk() method.
Name	Returns the name of a RemoteData object.
OrdinalPosition	Returns the relative position of an rdoColumn object within the rdoColumns collection.
BatchConflictValue	Returns a value currently in the database that is newer than the Value property, as determined by an optimistic batch-update conflict.
KeyColumn	Returns or sets a value that specifies whether this column is part of the primary key.
Status	Returns or sets the status of the current row or column. If set to rdRowUnmodified — the row or column hasn't been modified or has been updated successfully. If set to rdRowModified — the row or column has been modified, but not updated in the database. If set to rdRowNew — the row or column has been inserted with the AddNew() method, but hasn't been inserted yet into the database. If set to rdRowDeleted — the row or column has been deleted, but hasn't been deleted yet in the database. If set to rdRowDBDeleted — the row or column has been deleted locally and in the database.
OriginalValue	Returns the value of the column as first fetched from the database.

Property	Description
`Required`	Returns a value that indicates whether an `rdoColumn` requires a non-`Null` value.
`Size`	Returns a value that indicates the maximum size, in bytes, of the underlying data of an `rdoColumn` object that contains text, or the fixed size of an `rdoColumn` object that contains text or numeric values.
`SourceColumn`	Returns a value that indicates the name of the column that is the original source of the data for an `rdoColumn` object.
`SourceTable`	Returns a value that indicates the name of the table that is the original source of the data for an `rdoColumn` object.
`Type`	Returns or sets a value that indicates the type or data type of an object.
`Updatable`	Returns a Boolean value that indicates whether changes can be made to a remote data object.
`Value`	Returns or sets the value of an object.

TABLE **B-2** THE RDOCOLUMN OBJECT METHODS

Method	Syntax	Parameters	Description
Append Chunk()	`object ! column. AppendChunk source`	`Object`: An object expression that evaluates to the `rdoResultset` object containing the `rdoColumns` collection. `Column`: An object expression that evaluates to an `rdoColumn` object whose `Chunk Required` property is set to `True`. Source: A string	Appends data from a Variant expression to an `rdoColumn` object with a data type of `rdTypeLONGVARBINARY` or `rdTypeLONGVARCHAR`.

Continued

TABLE **B-2 THE RDOCOLUMN OBJECT METHODS** *(continued)*

Method	Syntax	Parameters	Description
		expression or variable containing the data that you want to append to the rdo Column object specified by column.	
Column Size()	varname = object ! column. Column Size( )	Varname: The name of a Long or Variant variable. Object: An object expression that evaluates to the rdoResultset object containing the rdoColumns collection. Column: The name of an rdo Column object whose ChunkRequired property is set to True.	Returns the number of bytes in an rdoColumn object with a data type of rdTypeLONGVARBINARY or rdTypeLONGVARCHAR.
GetChunk()	varname = object ! column. GetChunk (numbytes)	Varname: The name of a Variant that receives the data from the rdo Column object named by column. Object: An object expression that evaluates to an rdoResultset object containing the rdo Columns collection. Column: An object expression that evaluates to an rdoColumn object whose Chunk	Returns all or a portion of the contents of an rdoColumn object with a data type of rdTypeLONGVARBINARY or rdTypeLONGVARCHAR.

Method	Syntax	Parameters	Description
		Required property is True. Numbytes: A numeric expression that is the number of bytes that you want to return.	

rdoColumns

The rdoTable, or rdoResultset object's rdoColumns collection, represents the rdoColumn objects in a row of data. You use the rdoColumn object in an rdoResultset to read and set values for the data columns in the current row of the object. Table B-3 lists and describes the properties of the rdoColumns object.

TABLE B-3 THE RDOCOLUMNS OBJECT PROPERTIES

Property	Description
Item	Returns a specific member of an RDO collection object, either by position or by key.
Count	Returns the number of objects in a collection.

The rdoColumns object has one method, Refresh(), whose syntax is Refresh. It has no parameters, and it either closes (and rebuilds the rdoResultset object created by a RemoteData control) or it refreshes the members of the collections in the Applies To list.

rdoConnection

Generally, an rdoConnection object represents a physical connection to the remote data source and corresponds to a single ODBC hDbc handle. A connection to a remote data source is required before you can access its data. You can open connections to remote ODBC data sources and create `rdoConnection` objects with either the `RemoteData` control or the `OpenConnection()` method of an `rdoEnvironment` object. Table B-4 lists and describes the properties of the `rdoConnection` object. Table B-5 lists and describes the methods of the `rdoConnection` object.

TABLE B-4 THE RDOCONNECTION OBJECT PROPERTIES

Property	Description
CursorDriver	Returns or sets a value that specifies the type of cursor to be created. If set to `rdUseIfNeeded` — the ODBC driver will choose the appropriate style of cursors. Server-side cursors are used if they are available. If set to `rdUseOdbc` — the ODBC cursor library is used. If set to `rdUseServer` — server-side cursors are used. If set to `rdUseClientBatch` — RDO uses the optimistic batch cursor library.
HEnv	Returns a value corresponding to the ODBC `environment` handle.
LoginTimeout	Returns or sets a value that specifies the number of seconds that the ODBC Driver Manager waits before a timeout error occurs when a connection is opened.
Name	Returns the name of a `RemoteData` object.
Password	Represents the password used during creation of an `rdoEnvironment` object.
UserName	Returns or sets a value that represents a user of an `rdoEnvironment` object. Use the `UserName` property with the `Password` property to connect to an ODBC data source.
Item	Returns a specific member of an RDO collection object, either by position or by key.
RdoConnections	Returns a specific member of an `rdoConnections` collection, either by position or by key.

TABLE **B-5** THE RDOCONNECTION OBJECT METHODS

Method	Syntax	Parameters	Description
Begin Trans()	BeginTrans	None	Begins a new transaction.
Commit Trans()	Commit Trans	None	Ends the current transaction and saves the changes.
Rollback Trans()	Rollback Trans	None	Ends the current transaction and restores the databases in the rdoEnvironment object to the state they were in when the current transaction began.
Close()	Close	None	Closes an open remote data object.
Open Connection ()	Set connection = environ- ment.Open Connection (dsName[, prompt[, readonly[, connect[, options]]]])	connection: An object expression that evaluates to an rdoConnection object that you're opening. Environment: An object expression that evaluates to an existing rdoEnviron- ment object. DsName: A string expression that is the name of a registered ODBC DSN. Prompt: A Variant or constant that determines how the operation is carried out. Readonly: A Boolean value that is True if the connection is to be opened for read-only access, and False if the connection is to be opened for read/write	Opens a connection to an ODBC data source and returns a reference to the rdoConnection object that represents a specific database.

Continued

TABLE **B-5** **THE RDOCONNECTION OBJECT METHODS** *(continued)*

Method	Syntax	Parameters	Description
		access. `Options:` A Variant or constant that determines how the operation is carried out, as specified in `Settings`. If set to `rdAsyncEnable` — executes operation asynchronously.	
`Add()`	`object.Add item, key, before, after`	`Object:` An object expression that evaluates to an object in the Applies To list. `Item:` An expression of any type that specifies the member to add to the collection. `Key:` A unique string expression that specifies a key string that can be used. `Before:` An expression that specifies a relative position in the collection.	Adds a member to a `Collection` object.
`Remove()`	`object. Remove index`	`object:` An object expression that evaluates to an object in the Applies To list. `Index:` An expression that specifies the position of a member of the collection.	Removes a member from a `Collection` object.

rdoEngine

The `rdoEngine` object can represent a remote database engine or another data source managed by the ODBC Driver Manager as a database. The `rdoEngine` object is a predefined object; therefore, you can't create additional `rdoEngine` objects, and it isn't a member of any collection. Table B-6 lists and describes the properties of the `rdoEngine` object. Table B-7 lists and describes the methods of the `rdoEngine` object.

TABLE B-6 THE RDOENGINE OBJECT PROPERTIES

Property	Description
AbsolutePosition	Returns or sets the absolute row number of an `rdoResultset` object's current row.
rdoDefaultCursorDriver	Returns or sets the cursor library used by the ODBC Driver Manager. If set to `rdUseIfNeeded` — RDO chooses the style of cursors most appropriate for the driver. Server-side cursors are used if they are available. If set to `rdUseODBC` — RDO uses the ODBC cursor library. This option gives better performance for small result sets, but degrades quickly for larger result sets. If set to `rdUseServer` — RDO uses server-side cursors. For most large operations, this gives better performance, but might cause more network traffic. If set to `rdUseClientBatch` — RDO uses the optimistic batch cursor library, as required by all batch mode operations and dissociate `rdoResultset` objects. If set to `rdUseNone` — RDO does not create a scrollable cursor. Basically, this is a forward-only, read-only result set with a `RowsetSize` set to 1. This type of result set performs faster than those that require creation of a cursor.
rdoDefaultUser	Returns or sets the default username assigned to any new `rdoEnvironment`.
rdoDefaultPassword	Returns or sets the default password assigned to any new `rdoEnvironment`.

Continued

TABLE B-6 THE RDOENGINE OBJECT PROPERTIES *(continued)*

Property	Description
rdoDefaultErrorThreshold	Returns or sets a value that indicates the default value for the ErrorThreshold property for rdoQuery objects.
rdoDefaultLoginTimeout	Returns or sets a default value that determines the number of seconds the ODBC driver waits before abandoning an attempt to connect to a data source.
rdoLocaleID	Returns or sets a value that indicates the locale of the RDO library. If set to rdLocaleSystem — System. If set to rdLocaleEnglish — English. If set to rdLocaleFrench — French. If set to rdLocaleGerman — German. If set to rdLocaleItalian — Italian. If set to rdLocaleJapanese — Japanese. If set to rdLocaleSpanish — Spanish. If set to rdLocaleChinese — Chinese. If set to rdLocaleSimplifiedChinese — Simplified Chinese. If set to rdLocaleKorean — Korean.
rdoVersion	Returns a value that indicates the version of the RDO library associated with the object.

TABLE B-7 THE RDOENGINE OBJECT METHODS

Method	Syntax	Parameters	Description
RdoCreate Environment ()	Set variable = rdoCreate Environment (name, user, password)	Variable: An object expression that evaluates to an rdoEnvironment object. Name: A String variable that uniquely names the new rdoEnviron- ment object. See the Name property for	Creates a new rdoEnvironment object.

Method	Syntax	Parameters	Description
		details on valid `rdo Environment` names. `User:` A String variable that identifies the owner of the new `rdo Environment` object. See the `UserName` property for more information. `Password:` A String variable that contains the password for the new `rdoEnvironment` object. The password can be up to 14 characters long and can include any characters except ASCII character 0 (null).	
`RdoRegister DataSource()`	`rdoRegister DataSource DSN, driver, silent, attributes`	`DSN:` A string expression that is the name used in the `Open Connection()` method that refers to a block of descriptive information about the data source. `Driver:` A string expression that is the name of the ODBC driver. This isn't the name of	Enters connection information for an ODBC data source into the Windows Registry.

Continued

TABLE B-7 THE RDOENGINE OBJECT METHODS *(continued)*

Method	Syntax	Parameters	Description
		the ODBC driver DLL file. Silent: A Boolean value that is True if you don't want to display the ODBC driver dialog boxes that prompt for driver-specific information, or False if you do want to display the ODBC driver dialog boxes. Attributes: A string expression that is a list of keywords to be added to the ODBC.INI file. The keywords are in a carriage-return-delimited string.	

rdoEnvironment

An rdoEnvironment object defines a logical set of connections and transaction scope for a particular username. It contains both open and allocated-but-unopened connections, provides mechanisms for simultaneous transactions, and provides a security context for data manipulation language (DML) operations on the database. Table B-8 lists and describes the properties of the rdoEnvironment object. Table B-9 lists and describes the methods of the rdoEngine object.

TABLE B-8 THE RDOENVIRONMENT OBJECT PROPERTIES

Property	Description
CursorDriver	Returns or sets a value that specifies the type of cursor to be created. If set to rdUseIfNeeded — the ODBC driver chooses the appropriate style of cursors. Server-side cursors are used if they are available. If set to rdUseOdbc — the ODBC cursor library is used. If set to rdUseServer — server-side cursors are used. If set to rdUseClientBatch — RDO uses the optimistic batch cursor library.
hEnv	Returns a value corresponding to the ODBC environment handle.
LoginTimeout	Returns or sets a value that specifies the number of seconds the ODBC Driver Manager waits before a timeout error occurs when a connection is opened.
Name	Returns the name of a RemoteData object.
Password	Represents the password used during creation of an rdoEnvironment object.
UserName	Returns or sets a value that represents a user of an rdoEnvironment object. Use the UserName property with the Password property to connect to an ODBC data source.
Item	Returns a specific member of an RDO collection object, either by position or by key.
RdoConnections	Returns a specific member of an rdoConnections collection, either by position or by key.

TABLE B-9 THE RDOENVIRONMENT METHODS

Method	Syntax	Parameters	Description
BeginTrans()	BeginTrans	None	Begins a new transaction.

Continued

TABLE **B-9** **THE RDOENVIRONMENT METHODS** *(continued)*

Method	Syntax	Parameters	Description
Commit Trans()	Commit Trans	None	Ends the current transaction and saves the changes.
Rollback Trans()	Rollback Trans	None	Ends the current transaction and restores the databases in the rdoEnvironment object to the state they were in when the current transaction began.
Close()	Close	None	Closes an open remote data object.
Open Connection()	Set connection = environment.Open Connection (dsName[, prompt[, readonly[, connect[, options]]]])	connection: An object expression that evaluates to an rdoConnection object that you're opening. Environment: An object expression that evaluates to an existing rdoEnvironment object. DsName: A string expression that is the name of a registered ODBC DSN or a zero-length string (""). Prompt: A Variant or constant that determines how the operation is carried out. readonly: A Boolean value that is True if the connection is to be opened for read-only access, and False if the connection is to be opened for read/write	Opens a connection to an ODBC data source and returns a reference to the rdoConnection object that represents a specific database.

Method	Syntax	Parameters	Description
		access. `Connect`: A string expression used to pass arguments to the ODBC Driver Manager for opening the database. `options`: A Constant that determines how the operation is carried out.	
`Add()`	`object.Add item, key, before, after`	`object`: An object expression that evaluates to an object in the Applies To list. `Item`: Required. An expression of any type that specifies the member to add to the collection. `Key`: A unique string expression that specifies a key string that can be used. `Before`: An expression that specifies a relative position in the collection. `After`: An expression that specifies a relative position in the collection.	Adds a member to a `Collection` object.
`Remove()`	`object. Remove index`	`object`: An object expression that evaluates to an object in the Applies To list. `Index`: Required. An expression that specifies the position	Removes a member from a `Collection` object.

Continued

TABLE B-9 THE RDOENVIRONMENT METHODS *(continued)*

Method	Syntax	Parameters	Description
		of a member of the collection. If a numeric expression, `index` must be a number from 1 to the value of the collection's `Count` property. If a string expression, `index` must correspond to the key argument specified when the member referred to was added to the collection.	

rdoEnvironments

`rdoEnvironment` objects are created with the `rdoCreateEnvironment()` method of the `rdoEngine` object. Newly created `rdoEnvironment` objects are automatically appended to the `rdoEnvironments` collection, unless you either don't provide a name for the new object when using the `rdoCreateEnvironment()` method or simply declare a new `rdoEnvironment` object in code. The `rdoEnvironments` collection is automatically initialized with a default `rdoEnvironment` object, based on the default properties set in the `rdoEngine` object. Table B-10 lists and describes the properties of the `rdoEnvironments` object. Table B-11 lists and describes the methods of the `rdoEnvironments` object.

TABLE B-10 THE RDOENVIRONMENTS OBJECT PROPERTIES

Property	Description
Item	Returns a specific member of an RDO collection object, either by position or by key.
Count	Returns the number of objects in a collection.

TABLE B-11 THE RDOENVIRONMENTS OBJECT METHODS

Method	Syntax	Parameters	Description
Add()	object.Add item, key, before, after	Object: An object expression that evaluates to an object in the Applies To list. Item: An expression of any type that specifies the member to add to the collection. Key: A unique string expression that specifies a key string that can be used. Before: An expression that specifies a relative position in the collection. After: An expression that specifies a relative position in the collection.	Adds a member to a Collection object.
Remove()	object. Remove index	Object: An object expression that evaluates to an object in the Applies To list. Index: An expression that specifies the position of a member of the collection. If a numeric expression, index must be a number from 1 to the value of the collection's Count property. If a string expression, index must correspond to	Removes a member from a Collection object.

Continued

TABLE B-11 THE RDOENVIRONMENTS OBJECT METHODS *(continued)*

Method	Syntax	Parameters	Description
		the key argument specified when the member referred to was added to the collection.	

rdoErrors

Any operation involving remote data objects can generate one or more errors. As each error occurs, one or more rdoError objects are placed in the rdoErrors collection of the rdoEngine object. When another RDO operation generates an error, the rdoErrors collection is cleared, and the new set of rdoError objects is placed in the rdoErrors collection. RDO operations that don't generate an error have no effect on the rdoErrors collection. Table B-12 lists and describes the properties of the rdoErrors object. The rdoErrors object supports just one method, Clear(), which clears all members from the rdoErrors collection. The Clear() method doesn't take any parameters.

TABLE B-12 THE RDOERRORS OBJECT PROPERTIES

Property	Description
Item	Returns a specific member of an RDO collection object, either by position or by key.
Count	Returns the number of objects in the rdoErrors collection.

rdoError

Any operation involving remote data objects can potentially generate one or more ODBC errors or informational messages. As each error occurs, or as messages are generated, one or more rdoError objects are placed in the rdoErrors collection of the `rdoEngine` object. When a subsequent RDO operation generates an error, the `rdoErrors` collection is cleared, and the new set of `rdoError` objects is placed in the `rdoErrors` collection. RDO operations that don't generate an error have no effect on the `rdoErrors` collection. To make error handling easier, you can use the `Clear()` method to purge the `rdoErrors` collection between operations. Table B-13 lists and describes the properties of the `rdoError` object.

TABLE B-13 THE RDOERRORS OBJECT PROPERTIES

Property	Description
Description	Returns a descriptive string associated with an error.
HelpContext	Returns a context ID for a topic in a Microsoft Windows Help file.
HelpFile	Returns as a variable a fully qualified path to the Help file.
Number	Returns a numeric value specifying a native error.
Source	Returns a value that indicates the source of a remote data access error.
SQLRetCode	Returns the ODBC error return code from the most recent RDO operation. If set to `rdSQLSuccess` — the operation is successful. If set to `rdSQLSuccessWithInfo` — the operation is successful and additional information is available. If set to `rdSQLNoDataFound` — no additional data is available. If set to `rdSQLError` — an error occurred performing the operation. If set to `rdSQLInvalidHandle` — the handle supplied is invalid.
SQLState	Returns a value corresponding to the type of error, as defined by the X/Open and SQL standards.

rdoParameters

The `rdoParameters` collection provides information only about marked parameters in an `rdoQuery` object or stored procedure. You can't append objects to or delete objects from the `rdoParameters` collection.

When the `rdoParameters` collection is first referenced, RDO and the ODBC interface parse the query, searching for parameter markers – the question mark (?). For each marker found, RDO creates an `rdoParameter` object and places it in the `rdoParameters` collection. However, if the query cannot be compiled or otherwise processed, the `rdoParameters` collection isn't created and your code will trigger a trappable error indicating that the object doesn't exist. In this case, check the query for improper syntax, permissions on underlying objects, and proper placement of parameter markers. Table B-14 lists and describes the properties of the `rdoParameters` object.

TABLE B-14 THE RDOPARAMETERS OBJECT PROPERTIES

Property	Description
Item	Returns a specific member of an RDO collection object, either by position or by key.
Count	Returns the number of objects in a collection.

rdoParameter

When you work with stored procedures or SQL queries that require use of arguments that change from execution to execution, you should create an `rdoQuery` object to manage the query and its parameters. For example, if you submit a query that includes information provided by the user, such as a date range or part number, RDO and the ODBC interface can insert these values into the SQL statement automatically at specific positions in the query. Table B-15 lists and describes the properties of the `rdoParameter` object. The `rdoParameter` object supports just one method, `AppendChunk()`, which appends data from a Variant expression to an `rdoColumn` object with a data type of `rdTypeLONGVARBINARY` or `rdTypeLONGVARCHAR`. The `AppendChunk` method has the following syntax:

```
object ! column.AppendChunk source
```

The `Object` parameter is an object expression that evaluates to the `rdoResultset` object containing the `rdoColumns` collection. `Column` is an object expression that evaluates to an `rdoColumn` object whose `ChunkRequired` property is set to `True`. The `Source` parameter is a string expression or variable containing the data that you want to append to the `rdoColumn` object specified by `column`.

TABLE B-15 THE RDOPARAMETER OBJECT PROPERTIES

Property	Description
Direction	Returns or sets a value indicating how a parameter is passed to or from a procedure. If set to rdParamInput — the parameter is used to pass information to the procedure. If set to rdParamInputOutput — the parameter is used to pass information both to and from the procedure. If set to rdParamOutput — the parameter is used to return information from the procedure as output parameter in SQL. If set to rdParamReturnValue — the parameter is used to return the return status value from a procedure.
Name	Returns the name of a RemoteData object.
Type	Returns or sets a value that indicates the type or data type of an object.
Value	Returns or sets the value of an object.

rdoPreparedStatement

An rdoPreparedStatement object is a prepared query definition. Table B-16 lists and describes the properties of the rdoPreparedStatement object. Table B-17 lists and describes the methods of the rdoPreparedStatement object.

TABLE B-16 THE RDOPREPAREDSTATEMENT OBJECT PROPERTIES

Name	Description
BindThreshold	Returns or sets a value specifying the largest column that will be automatically bound under ODBC.
Connect	Returns or sets a value that provides information about the source of an open rdoConnection. The Connect property contains the ODBC connect string. This property is always readable, but can't be changed after the connection is established.

Continued

TABLE **B-16** **THE RDOPREPAREDSTATEMENT OBJECT PROPERTIES** *(continued)*

Name	Description
ErrorThreshold	Returns or sets a value that determines the severity level that constitutes a fatal error.
HStmt	Returns a value corresponding to the ODBC `statement` handle.
KeysetSize	Returns or sets a value indicating the number of rows in the keyset buffer.
LockType	Returns or sets a Long integer value indicating the type of concurrency handling.
LogMessages	Enables ODBC trace logging and returns or sets a value that indicates the path of the ODBC trace file that was created by the ODBC Driver Manager to record all ODBC operations.
MaxRows	Returns or sets a value indicating the maximum number of rows to be returned from a query or processed in an action query.
Name	Returns the name of a `RemoteData` object.
QueryTimeout	Returns or sets a value that specifies the number of seconds the ODBC Driver Manager waits before a timeout error occurs when a query is executed.
RowsAffected	Returns the number of rows affected by the most recently invoked `Execute()` method.
RowsetSize	Returns or sets a value that determines the number of rows in an `rdoResultset` cursor.
SQL	Returns or sets the SQL statement that defines the query executed by an `rdoQuery`.
StillExecuting	Returns a Boolean value that indicates whether a query is still executing.
Type	Returns or sets a value that indicates the type or data type of an object.
Updatable	Returns a Boolean value that indicates whether changes can be made to a remote data object.

TABLE B-17 THE RDOPREPAREDSTATEMENT OBJECT METHODS

Method	Syntax	Parameters	Description
Cancel()	Cancel	None	Cancels the processing of a query running in asynchronous mode, or cancels any pending results against the specified RDO object.
Close()	Close	None	Closes an open remote data object.
Execute()	query.Execute source[, options]	Query: An object expression that evaluates to the rdo Query object whose SQL property setting specifies the SQL statement to execute. Source: A string expression that contains the action query to execute or the name of an rdoQuery. Options: A Variant or constant that determines how the query is run.	Runs an action query or executes an SQL statement that doesn't return rows.
Open Resultset ()	Set variable = object.Open Resultset ([type [,lock type [, option]]])	Variable: An object expression that evaluates to an rdoResultset object. Object: An object expression that evaluates to an existing rdoQuery or rdoTable object that you want to use to	Creates a new rdoResultset object.

Continued

TABLE B-17 THE RDOPREPAREDSTATEMENT OBJECT METHODS *(continued)*

Method	Syntax	Parameters	Description
		create the new rdo Resultset. Name: A String that specifies the source of the rows for the new rdo Resultset. Type: A Variant or constant that specifies the type of cursor to create. Locktype: A Variant or constant that specifies the type of concurrency control. Option: A Variant or constant that specifies characteristics of the new rdoResultset.	

rdoPreparedStatements

An rdoPreparedStatements collection contains all the rdoPreparedStatement objects in an rdoConnection. Table B-18 lists and describes the properties of the rdoPreparedStatements object.

TABLE B-18 THE RDOPREPAREDSTATEMENTS OBJECT PROPERTIES

Property	Description
Item	Returns a specific member of an RDO collection object, either by position or by key.
Count	Returns the number of objects in a collection.

rdoQueries

Contains rdoQuery objects that have been added to the rdoQueries collection, either automatically via the CreateQuery() method or with the Add() method. Table B-19 lists and describes the properties of the rdoQueries object.

TABLE **B-19** THE RDOQUERIES OBJECT PROPERTIES

Property	Description
Item	Returns a specific member of an RDO collection object, either by position or by key.
Count	Returns the number of objects in a collection.

rdoQuery

The rdoQuery object is used to manage SQL queries that require the use of input, output, or input/output parameters. Basically, an rdoQuery functions as a compiled SQL statement. When you work with stored procedures or queries that require use of arguments that change from execution to execution, you can create an rdoQuery object to manage the query parameters. If your stored procedure returns output parameters or a return value, or you want to use rdoParameter objects to handle the parameters, you must use an rdoQuery object to manage it. For example, if you submit a query that includes information provided by the user, such as a date range or part number, RDO can substitute these values into the SQL statement automatically when the query is executed. Table B-20 lists and describes the properties of the rdoQuery object. Table B-21 lists and describes the methods of the rdoQuery object.

TABLE **B-20** THE RDOQUERY OBJECT PROPERTIES

Property	Description
BindThreshold	Returns or sets a value specifying the largest column that will be automatically bound under ODBC.

Continued

TABLE B-20 THE RDOQUERY OBJECT PROPERTIES *(continued)*

Property	Description
HStmt	Returns a value corresponding to the ODBC statement handle.
KeysetSize	Returns or sets a value indicating the number of rows in the keyset buffer.
LockType	Returns or sets a Long integer value indicating the type of concurrency handling. If set to rdConcurReadOnly — Cursor is read-only. No updates are allowed. If set to rdConcurLock — Pessimistic concurrency. If set to rdConcurRowVer — Optimistic concurrency based on row ID. If set to rdConcurValues — Optimistic concurrency based on row values. If set to rdConcurBatch — Optimistic concurrency using batch mode updates. Status values returned successfully for each row are updated.
MaxRows	Returns or sets a value indicating the maximum number of rows to be returned from a query or processed in an action query.
Name	Returns the name of a RemoteData object.
QueryTimeout	Returns or sets a value that specifies the number of seconds the ODBC Driver Manager waits before a timeout error occurs when a query is executed.
CursorType	Returns or sets a value that specifies the default type of cursor to use when opening a result set from the specified query. If set to rdOpenForwardOnly — Fixed set, non-scrolling. If set to rdOpenKeyset — Updatable, fixed set, scrollable query result set cursor. If set to rdOpenDynamic — Updatable, dynamic set, scrollable query result set cursor. If set to rdOpenStatic — Read-only, fixed set.
Prepared	Returns or sets a value that determines whether the query should be prepared using the SQLPrepare or SQLExecDirect ODBC API function.
RowsAffected	Returns the number of rows affected by the most recently invoked Execute() method.
RowsetSize	Returns or sets a value that determines the number of rows in an rdoResultset cursor.

Property	Description
SQL	Returns or sets the SQL statement that defines the query executed by an rdoQuery object.
StillExecuting	Returns a Boolean value that indicates whether a query is still executing.
Type	Returns or sets a value that indicates the type or data type of an object.
ActiveConnection	Returns or sets an object reference indicating the connection this query should be associated with.

TABLE **B-21 THE RDOQUERY OBJECT METHODS**

Method	Syntax	Parameters	Description
Cancel()	Cancel	None	Cancels the processing of a query running in asynchronous mode, or cancels any pending results against the specified RDO object.
Close()	Close	None	Closes an open remote data object.
Execute()	query.Execute [options]	Query: An object expression that evaluates to the rdoQuery object whose SQL property setting specifies the SQL statement to execute. Options: A Variant or constant that determines how the query is run, if set to rdAsyncEnable — execute operation	Runs an action query or executes an SQL statement that doesn't return rows.

Continued

TABLE B-21 THE RDOQUERY OBJECT METHODS *(continued)*

Method	Syntax	Parameters	Description
		asynchronously; if set to rdExecDirect — Bypass creation of a stored procedure to execute the query.	
Open Resultset()	Set variable = object. OpenResultset ([type [, locktype [, option]]])	variable: An object expression that evaluates to an rdoResultset object. Object: An object expression that evaluates to an existing rdoQuery or rdoTable object you want to use to create the new rdo Resultset. Type: A Variant or constant that specifies the type of cursor to create. Locktype: A Variant or constant that specifies the type of concurrency control. Option: A Variant or constant that specifies characteristics of the new rdoResultset.	Creates a new rdoResultset object.

rdoResultset

When you use remote data objects, you interact with data almost entirely using rdoResultset objects. rdoResultset objects are created using the RemoteData control, or the OpenResultset() method of the rdoQuery, rdoTable, or rdoConnection object.

When you execute a query that contains one or more SQL SELECT statements, the data source returns zero or more rows in an rdoResultset object. All rdoResultset objects are constructed using rows and columns.

A single rdoResultset can contain zero or any number of result sets – so-called "multiple" result sets. Once you have completed processing the first result set in an rdoResultset object, use the MoreResults() method to discard the current rdoResultset rows and activate the next rdoResultset. You can process individual rows of the new result set just as you processed the first rdoResultset. You can repeat this until the MoreResults() method returns False. Table B-22 lists and describes the properties of the rdoResultset object. Table B-23 lists and describes the methods of the rdoResultset object.

TABLE B-22 THE RDORESULTSET OBJECT PROPERTIES

Property	Description
AbsolutePosition	Returns or sets the absolute row number of an rdoResultset object's current row.
BOF	Returns a value that indicates whether the current row position is before the first row in an rdoResultset.
EOF	Returns a value that indicates whether the current row position is after the last row in an rdoResultset.
Bookmark	Returns or sets a bookmark that uniquely identifies the current row in an rdoResultset object. If you have a valid bookmark, you can use it to reposition the current row in an rdoResultset.
Bookmarkable	Returns a value that indicates whether an rdoResultset object supports bookmarks, which you can set using the Bookmark property.
EditMode	Returns a value that indicates the state of editing for the current row. If set to rdEditNone – no editing operation is in progress. If set to rdEditInProgress – the Edit() method has been invoked, and the current row is in the copy buffer. If set to rdEditAdd – the AddNew() method has been invoked, and the current row in the copy buffer is a new row that hasn't been saved in the database.

Continued

TABLE **B-22** THE RDORESULTSET OBJECT PROPERTIES *(continued)*

Property	Description
HStmt	Returns a value corresponding to the ODBC statement handle.
LastModified	Returns a bookmark indicating the most recently added or changed row.
LockType	Returns or sets a Long integer value indicating the type of concurrency handling. If set to rdConcurReadOnly — cursor is read-only; no updates are allowed. If set to rdConcurLock — pessimistic concurrency. If set to rdConcurRowVer — optimistic concurrency based on row ID. If set to rdConcurValues — optimistic concurrency based on row values. If set to rdConcurBatch — optimistic concurrency using batch-mode updates.
LockEdits	Returns a Boolean value indicating the type of locking that is in effect.
Name	Returns the name of a RemoteData object.
PercentPosition	Returns or sets a value that indicates or changes the approximate location of the current row in the rdoResultset object, based on a percentage of the rows in the rdoResultset.
BatchCollisionCount	Returns a value that specifies the number of rows that didn't complete the last batch-mode update.
BatchCollisionRows	Returns an array of bookmarks indicating the rows that generated collisions in the last batch-update operation.
BatchSize	Returns or sets a value that specifies the number of statements sent back to the server in each batch.
Status	Returns or sets the status of the current row or column. If set to rdRowUnmodified — the row or column hasn't been modified or has been updated successfully. If set to rdRowModified — the row or column has been modified, but not updated in the database. If set to rdRowNew — the row or column has been inserted with the AddNew() method, but hasn't been inserted yet into the database. If set to rdRowDeleted — the row or column has been deleted, but hasn't been deleted yet in the database. If set to rdRowDBDeleted — the row or column has been deleted locally and in the database.

Property	Description
UpdateCriteria	Returns or sets a value that specifies how the WHERE clause is constructed for each row during an optimistic batch-update operation. If set to rdCriteriaKey — uses just the key column(s) in the WHERE clause. If set to rdCriteriaAllCols — uses the key column(s) and all updated columns in the WHERE clause. If set to rdCriteriaUpdCols — uses the key column(s) and all the columns in the WHERE clause. If set to rdCriteriaTimeStamp — uses just the timestamp column, if available.
UpdateOperation	Returns or sets a value that specifies whether the optimistic batch update should use an Update statement or a Delete followed by an Insert. If set to rdOperationUpdate — uses an Update statement for each modified row. If set to rdOperationDelIns — uses a pair of Delete and Insert statements for each modified row.
Restartable	Returns a value that indicates whether an rdoResultset object supports the Requery() method, which re-executes the query that the rdoResultset is based on.
RowCount	Returns the number of rows accessed in an rdoResultset object.
StillExecuting	Returns a Boolean value that indicates whether a query is still executing.
Transactions	Returns a value that indicates whether an object supports the recording of a series of changes that can later be rolled back (undone) or committed (saved).
Type	Returns or sets a value that indicates the type or data type of an object.
Updatable	Returns a Boolean value that indicates whether changes can be made to a remote data object.
ActiveConnection	Returns or sets an object reference indicating the connection that this query should be associated with.

TABLE **B-23** **THE RDORESULTSET OBJECT METHODS**

Method	Syntax	Parameters	Description
AddNew()	AddNew	None	Creates a new row for an updatable rdoResultset object.
Cancel()	Cancel	None	Cancels the processing of a query running in asynchronous mode, or cancels any pending results against the specified RDO object.
Cancel Update()	Cancel Update	None	Cancels any pending updates to an rdoResultset object.
Close()	Close	None	Closes an open remote data object.
Delete()	Delete	None	Deletes the current row in an updatable rdoResultset object.
Edit()	Edit	None	Enables changes to data values in the current row of an updatable rdoResultset object.
GetRows()	array = object. GetRows (rows)	Array: The name of a Variant type variable to store the returned data. Object: An object expression that evaluates to an object in the Applies To list. Rows: A Long value indicating the number of rows to retrieve.	Retrieves multiple rows of an rdoResultset into an array.

Method	Syntax	Parameters	Description
MoreResults()	MoreResults	None	Clears the current result set of any pending rows and returns a Boolean value that indicates whether one or more additional result sets are pending.
Move()	object.Move rows[, start]	Object: An object expression that evaluates to an object in the Applies To list. Rows: A signed Long value that specifies the number of rows the position will move, as described in Settings. Start: A Variant value that identifies a bookmark, as described in Settings.	Repositions the current row pointer in an rdoResultset object.
MoveFirst()	MoveFirst	None	Move to the first record in the result set.
MoveLast()	MoveLast	None	Move to the last record in the result set.
MoveNext()	MoveNext	None	Move to the next record in the result set.
Move Previous()	Move Previous	None	Move to the previous record in the result set.
Requery()	object. Requery [options]	Object: The object placeholder represents an object expression that evaluates to an object in the Applies To list. Options: A Variant or constant that determines how the query is run; if set	Re-run the previous query.

Continued

TABLE B-23 **THE RDORESULTSET OBJECT METHODS** *(continued)*

Method	Syntax	Parameters	Description
		to `rdAsyncEnable` — execute operation asynchronously.	
Update()	Update	None	Saves the contents of the copy buffer row to a specified updatable `rdoResultset` object and then discards the copy buffer.
Batch Update()	`object.` `BatchUpdate` `(SingleRow,` `Force)`	`Object:` An object expression that evaluates to an object in the Applies To list. `SingleRow:` A Boolean value that is `True` if the update is done only for the current row, or `False` if the update applies to all rows in the batch. Default is `False`. `Force:` A Boolean value that is `True` if the row or batch of rows will overwrite existing rows in the database regardless of whether they cause collisions.	Performs a batch optimistic update.

Method	Syntax	Parameters	Description
Cancel Batch()	object. CancelBatch (SingleRow)	Object: An object expression that evaluates to an object in the Applies To list. SingleRow: A Boolean value that is True if the cancel action is done only for the current row, or False if the cancel action applies to all rows in the batch.	Cancels all uncommitted changes in the local cursor (used in batch mode).
GetClip String()	Resulset String = object.Get ClipString (NumRows, [Column Delimiter], [Row Delimiter], NullExpr])	A variable used to reference the entire result set as a delimited string. Object: An object expression that evaluates to an rdoResultset object. NumRows: Number of rows to copy into the clip string. Column Delimiter: String expression used to separate data columns. RowDelimiter: String expression used to separate data rows, as described in Settings. NullExpr: String expression used when NULL values are encountered.	The GetClipString() method returns a delimited string for 'n' rows in a result set.

rdoResultsets

The `rdoResultsets` collection contains all open `rdoResultset` objects in an `rdoConnection`. A new `rdoResultset` is automatically added to the `rdoResultsets` collection when you open the object, and it's automatically removed when you close it. Several `rdoResultset` objects might be active at any one time. Table B-24 lists and describes the properties of the `rdoResultsets` object.

TABLE B-24 THE RDORESULTSETS OBJECT PROPERTIES

Property	Description
Item	Returns a specific member of an RDO collection object, either by position or by key.
Count	Returns the number of objects in a collection.

rdoTables

The `rdoTables` collection contains all stored `rdoTable` objects in a database. Table B-25 lists and describes the properties of the `rdoTables` object. The `rdoTables` object supports just one method, `Refresh()`, which either closes and rebuilds the `rdoResultset` object created by a `RemoteData` control or refreshes the members of the collections in the Applies To list. The `Refresh()` method doesn't take any parameters.

TABLE B-25 THE RDOTABLES OBJECT PROPERTIES

Property	Description
Item	Returns a specific member of an RDO collection object, either by position or by key.
Count	Returns the number of objects in a collection.

rdoTable

An rdoTable object represents the stored definition of a base table or an SQL view. Table B-26 lists and describes the properties of the rdoTable object. The rdoTable object supports just one method, OpenResultset(), which opens a new record set. It has the following syntax:

```
Set variable = object.OpenResultset([type [,locktype [, option]]])
```

The Variable parameter is an object expression that evaluates to an rdoResultset object. The Object parameter is an object expression that evaluates to an existing rdoQuery or rdoTable object that you want to use to create the new rdoResultset. The Name parameter is a String that specifies the source of the rows for the new rdoResultset. This argument can specify the name of an rdoTable object, the name of an rdoQuery, or an SQL statement that might return rows. The Type parameter is a Variant or constant that specifies the type of cursor to create. The Locktype parameter is a Variant or constant that specifies the type of concurrency control. The Option parameter is a Variant or constant that specifies characteristics of the new rdoResultset.

TABLE **B-26** THE RDOTABLE OBJECT PROPERTIES

Property	Description
Name	Returns the name of a RemoteData object.
RowCount	Returns the number of rows accessed in an rdoResultset object.
Type	Returns or sets a value that indicates the type or data type of an object.
Updatable	Returns a Boolean value that indicates whether changes can be made to a remote data object.

Appendix C

ADO API Reference

ADO CONSISTS OF the following objects: Command, Connection, Error, Field, Parameter, and Recordset. The ADO objects do not function in a strict hierarchy. This makes ADO much easier to use, because all the ADO objects, except for the Error and Field objects, can be created independently. The Command, Error, and Parameter objects are optional. This appendix details the properties and methods of each of these objects.

Connection Object

The Connection object encapsulates a connection to a data source and also allows commands to be executed using the Execute() method. The Execute() command returns a Recordset object. The Connection object is used to configure a connection, define the isolation level, execute commands and control their execution, manage transactions, and manage connection errors. Table C-1 lists the properties supported by the Connection object. Table C-2 lists the methods supported by the Connection object.

TABLE C-1 **CONNECTION OBJECT PROPERTIES**

Property	Read/Write	Description
Attributes	R/W	The Connection object attributes.
CommandTimeout	R/W	The number of seconds to wait for a command to execute; the default is 30 seconds.
ConnectionString	R/W	The string to use when connecting to a data source, when the ConnectString parameter is not passed to the Open() method.

Continued

819

TABLE C-1 **CONNECTION OBJECT PROPERTIES** *(continued)*

Property	Read/Write	Description
ConnectionTimeout	R/W	The number of seconds to wait when establishing a connection to a data source; the default is 15 seconds.
DefaultDatabase	R/W	The default name of the database currently connected to, or used in conjunction with the Open() method when not specified.
IsolationLevel	R/W	How the Connection object handles transactions.
Mode	R/W	The sharing mode used when opening a new data source.
Provider	R/W	The name of the current data provider, or used in conjunction with the Open() method when the data provider is not specified.
Version	R	Returns the current ADO version number.

TABLE C-2 **CONNECTION OBJECT METHODS**

Method	Description
BeginTrans()	Begins a new transaction with the data source.
Close()	Closes a data source connection. Any resources in use are also freed.
CommitTrans()	Saves any changes made to the data source since the current nesting level was started (not all data sources support nested transactions).
Execute()	Executes a query or command that is supported by the data source and then returns a Recordset object.
Open()	Opens a data source connection.

Method	Description
RollbackTrans()	Throws away any changes made to the data source since the current nesting level was started (not all data sources support nested transactions).

Command Object

The Command object encapsulates a command that can be interpreted by the data source. Command objects can be created independently of a Connection object. You can use the Command object to issue data-manipulation commands that create Recordset objects. In addition, you can use it to perform batch updates, issue data-definition commands to modify the data source schema, open a connection to a data source, specify a command, execute stored procedures, and create prepared statements. The Command object can be used in conjunction with the Parameters object, to create parameterized commands. The application can add Parameter objects to the Parameters collection without requiring the data provider to fill the Parameters collection beforehand. The Command object is optional – supported only by OLE DB providers that support the command interface. Table C-3 lists the properties supported by the Command object. Table C-4 lists the methods supported by the Command object.

TABLE C-3 COMMAND OBJECT PROPERTIES

Property	Read/Write	Description
ActiveConnection	R/W	The connection associated with this command.
CommandText	R/W	The actual command text string.
CommandTimeout	R/W	The number of seconds to wait for the command to execute; by default, 30 seconds.
CommandType	R/W	The type of the command, as specified by one of the CommandTypeEnum constants.
Prepared	R/W	A Boolean value; if True, a prepared statement is created before the command is executed.

TABLE C-4 COMMAND OBJECT METHODS

Method	Description
CreateParameter()	Creates a new command Parameter object. Parameters can be used to specify a value that is passed to, or returned from, a command or stored procedure.
Execute()	Performs the specified command or stored procedure.

Error Object

The Error object encapsulates errors returned from the data source. The Error object is used to retrieve an error description, error number, the object that created the error, a Help file reference, and the current SQL state, if applicable. The Error object can support multiple errors. Before each ADO method is called, the Errors collection is automatically cleared. The Errors object provides two properties. The Count property returns the number of Error objects contained in the collection. The Item property returns the Error object at the specified index. You don't need to use the Item() method directly. The Errors collection object provides a single method, Clear(). The Clear() method is used to empty the Errors collection manually. Table C-5 lists the properties supported by the Error object. The Error object does not provide any methods.

TABLE C-5 ERROR OBJECT PROPERTIES

Property	Read/Write	Description
Description	R	Used to return a text message describing the error or warning.
HelpContext	R	Returns a Help file context that can be used to retrieve more information about the error that occurred.
HelpFile	R	Returns the name of the data source provider Help file.
NativeError	R	Used to return the data source error number that caused the error or warning. You must consult with your data source provider for more information.

Property	Read/Write	Description
Number	R	Returns the ADO error constant value.
Source	R	Returns the name of the ADO object that caused the error or warning.
SQLState	R	Returns the ANSI SQL error code value. Not all data providers conform to the ANSI SQL error state standards.

Field Object

The Field object is used to encapsulate a column of a Recordset. A Recordset consists of a collection of Field objects. The Field object can be used to access the name of a column, the value of a column, and the type, precision, scale, and size of a column. The Field object can also be used to change the value of a field and access Binary Large Object (BLOB) fields. The Field object can be accessed only from a Recordset object. Depending on the OLE DB data provider, the Field object's capability may be limited. The Fields object provides two properties. The Count property returns the number of Field objects contained in the collection. The Item property returns the Field object at the specified index. You don't need to use the Item() method directly. The Fields object provides a single method, Refresh(). The Refresh() method is used to update the Fields collection manually, to reflect the current columns. You shouldn't need to use the Refresh() method with the Fields collection. Table C-6 lists the properties supported by the Field object. The Field object provides two methods, which are used to store and retrieve large text and binary-type column data. The AppendChunk() method is used to store large field data, and the GetChunk() method is used to retrieve large field data. These methods can be used to manipulate this data one piece at a time.

TABLE C-6 FIELD OBJECT PROPERTIES

Property	Read/Write	Description
ActualSize	R	The actual length of the column, if it's known.
Attributes	R	The properties of the field. Can be used to determine whether the field has a fixed length or can be set to a null value.

Continued

TABLE C-6 FIELD OBJECT PROPERTIES *(continued)*

Property	Read/Write	Description
DefinedSize	R	The maximum length of the column.
Name	R	The name of the column.
NumericScale	R	The number of places to the right of the decimal in floating-point values.
OriginalValue	R	The original value of a column. This is the value that the column had before any changes.
Precision	R	The total number of digits used to represent a numeric value.
Type	R	The type of the column, which *must* be one of the DataTypeEnum constants.
UnderlyingValue	R	The current value the column actually has at the data source. Used when synchronizing a column with transactions.
Value	R/W	The value of the field. Used to set and retrieve the column value.

Parameter Object

The Parameter object encapsulates a command parameter. A command parameter can be an input, output, or input/output type. The Parameter object can be used to specify the parameter name, value, attribute, direction, precision, scale, size, and type. A Parameter object can also represent BLOB-type parameters. Parameters can be used with parameterized queries and stored procedures. The Parameters object provides two properties. The Count property returns the number of Parameter objects contained in the collection. The Item property returns the Parameter object at the specified index, without requiring the use of the Item() method; Table C-7 lists the properties supported by the Parameter object.

Table C-8 lists the methods supported by the Parameters object. The Parameter object provides just one method, the AppendChunk() method, which has already been reviewed. Parameters can be used to pass BLOB-type information to commands and queries. The AppendChunk() method is used to store large text and binary information in a parameter. Before the AppendChunk() method can be used, though, the Parameter object's Attribute property must have the adFldLong flag set.

TABLE **C-7** PARAMETER OBJECT PROPERTIES

Property	Read/Write	Description
Attributes	R/W	The properties of the parameter. Can be used to determine whether the field has a fixed length or can be set to a null value.
Direction	R/W	Specifies whether the property is used for input, output, or input and output.
Name	R/W	The name of the parameter. After a Parameter has been added to the Parameters collection, its name can't be changed.
NumericScale	R/W	The number of places to the right of the decimal in floating-point values.
Precision	R/W	The total number of digits used to represent a numeric value.
Size	R/W	The maximum size of the parameter (in bytes).
Type	R/W	The type of the parameter, which *must* be one of the DataTypeEnum constants.
Value	R/W	The value of the parameter. Used to set and retrieve the non-BLOB parameter values.

TABLE **C-8** PARAMETERS OBJECT METHODS

Method	Description
Refresh()	Retrieves provider parameter information for the stored procedure or parameterized query specified in the Command object.
Append()	Adds a new Parameter to the Parameters collection.
Delete()	Removes a Parameter from the Parameters collection.

Property Object

The Property object is used to determine whether a data provider supports an ADO object property, and then to set and retrieve its value. While some of the ADO object properties are required, some objects provide optional properties. A Property object encapsulates each ADO object property. Each of these property objects are contained in a Properties object collection. Table C-9 lists the properties that are supported by the Property object. The Property object doesn't provide any methods. The Properties object provides two properties. The Count property returns the number of Property objects contained in the collection. The Item property returns the Property object at the specified index. You don't need to use the Item() method directly. The Properties object provides one method, Refresh(), which can be used to synchronize an ADO object's optional properties with a data provider. Calling the Refresh() method fills the Properties collection. You don't need to call the Refresh() method explicitly, because accessing the Properties collection for the first time also causes the collection to be populated.

TABLE C-9 PROPERTY OBJECT PROPERTIES

Property	Read/Write	Description
Attribute	R	Describes the attributes of the property.
Name	R	Returns the name of the property.
Type	R	Returns the data type of the property value.
Value	R/W	Used to set or return the property's value.

Recordset Object

The Recordset object, which is the heart of ADO, can be created independently. The Recordset object can be used to access column-level data, specify a cursor, navigate a collection of records, update records in a batch mode, add and delete new records, and apply filters to records that are returned. The Recordset object can be used to establish a direct connection with a data provider The Recordset object encapsulates a collection of Field objects, which can be used to access column-level data. Table C-10 lists the properties supported by the Recordset object. Table C-11 lists the methods supported by the Recordset object.

TABLE C-10 RECORDSET OBJECT PROPERTIES

Property	Read/Write	Description
AbsolutePage	R/W	Used to set or determine the current record set page.
AbsolutePosition	R/W	Used to set or determine the current record position.
ActiveConnection	R/W	Used to set or determine the current Connection object.
BOF	R	Returns True if the current record position is at or before the beginning of the record set.
Bookmark	R/W	Used to set or return a bookmark to the current record.
CacheSize	R/W	Used to determine the number of records currently cached. When using forward-only-type cursors, this value is 1. With all other cursors, this value is 10.
CursorType	R/W	Used to set or determine the current cursor type.
EditMode	R	Used to determine the current edit mode.
EOF	R	Returns True if the current record position is after or at the end of the record set.
Filter	R/W	Used to specify a filter that is applied when navigating the record set.
LockType	R/W	Used to set or determine the current locking mode.
MaxRecords	R/W	Used to set or determine the maximum number of records returned by a query. By default, this value is 0, which indicates no limit.
PageCount	R	Used to determine the number of pages used by the record set.

Continued

TABLE C-10 RECORDSET OBJECT PROPERTIES *(continued)*

Property	Read/Write	Description
PageSize	R/W	Used to set or determine the number of records.
RecordCount	R	Returns the number of records contained in the record set.
Source	R	Returns the source of the records contained in the record set.
Status	R	Returns the status of the current record.

TABLE C-11 RECORDSET OBJECT METHODS

Method	Description
AddNew()	Adds a new record to a record set.
CancelBatch()	Cancels a batch update, before the UpdateBatch() is called.
CancelUpdate()	Cancels any changes made to a record, before the Update() method is called.
Clone()	Creates a new Recordset object that contains a copy of the current Recordset object.
Close()	Closes the current Recordset object connection.
Delete()	Deletes the current record.
GetRows()	Used to retrieve a number of rows from a record set into an array.
Move()	Used to move to a specific record.
MoveFirst()	Used to move to the first record of the record set.
MoveLast()	Used to move to the last record of the record set.
MoveNext()	Used to move to the next record of the record set.
MovePrevious()	Used to move to the previous record of the record set.

Method	Description
NextRecordset()	Retrieves the next record set of a query or stored procedure that returns multiple record sets.
Open()	Used to open a new Recordset object connection to a data source.
Requery()	Re-executes the current query.
Supports()	Determines whether a Recordset objects supports specific methods or properties.
Update()	Any changes to the current record are written back.
UpdateBatch()	Any changes to the current batch of records are written back.

Appendix D

SQL Server Error Codes

DATABASE APPLICATIONS THAT access Microsoft SQL Server can generate a variety of errors. Table D-1 lists and describes the errors that can be generated by Microsoft SQL Server 6.5. The severity column is used to determine the seriousness of the SQL Server error – the greater the value, the more serious the error.

TABLE **D-1** MICROSOFT SQL SERVER-GENERATED ERROR CODES

Error Number	Severity	Message Returned
1	10	Version Date of last upgrade: 10/11/90.
21	10	WARNING—Fatal Error %d occurred at %S_DATE. Please note the error and time, and contact your System Administrator.
101	15	Line %d: SQL syntax error.
102	15	Incorrect syntax near '%.*s'.
103	15	The %S_MSG that starts with '%.*s' is too long. Maximum length is %d.
104	15	Order-by items must appear in the select-list if the statement contains set operators.
105	15	Unclosed quote before the character string '%.*s'.
106	16	Too many table names in the query. The maximum allowable is %d.
107	15	The column prefix '%.*s' does not match with a table name or alias name used in the query.

Continued

TABLE D-1 MICROSOFT SQL SERVER-GENERATED ERROR CODES *(continued)*

Error Number	Severity	Message Returned
108	15	The order-by position number '%ld' is out of range of the number of items in the select-list.
109	15	There are more columns in the INSERT statement than values specified in the VALUES clause. The number of values in the VALUES clause must match the number of columns specified in the INSERT statement.
110	15	There are fewer columns in the INSERT statement than values specified in the VALUES clause. The number of values in the VALUES clause must match the number of columns specified in the INSERT statement.
111	15	%s must be the first command in a query batch.
112	15	Variables are not allowed in %s statement.
113	15	Missing end comment mark '*/'.
114	15	Browse mode is invalid for a statement that assigns values to a variable.
115	15	The offset '%d' given in a CONTROLROW command does not correspond to the beginning of a statement.
116	15	The symbol '*' can only be used for a subquery select list when the subquery is introduced with EXISTS or NOT EXISTS.
117	15	The %S_MSG name '%.*s' contains more than the maximum number of prefixes. The maximum is %d.
118	15	Only System Administrator can specify %s option for %s command.

Error Number	Severity	Message Returned
119	15	Must pass parameter number %d and subsequent parameters as '@name = value'. Once the form '@name = value' has been used, all subsequent parameters must be passed in the form '@name = value'.
120	15	The SELECT list for the INSERT statement contains fewer items than the INSERT list. The number of SELECT values must match the number of INSERT columns.
121	15	The SELECT list for the INSERT statement contains more items than the INSERT list. The number of SELECT values must match the number of INSERT columns.
122	15	The debug option '%d' is larger than the maximum allowed. The highest option available is %d.
123	15	Must attach a value to the binary prefix '0x'; zero-length binary value is not allowed.
124	15	CREATE PROCEDURE contains no statements.
125	15	Case expressions may only be nested to level %d.
126	15	Cannot nest CREATE PROCEDURE statements.
127	15	This CREATE may only contain 1 statement.
128	15	The name '%.*s' is illegal in this context. Only constants, constant expressions, or variables allowed here. Column names are illegal.
129	15	Fillfactor '%d' is not a valid percentage; fillfactor must be between 1 and 100.
130	16	Cannot perform an aggregate function on an expression containing an aggregate or a subquery.

Continued

TABLE D-1 MICROSOFT SQL SERVER-GENERATED ERROR CODES *(continued)*

Error Number	Severity	Message Returned
131	15	The size (%d) given to the %S_MSG '%.*s' exceeds the maximum. The largest size allowed is %d.
132	15	The label '%.*s': has already been declared. Label names must be unique within a query batch or stored procedure
133	15	A GOTO statement references the label '%.*s' but the label has not been declared.
134	15	The variable name '%.*s' has already been declared. Variable names must be unique within a query batch or stored procedure.
135	15	Cannot use a BREAK statement outside the scope of a WHILE statement.
136	15	Cannot use a CONTINUE statement outside the scope of a WHILE statement.
137	15	Must declare variable '%.*s'.
138	15	Illegal correlation clause in a subquery.
139	15	Cannot assign a default value to a local variable.
140	15	Can only use IF UPDATE within a CREATE TRIGGER.
141	15	A SELECT statement that assigns a value to a variable must not be combined with data-retrieval operations.
142	15	Incorrect syntax for definition of %s constraint.
143	15	A compute-by item was not found in the order-by list. All expressions in the compute-by list must also be present in the order-by list.

Error Number	Severity	Message Returned
144	15	Cannot use an aggregate or a subquery in an expression used for the by-list of a GROUP BY clause.
145	15	Order-by items must appear in the select-list if SELECT DISTINCT is specified.
146	16	Too many subqueries in the query. The maximum allowable is %d.
147	15	An aggregate may not appear in the WHERE clause unless it is in a subquery contained in a HAVING clause or a select list, and the column being aggregated is an outer reference.
148	15	Incorrect time syntax in time string '%.*s' used with WAITFOR.
149	15	Time value '%.*s' used with WAITFOR is not a legal value. Check date/time syntax.
150	15	Both terms of an outer join must contain columns.
151	15	'%.*s' is an invalid money value.
152	15	Subqueries that use DISTINCT with a GROUP BY clause are not currently supported.
153	15	Invalid usage of the option '%.*s' in '%s' statement.
154	15	%S_MSG is not allowed in %S_MSG.
155	15	'%.*s' is not a recognized %s option.
156	15	Incorrect syntax near the keyword '%.*s'.
157	15	An aggregate may not appear in the set list of an update statement.
158	15	Too many ORDER BY expressions. The maximum is %d.

Continued

TABLE D-1 MICROSOFT SQL SERVER-GENERATED ERROR CODES *(continued)*

Error Number	Severity	Message Returned
159	15	For DROP INDEX, must give both the table and the index name, in the form tablename.indexname.
160	15	Rule does not contain a variable.
161	15	Rule contains more than one variable.
162	15	The select list item identified by the order by number '%ld' is a '*', rather than a column name. When ordering by column number, a column name must appear in the select list position that corresponds to the order by number.
163	15	The COMPUTE BY list does not match the ORDER BY list.
164	15	GROUP BY expressions must refer to column names that appear in the SELECT list.
165	16	Privilege %s may not be GRANTed or REVOKEd.
166	15	%s does not allow specifying the database name as a prefix to the object name.
167	16	May not create a trigger on a temporary object.
168	15	The %S_MSG '%.*s' is out of the range of machine representation (%d bytes).
169	15	Column '%.*s' is specified more than once in the ORDER BY list. Columns in the ORDER BY list must be unique.
170	15	Line %d: Incorrect syntax near '%.*s'.
171	15	Can't use SELECT INTO in Browse Mode.
172	15	Can't use HOLDLOCK in Browse Mode
173	15	The definition for column '%.*s' must include a datatype.

Error Number	Severity	Message Returned
174	15	The function '%.*s' requires %d arguments.
175	15	Functions may only be nested to level %d.
176	15	Function '%.*s' is not yet implemented.
177	15	The IDENTITY function can only be used when the SELECT statement has an INTO clause.
178	15	A RETURN statement with a return status may only be used in a stored procedure.
179	15	Can't use the OUTPUT option when passing a constant to a stored procedure.
180	15	There are too many parameters in this CREATE PROCEDURE statement. The maximum number is %d.
181	15	Can't use the OUTPUT option in a DECLARE statement.
182	15	Table and column names must be supplied for the READTEXT or WRITETEXT utility.
183	15	The scale (%d) for column '%.*s' must be within the range %d to %d.
184	15	Invalid money datatype specification for column '%.*s'. Only money(19, 4) is allowed for non-external tables.
185	15	Data stream is invalid for WRITETEXT command in bulk form.
186	15	Data stream missing from WRITETEXT command.
187	15	Odd number of bytes in IMAGE data.
188	15	Can't specify a log-device in a CREATE DATABASE statement without also specifying at least one non-log-device.
189	15	Function '%.*s' requires %d to %d arguments.

Continued

TABLE **D-1 MICROSOFT SQL SERVER–GENERATED ERROR CODES** (continued)

Error Number	Severity	Message Returned
190	15	Cannot update the global variable '%.*s'.
191	15	Some part of your SQL statement is nested too deeply. Please re-write the query or break it up into smaller queries.
192	15	Constant expressions are not allowed in ORDER BY lists.
193	15	The object or column name starting with '%.*s' is too long. The maximum length is %d characters.
194	15	A SELECT INTO statement may not contain a SELECT statement that assigns values to a variable.
195	15	'%.*s' is not a recognized %S_MSG.
196	15	SELECT INTO must be the first query in a SQL statement containing set operators.
197	15	Set operators may not appear within the definition of a view.
198	15	Browse mode is invalid for statements containing set operators.
199	15	An INSERT statement may not contain a SELECT statement that assigns values to a variable.
201	16	Procedure %.*s expects parameter %.*s, which was not supplied.
202	11	Internal error—Unable to open table at query execution time.
203	16	The name '%.*s' is not a valid identifier.
204	20	Normalization error; node %s.
205	16	All queries in an SQL statement containing set operators must have an equal number of expressions in their target lists.

Error Number	Severity	Message Returned
206	16	Operand type clash: %s is incompatible with %s.
207	16	Invalid column name '%.*s'.
208	16	Invalid object name '%.*s'.
209	16	Ambiguous column name %.*s.
210	16	Syntax error converting DATETIME from BINARY/VARBINARY string.
211	16	Syntax error converting SMALLDATETIME from BINARY/VARBINARY string.
212	16	Expression result length exceeds maximum: max—%d found—%d.
213	16	Insert error: column name or number of supplied values does not match table definition.
214	16	Cannot convert parameter %.*s to type %.*s expected by procedure.
216	16	Attempt to drop temporary object(s) failed during cleanup processing.
217	16	Maximum stored procedure nesting level exceeded (limit %d).
218	16	Given parameter %.*s is too large; maximum size for this parameter is %d bytes.
219	16	Print format failed to match with a result column.
220	16	Arithmetic overflow error for type %s, value = %ld.
222	20	Unintelligible query plan step encountered.
223	11	Object %ld specified as a default for tabid %ld, colid %d is missing or not of type default.

Continued

TABLE **D-1** MICROSOFT SQL SERVER–GENERATED ERROR CODES *(continued)*

Error Number	Severity	Message Returned
224	11	Object %ld specified as a rule for tabid %ld, colid %d is missing or not of type default.
225	11	Cannot run query—referenced object (name %.*s) dropped during query optimization.
226	16	%s command not allowed within multi-statement transaction.
227	16	Maximum number of vector aggregates exceeded (%d max, %d found).
228	14	Query is based on a view that no longer exists (id = %ld)—cannot run.
229	14	%s permission denied on object %.*s, database %.*s, owner %.*s.
230	14	%s permission denied on column %.*s of object %.*s, database %.*s, owner %.*s.
231	11	Getdefault: no such default. id=%ld dbid=%d.
232	16	Arithmetic overflow error for type %s, value = %f.
233	16	The column %.*s in table %.*s may not be null.
234	16	There is insufficient result space to convert MONEY value to CHAR.
235	16	Cannot convert CHAR value to MONEY. The CHAR value has incorrect syntax.
236	16	The conversion from CHAR to MONEY resulted in a MONEY overflow error.
237	16	There is insufficient result space to convert MONEY value to %s.
238	16	There is insufficient result space to convert %s value (= %d) to MONEY.

Error Number	Severity	Message Returned
239	16	Table '%.*s' does not exist. Please refer to Sysobjects for correct name.
240	16	There is insufficient result space to convert DATETIME value to CHAR.
241	16	Syntax error converting DATETIME from character string.
242	16	The conversion of CHAR to DATETIME resulted in a DATETIME value out of range.
243	16	Type '%.*s' is not a defined system type.
244	16	The conversion of CHAR value '%.*s' overflowed an INT1 field, use a larger integer field.
245	16	Syntax error converting CHAR value '%.*s' to an INT1 field.
246	16	The conversion of CHAR value '%.*s' overflowed an INT2 field, use a larger integer field.
247	16	Syntax error converting CHAR value '%.*s' to an INT2 field.
248	16	The conversion of CHAR value '%.*s' overflowed an INT4 field. Maximum integer value exceeded.
249	16	Syntax error converting CHAR value '%.*s' to an INT4 field.
251	16	Unable to allocate ancillary table for query optimization. Maximum number of tables in a query (%d) exceeded.
252	16	Can't group by a bit field.
253	16	Maximum number of group-by expressions exceeded (16 max, %d found).
254	16	Maximum number of columns in a work table (%d) exceeded.

Continued

TABLE D-1 MICROSOFT SQL SERVER-GENERATED ERROR CODES *(continued)*

Error Number	Severity	Message Returned
255	16	Maximum row size (%d) for a work table exceeded.
256	16	The data type '%s' is invalid for the %s function. Allowed types are: CHAR/VARCHAR and BINARY/VARBINARY.
257	16	Implicit conversion from datatype '%s' to '%s' is not allowed. Use the CONVERT function to run this query.
258	20	Database '%.*s' missing during query recompile.
259	16	Ad-hoc updates to system catalogs not enabled. System Administrator must reconfigure system to allow this.
260	16	Disallowed implicit conversion from datatype '%s' to datatype '%s'%s Table: '%s', Column: '%s'%s. Use the CONVERT function to run this query.
261	16	'%.*s' is not a recognized global variable.
262	16	%s permission denied, database %.*s, owner %.*s.
263	16	Must specify table to SELECT * FROM.
264	16	Column name %.*s appears more than once in the result column list.
265	16	Syntax error converting CHAR value '%.*s' to a BIT field. Field contains non-numeric value(s).
266	16	Transaction count after EXECUTE indicates that a COMMIT or ROLLBACK TRAN is missing. Previous count = %ld, Current count = %ld.
267	16	Object '%.*s' cannot be found.

Error Number	Severity	Message Returned
268	16	You can't run SELECT INTO in this database. Please check with the Database Owner.
269	16	SETUSER with no name should be invoked from the database where the corresponding SETUSER with name was issued. Use database '%.*s'.
270	16	Table '%.*s' can't be modified.
272	16	Can't update a TIMESTAMP column.
273	16	The user can't INSERT a non-null value into a TIMESTAMP column. Use INSERT with a column list or with a default of NULL for the TIMESTAMP column.
274	20	A SYSTEM exception was raised with an unrecognized minor number %d.
275	16	TEXT and IMAGE datatypes may not be used in an aggregate expression.
276	16	The parameter '%.*s' in the procedure '%.*s' was not declared as an OUTPUT parameter.
277	23	A transaction begun in this stored procedure that did updates in tempdb is still active. This will cause a corruption of tempdb that will exist until the server is rebooted. All BEGIN TRANs must have matching COMMITs or ROLLBACKs.
278	16	TEXT and IMAGE datatypes may not be used in a GROUP BY clause.
279	16	TEXT and IMAGE datatypes are invalid in this subquery or aggregate expression.
280	16	Only TEXT and IMAGE datatypes are valid with the TEXTPTR function.

Continued

TABLE D-1 MICROSOFT SQL SERVER-GENERATED ERROR CODES *(continued)*

Error Number	Severity	Message Returned
281	16	%d is not a valid style number when converting from DATETIME to a character string.
282	10	Procedure '%.*s' attempted to return a status of NULL, which is not allowed. A status of 0 will be returned instead.
283	16	You can't use browse mode with DBLIB 2.0— you must upgrade to DBLIB 4.0 in order to run this query.
284	16	Rules may not be bound to TEXT or IMAGE datatypes.
285	16	READTEXT and WRITETEXT commands may not be used with views.
286	16	The logical tables INSERTED and DELETED may not be updated.
287	16	%s command not allowed within a trigger.
288	16	The PATINDEX function operates on CHAR, VARCHAR, and TEXT datatypes only.
290	16	Trace 3604 is illegal within a stored procedure.
292	16	There is insufficient result space to convert SMALLMONEY value to CHAR.
293	16	Cannot convert CHAR value to SMALLMONEY. The CHAR value has incorrect syntax.
294	16	The conversion from CHAR to SMALLMONEY resulted in a SMALLMONEY overflow error.
295	16	Syntax error converting SMALLDATETIME from character string.
296	16	The conversion of CHAR to SMALLDATETIME resulted in a SMALLDATETIME value out of range.

Error Number	Severity	Message Returned
297	16	There is insufficient result space to convert SMALLDATETIME value to CHAR.
298	16	The conversion from DATETIME to SMALLDATETIME resulted in a SMALLDATETIME overflow error.
299	16	The function DATEADD was called with bad type '%s'.
301	16	Query contains an illegal outer-join request.
303	16	The table '%.*s' is an inner member of an outer-join clause. This is not allowed if the table also participates in a regular join clause.
304	16	The table '%.*s' is outer-joined with itself.
305	16	The column '%.*s' (user type:%.*s) is joined with '%.*s' (user type:%.*s). The user types are not compatible: user types must be identical in order to join.
306	16	TEXT and IMAGE datatypes may not be used in the WHERE or HAVING clause, except with the LIKE predicate and the IS NULL predicate.
307	16	Index id %d on table '%.*s' (specified in the FROM clause) does not exist.
308	16	Index '%.*s' on table '%.*s' (specified in the FROM clause) does not exist.
309	16	Unable to allocate ancillary table for reformatting. Maximum number of tables in a query (%d) exceeded.
401	16	Unimplemented command or expression %s.
403	16	Invalid operator for datatype op: %s type: %s.

Continued

TABLE D-1 MICROSOFT SQL SERVER-GENERATED ERROR CODES *(continued)*

Error Number	Severity	Message Returned
404	19	Too many ANDs or ORs in expression (limit %d per expression level). Try splitting query or limiting ANDs and ORs.
405	20	Cannot route query results—query internal representation corrupted.
406	23	Ord_needed: Can't find index for varno=%d, objid=%ld.
407	19	Unable to allocate ancillary table for query optimization. Maximum number of tables in a query (%d) exceeded.
408	20	Is_var: Unknown data type %d.
409	16	The %s operation cannot take a %s datatype as an argument.
410	20	Compute clause #%d, 'by' expression #%d is not in the order-by list.
411	20	Compute clause #%d, aggregate expression #%d is not in the select list.
412	16	Cannot update more than 1 Sysindexes row at a time.
414	16	The current query would generate a key size of %d for a work table. This exceeds the maximum allowable limit of %d.
415	16	The current query would require an index on a work table to be built with %d keys. The maximum allowable number of keys is %d.
416	16	Create of work table failed because the row size would be %d. This exceeds the maximum allowable size of a row in a table, %ld.
418	20	Can't find the real column name corresponding to the column heading '%.*s'.

Error Number	Severity	Message Returned
420	16	TEXT and IMAGE datatypes may not be used in an ORDER BY clause.
421	16	TEXT and IMAGE datatypes may not be selected as DISTINCT.
422	19	Too many nested expressions or logical operators to compile. Try splitting query or limiting ANDs and ORs.
423	16	Too many substitution nodes in worktable. (MAX: %d, ACTUAL: %d). Try splitting query or limiting SELECT list.
425	16	Datatype '%s' of receiving variable not equal to datatype '%s' of column '%.*s'.
426	16	Length '%d' of receiving variable less than length '%d' of column '%.*s'.
427	20	Unable to load SYSPROCEDURES entries for constraint id '%d' in dbid '%d'.
428	20	Unable to find row in SYSCONSTRAINTS for constraint id '%d' in dbid '%d'.
429	20	Unable to find new constraint id '%d' in SYSCONSTRAINTS, dbid '%d' at compile time.
430	20	Unable to resolve table name for object id '%d', dbid '%d' when compiling foreign key.
431	19	Unable to bind foreign key constraint. Too many tables involved in query.
432	19	Unable to bind work table for foreign key constraint. Too many tables involved in query.
433	20	Unable to find CHECK constraint for '%.*s' though table is flagged as having one.
434	20	Insert into worktable for variable '%d' for deferred constraint check failed.

(Continued)

TABLE D-1 MICROSOFT SQL SERVER–GENERATED ERROR CODES *(continued)*

Error Number	Severity	Message Returned
435	20	Unable to open referencing table id '%d' in dbid '%d'.
436	20	Unable to open referenced table id '%d' in dbid '%d'.
437	20	Unable to resolve the referenced column name in table id '%d'.
438	20	Unable to resolve the referencing column name in table id '%d'.
439	20	Unable to find foreign key constraints for table '%.*s' in dbid '%d' though table is flagged as having them.
440	20	Unable to resolve column name for dbid '%d', object id, '%d', column id '%d' in constraint '%.*s'.
501	20	There is no result-list for a SELECT statement.
502	18	Internal error encountered in merging rows; resubmit query batch.
503	16	Stored procedure '%.*s' is a replication filter and cannot be executed.
504	11	Stored procedure '%.*s' not found.
505	16	Current user account was invoked with SETUSER. Changing databases is not allowed.
508	20	No begin-row pointer found in plan.
509	11	User name '%.*s' not found.
510	20	Bad eop type 0x%x.
511	16	Updated or inserted row is bigger than maximum size (%d bytes) allowed for this table.

Error Number	Severity	Message Returned
512	16	Subquery returned more than 1 value. This is illegal when the subquery follows =, !=, <, <= , >, >=, or when the subquery is used as an expression.
513	16	A column insert or update conflicts with a rule imposed by a previous CREATE RULE command. The command was aborted. The conflict occurred in database '%.*s', table '%.*s', column '%.*s'
514	16	Expression stack overflow. Usually this is because built-in functions have been nested too deeply. Try to rephrase the query using less deeply nested functions.
515	16	Attempt to insert the value NULL into column '%.*s', table '%.*s'; column does not allow nulls. %s fails.
516	18	Attempt to get system date/time failed.
517	16	Adding a value to a %s field caused overflow.
518	16	Cannot convert type '%s' to type '%s'.
519	16	Overflow resulted from MONEY multiplication.
520	16	Overflow resulted from MONEY division.
521	16	Overflow resulted from MONEY addition.
522	16	Overflow resulted from MONEY subtraction.
523	16	Overflow resulted from %s minus operation
524	16	Overflow resulted from MONEY remainder (modulo) operation.
526	18	SQL Server has run out of alarms. Re-run your command when there are fewer users running WAITFOR.
527	20	Cannot remove alarm.

Continued

TABLE D-1 MICROSOFT SQL SERVER-GENERATED ERROR CODES (continued)

Error Number	Severity	Message Returned
528	20	System error detected during attempt to use upsleep system call.
529	16	Explicit conversion from datatype '%s' to '%s' is currently unimplemented.
530	16	Attempt to insert NULL value into column %d in work table (table id %ld); column does not allow NULLS. %s fails.
532	16	The timestamp (changed to %.*s) shows that the row has been updated by another user.
533	20	Can't find a range table entry for range %d.
534	16	TEXT and IMAGE datatypes require DBLIB version 4.0 or greater.
535	16	Difference of two datetime fields caused overflow at runtime.
536	16	Invalid length parameter passed to the substring function.
537	16	Overflow resulted from a SMALLMONEY remainder operation.
538	16	'%.*s' cannot be found. This language might have been dropped. Please see your System Administrator.
540	1	Schema for table '%.*s' has changed since compilation of this query. Please re-execute query.
542	16	An invalid datetime value was encountered. Value exceeds year 9999.
544	16	Attempting to insert explicit value for identity column in table '%.*s' when IDENTITY_INSERT is set to OFF.

Error Number	Severity	Message Returned
545	16	Explicit value must be specified for identity column in table '%.*s' when IDENTITY_INSERT is set to ON.
546	16	Identity value overflow for column '%.*s' while inserting into table '%.*s'.
547	16	%s statement conflicted with %s %s constraint '%.*s'. The conflict occurred in database '%.*s', table '%.*s'%s%.*s%s.
548	16	Attempt to perform direct %s to range that is maintained by replication. The conflict occurred in database '%.*s', table '%.*s'%s%.*s%s.
549	16	Data exists in table '%.*s', database '%.*s', that violates %s constraint '%.*s' being added. ALTER command has been aborted.
550	16	The attempted insert or update failed because the target view either specifies WITH CHECK OPTION or spans a view which specifies WITH CHECK OPTION and one or more rows resulting from the operation did not qualify under the CHECK OPTION constraint.
601	21	Descriptor for system table '%ld' in database '%d' not found in the descriptor hash table.
602	21	Could not find row in Sysindexes for dbid '%d', object '%ld',index '%d'. Run DBCC CHECKTABLE on Sysindexes.
603	19	There are not enough system session descriptors available to run this query. The maximum number available to a process is %d. Split query and rerun.
604	21	Could not find row in Sysobjects for object '%ld' in database '%.*s'. Run DBCC checktable on Sysobjects.

Continued

TABLE D-1 MICROSOFT SQL SERVER–GENERATED ERROR CODES *(continued)*

Error Number	Severity	Message Returned
605	21	Attempt to fetch logical page %ld in database '%.*s' belongs to object '%.*s', not to object '%.*s'.
606	16	Error %d encountered while reading without locking, command is terminated.
607	21	Insufficient room was allocated in the session descriptor for object '%.*s' for search arguments. Only %d search arguments were anticipated.
608	21	Buffer holding logical page %ld of object '%.*s' in database '%.*s' was not kept in the first or second slot of the session descriptor for that object during a scan.
610	19	Maximum number of databases that may be accessed by a transaction is 8. This number has been exceeded by this query.
611	21	Attempt made to end a transaction that is idle or in the middle of an update.
612	21	Attempt made to log a row of unknown type %d.
613	21	Request made to retrieve more rows from an already completed scan of object '%.*s' in database '%.*s'.
614	21	A row on page %ld was accessed that has an illegal length of %d in database '%.*s'.
615	21	Unable to find database table id = %d, name = '%.*s'.
616	20	Attempt to hash a previously hashed descriptor for object '%.*s' in database '%.*s'.
617	20	Descriptor for object '%ld' in database '%d' not found in the hash table during attempt to unhash it.

Error Number	Severity	Message Returned
618	21	A varno of %d was passed to opentable— the largest valid value is %d.
619	20	A deferred update was requested but the query is not one of INSERT, DELETE, or UPDATE.
620	21	Log record encountered at deferred update time with either a row length of less than 2 or an invalid log type. The log type was %d and the row length was %d.
621	21	A log record was encountered of type %d that is not one of the valid deallocation types.
622	20	Opentable was passed a varno of %d. Object '%.*s' already has that session descriptor in use.
623	21	Attempt to retrieve row from page via RID failed because logical page %ld is not a data page. %S_RID. %S_PAGE.
624	21	Attempt to retrieve row from page via RID failed because the requested RID has a higher number than the last RID on the page. %S_RID.%S_PAGE.
625	21	Could not retrieve row from logical page %ld via RID because the entry in the offset table (= %d) for that RID (= %d) is less than or equal to 0.
626	21	Tried to read a data page instead of an index page. %S_PAGE.
627	20	A transaction tried to call beginupdate while in state 'prepare'.
628	13	Attempt to issue 'SAVE TRANsaction' when there is no active transaction.
629	21	Fatal attempt to delete clustered index entry for page %ld—index row contains page %ld

Continued

TABLE **D-1** MICROSOFT SQL SERVER–GENERATED ERROR CODES *(continued)*

Error Number	Severity	Message Returned
630	21	The end of page limit has been exceeded while building an offset table for object %ld on page %ld.
631	21	The length of %d passed to delete row routine for the row at offset %d is incorrect on the following page: %S_PAGE.
632	20	Memmove() was called with a length of %d—maximum allowed length is 2048.
633	21	The PG_DEALLOC bit set by recovery is on at runtime on the following page. %S_PAGE.
634	20	Memmove() was called with an address of 0x%lx and a length of %d—which would cross a 2k boundary.
635	20	Process %d tried to remove DES resource lock that it doesn't hold—%S_DES.
637	20	Index shrink program returned invalid status of 0.
638	20	Memmove() was called with an address of 0x%lx—which is not allocated memory.
639	21	Attempt to fetch logical page %ld dbid %d failed—page is not currently allocated.
640	21	Attempt to insert/delete row on wrong type of page. %S_PAGE.
641	21	Attempt to add BEGINUPDATE record in transaction %S_RID that already has an active CMD.
642	20	Attempt to begin update in transaction %S_RID which already has an active transaction.
643	20	Attempt to read page %d in database '%.*s' which is not allocated.

Error Number	Severity	Message Returned
644	21	The non_clustered leaf row entry for page %ld row %d was not found in index page %ld indexid %d database '%.*s'
649	21	Could not find the clustered index entry for Page %ld Objid %ld status 0x%x. Index page %ld was searched for this entry in database '%.*s'.
701	19	There is insufficient system memory to run this query.
702	20	Memory request for %d bytes exceeds the size of single page of %d bytes.
704	20	Tried to free procedure header 0x%lx, but it's still in use by procedure '%.*s' at procedure buffer 0x%lx.
705	19	There is no room for process %d to store PROC_HDR 0x%lx in Pss.
706	20	Process %d tried to remove PROC_HDR 0x%lx that it does not hold in Pss.
707	20	System error detected during attempt to free memory at address 0x%lx. Please consult the SQL Server error log for more details.
801	20	Process %d tried to remove resource lock it doesn't hold on buffer 0x%lx−%S_PAGE.
803	20	Unable to place buffer 0x%lx holding logical page %ld in sdes for object '%.*s'—either there is no room in sdes or buffer already in requested slot.
804	20	Unable to find buffer 0x%lx holding logical page %ld in sdes 0x%lx kept buffer pool for object '%.*s'.
805	21	Unable to find descriptor for object '%.*s' in database '%.*s' in hash table when marking buffer dirty or flushing Syslogs.

Continued

TABLE **D-1 MICROSOFT SQL SERVER–GENERATED ERROR CODES** *(continued)*

Error Number	Severity	Message Returned
806	21	Could not find virtual page for logical page %ld in database '%.*s'.
807	10	Logical page %ld in buffer 0x%lx already kept in SDES for object '%.*s' in database '%.*s'.
808	20	Alloc page buffer pool in Pss is full— logical pages %ld, %ld, and %ld in respective databases '%.*s', '%.*s', and '%.*s' are already held there. Cannot add logical page %ld in database '%.*s'.
809	20	Buffer 0x%lx, alloc pg %ld, in database '%.*s' not in alloc buf pool in Pss.
810	20	Attempt to pin log page buffer.
811	21	Attempt to grab buffer which is on descriptor chain.
812	21	Attempt to grab a pinned buffer.
813	20	Logical page 0x%lx in database %d is already hashed.
814	20	Keep count of buffer 0x%lx holding logical page %ld in database %.*s has become negative.
815	21	Unable to find buffer holding Sysindexes page in the cache—pageno = %ld dbid = %d.
816	20	Process %d tried to remove a buffer resource lock %S_BUF that it does not hold in SDES %S_SDES.
817	20	Process %d tried to remove a buffer resource lock %S_BUF that it does not hold in Pss 0x%lx.
818	19	There is no room to hold the buffer resource lock %S_BUF in SDES %S_SDES.
819	19	There is no room for process %d to hold buffer resource lock %S_BUF in Pss.

Error Number	Severity	Message Returned
820	21	Attempt to dirty non-log buffer %S_BUF which is in I/O.
821	20	Attempt to unhash buffer at 0x%lx with a buffer pageno of %ld and database id %d with HASHED status set failed—buffer was not found. %S_PAGE.
822	21	Could not start I/O for request %S_BLKIOPTR.
823	24	I/O error detected during %S_MSG for %S_BUF.
824	21	Attempt made to write page in buffer in database that has no entry in Sysdatabases. %S_BUF.
825	21	Attempt made to write page in buffer in database with no DBTABLE structure— Sysdatabases row marked as in use by process %d. %S_BUF.
826	20	Attempt made to hold allocation page %ld that is already in Pss pool. Database '%.*s'.
827	20	Attempt to dirty page %ld which is not kept in database '%.*s.
840	17	Device '%.*s' (with physical name '%.*s', and virtual device number %d) is not available. Please contact System Administrator for assistance.
901	21	Unable to find descriptor for database '%d' object '%ld' in hash table after hashing it.
902	24	Hardware error detected reading logical page %ld, virtual page %ld in database '%.*s'.

Continued

TABLE **D-1** MICROSOFT SQL SERVER–GENERATED ERROR CODES *(continued)*

Error Number	Severity	Message Returned
903	22	Unable to find row in Sysindexes for clustered index on system catalog %ld in database %d. This index should exist in all databases. Run DBCC CHECKTABLE on Sysindexes in the database.
904	22	Unable to find master database row in Sysdatabases. Cannot open master database.
905	17	Unable to allocate a DBTABLE descriptor to open database '%.*s'. Another database must be closed or dropped before opening this one.
906	22	Could not locate row in Sysobjects for system catalog '%.*s' in database '%.*s'. This system catalog should exist in all databases. Run DBCC CHECKTABLE on Sysobjects in this database.
908	22	Unable to find any entries in Sysusages for dbid '%d', database '%.*s'. Run DBCC CHECKTABLE on Sysusages in the master database.
909	21	More than %d entries required to build the logical-virtual translation table for database '%.*s'. The database is too fragmented.
910	17	Could not allocate a new object descriptor for required system catalog in database '%d'. Another database must be closed or objects in another database dropped in order to open this database.
911	16	Attempt to locate entry in Sysdatabases for database '%.*s' by name failed—no entry found under that name. Make sure that name is entered properly.

Error Number	Severity	Message Returned
912	21	DBTABLE descriptor cannot be found for database '%.*s' which is supposed to be already open.
913	22	Could not find row in Sysdatabases with database id %d. Run DBCC CHECKTABLE on Sysdatabases.
915	21	Descriptor for system catalog '%.*s' not found in DBTABLE chain for database '%.*s'—all system catalogs should reside permanently in this chain.
916	14	Server user id %d is not a valid user in database '%.*s'.
917	20	Illegal attempt to close the master database for the last time—this database must always be open.
918	14	Database '%.*s' has not yet been recovered—please wait before accessing this database.
919	21	Database '%.*s' has been marked 'suspect' by recovery. Please run DBCC to drop this database.
920	22	Could not find Syslogs row in Sysindexes for database '%.*s'. Run DBCC CHECKTABLE on this system catalog.
921	14	Database '%.*s' has not been recovered yet—please wait and try again.
922	14	Database '%.*s' is being recovered—will wait until recovery is finished.
923	14	User %d not allowed in database '%.*s'— only the owner of this database can access it.
924	14	Database '%.*s' is already open and can only have one user at a time.

Continued

TABLE **D-1 MICROSOFT SQL SERVER–GENERATED ERROR CODES** *(continued)*

Error Number	Severity	Message Returned
925	19	Maximum number of used databases for each query has been exceeded. The maximum allowed is %d.
926	14	Database '%.*s' cannot be opened—it has been marked SUSPECT by recovery. The SA can drop the database with DBCC.
927	14	Database '%.*s' cannot be opened—it is in the middle of a load.
928	14	Database '%.*s' cannot be opened—it is currently being created. Wait and try query again.
929	20	Attempting to close a database which is not open. Please report to Technical Support.
930	14	Database '%.*s' cannot be opened because an earlier system termination left LOAD DATABASE incomplete. Reload the database or notify the System Administrator.
931	21	Database '%.*s' cannot be opened because of a failure to initialize the global timestamp. This indicates that a problem exists in the log for the current database. Please contact Technical Support for assistance.
932	22	Database '%.*s' cannot be opened because the log for the current database is corrupt. Page %ld of the log is linked to a page that belongs to a database object with id %ld. Please contact Technical Support for assistance.
933	22	Logical page %ld of the log encountered while retrieving highest timestamp in database '%.*s' is not the last page of the log and we are not currently recovering that database.

Error Number	Severity	Message Returned
935	10	WARNING—the timestamp in database '%.*s' is approaching the maximum allowed.
1001	16	Line %d: Length or precision specification %d is invalid.
1002	16	Line %d: Specified scale %d is invalid.
1003	15	Line %d: %s clause allowed only for %s.
1004	15	Line %d: Use of %s not allowed; use %s.
1005	15	Line %d: Invalid procedure number (%d). Minimum procedure number is 1.
1006	15	CREATE TRIGGER contains no statements.
1007	15	The %S_MSG '%.*s' is out of the range for numeric representation (%d bytes).
1008	15	The select list item identified by the order by number '%d' contains a variable as part of the expression that identifies a column position. Variables are only allowed when ordering by an expression referencing a column name.
1101	17	Unable to allocate new page for database '%.*s'. There are no more pages available on valid allocation pages. Space can be created by dropping objects, extending the database, or dumping the log with no_log.
1102	22	Unable to locate allocation page %ld for database '%.*s'. This allocation page contains the extent that the target allocation page is in, but the allocation page is not in the translation table in the DBTABLE. Run DBCC CHECKTABLE on Sysusages.
1103	21	Allocation page %d in database '%.*s' has different segment id than that of the object to which we are allocating. Run DBCC CHECKALLOC.

(Continued)

TABLE **D-1** MICROSOFT SQL SERVER–GENERATED ERROR CODES *(continued)*

Error Number	Severity	Message Returned
1104	20	Conflict between number of extents marked in log record in the allocation bitmap and the allocation count. Allocation count is %d. Bitmap is 0x%lx %lx %lx %lx.
1105	17	Can't allocate space for object '%.*s' in database '%.*s' because the '%.*s' segment is full. If you ran out of space in Syslogs, dump the transaction log. Otherwise, use ALTER DATABASE or sp_extendsegment to increase the size of the segment.
1106	20	First pass through allocation page %d found %d free extents. After logging, only found %d free extents.
1108	21	Cannot deallocate extent %ld, database %d. Object id %ld, index id %d, status %d in extent does not match object id %ld, index id %d, status %d in object being deallocated. Run DBCC CHECKALLOC.
1109	21	Attempt to read allocation page %ld failed either because object ID is not correct (%ld) or the page ID is not correct (%ld).
1110	20	Attempt to resource lock allocation page %d in database '%.*s' by process %d while allocating to non-Syslogs object '%.*s'.
1111	20	Extent bitmap on allocation page %d in database '%.*s' does not have extents marked that are being removed.
1113	20	Extent %d already locked while allocating it in database '%.*s'.
1114	20	Attempt to resource lock page %d in database '%.*s' by process %d failed because lock is already held by process %d.

Error Number	Severity	Message Returned
1115	20	Attempt to transfer a resource lock to process ID 0 on allocation page %d in database '%.*s'.
1116	20	Attempt to back out the allocation of LOG page %ld, in database '%.*s'.
1117	21	Extent chain for object %ld is not correctly linked.
1118	17	Database %.*s is full. Cannot allocate space for object %.*s. All available pages are held by other transactions. Try your command again.
1201	20	Page_lock was called with illegal mode %d.
1202	20	Table_lock was called with illegal mode %d.
1203	20	Caller of lock manager is incorrectly trying to unlock an unlocked object. spid=%d locktype=%d dbid=%d lockid=%ld.
1204	19	SQL Server has run out of LOCKS. Re-run your command when there are fewer active users, or ask your System Administrator to reconfigure SQL Server with more LOCKS.
1205	13	Your server command (process id #%d) was deadlocked with another process and has been chosen as deadlock victim. Re-run your command.
1206	20	Locksleep was called with incorrect process id. Process %d is trying to sleep on itself.
1207	20	Locksleep called with bad process id %d.
1208	20	Extent_lock was called with illegal mode %d.

Continued

TABLE **D-1** MICROSOFT SQL SERVER–GENERATED ERROR CODES *(continued)*

Error Number	Severity	Message Returned
1209	20	Internal lock routine called with illegal mode %d.
1210	20	No matching xdes found for dbid %d. Lock was requested for objid %ld, by process %d. Lock requested was %s.
1211	13	Process %d was chosen as deadlock victim with P_BACKOUT bit set.
1501	20	Sort failure.
1503	20	Sort failure: too many sort keeps (%d).
1505	14	Create unique index aborted on duplicate key. Primary key is '%S_KEY'.
1507	10	Warning: deleted duplicate row. Primary key is '%S_KEY'.
1508	14	Create index aborted on duplicate rows. Primary key is '%S_KEY'.
1509	20	Row compare failure.
1510	17	Sort failed: Out of space or locks in database '%.*s'.
1511	20	Sort cannot be reconciled with transaction log.
1513	20	Reuse of extent failed in sort.
1514	21	Page allocated to sort found to be busy. Page number %ld. %S_BUF.
1515	20	Bad session descriptor for sort.
1519	20	An attempt was made to keep a sort buffer in a slot where a buffer was already kept. Buffer pointer: 0x%lx Slot: %d.
1520	18	Sort failed because dpages in the Sysindexes row for table '%.*s' in database '%.*s' had an incorrect value. Please run DBCC CHECKTABLE on this table to correct the value, then re-run your command.

Error Number	Severity	Message Returned
1521	18	Sort failed because a table in tempdb used for the processing of the query had a bad data page count. Tempdb should not have been damaged.
1522	20	Sort failure. Prevented overwriting of allocation page in database '%.*s' by aborting sort.
1523	20	Sort failure. Prevented incorrect extent deallocation by aborting sort.
1525	21	Sort Failure. Rollforward of sort encountered sort descriptor timestamps out of sequence. Old timestamp in log: %04x %08lx. New timestamp in log: %04x %08lx. Timestamp in sort descriptor: %04x %08lx.
1528	21	Character data comparison failure. An unrecognized Sort-Map-Element type (%d) was found in the server-wide default sort table at SMEL entry [%d].
1529	21	Character data comparison failure. A list of Sort-Map-Elements from the server-wide default sort table does not end properly. This list begins at SMEL entry [%d].
1530	16	Create index with sorted_data was aborted because of row out of order. Primary key of first out of order row is '%S_KEY'.
1531	16	The sorted_data option cannot be used for a nonclustered index if the keys are not unique within the table. Create index was aborted because of duplicate keys. Primary key is '%S_KEY'.
1601	21	No resources available to start '%s' process. Use sp_configure to increase the number of user connections.
1602	21	Unable to initialize network %d.

Continued

TABLE **D-1** MICROSOFT SQL SERVER–GENERATED ERROR CODES *(continued)*

Error Number	Severity	Message Returned
1603	21	Process priority %d invalid or no process slots available.
1604	21	Process not runnable or kpid %d not within range.
1605	21	Failed to open virtual socket for new connections.
1606	21	Failed to initialize network receive buffer.
1607	21	Failed to initialize network send buffer.
1608	21	A network error was encountered while sending results to the front end. Check the SQL Server error log for more information.
1609	21	Kpid %d out of range.
1610	21	Could not kill process %d.
1611	21	Could not install quit function.
1612	21	Could not install attention function.
1613	21	Could not close network %d connection for server process %d.
1614	21	Could not yield process.
1615	21	Process unable to sleep.
1616	21	Failed to flush receive stream buffer.
1617	21	Could not infect process %d.
1619	21	Could not open TEMPDB, unable to continue.
1620	21	Failure to open master db for the first time.
1621	18	Type '%c' not allowed before login.
1622	18	Type '%c' not implemented.

Error Number	Severity	Message Returned
1701	16	Creating table '%.*s' failed because row size would be %d. This exceeds the maximum allowable size of a row in a table, %d.
1702	16	Create table failed because column '%.*s' in table '%.*s' exceeds the maximum of 250 columns.
1703	17	Failed to allocate disk space for a work table in database '%.*s'. You may be able to free up space by using the DUMP TRANsaction command, or you may want to extend the size of the database by using the ALTER DATABASE command.
1704	16	Only the SA can create the system table '%.*s'.
1705	16	Must create system table '%.*s' in the Master Database.
1706	16	System table '%.*s' was not created, because ad-hoc updates to system catalogs are not enabled.
1707	18	Could not create system table '%.*s'.
1708	15	The total row size, %d, for table '%.*s' exceeds the maximum number of bytes per row, %d.
1750	10	Unable to create constraint. See previous errors.
1752	16	Unable to create DEFAULT for column '%.*s' as it is not a valid column in table '%.*s'.
1753	16	Column '%.*s.%.*s' is not of same length as referencing column '%.*s.%.*s' in foreign key '%.*s'.
1754	16	DEFAULTS cannot be created on columns with an IDENTITY attribute. Table '%.*s', column '%.*s'.

Continued

TABLE **D-1 MICROSOFT SQL SERVER–GENERATED ERROR CODES** *(continued)*

Error Number	Severity	Message Returned
1755	16	DEFAULTS cannot be created on columns of type TIMESTAMP. Table '%.*s', column '%.*s'.
1756	10	Skipping foreign key constraint '%.*s' definition for temporary table.
1757	10	Unable to create DEFAULT constraint. See previous errors.
1758	20	Unable to update category field for ADD constraint.
1759	16	Invalid column '%.*s' specified in constraint definition.
1760	16	Constraints of type %s cannot be created on columns of type %s.
1761	16	Foreign key '%.*s' references invalid database '%.*s'.
1762	16	'%.*s' is not a valid constraint.
1763	16	Cross database foreign key references are not supported. Foreign key '%.*s'.
1764	20	Unable to update category field for %s table.
1766	16	Foreign key references to temporary tables are not supported. Foreign key '%.*s'.
1767	16	Foreign key '%.*s' references invalid table '%.*s'.
1768	16	Foreign key '%.*s' references object '%.*s' which is not a user table.
1769	16	Foreign key '%.*s' references invalid column '%.*s' in referencing table '%.*s'.
1770	16	Foreign key '%.*s' references invalid column '%.*s' in referenced table '%.*s'.

Error Number	Severity	Message Returned
1771	16	Foreign key '%.*s' references object '%.*s' which is not a table.
1772	16	Foreign key '%.*s' defines invalid relationship between a user table and system table.
1773	16	Foreign key '%.*s' has implicit reference to object '%.*s' which does not have a PRIMARY KEY defined on it.
1774	16	Number of columns in referencing column list for foreign key '%.*s' does not match those of the PRIMARY KEY in the referenced table '%.*s'.
1775	16	Number of columns in referencing column list for foreign key '%.*s' does not match those of the referenced key in the referenced table '%.*s'.
1776	16	There are no primary or candidate keys in the referenced table '%.*s' that match the referencing column list in the foreign key '%.*s'.
1777	14	User does not have correct permissions on referenced table '%.*s' to create foreign key '%.*s'.
1778	16	Column '%.*s.%.*s' is not of same type as referencing column '%.*s.%.*s' in foreign key '%.*s'.
1779	16	Table '%.*s' already has a PRIMARY KEY defined on it.
1780	20	Could not find column '%d' in SYSCOLUMNS for object id '%d' in dbid '%d'.
1781	16	Column already has a DEFAULT bound to it.
1782	20	Unable to update syscolumns to bind constraint based DEFAULT.

Continued

TABLE **D-1 MICROSOFT SQL SERVER–GENERATED ERROR CODES** *(continued)*

Error Number	Severity	Message Returned
1783	20	Unable to open table '%s' in dbid '%d' for constraint processing.
1784	20	Unable to open system table '%s' in dbid '%d' for constraint processing. Ensure that this database has been correctly upgraded.
1801	16	Database '%.*s' already exists.
1802	11	CREATE DATABASE failed. Some disk names listed in command were not found. Check that names exist and are spelled correctly before re-running.
1803	17	CREATE DATABASE failed. Could not allocate enough disk space for a new database on the disks named in the command. Total space allocated must be at least %d Mbytes (%ld 2048-byte pages) to accommodate copy of Model Database.
1804	10	There is no disk named '%.*s'. Checking other disk names.
1805	10	CREATE DATABASE: allocating %ld pages on disk '%.*s'.
1807	17	MODEL database in use, cannot create new database. Check with your System Administrator before re-running CREATE DATABASE.
1808	21	Crdb_disk : default disk not found. Cannot complete create/alter database command.
1809	14	CREATE DATABASE must be preceded by a 'USE master' command. Check with your DBO (or System Administrator) if you do not have permission to USE master.

Error Number	Severity	Message Returned
1810	16	CREATE DATABASE failed because of incorrect size parameter(s). Total number of megabytes specified must be at least %d megabytes so that the Model Database can be copied to the new database.
1811	16	'%.*s' is the wrong type of device for CREATE or ALTER database. Please check Sysdevices. The CREATE or ALTER is aborted.
1813	16	Cannot open new database '%.*s'. CREATE DATABASE is aborted.
1814	10	Problem creating Temporary Database—if out of space, please extend and reboot. If some other problem, please contact Technical Support.
1816	16	CREATE DATABASE failed because the log device '%.*s' has no space available.
1819	16	Could not create database '%.*s'.
1901	16	Column '%.*s'—can't create index on a column of BIT data type.
1902	16	Cannot create more than one clustered index on table '%.*s'. Drop the existing clustered index '%.*s' before creating another.
1903	16	%d is the maximum allowable size of an index. Composite index specified is %d bytes.
1904	16	Cannot specify more than %d column names for index key list. %d specified.
1905	21	Could not find 'zero' row for index '%.*s' the table in Sysindexes.
1906	11	Cannot create an index on table '%.*s', because this table does not exist in database '%.*s'.

Continued

TABLE D-1 MICROSOFT SQL SERVER–GENERATED ERROR CODES *(continued)*

Error Number	Severity	Message Returned
1907	16	Create index on non-empty table not supported yet.
1908	16	Too many parameters—symbol table overflow.
1909	16	Can't use duplicate column names in index key list. Column name '%.*s' listed more than once.
1910	16	Cannot create more than %d indexes on one table.
1911	16	Column name '%.*s' does not exist in target table.
1913	16	There is already an index on table '%.*s' named '%.*s'.
1914	16	Cannot create index on object '%.*s' because it is not a user table.
1915	16	Only the owner of table '%.*s' or the System Administrator may create an index on it.
1916	16	CREATE INDEX options %s and %s are mutually exclusive.
1918	10	Non-clustered index (index id = %d) is being rebuilt.
1919	16	Column '%.*s'—can't create index on a column of TEXT or IMAGE data type.
2001	10	Cannot use duplicate parameter names. Parameter name '%.*s' listed more than once.
2002	10	Cannot use variable '%.*s' without first declaring it.
2004	16	Procedure '%.*s' has already been created with group number %d—create procedure with an unused group number.

Error Number	Severity	Message Returned
2007	11	Cannot add rows to Sysdepends for the current stored procedure because it depends on the missing object '%.*s'. The stored procedure will still be created.
2008	16	The object '%.*s' is not a procedure so you cannot create another procedure under that group name.
2103	16	Cannot create a trigger on a view, name: %.*s.
2106	11	Cannot create a trigger on table '%.*s', because this table does not exist in database '%.*s'.
2108	16	Cannot CREATE TRIGGER on table '%.*s', because you can only create a trigger on a table in the current database.
2109	16	Cannot CREATE TRIGGER on table '%.*s', that accesses 'inserted' or 'deleted' because the table was created with the no_log option.
2201	16	Could not open file/device %s OS/2 errno=%d. Check mode of db file.
2202	21	Could not translate virtual read address to device and seek vaddr=0x%x.
2203	24	Could not seek to vaddr 0x%x for read. Fd=%d errno =%d.
2204	24	Could not read complete record. Count=%d fd=%d errno =%d.
2205	21	Could not translate virtual write address to device and seek vaddr=0x%x.
2206	24	Could not seek to vaddr 0x%x for write. Fd=%d errno =%d.
2207	24	Could not write complete record. Count=%d fd=%d errno =%d.
2208	21	Tried to read unopened device vaddr=0x%x.

Continued

TABLE **D-1** MICROSOFT SQL SERVER–GENERATED ERROR CODES *(continued)*

Error Number	Severity	Message Returned
2209	21	Tried to write unopened device vaddr=0x%x.
2210	16	Tried to write database without using -w or -W flag.
2301	19	Operating System allocation call failed.
2501	16	Table named %.*s not found; check Sysobjects.
2502	16	Table Corrupt: A page is linked in more than one chain; check this page:page number=%ld allocation status=%d.
2503	16	Table Corrupt: Page linkage is not consistent; check the following pages: (current page#=%ld; page# pointing to this page=%ld; previous page# indicated in this page=%ld).
2504	16	Table Corrupt: The index id in alloc page does not match the index id in Sysindexes (alloc page#=%ld; extent id=%ld; index id in alloc=%d; index id in Sysindexes=%d).
2505	16	Table Corrupt: Free offset in page header is not reasonable; free offset should be >= 32 and <= 2048; check this page and offset (page#=%ld freeoffset on the page header=%d).
2506	16	Table Corrupt: The values in adjust table should be in ascending order starting from the end of the table (page#=%ld row#=%d); check adjust table in this row.
2507	16	Table Corrupt: Offset table is incorrect (page#=%ld row#=%d offset in offset table is=%d correct offset is=%d).
2508	16	Table Corrupt: Row length is incorrect (page#=%ld row#=%d minimum row length=%d row length=%d).

Error Number	Severity	Message Returned
2509	16	Table Corrupt: The row number and offset of each row in the page should have a matching entry in row number table; check this page (page#=%ld row#=%d offset in row number table=%d).
2510	16	Table Corrupt: Keys do not match between leaf page %ld and data page %ld; check row # %d on the data page.
2511	16	Table Corrupt: Keys in %S_MSG should be in ascending order; check page number %ld.
2512	16	Table Corrupt: The specified row number %d in index page %ld cannot be found on data page %ld.
2513	16	Table Corrupt: Object id %ld (object name = %.*s) does not match between %.*s and %.*s.
2514	16	Table Corrupt: Type id %ld (type name = %.*s) does not match between %.*s and %.*s.
2516	16	Table Corrupt: Segment number %d does not match between %.*s and %.*s.
2517	16	Table Corrupt: Procedure id %d (procedure name = %.*s) does not match between %.*s and %.*s.
2518	16	Database Corrupt: Incorrect last checkpoint in Syslogs.
2519	16	Database Corrupt: The last checkpoint in Sysdatabases is incorrect. Syslogs recorded a different checkpoint.
2520	16	Database named %.*s not found; check Sysdatabases.

Continued

TABLE D-1 MICROSOFT SQL SERVER-GENERATED ERROR CODES *(continued)*

Error Number	Severity	Message Returned
2521	16	Table Corrupt: Page is linked but not allocated; check the following pages and table: alloc page#=%ld extent id=%ld logical page#=%ld object id in extent=%ld (object name = %.*s) index id in extent=%d.
2522	16	Table Corrupt: The object id %ld (object name = %.*s) in page# %ld is different from the object id %ld (object name = %.*s) in Sysindexes.
2523	16	Table Corrupt: Page number %ld is out of range for this database %.*s. The maximum page number in this database is %ld.
2524	16	Table Corrupt: Row length is inconsistent between the computed row length and the recorded row length on page; check the following page and row: pageno=%ld row#=%d computed row length=%d row length on page=%d.
2525	16	Table Corrupt: Object id wrong; tables: alloc page %ld extent id=%ld l page#=%ld objid in ext=%ld (name = %.*s) objid in page=%ld (name = %.*s)objid in sysindexes=%ld (name = %.*s).
2526	16	Incorrect DBCC command. Please check the Commands Reference Manual for the correct DBCC syntax and options.
2527	10	DBCC detected internal database inconsistency; see your System Administrator.
2528	10	DBCC execution completed. If DBCC printed error messages, see your System Administrator.
2529	16	Table Corrupt: Page %ld not found.

Error Number	Severity	Message Returned
2531	16	Table Corrupt: Index id on extent should be 0; check the following page and ids: alloc page=%ld extent=%ld index id on extent=%d.
2532	16	Table Corrupt: No Syslogs entry in Sysindexes.
2533	16	Table Corrupt: Incorrect index key length %d in internal (sarg) structure.
2534	16	Table Corrupt: No keys found on index page %ld. Offset for the free space: (freeoff=%ld).
2535	16	Table Corrupt: Page# %ld belongs to object id %ld (object name = %.*s) not object id %ld (object name = %.*s).
2536	10	Checking %.*s.
2537	10	Checking %ld.
2538	10	Alloc page %ld (# of extent=%ld used pages=%ld ref pages=%ld).
2539	10	Total (# of extent=%ld used pages=%ld ref pages=%ld) in this database.
2540	16	Table Corrupt: Page is allocated but not linked; check the following pages and ids: allocation pg#=%ld extent id=%ld logical pg#=%ld object id on extent=%ld (object name = %.*s) indid on extent=%ld.
2541	16	Table Corrupt: object id does not match between extent in allocation page and Sysindexes; check the following extent: alloc pg#=%ld extent#=%ld object id on extent=%ld (object name = %.*s) object id in Sysindexes=%ld (object name = %.*s).
2542	16	Table Corrupt: Extent is linked in more than one chain. Check the following allocation page and extent: alloc pg#=%ld extent#=%ld status=%d.

Continued

TABLE D-1 MICROSOFT SQL SERVER–GENERATED ERROR CODES *(continued)*

Error Number	Severity	Message Returned
2543	16	Table Corrupt: Extent structures are linked incorrectly; check the following extent: alloc pg#=%ld extent#=%ld previous extent# on this extent=%ld previous extent should be=%ld.
2544	16	Table Corrupt: Extent id %ld on allocation pg# %ld had object id %ld (object name = %.*s) on but used bit off.
2545	16	Table Corrupt: Extent#=%ld on allocation pg#=%ld was used but object id was 0.
2546	16	Table Corrupt: Extent id %ld on allocation pg# %ld has objid %ld and used bit on, but reference bit off.
2547	16	Table Corrupt: Segment number %d specified for use in the segment map in Sysusages has no entry in Syssegments. The entry in Sysusages is for dbid %d (db name = %.*s), with a virtual starting address of %ld.
2548	16	There is no default segment specified in Syssegments.
2549	16	There is more than one default segment specified in Syssegments.
2550	16	Missing segment in Sysusages segmap.
2551	10	The following segments have been defined for database %d (database name %.*s).
2552	10	Virtual start addr size segments.
2556	20	Page #%lx of Sysindexes in database %d not found in cache after read.
2557	16	Must be owner of object '%.*s' to run DBCC %s on it.

Error Number	Severity	Message Returned
2558	16	Extent not within segment: Object %ld, indid %d includes extents on allocation page %ld which is not in segment %d.
2559	16	Data page number %ld is empty but is not the first page. Status = 0x%x.
2560	16	Incorrect parameter passed to DBCC command.
2561	16	Unable to open log for database %d.
2562	16	%s cannot access object '%.*s' because it is not a table.
2563	14	Only the DBO of database %.*s may run the DBCC CHECKCATALOG command.
2564	14	Only the DBO of database %.*s may run the DBCC CHECKDB command.
2565	14	Only the DBO of database %.*s may run the DBCC CHECKALLOC command.
2567	14	Only the DBO of database %.*s may run the DBCC DBREPAIR command.
2568	16	Page %ld is out of range for this database.
2570	10	Warning—Page %ld has DEALLOC bit on— indid %d, status 0x%x.
2571	10	Only the System Administrator may use the DBCC command '%.*s'.
2572	10	Database '%.*s' is not in single user mode—may find spurious allocation problems due to transactions in progress.
2573	16	Database '%.*s' is not marked suspect. You cannot drop it with DBCC.
2574	16	Index page number %ld is empty. Status = 0x%x.

Continued

TABLE **D-1** **MICROSOFT SQL SERVER–GENERATED ERROR CODES** *(continued)*

Error Number	Severity	Message Returned
2575	16	The last page %ld in Sysindexes for table '%.*s' has next page # %ld in its page header. The next page # should be NULL. Please check Sysindexes.
2576	16	The %S_MSG page %ld specified in Sysindexes for table '%.*s' cannot be found. Please check Sysindexes.
2577	16	The root page %ld in Sysindexes for table '%.*s' has next page # %ld and previous page # %ld in its page header. Both the next page # and the previous page # should be NULL. Please check Sysindexes.
2578	16	The first page %ld in Sysindexes for table '%.*s' has previous page # %ld in its page header. The previous page # should be NULL. Please check Sysindexes.
2579	10	The total number of data pages in this table is %ld.
2580	16	The clustered index page (%S_PAGE) has an unexpected key pointer to an overflow data page (%S_PAGE). Please check page status.
2581	16	Data page (%S_PAGE) indicates that an overflow page is linked to it; however, the next page (%S_PAGE) has not been marked as an overflow page. Please check page status.
2582	16	Data page (%S_PAGE) has been marked as an overflow page; however, the previous page (%S_PAGE) does not indicate that there is an overflow page linked to it.
2584	16	The last key in the previous page (%S_PAGE) is equal to the first key in the current page (%S_PAGE); however, the status of current page does not indicate that it is an overflow page.

Error Number	Severity	Message Returned
2585	16	The last key in the previous page (%S_PAGE) is equal to the first key in the current page (%S_PAGE); however, the status of previous page indicates that there is a disconnected overflow page.
2586	16	The last key in the previous page (%S_PAGE) is equal to the first key in the current page (%S_PAGE); however, the status of previous page indicates that there is no overflow page.
2587	16	The last key in the previous page (%S_PAGE) is not equal to the first key in the current page (%S_PAGE); the current page is an overflow page; however, the status of previous page indicates that there is no disconnected overflow page.
2588	16	Page %d was expected to be the first page of a TEXT/IMAGE value.
2589	16	Object '%.*s' must have its status updated in Sysobjects, to reflect the intent of repairing the index on it.
2590	16	DBCC option available for system tables only.
2591	16	Could not find index row which has id %d for table '%.*s'.
2592	10	%s index successfully restored for object '%.*s' in the '%.*s' database.
2593	10	There are %ld rows in %ld pages for object '%.*s'.
2594	16	Invalid index id specified (index id = %d).
2595	16	Database '%.*s' must be set to single user mode before executing this command.

Continued

TABLE **D-1 MICROSOFT SQL SERVER–GENERATED ERROR CODES** *(continued)*

Error Number	Severity	Message Returned
2596	16	%S_PAGE has an incorrect pgfreeoff value of %d. The offset should be %d.
2597	16	The database is not open. Please issue a 'use %.*s' and re-run the DBCC command.
2598	16	Indexes on Sysobjects and Sysindexes cannot be re-created.
2601	14	Attempt to insert duplicate key row in object '%.*s' with unique index '%.*s'.
2603	21	No space left on logical page %ld of index %d for object '%.*s' when inserting row on index page—this situation should have been taken care of while traversing the index.
2610	22	Could not find leaf row in nonclustered index '%.*s' that corresponds to data row from logical data page %ld, row offset %d during update index attempt after data page split.
2613	20	Attempt to remove resource lock on buffer holding logical page %d failed—the buffer was not resource locked.
2615	14	Attempt to insert duplicate row in table '%.*s' with index '%.*s' in database '%.*s'. Could drop and recreate index with ignore duprow or allow duprow.
2616	20	Buffer holding logical page %d cannot move to slot 1 since buffer holding logical page %d is already there.
2617	20	Buffer holding logical page %d not found in keep pool in SDES for object '%.*s'.
2618	20	Couldn't find dupkey group starting at offset %d on page 0x%x.

Error Number	Severity	Message Returned
2619	20	Keys did not match overflow page when inserting row at end of page that has overflow page that is not disconnected.
2620	21	The offset of the row number at offset %d does not match the entry in the offset table of the following page: %S_PAGE.
2621	20	Process %d already has the buffer we are using for an allocation resource locked: %S_PAGE.
2622	21	Insufficient room on this page to insert a row of length %d. %S_PAGE.
2623	21	The PG_DEALLOC bit is on in this page at runtime—should have been turned off by deallocating page in recovery. %S_PAGE.
2624	21	Insert into table %S_DES fails because rowlength %d is less than minlen %d.
2625	20	Deadlock encountered in log allocation for database '%.*s'. This state should not be reached.
2626	21	Illegal attempt to insert duplicate key row in the clustered index for object '%.*s' in database '%.*s'.
2627	14	Violation of %s constraint '%.*s': Attempt to insert duplicate key in object '%.*s'.
2701	10	Database name '%.*s' ignored, referencing object in Tempdb.
2702	16	Database '%.*s' does not exist.
2703	16	Segment '%.*s' does not exist.
2705	16	Column names in each table must be unique. Column name '%.*s' in table '%.*s' is specified more than once.
2706	11	Table '%.*s' does not exist.

Continued

TABLE D-1 MICROSOFT SQL SERVER-GENERATED ERROR CODES *(continued)*

Error Number	Severity	Message Returned
2710	16	You are not the owner specified for the object named '%.*s' in this command (CREATE, ALTER, TRUNCATE, UPDATE STATISTICS, or BULK INSERT). The database owner can use the SETUSER command to assume the identity of another user.
2714	16	There is already an object named '%.*s' in the database.
2715	16	Column or parameter #%d: Can't find type '%.*s'.
2716	16	Column or parameter #%d:−can't specify a column width on type '%.*s'.
2717	16	Column or parameter #%d:−specified column width too large for type '%.*s'.
2718	16	Column or parameter #%d:−can't specify Null values on a column of type BIT.
2721	11	Could not find a default segment to create the table on. Ask your System Administrator to specify a default segment in Syssegments.
2724	10	Parameter '%.*s' has an invalid data type.
2727	11	Cannot find index '%.*s'.
2728	21	Could not find Sysobjects row for table '%.*s'.
2729	16	Object '%.*s' group number 1 already exists in the database. Choose another procedure name.
2730	11	Cannot create procedure '%.*s' with a group number of %d because a procedure with the same name and a group number of 1 does not currently exist in the database. Must CREATE PROCEDURE '%.*s';1 first.

Error Number	Severity	Message Returned
2731	16	Column or parameter #%d:—can't specify column width of zero for '%.*s'.
2732	16	User error number %ld is invalid. Number must be between %ld and %ld.
2734	16	User name %.*s does not exist in Sysusers.
2735	16	Object text is too long—can only support 255 rows in Syscomments. Shorten the object text or split into multiple objects. Text which caused overflow starts at: '%.*s'.
2736	16	Owner name that was specified is a group name. Objects cannot be owned by groups.
2737	16	Message passed to %s must be of type CHAR or VARCHAR.
2738	16	A table can only have one timestamp column. Since table '%.*s' already has one, you can't add the column '%.*s'.
2739	16	TEXT and IMAGE datatypes are invalid for local variables.
2740	16	SET LANGUAGE failed because '%.*s' is not an official language name or a language alias on this SQL Server.
2741	16	SET DATEFORMAT date order '%.*s' is invalid.
2742	16	SET DATEFIRST %d is out of range.
2743	16	%s command requires %S_MSG parameter.
2744	16	Multiple identity columns specified for table '%.*s', only one identity column per table.
2745	10	Process %d has raised user error %d, severity %d. SQL Server is terminating this process.

Continued

TABLE **D-1** **MICROSOFT SQL SERVER–GENERATED ERROR CODES** (continued)

Error Number	Severity	Message Returned
2746	16	Cannot specify user error format string with length exceeding %d bytes.
2747	16	Too many substitution parameters for raiserror. Cannot exceed %d substitution parameters.
2748	16	Cannot specify %s datatype(raiserror parameter %d) as substitution parameter for raiserror.
2749	16	Identity column '%.*s' must be of type int, smallint, tinyint, decimal, or numeric with scale of 0 and constrained to be non-nullable.
2750	16	Column or parameter #%d:–specified column precision %d is greater than the maximum precision of %d.
2751	16	Column or parameter #%d:–specified column scale %d is greater than the specified precision of %d.
2752	16	Identity column '%.*s' contains invalid SEED.
2753	16	Identity column '%.*s' contains invalid INCREMENT.
2754	16	Error severity greater than %d can be specified only by System Administrator by using the WITH LOG option.
2755	16	SET DEADLOCK_PRIORITY option '%.*s' is invalid.
2756	16	Invalid value %d for State; valid range is from %d to %d.
2757	16	Raiserror failed due to invalid parameter substitution(s) for error %d, severity %d, state %d.

Error Number	Severity	Message Returned
2758	16	%s could not locate entry for error %d in Sysmessages.
2802	20	Both the tree and plan pointer are set; ambiguous procedure.
2804	20	Stored procedure '%.*s' is out of sync with its own procedure header.
2805	20	Bad pointer 0x%lx encountered while remapping stored procedure '%.*s'. Must re-create procedure.
2806	20	Stored procedure '%.*s' is corrupted. Must re-create procedure.
2807	18	Process %d could not unlock stored procedure '%.*s' because the procedure is not currently locked by that process.
2808	18	Incorrect object structure returned from getobject.
2809	18	The request for %S_MSG '%.*s' failed because '%.*s' is a %S_MSG object.
2810	18	Cache reports negative usage count for procedure '%.*s'.
2811	18	Cannot create procedure dbid %d, objid %d, with a group number of %d.
2812	16	Stored procedure '%.*s' not found.
2813	20	Procedure %.*s in procedure buffer 0x%lx not properly linked with procedure header 0x%lx.
2814	20	Procedure %.*s in procedure buffer 0x%lx does not contain the same object id as procedure header 0x%lx.
2815	20	Procedure %.*s in procedure buffer 0x%lx contains page address 0x%lx which is not aligned on a 2K boundary.

Continued

Tᴀʙʟᴇ **D-1 MICROSOFT SQL SERVER-GENERATED ERROR CODES** *(continued)*

Error Number	Severity	Message Returned
2816	20	Procedure %.*s in procedure buffer 0x%1x contains page address 0x%1x which is not within any memory map.
2817	20	Procedure %.*s in procedure buffer 0x%1x contains page address 0x%1x which should be allocated.
2818	20	You must provide both name and object id in order to install a procedure.
2819	20	You must provide both name and object id in order to remove a procedure.
2821	16	You must drop and re-create procedure %.*s.
2822	20	Bad version number encountered for procedure %.*s.
2823	20	Process %d tried to remove a PROC_BUF 0x%1x named '%.*s' that it does not hold in the hold procedure linked list.
2824	19	Process %d cannot hold PROC_BUF 0x%1x named '%.*s' because it holds another PROC_BUF 0x%1x named '%.*s'. A process can only hold one view, rule, or default at a time.
2825	20	Process %d tried to remove a PROC_BUF 0x%1x named '%.*s' that it does not hold.
2826	20	Process %d has held the PROC_BUF 0x%1x named '%.*s' in the hold procedure linked list already; check your procedure cache.
2827	20	Procedure '%.*s' in procedure buffer 0x%1x is not properly hashed.
3001	21	Internal error. Could not find index for system catalog '%.*s', unable to dump database.

Error Number	Severity	Message Returned
3002	23	Attempt to dump database %.*s found logical page %ld when logical page %ld expected.
3004	10	%ld uninitialized pages encountered while dumping database %.*s. Run DBCC CHECKALLOC on this database for more information, then call Technical Support if there are any errors.
3005	16	DUMP DATABASE has been interrupted by a USER ATTENTION signal.
3101	16	Database in use. System Administrator must have exclusive use of database to run load.
3102	16	Specified file '%.*s' is not in valid dump database format.
3103	10	Unexpected end-of-dump while loading database, attempting to continue. Please verify database integrity.
3104	16	LOAD DATABASE encountered page with invalid logical page number 0x%lx.
3105	16	Data on dump will not fit into current database. Need %ld Mbyte database.
3106	16	Specified file '%.*s' is in an obsolete dump database format: version %d, expected version %d.
3107	20	Page #0x%lx of Sysindexes in database %d not found in cache after read.
3108	16	LOAD DATABASE must be used in single user mode if trying to restore the Master database.
3109	16	This dump was created from the Master database. A dump from Master can only be loaded as part of the Restore Master procedure.

Continued

TABLE **D-1 MICROSOFT SQL SERVER–GENERATED ERROR CODES** *(continued)*

Error Number	Severity	Message Returned
3110	14	You must be the DBO of database %.*s or the SA to run LOAD DATABASE.
3111	16	This dump was not created from the Master database. Master can only be loaded from a dump of the Master database.
3112	16	Cannot load any database other than Master when server in single-user mode.
3113	21	Database %.*s does not have an entry in Sysusers for the DBO.
3114	21	Database %.*s does not have an entry in Sysdatabases.
3115	10	User %.*s in database %.*s has suid %d, which is the same as the suid of the DBO (as defined in Sysdatabases). User %.*s will be given suid %d.
3116	10	When all load transactions have been completed for database %.*s, user %.*s should be given a unique suid.
3117	10	Database %.*s already has a user with suid %d. Please call Technical Support.
3118	16	LOAD DATABASE has been interrupted by a USER ATTENTION signal. A LOAD DATABASE must be completed in this database before it will be accessible.
3120	16	The database you are attempting to LOAD was DUMPed under a different sort order ID (%d) than the one currently running on this server (%d), and at least one of them is a non-binary sort order.
3121	16	The %sCLUSTERED index %s.%s (objid = %ld, indid = %d) may be invalid since it uses CHAR or VARCHAR columns in its key, and was created under a different sort order ID (%d) than the one currently running on this server (%d).

Error Number	Severity	Message Returned
3122	16	This master database dump was created from a 4.2x server and cannot be loaded.
3123	16	Multipart database names ('%.*s') are illegal for LOAD DATABASE.
3124	16	Must be an System Administrator to perform LOAD HEADERONLY.
3125	16	No devices specified for LOAD HEADERONLY.
3201	16	Can't open dump device '%.*s', device error, or device off line. Please consult the SQL Server error log for more details.
3202	16	Write on dump device '%.*s' failed, vsn=%ld return=%d status=%ld. Please consult the SQL Server error log for more details.
3203	16	Read on dump device '%.*s' failed, vsn=%ld return=%d status=%ld. Please consult the SQL Server error log for more details.
3204	16	Operator aborted Dump or Load.
3205	16	Too many dump devices specified for dump/load; only %d allowed.
3206	16	No entry in Sysdevices for dump device name '%.*s'. Update Sysdevices and re-run command.
3207	16	DUMP or LOAD via the network is not currently supported. Re-run your command specifying a dump device.
3208	16	Unexpected end of file while reading beginning of dump. Please confirm that dump media contains a valid SQL Server dump. The SQL Server error log may contain more information on the problem.
3209	16	'%.*s' is not a DUMP or LOAD device. Please check Sysdevices.

Continued

TABLE **D-1 MICROSOFT SQL SERVER–GENERATED ERROR CODES** *(continued)*

Error Number	Severity	Message Returned
3210	16	Read via host failed, vsn=%ld return=%d status=%ld. Please consult the SQL Server error log for more detail.
3211	10	%d percent %s.
3212	16	The load requires %d dump devices and %d have been specified.
3213	10	%d volume(s) of the current stripe set have been read; mount the next %d volume(s).
3214	16	The volume on %.*s does not belong to the current stripe set.
3215	16	Number of stripe dump devices(%d) can be at most one more than the system config parameter 'backup threads' (%d); reconfigure 'backup threads' to be at least %d, and restart the server to try again.
3216	16	%s expects '%s' type; '%s' type has been specified and is invalid.
3217	16	Invalid value '%s' specified for %s.
3218	16	Dump was done from a server with Processor type %d and cannot be loaded in a server with Processor type %d.
3219	16	The stripeset tape in device '%.*s' has already been loaded.
3301	21	Invalid log record found in Syslogs (logop %d)
3303	21	Failed to find SAVEPT in log for xact %S_RID, current number is %d, looking for %d.
3305	21	Page %ld in database '%.*s' read in during runtime or load xact was uninitialized.

Error Number	Severity	Message Returned
3306	21	Process %d was expected to hold logical lock on page %ld instead of process %d.
3307	21	Process %d was expected to hold logical lock on page %ld.
3308	21	Page %ld was expected to have %s lock on it.
3309	21	While in backout, process %d was chosen as deadlock victim while waiting for process %d to release lock on page %ld.
3310	21	Cannot find log record with RID: (%ld, %d).
3311	22	No space left on page %ld to move data of %d length.
3312	22	Free offset %d is invalid on page %ld.
3313	10	Error while redoing log row in database '%.*s'. %S_RID.
3314	10	Error while undoing log row in database '%.*s'. %S_RID.
3401	21	Rec_init: getnext SCAN_RID of last checkpoint failed on Rid from Sysdatabases. %S_RID.
3403	22	Rec_init: Found that page %d had non-log object id %d while checking Syslogs allocation.
3404	21	Rec_complete: Could not open controlling database (id %d) of controlling database in multi-db transaction.
3405	10	Recovering database '%.*s'
3406	10	%d transactions rolled forward in dbid %d.
3407	10	%d transactions rolled back in dbid %d.
3408	10	Recovery complete.

Continued

TABLE **D-1** **MICROSOFT SQL SERVER-GENERATED ERROR CODES** *(continued)*

Error Number	Severity	Message Returned
3409	10	Roll forward transaction '%s' in dbid %d.
3410	10	Roll back transaction '%s'—was aborted in dbid %d.
3411	10	Roll back transaction '%s'—no 'end transaction' in dbid %d.
3412	21	Database %d, table %ld. Attempt to mark table as suspect. Getnext SCAN_CLUST on Sysobjects.objid failed.
3413	21	Database %d. Attempt to mark database as suspect failed. Getnext NC scan on Sysdatabases.dbid failed.
3414	10	Database '%.*s' (dbid %d): Recovery failed. Please contact Technical Support for further instructions.
3417	21	Cannot recover the master database, exiting.
3418	21	Not enough descriptors to open model.
3419	16	Unable to proceed with the recovery of dbid <%d> because of previous errors. Continuing with the next database.
3421	21	Unable to recover database '%.*s' because of a failure to initialize the global timestamp. This indicates that a problem exists in the log for the current database. Please contact Technical Support for assistance.
3423	21	Error recovering database '%.*s'—could not find expected BEGIN TRANSACTION record at location: %S_RID.
3424	21	No more room in transaction table for transaction (%ld, %d).
3425	21	Transaction (%ld, %d) not found in transaction table.

Error Number	Severity	Message Returned
3426	10	Could not make log consistent during special recovery of database %d. Please run dbcc save_rebuild_log utility if you wish to attempt to create a new log for this database.
3429	21	Error recovering database '%.*s'—could not connect to commit service to check completion status of xact: %S_RID.
3430	16	Could not add a checkpoint record during special recovery of database %d. If you intend to do updates in this database, first free up space by running DUMP TRANSaction WITH NO_LOG, and then checkpoint the database.
3432	16	Warning: Syslanguages is missing.
3433	16	Name is truncated to '%.*s'. The maximum name length is %d.
3434	20	Cannot change sortorder. Server shutting down. Restart to continue with sortorder unchanged.
3435	20	Sortorder cannot be changed because user objects or user databases exist.
3436	20	Cannot rebuild index %d for the '%.*s' table in the '%.*s' database.
3501	21	Could not get Sysdatabases row for database '%d' at checkpoint time %S_RID.
3502	21	No checkpoint records found in Syslogs for database '%.*s'.
3504	21	Sysindexes page # 0x%1x in database '%.*s' is not in buffer cache at checkpoint after getindex call.
3505	14	Only the DBO of database %.*s may run the checkpoint command.

Continued

TABLE D-1 MICROSOFT SQL SERVER–GENERATED ERROR CODES *(continued)*

Error Number	Severity	Message Returned
3508	25	Attempt to set '%.*s' database to single user mode failed because the usage count is %ld. Make sure that no other users are currently using this database and rerun CHECKPOINT.
3509	14	Attempt to set database '%.*s' to read only user mode failed because transaction %d:%d is active. Make sure that no other users are currently using this database and rerun CHECKPOINT.
3604	10	Duplicate key was ignored.
3605	10	Duplicate row was ignored.
3606	10	Arithmetic overflow occurred.
3607	10	Divide by zero occurred.
3608	10	Null value used in an expression.
3609	10	Attempt to update a column in the fabricated row of an inner table in an outer join.
3612	10	%sSQL Server Execution Times:%s cpu time = %lu ms. elapsed time = %lu ms.
3613	10	SQL Server Parse and Compile Time:%s cpu time = %lu ms.
3615	10	Table: %.*s scan count %d, logical reads: %d, physical reads: %d.
3616	22	Non-leaf page %d in table %d, index %d is empty—please rebuild the index.
3618	10	Transaction has been aborted.
3619	10	Unable to write CHECKPOINT record in database %d because the log is out of space.

Error Number	Severity	Message Returned
3620	10	Automatic checkpointing is disabled in database '%.*s' because the log is out of space. It will continue when the DBO successfully checkpoints the database. Please free up some space or extend the database and then run CHECKPOINT.
3621	10	Command has been aborted.
3622	10	Domain error occurred.
3623	10	A transaction on a no_log table was undone. Check the errorlog file in the SQL Server directory for details.
3701	11	Cannot drop the %S_MSG '%.*s', because it doesn't exist in the system catalogs.
3702	16	Cannot drop the %S_MSG '%.*s' because it is currently in use.
3703	11	Cannot drop the %S_MSG with object-id %ld in database %d, because it doesn't exist in the system catalogs.
3704	16	Cannot drop the %S_MSG '%.*s' because you are not the owner or System Administrator.
3705	16	Cannot use DROP %s with '%.*s' because '%.*s' is a %S_MSG. Use DROP %s.
3706	11	DES not found while dropping %s '%.*s'.
3708	16	Cannot drop the %S_MSG '%.*s' because it is a system %S_MSG.
3709	16	Cannot drop '%.*s' because you are not currently in the master database.
3716	16	The %S_MSG '%.*s' cannot be dropped because it is bound to one or more %S_MSG.
3718	11	Could not drop index '%.*s' because the table/clustered index entry cannot be found in the Sysindexes system catalog.

Continued

Error Number	Severity	Message Returned
3723	16	Explicit DROP INDEX not allowed on index '%.*s'. It is being used for %s constraint enforcement.
3724	16	Cannot drop the %S_MSG '%.*s' because it is published for replication.
3725	16	Constraint '%.*s' is being referenced by table '%.*s', foreign key constraint '%.*s'.
3726	16	Could not drop object '%.*s'. It is being referenced by a foreign key constraint.
3727	10	Unable to drop constraint. See previous errors.
3728	16	'%.*s' is not a constraint.
3729	20	Unable to open table '%.*s' in dbid '%d'.
3730	20	Unable to locate entry in %s for constraint '%.*s'.
3731	16	'%.*s' is not a valid object.
3733	16	Constraint '%.*s' does not belong to table '%.*s'.
3734	20	Unable to update category field for DROP constraint.
3735	20	Primary key or unique constraint '%.*s' returned invalid indid:%d from sysconstraints.
3901	17	This transaction has referenced too many databases. The maximum allowed is %d. The transaction must be split into smaller sections.
3902	13	The commit transaction request has no corresponding BEGIN TRANSACTION.
3903	13	The rollback transaction request has no corresponding BEGIN TRANSACTION.

Error Number	Severity	Message Returned
3904	21	Can't unsplit logical page %ld in object '%.*s' in database '%.*s'—both pages together contain more data than will fit on one page.
3905	21	Can't unsplit logical page %ld in object '%.*s' in database '%.*s'—row number %d is used on both pages.
3906	16	Attempt to BEGIN TRANsaction in database '%.*s' failed because database is READ ONLY.
3907	21	Failed to receive results from PROBE. The distributed transaction named %.*s has not been committed and data may be inconsistent across databases.
3908	16	Attempt to BEGIN TRANsaction in database '%.*s' failed because database is in BYPASS RECOVERY mode.
4001	11	Cannot open default database '%.*s'.
4002	14	Login failed.
4013	14	Login failed—not a secure SQL Server.
4016	16	Language name in login record '%.*s' is not an official name on this SQL Server. Using default '%.*s' from Syslogins instead.
4017	16	Neither language name in login record '%.*s' nor language name in Syslogins '%.*s' is an official language name on this SQL Server. Using server-wide default '%.*s' instead.
4018	16	Your default language name from Syslogins '%.*s' is not an official language name on this SQL Server. Using server-wide default '%.*s' instead.
4019	16	Default date order '%.*s' for language '%.*s' is invalid. Using 'mdy' instead.

Continued

TABLE **D-1** **MICROSOFT SQL SERVER–GENERATED ERROR CODES** *(continued)*

Error Number	Severity	Message Returned
4027	16	Mount tape for %s of database '%s'.
4028	10	End of tape has been reached, remove tape '%s' and mount next tape for %s of database '%s'.
4029	10	Database '%s'%s(%d pages) dumped to file <%d> on tape '%s'.
4030	16	Tape '%s' expires on day '%s' year '%s' and cannot be overwritten.
4031	16	Creation date on tape '%s'(%s) does not match that of first volume(%s).
4032	16	Cannot find file %d on tape '%s'.
4033	16	File <%d> on tape '%s' is not an SQL Server %s dump.
4034	16	Warning, file <%d> on tape '%s' was dumped from database '%s'.
4035	10	Database '%s'%s(%d pages) dumped to file <%d> on device '%s'.
4036	16	Diskdump '%s'expires on day '%s' year '%s' and cannot be overwritten.
4037	16	User specified volume id '%s' does not match the volume id '%s' of the device '%.*s'.
4038	16	Cannot find file %d on device '%s'.
4039	10	Warning, file <%d> on device '%s' was dumped from database '%s'.
4040	16	File <%d> on device '%s' is not an SQL Server %s dump.
4041	16	Device '%s' has a stripe volume version; use INIT option for non-stripe dumps.
4042	16	Device '%s' has a non stripe volume version; use INIT option for stripe dumps.

Error Number	Severity	Message Returned
4043	16	Device '%.*s' has file number mismatch <%d> with stripe file number <%d>.
4044	10	Warning: EXPIREDATE or RETAINDAYS is enforced only for the first dump in the volume.
4202	21	Could not find BEGINXACT record in log while finding truncation page during dump transaction in database '%.*s'.
4203	21	Could not find checkpoint record after truncate page in dump transaction in database '%.*s'.
4204	10	Unable to continue logged version of DUMP TRANsaction. Please free up some space in database %d or use the NO_LOG option.
4205	16	Syslogs does not exist in its own segment in database '%d' with segmap '%ld' with logical start page number of '%ld'. You may not use DUMP TRAN in this case; use DUMP DATABASE instead.
4206	16	You cannot run DUMP TRANsaction WITH NO_LOG inside a user transaction.
4207	16	DUMP TRANsaction is not allowed while the select into/bulk copy option is enabled or if a non-logged operation has occurred: use DUMP DATABASE, or disable the option with sp_dboption.
4208	16	DUMP TRANsaction is not allowed while the trunc. log on chkpt. option is enabled: use DUMP DATABASE, or disable the option with sp_dboption.
4209	16	DUMP TRANsaction is not allowed because log was truncated or DUMP DATABASE was never run. Must run DUMP DATABASE.
4210	16	While attempting DUMP TRANsaction WITH NO_TRUNCATE, couldn't find database %.*s.

Continued

TABLE D-1 MICROSOFT SQL SERVER–GENERATED ERROR CODES *(continued)*

Error Number	Severity	Message Returned
4211	23	Couldn't complete DUMP TRANsaction WITH NO_TRUNCATE on database '%.*s', because the log pointer in Sysdatabases (page number %ld) is not accurate.
4301	16	Database in use. System Administrator must have exclusive use of DB to load transaction.
4302	16	Specified file '%.*s' is not in valid dump transaction format.
4305	16	Specified file '%.*s' is out of sequence. Current time stamp is %S_DATE while dump was from %S_DATE.
4306	16	There was activity on database since last load, unable to load. Must restart load sequence with the load database to continue.
4307	16	Specified file '%.*s' is not properly terminated.
4308	16	Premature end of file, unable to load.
4309	16	Loaded log page #%ld not free or allocated to log. File may be corrupted or internal error detected.
4310	16	Specified file '%.*s' is not in valid DUMP TRANsaction format.
4311	16	Specified file '%.*s' is in an obsolete DUMP TRANsaction format.
4312	16	You must be the DBO of database %.*s or the SA to run LOAD TRANsaction.
4313	16	Re-create index failed for table %ld, index %d. The table has been left in an inconsistent state, and the index is missing, so LOAD TRANSACTION errors may result. Run DBCC CHECKTABLE on the table if LOAD TRANSACTION succeeds.

Error Number	Severity	Message Returned
4314	20	Cannot find table %ld to re-create index %d.
4315	20	Log scan for re-create index failed.
4316	16	Can only LOAD TRANsaction in master if SQL Server is in single-user mode.
4317	16	Multipart database names ('%.*s') are illegal for LOAD TRANSACTION.
4401	16	View '%.*s' no longer exists.
4402	16	Infinite loop in view definition. Cannot resolve the view definitions in the query to the underlying tables.
4403	16	View '%.*s' is not updatable because it contains aggregates.
4404	16	View '%.*s' is not updatable because the definition contains DISTINCT.
4405	16	View '%.*s' is not updatable because the FROM clause names multiple tables.
4406	16	View '%.*s' is not updatable because a field of the view is derived or constant.
4408	19	The query and the views in it exceed the limit of %d tables.
4409	20	The columns in the query definition and the view definition do not match.
4412	16	View '%.*s's definition contains '%.*s', which is a temporary object. Views can only be based on permanent objects.
4413	16	View resolution could not succeed because the previously mentioned objects, upon which the view directly or indirectly relies, do not currently exist. These objects need to be re-created for the view to be usable.

Continued

TABLE **D-1 MICROSOFT SQL SERVER-GENERATED ERROR CODES** *(continued)*

Error Number	Severity	Message Returned
4414	16	Unable to allocate ancillary table for view resolution. Maximum number of tables in a query (%d) exceeded.
4415	16	View '%.*s' is not updatable because either it was created WITH CHECK OPTION or it spans a view created WITH CHECK OPTION and the target table is referenced multiple times in the resultant query.
4501	16	View '%.*s' has more columns defined than column names given.
4502	16	View '%.*s' has more column names specified than columns defined.
4503	20	The create view tree has a resdom with no right-hand side. View '%.*s', resdom '%.*s'.
4504	16	CREATE TABLE failed because there was not enough space to allocate memory for the table.
4505	16	CREATE VIEW failed because column '%.*s' in view '%.*s' exceeds the maximum of 250 columns.
4506	10	Column names in each view must be unique. Column name '%.*s' in view '%.*s' is specified more than once.
4507	16	Column '%.*s' specifies storage type %d, which does not currently exist.
4508	16	Views are not allowed on temporary tables. Table names that begin with '#' denote temporary tables.
4509	10	Column names in each view must be unique. An unnamed column is specified more than once in view '%.*s'.

Error Number	Severity	Message Returned
4510	16	Create view failed because WITH CHECK OPTION was specified and the view is not updatable.
4601	14	Only owner <%.*s> of object <%.*s>,in database %.*s can GRANT/REVOKE this permission.
4602	14	Only the System Administrator may GRANT or REVOKE the CREATE DATABASE permission.
4603	14	Only owner of current database may GRANT/REVOKE this permission.
4604	16	There is no such user %.*s.
4606	16	GRANTed/REVOKEd privilege %s not compatible with object.
4607	16	Privilege %s may not be GRANTed or REVOKEd.
4608	16	Only the System Administrator may GRANT/REVOKE ALTER DATABASE permission, and only to/from users with CREATE DATABASE permission.
4609	16	You cannot specify a column list with INSERT or DELETE.
4610	16	You may only GRANT or REVOKE permission on objects in the current database.
4701	11	Cannot truncate table '%.*s', because this table does not exist in database '%.*s'.
4706	17	Could not truncate table '%.*s' because there is not enough room in the log to record the deallocation of all of the index and data pages.
4708	16	Could not truncate object '%.*s' because it is not a table.
4709	16	You are not allowed to truncate the system table '%.*s'.

Continued

TABLE D-1 MICROSOFT SQL SERVER–GENERATED ERROR CODES *(continued)*

Error Number	Severity	Message Returned
4710	16	Cannot truncate table '%.*s' because you are not the owner or System Administrator.
4711	16	Cannot truncate table '%.*s' because it is published for replication.
4712	16	Cannot truncate table '%.*s' because it is being referenced by a foreign key constraint.
4801	20	Bulk_main: opentable on BULK INSERT table failed. Dbid=%d name='%.*s'.
4802	21	Bulk_main: getindex of primary index row failed on BULK INSERT table .
4804	21	Premature end-of-message while reading current row from host. Host program may have died.
4805	17	The front end tool you are using does not support the feature of bulk insert from host, please use the proper tools for this command.
4806	10	Warning, reverting to slow bulk copy on table '%.*s' because BULKCOPY option not set in database '%.*s'.
4808	10	The bulk copy of this table has been aborted because the CHECKPOINT record could not be written in the log. Please free up space in the database.
4810	16	Expected TEXT token in data stream for bulk copy of text data.
4811	16	Expected column offset in data stream for bulk copy of text data.
4812	16	Expected row offset in data stream for bulk copy of text data.

Error Number	Severity	Message Returned
4813	16	Expected text length in data stream for bulk copy of text data.
4814	16	Cannot perform an unlogged bulk copy into table '%.*s' because it is published for replication.
4901	16	ALTER TABLE only allows columns to be added which can contain nulls. Column '%.*s' cannot be added to table '%.*s' because it does not allow nulls.
4902	11	Cannot alter table '%.*s', because this table does not exist in database '%.*s'.
4905	21	ALTER TABLE failed because page %d of the system catalog Sysindexes in database '%.*s' is not in the cache.
4906	16	ALTER TABLE failed because adding all of the new columns to table '%.*s' would make the size of a row %d. %d is the maximum allowable size of a row in a table.
4909	16	Can't alter %.*s because it is not a table.
4910	16	Can't alter table '%.*s' because you are not the owner or System Administrator.
4912	16	The alter table statement contains multiple identity columns, alter table '%.*s' failed.
4913	16	Table '%.*s' already contains an identity column, cannot add new identity column via alter table.
4914	16	The number of existing rows (%ld) exceeds the maximum value for the specified datatype, cannot add new identity column to '%.*s'.

Continued

TABLE **D-1 MICROSOFT SQL SERVER–GENERATED ERROR CODES** *(continued)*

Error Number	Severity	Message Returned
4915	16	Maximum row width exceeded when adding identity column '%.*s' to table '%.*s'.
5001	16	User must be in Master Database.
5002	16	Database %.*s does not exist; check Sysdatabases.
5004	16	ALTER DATABASE failed. The size request must be positive.
5005	10	Extending database by %ld pages on disk %.*s.
5006	16	Could not find enough space on disks to extend database %.*s.
5008	16	System does not support Deextend Database currently.
5009	16	ALTER DATABASE failed. Some disk names listed in command were not found. Check that names exist and are spelled correctly before re-running command.
5011	14	Only the owner of database %.*s or the System Administrator may ALTER it.
5013	16	Cannot extend the MASTER database onto any device other than 'master'. The ALTER DATABASE was aborted.
5015	16	ALTER DATABASE failed. The total size specified must be 1 megabyte or greater.
5016	16	Incorrect database name or device name(s).
5017	16	ALTER DATABASE failed. Database %.*s not created with 'for load' option.
5018	16	The size of tempdb in RAM has exceeded the limit. The sum of 'memory size' and 'tempdb in ram' (configurable options) cannot exceed 2046 Megs.

Error Number	Severity	Message Returned
5101	15	Must give parameters for 'DISK %s' command. Usage: %s.
5102	15	No such command: 'DISK %.*s'.
5103	16	Illegal disk address range. The sum of VSTART and SIZE must be less than 16777216 (0x1000000).
5104	16	Device number %ld already used.
5105	16	Device activation error. The physical filename '%.*s' may be incorrect.
5106	15	Parameter '%s' requires value of type '%s'.
5107	15	Value is wrong type for parameter '%s' (requires type '%s').
5108	15	Parameter '%s' does not take a value.
5109	16	No such parameter: '%.*s'.
5114	20	Could not yield.
5115	16	I/O error during disk initialization. PHYSNAME '%.*s' may be incorrect or %ld (VSTART SIZE) may exceed the size of the device or permissions may be wrong for the device.
5116	14	Permission denied. Only the System Administrator may run DISK commands.
5117	16	Unable to run DISK command. Must be in master database to run this command.
5118	16	Unable to run DISK REFIT. SQL Server must be booted with the -m option. Please see your System Administration Guide about the Restore Master procedure.
5119	18	Unable to reserve a buffer, aborting DISK REFIT command. Please retry Restore Master procedure.

Continued

TABLE D-1 MICROSOFT SQL SERVER–GENERATED ERROR CODES *(continued)*

Error Number	Severity	Message Returned
5120	10	Bad segment map (%d) in Sysusages for row with Dbid = %d, Logical Start = 0x%lx, Virtual Start = 0x%lx, and Size = 0x%lx. Recommend you patch this value with correct information after Disk Refit completes.
5121	10	Warning: Disk Refit may not have the correct segment map information in Sysusages. Please review these after the command completes to verify their accuracy.
5122	10	The disk size must be >= 512.
5123	16	DISK INIT encountered an error while attempting to open/create the physical file. Please consult the SQL Server error log (in the SQL Server boot directory) for more details.
5124	10	Activating disk '%.*s'.
5125	10	Failed to complete unmirror of logical device '%.*s' after recovery of the master database.
5126	16	The logical device '%.*s' does not exist in SYSDEVICES.
5127	16	The device '%.*s' is already mirrored and mirroring is enabled.
5128	16	The device '%.*s' is already mirrored but mirroring is disabled. Use the DISK REMIRROR command to enable mirroring or unmirror the device.
5129	16	Syntax error detected in the value for parameter 'mirror'. You must provide a valid physical device/file name for this parameter.

Error Number	Severity	Message Returned
5130	16	The value for parameter 'mirror' translates to the same name as that for the primary device. Use another physical device for the mirror.
5131	16	The device '%.*s' is not currently mirrored.
5132	10	DISK MIRROR encountered an error while attempting to create the physical file '%.*s'. Please consult the SQL Server error log for more details.
5133	10	Unable to start i/o to '%.*s'. Please consult the SQL Server error log for details.
5134	10	Dynamic mirroring failed for logical device '%.*s'. Check the SQL Server error log for more information.
5135	10	Starting Dynamic Mirroring of %ld pages for logical device '%.*s'.
5136	10	%ld pages mirrored...
5137	10	Failed to mirror device '%.*s'.
5138	10	Failed to unmirror device '%.*s'.
5139	10	Failed to remirror device '%.*s'.
5140	10	Creating the physical file for the mirror...
5141	17	Unable to start Dynamic Mirroring because an i/o buffer is not currently available. Try the command again later.
5142	16	Mirroring for device '%.*s' is not currently enabled.
5143	10	The remaining %ld pages are currently unallocated and will be mirrored as they are allocated.

Continued

TABLE D-1 MICROSOFT SQL SERVER-GENERATED ERROR CODES *(continued)*

Error Number	Severity	Message Returned
5144	16	You can't remove the secondary physical device for virtual device '%.*s' since it is currently the only operational device. Use the SIDE=PRIMARY qualifier for the DISK UNMIRROR COMMAND.
5145	16	Error re-initializing device '%.*s'. Check SQL Server error log for more information.
5146	16	The %s of %d is out of range. It must be between %d and %d.
5147	10	Device size set to %ld blocks.
5148	16	Disk Resize can be used only to expand non-RAM devices.
5149	16	Disk Resize encountered an error while attempting to expand the physical file. Please consult the SQL Server error log for more details.
5150	16	Cannot find device '%.*s' in sysdevices.
5151	16	Cannot explicitly open or close the master device.
5152	16	Failed to close device '%.*s', see errorlog for details.
5153	16	Failed to open device '%.*s', see errorlog for details.
5154	16	Device '%.*s' is not open.
5155	16	Device '%.*s' is already open.
5156	16	Usage: DBCC DEVCONTROL(devname,ONLINE|OFFLINE).
5157	16	IO error in writelog during backout.
5158	10	Warning, media in device '%.*s' may have been changed.
5159	16	OS Error %.*s on device '%.*s' during %s.

Error Number	Severity	Message Returned
5160	16	Cannot take '%.*s' offline because usecount=%d.
5161	16	Database '%.*s' is marked offline.
5162	16	Cannot find '%.*s' in sysdatabases.
5163	16	Cannot open '%.*s' to take offline.
5164	16	Usage: DBCC DBCONTROL(dbname,ONLINE|OFFLINE).
5165	16	Cannot explicitly open or close master database.
5166	16	Database '%.*s' is not offline.
5167	16	Database '%.*s' is already offline.
5701	10	Changed database context to '%.*s'.
5702	10	The SQL Server is terminating this process.
5703	10	Changed language setting to '%.*s'.
5803	10	Unknown config number in Sysconfigures, config = %d.
5804	16	Too few databases specified, minimum = %d.
5805	16	Too few locks specified, minimum = %d.
5806	16	Too few descriptors specified, minimum = %d.
5807	16	Do not recommend recovery intervals above %d minutes—use override option to force this configuration.
5808	16	Do not recommend ad hoc updates to system catalogues, use override option to force this configuration.
5809	16	Do not recommend average time slices above %d milliseconds, use override option to force this configuration.

Continued

TABLE **D-1 MICROSOFT SQL SERVER–GENERATED ERROR CODES** *(continued)*

Error Number	Severity	Message Returned
5810	16	Legal values for fill factor is 0 to 100.
5811	16	Legal values for percent allocated to procedure cache is 1 to 99.
5812	14	Permission denied. Only the System Administrator may run reconfigure.
5813	16	Unable to run with specified memory size of %ld. Please see the System Administration Guide for more information on how to calculate this number.
5816	16	Legal values for the number of remote logins are 0 or positive numbers.
5817	16	Legal values for the number of remote sites are 0 or positive numbers.
5818	16	Legal values for the number of remote connections are 0 or positive numbers.
5819	16	Legal values for the number of pre-read packets per remote connection are 0 or positive numbers.
5820	16	Number of remote logins should be greater than the number of remote sites.
5821	16	Number of remote connections should be greater than the number of remote sites.
5822	16	Version number should be between 0 and 10000.
5823	16	Cannot reconfigure server to use sort order ID %d, because the row for that sort order does not exist in Syscharsets.
5824	16	Cannot reconfigure server to use sort order ID %d, because the row for its underlying character set (ID %d) does not exist in Syscharsets.

Error Number	Severity	Message Returned
5825	16	Cannot reconfigure the server's sort order since the Syscharsets table does not exist. You must upgrade your server prior to attempting this.
5826	10	You have just reconfigured SQL Server's default sort order. System table indexes will be rebuilt when you reboot the SQL server.
5827	10	In changing the default sort order, you have also reconfigured SQL Server's default character set.
5828	16	User connections are limited to %d.
5901	20	Was unable to get an alarm, the background checkpoint process is unable to run.
5902	20	Serious kernel error reported on upsleep call, unwilling to continue. Aborting the background checkpoint process.
5903	16	Unable to open database with id = %d, suspect inconsistency in sysdatabases table.
5904	17	Background checkpoint process suspended until locks are available.
6001	10	SHUTDOWN is waiting for %d process(es) to complete.
6002	10	A SHUTDOWN command is in progress. Please log off.
6003	10	This process terminated by SHUTDOWN command.
6004	10	The SHUTDOWN command may only be used by the system administrator.
6005	10	A SHUTDOWN is in progress.
6006	10	Server SHUTDOWN by request.

Continued

TABLE **D-1 MICROSOFT SQL SERVER–GENERATED ERROR CODES** *(continued)*

Error Number	Severity	Message Returned
6101	16	Process '%d' is not a valid process number. Choose a number between 1 and '%d'.
6102	14	Only the System Administrator may use the KILL command.
6103	17	Unable to do cleanup for the killed process; received Msg %d.
6104	16	You cannot use KILL to kill your own process.
6106	16	Process '%d' is not an active process number.
6107	14	Only User processes can be KILLed.
6201	10	STEP %d.
6202	10	The type of query is SELECT (into a worktable).
6203	10	The type of query is %s.
6204	10	The update mode is direct.
6205	10	The update mode is deferred.
6206	10	%*sGROUP BY.
6207	10	%*sVector Aggregate.
6208	10	Scalar Aggregate.
6209	10	This step involves sorting.
6210	10	Worktable created for ORDER BY.
6211	10	Worktable created for DISTINCT.
6212	10	Worktable created for REFORMATTING.
6213	10	Worktable created for SELECT INTO.
6214	10	%*sTO TABLE.
6215	10	%*sFROM TABLE.
6216	10	%*sWorktable %d.

Error Number	Severity	Message Returned
6217	10	%*s%.*s %.*s.
6219	10	%*sNested iteration.
6220	10	%*sEXISTS TABLE : nested iteration.
6221	10	Using GETSORTED Table Scan.
6222	10	%*sUsing Dynamic Index.
6223	10	%*sTable Scan.
6224	10	%*sUsing Clustered Index.
6225	10	%*sIndex : %.*s.
6226	10	%*sIndex name not found.
6227	10	%*sSUBQUERY : nested iteration.
6228	10	%*sAND EXISTS : nested iteration.
6229	10	%*sAND NOT EXISTS : nested iteration.
6230	10	%*sOR EXISTS : nested iteration.
6231	10	%*sOR NOT EXISTS : nested iteration.
6232	10	%*sRow estimate: %s.
6233	10	%*sCost estimate: %s.
6234	10	%*sJOINS WITH.
6235	10	WITH CHECK OPTION.
6401	16	Cannot rollback %.*s—no transaction or savepoint of that name found.
6402	20	Inconsistency in rollback logic. ROLLBACK finds no matching SAVE TRANsaction or BEGIN TRANsaction. ROLLBACK aborted.
6403	20	No matching savexact record found when rolling back the subordinate transaction %.*s.
6501	21	Logical page 0x%x in database '%.*s' missing from buffer cache after fetching the index row.

Continued

TABLE D-1 MICROSOFT SQL SERVER–GENERATED ERROR CODES *(continued)*

Error Number	Severity	Message Returned
6701	16	Could not open dbid %d, object %ld.
6901	21	Overflow on High component of timestamp occurred in database %d. Database table possibly corrupt.
6902	21	Page timestamp value falls between the old and new timestamps from log. Page #=%ld, object id = %ld, page timestamp=%04x %08lx. Log: old timestamp=%04x %08lx, new timestamp=%04x %08lx.
6903	21	High order of timestamp indicates that timestamp structure may be incorrect.
6904	21	Mismatch between database table passed and the one found in the system structure when requesting new database timestamp. Database id passed in : %d. System database id : %d.
7101	17	Unable to allocate new text value, dbid %d.
7102	19	Unexpected end-of-message found while reading from network.
7103	22	Read of text value failed for text pointer %lx%lx.
7104	22	Can't open the object containing text pointer %lx%lx.
7105	22	Page %ld for text value does not exist.
7106	22	Row %d for text value does not exist.
7107	22	Text pointer %lx%lx invalid. On page %d, row %d doesn't contain text value.
7108	20	Process %d already has the buffer we are using for an allocation resource locked: %S_PAGE.

Error Number	Severity	Message Returned
7109	22	Unexpected log record of type %d found while processing TEXT/IMAGE data.
7111	17	Can't log text value because log is out of space.
7112	17	Deadlock occurred while trying to lock page %ld, which is held by SQL Server process %d.
7113	22	Data size mismatch detected when transferring TEXT/IMAGE value. First fragment page number: %ld.
7114	22	Page %ld is not a valid text page.
7115	25	Page %ld expected to be first fragment value.
7116	25	Offset %d is not in range of available text data.
7117	16	Length %d is not in range of available text data.
7118	16	Object id %ld on page %ld is not the one expected which is %ld.
7120	22	Log record %ld:%d was not found in the LOG.
7121	22	Free offset %d is invalid on page %ld.
7122	20	Invalid source identified during TEXT/IMAGE transfer. Source id is: %d.
7123	16	Invalid text pointer value %s.
7124	16	The offset and length specified in the READTEXT command is greater than the actual data length of %ld.
7125	16	Text pointer value conflicts with the column name specified.
7126	16	Text pointer value references a data page with an invalid text status.

Continued

TABLE **D-1 MICROSOFT SQL SERVER–GENERATED ERROR CODES** *(continued)*

Error Number	Severity	Message Returned
7127	16	Text pointer value references a data page with an invalid time stamp.
7128	16	Text pointer value references a data page which is no longer allocated.
7129	16	Synchronization time stamp does not agree with text data page value.
7130	16	%s with no log is not valid at this time. Use sp_dboption to set the 'select into/bulk copy' option on for database %s.
7131	16	Invalid table and column name specified in textvalid function.
7132	16	Selection of TEXT and IMAGE datatypes require DBLIB 4.0 or greater.
7133	16	NULL textptr passed to %s function.
7134	16	The text table and the table referenced by the text pointer disagree.
7135	16	Deletion length %ld is not in the range of available text data.
7201	17	Can't open a connection to site '%.*s' because there are no remote sites available. Rerun when there are fewer active remote sites, or ask your System Administrator to reconfigure SQL Server with more 'remote sites'.
7202	17	Can't open a connection to site '%.*s' because there are no available PSS structures.
7203	17	Can't open a connection to site '%.*s' because SQL Server is not configured for enough user connections. See the error log file in the SQL Server boot directory.

Error Number	Severity	Message Returned
7204	18	Can't open a connection to site '%.*s' because the site is already active.
7205	18	Can't open a connection to site '%.*s'. See the error log file in the SQL Server boot directory.
7206	17	Can't open a connection to site '%.*s' because all channel numbers are in use.
7207	17	Can't open a connection to site '%.*s' because there are no remote connections available. Rerun when there are fewer remote users and/or fewer local users making remote accesses, or ask your SA to reconfigure SQL Server with more 'remote connections'.
7208	17	Can't open a connection to site '%.*s' because there are no remote logins available. Rerun when there are fewer local users making remote accesses, or ask your System Administrator to reconfigure SQL Server with more 'remote logins'.
7209	17	Cannot open a connection to site '%.*s' because %S_MSG buffer could not be initialized.
7210	18	Can't open a connection to site '%.*s' because 'set up channel' message could not be sent.
7211	18	Can't open a connection to site '%.*s' because 'set up channel' message was not acknowledged.
7212	11	Can't close connection %d on site '%.*s' because it is not active.
7213	18	Can't remove site '%.*s' from list of active sites because it is missing.

Continued

TABLE D-1 MICROSOFT SQL SERVER-GENERATED ERROR CODES *(continued)*

Error Number	Severity	Message Returned
7214	11	No site name received in server login packet. Server login rejected.
7215	18	Can't send to site '%.*s'.
7216	18	Can't read from site '%.*s'.
7217	18	Echo failed from site '%.*s'.
7218	11	Site '%.*s' not found in Sysservers.
7219	11	Site %d not found in Sysservers.
7220	11	Site '%s' not found in interfaces file.
7221	14	Login to site '%.*s' failed.
7222	18	Received bad token 0x%x from site '%.*s'.
7223	16	Cannot %S_MSG site '%.*s'.
7224	16	Unexpected end-of-message encountered in RPC response from site '%.*s'.
7225	16	Unknown datatype token %d '%s' encountered.
7226	16	Alternate row received for id %d with no corresponding format information.
7227	17	Can't open a connection to site '%.*s' because SQL Server is not configured for remote access. Ask your System Administrator to reconfigure SQL Server to allow remote access.
7901	16	Page %ld was expected to be the first page of a TEXT/IMAGE value.
7902	16	Data size mismatch occurred while checking TEXT/IMAGE values. The first page for this value is: %ld. There were %ld bytes found, which is different from the expected data length of %ld bytes.

Error Number	Severity	Message Returned
7903	16	Page %ld was expected to be a TEXT/IMAGE page. This occurred when link number %ld was examined.
7904	10	The total number of TEXT/IMAGE pages in this table is %ld.
7905	10	The number of rows in Sysindexes for this table was %ld. It has been corrected to %ld.
7906	10	The number of data pages in Sysindexes for this table was %ld. It has been corrected to %ld.
7907	16	The status in the first page (%ld) of the no_log table %.*s and the status in the sysobjects row, do not match.
7908	10	The table %.*s was created with the no_log option.
7909	10	A transaction involving the no_log table %.*s was undone. This may have left the table in an inconsistent state. Rebuild the table.
7910	16	Page %ld allocated (Alloc page: %ld Extent ID: %ld Alloc mask: 0x%x).
7911	16	Page %ld deallocated (Alloc page: %ld Extent ID: %ld Alloc mask: 0x%x).
7912	16	EXTID:%ld (Alloc page: %ld) is initialized. Extent follows.
7913	16	NEXT=%ld PREV=%ld OBJID=%ld ALLOC=0x%x DEALL=0x%x INDID=%d STATUS=0x%x.
7914	16	Allocation page %ld Extid %ld is not referenced, but there are referenced pages within this extent. Contact Tech Support for object %ld.

Continued

TABLE D-1 MICROSOFT SQL SERVER–GENERATED ERROR CODES (continued)

Error Number	Severity	Message Returned
7915	16	Allocation page %ld extid %ld is referenced, but there are no referenced pages within this extent. Contact Tech Support for object %ld.
7916	16	Total (# alloc pages= %ld, # of alloc pages modified=%ld).
7917	16	Total (# pages allocated=%ld pages deallocated=%ld extents deleted=%ld).
7918	16	Alloc page %ld (pgs allocated=%ld pgs deallocated=%ld extents deleted=%ld).
7919	16	Fix_al not processed. Database needs to be in SINGLE USER mode.
7920	16	Processed %ld entries in the Sysindexes for dbid %d.
7921	16	Found %ld bad entries in the Sysindexes.
7923	16	TABLE: %.*sOBJID = %ld.
7924	16	INDID=%ld FIRST=%ld ROOT=%ld DPAGES=%ld SORT=%d.
7925	16	Indid: %d. %ld Index Pages in %ld extents.
7926	16	Data level: %d. %ld Data Pages in %ld extents.
7927	16	TOTAL # of extents = %ld.
7928	16	Index %.*s is not consistent; found %ld leaf rows. Drop and re-create the index.
7929	16	Table has %ld data rows.
7930	16	Table Corrupt: keys in left child is not less than the parent key; check left child page %ld.
7931	16	Table Corrupt: keys in right child is less than parent key; check right child page %ld.

Error Number	Severity	Message Returned
7932	16	The indexes for '%.*s' are already correct. They will not be rebuilt.
7933	16	One or more indexes are corrupt. They will be rebuilt.
7934	16	The table '%.*s' has no indexes.
7935	16	REINDEX received an exception—command aborted.
7937	16	The data in table '%.*s' is possibly corrupt—REINDEX aborted. Run DBCC CHECKTABLE and report errors to your System Administrator.
7944	10	*** NOTICE: Space used on the log segment is %4.2f Mbytes, %4.2f%%.
7945	10	*** NOTICE: Space free on the log segment is %4.2f Mbytes, %4.2f%%.
7946	10	*** NOTICE: Notification of log space used/free cannot be reported because the log segment is not on its own device.
7947	16	The sortorder and character set IDs for index %d on this table were %d:%d in Sysindexes. They have been corrected to %d:%d.
7962	16	Upgrade requires the SQL Server to be booted in single user mode. Reboot the SQL Server with the -m flag.
7963	16	Upgrade encountered a fatal error. Please check the SQL Server error log.
7964	16	Allocation page SDES not open.
7965	16	Page is not an allocation page.
7966	10	WARNING: NOINDEX option of '%.*s' being used, checks on non-system indexes will be skipped.

Continued

TABLE D-1 MICROSOFT SQL SERVER-GENERATED ERROR CODES *(continued)*

Error Number	Severity	Message Returned
7967	16	DBCC %.*s command does not support the %.*s option.
7968	1	Transaction Information for database: %.*s.
7969	1	No active open transactions.
7970	1	%sOldest active transaction:
7971	1	SPID : %d.
7972	1	UID : %d.
7973	1	SUID : %d.
7974	1	Name : %.*s.
7975	1	RID : (%d , %d).
7976	1	Time Stamp : %04X %08X.
7977	1	Start Time : %.*s.
7979	1	%sReplicated Transaction Information:
7980	1	Oldest Distributed RID : (%d , %d).
7981	1	Time Stamp : %04X %08X.
7982	1	Oldest Non-Distributed RID : (%d , %d).
7983	14	Only the DBO of database %.*s may run the DBCC %s command.
7984	16	Invalid object name '%.*s'.
7985	16	The object name '%.*s' contains more than the maximum number of prefixes. The maximum is %d.
7986	16	WARNING: Pinning tables should be carefully considered. If a pinned table is larger or grows larger than the available data cache, the server may need to be restarted and the table unpinned.
7987	16	Switch to database '%.*s' before running this command.

Error Number	Severity	Message Returned
7988	16	This command cannot be run on the MASTER database when a size parameter is specified. Use the '%s' option.
7989	16	The size option cannot be specified for TEMPDB when it is on a RAM device.
7990	16	Database '%.*s' has status: 0x%x which is not a normal database state. (Mask: 0x%x).
7991	16	Unable to shrink database '%.*s' as it contains %d pages. Minimum pages %d.
7992	10	DBCC SHRINKDB running on database '%.*s'
7993	16	Unable to shrink database '%.*s' to %d pages as it only contains %d pages.
7994	16	Unable to shrink database '%.*s' to %d pages. Minimum new size %d pages.
7995	16	See prior errors. DBCC operation has been aborted.
7996	16	Extended stored procedures can only be created in the master database.
8002	15	Parameter number %d and subsequent parameters must be passed as '@name = value'. Once the form '@name = value' has been used, all subsequent parameters must be passed in the form '@name = value'.
8003	15	There are too many parameters in this CREATE PROCEDURE statement. The maximum number is %d.
8004	16	Received an unrecognized datatype %d from TDS datastream.
8005	15	Received a procedure name length of %d. The TDS datastream is incorrect.
8006	16	Maxlen %d invalid for datatype '%s'.

Continued

TABLE **D-1 MICROSOFT SQL SERVER–GENERATED ERROR CODES** *(continued)*

Error Number	Severity	Message Returned
8101	16	An explicit value for the identity column in table '%.*s' can only be specified when a column list is used and IDENTITY_INSERT is ON.
8102	16	Illegal attempt to update identity column '%.*s'.
8103	16	Table '%.*s' does not exist or cannot be opened for SET operation.
8104	16	Current user is not the DBO or object owner for table '%.*s', unable to perform SET operation.
8105	16	'%.*s' is not a user table, unable to perform SET operation.
8106	16	Table '%.*s' does not have the identity property, unable to perform SET operation.
8107	16	IDENTITY_INSERT is already ON for table '%.*s.%.*s.%.*s'.%sUnable to perform SET operation for table '%.*s'.
8108	16	Attempting to add identity column to table '%.*s', via select into, which already has column '%.*s' that inherits the identity property.
8109	16	Attempting to add multiple identity columns to table '%.*s', via select into.
8110	16	Attempting to add multiple primary key constraints to table '%.*s'.
8111	16	Attempting to define PRIMARY KEY constraint on nullable column in table '%.*s'.
8112	16	Attempting to add more than one clustered index for constraints on table '%.*s'.

Error Number	Severity	Message Returned
8113	16	Unable to recompile '%.*s', '%s %.*s' is illegal in an open transaction.
8114	16	Error converting type %s to type %s.
8115	16	Arithmetic overflow error converting %s to type %s.
8116	16	Argument type %s is invalid for argument %d of %s function.
8117	16	Operand data type %s is invalid for %s operator.
8118	16	Column '%.*s.%.*s' is invalid in the select list because it is not contained in an aggregate function and there is no GROUP BY clause.
8119	16	Column '%.*s.%.*s' is invalid in the HAVING clause because it is not contained in an aggregate function and there is no GROUP BY clause.
8120	16	Column '%.*s.%.*s' is invalid in the select list because it is not contained in either an aggregate function or the GROUP BY clause.
8121	16	Column '%.*s.%.*s' is invalid in the HAVING clause because it is not contained in either an aggregate function or the GROUP BY clause.
8122	16	Only the first query in the UNION statement is allowed to have a select with assignment.
8123	16	A correlated expression is invalid because it is not in a GROUP BY clause.

Continued

TABLE D-1 MICROSOFT SQL SERVER-GENERATED ERROR CODES *(continued)*

Error Number	Severity	Message Returned
8124	16	Multiple columns specified in an aggregated expression containing an outer reference. If an expression being aggregated contains an outer reference, then that outer reference must be the only column reference in the expression.
8125	16	An aggregated expression containing an outer reference must be contained in either the select list or a subquery of the HAVING clause of the query whose FROM clause contains the table containing the column being aggregated.
8126	16	Column name '%.*s.%.*s' is invalid in the ORDER BY clause because it is not contained in an aggregate function and there is no GROUP BY clause.
8127	16	Column name '%.*s.%.*s' is invalid in the ORDER BY clause because it is not contained in either an aggregate function or the GROUP BY clause.
8129	16	Shrinking of database devices is not allowed in the current version. The new disk size must be greater than %d.
8130	16	Device is not a database device. Only database devices can be expanded.
8131	16	Error occurred allocating resource during expansion of device TEMP_DB. Please consult the event log for details.
8132	16	The number of expansions of the device TEMP_DB has exceeded the system limit. In order to expand the device shutdown and restart the server.
8133	16	All the result expressions in a CASE specification must not be NULL.

Error Number	Severity	Message Returned
8134	16	Divide by zero error encountered.
8135	16	Table level constraint does not specify column list, table '%.*s'.
8136	16	Duplicate columns specified in %s constraint key list, table '%.*s'.
8137	16	Foreign key reference is missing target table name, table '%.*s'.
8138	16	More than 16 columns specified in foreign key column list, table '%.*s'.
8139	16	Number of referencing columns in foreign key differs from number of referenced columns, table '%.*s'.
8140	16	More than one key specified in column level %s constraint, table '%.*s'.
8141	16	Column %s constraint for column '%.*s' references another column, table '%.*s'.
8142	16	Subqueries are not supported in %s constraints, table '%.*s'.
8143	16	Parameter %.*s was supplied multiple times.
8144	16	Too many arguments supplied for procedure %.*s.
8145	16	%.*s is not a parameter for procedure %.*s.
8146	16	Procedure %.*s has no parameters and arguments were supplied.
8147	16	Attempt to create IDENTITY attribute on nullable column '%.*s', table '%.*s'.
8148	16	More than one column %s constraint specified for column '%.*s', table '%.*s'.
8149	16	Invalid column '%.*s' specified in %s definition, table '%.*s'.

Continued

TABLE **D-1** MICROSOFT SQL SERVER-GENERATED ERROR CODES *(continued)*

Error Number	Severity	Message Returned
8150	16	Multiple NULL constraints specified for column '%.*s', table '%.*s'.
8151	16	Both a primary key and unique constraint have been defined for column '%.*s', table '%.*s'. Only one is allowed.
13001	10	data page
13002	10	index page
13003	10	leaf page
13004	10	last
13005	10	root
13006	10	read from
13007	10	send to
13008	10	receive
13009	10	send
13010	10	read
13011	10	wait
13012	10	A USE DATABASE statement.
13013	10	A procedure or trigger.
13014	10	A DISTINCT clause.
13015	10	A view.
13016	10	An INTO clause.
13017	10	An ORDER BY clause.
13018	10	A COMPUTE clause.
13019	10	A SELECT INTO statement.
13020	10	option
13021	10	offset option
13022	10	statistics option

Error Number	Severity	Message Returned
13023	10	parameter option
13024	10	built-in function name
13025	10	field
13026	10	parameter
13027	10	convert specification
13028	10	index
13029	10	table
13030	10	database
13031	10	procedure
13032	10	trigger
13033	10	view
13034	10	default
13035	10	rule
13036	10	system
13037	10	unknown type
13038	10	SET command
13039	10	column
13040	10	type
13041	10	character string
13042	10	integer
13043	10	identifier
13044	10	number
13045	10	integer value
13046	10	floating point value
13047	10	object
13048	10	column heading
13076	10	An assignment.

Continued

TABLE **D-1** MICROSOFT SQL SERVER-GENERATED ERROR CODES *(continued)*

Error Number	Severity	Message Returned
13076	10	An assignment.
13077	10	A cursor declaration.
13078	10	replication filter
14001	16	The destination table must not be qualified.
14002	16	The 'Sync' subsystem with the Task id '%ld' was not found.
14003	16	You must supply a publication name.
14004	16	%s must be in the current database.
14005	16	Unable to drop publication. A subscription exists on it.
14006	16	Unable to drop the publication.
14007	16	You cannot change the destination database of a subscription unless it is inactive.
14008	11	There are no publications.
14009	11	There are no articles for publication '%s'.
14010	16	The remote server is not defined as a subscription server.
14011	16	The publication you have selected does not exist or you do not have permission to access it.
14012	16	The @status value must be either 'active' or 'inactive'.
14013	16	This database is not enabled for publication.
14014	16	The synchronization method (@sync_method) must be either '[bcp] native' or '[bcp] character'.

Error Number	Severity	Message Returned
14015	16	The replication frequency (@repl_freq) must be either 'continuous' or 'snapshot'.
14016	16	The publication '%s' already exists.
14017	16	Invalid @restricted value. Valid options are 'true' or 'false'.
14018	16	The publication could not be created.
14019	16	The @operation must be either 'add' or 'drop'.
14020	16	The column id for the specified column could not be obtained. The column was not correctly added to the article.
14021	16	The column was not correctly added to the article.
14022	16	The property must be 'name', 'description', 'sync_object', 'type', 'status', 'ins_cmd', 'del_cmd', 'upd_cmd', 'filter', 'dest_table', 'creation_script' or 'pre_creation_cmd'.
14023	16	The type must be 'logbased', 'logbased manualfilter', 'logbased manualview', or 'logbased manualboth'.
14024	16	The status must be 'active' or 'inactive'.
14025	10	The article was successfully updated.
14026	16	The synchronization method must be '[bcp] native', '[bcp] character', or 'dump/load'
14027	11	%s does not exist in the current database.
14028	11	User tables are the only objects that can be published.
14029	16	The vertical partition switch must be either 'true' or 'false'.

Continued

TABLE **D-1** MICROSOFT SQL SERVER-GENERATED ERROR CODES *(continued)*

Error Number	Severity	Message Returned
14030	16	The article '%s' already exists in publication '%s'.
14031	16	User tables and views are the only valid synchronization objects.
14032	16	The article name cannot be the keyword 'all'.
14034	16	The publication name @publication cannot be the keyword 'all'.
14035	10	Database '%s' is already enabled for publishing.
14036	16	Unable to enable database for publishing.
14037	16	Database '%s' is not enabled for publishing.
14038	16	Unable to disable database for publishing.
14039	16	Unable to construct column clause for article view. Reduce the number of columns or create the view manually.
14040	16	The server '%s' is already a subscriber.
14041	16	Unable to perform the command. The distribution server is not available.
14042	16	Unable to be create subscriber.
14043	16	%s cannot be NULL.
14044	16	Owner qualified %s names are not allowed.
14045	16	The task id must be unique. The specified @taskid has already been used.
14046	16	Unable to drop article. A subscription exists on it.
14047	16	Unable to drop %s.
14048	16	The server '%s' is not a subscriber.

Error Number	Severity	Message Returned
14049	16	Stored procedures are the only objects that can be used as a filter.
14050	11	You do not have a subscription on this publication/article.
14051	16	The property must be 'sync_type' or 'dest_db'.
14052	16	The sync_type must be 'manual', 'automatic', or 'none'.
14053	16	The subscription could not be updated at this time.
14054	10	The subscription was successfully updated.
14055	10	There is no subscription on article %s in publication %s for subscriber %s.
14056	16	The subscription could not be dropped at this time.
14057	16	The subscription could not be created.
14058	16	The subscription already exists.
14059	16	Unable to obtain information from the distribution server.
14060	16	Unable to update distribution subscriber table. The subscriber could not be removed at this time.
14061	16	The pre_creation_cmd must be 'none', 'drop', 'delete', or 'truncate'.
14062	10	The subscriber was dropped.
14063	11	The remote server does not exist or has not been designated as a valid subscriber.
14064	11	There are no subscribers registered.
14065	16	The status must be 'active', 'inactive', or 'subscribed'.

Continued

TABLE D-1 MICROSOFT SQL SERVER–GENERATED ERROR CODES (continued)

Error Number	Severity	Message Returned
14066	16	The previous status must be 'active', 'inactive', or 'subscribed'.
14067	16	The status value is the same as the previous status value.
14068	16	Unable to update sysobjects. The subscription status could not be changed.
14069	16	Unable to update sysarticles. The subscription status could not be changed.
14070	16	Unable to update the distribution database subscription table. The subscription status could not be changed.
14071	16	This distributor information could not be obtained.
14072	16	The publication you have selected is restricted. Contact your System Administrator or Database Owner to obtain permission to subscribe to this publication. The subscription was not created.
14073	16	This procedure must be executed from the subscriber.
14074	16	The server '%s' is already listed as a publisher.
14075	16	The publisher could not be created at this time.
14076	16	Unable to grant replication login privilege to '%s'.
14077	10	The publication was successfully updated.
14078	16	The property must be 'name', 'description', 'taskid', 'sync_method', 'status', 'repl_freq', or 'restricted'.

Error Number	Severity	Message Returned
14079	16	Do not qualify the destination table name with a database. Use the 'dest_db' property of sp_changesubscription to specify a destination database.
14080	11	The remote server does not exist or has not been designated as a valid publisher.
14081	16	@replicated must be either 'true' or 'false'.
14082	10	The object was successfully marked as a replicated object.
14083	16	The object was not successfully (un)marked as a replicated object.
14085	16	The subscriber information could not be obtained from the distributor.
14086	16	'%s' is not a valid @subscriber_db.
14087	16	No completed transactions found.
14088	16	The table '%s' must have a primary key in order to be published.
14089	10	'%ld' completed transactions for subscriber '%s' were removed from the distribution database.
14090	16	A distribution server already exists.
14091	16	The @type parameter passed to sp_helpreplicationdb must be either 'pub' or 'sub'.
14092	16	Unable to change article. A subscription exists on it.
14093	16	You must be System Administrator (SA) or the Database Owner (dbo) or a Replication Subscriber (repl_subscriber) to execute this stored procedure.
14150	10	Replication-%s: Task '%s' succeeded. %s.

Continued

TABLE **D-1** **MICROSOFT SQL SERVER-GENERATED ERROR CODES** *(continued)*

Error Number	Severity	Message Returned
14151	20	Replication-%s: Task '%s' failed. %s.
14152	18	Replication-%s: Task '%s' scheduled for retry after %d attempt(s). '%s'.
14153	10	Replication-%s: Task '%s' detected the potential for missing jobs on '%s'.
14200	16	Invalid frequency type.
14201	16	Invalid frequency subtype.
14202	16	Frequency interval invalid for this frequency type; consult your documentation.
14203	16	Invalid frequency relative interval; consult your documentation.
14204	16	Active end date cannot be less than active start date.
14205	16	Active end time cannot be less than active start time.
14206	16	Next run date must be between active start date and active end date.
14207	16	Next run time must be between active start time and active end time.
14208	16	You must specify a task name.
14209	16	Server '%s' is not a registered remote server.
14210	16	Task '%s' already exists.
14211	16	Database '%s' not found.
14212	16	Operator '%s' not found.
14213	16	Run priority must be one of: -15 (idle), -2 (lowest), -1(low), 0 (normal), 1 (high), 2 (highest), 15 (time critical).
14214	16	Invalid log history completion level.

Error Number	Severity	Message Returned
14215	16	Invalid email completion level.
14216	16	Invalid task id.
14217	16	You must be the SA or logged in as the owner of this task to update it.
14218	16	Invalid task name.
14219	16	You must be the SA or the owner of this task to drop it.
14220	16	Login '%s' not found.
14221	16	Administrator '%s' not found.
14222	16	Task '%s' not found.
14223	16	Task id '%ld' not found.
14224	16	You must be the SA, or specify a task for which you are the owner, to purge task histories.
14225	16	You must specify an Administrator name.
14226	16	Administrator '%s' already exists.
14227	16	You must specify an email address and/or a pager number for an Administrator.
14228	16	Invalid pager start time.
14229	16	Invalid pager end time.
14230	16	Pager end time must be later than pager end time.
14231	16	Pager days must be one or more of Sunday (day 1) thru Saturday (day 7).
14232	16	You must be the SA to add, drop, or update Administrators.
14233	16	Invalid admin id.
14234	16	Administrator '%s' is the Email Admin for one or more Tasks. You must reassign those Tasks before dropping the Administrator.

Continued

TABLE D-1 MICROSOFT SQL SERVER–GENERATED ERROR CODES (continued)

Error Number	Severity	Message Returned
14235	16	Administrator '%s' is the Email or Page Admin for one or more Alerts. You must reassign those Alerts before dropping the Administrator.
14236	16	Invalid active end date.
14237	16	Invalid active end time of day.
14238	16	Invalid active start date.
14239	16	Invalid active start time of day.
14240	16	Invalid next run date.
14241	16	Invalid next run time.
14244	16	You must be SA to reassign tasks.
14245	16	You must specify the task name or a login name to reassign or drop tasks.
14246	16	You must specify the name or id of the task to be updated.
14247	16	The username (%s) you have specified is not your username (%s) in the %s database. Only the SA or the DBO of %s may do this.
14500	16	You must supply either a zero (or NULL) for @message_id and a non-zero non-null value for @severity, or a zero (or NULL) for @severity and a non-zero non-null value for @message_id.
14501	16	The @task_name parameter you have supplied does not exist in systasks.
14502	16	The @severity parameter you have supplied is not valid.
14503	16	The @include_event_description_in parameter must be EMAIL, PAGER, BOTH, or NONE.

Error Number	Severity	Message Returned
14504	16	The @delay_between_responses parameter must be greater than or equal to 0.
14505	16	The @occurrence_count parameter must be greater than 0 or equal to 0.
14506	16	An Alert for this @message_id—or @severity—with the same @event_description_keyword and @database_name values already exists (id = %s).
14507	16	The @alert_name parameter you have supplied does not exist in sysalerts.
14508	16	The @operator_name parameter you have supplied does not exist in sysoperators.
14509	16	This Notification does not exist in sysnotifications.
14510	16	The @object_type parameter must be either ALERTS or OPERATORS.
14511	16	The @enum_type parameter must be either ALL, ACTUAL, or TARGET.
14512	16	The @notification_method parameter must be either EMAIL, PAGER, or BOTH.
14513	16	This Operator already exists.
14514	16	The @pager_days parameter you have supplied is invalid.
14515	16	This Notification already exists.
14516	16	The @enabled parameter must be either 0 or 1.
14517	16	The @notification_method parameter must be EMAIL, PAGER, or BOTH.
14518	16	The @message_id parameter you have supplied is not valid.

Continued

TABLE D-1 MICROSOFT SQL SERVER–GENERATED ERROR CODES *(continued)*

Error Number	Severity	Message Returned
14519	16	The @target_name parameter must be supplied when specifying an @enum_type of TARGET.
14520	16	The @target_name parameter should not be supplied when specifying an @enum_type of ALL or ACTUAL.
14521	16	The @target_name parameter does not exist in sys%s.
14522	16	The @weekday_pager_start_time parameter is invalid (must be in HHMMSS format).
14523	16	The @weekday_pager_end_time parameter is invalid (must be in HHMMSS format).
14524	16	The @saturday_pager_start_time parameter is invalid (must be in HHMMSS format).
14525	16	The @saturday_pager_end_time parameter is invalid (must be in HHMMSS format).
14526	16	The @sunday_pager_start_time parameter is invalid (must be in HHMMSS format).
14527	16	The @sunday_pager_end_time parameter is invalid (must be in HHMMSS format).
14528	16	The @name or @new_name parameter you have supplied is not unique.
14529	16	The @new_name parameter you have supplied is not unique.
14530	16	%s is the Fail-Safe Operator. You must make another operator the Fail-Safe operator before %s can be dropped.
14531	16	The @task_name parameter you have supplied is not an On-Demand task. Only On-Demand tasks may be fired in response to an Alert.

Error Number	Severity	Message Returned
15000	16	You must be System Administrator (SA) or the Database Owner (dbo) to execute this stored procedure.
15001	16	%s does not exist.
15002	16	The procedure '%s' cannot be executed from within a transaction.
15003	16	You must be System Administrator (SA) to execute this stored procedure.
15004	16	Name cannot be NULL.
15005	16	'%s' is not a valid name since it begins with an invalid character.
15006	16	'%s' is not a valid name since it contains invalid characters.
15007	16	The login '%s' does not exist.
15008	16	User '%s' does not exist in the current database.
15009	16	The object '%s' does not exist in database '%s'.
15010	16	The database '%s' does not exist. Use sp_helpdb to show available databases.
15011	16	Database option '%s' does not exist.
15012	16	The device '%s' does not exist. Use sp_helpdevice to show available devices.
15013	16	The device option '%s' does not exist or is not a settable option.
15014	16	The group '%s' does not exist in the current database.
15015	16	The server '%s' does not exist. Use sp_helpserver to show available servers.
15016	16	The default '%s' does not exist.
15017	16	The rule '%s' does not exist.

Continued

TABLE D-1 MICROSOFT SQL SERVER–GENERATED ERROR CODES *(continued)*

Error Number	Severity	Message Returned
15018	16	The segment '%s' does not exist.
15019	16	The extended stored procedure '%s' does not exist.
15020	16	The stored procedure '%s' does not exist in the current database.
15021	16	The report '%s' does not exist in the current database.
15022	16	The specified user name is already aliased.
15023	16	User '%s' already exists in the current database.
15024	16	The group '%s' already exists in the current database.
15025	16	The login '%s' already exists.
15026	16	Logical device '%s' already exists.
15027	16	The segment '%s' already exists.
15028	16	The server '%s' already exists.
15029	16	The type '%s' already exists in the current database.
15030	16	Physical device '%s' already exists.
15031	16	The object '%s' already exists in the current database.
15032	16	The database '%s' already exists.
15033	16	'%s' is not a valid official language name.
15034	16	The alias '%s' already exists in Syslanguages.
15035	16	'%s' is not a database device.
15036	16	The datatype '%s' does not exist.

Error Number	Severity	Message Returned
15037	16	The physical datatype '%s' does not allow NULLs.
15038	16	User-defined datatypes based on the 'timestamp' datatype are not allowed.
15039	16	The language '%s' already exists in Syslanguages.
15040	16	User defined error messages must have a number > 50000.
15041	16	User defined error messages must have a severity between 1 and 25.
15042	16	Only the System Administrator (SA) may add messages with severity > 18 or which set the WITH_LOG option to 'true'.
15043	16	You must specify 'REPLACE' to overwrite an existing message.
15044	16	'%s' is an unknown device type. Use 'disk', 'tape', 'diskette' or 'pipe'.
15045	16	Logical name may not be NULL.
15046	16	Physical name may not be NULL.
15047	16	The only legal options for a tape device are 'skip' and 'noskip'.
15048	16	'%s' is not a valid database device type. Please enter either 'system' or 'data'.
15049	16	Database already exists, specify 'data' instead of 'system' as the database device type to install additional data devices for an existing database.
15050	16	No such database. You must first create the database by defining its system device.
15051	16	The database size must be at least 1 Meg per device.

Continued

TABLE **D-1** MICROSOFT SQL SERVER-GENERATED ERROR CODES *(continued)*

Error Number	Severity	Message Returned
15052	16	A new location for the system device must be provided when installing the system database device.
15053	16	Objects exist which are not owned by the DBO.
15054	16	No more available device numbers.
15055	16	File '%s' cannot be opened.
15056	16	Error inserting into table '%s'. Database fragment not installed.
15057	16	List of %s name contains spaces, which are not allowed.
15058	16	List of %s has too few names.
15059	16	List of %s has too many names.
15060	16	List of %s names contains name(s) which have '%s' non-alphabetic characters.
15061	16	WARNING: physical device name '%s' is not unique.
15062	16	The 'guest' user may not be mapped to a login name.
15063	16	Login already has an account under a different user name.
15064	16	Primary Key constraints do not have space allocated.
15065	16	All user ids have been assigned.
15066	16	There is already a default-name mapping of a remote login from remote server '%s'.
15067	16	'%s' isn't a local user—remote login denied.
15068	16	There is already a remote user named '%s' for remote server '%s'.

Error Number	Severity	Message Returned
15069	16	One or more users is using the database. Cannot complete requested operation.
15070	16	The 'repl_subscriber' user may only be mapped to the 'repl_subscriber' login.
15071	16	usage: sp_addmessage <msgnum>,<severity>,<msgtext> [,REPLACE].
15072	16	Usage: sp_addremotelogin remoteserver [, loginame [,remotename]].
15073	16	The device '%s' is not used by database '%s'.
15074	16	'%s' is reserved exclusively as a log device.
15075	16	The maximum number of segments for the current database are already defined.
15076	16	Default and table or user datatype must be in the 'current' database.
15077	16	Rule and table or usertype must be in the 'current' database.
15078	16	Table or view name must be in the 'current' database.
15079	10	Queries processed: %d.
15080	17	Failure using SQLMapi, check SQL Server error log.
15081	16	The dependent table or view does not exist in the current database.
15082	16	Name must be in the 'current' database.
15083	16	Report must be in the 'current' database.
15084	16	Column or user datatype must be in the 'current' database.
15085	16	Usage: sp_addtype name, 'datatype' [,null | nonull].

Continued

TABLE D-1 MICROSOFT SQL SERVER–GENERATED ERROR CODES *(continued)*

Error Number	Severity	Message Returned
15086	16	Illegal precision specified—must be between 1 and 38.
15087	16	Illegal scale specified—must be less than precision and positive.
15088	16	Physical type is fixed length. You cannot specify the length.
15089	16	Usage: sp_addserver servername [, 'local'].
15090	16	There is already a local server.
15091	16	You must specify a length with this physical type.
15092	16	Illegal length specified—must be between 1 and 255.
15093	16	'%s' is not a valid date order.
15094	16	'%s' is not a valid first day.
15095	16	Insert into 'syslanguages' failed. Language not added.
15096	16	Only the System Administrator (SA) or '%s' can change '%s's default language.
15097	16	Can't drop '%s' because there are associated entries in master.dbo.sysmessages. Run sp_droplanguage with dropmessages flag.
15098	16	The only legal value for @dropmessages is 'dropmessages'.
15099	16	Update of 'syslanguages' failed. Language alias not changed.
15100	16	Usage: sp_bindefault defaultname, objectname [, 'futureonly'].
15101	16	You cannot bind a default to a column of datatype 'timestamp'.

Error Number	Severity	Message Returned
15102	16	You cannot bind a default to an identity column.
15103	16	You cannot bind a default to a column that was created with or altered to have a default value.
15104	16	You do not own a table named '%s' that has a column named '%s'.
15105	16	You do not own a datatype with that name.
15106	16	Usage: bindrule rulename, objectname [, 'futureonly'].
15107	16	You cannot bind a rule to a column of datatype 'text', 'image', or 'timestamp'.
15108	16	Only the System Administrator (SA) can change the owner of a database.
15109	16	The owner of the 'master' database may not be changed.
15110	16	The proposed new db owner already is a user in the database.
15111	16	The proposed new db owner already is aliased in the database.
15112	16	First table in the common key does not exist.
15113	16	Second table in the common key does not exist.
15114	16	Only the table owner may define its common keys.
15115	16	The tables have no such first column or the columns are of different types.
15116	16	The tables have no such second column or the columns are of different types.
15117	16	The tables have no such third column or the columns are of different types.

Continued

TABLE **D-1** **MICROSOFT SQL SERVER–GENERATED ERROR CODES** *(continued)*

Error Number	Severity	Message Returned
15118	16	The tables have no such fourth column or the columns are of different types.
15119	16	The tables have no such fifth column or the columns are of different types.
15120	16	The tables have no such sixth column or the columns are of different types.
15121	16	The tables have no such seventh column or the columns are of different types.
15122	16	The tables have no such eighth column or the columns are of different types.
15123	16	The configuration option does not exist.
15124	16	The configuration option '%s' is not unique.
15125	16	Only the System Administrator (SA) may change configuration parameters.
15126	16	You cannot set the number of devices to be less than the number of devices already defined in sysdevices.
15127	16	You cannot set the default language to a language ID that is not defined in Syslanguages.
15128	16	You cannot set the kernel language to a language ID that is not defined in Syslanguages.
15129	16	'%d' is not a valid value for configuration option '%s'.
15130	16	usage: sp_dbinstall <dbname>,<logical devname>,<physical devname>,<size>,{'system' | 'data'},['new location'].
15131	16	usage: sp_dbremove <dbname> [,dropdev].

Error Number	Severity	Message Returned
15132	16	You cannot change someone else's default database.
15133	16	Cannot change settings for 'master' device.
15134	16	No alias for specified user exists.
15135	16	Device option '%s' is not unique.
15136	16	usage: sp_devoption [devname, optname, {true | false}].
15137	16	Only the System Administrator (SA) may set device options.
15138	16	Cannot set device to 'read only' because it is used by non 'read only' database(s). Use sp_dboption to set database options.
15139	16	The device is a RAM disk and cannot be used as a default device.
15140	16	Usage: sp_diskdefault logicalname {defaulton | defaultoff}.
15141	16	Cannot drop device since it is being used by one or more databases.
15142	16	Cannot drop the group 'public'.
15143	16	'%s' is not a valid option for @updateusage. Please enter either 'true' or 'false'.
15144	16	Group has members. It must be empty before it can be dropped.
15145	16	Usage: sp_dropkey {primary | foreign | common}, tabname [,deptabname]. Type must be 'primary', 'foreign', or 'common'.
15146	16	You must be the owner of the table or view to drop its key.
15147	16	No primary key for the table or view exists.

Continued

TABLE **D-1** MICROSOFT SQL SERVER-GENERATED ERROR CODES *(continued)*

Error Number	Severity	Message Returned
15148	16	You need to supply the dependent table or view as the third parameter.
15149	16	No foreign key for the table or view exists.
15150	16	No common keys exist between the two tables or views supplied.
15151	16	Foreign key table does not exist.
15152	16	Primary key table does not exist.
15153	16	Only the owner of the table may define a foreign key.
15154	16	The table has no such first column.
15155	16	The table has no such second column.
15156	16	The table has no such third column.
15157	16	The table has no such fourth column.
15158	16	The table has no such fifth column.
15159	16	The table has no such sixth column.
15160	16	The table has no such seventh column.
15161	16	The table has no such eighth column.
15162	16	Primary key does not exist with the same number of columns as the foreign key.
15163	16	Primary key does not exist.
15164	16	Datatypes of the first column in the keys are different.
15165	16	Datatypes of the second column in the keys are different.
15166	16	Datatypes of the third column in the keys are different.
15167	16	Datatypes of the fourth column in the keys are different.

Error Number	Severity	Message Returned
15168	16	Datatypes of the fifth column in the keys are different.
15169	16	Datatypes of the sixth column in the keys are different.
15170	16	Datatypes of the seventh column in the keys are different.
15171	16	Datatypes of the eighth column in the keys are different.
15172	16	Only the owner of the table may define a primary key.
15173	16	Primary key already exists on table—drop key first.
15174	16	Login '%s' owns one or more database(s). Change the owner of the following database(s) before dropping login.
15175	16	Login '%s' is mapped to user: '%s' in database '%s'. Drop user before dropping login.
15176	16	Login '%s' is aliased to user: '%s' in database '%s'. Drop alias before dropping login.
15177	16	usage: sp_dropmessage <msg number>.
15178	16	Cannot drop a message with a number < 50000.
15179	16	Message number %u does not exist.
15180	16	Type is being used. You cannot drop it.
15181	16	You cannot drop the 'database owner'.
15182	16	You cannot drop the 'guest' user from master or tempdb.
15183	16	The user owns objects in the database and cannot be dropped.

Continued

TABLE **D-1** MICROSOFT SQL SERVER–GENERATED ERROR CODES *(continued)*

Error Number	Severity	Message Returned
15184	16	The user owns datatypes in the database and cannot be dropped.
15185	16	There is no remote user '%s' mapped to local user '%s' from the remote server '%s'.
15186	16	Cannot drop segment '%s' completely.
15187	16	The segment '%s' is being used.
15188	16	Segment '%s' does not reference device '%s'.
15189	16	There is only one unique device mapping for the segment '%s'—use sp_dropsegment with no device argument.
15190	16	There are still remote logins for the server '%s'.
15191	16	Usage: sp_dropserver server [, droplogins].
15192	16	Can't make the only segment on original device log-only.
15193	16	This procedure can be used on system tables only.
15194	16	Cannot re-create index on this table.
15195	16	The first table does not exist.
15196	16	The second table does not exist.
15197	16	There is no text for object '%s'
15198	16	The name supplied is not a user, group, or aliased.
15199	16	Only the System Administrator (SA) or the Database Owner (dbo) may move the syslogs table.
15200	16	There are no remote servers defined.

Error Number	Severity	Message Returned
15201	16	There are no remote logins for the remote server '%s'.
15202	16	There are no remote logins defined.
15203	16	There are no remote logins for '%s'.
15204	16	There are no remote logins for '%s' on remote server '%s'.
15205	16	There are no servers defined.
15206	16	Invalid Remote Server Option: '%s'.
15207	16	usage: sp_makestartup <procname>.
15208	16	The specified procedure must be owned by the SA.
15209	16	Procedure expects parameters. Cannot be used as a startup stored procedure.
15210	16	Only System Administrator (SA) can use loginame option—password not changed.
15211	16	Old (current) password incorrect for user—password not changed.
15212	16	Use sp_logdevice to move syslogs table.
15213	16	You cannot move system tables.
15214	16	You do not own a table named '%s'.
15215	16	There is no index named '%s' for table '%s'.
15216	16	'%s' is not a valid option for @delfile.
15217	16	'%s' is a system table. sp_recompile cannot be used on system tables.
15218	16	Object '%s' is not a table.
15219	16	You do not own table '%s'. Only the System Administrator (SA) or the table's owner may perform this action.

Continued

Error Number	Severity	Message Returned
15220	16	Usage: sp_remoteoption [remoteserver, loginame, remotename, optname, {true | false}].
15221	16	Remote login option does not exist or cannot be set by user. Run sp_remoteoption with no parameters to see options.
15222	16	Remote login option '%s' is not unique.
15223	16	A column named '%s' already exists in table '%s'.
15224	16	An index named '%s' already exists in table '%s'.
15225	16	Object name beginning with '#' is not allowed.
15226	16	Only the System Administrator (SA) can change the name of a database.
15227	16	The database '%s' cannot be renamed.
15228	16	The System Administrator (SA) must set database '%s' to single-user mode with sp_dboption before it can be renamed.
15229	16	usage: sp_serveroption [server, optname, {true | false}].
15230	16	Server option does not exist or cannot be set by user. Run sp_serveroption with no parameters to see options.
15231	16	Server option '%s' is not unique.
15232	16	Only the System Administrator (SA) may set server options.
15233	16	There is already a server network name '%s'.
15234	16	Object is stored in 'sysprocedures' and has no space allocated directly.

Error Number	Severity	Message Returned
15235	16	Views do not have space allocated.
15236	16	Column '%s' has no default.
15237	16	User datatype '%s' has no default.
15238	16	Column '%s' has no rule.
15239	16	User datatype '%s' has no rule.
15240	16	usage: sp_unmakestartup <procname>.
15241	16	usage: sp_dboption [dbname, optname, {true | false}].
15242	16	Database option '%s' is not unique.
15243	16	The option '%s' cannot be changed for the 'master' database.
15244	16	Only the System Administrator (SA) or the owner of the database may set db options.
15245	16	'DBCC DBCONTROL' error. Database not placed offline.
15246	16	Cannot bring database online due to problem opening device '%s'.
15247	16	The object name '%s' is ambiguous. Table '%s' has both a column and an index named '%s'. Please specify either 'COLUMN' or 'INDEX' after the new name.
15248	16	You cannot specify '%s' unless renaming a column or index.
15249	16	'%s' is an invalid option for object type. Please enter either 'COLUMN' or 'INDEX'.
15250	16	Database name component of object qualifier must be name of current database.
15251	16	Illegal '%s' specified—must be %s.

Continued

TABLE **D-1** MICROSOFT SQL SERVER–GENERATED ERROR CODES *(continued)*

Error Number	Severity	Message Returned
15252	16	PK table name or FK table name must be given.
15253	16	'%s' is not a column in table '%s'.
15254	16	Non-dbo/guest users exist in database. Please drop them before removing database.
15255	16	'%s' is not a valid value for @autofix. The only valid option is 'auto'.
15256	16	usage: sp_certify_removable <dbname> [,'auto'].
15257	16	You cannot be USEing the database that you are attempting to certify.
15258	16	The database must be owned by the System Administrator before it can be removed.
15259	16	The database must occupy at least three database devices (one each for the 'system' and 'log' segments and one or more for the 'data' segment(s)) before it can be removed.
15260	16	The database cannot be removed since it has noncontiguous fragments on one or more devices.
15261	16	usage: sp_create_removable <dbname>,<syslogical>,<sysphysical>, <syssize>,<loglogical>,<logphysical>, <logsize>,<datalogical1>,<dataphysical1>, <datasize1> [,<datalogical2>,<dataphysical2>, <datasize2>...<datalogical16>, <dataphysical16>,<datasize16>]
15262	16	Invalid device size entered. Database devices must be at least 1 Meg. in size.
15263	16	Could not create the '%s' device. See the error log for details.

Error Number	Severity	Message Returned
15264	16	Could not create the '%s' portion of the database.
15265	16	Could not update sysusages.segmap.
15266	16	Cannot make '%s' database removable.
15267	16	You must supply a physical device for logical data device '%s'.
15268	16	You must supply a size for logical data device '%s'.
15269	16	Logical data device '%s' not created.
15270	16	You may not specify a length for user types based on the 'sysname' type.
15271	16	Invalid @with_log value. Valid options are 'true' or 'false'.
15272	16	Procedure '%s' is not a valid startup procedure since startup procedures must be in the 'master' database.
15273	16	Cannot make '%s' a startup procedure since startup procedures must be in the 'master' database and the current database is '%s'.
15274	16	Procedure '%s' is not a valid startup procedure since startup procedures must be in the 'master' database and the current database is '%s'.
15275	16	Foreign Key constraints do not have space allocated.
16901	10	%s:This feature has not been implemented yet.
16902	10	%s: The parameter %s is invalid.
16903	10	%s procedure called with incorrect number of parameters.
16904	10	The cursor handle is invalid.

Continued

TABLE D-1 MICROSOFT SQL SERVER–GENERATED ERROR CODES *(continued)*

Error Number	Severity	Message Returned
16905	10	The cursor is already open.
16906	10	The cursor is not declared.
16907	10	%s is not allowed in cursor statements.
16909	10	%s: The cursor identifier value provided (%d) is not valid.
16910	10	%s: The fetch type %s can only be used with keyset driven cursors.
16911	10	%s: The fetch type %s cannot be used with forward only cursors.
16912	10	%s: This fetch type requires a rownumber.
16914	10	%s procedure called with too many parameters.
16915	10	A cursor with the name '%s' already exists.
16916	10	A cursor with the name '%s' does not exist.
16917	10	Cursor is not open.
16919	10	Cannot open cursor–referenced object (NAME NOT RECOVERABLE) dropped already.
16920	10	Stored procedure defining the cursor does not have a select statement.
16921	10	Cursorfetch: Must declare variable '%s'.
16922	10	Cursorfetch: Variable type of '%s' does not match that of selected column in the cursor.
16923	10	Cursorfetch: Maximum length of '%s' is incompatible with that of selected column in the cursor.
16924	10	Cursorfetch: Number of variables declared in the INTO list must match that of selected columns.

Error Number	Severity	Message Returned
16925	10	The fetch type %s cannot be used with dynamic cursors.
16926	10	sp_cursoroption: The column id (%d) does not correspond to a TEXT or IMAGE column.
16927	10	sp_cursoroption: The cursor already has a name.
16928	10	The column name '%s' specified in the FOR UPDATE list is invalid or ambiguous.
16929	10	Cursor is read only.
16930	10	Requested row is not in the fetch buffer.
16931	10	There are no rows in the current fetch buffer.
16932	10	Cursor has a 'FOR UPDATE' list and the requested column to be updated is not in this list.
16933	10	The cursor does not include the table being modified.
16934	10	Optimistic concurrency check failed, the row was modified outside of this cursor.
16935	10	No value parameters were specified for the sp_cursor-%s command.
16936	10	Cannot open cursor-referenced object '%s' (ID %d) during %s.
16937	10	Cannot open a cursor on a stored procedure that has anything other than a single select statement in it.
16938	10	sp_cursoropen: The statement parameter can only be a single select or a single stored procedure.
16939	10	Process has isolation level set to 0 (uncommitted reads), which can only support READ ONLY cursors.

Continued

TABLE **D-1** **MICROSOFT SQL SERVER-GENERATED ERROR CODES** *(continued)*

Error Number	Severity	Message Returned
16940	10	Table optimizer hint '%s' is not allowed with READ ONLY cursors.
16941	10	Cursor updates are not allowed on tables opened with NOLOCK option.
16942	10	Asynchronous keyset generation failed, the cursor has been deallocated.
16943	10	Cursor open failed because the size of the keyset row exceeded maximum allowed row size.
16944	10	The unique index used for the table needs to have smaller number of keys or keys with smaller sizes.
16945	10	Cursor open failed because the size of the table row is too large for optimistic checking based on values.
16946	10	Try using locking, readonly, or timestamp based optimistic checking for concurrency control on the table.

Appendix E

About the CD-ROM

THE CD-ROM CONTAINS all source code presented in this book. A directory is provided for each chapter, which contains the complete chapter source code. To run the examples presented in this book, you should have Microsoft Visual Basic 6 installed on your system.

The CD-ROM also includes the following Visual Basic 6 tools to help you with your application development:

- ◆ ActiveListBar – Sheridan Software, Inc.

- ◆ ActiveThreed – Sheridan Software, Inc.

- ◆ ActiveTreeView – Sheridan Software, Inc.

- ◆ ButtonMaker Demo – FarPoint Technologies, Inc.

- ◆ Calendar ObjX Demo – FarPoint Technologies, Inc.

- ◆ Calendar Widgets – Sheridan Software, Inc.

- ◆ Data Widgets – Sheridan Software, Inc.

- ◆ Designer Widgets – Sheridan Software, Inc.

- ◆ ListPro Spread Demo – FarPoint Technologies, Inc.

- ◆ TabPro Demo – FarPoint Technologies, Inc.

- ◆ InputPro Demo – FarPoint Technologies, Inc.

- ◆ VBAssist – Sheridan Software, Inc.

Each tool is provided in a separate directory on the CD-ROM. Refer to the README.TXT file in each tool directory for installation instructions.

Glossary

ActiveX Data Objects (ADO)   Data access methodology that provides access to OLE DB data sources.

American National Standards Institute (ANSI)   Responsible for defining computer industry standards.

application server   An application's business logic is moved from the client into a common, shared host server. The client is basically used for presentation services – not unlike the role that a terminal plays on a mainframe. For this reason, it is termed a thin client.

client/server computing   Logical extension of modular programming. Client/server computing recognizes that not all of those modules need to be executed within the same memory space. With this architecture, the calling module becomes the "client" (which requests a service), and the called module becomes the "server" (which provides the service).

cursor   When you access data from a database, you may retrieve one or more rows. You can access only one row of this set of data at a time – either for reading or updating. If you're using bound controls, such as a grid, you actually may be able to see more than one row at a time. When your application accesses a row of data from your database, the row is read into the *buffer*, a temporary storage location, where it is available for your application. If you make a change to a row, it is first changed in the buffer, and then changed in the database.

Data Access Object (DAO)   Data access methodology that is optimized for accessing single-user, standalone database sources.

data binding   Enables Visual Basic controls to interact directly with data sources.

database-level locking   Restricts access to the entire database to one user at a time.

Dynamic Link Library (DLL)   Allows executable routines to be stored separately as files with .DLL extensions and to be loaded only when needed by a program.

dynaset cursor   Stores the keys required to retrieve the row (as with the keyset cursor). Each time you access a row in the result set, the query is re-executed, which means you always see the most current data in the database. The downside of using dynamic cursors is slowed performance. Dynaset cursors typically are very slow, and expensive to implement. However, if you need access to the most current database data, they are the optimal choice.

keyset cursor Stores a set of keys, which permits a selected row to be retrieved according to the row-specific information stored in that set of keys, precisely when that information is actually required. The keyset cursor requires separate storage for the data in each of the keys that are its parts. This cursor's membership is fixed immediately after the result set is created, which means that any database changes made after the cursor is created can't be seen by this type of cursor until it is re-created.

messaging server A second-generation transaction-processing (TP) monitor that provides the same funneling process as a TP monitor. Messages are processed asynchronously, with the appropriate priority level. As with a TP monitor, a messaging server provides connectivity to data sources other than database servers.

multitier applications In multitier data access applications, you can store components of your applications in a centralized location – typically a transaction server. These components are executed on the transaction server, which enables you to centralize your application logic there and reuse that logic in other applications.

normalization Normalization can best be described as the process of eliminating duplicate data in your database. A normalized database can reduce the amount of data your application needs to retrieve, modify, and add to your database. Entire books have been dedicated to the subject of database normalization; we present the basic rules of normalization along with examples of their application.

optimistic locking Keeps pages locked for the shortest period of time, which can be very important when many users are accessing the database. The biggest disadvantage of optimistic locking is that two users can begin to make modifications on the same record, and they don't find out that the record is locked, or has already been changed, until they attempt to commit their changes.

page-level locking The base-level locking inherently provided by the Jet Database Engine. Restricts access to database records to one user at a time while the records are being modified.

pessimistic locking Ensures database integrity at the highest level. When a user attempts to add or modify database records, the associated data pages become locked. However, pessimistic locking can cause pages to remain locked for long periods of time, preventing other users from accessing the same table data.

Rapid Application Development (RAD) A platform-independent software-development approach, RAD offers potential reduction in the amount of time required to deliver high-quality software. Most client/server IS groups claim to use RAD. When asked how much success they are having using RAD, however, they often describe scenarios of best intentions being followed by impossible deadlines, hacked code, and stressed-out project teams.

Remote Data Objects (RDO)   Data access methodology that is optimized for accessing ODBC (Open Database Connectivity) server-side database sources.

replica   A copy of the database.

replication   Enables a native Jet/Access database to be split into multiple copies that can be kept in synchronization. Also enables a database to be used in a distributed environment, providing mechanisms to bring the distributed copies back into synchronization.

single-row buffer   Not a cursor, but functions the same way the keyset cursor does. With a single-row buffer, you can only see one row of a query's result set at a time. When you use a single-row buffer, data can be viewed in only one direction – as you move forward through the data contained in the result set.

snapshot cursor   A snapshot or *static* cursor uses the same key-set accessibility as the keyset cursor, but the data retrieved from the database is also stored on the client. After the query is run, the result is buffered on the client; any rows read as the result of the query are read from this buffer. If any changes are made to the database, even to rows that are members of the result set, these changes won't be seen by the client.

stored procedures   Most server-side databases (including Microsoft SQL Server and Oracle) enable you to create procedures that are stored and executed on the database server itself, which enables you to centralize your application logic on the database server and reuse that logic in other applications. The use of stored procedures is discussed in this book in conjunction with each data access model.

Structured Query Language (SQL)   A standardized language that enables users to manipulate a database and, more importantly, the data it contains. SQL was developed in the 1970s; its roots can be traced to E. F. Codd, the inventor of relational databases, and to work performed at IBM during the same period. Since that time, SQL has evolved into the standard for manipulating relational-database information.

synchronization   The process of distributing database updates.

table-level locking   Restricts access to a database table to one user at a time.

three-tier client/server   Architecture in which the middle layer can perform multiple functions – queuing, application execution, database staging, and so forth. The use of client/server technology with such a middle layer has proven to offer considerably more performance and flexibility than a two-tier approach.

transaction-processing (TP) monitor   Provides a message-queuing service. The client connects to the TP monitor instead of the database server. The transaction is accepted by the monitor, which queues it and then takes responsibility for managing it to correct completion.

transactions   Help to maintain database integrity. When you update many records spanning a few tables, if any errors occur during your processing, transaction processing can undo your changes before they are applied to the database.

two-tier client/server architecture   Remote calls or SQL typically are used to communicate between the client and server. The server is likely to have support for stored procedures and triggers, which means the server can be programmed to implement business rules that are better-suited to run on the server than on the client, resulting in a much more efficient overall system.

Index

Numbers and Symbols

* (asterisk)
    use of with . (period) operator, 84–85
    use of with LIKE comparison operator, 83
{} (braces), using in rdoPreparedStatements, 353
[] (bracket characters), using in SQL statements, 86
" (double quotes), enclosing string literals in, 83
. (period) operator, use of in SELECT statements, 84
? (question mark), use of with LIKE comparison
    operator, 83
' (single quotes), enclosing string literals in, 83

A

About tab, ODBC Data Source Administrator dialog
    box, 68
AbsolutePage property, Recordset object, 448
AbsolutePosition property
    moving to a specific location in a result set with,
      329–330
    rdoEngine object, 290
    rdoResultset object, 318
    Recordset object, 448
Access database
    opening a secured, 176–177
    sharing, 178
action parameter, Validate event, 255
    Remote Data Control, 381
    results of settings, 382
Active Server Pages, ADO support for, 11
ActiveConnection property
    ADO Command object, 464–465
    rdoResultset object, 320
ActiveRow property, DataRepeater control, 620
ActiveRowChanged event, Data Control, 621
ActiveScript plug-in (NCompass Labs) for Recordset
    object, Web site address for, 413
ActiveX
    mastering, 413–414
    support for in Visual Basic 6, 5
    technologies that are part of, 414
ActiveX controls, 414
    plug-ins available to be used Netscape Navigator,
      413
    support for under Internet Explorer Web browsers,
      413
    versus OCX controls, 9, 412
ActiveX Data Object (ADO)
    API Web site address, 422
    choosing over other methods, 43–44
    comparing to DAO, 417–418
    comparing to RDO, 418
    Command object, 457–467
    connect string parameters supported by, 428
    Connection and Recordset objects, 425–456
    Connection object properties, 433–434

converting RDO applications to, 421–422
data access model support, 4
error handling, 503–520
Error object, 505–511
error value constants returned by, 511–515
Errors collection, 503–505
exploring, 40–41
hierarchy, 415–417
including in your applications, 418–420
introduction to, 411–423
key features of, 41, 414–415
object hierarchy, 41
outline COM and DCOM, 411–413
Properties collection, 519–520
Property object, 515–518
Recordset fields, 473–474
typical object application configuration, 40, 415
understanding the components of, 414–417
using redistributable components, 420–421
using the Connection object Execute()
    method, 431
using the Connection object Open() and
    Close() methods, 427–428
using the Connection object transaction
    methods, 433
using to access ODBC data sources, 429
versus DAO and RDO, 40, 42
ActiveX documents, 414
ActiveX scripting, 414
ActiveX Server, 414
ActiveX/COM components, 414
ActualSize property, ADO Field object, 470, 471
Add() method, rdoEnvironment object, 297
AddNew() method
    rdoResultset object, 321
    Recordset object, 146, 438, 439–441
AddNewMode property, DataGrid control, 616
ADO (ActiveX Data Object), 707
    API Web site address, 422
    choosing over other methods, 43–44
    comparing to DAO, 417–418
    comparing to RDO, 418
    Command object, 457–467
    connect string parameters supported by, 428
    Connection and Recordset objects, 425–456
    Connection object properties, 433–434
    converting RDO applications to, 421–422
    data access model support, 4
    error handling, 503–520
    Error object, 505–511
    error value constants returned by, 511–515
    Errors collection, 503–505
    exploring, 40–41
    hierarchy, 415–417
    including in your applications, 418–420

IDG BOOKS WORLDWIDE, INC.
END-USER LICENSE AGREEMENT

4. <u>Restrictions on Use of Individual Programs</u>. You must follow the individual requirements and restrictions detailed for each individual program in the "About the CD-ROM" section of this Book. These limitations are also contained in the individual license agreements recorded on the Software Media. These limitations may include a requirement that after using the program for a specified period of time, the user must pay a registration fee or discontinue use. By opening the Software packet(s), you will be agreeing to abide by the licenses and restrictions for these individual programs that are detailed in the "About the CD-ROM" section and on the Software Media. None of the material on this Software Media or listed in this Book may ever be redistributed, in original or modified form, for commercial purposes.

5. <u>Limited Warranty</u>.

   (a) IDGB warrants that the Software and Software Media are free from defects in materials and workmanship under normal use for a period of sixty (60) days from the date of purchase of this Book. If IDGB receives notification within the warranty period of defects in materials or workmanship, IDGB will replace the defective Software Media.

   (b) IDGB AND THE AUTHORS OF THE BOOK DISCLAIM ALL OTHER WARRANTIES, EXPRESS OR IMPLIED, INCLUDING WITHOUT LIMITATION IMPLIED WARRANTIES OF MERCHANTABILITY AND FITNESS FOR A PARTICULAR PURPOSE, WITH RESPECT TO THE SOFTWARE, THE PROGRAMS, THE SOURCE CODE CONTAINED THEREIN, AND/OR THE TECHNIQUES DESCRIBED IN THIS BOOK. IDGB DOES NOT WARRANT THAT THE FUNCTIONS CONTAINED IN THE SOFTWARE WILL MEET YOUR REQUIREMENTS OR THAT THE OPERATION OF THE SOFTWARE WILL BE ERROR FREE.

   (c) This limited warranty gives you specific legal rights, and you may have other rights that vary from jurisdiction to jurisdiction.

6. <u>Remedies</u>.

   (a) IDGB's entire liability and your exclusive remedy for defects in materials and workmanship shall be limited to replacement of the Software Media, which may be returned to IDGB with a copy of your receipt at the following address: Software Media Fulfillment Department, Attn.: *Visual Basic 6 Database Programming*, IDG Books Worldwide, Inc., 7260 Shadeland Station, Ste. 100, Indianapolis, IN 46256, or call 1-800-762-2974. Please allow three to four weeks for delivery. This Limited Warranty is void if failure of the Software Media has resulted from accident, abuse, or misapplication. Any replacement Software Media will be warranted for the remainder of the original warranty period or thirty (30) days, whichever is longer.

(b) In no event shall IDGB or the authors be liable for any damages whatsoever (including without limitation damages for loss of business profits, business interruption, loss of business information, or any other pecuniary loss) arising from the use of or inability to use the Book or the Software, even if IDGB has been advised of the possibility of such damages.

(c) Because some jurisdictions do not allow the exclusion or limitation of liability for consequential or incidental damages, the above limitation or exclusion may not apply to you.

7. <u>U.S. Government Restricted Rights</u>. Use, duplication, or disclosure of the Software by the U.S. Government is subject to restrictions stated in paragraph (c)(1)(ii) of the Rights in Technical Data and Computer Software clause of DFARS 252.227-7013, and in subparagraphs (a) through (d) of the Commercial Computer – Restricted Rights clause at FAR 52.227-19, and in similar clauses in the NASA FAR supplement, when applicable.

8. <u>General</u>. This Agreement constitutes the entire understanding of the parties and revokes and supersedes all prior agreements, oral or written, between them and may not be modified or amended except in a writing signed by both parties hereto that specifically refers to this Agreement. This Agreement shall take precedence over any other documents that may be in conflict herewith. If any one or more provisions contained in this Agreement are held by any court or tribunal to be invalid, illegal, or otherwise unenforceable, each and every other provision shall remain in full force and effect.

my2cents.idgbooks.com

Register This Book — And Win!

Visit **http://my2cents.idgbooks.com** to register this book and we'll automatically enter you in our fantastic monthly prize giveaway. It's also your opportunity to give us feedback: let us know what you thought of this book and how you would like to see other topics covered.

Discover IDG Books Online!

The IDG Books Online Web site is your online resource for tackling technology — at home and at the office. Frequently updated, the IDG Books Online Web site features exclusive software, insider information, online books, and live events!

10 Productive & Career-Enhancing Things You Can Do at www.idgbooks.com

- Nab source code for your own programming projects.

- Download software.

- Read Web exclusives: special articles and book excerpts by IDG Books Worldwide authors.

- Take advantage of resources to help you advance your career as a Novell or Microsoft professional.

- Buy IDG Books Worldwide titles or find a convenient bookstore that carries them.

- Register your book and win a prize.

- Chat live online with authors.

- Sign up for regular e-mail updates about our latest books.

- Suggest a book you'd like to read or write.

- Give us your 2¢ about our books and about our Web site.

You say you're not on the Web yet? It's easy to get started with IDG Books' *Discover the Internet,* available at local retailers everywhere.

CD-ROM Installation Instructions

THIS BOOK'S CD-ROM CONTAINS all the source code presented in this book, as well as several Visual Basic 6 development tools. (See Appendix E for more information about the development tools provided.)

For each chapter in the book, a directory is provided that contains the complete chapter source code. To run the examples presented in this book, you should have Microsoft Visual Basic 6 installed on your system. To find a program that interests you, look on the CD-ROM to find the source code directory for the chapter in which the program appears. A file is provided for each listing number. You can open these code-listing files in a standard text editor; or include them in your own Visual Basic applications.

To install any of the development tools, run the installation application found in the Sheridan or FarPoint directories and check out the READ-ME files provided on the CD-ROM.